Computer-oriented Statistical Methods in Business

J. K. Sharma
Professor
Amity Business School
Amity University, Noida

Delhi • Chennai • Chandigarh

ISBN 978-81-317-6363-6

First Impression

Published by Dorling Kindersley (India) Pvt. Ltd, licencees of Pearson Education in South Asia.

Head Office: 7th Floor, Knowledge Boulevard, A-8(A), Sector 62, Noida 201 309, UP, India.
Registered Office: 11 Community Centre, Panchsheel Park, New Delhi 110 017, India.

Typeset by Sara Assignments, Delhi

Printed in India by Taj Press.

Contents

Syllabus *xi*
Preface *xiii*
About the Author *xiv*

CHAPTER 1 STATISTICS: AN OVERVIEW **1–11**

1.1 Reasons for Learning Statistics 1
1.2 Growth and Development of Statistics 2
1.3 Statistics Defined 2
1.4 Types of Statistical Methods 3
1.5 Importance and Scope of Statistics 4
1.5.1 Statistics and the State 4
1.5.2 Statistics in Economics 4
1.5.3 Statistics in Business Management 5
1.5.4 Statistics in Physical Sciences 5
1.5.5 Statistics in Social Sciences 5
1.5.6 Statistics in Medical Sciences 6
1.5.7 Statistics and Computers 6
1.6 Limitations of Statistics 6
1.6.1 Statistics Does Not Study Qualitative Phenomena 6
1.6.2 Statistics Does Not Study Individuals 7
1.6.3 Statistics Can Be Misused 7
Conceptual Questions 7
1.7 Need for Data 7
1.7.1 Types of Data 8

1.8 Sources of Data 8
1.8.1 Primary Data Sources 8
1.8.2 Secondary Data Sources 9
Chapter Concepts Quiz 10
Glossary of Terms 11

CHAPTER 2 DATA CLASSIFICATION, TABULATION AND PRESENTATION 12–57

2.1 Introduction 12
2.2 Classification of Data 12
2.2.1 Requisites of Ideal Classification 13
2.2.2 Basis of Classification 13
2.3 Organizing Data Using Data Array 15
2.3.1 Frequency Distribution 16
2.3.2 Methods of Data Classification 18
2.3.3 Bivariate Frequency Distribution 24
2.3.4 Types of Frequency Distributions 26
Conceptual Questions 2A 28
Self-Practice Problems 2A 29
Hints and Answers 30
2.4 Tabulation of Data 30
2.4.1 Objectives of Tabulation 31
2.4.2 Parts of a Table 31
Conceptual Questions 2B 33
Self-Practice Problems 2B 33
Hints and Answers 34
2.5 Graphical Presentation of Data 35
2.5.1 Functions of a Graph 35
2.5.2 Advantages and Limitations of Diagrams (Graphs) 36
2.5.3 General Rules for Drawing Diagrams 36
2.6 Types of Diagrams 37
2.6.1 One-Dimensional Diagrams 37
2.6.2 Two-Dimensional Diagrams 49
2.6.3 Three-Dimensional Diagrams 52
2.6.4 Pictograms or Ideographs 52
2.6.5 Cartograms of Statistical Maps 53
Conceptual Questions 2C 53
Self-Practice Problems 2C 54
Formulae Used 55
Chapter Concepts Quiz 55
Review Self-Practice Problems 56
Glossary of Terms 57

CHAPTER 3 MEASURES OF CENTRAL TENDENCY 58–116

3.1 Introduction 58
3.2 Objectives of Averaging 59
3.3 Requisites of a Measure of Central Tendency 59
3.4 Measures of Central Tendency 60
3.5 Mathematical Averages 61
3.5.1 Arithmetic Mean of Ungrouped (or Raw) Data 61
3.5.2 Arithmetic Mean of Grouped (or Classified) Data 64
3.5.3 Some Special Types of Problems and Their Solutions 68
3.5.4 Advantages and Disadvantages of Arithmetic Mean 74
3.5.5 Weighted Arithmetic Mean 76
Conceptual Questions 3A 79
Self-Practice Problems 3A 80
Hints and Answers 81
3.6 Geometric Mean 81
3.6.1 Combined Geometric Mean 85
3.6.2 Weighted Geometric Mean 85
3.6.3 Advantages, Disadvantages, and Applications of G.M. 87
Conceptual Questions 3B 88
Self-Practice Problems 3B 88
Hints and Answers 89
3.7 Harmonic Mean 90
3.7.1 Advantages, Disadvantages, and Applications of H.M. 93
3.8 Relationship among A.M., G.M., and H.M. 93
Self-Practice Problems 3C 93
Hints and Answers 94
3.9 Averages of Position 94
3.9.1 Median 94
3.9.2 Advantages, Disadvantages, and Applications of Median 97
3.10 Partition Values—Quartiles, Deciles, and Percentiles 97
3.10.1 Graphical Method for Calculating Partition Values 99
Conceptual Questions 3C 103
Self-Practice Problems 3D 103
Hints and Answers 104
3.11 Mode 104
3.11.1 Graphical Method for Calculating Mode Value 107
3.11.2 Advantages and Disadvantages of Mode Value 108
3.12 Relationship Between Mean, Median, and Mode 108
3.13 Comparison Between Measures of Central Tendency 109

Conceptual Questions 3D 110
Self-Practice Problems 3E 110
Hints and Answers 111
Formulae Used 112
Chapter Concepts Quiz 112
Review Self-Practice Problems 113
Hints and Answers 114
Glossary of Terms 115

CHAPTER 4 MEASURES OF DISPERSION 117–161

4.1 Introduction 117
4.2 Significance of Measuring Dispersion 118
4.2.1 Essential Requisites for a Measure of Variation 118
4.3 Classification of Measures of Dispersion 119
4.4 Distance Measures 120
4.4.1 Range 120
4.4.2 Interquartile Range or Deviation 122
Conceptual Questions 4A 124
Self-Practice Problems 4A 124
Hints and Answers 126
4.5 Average Deviation Measures 126
4.5.1 Mean Absolute Deviation 126
4.5.2 Variance and Standard Deviation 133
4.5.3 Mathematical Properties of Standard Deviation 140
4.5.4 Coefficient of Variation 148
Conceptual Questions 4B 151
Self-Practice Problems 4B 152
Hints and Answers 154
Formulae Used 155
Chapter Concepts Quiz 155
Review Self-Practice Problems 156
Hints and Answers 158
Glossary of Terms 161

CHAPTER 5 SKEWNESS AND KURTOSIS 162–186

5.1 Introduction 162
5.2 Measures of Skewness 163
5.2.1 Relative Measures of Skewness 164

Conceptual Questions 5A 171
Self-Practice Problems 5A 172
Hints and Answers 173
5.3 Kurtosis 174
5.3.1 Measures of Kurtosis 175
Conceptual Questions 5B 183
Self-Practice Problems 5B 183
Hints and Answers 184
Formulae Used 184
Review Self-Practice Problems 185
Hints and Answers 185
Glossary of Terms 186

CHAPTER 6 PROBABILITY AND PROBABILITY DISTRIBUTIONS 187–240

6.1 Introduction 187
6.2 Concepts of Probability 187
6.2.1 Random Experiment 188
6.2.2 Sample Space 188
6.2.3 Event Types 189
6.3 Definition of Probability 190
6.3.1 Classical Approach 190
6.3.2 Relative Frequency Approach 191
6.3.3 Subjective Approach 191
6.3.4 Fundamental Rules of Probability 191
6.3.5 Glossary of Probability Terms 192
6.4 Combinations and Permutations 192
Conceptual Questions 6A 195
Self-Practice Problems 6A 195
Hints and Answers 196
6.5 Rules of Probability and Algebra of Events 197
6.5.1 Rules of Addition 197
6.5.2 Rules of Multiplication 201
Self-Practice Problems 6B 206
Hints and Answers 207
6.6 Bayes' Theorem 209
Self-Practice Problems 6C 210
Hints and Answers 211
6.7 Probability Distributions 212
6.8 Expected Value and Variance of a Random Variable 213
6.8.1 Properties of Expected Value and Variance 214

Conceptual Questions 6B 215
Self-Practice Problems 6D 216
Hints and Answers 216
6.9 Discrete Probability Distributions 217
6.9.1 Binomial Probability Distribution 217
Conceptual Questions 6C 221
Self-Practice Problems 6E 222
Hints and Answers 222
6.9.2 Poisson Probability Distribution 223
Conceptual Questions 6D 226
Self-Practice Problems 6F 227
Hints and Answers 227
6.10 Continuous Probability Distributions 228
6.10.1 Normal Probability Distribution Function 229
Conceptual Questions 6E 233
Self-Practice Problems 6G 233
Hints and Answers 234
Formulae Used 235
Chapter Concepts Quiz 236
Review Self-Practice Problems 237
Hints and Answers 238
Glossary of Terms 239

CHAPTER 7 SAMPLING AND SAMPLING DISTRIBUTIONS 241–261

7.1 Introduction 241
7.2 Reasons of Sample Survey 242
7.3 Population Parameters and Sample Statistics 242
7.4 Sampling Methods 243
7.4.1 Probability Sampling Methods 243
7.4.2 Non-Random Sampling Methods 245
7.5 Sampling Distributions 246
Conceptual Questions 7A 246
7.6 Sampling Distribution of Sample Mean 247
7.6.1 Sampling Distribution of Mean When Population Has Normal Distribution 247
7.6.2 Sampling Distribution of Difference Between Two Sample Means 251
Self-Practice Problems 7A 253
Hints and Answers 253

7.7 Sampling Distribution of Sample Proportion 254
7.7.1 Sampling Distribution of the Difference of Two Proportions 255
Self Practice Problems 7B 257
Hints and Answers 257
Formulae Used 258
Chapter Concepts Quiz 259
Review Self-Practice Problems 259
Hints and Answers 260
Glossary of Terms 261

CHAPTER 8 HYPOTHESIS TESTING 262–299

8.1 Introduction 262
8.2 General Procedure for Hypothesis Testing 263
8.3 Direction of the Hypothesis Test 265
8.4 Errors in Hypothesis Testing 266
Conceptual Questions 8A 267
8.5 Hypothesis Testing for Single Population Mean 268
8.6 Hypothesis Testing for Difference Between Two Population Means 271
Self-Practice Problems 8A 274
Hints and Answers 275
8.7 Hypothesis Testing for Single Population Proportion 276
8.7.1 Hypothesis Testing for Difference Between Two Population Porportions 277
Self-Practice Problems 8B 281
Hints and Answers 281
8.8 Hypothesis Testing for Population Mean with Small Samples 283
8.8.1 Hypothesis Testing for Single Population Mean 283
Self-Practice Problems 8C 287
Hints and Answers 288
8.9 Hypothesis Testing Based on F-Distribution 289
8.9.1 Comparing Two Population Variances 290
Self-Practice Problems 8D 292
Hints and Answers 293
Formulae Used 294
Chapter Concepts Quiz 295
Review Self-Practice Problems 295
Hints and Answers 296
Glossary of Terms 299

CHAPTER 9 CORRELATION ANALYSIS **300–335**

9.1 Introduction 300
9.2 Significance of Measuring Correlation 301
9.3 Correlation and Causation 302
9.4 Types of Correlations 302
9.4.1 Positive and Negative Correlation 303
9.4.2 Linear and Non-Linear Correlation 303
9.4.3 Simple, Partial, and Multiple Correlation 303
9.5 Methods of Correlation Analysis 304
9.5.1 Scatter Diagram Method 304
9.5.2 Karl Pearson's Correlation Coefficient 307
9.5.3 Probable Error and Standard Error of Coefficient of Correlation 308
9.5.4 The Coefficient of Determination 311
Self-Practice Problems 9A 319
Hints and Answers 320
9.5.5 Spearman's Rank Correlation Coefficient 320
Self-Practice Problems 9B 330
Hints and Answers 331
Conceptual Questions 332
Formulae Used 332
Chapter Concepts Quiz 333
Review Self-Practice Problems 333
Hints and Answers 335

CHAPTER 10 REGRESSION ANALYSIS **336–365**

10.1 Introduction 336
10.2 Advantages of Regression Analysis 337
10.3 Parameters of Simple Linear Regression Model 338
10.3.1 Regression Coefficients 338
10.4 Methods to Determine Regression Coefficients 339
10.4.1 Least Squares Normal Equations 339
10.4.2 Deviations Method 342
Self-Practice Problems 10A 356
Hints and Answers 358
Conceptual Questions 361
Formulae Used 361
Chapter Concepts Quiz 362
Review Self-Practice Problems 362
Hints and Answers 363

Syllabus

Computer-oriented Statistical Methods in Business

BBA-204

UNIT-I

Measures of Central Tendency, Graphical Representation of Data, Dispersion and Skewness.

UNIT-II

Correlation and Regression Analysis, Partial Correlation.

UNIT-III

Theoretical Frequency Distribution – Binomial, Poisson and Normal Distribution.

UNIT-IV

Method of Least Square and Curve Fitting, Sampling of Data.

UNIT-V

Test of Significance: chi-Square and F-Test.

Preface

The primary objective in writing this book is to explain the concepts of business statistics lucidly along with solution procedures and analysis of results. Numerous solved business-oriented examples have been presented throughout the text. Unsolved *Self Practice Problems* with *Hints and Answers* and *Review Questions* have been added in each chapter to strengthen the conceptual as well as practical knowledge of the reader.

This book is designed to be self-contained and comprises 10 chapters. It is intended to serve as a core primary text for students of management and similar other undergraduate courses. It enables students to understand fundamental concepts of business statistics and apply formulae directly to business problems.

The presentation and sequence of chapters have made the text interesting and lucid. In writing this book, I have benefitted by referring many books and publications. I express my gratitude and acknowledgement to such authors, publishers and institutions.

I wish to acknowledge my sincere thanks to my well wishers, friends and students for their valuable suggestions and encouragement during the preparation of this book. I would like to thank the publisher – Pearson Education for cooperation and the manner in which this project was managed. Last but not the least, I thank my wife, son, daughters and daughter-in-law for the unflagging support they gave me while I worked on this book.

Suggestions and comments to improve the book in contents and style are always welcome and will be appreciated and acknowledged. The readers can directly in get in touch with me on jks_sharma@yahoo.com.

J. K. Sharma

About the Author

J. K. Sharma is a professor in Amity Business School, Amity University, Noida. He has also served as a professor at the Faculty of Management Studies, University of Delhi and has more than 30 years of teaching experience. He has taught subjects such as Operations Research, Business Statistics, Business Mathematics and Logistics Management. He was awarded the Madan Mohan Gold Medal for securing first position in M.Sc. (Mathematics) examination. He has been a visiting professor at Group ESSEC (A Graduate School of Management) in France during 1992-94. He has authored 18 books, which have been widely appreciated by the students of undergraduate and postgraduate classes of all the Indian universities/management institutes, and has also written more than 100 research papers/case studies. He is the member of Board of Studies/Academic Council of several schools of management and universities in the country. Professor Sharma is actively involved in research projects and in conducting management development programmes for both public and private sector companies.

Statistics: An Overview

LEARNING OBJECTIVES

After studying this chapter, you should be able to

- present a broad overview of statistics as a subject
- bring out applications of statistics and its usefulness in managerial decision making
- describe the data collection process
- understand basic concepts of questionnaire design and measurement scales

1.1 REASONS FOR LEARNING STATISTICS

H. G. Wells' statement that "statistical thinking will one day be as necessary as the ability to read and write" is valid in the context of today's competitive business environment where many organizations find themselves data-rich but information-poor. Thus, for decision makers, it is important to develop the ability to extract meaningful information from raw data to make better decisions. It is possible only through the careful analysis of data guided by statistical thinking.

The reason for analysis of **data** is an understanding of *variation and its causes* in any phenomenon. Since variation is present in all phenomena, therefore knowledge of it leads to better decisions about a phenomenon that produced the data. It is from this perspective that the learning of statistics enables the decision-maker to understand how to

- present and describe information (data) so as to improve decisions;
- draw conclusions about the large **population** based upon information obtained from samples;
- seek out relationship between pair of variables to improve processes;
- obtain reliable forecasts of statistical variables of interest;

Thus, a statistical study might be a simple exploration enabling us to gain insight into a virtually unknown situation or it might be a sophisticated analysis to produce numerical confirmation or a reflection of some widely held belief.

1.2 GROWTH AND DEVELOPMENT OF STATISTICS

The views commonly held about **statistics** are numerous, but often incomplete. It has different meanings to different people depending largely on its use. For example, (i) for a cricket fan, statistics refers to numerical information or data relating to the runs scored by a cricketer; (ii) for an environmentalist, statistics refers to information on the quantity of pollutants released into the atmosphere by all types of vehicles in different cities; (iii) for the census department, statistics consists of information about the birth rate and the sex ratio in different states; (iv) for a share broker, statistics is the information on changes in share prices over a period of time; and so on.

The average person perceives statistics as a column of figures, various types of graphs, tables and charts showing the increase and/or decrease in per capita income, wholesale price index, industrial production, exports, imports, crime rate and so on. The sources of such statistics for a common man are newspapers, magazines/journals, reports/bulletins, radio, and television. In all such cases, the relevant data are collected; numbers manipulated and information presented with the help of figures, charts, diagrams, and pictograms; probabilities are quoted, conclusions reached, and discussions held. Efforts to understand and find a solution (with certain degree of precision) to problems pertaining to social, political, economic, and cultural activities, seem to be unending. All such efforts are guided by the use of methods drawn from the field of statistics.

1.3 STATISTICS DEFINED

As Statistical Data The word statistics refers to a special discipline or a collection of procedures and principles useful as an aid in gathering and analysing numerical information for the purpose of drawing conclusions and making decisions. Since any numerical figure, or figures, cannot be called statistics owing to many considerations which decide its use, statistical data or mere data is a more appropriate expression to indicate numerical facts.

A few definitions which describe the characteristics of statistics are as follows:

- The classified facts respecting the condition of the people in a state . . . especially those facts which can be stated in numbers or in tables of numbers or in any tabular or classified arrangement. —Webster

This definition is quite narrow as it confines the scope of statistics only to such facts and figures which are related to the conditions of the people in a state.

- By statistics we mean **quantitative data** affected to a marked extent by multiplicity of causes. —Yule and Kendall
- By statistics we mean aggregates of facts affected to a marked extent by multiplicity of causes numerically expressed, enumerated, or estimated according to reasonable standards of accuracy, collected in a systematic manner for predetermined purpose and placed in relation to each other. —Horace Secrist

As Statistical Methods Methods adopted as aids in the collection and analysis of numerical information or statistical data for the purpose of drawing conclusions and making decisions are called *statistical methods*.

Statistical methods, also called statistical techniques, are sometimes loosely referred to cover 'statistics' as a subject in whole. There are two branches of statistics: (i) *Mathematical statistics* and (ii) *Applied statistics*. Mathematical statistics is a branch of mathematics and is theoretical. It deals with the basic theory about how a particular statistical method is developed. Applied statistics, on the other hand, uses statistical theory in formulating and solving problems in other subject areas such as economics, sociology, medicine, business/industry, education, and psychology.

The purpose of this book is limited to discussing the fundamental principles and methods of applied statistics in a simple and lucid manner so that readers with no previous formal knowledge of mathematics could acquire the ability to use statistical methods for making managerial decisions.

A few relevant definitions of statistical methods are given below:

- Statistics is the science which deals with the methods of collecting, classifying, presenting, comparing and interpreting numerical data collected to throw some light on any sphere of enquiry. —Seligman
- The science of statistics is the method of judging, collecting natural or social phenomenon from the results obtained from the analysis or enumeration or collection of estimates. —King

A. L. Bowley has given the following three definitions keeping in mind various aspects of statistics as a science:

- Statistics may be called the science of counting.
- Statistics may be called the science of average.
- Statistics is the science of the measurement of social organism regarded as a whole in all its manifestations.

These definitions confine the scope of statistical analysis only to 'counting, average, and application' in the field of sociology alone. Bowley realized this limitation and said that statistics cannot be confined to any science. Another definition of statistics given by Croxton and Cowden is as follows:

- Statistics may be defined as a science of collection, presentation, analysis and interpretation of numerical data. —Croxton and Cowden

This definition has pointed out four stages of statistical investigation, to which one more stage 'organization of data' rightly deserves to be added. Accordingly, *statistics may be defined as the science of collecting, organizing, presenting, analysing, and interpreting numerical data for making better decisions.*

1.4 TYPES OF STATISTICAL METHODS

Statistical methods, broadly, fall into the following two categories:

(i) Descriptive statistics
(ii) Inferential statistics

(i) **Descriptive statistics** includes statistical methods involving the collection, presentation, and characterization of a set of data in order to describe the various features of that set of data. In general, methods of descriptive statistics include graphic methods and numeric measures. Bar charts, line graphs, and pie charts comprise the graphic methods, whereas numeric measures include measures of central tendency, dispersion, skewness, and kurtosis.

(ii) **Inferential statistics** includes statistical methods which facilitate estimating the characteristics of a population or making decisions concerning a population on the basis of sample results. **Sample** and population are two relative terms. The larger group of units about which inferences are to be made is called the population or universe, while a sample is a fraction, subset, or portion of that universe.

The need for sampling arises because in many situations data are sought for a large group of elements such as individuals, companies, voters, households, products, customers, and so on to make inferences about the population that the sample represents. Thus, due to time, cost, and other considerations data are collected from only a small portion of the population called *sample*. The concepts derived from probability theory help to ascertain the likelihood that the analysis of the characteristics based on a sample do reflect the characteristics of the population from which the sample is drawn. This helps the decision-maker to draw conclusions about the characteristics of a large population under study.

1.5 IMPORTANCE AND SCOPE OF STATISTICS

The scope of application of statistics has assumed unprecedented dimensions these days. Statistical methods are applicable in diverse fields such as economics, trade, industry, commerce, agriculture, bio-sciences, physical sciences, education, astronomy, insurance, accountancy and auditing, sociology, psychology, meteorology, and so on. Bringing out its wide applications, Carrol D. Wright (1887), United States Commissioner of the Bureau of Labour, has explained the importance of statistics by saying:

> To a very striking degree our culture has become a statistical culture. Even a person who may never have heard of an index number is affected by those index numbers which describe the cost of living. It is impossible to understand Psychology, Sociology, Economics or a Physical Science without some general idea of the meaning of an average, of variation, of concomitance of sampling, of how to interpret charts and tables.

In the recent past, statistics has acquired its importance as a subject of study in the curricula of many other disciplines. According to the statistician Bowley, '*A knowledge of statistics is like a knowledge of foreign language or of algebra, it may prove of use at any time under any circumstances*'.

1.5.1 Statistics and the State

A state in the modern setup collects the largest amount of statistics for various purposes. It collects data relating to prices, production, consumption, income and expenditure, investments, and profits. Popular statistical methods such as time-series analysis, index numbers, forecasting, and demand analysis are extensively practised in formulating economic policies. Governments also collect data on population dynamics in order to initiate and implement various welfare policies and programmes.

In addition to statistical bureaus in all ministries and government departments in the Central and state governments, other important agencies in the field are the Central Statistical Organisation (CSO), National Sample Survey Organization (NSSO), and the Registrar General of India (RGI).

1.5.2 Statistics in Economics

Statistical methods are extensively used in all branches of economics. For example:

(i) Time-series analysis is used for studying the behaviour of prices, production and consumption of commodities, money in circulation, and bank deposits and clearings.

(ii) Index numbers are useful in economic planning as they indicate the changes over a specified period of time in (a) prices of commodities, (b) imports and exports, (c) industrial/agricultural production, (d) cost of living, and the like.

(iii) Demand analysis is used to study the relationship between the price of a commodity and its output (supply).

(iv) Forecasting techniques are used for curve fitting by the principle of least squares and exponential smoothing to predict inflation rate, unemployment rate, or manufacturing capacity utilization.

1.5.3 Statistics in Business Management

According to Wallis and Roberts, 'Statistics may be regarded as a body of methods for making wise decisions in the face of uncertainty.' Ya-Lin-Chou gave a modified definition over this, saying that 'Statistics is a method of decision-making in the face of uncertainty on the basis of numerical data and calculated risks.' These definitions reflect the applications of statistics in the development of general principles for dealing with uncertainty.

Statistical reports provide a summary of business activities which improves the capability of making more effective decisions regarding future activities. Discussed below are certain activities of a typical organization where statistics plays an important role in their efficient execution.

Marketing Before a product is launched, the market research team of an organization, through a pilot survey, makes use of various techniques of statistics to analyse data on population, purchasing power, habits of the consumers, competitors, pricing, and a hoard of other aspects. Such studies reveal the possible market potential for the product.

Analysis of sales volume in relation to the purchasing power and concentration of population is helpful in establishing sales territories, routing of salesman, and advertising strategies to improve sales.

Production Statistical methods are used to carry out R&D programmes for improvement in the quality of the existing products and setting quality control standards for new ones. Decisions about the quantity and time of either self-manufacturing or buying from outside are based on statistically analysed data.

Finance A statistical study through correlation analysis of profits and dividends helps to predict and decide probable dividends for future years. Statistics applied to analysis of data on assets and liabilities and income and expenditure helps to ascertain the financial results of various operations.

Financial forecasts, break-even analysis, investment decisions under uncertainty—all involve the application of relevant statistical methods for analysis.

Personnel In the process of manpower planning, a personnel department makes statistical studies of wage rates, incentive plans, cost of living, labour turnover rates, employment trends, accident rates, performance appraisal, and training and development programmes. Employer-employee relationships are studied by statistically analysing various factors—wages, grievances handling, welfare, delegation of authority, education and housing facilities, and training and development.

1.5.4 Statistics in Physical Sciences

Currently there is an increasing use of statistical methods in physical sciences such as astronomy, engineering, geology, meteorology, and certain branches of physics. Statistical methods such as sampling, estimation, and design of experiments are very effective in the analysis of quantitative expressions in all fields of most physical sciences.

1.5.5 Statistics in Social Sciences

The following definitions reflect the importance of statistics in social sciences.

- Statistics is the science of the measurement of social organism, regarded as a whole in all its manifestations. —Bowley
- The science of statistics is the method of judging collective, natural or social phenomenon from the results obtained from the analysis, enumeration or collection of estimates. —W. I. King

Some specific areas of applications of statistics in social sciences are as listed below:

(i) Regression and correlation analysis techniques are used to study and isolate all those factors associated with each social phenomenon which bring out the changes in data with respect to time, place, and object.

(ii) Sampling techniques and estimation theory are indispensable methods for conducting any social survey pertaining to any strata of society, and drawing valid inferences.

(iii) In sociology, statistical methods are used to study mortality (death) rates, fertility (birth rates) trends, population growth, and other aspects of vital statistics.

1.5.6 Statistics in Medical Sciences

The knowledge of statistical techniques in all natural sciences—zoology, botany, meteorology, and medicine—is of great importance. For example, for proper diagnosis of a disease, the doctor needs and relies heavily on factual data relating to pulse rate, body temperature, blood pressure, heart beats, and body weight.

An important application of statistics lies in using the *test of significance* for testing the efficacy of a particular drug or injection meant to cure a specific disease. Comparative studies for effectiveness of a particular drug/injection manufactured by different companies can also be made by using statistical techniques such as the t-test and F-test.

To study plant life, a botanist has to rely on data about the effect of temperature, type of environment, and rainfall, and so on.

1.5.7 Statistics and Computers

Computers and information technology, in general, have had a fundamental effect on most business and service organizations. Over the last decade or so, however, the advent of the personal computer (PC) has revolutionized both the areas to which statistical techniques are applied. PC facilities such as spreadsheets or common statistical packages have now made such analysis readily available to any business decision-maker. Computers help in processing and maintaining past records of operations involving payroll calculations, inventory management, railway/airline reservations, and the like. Use of computer softwares, however, presupposes that the user is able to interpret the computer outputs that are generated.

1.6 LIMITATIONS OF STATISTICS

Although statistics has its applications in almost all sciences—social, physical, and natural—it has its own limitations as well, which restrict its scope and utility.

1.6.1 Statistics Does Not Study Qualitative Phenomena

Since statistics deals with numerical data, it cannot be applied in studying those problems which can be stated and expressed quantitatively. For example, a statement like 'Export volume of India has increased considerably during the last few years' cannot be analysed statistically. Also, qualitative characteristics such as honesty, poverty, welfare, beauty, or health, cannot directly be measured quantitatively. However, these subjective concepts can be related in an indirect manner to numerical data after assigning particular scores or quantitative standards. For example, attributes of intelligence in a class of students can be studied on the basis of their Intelligence Quotients (IQ) which is considered as a quantitative measure of the intelligence.

1.6.2 Statistics Does Not Study Individuals

According to Horace Secrist '*By statistics we mean aggregate of facts affected to a marked extent by multiplicity of factors . . . and placed in relation to each other.*' This statement implies that a single or isolated figure cannot be considered as statistics, unless it is part of the aggregate of facts relating to any particular field of enquiry. For example, price of a single commodity or increase or decrease in the share price of a particular company does not constitute statistics. However, the aggregate of figures representing prices, production, sales volume, and profits over a period of time or for different places do constitute statistics.

1.6.3 Statistics Can Be Misused

Statistics are liable to be misused. For proper use of statistics one should have enough skill and experience to draw accurate and sensible conclusions. Further, valid results cannot be drawn from the use of statistics unless one has a proper understanding of the subject to which it is applied.

The greatest danger of statistics lies in its use by those who do not possess sufficient experience and ability to analyse and interpret statistical data and draw sensible conclusions. Bowley was right when he said that '*statistics only furnishes a tool though imperfect which is dangerous in the hands of those who do not know its use and deficiencies.*' For example, the conclusion that smoking causes lung cancer, since 90 per cent of people who smoke die before the age of 70 years, is statistically invalid because here nothing has been mentioned about the percentage of people who do not smoke and die before reaching the age of 70 years. According to W. I. King, '*statistics are like clay of which you can make a God or a Devil as you please.*' He also remarked, '*science of statistics is the useful servant but only of great value to those who understand its proper use.*'

Conceptual Questions

1. What is statistics? How do you think that the knowledge of statistics is essential in management decisions. Give examples.
2. (a) How far can statistics be applied for business decisions? Discuss briefly bringing out limitations, if any.
   (b) Define 'statistics' and give its main limitations.
3. (a) Explain how statistics plays an important role in management planning and decision-making?
   (b) Define statistics and statistical methods. Explain the uses of statistical methods in modern business.
4. Discuss briefly the applications of Business Statistics, pointing out their limitations, if any.
5. Describe the main areas of business and industry where statistics are extensively used.
6. With the help of few examples explain the role of statistics as a managerial tool.
7. 'Statistics are numerical statements of facts but all facts numerically stated are not statistics'. Comment upon the statement.
8. Bring out the applications of statistics in economics and business administration as a scientific tool. Also point out any two limitations of statistics.

1.7 NEED FOR DATA

Statistical data are the basic material needed to make an effective decision in a particular situation. The main reasons for collecting data are as listed below:

(i) To provide necessary inputs to a given phenomenon or situation under study.
(ii) To measure performance in an ongoing process such as production, service, and so on.

(iii) To enhance the quality of decision-making by enumerating alternative courses of action in a decision-making process, and selecting an appropriate one.
(iv) To satisfy the desire to understand an unknown phenomenon.
(v) To assist in guessing the causes and probable effects of certain characteristics in given situations.

For any statistical analysis to be useful, the collection and use of input data is extremely important. One can collect an enormous amount of data on a subject of interest in a compact and usuable form from the internet. However, the reliability of such data is always doubtful. Thus, before relying on any interpreted data, either from a computer, internet or other source, we should study answers to the following questions: (i) Have data come from an unbaised source, that is, source should not have an interest in supplying the data that lead to a misleading conclusion, (ii) Do data represent the entire population under study i.e. how many observations should represent the population, (iii) Do the data support other evidences already available. Is any evidence missing that may cause to arrive at a different conclusion? and (iv) Do data support the logical conclusions drawn. Have we made conclusions which are not supported by data.

In order to design an experiment or conduct a survey one must understand the different types of data and their measurement levels.

1.7.1 Types of Data

Statistical data are the outcome of a continuous process of measuring, counting, and/or observing. These may pertain to several aspects of a phenomenon (or a problem) which are measurable, quantifiable, countable, or classifiable. While conducting a survey or making a study, an investigator develops a method to ask several questions to deal with the variety of characteristics of the given population or universe. These characteristics which one intends to investigate and analyse are termed as *variables*. The data, which are the observed outcomes of these variables, may vary from response to response. Consumer behaviour (attitude), profit/loss to a company, job satisfaction, drinking and/or smoking habits, leadership ability, class affiliation or status are examples of a variable.

1.8 SOURCES OF DATA

The choice of a data collection method from a particular source depends on the facilities available, the extent of accuracy required in analyses, the expertise of the investigator, the time span of the study, and the amount of money and other resources required for data collection. When the data to be collected are very voluminous and require huge amounts of money, manpower, and time, reasonably accurate conclusions can be drawn by observing even a small part of the population provided the concept of sampling is used objectively.

Data sources are classified as (i) primary sources, and (ii) secondary sources.

1.8.1 Primary Data Sources

Individuals, focus groups, and/or panels of respondents specifically decided upon and set up by the investigator for data collection are examples of primary data sources. Any one or a combination of the following methods can be chosen to collect primary data:

(i) Direct personal observations
(ii) Direct or indirect oral interviews
(iii) Administrating questionnaires

The methods which may be used for primary data collection are briefly discussed below:

Observation In observational studies, the investigator does not ask questions to seek clarifications on certain issues. Instead, he records the behaviour, as it occurs, of an event in which he is interested. Sometimes mechanical devices are also used to record the desired data.

Studies based on observations are best suited for researches requiring non-self report descriptive data. That is, when respondents' behaviours are to be understood without asking them to part with the needed information. Diverse opinions in the diagnosis of a particular disease could be an example of an observational study.

Interviewing Interviews can be conducted either face-to-face or over telephone. Such interviews provide an opportunity to establish a rapport with the interviewer and help extract valuable information. Direct interviews are expensive and time-consuming if a big sample of respondents is to be personally interviewed. Interviewers' biases also come in the way. Such interviews should be conducted at the exploratory stages of research to handle concepts and situational factors.

Telephonic interviews help establish contact with interviewers spread over distantly separated geographic locations and obtain responses quickly. This method is effective only when the interviewer has specific questions to ask and the needs responses promptly. Since the interviewer in this case cannot observe the non-verbal responses at the other end, the respondent can unilaterally terminate the interview without warning or explanation.

Questionnaire It is a formalized set of questions for extracting information from the target respondents. The form of the questions should correspond to the form of the required information. The three general forms of questions are: *dichotomous* (yes/no response type), *multiple choice*, and *open-ended*. A questionnaire can be administered personally or mailed to the respondents. It is an efficient method of collecting primary data when the investigator knows what exactly is required and how to measure such variables of interest as:

- Behaviour—past, present, or intended.
- Demographic characteristics—age, sex, income, and occupation.
- Level of knowledge.
- Attitudes and opinions.

1.8.2 Secondary Data Sources

Secondary data refer to those data which have been collected earlier for some purpose other than the analysis currently being undertaken. Besides newspapers and business magazines, other sources of such data are as follows:

1. External secondary data sources

- Government publications, which include
  - (i) The National Accounts Statistics, published by the Central Statistical Organization (CSO). It contains estimates of national income for several years, growth rate, and rate on major economic activities such as agriculture, industry, trade, transport, and so on;
  - (ii) Wholesale Price Index, published by the office of the Economic Advisor, Ministry of Commerce and Industry;
  - (iii) Consumer Price Index;
  - (iv) Reserve Bank of India bulletins;
  - (v) Economic Survey.
- Non-Government publications include publications of various industrial and trade associations such as
  - (i) The Indian Cotton Mills Association
  - (ii) The various Chambers of Commerce

(iii) The Bombay Stock Exchange, which publishes a directory containing financial accounts, key profitability and other relevant data.

2. Internal secondary data sources The data generated within an organization in the process of routine business activities, are referred to as internal secondary data. Financial accounts, production, quality control, and sales records are examples of such data. However, data originating from one department of an organization may not be useful for another department in its original form. It is, therefore, desirable to condense such data into a form needed by the other.

Advantages and Disadvantages of Secondary Data

Secondary data have their own advantages and disadvantages. The advantages are that such data are easy to collect and involve relatively lesser time and cost. Deficiencies and gaps can be identified easily and steps can be taken promptly to overcome the same.

Their disadvantage is that the unit of measurement may not be the same as required by the users. For example, the size of a firm may be stated in terms of either number of employees, gross sales, gross profit, or total paid-up capital.

The scale of measurement may also be different from the one desired. For example, dividend declared by various companies may have breakup of 'less than 10 per cent'; '10–15 per cent'; '15–20 per cent,' and so on. For a study requiring to know the number of companies who may have declared dividend of '16 per cent and above', such secondary data are of no use.

Chapter Concepts Quiz

True or False

1. The scale of measurement of a variable is a nominal scale when data are labels to identify an attribute of the element.
2. The statistical method used to summarize data depends upon whether the data are qualitative or quantitative.
3. Statistical studies can be classified as either experimental or observational.
4. Learning statistics does not help to improve processes.
5. Statistics cannot be misused.
6. All facts numerically stated are not statistics.
7. Statistical thinking focuses on ways to understand, manage, and reduce variation.
8. An average value computed from the set of all observations in the population is called a statistic.
9. Inferential statistics help in generalizing the results of a sample to the entire population.
10. Descriptive statistical methods are used for presenting and characterizing data.
11. A statistic is a summary measure that describes the characteristic of a population.
12. A descriptive measure computed from a sample of the population is called a parameter.
13. Enumerative studies involve decision-making regarding a population and/or its characteristics.
14. Analytical studies involve taking some action on a process to improve performance in the future.
15. Data are needed to satisfy our curiosity.
16. A continuous variable can also be used for quantitative data when every value within some interval is a possible result.
17. A summary measure computed from sample data is called statistic.
18. The summary numbers for either a population or a sample are called descriptive statistics.

Concepts Quiz Answers

1. T	**2.** T	**3.** T	**4.** F	**5.** F	**6.** T	**7.** T	**8.** F
9. T	**10.** T	**11.** F	**12.** F	**13.** T	**14.** T	**15.** T	**16.** T
17. T	**18.** T						

Glossary of Terms

Data: A collection of observations of one or more variables of interest.
Population: A collection of all elements (units or variables) of interest.
Statistics: The art and science of collecting, analysing, presenting, and interpreting data.
Quantitative data: Numerical data measured on an interval or ratio scales to describe 'how much' or 'how many'.
Descriptive statistics: It consists of procedures used to summarize and describe the characteristics of a set of data.
Inferential statistics: It consists of procedures used to make inferences about population characteristics on the basis of sample results.
Sample: A subset (portion) of the population.

Data Classification, Tabulation and Presentation

LEARNING OBJECTIVES

After studying this chapter, you should be able to

- understand types of data and the basis of their classification
- use techniques of organizing data in tabular and graphical form in order to enhance data analysis and interpretation

2.1 INTRODUCTION

In Chapter 1, we learned how to collect data through primary and/or secondary sources. Whenever a set of data that we have collected contains a large number of observations, the best way to examine such data is to present it in some compact and orderly form. Such a need arises because data contained in a questionnaire are in a form which does not give any idea about the salient features of the problem under study. Such data are not directly suitable for *analysis* and *interpretation*. For this reason the data set is organized and summarized in such a way that patterns are revealed and are more easily interpreted. Such an arrangement of data is known as the *distribution* of the data. Distribution is important because it reveals the pattern of variation and helps in a better understanding of the phenomenon the data present.

2.2 CLASSIFICATION OF DATA

Classification of data is the process of arranging data in groups/classes on the basis of certain properties. The classification of statistical data serves the following purposes:

(i) It condenses the raw data into a form suitable for statistical analysis.
(ii) It removes complexities and highlights the features of the data.
(iii) It facilitates comparisons and drawing inferences from the data. For example, if university students in a particular course are divided according to sex, their results can be compared.

(iv) It provides information about the mutual relationships among elements of a data set. For example, based on literacy and criminal tendency of a group of people, it can be established whether literacy has any impact or not on criminal tendency.

(v) It helps in statistical analysis by separating elements of the data set into homogeneous groups and hence brings out the points of similarity and dissimilarity.

2.2.1 Requisites of Ideal Classification

The classification of data is decided after taking into consideration the nature, scope, and purpose of the investigation. However, an ideal classification should have following characteristics:

It should be unambiguous It is necessary that the various classes should be so defined that there is no room for confusion. There must be only one class for each element of the data set. For example, if the population of the country is divided into two classes, say literates and illiterates, then an exhaustive definition of the terms used would be essential.

Classes should be exhaustive and mutually exclusive Each element of the data set must belong to a class. For this, an extra class can be created with the title 'others' so as to accommodate all the remaining elements of the data set.

Each class should be mutually exclusive so that each element must belong to only one class. For example, classification of students according to the age: below 25 years and more than 20 years, is not correct because students of age 20 to 25 may belong to both the classes.

It should be stable The classification of a data set into various classes must be done in such a manner that if each time an investigation is conducted, it remains unchanged and hence the results of one investigation may be compared with that of another. For example, classification of the country's population by a census survey based on occupation suffers from this defect because various occupations are defined in different ways in successive censuses and, as such, these figures are not strictly comparable.

It should be flexible A classification should be flexible so that suitable adjustments can be made in new situations and circumstances. However, flexibility does not mean instability. The data should be divided into few major classes which must be further subdivided. Ordinarily there would not be many changes in the major classes. Only small sub-classes may need a change and the classification can thus retain the merit of stability and yet have flexibility.

2.2.2 Basis of Classification

Statistical data are classified after taking into account the nature, scope, and purpose of an investigation. Generally, data are classified on the basis of the following four bases:

Geographical Classification In geographical classification, data are classified on the basis of geographical or locational differences such as—cities, districts, or villages between various elements of the data set. The following is an example of a geographical distribution:

City	:	Mumbai	Kolkata	Delhi	Chennai
Population density (per square km)	:	654	685	423	205

Such a classification is also known as *spatial classification*. Geographical classifications are generally listed in alphabetical order. Elements in the data set are also listed by the frequency size to emphasize the importance of various geographical regions as in ranking the metropolitan cities by population density. The first approach is followed in case of reference tables while the second approach is followed in the case of summary tables.

Chronological Classification When data are classified on the basis of time, the classification is known as chronological classification. Such classifications are also called *time series* because data are usually listed in chronological order starting with the earliest period. The following example would give an idea of chronological classification:

Year	:	1941	1951	1961	1971	1981	1991	2001
Population (crore)	:	31.9	36.9	43.9	54.7	75.6	85.9	98.6

Qualitative Classification In qualitative classification, data are classified on the basis of descriptive characteristics or on the basis of attributes like sex, literacy, region, caste, or education, which cannot be quantified. This is done in two ways:

(i) *Simple classification:* In this type of classification, each class is subdivided into two sub-classes and only one attribute is studied such as: male and female; blind and not blind, educated and uneducated, and so on.

(ii) *Manifold classification:* In this type of classification, a class is subdivided into more than two sub-classes which may be sub-divided further. An example of this form of classification is shown in the box.

Quantitative Classification In this classification, data are classified on the basis of some characteristics which can be measured such as height, weight, income, expenditure, production, or sales.

Quantitative variables can be divided into the following two types. The term variable refers to any quantity or attribute whose value varies from one investigation to another.

(i) *Continuous variable* is the one that can take any value within the range of numbers. Thus the height or weight of individuals can be of any value within the limits. In such a case, data are obtained by measurement.

(ii) *Discrete* (also called *discontinuous*) *variable* is the one whose values change by steps or jumps and can not assume a fractional value. The number of children in a family, number of workers (or employees), number of students in a class, are few examples of a discrete variable. In such a case data are obtained by counting.

The following are examples of continuous and discrete variables in a data set (Table 2.1).

Table 2.1

Discrete Series		*Continuous Series*	
Number of Children	*Number of Families*	*Weight (kg)*	*Number of Persons*
0	10	100 to 110	10
1	30	110 to 120	20
2	60	120 to 130	25
3	90	130 to 140	35
4	110	140 to 150	50
5	20		
	320		140

2.3 ORGANIZING DATA USING DATA ARRAY

The best way to examine a large set of numerical data is first to organize and present it in an appropriate tabular and graphical format.

Table 2.2 presents the total number of overtime hours worked for 30 consecutive weeks by machinists in a machine shop. The data displayed here are in *raw form*, that is, the numerical observations are not arranged in any particular order or sequence.

Table 2.2 Raw Data Pertaining to Total Time Hours Worked by Machinists

94	89	88	89	90	94	92	88	87	85
88	93	94	93	94	93	92	88	94	90
93	84	93	84	91	93	85	91	89	95

These raw data are not amenable even to a simple reading and do not highlight any characteristic/trend, such as the highest, the lowest, and the average weekly hours. Even a careful look at these data do not easily reveal any significant trend regarding the nature and pattern of variations therein. As such no meaningful inference can be drawn, unless these data are reorganized to make them more useful. For example, if we are to ascertain a value around which most of the overtime hours cluster, such a value is difficult to obtain from the raw data.

Moreover, as the number of observations gets large, it becomes more and more difficult to focus on the specific features in a set of data. Thus we need to organize the observation so that we can better understand the information that the data are revealing.

The raw data can be reorganized in a data array and frequency distribution. Such an arrangement enables us to see quickly some of the characteristics of the data we have collected.

When a raw data set is arranged in rank order, from the smallest to the largest observation or vice versa, the ordered sequence obtained is called an *ordered array*. Table 2.3 reorganizes data given in Table 2.2 in the ascending order.

Table 2.3 Ordered Array of Total Overtime Hours Worked by Machinists

84	84	85	85	87	88	88	88
88	89	89	89	90	90	91	91
92	92	93	93	93	93	93	93
94	94	94	94	94	95		

It may be observed that an ordered array does not summarize the data in any way as the number of observations in the array remains the same. However, a few advantages of ordered arrays are as under:

Advantages and Disadvantages of Ordered Array

Advantages The following are a few advantages of an ordered array:

(i) It provides a quick look at the highest and lowest observations in the data within which individual values vary.

(ii) It helps in dividing the data into various sections or parts.

(iii) It enables us to know the degree of concentration around a particular observation.

(iv) It helps to identify whether any values appear more than once in the array.

Disadvantages In spite of various advantages of converting a set of raw data into an ordered array, an array is a cumbersome form of presentation which is tiresome to construct. It neither summarizes nor organizes the data to present them in a more meaningful way. It also fails to highlight the salient characteristics of the data which may be crucial in terms of their relevance to decision-making.

The above task cannot be accomplished unless the observations are appropriately condensed. The best way to do so is to display them into a convenient number of groupings with the number of observations falling in different groups indicated against each. Such tabular summary presentation showing the number (frequency) of observations in each of several non-overlapping classes or groups is known as *frequency distribution* (also referred to as *grouped data*).

2.3.1 Frequency Distribution

A **frequency distribution** divides observations in the data set into conveniently established, numerically ordered classes (groups or categories). The number of observations in each class is referred to as *frequency* denoted as f.

Few examples of instances where frequency distributions would be useful are when (i) a marketing manager wants to know how many units (and what proportions or percentage) of each product sells in a particular region during a given period, (ii) a tax consultant desires to keep count of the number of times different size of firs are audited, and (iii) a financial analyst wants to keep track of the number of times the shares of manufacturing and service companies to be or gain order a period of time.

Advantages and Disadvantages of Frequency Distribution

Advantages The following are a few advantages of grouping and summarizing raw data in this compact form:

(i) The data are expressed in a more compact form. One can get a deeper insight into the salient characteristics of the data at the very first glance.
(ii) One can quickly note the pattern of distribution of observations falling in various classes.
(iii) It permits the use of more complex statistical techniques which help reveal certain other obscure and hidden characteristics of the data.

Disadvantages A frequency distribution suffers from some disadvantages as stated below:

(i) In the process of grouping, individual observations lose their identity. It becomes difficult to notice how the observations contained in each class are distributed. This applies more to a frequency distribution which uses the tally method in its construction.
(ii) A serious limitation inherent in this kind of grouping is that there will be too much clustering of observations in various classes in case the number of classes is too small. This will cause some of the essential information to remain unexposed.

Hence, it is important that summarizing data should not be at the cost of losing essential details. The purpose should be to seek an appropriate compromise between having too much of details or too little. To be able to achieve this compromise, certain criteria are discussed for constructing a frequency distribution.

The frequency distribution of the number of hours of overtime given in Table 2.2 is shown in Table 2.4.

Table 2.4 Array and Tallies

Number of Overtime Hours	*Tally*	*Number of Weeks (Frequency)*
84	||	2
85	||	2
86	—	0
87	|	1
88	||||	4
89	|||	3
90	||	2
91	||	2
92	||	2
93	~~||||~~ |	6
94	~~||||~~	5
95	|	1
		30

Constructing a Frequency Distribution As the number of observations obtained gets larger, the method discussed above to condense the data becomes quite difficult and time-consuming. Thus to further condense the data into frequency distribution tables, the following steps should be taken:

(i) Select an appropriate number of non-overlapping class intervals
(ii) Determine the width of the class intervals
(iii) Determine class limits (or boundaries) for each class interval to avoid overlapping.

1. *Decide the number of class intervals* The decision on the number of class groupings depends largely on the judgment of the individual investigator and/or the range that will be used to group the data, although there are certain guidelines that can be used. As a general rule, a frequency distribution should have at least five class intervals (groups), but not more than fifteen. The following two rules are often used to decide approximate number of classes in a frequency distribution:

(i) If k represents the number of classes and N the total number of observations, then the value of k will be the smallest exponent of the number 2, so that $2^k \geq N$.

In Table 2.3 we have N = 30 observations. If we apply this rule, then we shall have

$$2^3 = 8\ (< 30); \qquad 2^4 = 16\ (< 30); \qquad 2^5 = 32\ (> 30)$$

Thus we may choose $k = 5$ as the number of classes.

(ii) According to Sturge's rule, the number of classes can be determined by the formula

$$k = 1 + 3.222 \log_e N$$

where k is the number of classes and $\log_e N$ is the logarithm of the total number of observations.

Applying this rule to the data given in Table 2.3, we get

$$k = 1 + 3.222 \log 30 = 1 + 3.222\,(1.4771) = 5.759 \cong 5$$

2. *Determine the width of class intervals* When constructing the frequency distribution it is desirable that the width of each class interval should be equal in size. The size (or width) of each class interval can be determined by first taking the difference between the largest and smallest numerical values in the data set and then dividing it by the number of class intervals desired.

$$\text{Width of class interval } (h) = \frac{\text{Largest numerical value} - \text{Smallest numerical value}}{\text{Number of classes desired}}$$

The value obtained from this formula can be rounded off to a more convenient value based on the investigator's preference.

From the ordered array in Table 2.3, the range is: 95 – 84 = 11 hours. Using the above formula with 5 classes desired, the width of the class intervals is approximated as:

$$\text{Width of class interval} = \frac{11}{5} = 2.2 \text{ hours}$$

For convenience, the selected width (or interval) of each class is rounded to 3 hours.

3. *Determine Class Limits (Boundaries)* The limits of each class interval should be clearly defined so that each observation (element) of the data set belongs to one and only one class.

Each class has two limits—*a lower limit* and an *upper limit*. The usual practice is to let the lower limit of the first class be a convenient number slightly below or equal to the lowest value in the data set. In Table 2.3, we may take the lower class limit of the first class as 82 and the upper class limit as 85. Thus the class would be written as 82–85. This class interval includes all overtime hours ranging from 82 upto but not including 85 hours. The various other classes can be written as:

Overtime Hours (Class intervals)	*Tallies*	*Frequency*
82 but less than 85	||	2
85 but less than 88	|||	3
88 but less than 91	~~||||~~ ||||	9
91 but less than 94	~~||||~~ ~~||||~~	10
94 but less than 97	~~||||~~ |	6
		30

Mid-point of Class Intervals The main advantage of using the above summary table is that the major data characteristics become clear to the decision-maker. However, it is difficult to know how the individual values are distributed within a particular class interval without access to the original data. The **class mid-point** is the point halfway between the boundaries (both upper and lower class limits) of each class and is representative of all the observations contained in that class.

Arriving at the correct class mid-points is important, for these are used as representative of all the observations contained in their respective class while computing many important statistical measures. A mid-point is obtained by dividing the sum of the upper and lower class limits by two. Problems in computing mid-points arise when the class limits are ambiguous and not clearly defined.

The width of the class interval should, as far as possible, be equal for all the classes. If this is not possible to maintain, the interpretation of the distribution becomes difficult. For example, it will be difficult to say whether the difference between the frequencies of the two classes is due to the difference in the concentration of observations in the two classes or due to the width of the class intervals being different.

The width of the class intervals should preferably be not only the same throughout, but should also be a convenient number such as 5, 10, or 15. A width given by integers 7, 13, or 19 should be avoided.

2.3.2 Methods of Data Classification

There are two ways in which observations in the data set are classified on the basis of class intervals, namely

(i) Exclusive method, and
(ii) Inclusive method

Exclusive Method When the data are classified in such a way that the upper limit of a class interval is the lower limit of the succeeding class interval (i.e. no data point falls into more than one class interval), then it is said to be the exclusive method of classifying data. This method is illustrated in Table 2.5.

Table 2.5 Exclusive Method of Data Classification

Dividends Declared in per cent (Class Intervals)	*Number of Companies (Frequencies)*
0–10	5
10–20	7
20–30	15
30–40	10

Such classification ensures continuity of data because the upper limit of one class is the lower limit of succeeding class. As shown in Table 2.5, 5 companies declared dividends ranging from 0 to 10 per cent, this means a company which declared exactly 10 per cent dividend would not be included in the class 0–10 but would be included in the next class 10–20. Since this point is not always clear, therefore to avoid confusion data are displayed in a slightly different manner, as given in Table 2.6.

Table 2.6

Dividends Declared in per cent (Class Intervals)	*Number of Companies (Frequencies)*
0 but less than 10	5
10 but less than 20	7
20 but less than 30	15
30 but less than 40	10

Inclusive Method When the data are classified in such a way that both lower and upper limits of a class interval are included in the interval itself, then it is said to be the inclusive method of classifying data. This method is shown in Table 2.7.

Table 2.7 Inclusive Method of Data Classification

Number of Accidents (Class Intervals)	*Number of Weeks (Frequencies)*
0–4	5
5–9	22
10–14	13
15–19	8
20–24	2

Remarks: 1. An exclusive method should be used to classify a set of data involving continuous variables and an inclusive method should be used to classify a set of data involving discrete variables.

2. If a continuous variable is classified according to the inclusive method, then certain adjustment in the class interval is needed to obtain continuity as shown in Table 2.8.

Table 2.8

Class Intervals	*Frequency*
30 – 44	28
45 – 59	32
60 – 74	45
75 – 89	50
90 – 104	35

To ensure continuity, first calculate correction factor as:

$$x = \frac{\text{Upper limit of a class} - \text{Lower limit of the next higher class}}{2}$$

and then subtract it from the lower limits of all the classes and add it to the upper limits of all the classes.

From Table 2.8, we have $x = (45 - 44) \div 2 = 0.5$. Subtract 0.5 from the lower limits of all the classes and add 0.5 to the upper limits. The adjusted classes would then be as shown in Table 2.9.

Table 2.9

Class Intervals	*Frequency*
29.5 – 44.5	28
44.5 – 59.5	32
59.5 – 74.5	45
74.5 – 89.5	50
89.5 – 104.5	35

3. Class intervals should be of equal size to make meaningful comparison between classes. In a few cases, extreme values in the data set may require the inclusion of *open-ended classes* and this distribution is known as an *open-ended distribution*. Such open-ended classes do not pose any problem in data analysis as long as only a few frequencies (or values) lie in these classes. However, an open-ended distribution is not fit for further mathematical calculations because *mid-value* which is used to represent the class, cannot be determined for an open-ended class. An example of an open-ended distribution is given in Table 2.10.

Table 2.10

Age (Years)	*Population (Millions)*
Under 5	17.8
5–17	44.7
18–24	29.9
25–44	69.6
45–64	44.6
65 and above	27.4
	234.0

Table 2.11 provides a tentative guide to determine an adequate number of classes.

Table 2.11 Guide to Determine the Number of Classes to Use

Number of Observations, N	*Suggested Number of Classes*
20	5
50	7
100	8
200	9
500	10
1000	11

Example 2.1: The following set of numbers represents mutual fund prices reported at the end of a week for selected 40 nationally sold funds.

10	17	15	22	11	16	19	24	29	18
25	26	32	14	17	20	23	27	30	12
15	18	24	36	18	15	21	28	33	38
34	13	10	16	20	22	29	29	23	31

Arrange these prices into a frequency distribution having a suitable number of classes.

Solution: Since the number of observations are 40, it seems reasonable to choose 6 ($2^6 > 40$) class intervals to summarize values in the data set. Again, since the smallest value is 10 and the largest is 38, therefore the class interval is given by

$$h = \frac{\text{Range}}{\text{Number of classes}} = \frac{38-10}{6} = \frac{28}{6} = 4.66 \simeq 5$$

Now performing the actual tally and counting the number of values in each class, we get the frequency distribution by exclusive method as shown in Table 2.12:

Table 2.12 Frequency Distribution

Class Interval (Mutual Fund Prices, Rs.)	*Tally*	*Frequency (Number of Mutual Funds)*
10–15	~~IIII~~ I	6
15–20	~~IIII~~ ~~IIII~~ I	11
20–25	~~IIII~~ IIII	9
25–30	~~IIII~~ II	7
30–35	~~IIII~~	5
35–40	II	2
		40

Example 2.2: The take-home salary (in Rs.) of 40 unskilled workers from a company for a particular month was.

2482	2392	2499	2412	2440	2444
2446	2540	2394	2365	2412	2458
2482	2394	2450	2444	2440	2494
2460	2425	2500	2390	2414	2365
2390	2460	2422	2500	2470	2428

Construct a frequency distribution having a suitable number of classes.

Solution: Since the number of observations are 30, we choose $5(2^5 > 30)$ class intervals to summarize values in the data set. In the data set the smallest value is 2365 and the largest is 2500, so the width of each class interval will be

$$h = \frac{\text{Range}}{\text{Number of classes}} = \frac{2540 - 2365}{5} = \frac{175}{5} = 35$$

Sorting the data values into classes and counting the number of values in each class, we get the frequency distribution by exclusive method as shown in Table 2.13.

Table 2.13 Frequency Distribution

Class Interval (Salary, Rs.)	*Tally*	*Frequency (Number of Workers)*
2365–2400	卌 |	6
2400–2435	卌 ||	7
2435–2470	卌 ||||	10
2470–2505	卌 |	6
2505–2540	|	1
		30

Example 2.3: A computer company received a rush order for as many home computers as could be shipped during a six-week period. Company records provide the following daily shipments:

22	65	65	67	55	50	65
77	73	30	62	54	48	65
79	60	63	45	51	68	79
83	33	41	49	28	55	61
65	75	55	75	39	87	45
50	66	65	59	25	35	53

Group these daily shipments figures into a frequency distribution having the suitable number of classes.

Solution: Since the number of observations are 42, it seems reasonable to choose 6 $(2^6 > 42)$ classes. Again, since the smallest value is 22 and the largest is 87, therefore the class interval is given by

$$h = \frac{\text{Range}}{\text{Number of classes}} = \frac{87 - 22}{6} = \frac{65}{6} = 10.833 \text{ or } 11$$

Now performing the actual tally and counting the number of values in each class, we get the following frequency distribution by inclusive method as shown in Table 2.14.

Table 2.14 Frequency Distribution

Class Interval (Number of Computers)	*Tally*	*Frequency (Number of Days)*
22 – 32	||||	4
33 – 43	||||	4
44 – 54	卌 ||||	9
55 – 65	卌 卌 ||||	14
66 – 76	卌 |	6
77 – 87	卌	5
		42

Example 2.4: Following is the increase of D.A. in the salaries of employees of a firm at the following rates.

Rs. 250 for the salary range up to Rs. 4749
Rs. 260 for the salary range from Rs. 4750
Rs. 270 for the salary range from Rs. 4950
Rs. 280 for the salary range from Rs. 5150
Rs. 290 for the salary range from Rs. 5350

No increase of D.A for salary of Rs. 5500 or more. What will be the additional amount required to be paid by the firm in a year which has 32 employees with the following salaries (in Rs.)?

5422	4714	5182	5342	4835	4719	5234	5035
5085	5482	4673	5335	4888	4769	5092	4735
5542	5058	4730	4930	4978	4822	4686	4730
5429	5545	5345	5250	5375	5542	5585	4749

Solution: Performing the actual tally and counting the number of employees in each salary range (or class), we get the following frequency distribution as shown in Table 2.15.

Table 2.15 Frequency Distribution

Class Interval (Pay Range)	*Tally*	*Frequency, f (Number of Employees)*	*Rate of D.A. (Rs. x)*	*Total Amount Paid (Rs. f x)*
upto 4749	~~||||~~ |||	8	250	2000
4750 – 4949	~~||||~~	5	260	1300
4950 – 5149	~~||||~~	5	270	1350
5150 – 5349	~~||||~~ |	6	280	1680
5350 – 5549	~~||||~~ |||	8	290	2320
32		8650		

Hence additional amount required by the firm for payment of D.A. is Rs. 8650.

Example 2.5: Following are the number of items of similar type produced in a factory during the last 50 days.

21	22	17	23	27	15	16	22	15	23
24	25	36	19	14	21	24	25	14	18
20	31	22	19	18	20	21	20	36	18
21	20	31	22	19	18	20	20	24	35
25	26	19	32	22	26	25	26	27	22

Arrange these observations into a frequency distribution with both inclusive and exclusive class intervals choosing a suitable number of classes.

Solution: Since the number of observations are 50, it seems reasonable to choose 6 ($2^6 > 50$) or less classes. Since smallest value is 14, and the largest is 36 therefore the class interval is given by

$$h = \frac{\text{Range}}{\text{Number of classes}} = \frac{36 - 14}{6} = \frac{22}{6} = 3.66 \text{ or } 4$$

Performing the actual tally and counting the number of observations is each class, we get the following frequency distribution with inclusive class intervals as shown in Table 2.16.

Table 2.16 Frequency Distribution with Inclusive Class Intervals

Class Intervals	*Tally*	*Frequency (Number of Items Produced)*
14 – 17	𝍸 |	6
18 – 21	𝍸 𝍸 𝍸 |||	18
22 – 25	𝍸 𝍸 𝍸	15
26 – 29	𝍸	5
30 – 33	|||	3
34 – 33	|||	3
		50

Converting the class intervals shown in Table 2.16 into exclusive class intervals is shown in Table 2.17.

Table 2.17 Frequency Distribution with Exclusive Class Intervals

Class Intervals	*Mid-Value of Class Intervals*	*Frequency (Number of Items Produced)*
13.5 – 17.5	15.5	6
17.5 – 21.5	19.5	18
21.5 – 25.5	23.5	15
25.5 – 29.5	27.5	5
29.5 – 33.5	31.5	3
33.5 – 37.5	34.5	3

2.3.3 Bivariate Frequency Distribution

The frequency distributions discussed so far involved only one variable and therefore called *univariate frequency distributions*. In case the data involve two variables (such as profit and expenditure on advertisements of a group of companies, income and expenditure of a group of individuals, supply and demand of a commodity, etc.), then frequency distribution so obtained as a result of cross classification is called *bivariate frequency distribution*. It can be summarized in the form of a *two-way (bivariate) frequency table* and the values of each variable are grouped into various classes (not necessarily same for each variable) in the same way as for univariate distributions.

If the data corresponding to one variable, say x, is grouped into m classes and the data corresponding to another variable, say y, is grouped into n classes, then bivariate frequency table will have $m \times n$ cells.

Frequency distribution of variable x for a given value of y is obtained by the values of x and vice versa. Such frequencies in each cell are called *conditional frequencies*. The frequencies of the values of variables x and y together with their frequency totals are called the *marginal frequencies*.

Example 2.6: The following figures indicate income (x) and percentage expenditure on food (y) of 25 families. Construct a bivariate frequency table classifying x into intervals 200 – 300, 300 – 400, . . . and y into 10 – 15, 15 – 20, . . .

Write the marginal distribution of x and y and the conditional distribution of x when y lies between 15 and 20.

x	y	x	y	x	y	x	y	x	y
550	12	225	25	680	13	202	29	689	11
623	14	310	26	300	25	255	27	523	12
310	18	640	20	425	16	492	18	317	18
420	16	512	18	555	15	587	21	384	17
600	15	690	12	325	23	643	19	400	19

Solution: The two-way frequency table showing income (in Rs.) and percentage expenditure on food is shown in Table 2.18.

Table 2.18

Expenditure (y) (Percentage)	*Income (x)*					*Marginal Frequencies, f_y*
	200–300	*300–400*	*400–500*	*500–600*	*600–700*	
10 – 15				|| (2)	|||| (4)	6
15 – 20		||| (3)	|||| (4)	|| (2)	|| (2)	11
20 – 25		| (1)		| (1)	| (1)	3
25 – 30	||| (3)	|| (2)				5
Marginal Frequencies, f_x	3	6	4	5	7	25

The conditional distribution of x when y lies between 15 and 20 per cent is as follows:

Income (x) :	200–300	300–400	400–500	500–600	600–700
15%–20% :	0	3	4	2	2

Example 2.7: The following data give the points scored in a tennis match by two players X and Y at the end of twenty games:

(10, 12) (7, 11) (7, 9) (15, 19) (17, 21) (12, 8) (16, 10) (14, 14) (22, 18) (16, 7)
(15, 16) (22, 20) (19, 15) (7, 18) (11, 11) (12, 18) (10, 10) (5, 13) (11, 7) (10, 10)

Taking class intervals as: 5–9, 10–14, 15–19 . . ., for both X and Y, construct

(i) Bivariate frequency table.
(ii) Conditional frequency distribution for Y given X > 15.

Solution: (i) The two-way frequency distribution is shown in Table 2.19.

Table 2.19 Bivariate Frequency Table

Player Y	*Player X*				*Marginal Frequencies, f_y*
	5–9	*10–14*	*15–19*	*20–24*	
5– 9	| (1)	|| (2)	| (1)	—	4
10–14	|| (2)	~~||||~~ (5)	| (1)	—	8
15–19	| (1)	| (1)	||| (3)	| (1)	6
20–24	—	—	| (1)	| (1)	2
Marginal Frequencies, f_x	4	8	6	2	20

(ii) Conditional frequency distribution for Y given X > 15.

Player Y	*Player X*	
	15–19	*20–24*
5–9	1	—
10–14	1	—
15–19	3	1
20–24	1	1
	6	2

2.3.4 Types of Frequency Distributions

Cumulative Frequency Distribution Sometimes it is preferable to present data in a **cumulative frequency (cf) distribution** or simply a distribution which shows the cumulative number of observations below the upper boundary (limit) of each class in the given frequency distribution. A cumulative frequency distribution is of two types: (i) *more than* type and (ii) *less than* type.

In a *less than* cumulative frequency distribution, the frequencies of each class interval are added successively from top to bottom and represent the cumulative number of observations less than or equal to the class frequency to which it relates. But in the *more than* cumulative frequency distribution, the frequencies of each class interval are added successively from bottom to top and represent the cumulative number of observations greater than or equal to the class frequency to which it relates.

The frequency distribution given in Table 2.20 illustrates the concept of cumulative frequency distribution.

Table 2.20 Cumulative Frequency Distribution

Number of Accidents	*Number of Weeks (Frequency)*	*Cumulative Frequency (less than)*	*Cumulative Frequency (more than)*
0– 4	5	5	45 + 5 = 50
5– 9	22	5 + 22 = 27	23 + 22 = 45
10–14	13	27 + 13 = 40	10 + 13 = 23
15–19	8	40 + 8 = 48	2 + 8 = 10
20–24	2	48 + 2 = 50	2

From Table 2.20 it may be noted that cumulative frequencies are corresponding to the lower limit and upper limit of class intervals. The 'less than' cumulative frequencies are corresponding to the upper limit of class intervals and 'more than' cumulative frequencies are corresponding to the lower limit of class intervals shown in Table 2.21(a) and (b).

Table 2.21(a)

Upper Limits	*Cumulative Frequency (less than)*
less than 4	5
less than 9	27
less than 14	40
less than 19	48
less than 24	50

Table 2.21(b)

Lower Limits	*Cumulative Frequency (more than)*
0 and more	50
5 and more	45
10 and more	23
15 and more	10
20 and more	2

Relative Frequency Distribution To enrich data analysis it is sometimes important to show what percentage of observations fall within each class of a distribution instead of showing the actual class frequencies. To convert a frequency distribution into a corresponding **relative frequency distribution**, we divide each class frequency by the total number of observations in the entire distribution. Each relative frequency is thus a proportion as shown in Table 2.22.

Table 2.22 Relative and Percentage Frequency Distributions

Number of Accidents	*Number of Weeks (Frequency)*	*Relative Frequency*	*Percentage Frequency*
0–4	5	$\frac{5}{50} = 0.10$	$\frac{5}{50} \times 100 = 10$
5–9	22	$\frac{22}{50} = 0.44$	$\frac{22}{50} \times 100 = 44$
10–14	13	$\frac{13}{50} = 0.26$	$\frac{13}{50} \times 100 = 26$
15–19	8	$\frac{8}{50} = 0.16$	$\frac{8}{50} \times 100 = 16$
20–24	2	$\frac{2}{50} = 0.04$	$\frac{2}{50} \times 100 = 4$
	50	1.00	100

Percentage Frequency Distribution A **percentage frequency distribution** is one in which the number of observations for each class interval is converted into a percentage frequency by dividing it by the total number of observations in the entire distribution. The quotient so obtained is then multiplied by 100, as shown in Table 2.22.

Example 2.8: Following are the number of two wheelers sold by a dealer during eight weeks of six working days each.

13	19	22	14	13	16	19	21
23	11	27	25	17	17	13	20
23	17	26	20	24	15	20	21
23	17	29	17	19	14	20	20
10	22	18	25	16	23	19	20
21	17	18	24	21	20	19	26

(a) Group these figures into a table having the classes 10–12, 13–15, 16–18, . . ., and 28–30.

(b) Convert the distribution of part (i) into a corresponding percentage frequency distribution and also a percentage cumulative frequency distribution.

Solution: (a) Frequency distribution of the given data is shown in Table 2.23.

Table 2.23 Frequency Distribution

Number of Automobiles Sold (Class Intervals)	*Tally*	*Number of Days (Frequency)*
10 – 12	||	2
13 – 15	~~||||~~ |	6
16 – 18	~~||||~~ ~~||||~~	10
19 – 21	~~||||~~ ~~||||~~ ~~||||~~ |	16
22 – 24	~~||||~~ |||	8
25 – 27	~~||||~~	5
28 – 30	|	1
		48

(b) Percentage and More Than Cumulative Percentage Distribution (Table 2.24).

Table 2.24

Number of Automobiles Sold (Class Intervals)	*Number of Days (Frequency)*	*Cumulative Frequency*	*Percentage Frequency*	*Percentage Cumulative Frequency*
10 – 12	2	2	4.17	4.17
13 – 15	6	8	12.50	16.67
16 – 18	10	18	20.83	37.50
19 – 21	16	34	33.34	70.84
22 – 24	8	42	16.67	87.51
25 – 27	5	47	10.41	97.92
28 – 30	1	48	2.08	100.00
	48		100.00	

Conceptual Questions 2A

1. Explain the characteristics of a frequency distribution.
2. Illustrate two methods of classifying data in class-intervals.
3. What are the advantages of using a frequency distribution to describe a body of raw data? What are the disadvantages?
4. When constructing a grouped frequency distribution, should equal intervals always be used? Under what circumstances should unequal intervals be used instead?
5. What are the advantages and disadvantages of using open-end intervals when constructing a group frequency distribution?
6. When constructing a group frequency distribution, is it necessary that the resulting distribution be symmetric? Explain.
7. Why is it necessary to summarize data? Explain the approaches available to summarize data distributions.
8. What are the objections to unequal class and open class intervals? State the conditions under which the use of unequal class intervals and open class intervals are desirable and necessary.
9. (a) What do you understand by cumulative frequency distribution?

   (b) What do you understand by bivariate or two-way frequency distribution?

Self-Practice Problems 2A

2.1 A portfolio contains 51 stocks whose prices are given below:

67	34	36	48	49	31	61	34
43	45	38	32	27	61	29	47
36	50	46	30	40	32	30	33
45	49	48	41	53	36	37	47
47	30	50	28	35	35	38	36
46	43	34	62	69	50	28	44
43	60	39					

Summarize these stock prices in the form of a frequency distribution.

2.2 Construct a frequency distribution of the data given below, where class interval is 4 and the mid-value of one of the classes is zero.

−8	−7	10	12	6	4	3	0	7
−4	−3	−2	2	3	4	7	5	6
10	12	9	13	11	−10	−7	1	0
5	3	2	6	10	−6	−4		

2.3 Form a frequency distribution of the following data. Use an equal class interval of 4 where the lower limit of the first class is 10.

10	17	15	22	11	16	19	24	29
18	25	26	32	14	17	20	23	27
30	12	15	18	24	36	18	15	21
28	33	38	34	13	10	16	20	22
29	29	23	31					

2.4 If class mid-points in a frequency distribution of the ages of a group of persons are: 25, 32, 39,. 46, 53, and 60, find:

(a) the size of the class-interval
(b) the class boundaries
(c) the class limits, assuming that the age quoted is the age completed on the last birthdays

2.5 The distribution of ages of 500 readers of a nationally distributed magazine is given below:

Age (in Years)	*Number of Readers*
Below 14	20
15–19	125
20–24	25
25–29	35
30–34	80
35–39	140
40–44	30
45 and above	45

Find the relative and cumulative frequency distributions for this distribution.

2.6 The distribution of inventory to sales ratio of 200 retail outlets is given below:

Inventory to Sales Ratio	*Number of Retail Outlets*
1.0–1.2	20
1.2–1.4	30
1.4–1.6	60
1.6–1.8	40
1.8–2.0	30
2.0–2.2	15
2.2–2.4	5

Find the relative and cumulative frequency distributions for this distribution.

2.7 A wholesaler's daily shipments of a particular item varied from 1,152 to 9,888 units per day. Indicate the limits of nine classes into which these shipments might be grouped.

2.8 The class marks of distribution of the number of electric light bulbs replaced daily in an office building are 5, 10, 15, and 20. Find (a) the class boundaries and (b) class limits.

2.9 Classify the following data by taking class intervals such that their mid-values are 17, 22, 27, 32, and so on:

30	42	30	54	40	48	15	17	51
42	25	41	30	27	42	36	28	26
37	54	44	31	36	40	36	22	30
31	19	48	16	42	32	21	22	46
33	41	21						

2.10 In degree colleges of a city, no teacher is less than 30 years or more than 60 years in age. Their cumulative frequencies are as follows:

Less than	:	60	55	50	45
		40	35	30	25
Total frequency	:	980	925	810	675
		535	380	220	75

Find the frequencies in the class intervals 25–30, 30–35, . . .

Hints and Answers

2.3 The classes for preparing frequency distribution by inclusive method will be 10–13, 14–17, 18–21, . . ., 34–37, 38–41

2.4 (a) Size of the class interval = Difference between the mid-values of any two consecutive classes = 7

(b) The class boundaries for different classes are obtained by adding (for upper class boundaries or limits) and subtracting (for lower class boundaries or limits) half the magnitude of the class interval that is, 7 ÷ 2 = 3.5 from the mid-values.

Class Intervals :	21.5–28.5	28.5–35.5	35.5–42.5
Mid-Values :	25	32	39
Class Intervals :	42.5–49.5	49.5–56.5	56.5–63.5
Mid-Values :	46	53	60

(c) The distribution can be expressed in inclusive class intervals with width of 7 as: 22–28, 29–35, . . ., 56–63.

2.7 One possibility is 1000–1999, 2000–2999, 3000–3999, . . . 9000–9999 units of the item.

2.10

Age (year)	*Cumulative Frequency*	*Age*	*Frequency*
Less than 25	75	20–25	75
Less than 30	220	25–30	220 – 75 = 145
Less than 35	380	30–35	380 – 220 = 160
Less than 40	535	35–40	535 – 380 = 155
Less than 45	675	40–45	675 – 535 = 140
Less than 50	810	45–50	810 – 675 = 135
Less than 55	925	50–55	925 – 810 = 115
Less than 60	980	55–60	980 – 925 = 55

2.4 TABULATION OF DATA

Meaning and Definition Tabulation is another way of summarizing and presenting the given data in a systematic form in rows and columns. Such presentation facilitates comparisons by bringing related information close to each other and helps in further statistical analysis and interpretation. Tabulation has been defined by two statisticians as:

- The logical listing of related quantitative data in vertical columns and horizontal rows of numbers with sufficient explanatory and qualifying words, phrases and statements in the form of titles, headings and explanatory notes to make clear the full meaning, context and the origin of the data.

—Tuttle

This definition gives an idea of the broad structure of statistical tables and suggests that tabulation helps organize a set of data in an orderly manner to highlight its basic characteristics.

- Tables are means of recording, in permanent form, the analysis that is made through classification and by placing in a position just the things that are similar and should be compared.

—Secrist

This definition defines tabulation as the process of classifying the data in a systematic form which facilitates comparative studies of data sets.

2.4.1 Objectives of Tabulation

The above two definitions indicate that tabulation is meant to summarize data in a simplest possible form so that the same can be easily analysed and interpreted. A few objectives of tabulation defined by few statisticians are as follows:

- Tabulation is the process of condensing classified data in the form of a table so that it may be more easily understood, and so that any comparison involved may be more readily made.
—D. Gregory and H. Ward
- It is a medium of communication of great economy and effectiveness for which ordinary prose is inadequate. In addition to its formation in simple presentation, the statistical table is also a useful tool of analysis. —D. W. Paden and E. F. Lindquist

The major objectives of tabulation are:

1. *To simplify the complex data:* Tabulation presents the data set in a systematic and concise form avoiding unnecessary details. The idea is to reduce the bulk of information (data) under investigation into a simplified and meaningful form.
2. *To economize space:* By condensing data in to a meaningful form, space is saved without sacrificing on the quality and quantity of data.
3. *To depict trend:* Data condensed in the form of a table reveal the trend or pattern of data which otherwise cannot be understood in a descriptive form of presentation.
4. *To facilitate comparisons:* Data presented in a tabular form, having rows and columns, facilitate quick comparisons among its observations.
5. *To facilitate statistical comparisons:* Tabulation is a phase between classification of data and its presentation. Various statistical techniques such as measures of average and disperson, correlation and regression, time series, and so on can be applied to analyse data and then interpret the results.
6. *To help as a reference:* When data are arranged in tables in a suitable form, they can easily be identified and can also be used as a reference for future needs.

2.4.2 Parts of a Table

Presenting data in a tabular form is an art. A statistical table should contain all the requisite information in a limited space but without any loss of clarity. There are variations in practice, but explained below are certain accepted rules for the construction of an ideal table:

1. **Table number:** A table should be numbered for easy identification and reference in future. The table number may be given either in the centre or side of the table but above the top of the title of the table. If the number of columns in a table is large, then these can also be numbered so that easy reference to these is possible.
2. **Title of the table:** Each table must have a brief, self-explanatory and complete title so that
   (a) it should be able to indicate *nature* of data contained.
   (b) it should be able to explain the *locality* (i.e. geographical or physical) of data covered.
   (c) it should be able to indicate the *time* (or period) of data obtained.
   (d) it should contain the *source* of the data to indicate the authority for the data, as a means of verification and as a reference. The source is always placed below the table.
3. **Caption and stubs:** The heading for columns and rows are called caption and stub, respectively. They must be clear and concise.

   Two or more columns or rows with similar headings may be grouped under a common heading to avoid repetition. Such arrangements are called sub-captions or sub-stubs. Each row and column can also be numbered for reference and to facilitate comparisons. The caption should be written at the middle of the column in small letters to save space. If different columns are expressed in different units, then the units should be specified along with the captions.

The stubs are usually wider than column headings but must be kept narrow without sacrificing precision or clarity. When a stub occupies more than one line, the figures of the table should be written in the last line.

4. **Body:** The body of the table should contain the numerical information. The numerical information is arranged according to the descriptions given for each column and row.
5. **Prefactory or head note:** If needed, a prefactory note is given just below the title for its further description in a prominent type. It is usually enclosed in brackets and is about the unit of measurement.
6. **Footnotes:** Anything written below the table is called a footnote. It is written to further clarify either the title captions or stubs. For example if the data described in the table pertain to profits earned by a company, then the footnote may define whether it is profit before tax or after tax. There are various ways of identifying footnotes:
   (a) Numbering footnotes consecutively with small number 1, 2, 3, ... or letters a, b, c ... or star *, **, . . .
   (b) Sometimes symbols like @ or $ are also used to identify footnotes.

   A blank model table is given below:

Table Number and Title [Head or Prefactory Note (if any)]

Stub Heading	*Caption*				*Total (Rows)*
	Subhead		*Subhead*		
	Column-head	*Column-head*	*Column-head*	*Column-head*	
Stub Entries					
Total (Columns)					

Footnote :

Source Note :

Remarks: 1. Information which is not available should be indicated by the letter N.A. or by dash (–) in the body of the table.

2. Ditto marks ("), 'etc.' and use of the abbreviated forms should be avoided in the table.

3. The requisites of a good statistical table given by various people are as flows:

- In the final analysis, there are only two rules in tabular presentation that should be applied rigidly. First, the use of common sense when planning a table, and second the viewing of the proposed table from the stand point of user. The details of mechanical arrangement must be governed by a single objective, that is, to make the statistical table as easy to read and to understand as the nature of the material will permit. —J. C. Capt

- A good statistical table is not a mere careless grouping of columns and rows of figures, it is a triumph of ingenuity and technique, a master-piece of economy of space combined with a maximum of clearly presented information. To prepare a first class table, one must have a clear idea of the facts to be presented, the contrasts to be stressed, the points upon which emphasis is to be placed and lastly a familiarity with the technique of preparation. —Harry Jerome
- In collection and tabulation, commonsense is the chief requisite and experience, the chief teacher. —A. L. Bowley

Conceptual Questions 2B

10. What is a statistical table? Explain clearly the essentials of a good table.

11. Explain the role of tabulation in presenting business data, and discuss briefly the different methods of presentation.

12. In classification and tabulation, common sense is the chief requisite and experience the chief teacher. Comment.

13. What are the requisites of a good table? State the rules that serve as a guide in tabulating statistical data.

14. Distinguish between classification and tabulation. Mention the requisites of a good statistical table.

Self-Practice Problems 2B

2.11 Draw a blank table to show the number of candidates sex-wise appearing in the pre-university, first year, second year, and third year examinations of a university in the faculties of Arts, Science, and Commerce in a certain year.

2.12 Let the national income of a country for the years 2000–01 and 2001–02 at current prices be 80,650, 90,010, and 90,530 crore of rupees respectively, and per capita income for these years be 1050, 1056, and 1067 rupees. The corresponding figures of national income and per capita income at 1999–2000 prices for the above years were 80,650, 80,820, and 80,850 crore of rupees and 1050, 1051 and 1048 respectively. Present this data in a table.

2.13 Present the following information in a suitable form supplying the figure not directly given. In 2004, out of a total of 4000 workers in a factory, 3300 were members of a trade union. The number of women workers employed was 500 out of which 400 did not belong to any union.

In 2003, the number of workers in the union was 3450 of which 3200 were men. The number of non-union workers was 760 of which 330 were women.

2.14 Of the 1125 students studying in a college during a year, 720 were SC/ST, 628 were boys, and 440 were science students; the number of SC/ST boys was 392, that of boys studying science 205, and that of SC/ST students studying science 262; finally the number of science students among the SC/ST boys was 148. Enter these frequencies in a three-way table and complete the table by obtaining the frequencies of the remaining cells.

2.15 A survey of 370 students from the Commerce Faculty and 130 students from the Science Faculty revealed that 180 students were studying for only C.A. Examinations, 140 for only Costing Examinations, and 80 for both C.A. and Costing Examinations. The rest had opted for part-time Management Courses. Of those studying for Costing only, 13 were girls and 90 boys belonged to the Commerce Faculty. Out of the 80 studying for both C.A. and Costing, 72 were from the Commerce Faculty amongst whom 70 were boys. Amongst those who opted for part-time Management Courses, 50 boys were from the Science Faculty and 30 boys and 10 girls from the Commerce

Faculty. In all, there were 110 boys in the Science Faculty.

Present this information in a tabular form.

Find the number of students from the Science Faculty studying for part-time Management Courses.

Hints and Answers

2.11 Distribution of candidates appearing in various university examinations

	Boys					Girls				
Faculty	*Pre-Univ.*	*First year*	*Second year*	*Third year*	*Total*	*Pre-Univ.*	*First year*	*Second year*	*Third year*	*Total*
Arts										
Science										
Commerce										
Total										

2.12 National income and per capita income of the country

For the year 1999-2000 to 2001-2002

Year	*National Income*		*Per Capita Income*	
	At Current Prices (Rs. in crore)	*At 1999–2000 Prices (Rs. in crore)*	*At Current Prices*	*At 1999–2000 Prices*
1999–2000	80,650	80,650	1050	1050
2000–2001	90,010	80,820	1056	1051
2001–2002	90,530	80,850	1067	1048

2.13 Members of union by sex

Year	*2003*			*2004*		
	Males	*Females*	*Total*	*Males*	*Females*	*Total*
Member	3300	250	3450	3200	100	3300
Non-member	430	330	760	300	400	700
Total	3630	580	4210	3500	500	4000

2.14 Distribution of College Students by Caste and Faculty

Faculty	*Boys*			*Girls*		
	SC/ST	*Non-SC/ST*	*Total*	*SC/ST*	*Non-SC/ST*	*Total*
Science	148	57	205	114	121	235
Arts	244	179	423	214	48	262
Total	392	236	628	328	169	497

2.15 Distribution of students according to Faculty and Professional Courses

Faculty / *Courses*	*Commerce*			*Science*			*Total*		
	Boys	*Girls*	*Total*	*Boys*	*Girls*	*Total*	*Boys*	*Girls*	*Total*
Part-time Management	30	10	40	50	10	60	80	20	100
CA only	150	8	158	16	6	22	166	14	180
Costing only	90	10	100	37	3	40	127	13	140
CA and Costing	70	2	72	7	1	8	77	3	80
Total	340	30	370	110	20	130	450	50	500

2.5 GRAPHICAL PRESENTATION OF DATA

It has already been discussed that one of the important functions of statistics is to present complex and unorganized (raw) data in such a manner that they would easily be understandable. According to King, '*One of the chief aims of statistical science is to render the meaning of masses of figures clear and comprehensible at a glance*.' This is often best accomplished by presenting the data in a pictorial (or graphical) form.

The graphical (diagrammatical) presentation of data has many advantages. The following persons rightly observed that

- With but few exceptions, memory depends upon the faculty of our brains possess of forming visual images and it is this power of forming visual images which lies at the root of the utility of diagrammatic presentation. —R. L. A. Holmes
- Cold figures are uninspiring to most people. Diagrams help us to see the pattern and shape of any complex situation. Just as a map gives us a bird's eye-view of the wide stretch of a country, so diagrams help as visualise the whole meaning of the numerical complex at a single glance. —M. J. Moroney

According to Calvin F. Schmid, 'Charts and graphs represent an extremely useful and flexible medium for explaining, interpreting and analysing numerical facts largely by means of points, lines, areas and other geometric forms and symbols. They make possible the presentation of quantitative data in a simple, clear, and effective manner and facilitate comparison of values, trends and relationships.'

2.5.1 Functions of a Graph

Graphic presentation of frequency distributions facilitate easy understanding of data presentation and interpretation. The shape of the graph offers easy answers to several questions. The same information can also be obtained from tabular presentation of a frequency distribution, but the same is not as effective in highlighting the essential characteristics as explicitly as is possible in the case of graphic presentation.

The shape of the graph gives an exact idea of the variations of the distribution trends. Graphic presentation, therefore, serves as an easy technique for quick and effective comparison between two or more frequency distributions. When the graph of one frequency distribution is superimposed on the other, the points of contrast regarding the type of distribution and the pattern of variation become quite obvious. All these advantages necessitate a clear understanding of the various forms of graphic representation of a frequency distribution.

2.5.2 Advantages and Limitations of Diagrams (Graphs)

According to P. Maslov, 'Diagrams are drawn for two purposes (i) to permit the investigator to graph the essence of the phenomenon he is observing, and (ii) to permit others to see the results at a glance, i.e. for the purpose of popularisation.'

Advantages Few of the advantages and usefulness of diagrams are as follows:

(i) *Diagrams give an attractive and elegant presentation:* Diagrams have greater attraction and effective impression. People, in general, avoid figures, but are always impressed by diagrams. Since people see pictures carefully, their effect on the mind is more stable. Thus, diagrams give delight to the eye and add the spark of interest.

(ii) *Diagrams leave good visual impact:* Diagrams have the merit of rendering any idea readily. The impression created by a diagram is likely to last longer in the minds of people than the effect created by figures. Thus diagrams have greater memorizing value than figures.

(iii) *Diagrams facilitate comparison:* With the help of diagrams, comparisons of groups and series of figures can be made easily. While comparing absolute figures, the significance is not clear but when these are presented by diagrams, the comparison is easy. The technique of diagrammatic representation should not be used when comparison is either not possible or is not necessary.

(iv) *Diagrams save time:* Diagrams present the set of data in such a way that their significance is known without loss of much time. Moreover, diagrams save time and effort which are otherwise needed in drawing inferences from a set of figures.

(v) *Diagrams simplify complexity and depict the characteristics of the data:* Diagrams, besides being attractive and interesting, also highlight the characteristics of the data. Large data can easily be represented by diagrams and thus, without straining one's mind, the basic features of the data can be understood and inferences can be drawn in a very short time.

Limitations We often find tabular and graphical presentations of data in annual reports, newspapers, magazines, bulletins, and so on. But, inspite their usefulness, diagrams can also be misused. A few limitations of these as a tool for statistical analysis are as under:

(i) They provide only an approximate picture of the data.

(ii) They cannot be used as alternative to tabulation of data.

(iii) They can be used only for comparative study.

(iv) They are capable of representing only homogeneous and comparable data.

2.5.3 General Rules for Drawing Diagrams

To draw useful inferences from graphical presentation of data, it is important to understand how they are prepared and how they should be interpreted. When we say that 'one picture is worth a thousand words', it neither proves (nor disproves) a particular fact, nor is it suitable for further analysis of data. However, if diagrams are properly drawn, they highlight the different characteristics of data. The following general guidelines are taken into consideration while preparing diagrams:

Title: Each diagram should have a suitable title. It may be given either at the top of the diagram or below it. The title must convey the main theme which the diagram intends to portray.

Size: The size and portion of each component of a diagram should be such that all the relevant characteristics of the data are properly displayed and can be easily understood.

Proportion of length and breadth: An appropriate proportion between the length and breadth of the diagram should be maintained. As such there are no fixed rules about the ratio of length to width. However, a ratio of $\sqrt{2}$: 1 or 1.414 (long side) : 1 (short side) suggested by Lutz in his book *Graphic Presentation* may be adopted as a general rule.

Proper scale: There are again no fixed rules for selection of scale. The diagram should neither be too small nor too large. The scale for the diagram should be decided after taking into consideration the magnitude of data and the size of the paper on which it is to be drawn. The scale showing the values as far as possible, should be in even numbers or in multiples of 5, 10, 20, and so on. The scale should specify the size of the unit and the nature of data it represents, for example, 'millions of tonnes', in Rs. thousand, and the like. The scale adopted should be indicated on both vertical and horizontal axes if different scales are used. Otherwise, it can be indicated at some suitable place on the graph paper.

Footnotes and source note: To clarify or elucidate any points which need further explanation but cannot be shown in the graph, footnotes are given at the bottom of the diagrams.

Index: A brief index explaining the different types of lines, shades, designs, or colours used in the construction of the diagram should be given to understand its contents.

Simplicity: Diagrams should be prepared in such a way that they can be understood easily. To keep it simple, too much information should not be loaded in a single diagram as it may create confusion. Thus if the data are large, then it is advisible to prepare more than one diagram, each depicting some identified characteristic of the same data.

2.6 TYPES OF DIAGRAMS

There are a variety of diagrams used to represent statistical data. Different types of diagrams, used to describe sets of data, are divided into the following categories:

- **Dimensional diagrams**
  - (i) One dimensional diagrams such as histograms, frequency polygones, and pie charts.
  - (ii) Two-dimensional diagrams such as rectangles, squares, or circles.
  - (iii) Three dimensional diagrams such as cylinders and cubes.
- **Pictograms or Ideographs**
- **Cartographs or Statistical maps**

2.6.1 One-Dimensional Diagrams

These diagrams are most useful, simple, and popular in the diagrammatic presentation of frequency distributions. These diagrams provides a useful and quick understanding of the *shape* of the distribution and its characteristics. According to Calvin F. Schmid, 'The simple bar chart with many variations is particularly appropriate for comparing the magnitude (or size) of coordinate items or of parts of a total. The basis of comparison in the bar is linear or one-dimensional.'

These diagrams are called one-dimensional diagrams because only the length (height) of the bar (not the width) is taken into consideration. Of course, width or thickness of the bar has no effect on the diagram, even then the thickness should not be too much otherwise the diagram would appear like a two-dimensional diagram.

Tips for Constructing a Diagram The following tips must be kept in mind while constructing one-dimensional diagrams:

(i) The width of all the bars drawn should be same.

(ii) The gap between one bar and another must be uniform.

(iii) There should be a common base to all the bars.

(iv) It is desirable to write the value of the variable represented by the bar at the top end so that the reader can understand the value without looking at the scale.

(v) The frequency, relative frequency, or per cent frequency of each class interval is shown by drawing a rectangle whose base is the class interval on the horizontal axis and whose height is the corresponding frequency, relative frequency, or per cent frequency.

(vi) The value of variables (or class boundaries in case of grouped data) under study are scaled along the horizontal axis, and the number of observations (frequencies, relative frequencies or percentage frequencies) are scaled along the vertical axis.

The one-dimensional diagrams (charts) used for graphical presentation of data sets are as follows:

- Histogram
- Frequency polygon
- Frequency curve
- Cumulative frequency distribution (Ogive)
- Pie diagram

Histograms (Bar Diagrams) These diagrams are used to graph both ungrouped and grouped data. In the case of an ungrouped data, values of the variable (the characteristic to be measured) are scaled along the horizontal axis and the number of observations (or frequencies) along the vertical axis of the graph. The plotted points are then connected by straight lines to enhance the shape of the distribution. The height of such boxes (rectangles) measures the number of observations in each of the classes.

Listed below are the various types of histograms:

(i) Simple bar charts
(ii) Grouped (or multiple) charts
(iii) Deviation bar charts
(iv) Subdivided bar charts
(v) Paired bar charts
(vi) Sliding bar charts
(vii) Relative frequency bar charts
(viii) Percentage bar charts

For plotting a histogram of a grouped frequency distribution, the end points of class intervals are specified on the horizontal axis and the number of observations (or frequencies) are specified on the vertical axis of the graph. Often class mid-points are posted on the horizontal axis rather than the end points of class intervals. In either case, the width of each bar indicates the class interval while the height indicates the frequency of observations in that class. Figure 2.1 is a histogram for the frequency distribution given in Table 2.12 of Example 2.1.

Remarks: Bar diagrams are not suitable to represent long period time series.

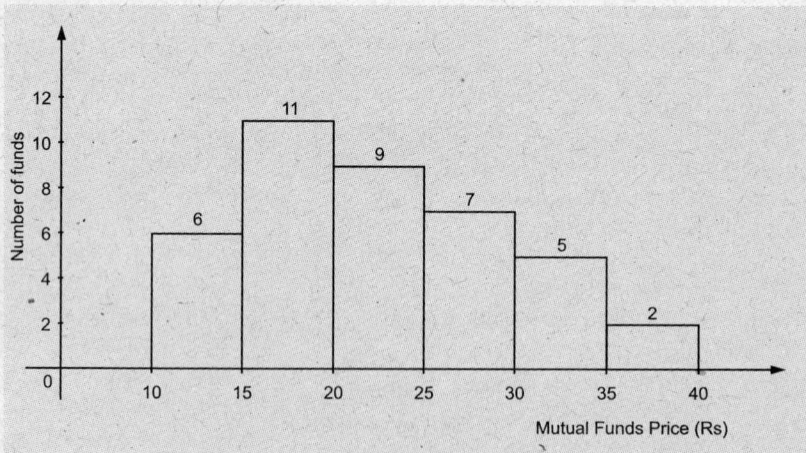

Figure 2.1 Histogram for Mutual Funds

Simple Bar Charts The graphic techniques described earlier are used for group frequency distributions. The graphic techniques presented in this section can also be used for displaying values of categorical variables. Such data is first tallied into summary tables and then graphically displayed as either *bar charts* or *pie charts*.

Bar charts are used to represent only one characteristic of data and there will be as many bars as number of observations. For example, the data obtained on the production of oil seeds in a particular year can be represented by such bars. Each bar would represent the yield of a particular oil seed in that year. Since the bars are of the same width and only the length varies, the relationship among them can be easily established.

Sometimes only lines are drawn for comparison of given variable values. Such lines are not thick and their number is sufficiently large. The different measurements to be shown should not have too much difference, so that the lines may not show too much dissimilarity in their heights.

Such charts are used to economize space, specially when observations are large. The lines may be either vertical or horizontal depending upon the type of variable—numerical or categorical.

Example 2.9: The data on the production of oil seeds in a particular year is presented in Table 2.25.

Table 2.25

Oil Seed	*Yield (Million tonnes)*	*Percentage Production (Million tonnes)*
Ground nut	5.80	43.03
Rapeseed	3.30	24.48
Coconut	1.18	8.75
Cotton	2.20	16.32
Soyabean	1.00	7.42
	13.48	100.00

Represent this data by a suitable bar chart.

Solution: The information provided in Table 2.25 is expressed graphically as the frequency bar chart as shown in Fig. 2.2. In this figure, each type of seed is depicted by a bar, the length of which represents the frequency (or percentage) of observations falling into that category.

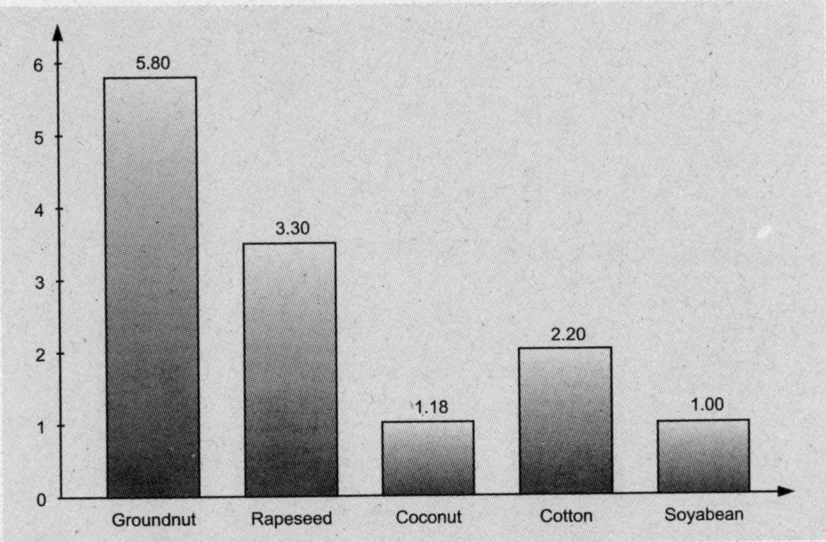

Figure 2.2 Bar Chart Pertaining to Production of Oil Seeds

Remark: The bars should be constructed vertically (as shown in Fig. 2.2) when categorized observations are the outcome of a numerical variable. But if observations are the outcome of a categorical variable, then the bars should be constructed horizontally.

Example 2.10: An advertising company kept an account of response letters received each day over a period of 50 days. The observations were:

0	2	1	1	1	2	0	0	1	0	1	0	0	1	0	1	1	0
2	0	0	2	0	1	0	1	0	1	0	3	1	0	1	0	1	0
2	5	1	2	0	0	0	0	5	0	1	1	2	0				

Construct a frequency table and draw a line chart (or diagram) to present the data.

Solution: The observations are tallied into the summary table as shown in Table 2.26.

Figure 2.3 depicts a frequency bar chart for the number of letters received during a period of 50 days presented in Table 2.26.

Table 2.26 Frequency Distribution of Letters Received

Number of Letters Received	*Tally*	*Number of Days (Frequency)*
0	~~IIII~~ ~~IIII~~ ~~IIII~~ ~~IIII~~ III	23
1	~~IIII~~ ~~IIII~~ ~~IIII~~ II	17
2	~~IIII~~ II	7
3	II	2
4	—	0
5	I	1
		50

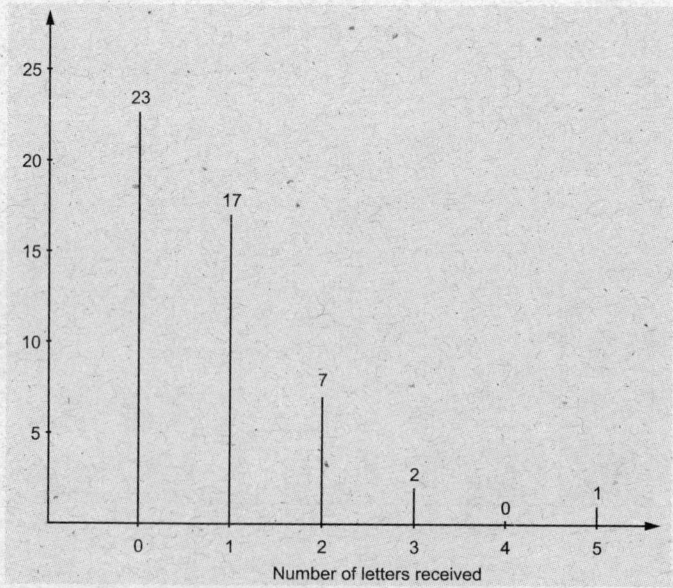

Figure 2.3 Number of Letters Received

Multiple Bar Charts A multiple bar chart is also known as grouped (or compound) bar chart. Such charts are useful for direct comparison between two or more sets of data. The technique of drawing such a chart is same as that of a single bar chart with a difference that each set of data is represented in different shades or colours on the same scale. An index explaining shades or colours must be given.

Example 2.11: The data on fund flow (in Rs. crore) of an International Airport Authority during financial years 2001–02 to 2003–04 are given below:

	2001–02	*2002–03*	*2003–04*
Non-traffic revenue	40.00	50.75	70.25
Traffic revenue	70.25	80.75	110.00
Profit before tax	40.15	50.50	80.25

Represent this data by a suitable bar chart.
Solution: The multiple bar chart of the given data is shown in Fig. 2.4.

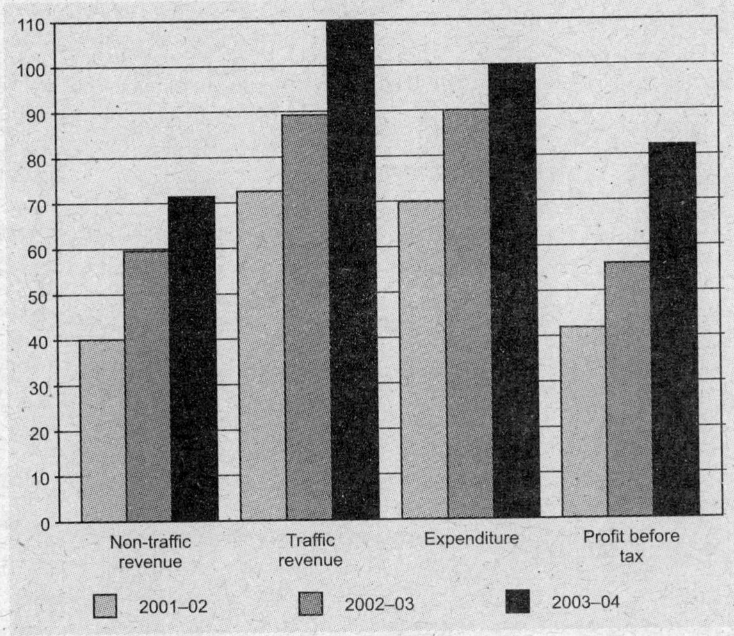

Figure 2.4 Multiple Bar Chart Pertaining to Performance of an International Airport Authority

Deviation Bar Charts Deviation bar charts are suitable for presentation of net quantities in excess or deficit such as profit, loss, import, or exports. The excess (or positive) values and deficit (or negative) values are shown above and below the base line.

Example 2.12: The following are the figures of sales and net profits of a company over the last three years.

(Per cent change over previous year)

Year	*Sales Growth*	*Net Profit*
2002–2003	15	30
2003–2004	12	53
2004–2005	18	– 72

Present this data by a suitable bar chart.

Solution: Figure 2.5 depicts deviation bar charts for sales and per cent change in sales over previous year's data.

Subdivided Bar Chart Subdivided bar charts are suitable for expressing information in terms of ratios or percentages. For example, net per capita availability of food grains, results of a college faculty-wise in last few years, and so on. While constructing these charts the various components in each bar should be in the same order to avoid confusion. Different shades must be used to represent various ratio values but the shade of each component should remain the same in all the other bars. An index of the shades should be given with the diagram.

A common arrangement while making these charts is that of presenting each bar in order of magnitude from the largest component at the base of the bar to the smallest at the end.

Since the different components of the bars do not start on the same scale, the individual bars are to be studied properly for their mutual comparisons.

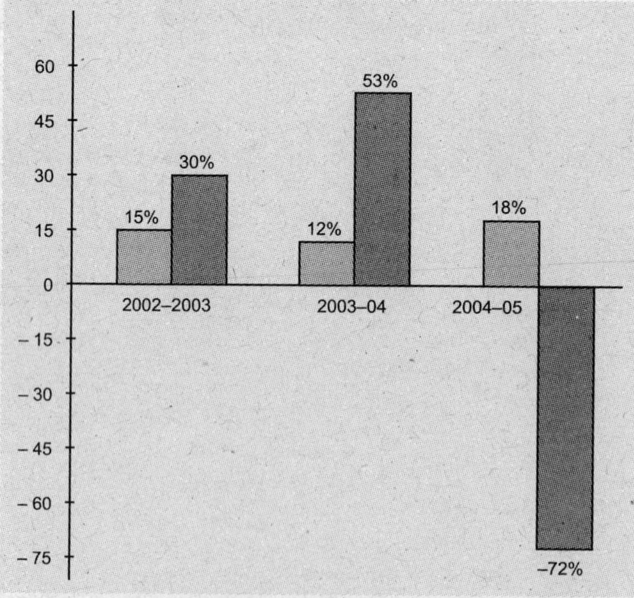

Figure 2.5 Deviation Bar Chart Pertaining to Sales and Profits

Example 2.13: The data on sales (Rs. in million) of a company are given below:

	2005	*2006*	*2007*
Export	1.4	1.8	2.29
Home	1.6	2.7	2.9
Total	3.0	4.5	5.18

Solution: Figure 2.6 depicts a subdivided bar chart for the given data.

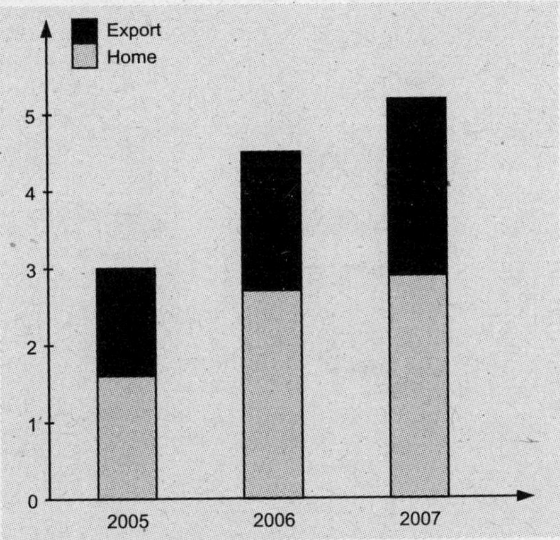

Figure 2.6 Subdivided Bar Chart Pertaining to Sales

Percentage Bar Charts When the relative proportions of components of a bar are more important than their absolute values, then each bar can be constructed with same size to represent 100%. The component values are then expressed in terms of percentage of the total to obtain the necessary length for each of these in the full length of the bars. The other rules regarding the shades, index, and thickness are the same as mentioned earlier.

Example 2.14: The following table shows the data on cost, profit, or loss per unit of a good produced by a company during the year 2006–07.

Particulars	*2006*			*2007*		
	Amount (Rs.)	*Percentage*	*Cumulative Percentage*	*Amount (Rs.)*	*Percentage*	*Cumulative Percentage*
Cost per unit						
(a) Labour	25	41.67	41.67	34	40.00	40.00
(b) Material	20	33.33	75.00	30	35.30	75.30
(c) Miscellaneous	15	25.00	100.00	21	24.70	100.00
Total cost	60	100		85	100	
Sales proceeds per unit	80	110		80	88	
Profit (+) or loss (–) per item	+ 20	+ 10		– 5	– 12	

Represent diagrammatically the data given above on percentage basis.

Solution: The cost, sales, and profit/loss data expressed in terms of percentages have been represented in the bar chart as shown in Fig. 2.7.

Frequency Polygon As shown in Fig. 2.8, the frequency polygon is formed by marking the mid-point at the top of horizontal bars and then joining these dots by a series of straight lines. The frequency polygons are formed as a closed figure with the horizontal axis, therefore a series of straight lines are drawn from the mid-point of the top base of the first and the last rectangles to the mid-point falling on the horizontal axis of the next outlaying interval with zero frequency. The frequency polygon is sometimes jagged in appearance.

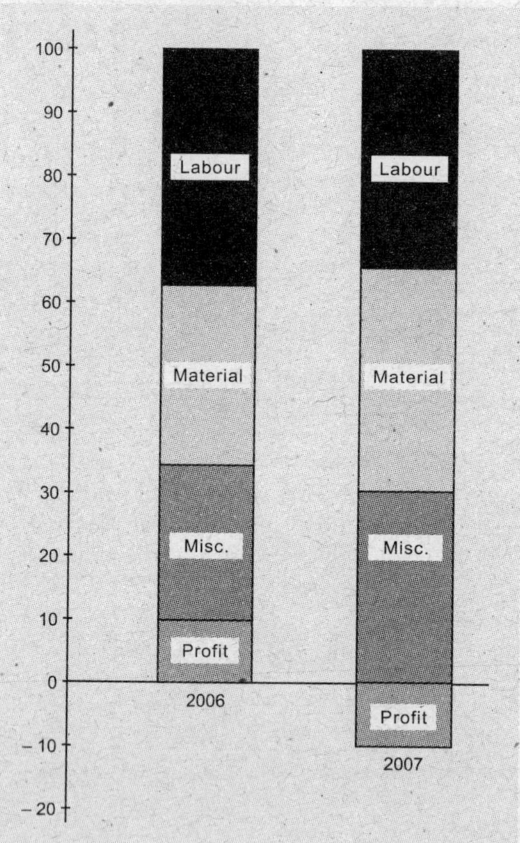

Figure 2.7 Percentage Bar Chart Pertaining to Cost, Sales, and Profit/Loss

A frequency polygon can also be converted back into a histogram by drawing vertical lines from the bounds of the classes shown on the horizontal axis, and then connecting them with horizontal lines at the heights of the polygon at each mid-point.

Drawing a frequency polygon does not necessarily require constructing a histogram first. A frequency polygon can be obtained directly on plotting points above each class mid-point at heights equal to the corresponding class frequency. The points so drawn are then joined by a series of straight lines and the polygon is closed as explained earlier. In this case, horizontal x-axis measures the successive class mid-points and not the lower class limits. Figure 2.8 shows the frequency polygon for the frequency distribution presented by histogram in Fig. 2.1.

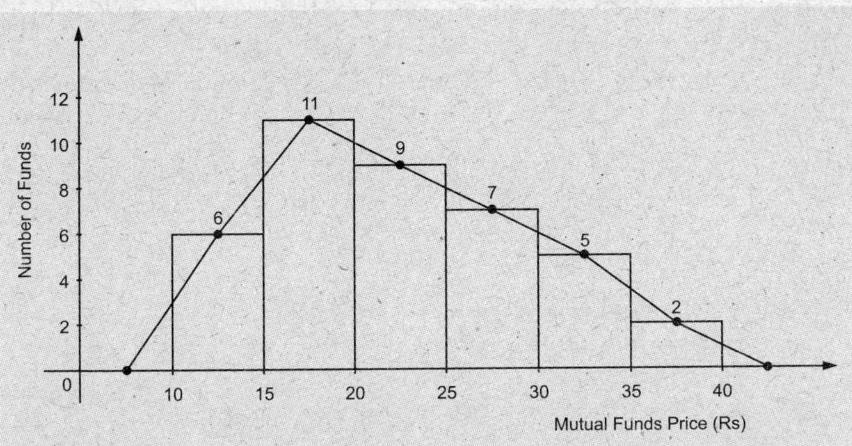

Figure 2.8 Frequency Polygon for Mutual Fund

Frequency Curve It is described as a smooth frequency polygon as shown in Fig. 2.9. A frequency curve is described in terms of its (i) symmetry (skewness) and its (ii) degree of peakedness (kurtosis). The concepts of skewness and kurtosis describing a frequency distribution will be discussed in Chapter 5.

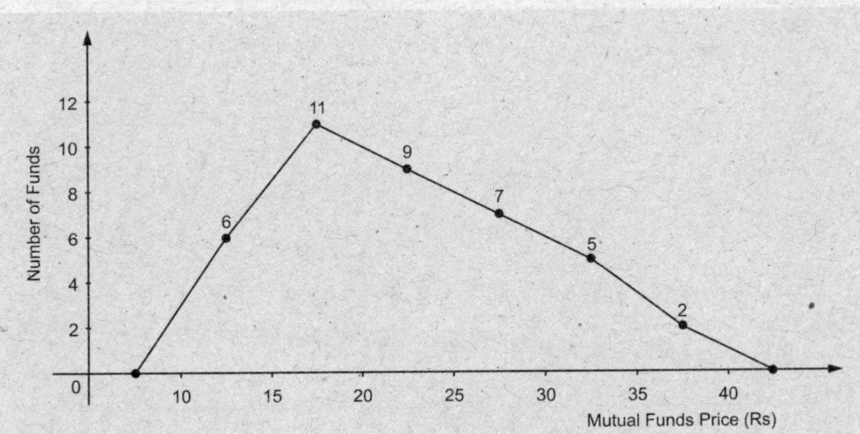

Figure 2.9 Frequency Curve

Two frequency distributions can also be compared by superimposing two or more frequency curves provided the width of their class intervals and the total number of frequencies are equal for the given distributions. Even if the distributions to be compared differ in terms of total frequencies, they still can be compared by drawing per cent frequency curves where the vertical axis measures the per cent class frequencies and not the absolute frequencies.

Cumulative Frequency Distribution (Ogive) It enables us to see how many observations lie above or below certain values rather than merely recording the number of observations within intervals. Cumulative frequency distribution is another method of data presentation that helps in data analysis and interpretation. Table 2.37 shows the cumulative number of observations below and above the upper boundary of each class in the distribution.

A cumulative frequency curve popularly known as *Ogive* is another form of graphic presentation of a cumulative frequency distribution. The ogive for the cumulative frequency distribution given in Table 2.27 is presented in Fig. 2.10.

Once cumulative frequencies are obtained, the remaining procedure for drawing curve called ogive is as usual. The only difference being that the y-axis now has to be so scaled that it accommodates the total frequencies. The x-axis is labelled with the upper class limits in the case of less than ogive, and the lower class limits in case of more than ogive.

Table 2.27 Calculation of Cumulative Frequencies

Mutual Funds Price (Rs.)	*Upper Class Boundary*	*Number of Funds (f)*	*Cumulative Frequency*	
			Less than	*More than*
10–15	15	6	6	40
15–20	20	11	6 + 11 = 17	40 – 6 = 34
20–25	25	9	17 + 9 = 26	34 – 11 = 23
25–30	30	7	26 + 7 = 33	23 – 9 = 14
30–35	35	5	33 + 5 = 38	14 – 7 = 7
35–40	40	2	38 + 2 = 40	7 – 5 = 2

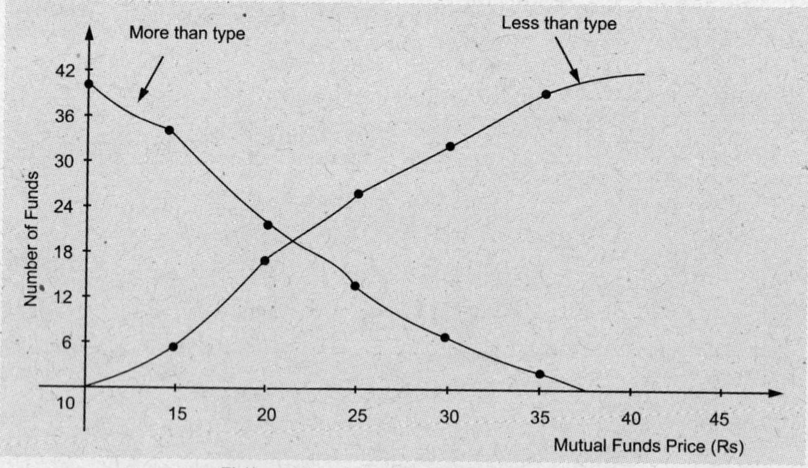

Figure 2.10 Ogive for Mutual Funds Prices

To draw a cumulative 'less than ogive', points are plotted against each successive upper class limit and a corresponding less than cumulative frequency value. These points are then joined by a series of straight lines and the resultant curve is closed at the bottom by extending it so as to meet the horizontal axis at the real lower limit of the first class interval.

To draw a cumulative 'more than ogive', points are plotted against each successive lower class limit and the corresponding more than cumulative frequency. These points are joined by a series of straight lines and the curve is closed at the bottom by extending it to meet the horizontal axis at the upper limit of the last class interval. Both the types of ogives so drawn are shown in Fig. 2.10.

It may be mentioned that a line drawn parallel to the vertical axis through the point of intersection of the two types of ogives will meet the x-axis at its middle point, and the value corresponding to this point will be the median of the distribution. Similarly, the perpendicular drawn from the point of intersection of the two curves on the vertical axis will divide the total frequencies into two equal parts.

Two ogives, whether *less than* or *more than* type, can be readily compared by drawing them on the same graph paper. The presence of unequal class intervals poses no problem in their comparison, as it does in the case of comparison of two frequency polygons. If the total frequencies are not the same in the two distributions, they can be first converted into per cent frequency distributions and then ogives drawn on a single graph paper to facilitate comparison.

Pie Diagram These diagrams are normally used to show the total number of observations of different types in the data set on a percentage basic rather than on an absolute basis through a circle. Usually the largest percentage portion of data in a pie diagram is shown first at 12 o'clock position on the circle, whereas the other observations (in per cent) are shown in clockwise succession in descending order of magnitude. The steps to draw a pie diagram are summarized below:

(i) Convert the various observations (in per cent) in the data set into corresponding degrees in the circle by multiplying each by 3.6 (360 ÷ 100).

(ii) Draw a circle of appropriate size with a compass.

(iii) Draw points on the circle according to the size of each portion of the data with the help of a protractor and join each of these points to the center of the circle.

The pie chart has two distinct advantages: (i) it is aesthetically pleasing and (ii) it shows that the total for all categories or slices of the pie adds to 100%.

Example 2.15: The data shows market share (in per cent) by revenue of the following companies in a particular year:

Batata–BPL	30	Escorts-First Pacific	5
Hutchison–Essar	26	Reliance	3
Bharti–Sing Tel	19	RPG	2
Modi Dista Com	12	Srinivas	2
		Shyam	1

Draw a pie diagram for the above data.

Solution: Converting percentage figures into angle outlay by multiplying each of them by 3.6 as shown in Table 2.28.

Table 2.28

Company	*Market Share (Per cent)*	*Angle Outlay (Degree)*
Batata–BPL	30	108.0
Hutchison–Essar	26	93.6
Bharti–Sing Tel	19	68.4
Modi Dista Com	12	43.2
Escorts First Pacific	5	18.0
Reliance	3	10.8
RPG	2	7.2
Srinivas	2	7.2
Shyam	1	3.6
Total	100	360.0

Using the data given in Table 2.38 construct the pie chart displayed in Fig. 2.11 by dividing the circle into 9 parts according to degrees of angle at the centre.

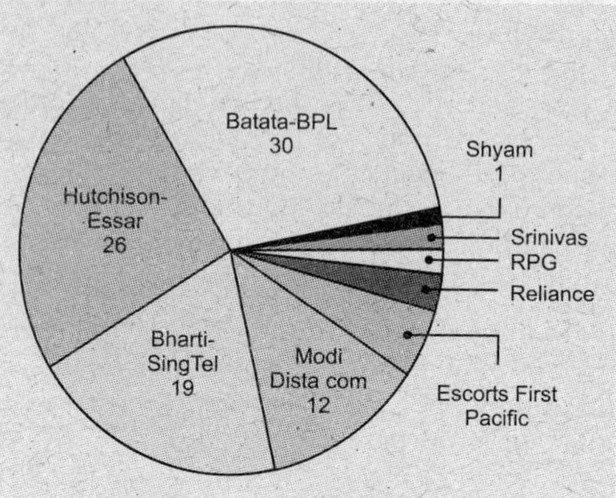

Figure 2.11 Percentage Pie Chart

Example 2.16: The following data relate to area in millions of square kilometer of oceans of the world.

Ocean	*Area (Million sq. km)*
Pacific	70.8
Atlantic	41.2
Indian	28.5
Antarctic	7.6
Arctic	4.8

Solution: Converting given areas into angle outlay as shown in Table 2.29.

Table 2.29

Ocean	*Area (Million sq km)*	*Angle Outlay (Degrees)*
Pacific	70.8	$\frac{70.8}{152.9} \times 360 = 166.70$
Atlantic	41.2	$\frac{41.2}{152.9} \times 360 = 97.00$
Indian	28.5	67.10
Antarctic	7.6	17.89
Arctic	4.8	11.31
Total	152.9	360.00

Pie diagram is shown in Fig. 2.12.

2.6.2 Two-Dimensional Diagrams

In one-dimensional diagrams or charts, only the length of the bar is taken into consideration. But in two-dimensional diagrams, both its height and width are taken into account for presenting the data. These diagrams, also known as *surface diagrams* or *area diagrams*, are:

- Rectangles
- Squares
- Circles

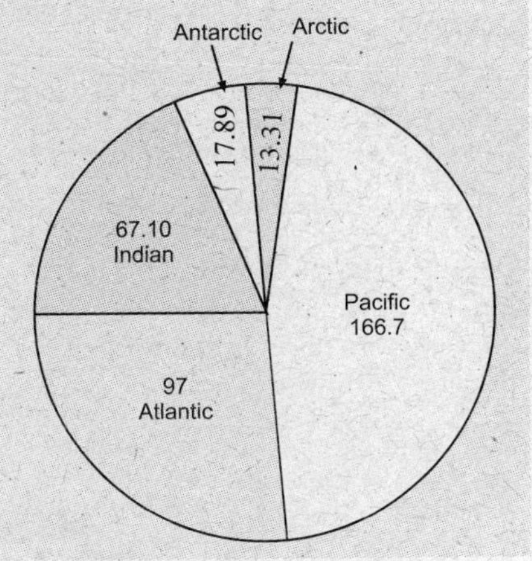

Figure 2.12 Per cent Pie Diagram

Rectangles Since area of a rectangle is equal to the product of its length and width, therefore while making such type of diagrams both length and width are considered.

Rectangles are suitable for use in cases where two or more quantities are to be compared and each quantity is sub-divided into several components.

Example 2.17: The following data represent the income of two families A and B. Construct a rectangular diagram.

Item of Expenditure	*Family A (Monthly Income Rs. 30,000)*	*Family B (Monthly Income Rs. 40,000)*
Food	5550	7280
Clothing	5100	6880
House rent	4800	6480
Fuel and light	4740	6320
Education	4950	6640
Miscellaneous	4860	6400
Total	30,000	40,000

Solution: Converting individual values into percentages taking total income as equal to 100 as shown in Table 2.30.

Table 2.30 Percentage Summary Table Pertaining to Expenses Incurred by Two Families

Item of Expenditure	*Family A (Monthly Income Rs. 3000)*			*Family B (Monthly Income Rs. 4000)*		
	Actual Expenses	*Percentage of Expenses*	*Cumulative Percentage*	*Actual Expenses*	*Percentage of Expenses*	*Cumulative Percentage*
Food	5550	18.50	18.50	7280	18.20	18.20
Clothing	5100	17.00	35.50	6880	17.20	35.40
House rent	4800	16.00	51.50	6480	16.20	51.60
Fuel and light	4740	15.80	6.78	6320	15.80	67.40
Education	4950	16.50	83.80	6640	16.60	84.00
Miscellaneous	4860	16.20	100.00	6400	16.00	100.00
Total		30,000	100.00		40,000	100.00

The height of the rectangles shown in Fig. 2.13 is equal to 100. The difference in the total income is represented by the difference on the base line which is in the ratio of 3 : 4.

Squares Squares give a better comparison than rectangular bars when the difference of totals to be compared is large. For example, if in Example 2.17 the total expenses of families A and B are Rs. 2000 and 20,000 respectively, then the width of the rectangles would be in the ratio 1 : 10. If such a ratio is taken, the diagram would look very unwieldy. Thus to overcome this difficulty, squares are constructed to make use of their areas to represent given data for comparison.

To construct a square diagram, first take the square-root of the values of various figures to be represented and then these values are divided either by the lowest figure or by some other common figure to obtain proportions of the sides of the squares. The squares constructed on these proportionate lengths must have either the base or the centre on a straight line. The scale is attached with the diagram to show the variable value represented by one square unit area of the squares.

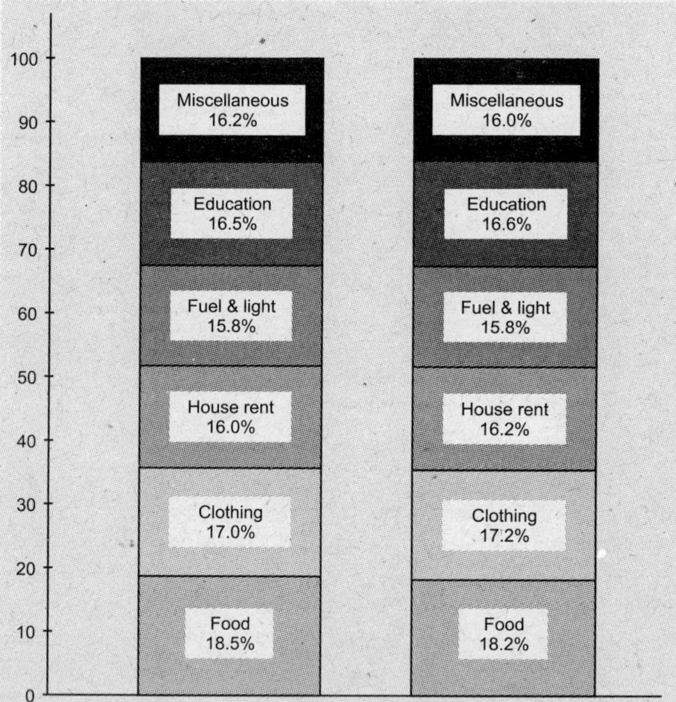

Figure 2.13 Percentage of Expenditure by Two Families

Example 2.18: The following data represent the production (in million tonnes) of coal by different countries in a particular year.

Country	*Production*
USA	130.1
USSR	44.0
UK	16.4
India	3.3

Represent the data graphically by constructing a suitable diagram.

Solution: The given data can be represented graphically by square diagrams. For constructing the sides of the squares, the necessary calculations are shown in Table 2.31.

Table 2.31 Side of a Square Pertaining to Production of Coal

Country	*Production (Million tonnes)*	*Square Root of Production Amount*	*Side of a Square (One square inch)*
USA	130.1	11.406	1.267
USSR	44.0	6.633	0.737
UK	16.4	4.049	0.449
India	3.3	1.816	0.201

The squares representing the amount of coal production by various countries are shown in Fig. 2.14.

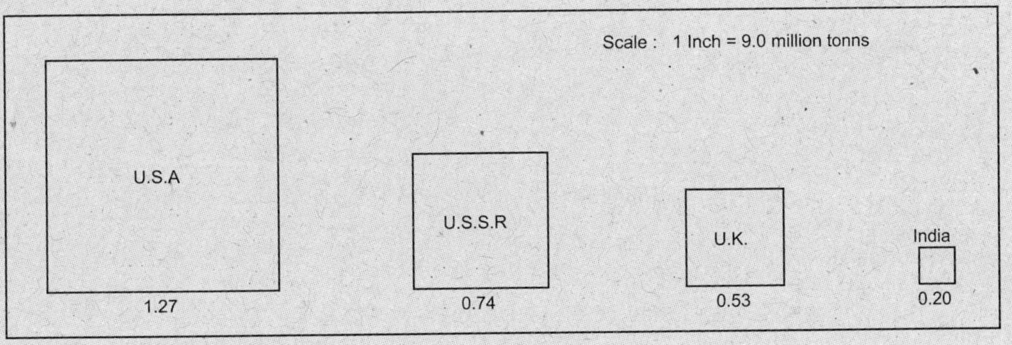

Figure 2.14 Coal Production in Different Countries

Circles Circles are alternatives, to squares to represent data graphically. The circles are also drawn such that their areas are in proportion to the figures represented by them. The circles are constructed in such a way that their centres lie on the same horizontal line and the distance between the circles are equal.

Since the area of a circle is directly proportional to the square of its radius, therefore the radii of the circles are obtain in proportion to the square root of the figures under representation. Thus, the lengths which were used as the sides of the square can also be used as the radii of circles.

Example 2.19: The following data represent the land area in different countries. Represent this data graphically using suitable diagram.

Country	*Land Area (crore acres)*
USSR	590.4
China	320.5
USA	190.5
India	81.3

Solution: The data can be represented graphically using circles. The calculations for constructing radii of circles are shown in Table 2.32.

Table 2.32 Radii of Circles Pertaining to Land Area of Countries

Country	*Land Area (crore acres)*	*Square Root of Land Area*	*Radius of Circles (Inches)*
USSR	590.4	24.3	0.81
China	320.5	17.9	0.60
USA	190.5	13.8	0.46
India	81.3	9.0	0.30

The various circles representing the land area of respective countries are shown in Fig. 2.15.

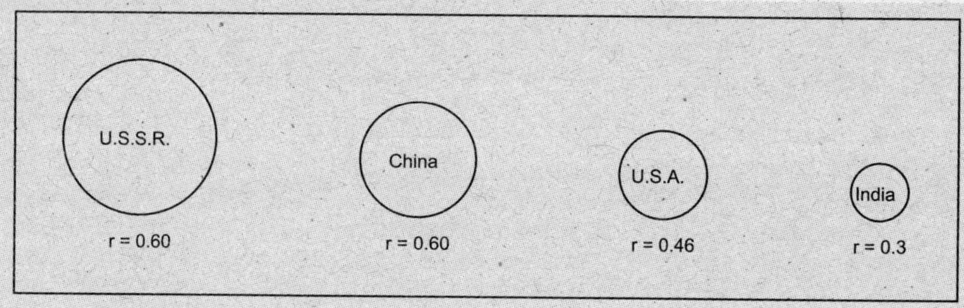

Figure 2.15 Land Area of Different Countries

2.6.3 Three-Dimensional Diagrams

Cylinders, spheres, cubes, and so on are known as three-dimensional diagrams because three dimensions—length, breadth, and depth, are taken into consideration for representing figures. These diagrams are used when only one point is to be compared and the ratio between the highest and the lowest measurements is more than 100 : 1. For constructing these diagrams, the cube root of various measurements is calculated and the side of each cube is taken in proportion to the cube roots.

Amongst the three-dimensional diagrams, cubes are the easiest and should be used only in those cases where the figures cannot be adequately presented through bar, square, or circle diagrams.

2.6.4 Pictograms or Ideographs

A pictogram is another form of pictorial bar chart. Such charts are useful in presenting data to people who cannot understand charts. Small symbols or simplified pictures are used to represent the size of the data. To construct pictograms or ideographs, the following suggestions are made:

(i) The symbols must be simple and clear.
(ii) The quantity represented by a symbol should be given.
(iii) Larger quantities are shown by increasing the number of symbols, and not by increasing the size of the symbols. A part of a symbol can be used to represent a quantity smaller than the whole symbol.

Example 2.20: Make a pictographic presentation of the output of vans during the year by a van manufacturing company.

Year :	1999	2000	2001	2002
Output :	2004	2996	4219	5324

Solution: Dividing the van output figures by 1000, we get 2.004, 2.996, 4.219, and 5.324, respectively.

Representing these figures by pictures of vans as shown in Fig. 2.16.

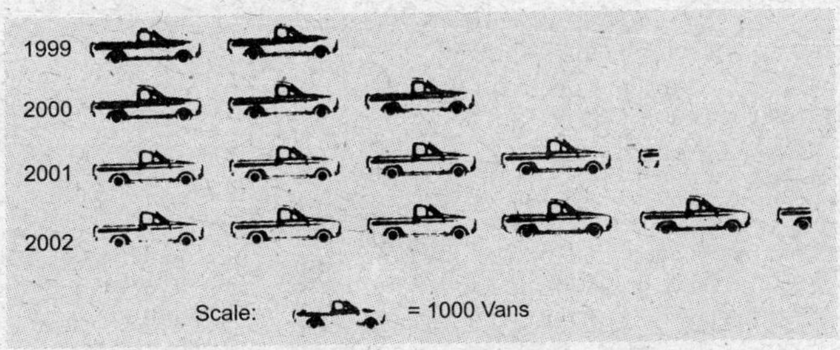

Figure 2.16 Output of Vans

2.6.5 Cartograms or Statistical Maps

Cartograms are used to represent graphical distribution of data on maps. The various figures in different regions on maps are shown either by (i) shades or colours, (ii) dots or bars, (iii) diagrams or pictures, or (iv) by putting numerical figures in each geographical area.

The following maps show the location of a particular type of soil, refineries, and aircraft industry in the country.

Conceptual Questions 2C

15. What are the different types of charts known to you? What are their uses?
16. Point out the role of diagrammatic presentation of data. Explain briefly the different types of bar diagrams known to you.
17. Charts are more effective in attracting attention than other methods of presenting data. Do you agree? Give reasons for your answer.
18. Discuss the utility and limitations (if any) of diagrammatic presentation of statistical data.
19. Diagrams are meant for a rapid view of the relation of different data and their comparisons. Discuss.
20. Write short notes on pictographic and cartographic representations of statistical data.
21. What are the advantages of using a graph to describe a frequency distribution?
22. When constructing a graph of a grouped frequency distribution, is it necessary that the resulting distribution be symmetric ? Explain.
23. Explain what is meant by a frequency polygon, a histogram, and a frequency curve.
24. Define the terms relative frequency and cumulative frequency. How are these related to a frequency distribution?
25. The distribution of heights of all students in the commerce department of the university has two peaks or is bimodal. The distribution of the IQs of the same students, however, has only one peak. How is this possible since the same students are considered in both cases? Explain.

Self-Practice Problems 2C

2.16 The following data represent the gross income, expenditure (in Rs. lakh), and net profit (in Rs. lakh) during the years 1999 to 2002.

	1999–2000	2000–2001	2001–2002
Gross income	570	592	632
Gross expenditure	510	560	610
Net income	60	32	22

Construct a diagram or chart you prefer to use here.

2.17 Which of the charts would you prefer to represent the following data pertaining to the monthly income of two families and the expenditure incurred by them.

Expenditure on	*Family A (Income Rs. 17,000)*	*Family B (Income Rs. 10,000)*
Food	4000	5400
Clothing	2800	3600
House rent	3000	3500
Education	2300	2800
Miscellaneous	3000	5000
Saving or deficits	+1900	– 300

2.18 The following data represent the outlays (Rs. crore) by heads of development.

Heads of Development	*Centre*	*States*
Agriculture	4765	7039
Irrigation and Flood control	6635	11,395
Energy	9995	8293
Industry and Minerals	12,770	2985
Transport and Communication	12,200	5120
Social services	8216	1420
Total	54,581	36,252

Represent the data by a suitable diagram and write a report on the data bringing out the silent features.

2.19 Make a diagrammatic representation of the following textile production and imports.

	Value (in crore)	*Length (in hundredyards)*
Mill production	116.4	426.9
Handloom production	106.8	192.8
Imports	319.7	64.7

What conclusions do you draw from the diagram?

2.20 Make a diagrammatic representation of the following data:

Country	*Production of Sugar in a Certain Year in Quintals (10,00,000)*
Cuba	32
Australia	30
India	20
Japan	5
Java	1
Egypt	1

2.21 The following data represent the estimated gross area under different cereal crops during a particular year.

Crop	*Gross Area ('000 hectares)*	*Crop*	*Gross Areas ('000 hectares)*
Paddy	34,321	Ragi	2656
Wheat	18,287	Maize	6749
Jowar	22,381	Barley	4422
Bajra	15,859	Small millets	6258

Draw a suitable chart to represent the data.

2.22 The following data indicate the rupee sales (in '000) of three products according to region.

Product Group	*Sales (in Rs. '000)*			*Total Sales*
	North	*South*	*East*	*(Rs. '000)*
A	70	75	90	135
B	90	60	100	250
C	50	60	40	150
	210	195	230	533

(i) Using vertical bars, construct a bar chart depicting total sales region-wise.

(ii) Construct a component chart to illustrate the product breakdown of sales region-wise by horizontal bars.

(iii) Construct a pie chart illustrating total sales.

Formulae Used

1. Class interval for a class in a frequency distribution
$$h = \text{Upper limit} - \text{Lower limit}$$
2. Midpoint of a class in a frequency distribution
$$m = \frac{\text{Upper limit} + \text{Lower limit}}{2}$$
3. Approximate interval size to be used in constructing a frequency distribution
$$h = \frac{\text{Largest data value} - \text{Smallest data value}}{\text{Number of class intervals}}$$
4. Approximate number of class intervals for constructing a frequency distribution: $2^k \geq N$, where k and N represent the number of classes and total number of observations, respectively.

Chapter Concepts Quiz

True or False

1. The midpoint of a class interval is h.
2. Frequency distribution of continuous data can be presented graphically as histograms or frequency polygons.
3. A frequency polygon is appropriate for graphing continuously distributed variables.
4. The percentile rank of a score is equal to the frequency of the scores falling up to and including the score.
5. Simple bar diagram is used only for one-dimensional comparisons.
6. Pie diagram is a circle divided into sections with areas equal to the corresponding component.
7. A pie diagram is inappropriate for representing nominally scaled data.
8. The height of a bar represents the frequency rather than the value of a variable.
9. The wider the class interval, the more specific information is lost about the actual data.
10. We cannot construct frequency distribution tables for nominally or ordinally scaled data.
11. The frequency distribution represents data in a compressed form.
12. The classes in any frequency distribution are all-inclusive and mutually exclusive.
13. A frequency polygon can always be used to construct a histogram.
14. A histogram shows each separate class in the distribution more clearly than a frequency polygon.
15. The data array does not allow us to locate the highest and lowest values in the data set.

Concepts Quiz Answers

1. F	**2.** T	**3.** F	**4.** T	**5.** T	**6.** T	**7.** T	**8.** F
9. F	**10.** F	**11.** T	**12.** T	**13.** T	**14.** T	**15.** F	

Review Self-Practice Problems

2.23 If the price of a two-bed room flat in Gurgaon varies from Rs. 9,00,000 to Rs. 12,00,000, then

(a) Indicate the class boundaries of 10 classes into which these values can be grouped

(b) What class interval width did you choose?

(c) What are the 10 class midpoints?

2.24 The raw data displayed here are the scores (out of 100 marks) of a market survey regarding the acceptability of a new product launch by a company for a random sample of 50 respondents

40	45	41	45	45	30	39	8	48
25	26	9	23	24	26	29	8	40
41	42	39	35	18	25	35	40	42
43	44	36	27	32	28	27	25	26
38	37	36	35	32	28	40	41	43
44	45	40	39	41				

(a) Form a frequency distribution having 9 class intervals

(b) Form a percentage distribution from the frequency distribution in part (a)

(c) Form a histogram of the frequency distribution in part (a)

2.25 State whether each of the following variables is qualitative or quantitative and indicate the measurement scale that is appropriate for each:

(a) Age (b) Gender
(c) Class rank (d) Annual sales
(e) Method of payment
(f) Earnings per share

2.26 The following data represent the sales of car tyres of various brands by a retail showroom of tyres during the year 2001–02.

Brand of Tyre	*Tyres Sold*
Dunlop	136
Modi	221
Firestone	138
Ceat	84
Goodyear	101
JK	120

(a) Construct a bar chart and pie chart.

(b) Which of these charts do you prefer to use? Why?

2.27 The following data represent the expenditure incurred on following heads by a company during the year 2002

Expenditure Head	*Amount (Rs. in lakh)*
Raw materials	1,689
Taxes	582
Manufacturing expenses	543
Employees salary	470
Depreciation	94
Dividend	75
Misc. expenses	286
Retained income	51

(a) Construct a bar chart and pie chart.

(b) Which of these charts do you prefer to use? Why?

2.28 Draw an ogive by less than method and determine the number of companies earning profits between Rs. 45 crore and Rs. 75 crore:

Profit (Rs. in crore)	*Number of Companies*
10–20	8
20–30	12
30–40	20
40–50	24
50–60	15
60–70	10
70–80	7
80–90	3
90–100	1

2.29 The following data represent the hottest career options in marketing:

Career Option	*Percentage*
Product Manager	23
Market Research Executive	10
Direct Marketing Manager	20
Manager-Events and Productions	10
VP Marketing	16
Other Marketing Careers	21

Develop the appropriate display(s) and thoroughly analyse the data.

2.30 The data represent the closing prices of 40 common stocks.

29	34	43	8	37	8	7	30	35
19	9	16	38	53	16	1	48	18
9	9	10	37	18	8	28	24	21
18	33	31	32	29	79	11	38	11
52	14	9	33					

(a) Construct frequency and relative frequency distributions for the data.

(b) Construct cumulative frequency and cumulative relative frequency distributions of the data.

2.31 The distribution of disability adjusted life year (DALY) loss by certain causes in in certain year (in percentage) is given below:

Cause	*India*	*China*	*World*
• Communicable diseases	50.00	25.30	45.80
• Non-communicable diseases	40.40	58.00	42.80
• Injuries	9.10	16.70	12.00

Depict this data by pie chart and bar chart.

2.32 A government hospital has the following data representing weight in kg at birth of 200 premature babies:

Weight	*Number of Babies*
0.5–0.7	14
0.8–1.0	16
1.1–1.3	25
1.4–1.6	26
1.7–1.9	28
2.0–2.2	36
2.3–2.5	37
2.6–2.8	18

(a) Develop an appropriate display(s).

(b) Calculate the approximate middle value in the data set.

(c) If a baby below 2 kg is kept in the ICU as a precaution, then what percentage of premature babies need extra care in the ICU?

2.33 The medical superintendent of a hospital is concerned about the amount of waiting time for a patient before being treated in the OPD. The following data of waiting time (in minutes) were collected during a typical day:

Waiting Time	*Number of Patients*
30–40	125
40–50	195
50–60	305
60–70	185
70–80	120
80–90	70

(a) Use the data to construct 'more than' and 'less than' frequency distributions and ogive.

(b) Use the ogive to estimate how long 75 per cent of the patients should expect to wait.

Glossary of Terms

Frequency distribution: A tabular summary of data showing the number (frequency) of observations in each of several non-overlapping class intervals.

Class mid-point: The point in each class that is halfway between the lower and upper class limits.

Cumulative frequency distribution: The cumulative number of observations less than or equal to the upper class limit of each class.

Cumulative relative frequency distribution: The cumulative number of observations less than or equal to the upper class limit of each class.

Cumulative percentage frequency distribution: The cumulative percentage of observations less than or equal to the upper class limit of each class.

Bar graph: A graphical device for depicting data that have been summarized in a frequency distribution, relative frequency distribution, or per cent frequency distribution.

Chapter 3

Measures of Central Tendency

LEARNING OBJECTIVES

After studying this chapter, you should be able to

- understand the role of descriptive statistics in summarization, description and interpretation of the data
- understand the importance of summary measures to describe characteristics of a data set
- use several numerical methods belonging to measures of central tendency to describe the characteristics of a data set

3.1 INTRODUCTION

In Chapter 2, we discussed how raw data can be organized in terms of tables, charts, and frequency distributions in order to be easily understood and analysed. Although frequency distributions and corresponding graphical representations make raw data more meaningful, yet they fail to identify three major properties that describe a set of quantitative data. These three major properties are:

(i) The numerical value of an observation (also called *central value*) around which most numerical values of other observations in the data set show a tendency to cluster or group, called the *central tendency*.

(ii) The extent to which numerical values are dispersed around the central value, called *variation*.

(iii) The extent of departure of numerical values from symmetrical (normal) distribution around the central value, called *skewness*.

These three properties—*central tendency*, *variation*, and *shape* of the frequency distribution—may be used to extract and summarize major features of the data set by the application of certain statistical methods called *descriptive measures* or *summary measures*. There are three types of summary measures:

(i) Measures of central tendency
(ii) Measures of dispersion or variation
(iii) Measure of symmetry—skewness

These measures can also be used for comparing two or more populations in terms of the properties mentioned in the previous page to draw useful inferences.

The term 'central tendency' was coined because observations (numerical values) in most data sets show a distinct tendency to group or cluster around a value of an observation located somewhere in the middle of all observations. It is necessary to identify or calculate this typical *central value* (also called *average*) to describe or project the characteristic of the entire data set. This descriptive value is the measure of the *central tendency* or *location* and methods of computing this central value are called *measures of central tendency*.

If the descriptive summary measures are computed using data of samples, then these are called **sample statistic** or simply *statistic* but if these measures are computed using data of the population, they are called **population parameters** or simply *parameters*. The population parameter is represented by the Greek letter μ (read : mu) and sample statistic is represented by the Roman letter $\bar{x}$ (read : x bar).

3.2 OBJECTIVES OF AVERAGING

A few of the objectives to calculate a typical central value or average in order to describe the entire data set are given below:

(i) It is useful to extract and summarize the characteristics of the entire data set in a precise form. For example, it is difficult to understand individual families' need for water during summers. Therefore knowledge of the average quantity of water needed for the entire population will help the government in planning for water resources.
(ii) Since an 'average' represents the entire data set, it facilitates comparison between two or more data sets. Such comparison can be made either at a point of time or over a period of time. For example, average sales figures of any month can be compared with the preceding months, or even with the sales figures of competitive firms for the same months.
(iii) It offers a base for computing various other measures such as dispersion, skewness, kurtosis that help in many other phases of statistical analysis.

3.3 REQUISITES OF A MEASURE OF CENTRAL TENDENCY

The following are the few requirements to be satisfied by an average or a measure of central tendency:

(i) **It should be rigidly defined** The definition of an average should be clear and rigid so that there must be uniformity in its interpretation by different decision-makers or investigators. There should not be any chance for applying discretion; rather it should be defined by an algebraic formula.

(ii) **It should be based on all the observations** To ensure that it should represent the entire data set, its value should be calculated by taking into consideration the entire data set.

(iii) **It should be easy to understand and calculate** The value of an average should be computed by using a simple method without reducing its accuracy and other advantages.

(iv) **It should have sampling stability** The value of an average calculated from various independent random samples of the same size from a given population should not vary much from another. The least amount of difference (if any) in the values is considered to be the sampling error.

(v) **It should be capable of further algebraic treatment** The nature of the average should be such that it could be used for statistical analysis of the data set. For example, it should be possible to determine the average production in a particular year by the use of average production in each month of that year.

(vi) **It should not be unduly affected by extreme observations** The value of an average should not be unduly affected by very small or very large observations in the given data. Otherwise the average value may not truly represent characteristics of the entire set of data.

3.4 MEASURES OF CENTRAL TENDENCY

The various measures of central tendency or averages commonly used can be broadly classified in the following categories:

(i) Mathematical Averages

(a) Arithmetic Mean commonly called the mean or average
- Simple
- Weighted

(b) Geometric Mean
(c) Harmonic Mean

(ii) Averages of Position

(a) Median
(b) Quartiles
(c) Deciles
(d) Percentiles
(e) Mode

Notations

m_i = mid-point for the ith class in the data set
f_i = number of observations (or frequency) in the ith class; (i = 1, 2, . . ., N)
N = total number of observations in the population
n = number of observations in the sample (sample size)
l = lower limit of any class interval
h = width (or size) of the class interval
cf = cumulative frequency
Σ = summation (read: sigma) of all values of observations

3.5 MATHEMATICAL AVERAGES

Various methods of calculating mathematical averages of a data set are classified in accordance of the nature of data available, that is, ungrouped (unclassified or raw) or grouped (classified) data.

3.5.1 Arithmetic Mean of Ungrouped (or Raw) Data

There are two methods for calculating **arithmetic mean (A.M.)** for ungrouped or unclassified data:

(i) Direct method, and
(ii) Indirect or Short-cut method.

Direct Method

In this method A.M. is calculated by adding the values of all observations and dividing the total by the number of observations. Thus if $x_1, x_2, \ldots, x_N$ represent the values of N observations, then A.M. for a population of N observations is:

$$\text{Population mean, } \mu = \frac{x_1 + x_2 + \ldots + x_N}{N} = \frac{1}{N}\sum_{i=1}^{N} x_i \tag{3-1a}$$

However, for a sample containing n observations $x_1, x_2, \ldots, x_n$, the sample A.M. can be written as:

$$\text{Sample mean, } \bar{x} = \frac{x_1 + x_2 + \ldots + x_n}{n} = \frac{1}{n}\sum_{i=1}^{n} x_i \tag{3-1b}$$

The denominator of above two formulae is different because in statistical analysis the uppercase letter N is used to indicate the number of observations in the population, while the lower case letter n is used to indicate the number of observations in the sample.

Example 3.1: In a survey of 5 cement companies, the profit (in Rs. lakh) earned during a year was 15, 20, 10, 35, and 32. Find the arithmetic mean of the profit earned.

Solution: Applying the formula (3-1b), we have

$$\bar{x} = \frac{1}{n}\sum_{i=1}^{5} x_i = \frac{1}{5}(15 + 20 + 10 + 35 + 32) = 22.4$$

Thus the arithmetic mean of the profit earned by these companies during a year was Rs. 22.4 lakh.

Alternative Formula In general, when observations x_i (i = 1, 2, . . ., n) are grouped as a frequency distribution, then A.M. formula (3-1b) should be modified as:

$$\bar{x} = \frac{1}{n}\sum_{i=1}^{n} f_i x_i \tag{3-2}$$

where f_i represents the frequency (number of observations) with which variable x_i occurs in the given data set, i.e. $n = \sum_{i=1}^{n} f_i$.

Example 3.2: If A, B, C, and D are four chemicals costing Rs. 15, Rs. 12, Rs. 8 and Rs. 5 per 100 g, respectively, and are contained in a given compound in the ratio of 1, 2, 3, and 4 parts, respectively, then what should be the price of the resultant compound.

Solution: Using the formula (3-2), the sample arithmetic mean is

$$\bar{x} = \frac{1}{n}\sum_{i=1}^{4} f_i x_i = \frac{1\times 15 + 2\times 12 + 3\times 8 + 4\times 5}{1+2+3+4} = \text{Rs. } 8.30$$

Thus the average price of the resultant compound should be Rs. 8.30 per 100 g.

Example 3.3: The number of new orders received by a company over the last 25 working days were recorded as follows: 3, 0, 1, 4, 4, 4, 2, 5, 3, 6, 4, 5, 1, 4, 2, 3, 0, 2, 0, 5, 4, 2, 3, 3, 1. Calculate the arithmetic mean for the number of orders received over all similar working days (Table 3.1).

Solution: Applying the formula (3-1b), the arithmetic mean is:

$$\bar{x} = \frac{1}{n}\sum_{i=1}^{25} x_i = \frac{1}{25}\,[3 + 0 + 1 + 4 + 4 + 4 + 2 + 5 + 3 + 6 + 4$$

$$+ 5 + 1 + 4 + 2 + 3 + 0 + 2 + 0 + 5 + 4 + 2 + 3 + 3 + 1]$$

$$= \frac{1}{25}\,(71) = 2.84 \cong 3 \text{ orders (approx.)}$$

Alternative approach: Use of formula (3-2)

Table 3.1 Calculations of Mean ($\bar{x}$) Value

Number of Orders (x_i)	*Frequency* (f_i)	$f_i x_i$
0	13	10
1	13	13
2	14	18
3	15	15
4	16	24
5	13	15
6	1	6
	25	71

$$\text{Arithmetic mean, } \bar{x} = \frac{1}{n}\sum f_i x_i = \frac{71}{25} = 2.8 \cong 3 \text{ orders (approx.)}$$

Example 3.4: From the following information on the number of defective components in 1000 boxes;

Number of defective components	:	0	1	2	3	4	5	6
Number of boxes	:	25	306	402	200	51	10	6

Calculate the arithmetic mean of defective components for the whole of the production line.

Solution: The calculations of mean defective components for the whole production line are shown in Table 3.2.

Table 3.2 Calculations of $\bar{x}$ for Ungrouped Data

Number of Defective Components (x_i)	*Number of Boxes* (f_i)	$f_i x_i$
0	25	0
1	306	306
2	402	804
3	200	600
4	51	204
5	10	50
6	6	36
	1000	2000

Applying the formula (3-2), the arithmetic mean is

$$\bar{x} = \frac{1}{n}\sum_{i=0}^{6} f_i x_i = \frac{1}{1000}(2000) = 2 \text{ defective components.}$$

Short-Cut Method (Ungrouped Data)

In this method an arbitrary *assumed mean* is used as a basis for calculating deviations from individual values in the data set. Let A be the arbitrary assumed A.M. and let

$$d_i = x_i - \text{A} \quad \text{or} \quad x_i = \text{A} + d_i$$

Substituting the value of x_i in formula (3-1b), we have

$$\bar{x} = \frac{1}{n}\sum_{i=1}^{n} x_i = \frac{1}{n}\sum_{i=1}^{n}(\text{A} + d_i) = \text{A} + \frac{1}{n}\sum_{i=1}^{n} d_i \qquad (3\text{-}3)$$

If frequencies of the numerical values are also taken into consideration, then the formula (3-3) becomes:

$$\bar{x} = \text{A} + \frac{1}{n}\sum_{i=1}^{n} f_i d_i \qquad (3\text{-}4)$$

where $n = \sum_{i=1}^{n} f_i$ = total number of observations in the sample.

Example 3.5: The daily earnings (in rupees) of employees working on a daily basis in a firm are:

Daily earnings (Rs.) :	100	120	140	160	180	200	220
Number of employees :	3	6	10	15	24	42	75

Calculate the average daily earning for all employees.

Solution: The calculations of average daily earning for employees are shown in Table 3.3.

Table 3.3 Calculations of $\bar{x}$ for Ungrouped Data

Daily Earnings (in Rs) (x_i)	*Number of Employees* (f_i)	$d_i = x_i - A$ $= x_i - 160$	$f_i d_i$
100	3	– 60	– 180
120	6	– 40	– 240
140	10	– 20	– 200
(160) ← A	15	0	0
180	24	20	480
200	42	40	1680
220	75	60	4500
	175		6040

Here A = 160 is taken as assumed mean. The required A.M. using the formula (3-4) is given by

$$\bar{x} = \text{A} + \frac{1}{n}\sum_{i=1}^{7} f_i d_i = 160 + \frac{6040}{175} = \text{Rs. } 194.51$$

Example 3.6: The human resource manager at a city hospital began a study of the overtime hours of the registered nurses. Fifteen nurses were selected at random, and following overtime hours during a month were recorded:

13 13 12 15 7 15 5 12 6 7 12 10 9 13 12
5 9 6 10 5 6 9 6 9 12

Calculate the arithmetic mean of overtime hours during the month.

Solution: Calculations of arithmetic mean of overtime hours are shown in Table 3.4.

Table 3.4 Calculations of $\overline{x}$ for Ungrouped Data

Overtime Hours (x_i)	*Number of Number* (f_i)	$d_i = x_i - A$ $= x_i - 10$	$f_i d_i$
5	3	– 5	– 15
6	4	– 4	– 16
7	2	– 3	– 6
9	4	– 1	– 4
(10) ← A	2	0	0
12	5	2	10
13	3	3	9
15	2	5	10
	25		– 12

Here A=10 is taken as assumed mean. The required arithmetic mean of overtime using the formula (3-4) is as follows:

$$\overline{x} = A + \frac{1}{n}\sum_{i=1}^{25} f_i d_i = 10 - \frac{12}{25} = 9.52 \text{ hours}$$

3.5.2 Arithmetic Mean of Grouped (or Classified) Data

Arithmetic mean for grouped data can also be calculated by applying any of the following methods:

(i) Direct method, and
(ii) Indirect or Step-deviation method

For calculating arithmetic mean for a grouped data set, the following assumptions are made:

(i) The class intervals must be closed.
(ii) The width of each class interval should be equal.
(iii) The values of the observations in each class interval must be uniformly distributed between its lower and upper limits.
(iv) The mid-value of each class interval must represent the average of all values in that class, that is, it is assumed that all values of observations are evenly distributed between the lower and upper class limits.

Direct Method

The formula used in this method is same as formula (3-2) except that x_i is replaced with the mid-point value m_i of class intervals. The new formula becomes:

$$\overline{x} = \frac{1}{n}\sum_{i=1}^{n} f_i m_i \quad (3\text{-}5)$$

where m_i = mid-value of ith class interval.
f_i = frequency of ith class interval.
$n = \Sigma f_i$, sum of all frequencies

Example 3.7: A company is planning to improve plant safety. For this, accident data for the last 50 weeks was compiled. These data are grouped into the frequency distribution as shown below. Calculate the A.M. of the number of accidents per week.

Number of accidents :	0–4	5–9	10–14	15–19	20–24
Number of weeks :	5	22	13	8	2

Solution: The calculations of A.M. are shown in Table 3.5 using formula (3-5).

Table 3.5 Arithmetic Mean of Accidents

Number of Accidents	*Mid-value* (m_i)	*Number of Weeks* (f_i)	$f_i m_i$
0–4	2	5	10
5–9	7	22	154
10–14	12	13	156
15–19	17	8	136
20–24	22	2	44
		50	500

The A.M. of the number of accidents per week is:

$$\bar{x} = \frac{1}{n}\sum_{i=1}^{5} f_i m_i = \frac{500}{50} = 10 \text{ accidents per week.}$$

Step-deviation Method The formula (3-5) for calculating A.M. can be improved as formula (3-6). This improved formula is also known as the *step-deviation method:*

$$\bar{x} = A + \frac{\Sigma\, f_i d_i}{n} \times h \qquad (3\text{-}6)$$

where A = assumed value for the A.M.
$n = \Sigma f_i$, sum of all frequencies
h = width of the class intervals
m_i = mid-value of ith class-interval
$d_i = \dfrac{m_i - A}{h}$, deviation from the assumed mean

The formula (3-6) is very useful in those cases where mid-values (m_i) and/or frequencies (f_i) are in three or more digits. The calculation of d_i from m_i involves reducing each m_i by an amount A (called assumed arithmetic mean) and then dividing the reduced values by h (width of class intervals). This procedure is usually referred to as *change of location and scale* or *coding*.

Example 3.8: Calculate the arithmetic mean of accidents per week by the short cut method using the data of Example 3.7.

Solution: The calculations of the average number of accidents are shown in the Table 3.6.

Table 3.6 Arithmetic Mean of Accidents

Number of Accidents	*Mid-value* (m_i)	$d_i = (m_i - A)/h$ $= (m_i - 12)/5$	*Number of Weeks* (f_i)	$f_i d_i$
0–14	2	−2	5	−10
5–19	7	−1	22	−22
10–14	(12) ← A	0	13	0
15–19	17	1	8	8
20–24	22	2	2	4
			50	−20

The arithmetic mean $\bar{x} = A + \left(\frac{1}{n}\Sigma f_i d_i\right)h$

$$= 12 + \left(\frac{1}{50}(-20)\right)5 = 10 \text{ accidents per week}$$

Example 3.9: The following distribution gives the pattern of overtime work done by 100 employees of a company. Calculate the average overtime work done per employee.

Overtime hours :	10–15	15–20	20–25	25–30	30–35	35–40
Number of employees :	11	20	35	20	8	6

Solution: The calculations of the average overtime work done per employee with assumed mean, A = 22.5 and h = 5 are given in Table 3.7.

Table 3.7 Calculations of Average Overtime

Overtime (hrs) x_i	*Number of Employees*, f_i	*Mid-value* (m_i)	$d_i = (m_i - 22.5)/5$	$f_i d_i$
10–15	11	12.5	−2	−22
15–20	20	17.5	−1	−20
20–25	35	(22.5) ← A	0	0
25–30	20	27.5	1	20
30–35	8	32.5	2	16
35–40	6	37.5	3	18
	100			12

The required A.M. is, $\bar{x} = A + \frac{\Sigma f_i d_i}{n} \times h = 22.5 + \frac{12}{100} \times 5 = 23.1$ hrs

Example 3.10: The following is the age distribution of 1000 persons working in an organization:

Age Group	*Number of Persons*	*Age Group*	*Number of Persons*
20–25	30	45–50	105
25–30	160	50–55	70
30–35	210	55–60	60
35–40	180	60–65	40
40–45	145		

Due to continuous losses, it is desired to bring down the manpower strength to 30 per cent of the present number according to the following scheme:

(a) Retrench the first 15 per cent from the lower age group.

(b) Absorb the next 45 per cent in other branches.

(c) Make 10 per cent from the highest age group retire permanently, if necessary.

Calculate the age limits of the persons retained and those to be transferred to other departments. Also find the average age of those retained.

Solution: (a) The first 15 per cent persons to be retrenched from the lower age groups are $(15/100)\times 1000 = 150$. But the lowest age group 20–25 has only 30 persons and therefore the remaining, $150 - 30 = 120$ will be taken from next higher age group, that is, 25–30, which has 160 persons.

(b) The next 45 per cent, that is, $(45/100)\times 1000 = 450$ persons who are to be absorbed in other branches, belong to the following age groups:

Age Groups	*Number of Persons*
25–30	(160 – 120) = 40
30–35	210
35–40	180
40–45	(450 – 40 – 210 – 180) = 20

(c) Those who are likely to be retired are 10 per cent, that is, $(10/100)\times 1000 = 100$ persons and belong to the following highest age groups:

Age Group	*Number of Persons*
55–60	(100 – 40) = 60
60–65	40

Hence, the calculations of the average age of those retained and/or to be transferred to other departments are shown in Table 3.8.

Table 3.8 Calculations of Average Age

Age Group (x_i)	*Mid value,* (m_i)	*Number of Persons* (f_i)	$d_i = (x_i - 47.5)/5$	$f_i d_i$
40–45	42.5	145 – 20 = 125	– 1	– 125
45–50	(47.5) ← A	105	0	0
50–55	52.5	70	1	70
		300		– 55

The required average age is, $\bar{x} = A + \frac{\sum d_i f_i}{n} \times h = 47.5 - \frac{55}{300} \times 5 = 46.58 = 47$ years (approx.).

3.5.3 Some Special Types of Problems and Their Solutions

Case 1: Frequencies are Given in Cumulative Form, that is, either 'More Than Type' or 'Less Than Type'

As we know that the 'more than type' cumulative frequencies are calculated by adding frequencies from bottom to top, so that the first class interval has the highest cumulative frequency and it goes on decreasing in subsequent classes. But in casc of 'less than cumulative frequencies', the cumulation is done downward so that the first class interval has the lowest cumulative frequency and it goes on increasing in the subsequent classes.

In both of these cases, data are first converted into inclusive class intervals or exclusive class intervals. Then the calculations for $\bar{x}$ are done in the usual manner as discussed earlier.

Example 3.11: Following is the cumulative frequency distribution of the preferred length of kitchen slabs obtained from the preference study on housewives:

Length (in metres) more than :	1.0	1.5	2.0	2.5	3.0	3.5
Preference of housewives :	50	48	42	40	10	5

A manufacturer has to take a decision on what length of slabs to manufacture. What length would you recommend and why?

Solution: The given data are converted into exclusive class intervals as shown in Table 3.9. The frequency of each class has been found out by deducting the given cumulative frequency from the cumulative frequency of the previous class:

Table 3.9 Conversion into Exclusive Class Intervals

Length (in metres)	*Preference of Housewives more than*	*Class Interval*	*Frequency*
1.0	50	1.0–1.5	(50 – 48) = 2
1.5	48	1.5–2.0	(48 – 42) = 6
2.0	42	2.0–2.5	(42 – 40) = 2
2.5	40	2.5–3.0	(40 – 10) = 30
3.0	10	3.0–3.5	(10 – 5) = 5
3.5	5		

The calculations for mean length of slab are shown in Table 3.10.

Table 3.10 Calculations of Mean Length of Slab

Class Interval	*Mid-value* (m_i)	*Preference of Housewives* (f_i)	$d_i = \frac{m_i - 2.25}{0.5}$	$f_i d_i$
1.0–1.5	1.25	2	– 2	– 4
1.5–2.0	1.75	6	– 1	– 6
2.0–2.5	(2.25) ← A	2	0	0
2.5–3.0	2.75	30	1	30
3.0–3.5	3.25	5	2	10
		45		30

The mean length of the slab is $\bar{x} = A + \frac{\Sigma f_i d_i}{n} \times h = 2.25 + \frac{30}{45} \times 0.5 = 2.58$ metres.

Example 3.12: In an examination of 675 candidates, the examiner supplied the following information:

Marks Obtained (Percentage)	*Number of Candidates*	*Marks Obtained (Percentage)*	*Number of Candidates*
Less than 10	7	Less than 50	381
Less than 20	39	Less than 60	545
Less than 30	95	Less than 70	631
Less than 40	201	Less than 80	675

Calculate the mean percentage of marks obtained.

Solution: Arranging the given data into inclusive class intervals as shown in Table 3.11.

Table 3.11 Calculations of Mean Percentage of Marks

Marks Obtained (Percentage)	*Cumulative Frequency*	*Class-intervals*	*Frequency*
Less than 10	7	0–10	7
Less than 20	39	10–20	(39 – 7) = 32
Less than 30	95	20–30	(95 – 39) = 56
Less than 40	201	30–40	(201 – 95) = 106
Less than 50	381	40–50	(381 – 201) = 180
Less than 60	545	50–60	(545 – 381) = 164
Less than 70	631	60–70	(631 – 545) = 86
Less than 80	675	70–80	(675 – 631) = 44

The calculations for mean percentage of marks obtained by the candidates are shown in Table 3.12.

Table 3.12 Calculations of Mean Percentage of Marks

Class Intervals	*Mid-value* (m_i)	*Number of Candidates* (f_i)	$d_i = \frac{m_i - 35}{10}$	$f_i d_i$
0–10	5	7	– 3	– 21
10–20	15	32	– 2	– 64
20–30	25	56	– 1	– 56
30–40	(35) ← A	106	0	0
40–50	45	180	1	180
50–60	55	164	2	328
60–70	65	86	3	258
70–80	75	44	4	176
		675		801

The mean percentage of marks obtained is:

$$\overline{x} = A + \frac{\sum f_i d_i}{n} \times h = 35 + \frac{801}{675} \times 10 = 46.86 \text{ marks}$$

Case 2: Frequencies are not Given but have to be Calculated From the Given Data

Example 3.13: 168 handloom factories have the following distribution of average number of workers in various income groups:

Income groups	:	800–1000	1000–1200	1200–1400	1400–1600	1600–1800
Number of firms	:	40	32	26	28	42
Average number of workers	:	8	12	8	8	4

Find the mean salary paid to the workers.

Solution: Since the total number of workers (i.e. frequencies) working in different income groups are not given, therefore these have to be determined as shown in Table 3.13.

Table 3.13

Income Group (x_i) (1)	*Mid-values* (m_i) (2)	$d_i = \frac{m_i - A}{h} = \frac{m_i - 1300}{200}$	*Number of Firms* (3)	*Average Number of Workers* (4)	*Frequencies* (f_i) (5) = (3) × (4)	$m_i f_i$
800–1000	900	– 2	40	8	320	– 640
1000–1200	1100	– 1	32	12	384	– 384
1200–1400	(1300) ← A	0	26	8	208	0
1400–1600	1500	1	28	8	224	224
1600–1800	1700	2	42	4	168	336
			168	40	1304	– 464

The required A.M. is given by

$$\bar{x} = A + \frac{\Sigma\ m_i f_i}{n} \times h = 1300 - \frac{464}{1304} \times 200 = 1228.84$$

Example 3.14: Find the missing frequencies in the following frequency distribution. The A.M. of the given data is 11.09.

Class Interval	*Frequency*	*Class*	*Frequency*
9.3–9.7	2	11.3–11.7	14
9.8–10.2	5	11.8–12.2	6
10.3–10.7	f_3	12.3–12.7	3
10.8–11.2	f_4	12.8–13.2	1
			60

Solution: The calculations for A.M. are shown in Table 3.14.

Table 3.14

Class Interval	*Frequency* (f_i)	*Mid-value* (m_i)	$d_i = \dfrac{m_i - 11.0}{0.5}$	$f_i d_i$
9.3–9.7	2	9.5	–3	–6
9.8–10.2	5	10.0	–2	–10
10.3–10.7	f_3	10.5	–1	$-f_3$
10.8–11.2	f_4	(11.0)	← A	0 0
11.3–11.7	14	11.5	1	14
11.8–12.2	6	12.0	2	12
12.3–12.7	3	12.5	3	9
12.8–13.2	1	13.0	4	4
	60			$23 - f_3$

where the assumed mean is, A = 11. Applying the formula

$$\bar{x} = A + \frac{\Sigma\ f_i\ d_i}{n} \times h$$

we get $$11.09 = 11.0 + \frac{23 - f_3}{60} \times 0.5$$

or $$0.09 = \frac{23 - f_3}{120} \quad \text{or} \quad f_3 = 23 - 0.09 \times 120 = 12.2$$

Since the total of the frequencies is 60 and f_3 = 12.2, therefore

$$f_4 = 60 - (2 + 5 + 12.2 + 14 + 6 + 3 + 1) = 16.8$$

Case 3: Complete Data are Not Given

Example 3.15: The pass result of 50 students who took a class test is given below:

Marks :	40	50	60	70	80	90
Number of students :	8	10	9	6	4	3

If the mean marks for all the students was 51.6, find out the mean marks of the students who failed.

Solution: The marks obtained by 40 students who passed are given in Table 3.15.

Table 3.15

Marks	*Frequency* (f_i)	$f_i x_i$
40	8	320
50	10	500
60	9	540
70	6	420
80	4	320
90	3	270
	40	2370

Total marks of all the students = 50 × 51.6 = 2580

Total marks of 40 students who passed = $\Sigma f_i x_i$ = 2370

Thus, marks of the remaining 10 students = 2580 – 2370 = 210. Hence, the average marks of 10 students who failed are 210/10 = 21 marks.

Case 4: Incorrect Values have been used for the Calculation of Arithmetic Mean

Example 3.16: (a) The average dividend declared by a group of 10 chemical companies was 18 per cent. Later on, it was discovered that one correct figure, 12, was misread as 22. Find the correct average dividend.

(b) The mean of 200 observations was 50. Later on, it was found that two observations were misread as 92 and 8 instead of 192 and 88. Find the correct mean.

Solution: (a) Given n = 10 and $\bar{x}$ = 18 per cent. We know that

$$\bar{x} = \frac{\Sigma x}{n} \quad \text{or} \quad \Sigma x = n\bar{x} = 10 \times 18 = 180$$

Since one numerical value 12 was misread as 22, therefore after subtracting the incorrect value and then adding the correct value in the total $n\bar{x}$, we have 180 – 22 + 12 = 170. Hence, correct mean is $\bar{x} = \Sigma x/n$ = 170/10 = 17 per cent.

(b) Given that n = 200, $\bar{x}$ = 50. We know that

$$\bar{x} = \frac{\Sigma x}{n} \quad \text{or} \quad \Sigma x = n\bar{x} = 200 \times 50 = 10{,}000$$

Since two observations were misread, therefore the correct total $\Sigma x = n\bar{x}$ can be obtained as:

$$\Sigma x = 10{,}000 - (92 + 8) + (192 + 88) = 10{,}180$$

Hence, correct mean is : $\bar{x} = \dfrac{\Sigma x}{n} = \dfrac{10{,}180}{200} = 50.9$

Case 5: Frequency Distributions have Open-Ended Class Intervals

Example 3.17: The annual salaries (in rupees thousands) of employees in an organization are given below: The total salary of 10 employees in the class over Rs. 40,000 is Rs. 9,00,000. Compute the mean salary. Every employee belonging to the top 25 per cent of earners has to pay 5 per cent of his salary to the workers' relief fund. Estimate the contribution to this fund.

Salary (Rs '000)	*Number of Employees*
below 10	4
10–20	6
20–30	10
30–40	20
40 and above	10

Solution: Since class intervals are uniform, therefore we can take some width for open-end class intervals also. Calculations of mean are shown in Table 3.16.

Table 3.16

Salary (Rs '000)	*Mid-value* (m_i)	*Number of Employees* (f_i)	$d_i = \frac{m_i - 25}{10}$	$f_i d_i$
0–10	5	4	−2	−8
10–20	15	6	−1	−6
20–30	(25) ← A	10	0	0
30–40	35	20	1	20
40 and above	45 (given)	10	2	20
		50		26

where mid-value 25 is considered as the assumed mean. Applying the formula, we get

$$\bar{x} = \text{A} + \frac{\sum f_i d_i}{n} \times h = 25 + \frac{26}{50} \times 10 = \text{Rs. } 30.2$$

The number of employees belonging to the top 25 per cent of the earners are $0.25 \times 50 = 13$ employees and the distribution of these top earners would be as follows:

Salary (Rs '000)	*Number of Employees*
40 and above	10
30–40	3

This calculation implies that 3 employees have been selected from the salary range 30–40. Under the assumption that frequencies are equally distributed between lower and upper limits of a class interval, the calculations would be as follows:

Since 20 employees have salary in the range 30–40 = 10 or Rs. 10,000, therefore 3 employees will have income in the range $(10/20) \times 3 = 1.5$ or Rs. 1,500. But we are interested in the top 3 earners in the range 30–40, their salaries will range from (40 – 1.5) to 40, i.e., 38.5 to 40. Thus, the distribution of salaries of the top 25 persons is as follows:

Salary (Rs '000)	*Mid-value* (m_i)	*Number of Employees* (f_i)	*Total Salary* ($m_i f_i$)
40 and above	—	10	9,00,000 (given)
30–40	35	3	1,05,000
		13	10,05,000

This shows that the total income of the top 25 per cent of earners is Rs. 10,05,000. Hence 5 per cent contribution to the fund is $0.05 \times 10{,}05{,}000$ = Rs. 50,250.

Remark: If the width of class intervals is not same, then in accordance with the magnitude of change in the width, fix the width of last class interval.

3.5.4 Advantages and Disadvantages of Arithmetic Mean

Advantages

(i) The calculation of arithmetic mean is simple and it is unique, that is, every data set has one and only one mean.

(ii) The calculation of arithmetic mean is based on all values given in the data set.

(iii) The arithmetic mean is reliable single value that reflects all values in the data set.

(iv) The arithmetic mean is least affected by fluctuations in the sample size. In other words, its value, determined from various samples drawn from a population, varies by the least possible amount.

(v) It can be readily put to algebraic treatment. Some of the algebraic properties of arithmetic mean are as follows:

(a) *The algebraic sum of deviations of all the observations x_i $(i = 1, 2 \ldots, n)$ from the A.M. is always zero, that is,*

$$\sum_{i=1}^{n} (x_i - \bar{x}) = \sum_{i=1}^{n} x_i - n\bar{x} = \sum_{i=1}^{n} x_i - n\left(\frac{1}{n}\right) \sum_{i=1}^{n} x_i = 0$$

Here the difference $x_i - \bar{x}$ $(i = 1, 2, \ldots, n)$ is usually referred to as *deviation from the arithmetic mean*. This result is also true for grouped data.

Due to this property, the mean is characterized as a *point of balance*, i.e. sum of the positive deviations from mean is equal to the sum of the negative deviations from mean.

(b) *The sum of the squares of the deviations of all the observations from the A.M. is less than the sum of the squares of all the observations from any other quantity.*

Let x_i $(i = 1, 2, \ldots, n)$ be the given observations and $\bar{x}$ be their arithmetic mean. Then this property implies that

$$\sum_{i=1}^{n} (x_i - \bar{x})^2 \leq \sum_{i=1}^{n} (x_i - a)^2$$

where 'a' is any constant quantity.

This property of A.M. is also known as the *least square property* and shall be quite helpful in defining the concept of standard deviation.

(c) *It is possible to calculate the combined (or pooled) arithmetic mean of two or more than two sets of data of the same nature.*

Let $\bar{x}_1$ and $\bar{x}_2$ be arithmetic means of two sets of data of the same nature, of size n_1 and n_2 respectively. Then their *combined A.M.* can be calculated as:

$$\bar{x}_{12} = \frac{n_1 \bar{x}_1 + n_2 \bar{x}_2}{n_1 + n_2} \qquad (3\text{-}7)$$

The result (3-7) can also be generalized in the same way for more than two sets of data of different sizes having different arithmetic means.

(d) While compiling the data for calculating arithmetic mean, it is possible that we may wrongly read and/or write certain number of observations. In such a case, the correct value of A.M. can be calculated first by subtracting the sum of observations wrongly recorded from Σx_i (total of all observations) and then adding the sum of the correct observations to it. The result is then divided by the total number of observations.

Disadvantages

(i) The value of A.M. cannot be calculated accurately for unequal and open-ended class intervals either at the beginning or end of the given frequency distribution.

(ii) The A.M. is reliable and reflects all the values in the data set. However, it is very much affected by the extreme observations (or outliers) which are not representative of the rest of the data set. Outliers at the high end will increase the mean, while outliers at the lower end will decrease it. For example, if monthly income of four persons is 50, 70, 80, and 1000, then their A.M. will be 300, which does not represent the data.

(iii) The calculation of A.M. sometime becomes difficult because every data element is used in the calculation (unless the short cut method for grouped data is used to calculate the mean). Moreover, the value so obtained may not be among the observations included in the data.

(iv) The mean cannot be calculated for qualitative characteristics such as intelligence, honesty, beauty, or loyalty.

(v) The mean cannot be calculated for a data set that has open-ended classes at either the high or low end of the scale.

Example 3.18: The mean salary paid to 1500 employees of an organization was found to be Rs. 12,500. Later on, after disbursement of salary, it was discovered that the salary of two employees was wrongly entered as Rs. 15,760 and 9590. Their correct salaries were Rs. 17,760 and 8590. Calculate correct mean.

Solution: Let x_i (i = 1, 2, . . ., 1500) be the salary of ith employee. Then we are given that

$$\bar{x} = \frac{1}{1500} \sum_{i=1}^{1500} x_i = 12{,}500$$

or

$$\sum_{i=1}^{1500} x_i = 12{,}500 \times 1500 = \text{Rs. } 1{,}87{,}50{,}000$$

This gives the total salary disbursed to all 1500 employees. Now after adding the correct salary figures of two employees and subtracting the wrong salary figures posted against two employees, we have

$$\begin{aligned} \sum x_i &= 1{,}87{,}50{,}000 + (\text{Sum of correct salaries figures}) \\ &\quad - (\text{Sum of wrong salaries figures}) \\ &= 18{,}75{,}000 + (17{,}760 + 8590) - (15{,}760 + 9590) \\ &= 1{,}87{,}50{,}000 + 26{,}350 - 25{,}350 = 1{,}88{,}01{,}700 \end{aligned}$$

Thus the correct mean salary is given by

$$\bar{x} = 1{,}88{,}01{,}700 \div 1500 = \text{Rs. } 12{,}534.46$$

Example 3.19: There are two units of an automobile company in two different cities employing 760 and 800 persons, respectively. The arithmetic means of monthly salaries paid to persons in these two units are Rs. 18,750 and Rs. 16,950 respectively. Find the combined arithmetic mean of salaries of the employees in both the units.

Solution: Let n_1 and n_2 be the number of persons working in unit 1 and 2 respectively, and $\bar{x}_1$ and $\bar{x}_2$ be the arithmetic mean of salaries paid to these persons respectively. We are given that:

Unit 1: $n_1 = 760$; $\bar{x}_1$ = Rs. 18,750

Unit 2: $n_2 = 800$; $\bar{x}_2$ = Rs. 16,950

Thus the combined mean of salaries paid by the company is:

$$\bar{x}_{12} = \frac{n_1\bar{x}_1 + n_2\bar{x}_2}{n_1 + n_2} = \frac{760 \times 18750 + 800 \times 16950}{760 + 800}$$

$$= \text{Rs. } 17{,}826.92 \text{ per month}$$

Example 3.20: The mean yearly salary paid to all employees in a company was Rs. 24,00,000. The mean yearly salaries paid to male and female employees were Rs. 25,00,000 and Rs. 19,00,000, respectively. Find out the percentage of male to female employees in the company.

Solution: Let n_1 and n_2 be the number of employees as male and female, respectively. We are given that

Characteristics	*Groups*		*Combined Group (Total Employees)*
	Male	*Female*	
Number of employees	$n_1 = ?$	$n_2 = ?$	$n = n_1 + n_2$
Mean salary (Rs)	$\bar{x}_1 = 25{,}00{,}000$	$\bar{x}_2 = 19{,}00{,}000$	$\bar{x}_{12} = 24{,}00{,}000$

Applying the formula for mean of combined group:

$$\bar{x}_{12} = \frac{n_1\bar{x}_1 + n_2\bar{x}_2}{n_1 + n_2}$$

or

$$(n_1 + n_2)\,\bar{x}_{12} = n_1\,\bar{x}_1 + n_2\,\bar{x}_2$$

$$(n_1 + n_2)\; 24{,}00{,}000 = 25{,}00{,}000\, n_1 + 19{,}00{,}000\, n_2$$

$$1000\, n_1 = 5000\, n_2$$

$$\frac{n_1}{n_2} = \frac{5000}{1000} = \frac{5}{1} \quad \text{or} \quad n_1 : n_2 = 5 : 1$$

Hence, male employees in the company are $\{5 \div (5 + 1)\} \times 100 = 83.33$ per cent and female employees are $\{1 \div (5 + 1)\} \times 100 = 16.67$ per cent.

3.5.5 Weighted Arithmetic Mean

The arithmetic mean, as discussed earlier, gives equal importance (or weight) to each observation in the data set. However, there are situations in which values of individual observations in the data set are not of equal importance. If values occur with different frequencies, then computing A.M. of values (as opposed to the A.M. of observations) may not be a true representative of the data set characteristic and thus may be misleading. Under these circumstances, we may attach to each observation value a 'weight' $w_1, w_2, \ldots, w_N$ as an indicator of their importance perhaps because of size or importance and compute a weighted mean or average denoted by $\bar{x}_w$ as:

$$\mu_w \text{ or } \bar{x}_w = \frac{\sum x_i w_i}{\sum w_i}$$

This is similar to the method for dealing with frequency data when the value is multiplied by the frequency, within each class, totalled and divided by the total number of values.

Remark: The **weighted arithmetic mean** should be used

(i) when the importance of all the numerical values in the given data set is not equal.
(ii) when the frequencies of various classes are widely varying
(iii) where there is a change either in the proportion of numerical values or in the proportion of their frequencies.
(iv) when ratios, percentages, or rates are being averaged.

Example 3.21: An examination was held to decide the awarding of a scholarship. The weights of various subjects were different. The marks obtained by 3 candidates (out of 100 in each subject) are given below:

Subject	*Weight*	*Students*		
		A	*B*	*C*
Mathematics	4	60	57	62
Physics	3	62	61	67
Chemistry	2	55	53	60
English	1	67	77	49

Calculate the weighted A.M. to award the scholarship.

Solution: The calculations of the weighted arithmetic mean is shown in Table 3.17

Table 3.17 Calculations of Weighted Arithmetic Mean

Subject	*Weight* (w_i)	*Students*					
		Student A		*Student B*		*Student C*	
		Marks (x_i)	$x_i w_i$	*Marks* (x_i)	$x_i w_i$	*Marks* (x_i)	$x_i w_i$
Mathematics	4	60	240	57	228	62	248
Physics	3	62	186	61	183	67	201
Chemistry	2	55	110	53	106	60	120
English	1	67	67	77	77	49	49
	10	244	603	248	594	238	618

Applying the formula for weighted mean, we get

$$\bar{x}_{wA} = \frac{603}{10} = 60.3\ ; \quad \bar{x}_A = \frac{244}{4} = 61$$

$$\bar{x}_{wB} = \frac{594}{10} = 59.4\ ; \quad \bar{x}_B = \frac{248}{4} = 62$$

$$\bar{x}_{wC} = \frac{618}{10} = 61.8\ ; \quad \bar{x}_c = \bar{x}_c = 59.5$$

From the above calculations, it may be noted that student B should get the scholarship as per simple A.M. values, but according to weighted A.M., student C should get the scholarship because all the subjects of examination are not of equal importance.

Example 3.22: The owner of a general store was interested in knowing the mean contribution (sales price minus variable cost) of his stock of 5 items. The data is given below:

Product	*Contribution per Unit*	*Quantity Sold*
1	6	160
2	11	60
3	8	260
4	4	460
5	14	110

Solution: If the owner ignores the values of the individual products and gives equal importance to each product, then the mean contribution per unit sold will be

$$\bar{x} = (1 \div 5)\ \{6 + 11 + 8 + 4 + 14\} = \text{Rs. } 8.6$$

This value, Rs. 8.60 may not necessarily be the mean contribution per unit of different quantities of the products sold. In this case the owner has to take into consideration the number of units of each product sold as different weights. Computing weighted A.M. by multiplying units sold (w) of a product by its contribution (x). That is,

$$\bar{x}_w = \frac{6(160) + 11(60) + 8(260) + 4(460) + 14(110)}{160 + 60 + 260 + 460 + 110} = \frac{7{,}080}{1{,}050} = \text{Rs. } 6.74$$

This value, Rs. 6.74, is different from the earlier value, Rs. 8.60. The owner must use the value Rs. 6.74 for decision-making purpose.

Example 3.23: A management consulting firm, has four types of professionals on its staff: managing consultants, senior associates, field staff, and office staff. Average rates charged to consulting clients for the work of each of these professional categories are Rs. 3150/hour, Rs. 1680/hour, Rs. 1260/hour, and 630/hour respectively. Office records indicate the following number of hours billed last year in each category: 8000, 14,000, 24,000, and 35,000 respectively. If the firm is trying to come up with an average billing rate for estimating client charges for next year, what would you suggest they do and what do you think is an appropriate rate?

Solution: The data given in the problem are as follows:

Staff	*Consulting Charges (Rs per hour)* x_i	*Hours Billed* w_i
Managing consultants	3150	8000
Senior associates	1680	14,000
Field staff	1260	24,000
Office staff	630	35,000

Applying the formula for weighted mean, we get,

$$\bar{x}_w = \frac{\Sigma x_i w_i}{\Sigma w_i} = \frac{3150(8000) + 1680\,(14{,}000) + 1260\,(24{,}000) + 630\,(35{,}000)}{8000 + 14{,}000 + 24{,}000 + 35{,}000}$$

$$= \frac{2{,}52{,}00{,}000 + 2{,}35{,}20{,}000 + 3{,}02{,}40{,}000 + 2{,}20{,}50{,}000}{81{,}000}$$

$$= \text{Rs. } 1247.037 \text{ per hour}$$

However, the firm should cite this as an average rate for clients who use the four professional categories for approximately 10 per cent, 17 per cent, 30 per cent and 43 per cent of the total hours billed.

Example 3.24: Calculate arithmetic mean from the data given below :

Marks :	0 – 10	10 – 20	20 – 30	30 – 40	40 – 50
No. of Students :	7	6	15	12	10

[*GJ Univ., BBA, 2005*]

Solution: Calculations required to find arithmetic mean from a classified data are shown below:

Marks	*Mid-values (m)*	*No. of Students (f)*	*fm*
0 – 10	5	7	25
10 – 20	15	6	90
20 – 30	25	15	375
30 – 40	35	12	420
40 – 50	45	10	450
		$\Sigma f = 50$	$\Sigma fm = 1370$

$$A.M., (\bar{x}) = \frac{\Sigma fm}{\Sigma f} = \frac{1370}{50} = 27.4$$

Conceptual Questions 3A

1. Explain the term *average*. What are the merits of a good average? Explain with examples.
2. What are the measures of central tendency? Why are they called measures of central tendency?
3. What are the different measures of central tendency? Mention the advantages and disadvantages of arithmetic mean.
4. What are the different measures of central tendency? Discuss the essentials of an ideal average.
5. Give a brief description of the various measures of central tendency. Why is arithmetic mean so popular?
6. What information about a body of data is provided by an average? How are averages useful as a descriptive measure?
7. It is said that the weighted mean is commonly referred to as a 'weighted average'. How is the use of this phrase inconsistent with the definition of an average?
8. How is an average considered as a representative measure or a measure of central tendency? How is the ability of an average to measure central tendency related to other characteristics of data?
9. What is statistical average? What are the desirable properties for an average to possess? Mention the different types of averages and state why arithmetic mean is the most commonly used amongst them.

Self-Practice Problems 3A

3.1 An investor buys Rs. 12,000 worth of shares of a company each month. During the first 5 months he bought the shares at a price of Rs. 100, Rs. 120, Rs. 150, Rs. 200, and Rs. 240 per share respectively. After 5 months what is the average price paid for the shares by him?

3.2 A company wants to pay bonus to members of the staff. The bonus is to be paid as under:

Monthly Salary (in Rs.)	*Bonus*
3000–4000	1000
4000–5000	1200
5000–6000	1400
6000–7000	1600
7000–8000	1800
8000–9000	2200
9000–10,000	2200
10,000–11,000	2400

Actual amount of salary drawn by the employees is given below:

3250 3780 4200 4550 6200 6600
6800 7250 3630 8320 9420 9520
8000 10,020 10,280 11,000 6100 6250
7630 3820 5400 4630 5780 7230
6900

How much would the company need to pay by way of bonus? What shall be the average bonus paid per member of the staff?

3.3 Calculate the simple and weighted arithmetic mean price per tonne of coal purchased by a company for the half year. Account for difference between the two:

Month	*Price/ tonne*	*Tonnes Purchased*	*Month*	*Price/ tonne*	*Tonnes Purchased*
January	4205	25	April	5200	52
February	5125	30	May	4425	10
March	5000	40	June	5400	45

3.4 Salary paid by a company to its employees is as follows:

Designation	*Monthly Salary (in Rs.)*	*Number of Persons*
Senior Manager	35,000	1
Manager	30,000	20
Executives	25,000	70
Jr Executives	20,000	10
Supervisors	15,000	150

Calculate the simple and weighted arithmetic mean of salary paid.

3.6 The mean monthly salary paid to all employees in a company is Rs. 16,000. The mean monthly salaries paid to technical and non-technical employees are Rs. 18,000 and Rs. 12,000 respectively. Determine the percentage of technical and non-technical employees in the company.

3.7 The mean marks in statistics of 100 students in a class was 72 per cent. The mean marks of boys was 75 per cent, while their number was 70 per cent. Find out the mean marks of girls in the class.

3.8 The arithmetic mean height of 50 students of a college is 5'8". The height of 30 of these is given in the frequency distribution below. Find the arithmetic mean height of the remaining 20 students.

Height in inches :	5'4"	5'6"	5'8"	5'10"	6'0"
Frequency :	4	12	4	8	2

3.9 An applicances manufacturing company is forecasting regional sales for next year. The Delhi branch, with current yearly sales of Rs. 387.6 million, is expected to achieve a sales growth of 7.25 percent; the Kolkata branch, with current sales of Rs. 158.6 million, is expected to grow by 8.20 per cent; and the Mumbai branch, with sales of Rs. 115 million, is expected to increase sales by 7.15 per cent. What is the average rate of growth forecasted for next year?

Hints and Answers

3.1 x = Rs. 146.30

3.2 Rs. 42,000 to pay bonus; Average bonus paid per member = 42,000/25 = Rs. 1,680

3.3 $\bar{x}$ = Rs. 4892.5 tonne; $\bar{x}_w$ = 5032.30

3.4 $\bar{x}$ = Rs. 25,000; $\bar{x}_w$ = Rs. 19,262.94

3.6 Percentage of technical personnal = 66.67 per cent ; Non-technical = 33.33 per cent

3.7 Mean marks of grils, $\bar{x}_2$ = 65 per cent

3.8 $\bar{x}_1$ (mean height of n_1 = 30 students) = 5'6".

Given $n_2 = 50 - 30 = 20$, $\bar{x}$ (mean height of 50 students) = 68". Thus

$$\bar{x} = \frac{n_1\bar{x}_1 + n_2\bar{x}_2}{n_1 + n_2} = 5'\,9''$$

3.9

$$\bar{x}_w = \frac{\Sigma x_i w_i}{\Sigma w_i}$$

$$= \frac{387.6 \times 7.25 + 158.6 \times 8.20 + 115 \times 7.15}{387.6 + 158.6 + 115}$$

$$= \frac{2810.10 + 1300.52 + 822.25}{661.20}$$

$$= \frac{4932.87}{661.20} = 7.46 \text{ per cent}$$

3.6 GEOMETRIC MEAN

In many business and economics problems, we deal with quantities (variables) that change over a period of time. In such cases the aim is to know an average percentage change rather than simple average value to represent the average growth or declining rate in the variable value over a period of time. Thus we need to calculate another measure of central tendency called **geometric mean** (*G.M.*). The specific application of G.M. is to show multiplicative effects over time in compound interest and inflation calculations.

Consider, for exàmple, the annual rate of growth of output of a company in the last five years.

Year	*Growth Rate (Per cent)*	*Output at the End of the Year*
1998	5.0	105
1999	7.5	112.87
2000	2.5	115.69
2001	5.0	121.47
2002	10.0	133.61

The simple arithmetic mean of the growth rate is:

$$\bar{x} = \frac{1}{5}(5 + 7.5 + 2.5 + 5 + 10) = 6$$

This value of 'mean' implies that if 6 per cent is the growth rate, then output at the end of 2002 should be 133.81, which is slightly more than the actual value, 133.61. Thus the correct growth rate should be slightly less than 6.

To find the correct growth rate, we apply the formula of geometic mean:

$$\text{G.M.} = \sqrt[n]{\text{Product of all the } n \text{ values}}$$

$$= \sqrt[n]{x_1 \cdot x_2 \ldots x_n} = (x_1 \cdot x_2 \cdot \ldots x_n)^{\frac{1}{n}} \qquad (3\text{-}8)$$

In other words, *G.M. of a set of n observations is the* n*th root of their product.*

For the above example, substituting the values of growth rate in the given formula, we have

$$\text{G.M.} = \sqrt[5]{5 \times 7.5 \times 2.5 \times 5 \times 10} = \sqrt[5]{4687.5}$$
$$= 5.9 \text{ per cent average growth.}$$

Calculation of G.M. When the number of observations are more than three, the G.M. can be calculated by taking logarithm on both sides of the equation. The formula (3-8) for G.M. for ungrouped data can be expressed in terms of logarithm as shown below:

$$\text{Log (G.M.)} = \frac{1}{n} \log (x_1 \cdot x_2 \cdot \ldots \cdot x_n)$$
$$= \frac{1}{n} \{\log x_1 + \log x_2 + \ldots + \log x_n\} = \frac{1}{n} \sum_{i=1}^{n} \log x_i$$

and therefore
$$\text{G.M.} = \text{Antilog} \left\{ \frac{1}{n} \sum \log x_i \right\} \tag{3-9}$$

If the observations $x_1, x_2, \ldots, x_n$ occur with frequencies $f_1, f_2, \ldots, f_n$, respectively, and the total of frequencies is $n = \sum f_i$, then the G.M. for such data is given by

$$\text{G.M.} = \left(x_1^{f_1} \cdot x_2^{f_2} \cdot \ldots \cdot x_n^{f_n} \right)^{1/n}$$

or
$$\log \text{(G.M.)} = \frac{1}{n} \{ f_1 \log x_1 + f_2 \log x_2 + \ldots + f_n \log x_n \}$$
$$= \frac{1}{n} \sum_{i=1}^{n} f_i \log x_i$$

or
$$\text{G.M.} = \text{Antilog} \left\{ \frac{1}{n} \sum f_i \log x_i \right\} \tag{3-10}$$

Example 3.25: The rate of increase in population of a country during the last three decades is 5 per cent, 8 per cent, and 12 per cent. Find the average rate of growth during the last three decades.

Solution: Since the data is given in terms of percentage, therefore geometric mean is a more appropriate measure.

The calculations of geometric mean are shown in Table 3.18.

Table 3.18 Calculations of G.M.

Decade	*Rate of Increase in Population (%)*	*Population at the End of Decade (x) Taking Preceding Decade as 100*	$\log_{10} x$
1	5	105	2.0212
2	8	108	2.0334
3	12	112	2.0492

Using the formula (3-10), we have

$$\text{G.M.} = \text{Antilog} \left\{ \frac{1}{n} \sum \log x \right\} = \text{Antilog} \left\{ \frac{1}{3} (6.1038) \right\}$$
$$= \text{Antilog } (2.0346) = 108.2$$

Hence the average rate of increase in population over the last three decades is 108.2 – 100 = 8.2 per cent.

Example 3.26: A given machine is assumed to depreciate 40 per cent in value in the first year, 25 per cent in the second year, and 10 per cent per year for the next three years, each percentage being calculated on the diminishing value. What is the average depreciation recorded on the diminishing value for the period of five years?

Solution: The calculation of geometric mean is shown in Table 3.19.

Table 3.19 Calculation of G.M.

Rate of Depreciation (x_i) *(in percentage)*	*Number of Years* (f_i)	$\log_{10} x_i$	$f_i \log_{10} x_i$
40	1	1.6021	1.6021
25	1	1.3979	1.3979
10	3	1.0000	3.0000
			6.0000

Using formula (3-11), we have

$$\text{G.M.} = \text{Antilog}\left\{\frac{1}{n}\Sigma f \log x\right\} = \text{Antilog}\left\{\frac{1}{5}(6.0000)\right\}$$

$$= \text{Antilog}\ (1.2) = 15.85$$

Hence, the average rate of depreciation for first five years is 15.85 per cent.

Example 3.27: A candidate obtained the following percentage of marks in different subjects in the half-yearly examination :

English : 46%, Statistics : 67%, Cost Accountancy : 72%,

Economics : 58%, Income Tax : 53%

It is agreed to give double weights to marks in English and Statistics as compared to other subjects. What is the simple and weighted arithmetic mean ?

Solution: The calculations for simple and weighted mean are shown in the table below:

Examination	*Percentage of Marks (x)*	*Weights (w)*	*wx*
English	46	2	92
Statistics	67	2	134
Cost Accountancy	72	1	72
Economics	58	1	58
Income Tax	53	1	53
$N = 5$	$\Sigma x = 296$	$\Sigma w = 7$	$\Sigma wx = 409$

$$\text{Simple Mean, } \bar{x} = \frac{\Sigma x}{N} = \frac{296}{5} = 59.2\%$$

$$\text{Weighted Mean, } \bar{x}_w = \frac{\Sigma WX}{\Sigma W} = \frac{409}{7} = 58.43\% \text{ (Approx)}$$

Example 3.28: The annual rate of growth of output of a factory in five years are 5.0, 6.5, 4.5, 8.5, 7.5 per cent respectively? What is the compound rate of growth of output per annum for the period?

[*Delhi Univ., BCom(Hons), 1990*]

Solution: Since the question involves the average rate of growth in percentages, so we need to calculate G.M. Let the output be 100 initially. Then,

Year	*Percentage*	*x*	*log x*
I	5.0	105.0	2.0212
II	6.5	106.5	2.0273
III	4.5	104.5	2.0191
IV	8.5	108.5	2.0354
V	7.5	107.5	2.0314
			$\Sigma \log x = 10.1344$

$$\text{G.M.} = \text{Antilog}\left(\frac{\Sigma \log X}{N}\right) = \text{Antilog}\left(\frac{10.1344}{5}\right) = \text{Antilog } (2.0269) = 106.38.$$

Hence, per cent growth (increase) of output is, 106.38 – 100 = 6.38%

Example 3.29: The number of divorces per 1000 marriages in a big city in India increased from 96 in 1980 to 120 in 1990. Find the annual rate of increase of the divorce rate for the period 1980 to 1990. [*Delhi Univ., BCom.(Hons)*, 1994]

Solution: Let the rate of growth in divorce be r. Then

$$P_n = P_0\left(1+\frac{r}{100}\right)^n \quad \text{or } 120 \quad = 96\left(1+\frac{r}{100}\right)^{10}$$

$$\frac{120}{96} = \left(1+\frac{r}{100}\right)^{10}$$

Taking log on both sides, we get

$$\log 120 - \log 96 = 10 \log\left(1+\frac{r}{100}\right)$$

$$10 \log\left(1+\frac{r}{100}\right) = 2.0792 - 1.9823 = 0.0969$$

$$1+\frac{r}{100} = \text{Antilog } (0.00969) = 1.0226$$

$$\frac{r}{100} = 0.0226 \quad \text{or} \quad r = 0.0226 \times 100 = 2.26\%.$$

Example 3.30: A machinery depreciates by 40 per cent in the first year, 25 per cent in second year and 10 per cent p.a. for the next three years, each percentage being calculated as a dimensing value. What is the average of depreciation for the entire period ?

Solution: The calculations of average percentage of depreciation are shown below in the table.

Year	*Depreciation (d)*	*x = 100 – d*	*log x*
1	40%	60	1.7782
2	25%	75	1.8751
3	10%	90	1.9542
4	10%	90	1.9542
5	10%	90	1.9542
			$\Sigma \log x = 9.5159$

$$\text{Geometric Mean} = \text{Antilog}\left(\frac{\Sigma \log x}{n}\right) = \text{Antilog}\left(\frac{9.5159}{5}\right) = \text{Antilog}\ (1.90318) = 80$$

Thus, the average depreciation is = 100 – 80 = 20%.

Example 3.31: The G.M. of four values was calculated as 16. It was later discovered that one of the values was recorded wrongly as 32 when in fact it was 162. Calculate correct GM.

[Delhi Univ., BCom, 2004]

Solution: Since G.M. = $(x_1 \cdot x_2 \cdot x_3 \cdot x_4)^{1/4}$, therefore

$$16 = (x_1 \cdot x_2 \cdot x_3 \cdot x_4)^{1/4} \quad \text{or} \quad (16)^4 = x_1 \cdot x_2 \cdot x_3 \cdot x_4$$

Wrong product, $x_1\, x_2\, x_3\, x_4$ = 65536 (given). Thus,

$$\text{Correct product} = \frac{65536 \times \text{Correct item}}{\text{Wrong item}} = \frac{65536 \times 162}{32} = 331776$$

Hence, correct Geometric Mean (GM) = $(331776)^{1/4}$ = 24.

3.6.1 Combined Geometric Mean

The combined geometric mean of observations formed by pooling the geometric means of different sets of data is defined as:

$$\log \text{G.M.} = \frac{\sum_{i=1}^{n} n_i \log G_i}{\sum_{i=1}^{n} n_i} \qquad \text{(3-11)}$$

where G_i is the geometric mean of the ith data set having n_i number of observations.

3.6.2 Weighted Geometric Mean

If different observations x_i (i = 1, 2, . . ., n) are given different weights (importance), say w_i (i = 1, 2, . . ., n) respectively, then their weighted geometric mean is defined as:

$$\text{G.M.}\ (w) = \text{Antilog}\left[\left(\frac{1}{n}\right)\Sigma\ w \log x\right] = \text{Antilog}\left[\left(\frac{1}{\Sigma\ w}\right)\Sigma\ w \log x\right] \qquad \text{(3-12)}$$

Example 3.32: Three sets of data contain 8, 7, and 5 observations and their geometric means are 8.52, 10.12, and 7.75, respectively. Find the combined geometric mean of 20 observations.

Solution: Applying the formula (3-12), the combined geometric mean can be obtained as follows:

$$\text{G.M.} = \text{Antilog}\left[\frac{n_1 \log G_1 + n_2 \log G_2 + n_3 \log G_3}{n_1 + n_2 + n_3}\right]$$

$$= \text{Antilog}\left[\frac{8 \log (8.52) + 7 \log (10.12) + 5 \log (7.75)}{8 + 7 + 5}\right]$$

$$= \text{Antilog}\left[\frac{(8 \times 0.9304) + (7 \times 1.0051) + (5 \times 0.8893)}{20}\right]$$

$$= \text{Antilog}\left(\frac{18.9254}{20}\right) = \text{Antilog}\ (0.94627) = 8.835$$

Hence, the combined G.M. of 20 observations is 8.835.

Example 3.33: The weighted geometric mean of four numbers 8, 25, 17, and 30 is 15.3. If the weights of the first three numbers are 5, 3, and 4 respectively, find the weight of fourth number.

Solution: Let weight of fourth number be w. Then the weighted geometric mean of four numbers can be calculated as shown in Table 3.20.

Table 3.20 Calculations of Weighted G.M.

Numbers (*x*)	*Weight of Each Number* (*w*)	$\log_{10} x$	$w \log_{10} x$
8	5	0.9031	4.5155
25	3	1.3979	4.1937
17	4	1.2304	4.9216
30	w	1.4771	$1.4771w$
	$12 + w$		$13.6308 + 1.4771w$

Thus the weighted G.M. is

$$\log \{\text{G.M.}\ (w)\} = \left[\left(\frac{1}{\sum w}\right)\sum w \log x\right]$$

or

$$\log (15.3) = \left[\left(\frac{1}{12 + w}\right)(13.6308 + 1.4771w)\right]$$

$$(1.1847)\ (12 + w) = 13.6308 + 1.4771w$$

$$14.2164 + 1.1847w = 13.6308 + 1.4771w$$

$$0.5856 = 0.2924\ w; \quad w = \frac{0.5856}{0.2924} = 2 \text{ (approx.)}$$

Thus the weight of fourth number is 2.

Example 3.34: A distribution consists of three components with total frequencies of 200, 250 and 300 having means 25, 10 and 15 respectively. Find mean of combined distribution.

[*Delhi Univ., BCom 2006*]

Solution: Given that

$n_1 = 200,\ \bar{x}_1 = 25,\quad n_2 = 250,\ \bar{x}_2 = 10,\quad n_3 = 300,\ \bar{x}_3 = 15$. The combined mean is given by

$$\text{Combined mean, } \bar{x} = \frac{n_1\bar{x}_1 + n_2\bar{x}_2 + n_3\bar{x}_3}{n_1 + n_2 + n_3} = \frac{200(25) + 250(10) + 300(15)}{200 + 250 + 300}$$

$$= \frac{5000 + 2500 + 4500}{750} = \frac{12000}{750} = 16$$

Example 3.35: The weighted G.M. of 5 number — 10,15, 25,12 and 20 is 18.15. If the weights of the first four numbers are 2, 3, 5, 2 respectively, find the weight of the 5th number.

Solution: Let the weight of 5th number be x. Then other calculations are as follows:

x	W	$log\ x$	$W\ log\ x$
10	2	1.0000	2.0000
15	3	1.1761	3.5283
25	5	1.3979	6.9895
12	2	1.0792	2.1584
20	x	1.3010	$1.3010x$
Total	$12+x$		$14.6762+1.3010x$

$$\text{Weighted G.M.} = \text{Antilog}\left(\frac{\Sigma W \log x}{\Sigma W}\right)$$

$$18.15 = \text{Antilog}\left(\frac{14.6762 + 1.301x}{12 + x}\right)$$

$$\log 18.15 = \frac{14.6762 + 1.301x}{12 + x}$$

$$1.2343 = \frac{14.6762 + 1.301x}{12 + x}$$

$$(1.2343)\ (12 + x) = 14.6751 + 1.301x$$

$$14.8116 + 1.2343x = 14.6762 + 1.301x$$

$$1.2343x - 1.301x = 14.6762 - 14.8116$$

$$-0.0667x = -0.1354 \text{ or } x = 2$$

Thus, the weight of 5th number is 2.

3.6.3 Advantages, Disadvantages, and Applications of G.M.

Advantages

(i) The value of G.M. is not much affected by extreme observations and is computed by taking all the observations into account.

(ii) It is useful for averaging ratio and percentage as well as in determining rate of increase and decrease.

(iii) In the calculation of G.M. more weight is given to smaller values and less weight to higher values. For example, it is useful in the study of price fluctuations where the lower limit can touch zero whereas the upper limit may go upto any number.

(iv) It is suitable for algebraic manipulations. The calculation of weighted G.M. and combined G.M. are two examples of algebraic manipulations of the original formula of geometric mean.

Disadvantages

(i) The calculation of G.M. as compared to A.M., is more difficult and intricate.

(ii) The value of G.M. cannot be calculated when any of the observations in the data set is either negative or zero.

(iii) While calculating weighted geometric, mean equal importance (or weight) is not given to each observation in the data set.

Applications

(i) The concept of G.M. is used in the construction of index numbers.

(ii) Since G.M. ≤ A.M., therefore G.M. is useful in those cases where smaller observations are to be given importance. Such cases usually occur in social and economic areas of study.

(iii) The G.M. of a data set is useful in estimating the average rate of growth in the initial value of an observation per unit per period. For example, it is useful in finding the percentage increase in sales, profit, production, population, and so on. It is also useful in calculating the amount of money accumulated at the end of n periods, with an original principal amount of P_0. The formula is as follows:

$$P_n = P_0 (1 + r)^n \quad \text{or} \quad r = \left(\frac{P_n}{P_0}\right)^{\frac{1}{n}} - 1$$

where r = interest rate (rate of growth) per unit period
n = number of years or length of the period.

Conceptual Questions 3B

10. Define simple and weighted geometric mean of a given distribution. Under what circumstances would you recommend its use?

11. Discuss the advantages, disadvantages, and uses of geometric mean.

Self-Practice Problems 3B

3.10 Find the geometric mean of the following distribution of data:

Dividend declared (%)	:	0–10	10–20	20–30	30–40	40–45
Number of companies	:	5	7	15	25	8

3.11 The weighted geometric mean of the four numbers 20, 18, 12, and 4 is 11.75. If the weights of the first three numbers are 1, 3, and 4 respectively, find the weight of the fourth number.

3.12 A machinery is assumed to depreciate 44 per cent in value in the first year, 15 per cent in the second year, and 10 per cent per year for the next three years, each percentage being calculated on diminishing value. What is the average percentage of depreciation for the entire period?

3.13 A manufacturer of electrical circuit borads, has manufactured the following number of units over the past 5 years:

2000	2001	2002	2003	2004
14,300	15,150	16,110	17,540	19,430

Calculate the average percentage increase in units produced over this time period, and use this to estimate production for 2006.

3.14 The owner of a warehouse is calculating the average growth factor for his warehouse over the last 6 years. Using a geometric mean, he comes up with an answer of 1.42. Individual growth factors for the first 5 years were 1.91, 1.53, 1.32, 1.91, and 1.40, but he lost the records for the sixth year, after he calculated the mean. What was it?

3.15 Industrial Gas Supplier keeps records on the cost of processing a purchase order. Over the last 5 years, this cost has been Rs. 355, 358, 361, 365 and 366. What has supplier's average percentage increase been over this period? If this average rate stays the same for 3 more years, what will cost supplier to process a purchase order at that time?

3.16 A sociologist has been studying the yearly changes in the number of convicts assigned to the largest correctional facility in the state. His data are expressed in terms of the percentage increase in the number of prisoners (a negative number indicates a percentage decrease). The sociologist's most recent data are as follows:

1999	2000	2001	2002	2003	2004
5%	6%	9%	4%	7%	6%

(a) Calculate the average percentage increase using only the 1999-2002 data.

(b) A new penal code was passed in 1998. Previously, the prison population grew at a rate of about 2 percent per year. What seems to be the effect of the new penal code?

Hints and Answers

3.10 G.M. = 25.64 per cent.

3.11 Apply log G.M. = $\frac{\Sigma\, w \log w}{\Sigma\, w}$ or log 11.75

$= \frac{9.4974 + 0.6021 w_4}{8 + w_4}$ or $w_4 = 0.850$ (approx.).

3.12 Depreciation rate : 44 15 10 10 10

Diminishing value taking 100 as base (x) : 56 85 90 90 90

Log x: 1.7582 1.9294 1.9542 1.9542 1.9542 = 9.5502

G.M. = Antilog ($\Sigma \log x/N$)

= Antilog (9.5502/5)

=Antilog (1.91004) = 81.28

The diminishing value is Rs. 81.28 and average depreciation is 18.72 per cent.

3.13 G.M.: $\sqrt[4]{19430/14300} = \sqrt[4]{1.3587} = 1.07964$. So the average increase is 7.96 per cent per year.In 2006, the estimated production will be $19430\ (1.0796)^2 = 22{,}646$ units (approx.)

3.14 Since G.M:

$$1.42 = x \times \sqrt[6]{1.91 \times 1.53 \times 1.32 \times 1.91 \times 1.40}$$

$$x = (1.42)^6/(1.91 \times 1.53 \times 1.32 \times 1.91 \times 1.40)$$
$$= 8.195/10.988 = 0.7458$$

3.15 G.M. = $\sqrt[4]{366/355} = \sqrt[4]{1.0309} = 1.00765$. So the average increase is 0.765 per cent per year. In three more years the estimated cost will be $366\ (1.00765)^3$ = Rs. 757.600

3.16 (a) G.M: $\sqrt[4]{0.95 \times 1.06 \times 1.09 \times 1.04}$

$= \sqrt[4]{2.5132} = 1.03364$.

So the average rate of increase from 1999-2002 was 3.364 per cent per year.

(b) G.M.: $\sqrt[6]{0.95\times1.06\times1.09\times1.04\times1.07\times0.94}$

$= \sqrt[6]{1.148156} = 1.01741$. So the new code appears to have slight effect on the rate of growth of convicts, which has decrease from 2 per cent to 1.741 per cent per year.

3.7 HARMONIC MEAN

The **harmonic mean** (H.M.) of a set of observations is defined as the reciprocal of the arithmetic mean of the reciprocal of the individual observations, that is,

$$\frac{1}{\text{H.M}} = \frac{1}{n}\sum_{i=1}^{n}\frac{1}{x_i}$$

or

$$\text{H.M.} = \frac{n}{\sum_{i=1}^{n}\left(\frac{1}{x_i}\right)} \quad \text{(For ungrouped data)} \qquad (3\text{-}13)$$

If $f_1, f_2, \ldots, f_n$ are the frequencies of observations $x_1, x_2, \ldots, x_n$, then the harmonic mean is defined as:

$$\text{H.M.} = \frac{n}{\sum_{i=1}^{n} f_i\left(\frac{1}{x_i}\right)} \quad \text{(For grouped data)} \qquad (3\text{-}14)$$

where $n = \sum_{i=1}^{n} f_i$.

Example 3.36: An investor buys Rs. 20,000 worth of shares of a company each month. During the first 3 months he bought the shares at a price of Rs. 120, Rs. 160, and Rs. 210. After 3 months what is the average price paid by him for the shares?

Solution: Since the value of shares is changing after every one month, therefore the required average price per share is the harmonic mean of the prices paid in first three months.

$$\text{H.M.} = \frac{3}{(1\div120)+(1\div160)+(1\div210)} = \frac{3}{0.008+0.006+0.004}$$

$$= 3/0.018 = \text{Rs. } 166.66$$

Example 3.37: Find the harmonic mean of the following distribution of data:

Dividend yield (per cent)	:	2–6	6–10	10–14
Number of companies	:	10	12	18

Solution: The calculation of harmonic mean is shown in Table 3.21.

Table 3.21 Calculation of H.M.

Class Intervals (Dividend yield)	*Mid-value* (m_i)	*Number of Companies (frequency,* f_i*)*	*Reciprocal* $\left(\frac{1}{m_i}\right)$	$f_i\left(\frac{1}{m_i}\right)$
2–6	4	10	1/4	2.5
6–10	8	12	1/8	1.5
10–14	12	18	1/12	1.5
		N = 40		5.5

The harmonic mean is: $\text{H.M.} = \dfrac{n}{\sum_{i=1}^{3} f_i\left(\dfrac{1}{m_i}\right)} = \dfrac{40}{5.5} = 7.27$

Hence the average dividend yield of 40 companies is 7.27 per cent.

Example 3.38: A certain store's profits were Rs. 50000, Rs. 100000, Rs. 800000 in 2002, 2003 and 2004 respectively. Determine the average rate of growth of the store's point.

[Delhi Univ., B.Com(Hons), 2005]

Solution: Using compound interest formula of geometric mean, we have

$$P_n = P_0\,(1 + r)^n$$

Since, given that $P_n = 8{,}00{,}000$, $P_0 = 50{,}000$, $r = ?$, $n = 2$, therefore

$$\therefore \quad 800000 = 50000\,(1 + r)^2 \quad \text{or} \quad \frac{800000}{50000} = (1 + r)^2$$

$$16 = (1 + r)^2 \quad \text{or} \quad 4 = 1 + r \text{ i.e. } r = 3 \text{ per cent}$$

Example 3.39: A piece of property was purchased for Rs. 20 lakhs and sold for Rs. 32.60 lakhs after 10 years. What is the average annual rate of return on the original investment?

[Delhi Univ., B.Com (Pass), 2004]

Solution: To compute the average rate of return, apply the following formula:

where P_0 = Value at the beginning of the period = Rs. 32.60 lakh

P_n = Value at the end of the period n = Rs. 20.00 lakh

r = rate of return, 10 per cent

n = Length of time period, 10 years

$$P_0 = P_n(1 + r)^n \text{ or } \frac{P_0}{P_n} = (1 + r)^{10}, \text{ i.e., } \frac{32.60}{20} = (1 + r)^{10}$$

Taking logarithm on both sides, we get

$$\log 32.60 - \log 20 = 10 \log (1 + r)$$

$$\log (1 + r) = \frac{\log 32.60 - \log 20}{10} = \frac{1.5132 - 1.3010}{10} = \frac{0.2122}{10} = 0.02122$$

$$\therefore \quad 1 + r = \text{Antilog } (0.02122)$$

$$1 + r = 1.050 \quad \text{or} \quad r = 0.05 = 5\%.$$

Example 3.40: A certain store made weekly profits of Rs. 5000, Rs. 10000, Rs. 18000 in 1998, 1999 and 2000 respectively. Determine the average rate of growth of this store's profit.

[GJ Univ., BBA, 2004]

Solution: To determine the average rate of growth, apply the following formula:

$$P_n = P_0\,(1 + r)^n$$

Then, $18000 = 5000\,(1 + r)^2$; since $P_n = 18000$, $P_0 = 5000$, $n = 2$

$$(1 + r)^2 = \frac{18000}{5000} = 3.6$$

$$1 + r = \sqrt{3.6} = 1.897, \quad \text{i.e. } r = 0.897$$

Thus average rate of growth is 0.897%.

Example 3.41: The per piece price of banana is Rs. 1.50 and that of orange is Rs. 3. Mr Ram spends Rs. 10 each on banana and orange. The average price per piece is not Rs 2.25 but Rs. 2.00. Comment.

Solution: Average price $= \frac{1.50+3}{2}$ = Rs. 2.25, but it is not true. Since this questions involves the ratio of two quantities, we need to. Applying the formula of H.M., we have find H.M.

$$\text{Average price} = \frac{2}{\frac{1}{1.50}+\frac{1}{23}} = \text{Rs. } 2$$

Example 3.42: Three men takes 12, 8, 6 hrs respectively to husk an acre of corn. Determine the average number of hours to husk an acre of corn. [*GJ Univ., BBA, 2004*]

Solution: The H.M. of digits: 12, 8, 6 is

$$\text{H.M.} = \frac{n}{\Sigma(1/x)} = \frac{3}{\frac{1}{12}+\frac{1}{8}+\frac{1}{6}} = \frac{3\times 24}{9} = 8 \text{ hours.}$$

Thus, the average number of hours to husk an acre is 8 hrs.

Example 3.43: If X travels 8 km at 4 km/h, 6km at 3km/h and 4km at 2km/h, what would be the average rate per hour at which he travelled ? Verify your answer.

Solution: Since this question involves the ratio of two quantities—speed and distance, we calculate weighted harmonic mean as shown below:

Speed x	*Distance (w)*	*w/x*
4	8	8/4 = 2
3	6	6/3 = 2
2	4	4/2 = 2

$$\text{H.M.} = \frac{\Sigma w}{\Sigma(w/x)} = \frac{18}{6} = 3\text{km/h}$$

Example 3.44: An investor buys Rs. 1200 worth of shares of a company each month. During the first five months he bought the shares at a price of Rs.10, Rs.12, Rs. 15 Rs. 20, and Rs. 24 per share. After five months what is the average price paid for the shares by him.

Solution: Since shares are bought with varying prices by investing the same amount of money each time, the average price per share is given by harmonic mean of 10, 12, 15, 20, 24. The formula for H.M. is as follows:

$$\text{H.M.} = \frac{n}{\Sigma(1/x)} = \frac{5}{\frac{1}{10}+\frac{1}{12}+\frac{1}{15}+\frac{1}{20}+\frac{1}{24}} = \frac{5\times 120}{41} = \text{Rs. } 14.63.$$

Example 3.45: The rate of a certain commodity in the first week is 0.4 kg/rupee. It is 0.6 kg/rupee in second week and is 0.5 kg per rupee in the third week. Is it correct to say that the average price is 0.5 kg per rupee? Justify.

Solution: Since it involves the ratio of two quantities i.e., kg and rupees, we need to calculate H.M. as shown below:

$$\text{H.M.} = \frac{n}{\Sigma(1/x)} = \frac{3}{\frac{3}{0.4}+\frac{1}{0.6}+\frac{1}{0.5}} = \frac{3}{10\left(\frac{1}{4}+\frac{1}{6}+\frac{1}{5}\right)} = 0.486.$$

Thus average price is 0.486 kg/rupee rather than 0.5 kg/rupee.

Example 3.46: Cities A, B and C are equidistant from each other. A motorist travels from A to B at 30 km/hr, from B to C at 40 km/hr and from C to A at 50 km/hr. Determine the average speed for the entire trip. [*Delhi Univ., B.Com (Hons), 2006*]

Solution: Average speed is calculated using formula of harmonic mean.

$$\text{H.M.} = \frac{n}{\Sigma(1/x)} = \frac{3}{\frac{1}{30}+\frac{1}{40}+\frac{1}{50}} = 38.3 \text{ km/h}$$

3.7.1 Advantages, Disadvantages, and Applications of H.M.

Advantages

(i) The H.M. of the given data set is also computed based on its every element.
(ii) While calculating H.M., more weightage is given to smaller values in a data set because in this case, the reciprocal of given values is taken for the calculation of H.M.
(iii) The original formula of H.M. can be extended to accommodate further analysis of data by certain algebraic manipulations.

Disadvantages

(i) The H.M. is not often used for analysing business problems.
(ii) The H.M. of any data set cannot be calculated if it has negative and/or zero elements.
(iii) The calculation of H.M. involves complicated calculations. For calculating the H.M. of a data set, the largest weight is given to smaller values of elements, therefore it does not represent the true characteristic of the data set.

Applications

The harmonic mean is particularly useful for computation of average rates and ratios. Such rates and ratios are generally used to express relations between two different types of measuring units that can be expressed reciprocally. For example, distance (in km), and time (in hours).

3.8 RELATIONSHIP AMONG A.M., G.M., AND H.M.

For any set of observations, its A.M., G.M., and H.M. are related to each other in the relationship

$$\text{A.M.} \geq \text{G.M.} \geq \text{H.M.}$$

The sign of '=' holds if and only if all the observations are identical.

If observations in a data set take the values $a, ar, ar^2, \ldots, ar^{n-1}$, each with single frequency, then

$$(\text{G.M.})^2 = \text{A.M.} \times \text{H.M.}$$

Self-Practice Problems 3C

3.17 In a certain factory, a unit of work is completed by A in 4 minutes, by B in 5 minutes, by C in 6 minutes, by D in 10 minutes, and by E in 12 minutes (a) What is the average rate of completing the work? (b) What is the average number of units of work completed per minute? (c) At this rate how many units will they complete in a six-hour day?

3.18 An investor buys Rs. 12,000 worth of shares of a company each month. During the first 5 months he bought the shares at a price of Rs. 100, Rs. 120, Rs. 150, Rs. 200, and Rs. 240 per share respectively. After 5 months what is the average price paid by him for the shares?

3.19 Calculate the A.M., G.M., and H.M. of the following observations and show that A.M. > G.M. > H.M.

32 35 36 37 39 41 43

3.20 The profit earned by 18 companies is given below:

Profit (in Rs. lakh)	:	20	21	22	23	24	25
No. of companies	:	4	2	7	1	3	1

Calculate the harmonic mean of profit earned.

3.21 Find the harmonic mean for the following distribution of data:

Class interval	:	0–10	10–20	20–30	30–40
Frequency	:	5	8	3	4

Hints and Answers

3.17 (a) Average rate of completing the work per minute = 6.25

(b) Average units/minute = 1 ÷ 6.25 = 0.16;

(c) Units completed in six-hours (360 minutes) day by all 5 workers = 360 × 0.16 = 288 units

3.18 Average price paid for shares = Rs. 146.30

3.19 A.M. = 37.56; G.M. = 37.52; H.M. = 37.25

3.20 H.M. = Rs. 21.9 lakh

3.21 H.M. = 9.09

3.9 AVERAGES OF POSITION

Different from mathematical averages—arithmetic mean, geometric mean, and harmonic mean, which are mathematical in nature and deal with those characteristics of a data set which can be directly measured quantitatively, such as: income, profit, level of production, rate of growth, etc. However, in cases where we want to guard against the influence of a few outlying observations (called outliers), and/or we need to measure qualitative characteristics of a data set, such as: honesty, intelligence, beauty, consumer acceptance, and so on, other measures of central tendency namely *median*, *quartiles*, *deciles*, *percentiles*, and *mode* are used. These measures are also called *positional averages*. The term 'position' refers to the place of the value of an observation in the data set. These measures help in identifying the value of an observation of interest rather than computing it.

3.9.1 Median

Median may be defined as the *middle value* in the data set when its elements are arranged in a sequential order, that is, in either ascending or decending order of magnitude. It is called a middle value in an ordered sequence of data in the sense that half of the observations are smaller and half are larger than this value. The **median** is thus a measure of the *location* or *centrality* of the observations.

The median can be calculated for both ungrouped and grouped data sets.

Ungrouped Data

In this case, the data is arranged in either ascending or decending order of magnitude.

(i) If the number of observations (n) is an *odd number*, then the median (Med) is represented by the numerical value corresponding to the positioning point of $(n + 1)/2$ ordered observation. That is,

$$\text{Med} = \text{Size or value of } \left(\frac{n+1}{2}\right)\text{th observation in the data array}$$

(ii) If the number of observations (n) is an *even number*, then the median is defined as the arithmetic mean of the numerical values of $n/2$th and $(n/2 + 1)$th observations in the data array. That is,

$$\text{Med} = \frac{\frac{n}{2}\text{th observation} + \left(\frac{n}{2}+1\right)\text{th observation}}{2}$$

Example 3.47: Calculate the median of the following data that relates to the service time (in minutes) per customer for 7 customers at a railway reservation counter: 3.5, 4.5, 3, 3.8, 5.0, 5.5, 4

Solution: The data are arranged in ascending order as follows:

Observations in the data array	:	1	2	3	4	5	6	7
Service time (in minutes)	:	3	3.5	3.8	4	4.5	5	5.5

The median for this data would be

Med = value of $(n + 1)/2$ th observation in the data array

= $\{(7 + 1) \div 2\}$th = 4th observation in the data array = 4

Thus, the median service time is 4 minutes per customer.

Example 3.48: Calculate the median of the following data that relates to the number of patients examined per hour in the outpatient ward (OPD) in a hospital: 10, 12, 15, 20, 13, 24, 17, 18

Solution: The data are arranged in ascending order as follows:

Observations in the data array	:	1	2	3	4	5	6	7	8
Number of patients	:	10	12	13	15	17	18	20	24

Since the number of observations in the data array are even, the average of $(n/2)$th = 4th observation, i.e. 15 and $(n/2) + 1$ = 5th observation, i.e. 17, will give the median, that is,

Med = $(15 + 17) \div 2 = 16$

Thus median number of patients examined per hour in OPD in a hospital are 16.

Grouped Data

To find the median value for grouped data, first identify the class interval which contains the median value or $(n/2)$th observation of the data set. To identify such class interval, find the cumulative frequency of each class until the class for which the cumulative frequency is equal to or greater than the value of $(n/2)$th observation. The value of the median within that class is found by using interpolation. That is, it is assumed that the observation values are evenly spaced over the entire class interval. The following formula is used to determine the median of grouped data:

$$\text{Med} = l + \frac{(n/2) - cf}{f} \times h$$

where l = lower class limit (or boundary) of the median class interval

cf = cumulative frequency of the class prior to the median class interval, that is, the sum of all the class frequencies upto, but not including, the median class interval

f = frequency of the median class

h = width of the median class interval

n = total number of observations in the distribution.

Example 3.49: A survey was conducted to determine the age (in years) of 120 automobiles. The result of such a survey is as follows:

Age of auto :	0–4	4–8	8–12	12–16	16–20
Number of autos :	13	29	48	22	8

What is the median age for the autos?

Solution: Finding the cumulative frequencies to locate the median class as shown in Table 3.22.

Table 3.22 Calculations for Median Value

Age of Auto (in years)	*Number of Autos (f)*	*Cumulative Frequency (cf)*
0–4	13	13
4–8	29	42
8–12	48	(90) ← Median class
12–16	22	112
16–20	8	120
	$n = 120$	

Here the total number of observations (frequencies) are $n = 120$. Median is the size of $(n/2)$th $= 120 \div 2 = 60$th observation in the data set. This observation lies in the class interval 8–12. Applying the formula (3-16), we have

$$\text{Med} = l + \frac{(n/2) - cf}{n} \times h = 8 + \frac{(120 \div 2) - 42}{48} \times 4 = 8 + 1.5 = 9.5$$

Example 3.50: In a factory employing 3000 persons, 5 per cent earn less than Rs. 150 per day, 580 earn from Rs. 151 to Rs. 200 per day, 30 per cent earn from Rs. 201 to Rs. 250 per day, 500 earn from Rs. 251 to Rs. 300 per day, 20 per cent earn from Rs. 301 to Rs. 350 per day, and the rest earn Rs. 351 or more per day. What is the median wage?

Solution: Calculation of median wage per day are shown in Table 3.23.

Table 3.23 Calculation of Median Wage

Earnings (Rs)	*Percentage of Workers (Per cent)*	*Number of Persons (f)*	*Cumulative Frequency (cf)*
Less than 150	5	150	150
151–200	—	580	730
201–250	30	900	(1630) ← Median class
251–300	—	500	2130
301–350	20	600	2730
351 and above	—	270	3000
		$n = 3000$	

Median observation $= (n/2)$th $= (3000) \div 2 = 1500$th observation. This observation lies in the class interval 201–250.

Now applying the formula (3-16), we have

$$\text{Med} = l + \frac{(n/2) - cf}{f} \times h$$

$$= 201 + \frac{1500 - 730}{900} \times 50 = 201 + 42.77 = \text{Rs. } 243.77$$

Hence, the median wage is Rs. 243.77 per day.

3.9.2 Advantages, Disadvantages, and Applications of Median

Advantages

(i) Median is unique, i.e. like mean, there is only one median for a set of data.

(ii) The value of median is easy to understand and may be calculated from any type of data. The median in many situations can be located simply by inspection.

(iii) The sum of the absolute differences of all observations in the data set from median value is minimum. In other words, the absolute difference of observations from the median is less than from any other value in the distribution. That is, $\sum |x - \text{Med}| =$ a minimum value.

(iv) The extreme values in the data set does not affect the calculation of the median value and therefore it is the useful measure of central tendency when such values do occur.

(v) The median is considered the best statistical technique for studying the qualitative attribute of an observation in the data set.

(vi) The median value may be calculated for an open-ended distribution of data set.

Disadvantages

(i) The median is not capable of algebraic treatment. For example, the median of two or more sets of data cannot be determined.

(ii) The value of median is affected more by sampling variations, that is, it is affected by the number of observations rather than the values of the observations. Any observation selected at random is just as likely to exceed the median as it is to be exceeded by it.

(iii) Since median is an average of position, therefore arranging the data in ascending or descending order of magnitude is time consuming in case of a large number of observations.

(iv) The calculation of median in case of grouped data is based on the assumption that values of observations are evenly spaced over the entire class interval.

Applications

The median is helpful in understanding the characteristic of a data set when

(i) observations are qualitative in nature

(ii) extreme values are present in the data set

(iii) a quick estimate of an average is desired.

3.10 PARTITION VALUES—QUARTILES, DECILES, AND PERCENTILES

The basic purpose of all the measures of central tendency discussed so far was to know more and more about the characteristics of a data set. Another method to analyse a data set is by arranging all the observations in either ascending or descending order of their magnitude and then dividing this ordered series into two equal parts by applying the concept of median. However, to have more knowledge about the data set, we may decompose it into more parts of equal size. The measures of central tendency which are used for dividing the data into several equal parts are called *partition values*.

In this section, we shall discuss data analysis by dividing it into *four*, *ten*, and *hundred* parts of equal size and the corresponding partition values are called *quartiles*, *deciles*, and *percentiles*. All these values can be determined in the same way as median. The only difference is in their location.

Quartiles The values of observations in a data set, when arranged in an ordered sequence, can be divided into four equal parts, or quarters, using three quartiles namely Q_1, Q_2, and Q_3. The first quartile Q_1 divides a distribution in such a way that 25 per cent $(=n/4)$ of observations have a value less than Q_1 and 75 per cent $(= 3n/4)$ have a value more than Q_1, i.e. Q_1 is the median of the ordered values that are below the median.

The second quartile Q_2 has the same number of observations above and below it. It is therefore same as median value.

The quartile Q_3 divides the data set in such a way that 75 per cent of the observations have a value less than Q_3 and 25 per cent have a value more than Q_3, i.e. Q_3 is the median of the order values that are above the median.

The generalized formula for calculating quartiles in case of grouped data is:

$$Q_i = l + \left[\frac{i\,(n/4) - cf}{f}\right] \times h\,; \quad i = 1, 2, 3 \tag{3-15}$$

where cf = cumulative frequency prior to the quartile class interval
l = lower limit of the quartile class interval
f = frequency of the quartile class interval
h = width of the class interval

Deciles The values of observations in a data set when arranged in an ordered sequence can be divided into ten equal parts, using nine deciles, D_i $(i = 1, 2, \ldots, 9)$. The generalized formula for calculating deciles in case of grouped data is:

$$D_i = l + \left[\frac{i\,(n/10) - cf}{f}\right] \times h\,; \quad i = 1, 2, \ldots, 9 \tag{3-16}$$

where the symbols have their usual meaning and interpretation.

Percentiles The values of observations in a data when arranged in an ordered sequence can be divided into hundred equal parts using ninety nine percentiles, P_i $(i = 1, 2, \ldots, 99)$. In general, the ith percentile is a number that has i% of the data values at or below it and $(100 - i)$% of the data values at or above it. The lower quartile (Q_1), median and upper quartile (Q_3) are also the 25th percentile, 50th percentile and 75th percentile, respectively. For example, if you are told that you scored 90th percentile in a test (like the CAT), it indicates that 90% of the scores were at or below your score, while 10% were at or above your score. The generalized formula for calculating percentiles in case of grouped data is:

$$P_i = l + \left[\frac{i\,(n/100) - cf}{f}\right] \times h\,; \quad i = 1, 2, \ldots, 99 \tag{3-17}$$

where the symbols have their usual meaning and interpretation.

3.10.1 Graphical Method for Calculating Partition Values

The graphical method of determining various partition values can be summarized into following steps:

(i) Draw an ogive (cumulative frequency curve) by 'less than' method.

(ii) Take the values of observations or class intervals along the horizontal scale (i.e. x-axis) and cumulative frequency along vertical scale (i.e., y-axis).

(iii) Determine the median value, that is, value of $(n/2)$th observation, where n is the total number of observations in the data set.

(iv) Locate this value on the y-axis and from this point draw a line parallel to the x-axis meeting the ogive at a point, say P. Draw a perpendicular on x-axis from P and it meets the x-axis at a point, say M.

The other partition values such as quartiles, deciles, and percentiles can also be obtained by drawing lines parallel to the x-axis to the distance $i\ (n/4)\ (i = 1, 2, 3)$; $i\ (n/10)\ (i = 1, 2, \ldots, 9)$, and $i\ (n/100)\ (i = 1, 2, \ldots, 99)$, respectively.

Example 3.51: The following is the distribution of weekly wages of 600 workers in a factory:

Weekly Wages (in Rs)	*Number of Workers*	*Weekly Wages (in Rs)*	*Number of Workers*
Below 875	69	1100 – 1175	58
875 – 950	167	1175 – 1250	24
950 –1025	207	1250 – 1325	10
1025 –1100	65		600

(a) Draw an ogive for the above data and hence obtain the median value. Check it against the calculated value.

(b) Obtain the limits of weekly wages of central 50 per cent of the workers.

(c) Estimate graphically the percentage of workers who earned weekly wages between 950 and 1250.

Solution: (a) The calculations of median value are shown in Table 3.24.

Table 3.24 Calculations of Median Value

Weekly Wages (in Rs)	*Number of Workers (f)*	*Cumulative Frequency (Less than type)*	*Percent Cumulative Frequency*
Less than 875	69	69	11.50
Less than 950	167	236 ← Q_1 class	39.33
Less than 1025	207	443 ← Median class	73.83
Less than 1100	65	508 ← Q_3 class	84.66
Less than 1175	58	566	94.33
Less than 1250	24	590	98.33
Less than 1325	10	600	100.00

Since a median observation in the data set is the $(n/2)$th observation = $(600 \div 2)$th observation, that is, 300th observation. This observation lies in the class interval 950–1025. Applying the formula (3-16) to calculate median wage value, we have

$$\text{Med} = l + \frac{(n/2) - cf}{f} \times h$$

$$= 950 + \frac{300 - 236}{207} \times 75 = 950 + 23.2 = \text{Rs. } 973.2 \text{ per week}$$

The median wage value can also be obtained by applying the graphical method as shown in Fig. 3.1.

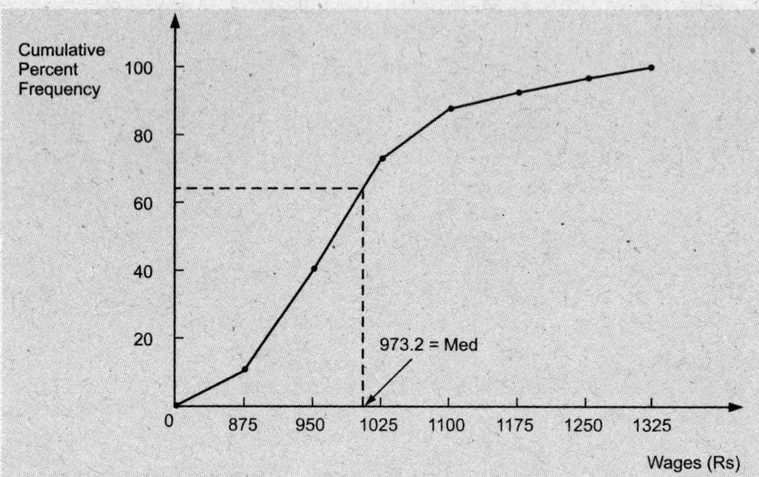

Fig. 3.1 Cumulative Frequency Curve

$$Q_1 = \text{value of } (n/4)\text{th observation}$$
$$= \text{value of } (600/4)\text{th} = 150\text{th observation}$$

(b) The limits of weekly wages of central 50 per cent of the workers can be calculated by taking the difference of Q_1 and Q_3. This implies that Q_1 lies in the class interval 875–950. Thus

$$Q_1 = l + \frac{(n/4) - cf}{f} \times h$$

$$= 875 + \frac{150 - 69}{167} \times 75 = 875 + 36.38 = \text{Rs. } 911.38 \text{ per week}$$

Similarly, Q_3 = Value of $(3n/4)$th observation

$$= \text{Value of } (3 \times 600/4)\text{th} = 450\text{th observation}$$

This value of Q_3 lies in the class interval 1025–1100. Thus

$$Q_3 = l + \frac{(3n/4) - cf}{f} \times h$$

$$= 1025 + \frac{450 - 443}{65} \times 75 = 1025 + 8.08 = \text{Rs. } 1033.08 \text{ per week}$$

Hence the limits of weekly wages of central 50 per cent workers are Rs. 411.38 and Rs. 533.08.

(c) The percentage of workers who earned weekly wages less than or equal to Rs. 950 is 39.33 and who earned weekly wages less than or equal to Rs. 1250 is 98.33. Thus the percentage of workers who earned weekly wages between Rs. 950 and Rs. 1250 is (98.33–39.33) = 59.

Example 3.52: You are working for the transport manager of a 'call centre' which hires cars for the staff. You are interested in the weekly distances covered by these cars. Kilometers recorded for a sample of hired cars during a given week yielded the following data:

Kilometers Covered	*Number of Cars*	*Kilometers Covered*	*Number of Cars*
100–110	4	150–160	8
110–120	0	160–170	5
120–130	3	170–180	0
130–140	7	180–190	2
140–150	11		40

(a) Form a cumulative frequency distribution and draw a cumulative frequency ogive.
(b) Estimate graphically the number of cars which covered less than 165 km in the week.
(c) Calculate Q_1, Q_2, Q_3 and P_{75}

Solution: (a) The calculations to obtain a cumulative frequency distribution and to draw ogive are shown in Table 3.25.

Table 3.25

Kilometers Covered Less than	*Number of Cars*	*Cumulative Frequency*	*Percent Cumulative Frequency*
110	4	4	10.0
120	0	4	10.0
130	3	7	17.5
140	7	14 $\leftarrow Q_1$	35.0
150	11	25 $\leftarrow$ Me $= Q_2$	62.5
160	8	33 $\leftarrow Q_3$	82.5 $\leftarrow P_{75}$
170	5	38	95.0
180	0	38	95.0
190	2	40	100.0

Plotting cumulative frequency values on the graph paper, frequency polygon is as shown in Fig. 3.2.

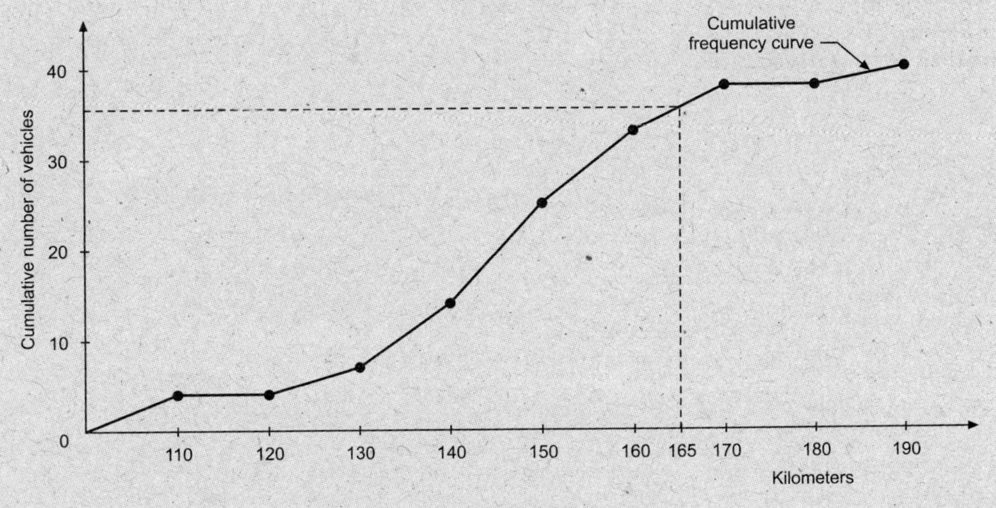

Fig. 3.2 Cumulative Frequency Curve

(b) The number of cars which covered less than 165 km in the week are 35 as shown in the Fig. 3.2.

(c) Since there are 40 observations in the data set, we can take 10th, 20th and 30th cumulative values to corresponds to Q_1, Q_2 and Q_3 respectively. These values from the graph gives $Q_1 = 134$, $Q_2 = 146$ and $Q_3 = 156$.

$$P_{75} = \frac{(75n/100) - cf}{f} \times h = 150 + \frac{30-25}{8} \times 10 = 156.25$$

This implies that 75 per cent of cars covered less than or equal to 156.25 kilometers.

Example 3.53: The following distribution gives the pattern of overtime work per week done by 100 employees of a company. Calculate median, first quartile, and seventh decile.

Overtime hours :	10–15	15–20	20–25	25–30	30–35	35–40
No. of employees :	11	20	35	20	8	6

Calculate Q_1, D_7 and P_{60}.

Solution: The calculations of median, first quartile (Q_1), and seventh decile (D_7) are shown in Table 3.26.

Table 3.26

Overtime Hours	*Number of Employees*	*Cumulative Frequency (Less than type)*
10–15	11	11
15–20	20	31 ← Q_1 class
20–25	35	66 ← Median and P_{60} class
25–30	20	86 ← D_7 class
30–35	8	94
35–40	6	100
	100	

Since the number of observations in this data set are 100, the median value is $(n/2)$th = $(100 \div 2)$th = 50th observation. This observation lies in the class interval 20–25. Applying the formula (3-16) to get median overtime hours value, we have

$$\text{Med} = l + \frac{(n/2) - cf}{f} \times h$$

$$= 20 + \frac{50-31}{35} \times 5 = 20 + 2.714 = 22.714 \text{ hours}$$

Q_1 = value of $(n/4)$ th observation = value of (100/4)th = 25th observation

$$\text{Thus}\quad Q_1 = l + \frac{(n/4) - cf}{f} \times h = 15 + \frac{25-11}{20} \times 5 = 15 + 3.5 = 18.5 \text{ hours}$$

D_7 = value of $(7n/10)$th observation = value of $(7 \times 100)/10$ = 70th observation

$$\text{Thus}\quad D_7 = l + \frac{(7n/10) - cf}{f} \times h = 25 + \frac{70-66}{20} \times 5 = 25 + 1 = 26 \text{ hours}$$

P_{60} = Value of $(60n/100)$ th observation = $60 \times (100/100)$ = 60th observation

$$\text{Thus}\quad P_{60} = l + \frac{(60 \times n/100) - cf}{f} \times h = 20 + \frac{60-31}{35} \times 5 = 24.14 \text{ hours}$$

Conceptual Questions 3C

12. Define median and discuss its advantages and disadvantages.
13. When is the use of median considered more appropriate than mean?
14. Write a short criticism of the following statement: 'Median is more representative than mean because it is relatively less affected by extreme values'.
15. What are quartiles of a distribution? Explain their uses.
16. It has been said that the same percentage of frequencies falls between the first and ninth decile for symmetric and skewed distributions. Criticize or explain this statement. Generalize your answer to other percentiles.
17. Describe the similarities and differences among median, quartiles, and percentiles as descriptive measures of position.

Self-Practice Problems 3D

3.22 On a university campus 200 teachers are asked to express their views on how they feel about the performance of their Union's president. The views are classified into the following categories:

Disapprove strongly = 94
Disapprove = 52
Approve = 43
Approve strongly = 11

What is the median view?

3.23 The following are the profit figures earned by 50 companies in the country:

Profit (in Rs. lakh)	*Number of Companies*
10 or less	4
20 or less	10
30 or less	30
40 or less	40
50 or less	47
60 or less	50

Calculate

(a) the median, and

(b) the range of profit earned by the middle 80 per cent of the companies. Also verify your results by graphical method.

3.24 A number of particular items has been classified according to their weights. After drying for two weeks the same items have again been weighted and similarly classified. It is known that the median weight in the first weighting was 20.83 g, while in the second weighing it was 17.35 g. Some frequencies, a and b, in the first weighing and x and y in the second weighing are missing. It is known that $a = x/3$ and $b = y/2$. Find out the values of the missing frequencies.

Class	*Frequencies*		*Class*	*Frequencies*	
	I	*II*		*I*	*II*
0–5	a	x	15–20	52	50
5–10	b	y	20–25	75	30
10–15	11	40	25–30	22	28

3.25 The length of time taken by each of 18 workers to complete a specific job was observed to be the following:

Time (in min) :	5–9	10–14	15–19	20–24	25–29
Number of workers :	3	8	4	2	1

(a) Calculate the median time

(b) Calculate Q_1 and Q_3

3.26 The following distribution is with regard to weight (in g) of mangoes of a given variety. If mangoes less than 443 g in weight be considered unsuitable for the foreign market, what is the percentage of total yield suitable for it? Assume the given frequency distribution to be typical of the variety.

Weight (in g)	*Number of Mangoes*	*Weight (in g)*	*Number of Mangoes*
410–419	10	450–459	45
420–429	20	460–469	18
430–439	42	470–479	7
440–449	54		

Draw an ogive of 'more than' type of the above data and deduce how many mangoes will be more than 443 g.

3.27 Given the following frequency distribution with some missing frequencies:

Class	*Frequency*	*Class*	*Frequency*
10–20	185	50–60	136
20–30	—	60–70	—
30–40	34	70–80	50
40–50	180		

If the total frequency is 685 and median is 42.6, find out the missing frequencies.

Hints and Answers

3.22 Disapprove
3.23 Med = 27.5; $P_{90} - P_{10} = 47.14 - 11.67 = 35.47$
3.24 $a = 3, b = 6; x = 9, y = 12$
3.25 (a) 13.25 (b) $Q_3 = 17.6, Q_1 = 10.4$
3.26 52.25%; 103
3.27 20–30(77)

3.11 MODE

The **mode** is that value of an observation which occurs most frequently in the data set, that is, the point (or class mark) with the highest frequency.

The concept of mode is of great use to large scale manufacturers of consumable items such as ready-made garments, shoe-makers, and so on. In all such cases it is important to know the size that fits most persons rather than 'mean' size.

There are many practical situations in which arithmetic mean does not always provide an accurate characteristic (reflection) of the data due to the presence of extreme values. For example, in all such statements like 'average man prefers . . . brand of cigarettes', 'average production of an item in a month', or 'average service time at the service counter'. The term 'average' means majority (i.e. mode value) and not the arithmetic mean. Similarly, the median may not represent the characteristics of the data set completely owing to an uneven distribution of the values of observations. For example, suppose in a distribution the values in the lower half vary from 10 to 100 (say), while the same number of observations in the upper half vary from 100 to 7000 (say) with most of them close to the higher limit. In such a distribution, the median value of 100 will not provide an indication of the true nature of the data. Such shortcomings stated above for mean and median are removed by the use of *mode*, the third measure of central tendency.

The mode is a poor measure of central tendency when most frequently occurring values of an observation do not appear close to the centre of the data. The mode need not even be a unique value. Consider the frequency distributions shown in Fig. 3.3(a) and (b). The distribution in Fig. 3.3(a) has its mode at the lowest class and certainly cannot be considered representative of central location. The distribution shown in Fig. 3.3(b) has two modes. Obviously neither of these values appear to be representative of the central location of the data. For these reasons the mode has limited use as a measure of central tendency for decision-making. However, for descriptive analysis, mode is a useful measure of central tendency.

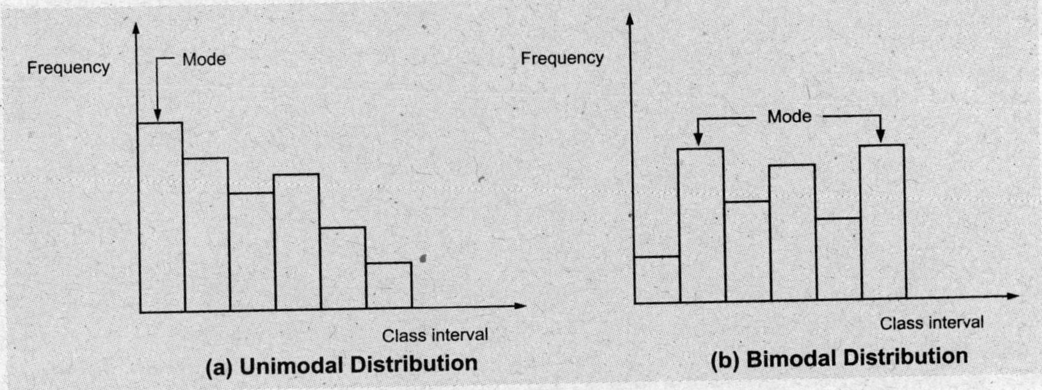

Fig. 3.3 Frequency Distribution

Calculation of Mode It is always preferable to calculate mode from grouped data. Table 3.27, for example, shows the sales per day of an item for 20 days period. The mode of this data is 71 since this value occurs more frequently (four times than any other value). However, it fails to reveal the fact that most of the values are under 70.

Table 3.27 Sales During 20 Days Period
(Data arranged in ascending order)

53,	56,	57,	58,	58,	60,	61,	63,	63,	64
64,	65,	65,	67,	68,	71,	71,	71,	71,	74

Converting this data into a frequency distribution as shown in Table 3.28:

Table 3.28 Frequency Distribution of Sales Per Day

Sales volume (Class interval)	:	53–56	57–60	61–64	65–68	69–72	72 and above
Number of days (Frequency)	:	2	4	5	4	4	1

Table 3.28 shows that a sale of 61–64 units of the item was achieved on 5 days. Thus this class is more representative of the sales per day.

In the case of grouped data, the following formula is used for calculating mode:

$$\text{Mode} = l + \frac{f_m - f_{m-1}}{2f_m - f_{m-1} - f_{m+1}} \times h$$

where l = lower limit of the model class interval
f_{m-1} = frequency of the class preceding the mode class interval
f_{m+1} = frequency of the class following the mode class interval
h = width of the mode class interval

Example 3.54: Find the missing frequency for the following incomplete distribution by using appropriate formula when mode is 36.

Marks	*No. of Students*
0 – 10	5
10 – 20	7
20 – 30	–
30 – 40	–
40 – 50	10
50 – 60	6
	50

Solution: Let the missing frequency corresponding to class 20 – 30 be x. Then missing frequency corresponding to class 30 – 40 will be 50 – (5 + 7 + x + 10 + 6) = 22 – x

Since mode is 36, therefore model class is 30 – 40. Then

$$\text{Mode} = l + \frac{f_m - f_{m-1}}{2f_m - f_{m_{-1}} - f_{m+1}} \times h = 30 + \frac{22 - x - x}{2(22 - x) - x - 10}$$

$$36 = 30 + \frac{22 - 2x}{34 - 3x} \times 10$$

$$6(34 - 3x) = (22 - 2x)(10)$$

$$204 - 18x = 220 - 20x$$

$$2x = 16, \text{ i.e., } x = 8$$

Missing frequency is x = 8 and 22 – x = 22 – 8 = 14.

Example 3.55: Median and mode are not affective by extreme values. Give examples in support of your answer.

[*Delhi Univ., BCom (Hons), 2006*]

Solution: For calculating median consider the following five figures: 2500, 3000, 4000, 4500, 11,500

$$\text{Median value} = \text{Size of} \left(\frac{n+1}{2}\right)^{\text{th}} \text{ item} = \text{Size of 3rd item} = 4000$$

If values of the first and last figure is changed to 1500 and 9500, then median value again be 3500. This is because position of the third observation remains unchanged.

for modal value, consider an example : 115, 120, 125, 130,135, 140, 130, 130, 142, 132. The value 130 is occurring more number of times than others. Thus mode value does not change with the change in extreme values:

Example 3.56: Using the data of Table 3.28, calculate the mode of sales distribution of the units of item during the 20 days period.

Solution: Since the largest frequency corresponds to the class interval 61–64, therefore it is the mode class. Then we have, l = 61, f_m = 5, f_{m-1} = 4, f_{m+1} = 4 and h = 3. Thus

$$M_0 = l + \frac{f_m - f_{m-1}}{2f_m - f_{m-1} - f_{m+1}} \times h$$

$$= 61 + \frac{5 - 4}{10 - 4 - 4} \times 3 = 61 + 1.5 = 62.5$$

Hence, the modal sale is of 62.5 units.

Example 3.57: In 500 small-scale industrial units, the return on investment ranged from 0 to 30 per cent; no unit sustaining loss. Five per cent of the units had returns ranging from zero per cent to (and including) 5 per cent, and 15 per cent of the units earned returns exceeding 5 per cent but not exceeding 10 per cent. The median rate of return was 15 per cent and the upper quartile 2 per cent. The uppermost layer of returns exceeding 25 per cent was earned by 50 units.

(a) Present the information in the form of a frequency table as follows:

Exceeding 0 per cent but not exceeding 5 per cent
Exceeding 5 per cent but not exceeding 10 per cent
Exceeding 10 per cent but not exceeding 15 per cent
and so on.

(b) Find the rate of return around which there is maximum concentration of units.

Solution: (a) The given information is summarized in the form of a frequency distribution as shown in Table 3.29.

Table 3.29

Rate of Return	*Industrial Units*
Exceeding 0 per cent but not exceeding 5 per cent	$500 \times \frac{5}{100} = 25$
Exceeding 5 per cent but not exceeding 10 per cent	$500 \times \frac{15}{100} = 75$
Exceeding 10 per cent but not exceeding 15 per cent	250 – 100 = 150
Exceeding 15 per cent but not exceeding 20 per cent	375 – 250 = 125
Exceeding 20 per cent but not exceeding 25 per cent	500 – 375 – 50 = 75
Exceeding 25 per cent but not exceeding 30 per cent	50

(b) Calculating mode to find out the rate of return around which there is maximum concentration of the units. The mode lies in the class interval 10–15. Thus

$$M_o = l + \frac{f_m - f_{m-1}}{2f_m - f_{m-1} - f_{m+1}}$$

$$= 10 + \frac{150 - 75}{2 \times 150 - 75 - 125} \times 5 = 10 + 3.75 = 13.75 \text{ per cent}$$

3.11.1 Graphical Method for Calculating Mode Value

The procedure of calculating mode using the graphical method is summarized below:

(i) Draw a histogram of the data, the tallest rectangle will represent the modal class.
(ii) Draw two diagonal lines from the top right corner and left corner of the tallest rectangle to the top right corner and left corner of the adjacent rectangles.
(iii) Draw a perpendicular line from the point of intersection of the two diagonal lines on the x-axis. The value on the x-axis marked by the line will represent the modal value.

Example 3.58: Calculate the mode using the graphical method for the following distribution of data:

Sales (in units) :	53–56	57–60	61–64	65–68	69–72	73–76
Number of days :	2	4	5	4	4	1

Solution: Construct a histogram of the data shown in Fig. 3.4 and draw other lines for the calculation of mode value.

The mode value from Fig. 3.4 is 62.5 which is same as calculated in Example 3.37.

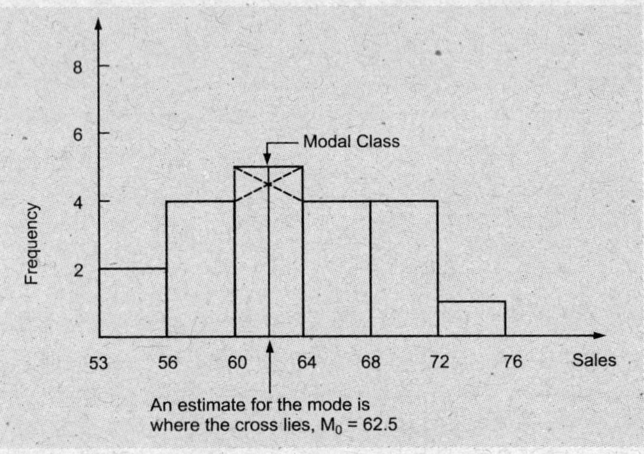

Figure 3.4 Graph for Modal Value

3.11.2 Advantages and Disadvantages of Mode Value

Advantages

(i) Mode value is easy to understand and to calculate. Mode class can also be located by inspection.
(ii) The mode is not affected by the extreme values in the distribution. The mode value can also be calculated for open-ended frequency distributions.
(iii) The mode can be used to describe quantitative as well as qualitative data. For example, its value is used for comparing consumer preferences for various types of products, say cigarettes, soaps, toothpastes, or other products.

Disadvantages

(i) Mode is not a rigidly defined measure as there are several methods for calculating its value.
(ii) It is difficult to locate modal class in the case of multi-modal frequency distributions.
(iii) Mode is not suitable for algebraic manipulations.
(iv) When data sets contain more than one modes, such values are difficult to interpret and compare.

3.12 RELATIONSHIP BETWEEN MEAN, MEDIAN, AND MODE

In a *unimodal* and symmetrical distribution, the values of mean, median, and mode are equal as indicated in Fig. 3.5. In other words, when all these three values are not equal to each other, the distribution is not symmetrical.

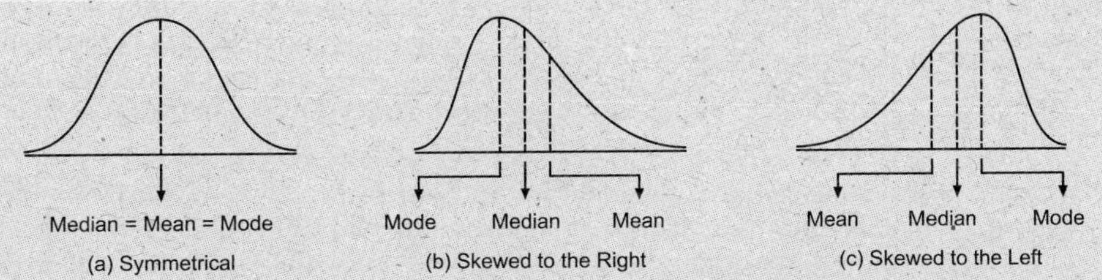

Figure 3.5 A comparison of Mean, Median, and Mode for three Distributional Shapes

A distribution that is not symmetrical, but rather has most of its values either to the right or to the left of the mode, is said to be *skewed*. For such asymmetrical distribution, Karl Pearson has suggested a relationship between these three measures of central tendency as:

$$\text{Mean} - \text{Mode} = 3\,(\text{Mean} - \text{Median}) \qquad (3\text{-}18)$$

or

$$\text{Mode} = 3\,\text{Median} - 2\,\text{Mean}$$

This implies that the value of any of these three measures can be calculated provided we know any two values out of three. The relationship (3-18) is shown in Fig. 3.5(b) and (c).

If most of the values of observations in a distribution fall to the right of the mode as shown in Fig. 3.5(b), then it is said to be skewed to the right *or positively skewed*. Distributions that are skewed right contain a few unusually large values of observations. In this case, mode remains under the peak (i.e., representing highest frequency) but the median (value that depends on the number of observations) and mean move to the right (value that is affected by extreme values). The order of magnitude of these measures will be

$$\text{Mean} > \text{Median} > \text{Mode}$$

But if the distribution is skewed to the left or *negatively skewed* (i.e., values of lower magnitude are concentrated more to the left of the mode) then mode is again under the peak whereas median and mean move to the left of mode. The order of magnitude of these measures will be

$$\text{Mean} < \text{Median} < \text{Mode}$$

In both these cases, the difference between mean and mode is 3 times the difference between mean and median.

In general, for a single-peaked skewed distribution (non-symmetrical), the median is preferred to the mean for measuring location because it is neither influenced by the frequency of occurrence of a single observation value as mode nor it is affected by extreme values.

3.13 COMPARISON BETWEEN MEASURES OF CENTRAL TENDENCY

In this chapter, we have already presented three methods to understand the characteristics of a data set. However, the choice of which method to use for describing a distribution of values of observations in a data set is not always easy. The choice to use any one of these three is mainly guided by their characteristics. The characteristics of these three differ from each other with regard to three factors:

(i) Presence of outlier data values
(ii) Shape of the frequency distribution of data values
(iii) Status of theoretical development

(i) ***The Presence of Outlier Data Values:*** The data values that differ in a big way from the other values in a data set are known as *outliers* (either very small or very high values). As mentioned earlier, the median is not sensitive to outlier values because its value depend only on the number of observations and the value always lies in the middle of the ordered set of values, whereas mean, which is calculated using all data values is sensitive to the outlier values in a data set. Obviously, smaller the number of observations in a data set, greater the influence of any outliers on the mean. The median is said to be *resistant* to the presence of outlier data values, but the mean is not.

(ii) ***Shape of Frequency Distribution:*** The effect of the shape of frequency distribution on mean, median, and mode is shown in Fig. 3.5. In general, the median is preferred to the mean as a way of measuring location for single peaked, skewed distributions. One of the reasons is that it satisfies the criterion that the *sum of absolute* difference (i.e., absolute error of judgment) of median from values in the data set is minimum, that is, $\Sigma \mid x - \text{Med} \mid = \text{min}$. In other words, the smallest sum of the absolute errors is associated with the median value is the data set as compared to either mean or mode. When data is multi-modal, there is no single measure of central location and the mode can vary dramatically from one sample to another, particularly when dealing with small samples.

(iii) ***The Status of Theoretical Development:*** Although the three measures of central tendency—Mean, Median, and Mode, satisfy different mathematical criteria but the objective of any statistical analysis in *inferential statistics* is always to minimize the *sum of squared deviations (errors)* taken from these measures to every value in the data set. The criterion of the sum of squared deviations is also called *least squares criterion*. Since A.M. satisfies the least squares criterion, it is mathematically consistent with several techniques of statistical inference.

As with the median, it can not be used to develop theoretical concepts and models and so is only used for basic descriptive purposes.

Conceptual Questions 3D

18. Give a brief description of the different measures of central tendency. Why is arithmetic mean so popular?

19. What are the advantages and disadvantages of the three common averages: Mean, Median, and Mode?

20. Identify the mathematical criteria associated with mean, median, and mode and briefly explain the meaning of each criterion.

21. What is a statistical average? What are the desirable properties for an average to possess? Mention the different types of averages and state why arithmetic mean is most commonly used amongst them.

22. What is the relationship between mean, median, and mode? Under what circumstances are they equal?

23. Which measure of central tendency is usually preferred if the distribution is known to be single peaked and skewed? Why?

Self-Practice Problems 3E

3.28 Given below is the distribution of profits (in '000 rupees) earned by 94 per cent of the retail grocery shops in a city.

Profits	*Number of Shops*	*Profit*	*Number of Shops*
0–10	0	50–60	68
10–20	5	60–70	83
20–30	14	70–80	91
30–40	27	80–90	94
40–50	48		

Calculate the modal value.

3.29 Compute mode value from the following data relating to dividend paid by companies in a particular financial year.

Dividend (in per cent) Value	*Number of Companies (in per cent)*	*Dividend of the Share of the Share Value*	*Number of Companies*
5.0–7.5	182	15.0–17.5	280
7.5–10.0	75	17.5–20.0	236
10.0–12.5	59	20.0–22.5	378
12.5–15.0	127	22.5–25.0	331

3.30 Following is the cumulative frequency distribution of the preferred length of kitchen slabs obtained from the preference study on 50 housewives:

Length (metres) more than	*Number of Housewives*
1.0	50
1.5	46
2.0	40
2.5	42
3.0	10
3.5	3

A manufacturer has to take a decision on what length of slabs to manufacture. What length would you recommend and why?

3.31 The number of solar heating systems available to the public is quite large, and their heat storage capacities are quite varied. Here is a distribution of heat storage capacity (in days) of 28 systems that were tested recently by a testing agency

Days	*Frequency*	*Days*	*Frequency*
0–0.99	2	4–4.99	5
1–1.99	4	5–5.99	3
2–2.99	6	6–6.99	1
3–3.99	7		

The agency knows that its report on the tests will be widely circulated and used as the basis for solar heat allowances.

Compute the mean, median, and mode of these data.

3.32 Mr Pandey does statistical analysis for an automobile racing team. The data on fuel consumption (in km per litre) for the team's cars in recent races are as follows:

14.77 16.11 16.11 15.05 15.99 14.91
15.27 16.01 15.75 14.89 16.05 15.22
16.02 15.24 16.11 15.02

(a) Calculate the mean and median fuel consumption.

(b) Group the data into five equally-sized classes. What is the fuel consumption value of the modal class?

(c) Which of the three measures of central tendency is best to use? Explain.

3.33 An agriculture farm sells grab bags of flower bulbs. The bags are sold by weight; thus the number of bulbs in each bag can vary depending on the varieties included. Below are the number of bulbs in each of the 20 bags sampled:

21 33 37 56 47 25 33 32 47 34
36 23 26 33 37 26 37 37 43 45

(a) What are the mean and median number of bulbs per bag?

(b) Based on your answer, what can you conclude about the shape of the distribution of number of bulbs per bag?

3.34 The table below is the frequency distribution of ages to the nearest birthday for a random sample of 50 employees in a large company.

Age to nearest birthday :	20–29	30–39	40–49	50–59	60–69
Number of employees :	5	12	13	8	12

Compute the mean, median, and mode for these data.

Hints and Answers

3.28 $M_0 = 3\text{ Med} - 2\bar{x}$ = Rs. 50.04 thousand

3.29 M_0 = 21.87 (per cent of the share value)

Formulae Used

1. Summation of n numbers

$$\sum_{i=1}^{n} x_i = x_1 + x_2 + \ldots + x_n$$

Simplified expression for the summation of n numbers

$$\sum x_i = x_1 + x_2 + \ldots + x_n$$

2. Sample mean, $\bar{x} = \dfrac{\sum x_i}{n}$

Population mean, $\mu = \dfrac{\sum x_i}{N}$

Sample mean for grouped data, $\bar{x} = \dfrac{\sum f_i m_i}{n}$

where $n = \sum f_i$ and m_i = mid-value of class intervals

3. Weighted mean for a population or a sample,

$$\bar{x}_w \text{ or } \mu_w = \frac{\sum w_i x_i}{\sum w_i}$$

where w_i = weight for observation i

4. Position of the median in an ordered set of observation belong to a population or a sample is, Med = $x_{(n/2)+(1/2)}$

Median for grouped data,

$$\text{Med} = l + \left[\frac{(n/2) - cf}{f}\right]h$$

5. Quartile for a grouped data

$$Q_i = l + \left[\frac{i(n/4) - cf}{f}\right]h; \quad i = 1, 2, 3$$

Decile for a grouped data

$$D_i = l + \left[\frac{i(n/10) - cf}{f}\right]h; \quad i = 1, 2, \ldots, 9$$

Percentile for a grouped data

$$P_i = l + \left[\frac{i(n/100) - cf}{f}\right]h; \quad i = 1, 2, \ldots, 99$$

6. Mode for a grouped data

$$M_0 = l + \left[\frac{f_m - f_{m-1}}{2f_m - f_{m-1} - f_{m+1}}\right]h$$

Mode for a multimode frequency distribution

$$M_0 = 3 \text{ Median} - 2 \text{ Mean}$$

Chapter Concepts Quiz

True or False

1. Inferential statistics are used to describe specific characteristics of the data.
2. With nominal data, the mean should be used as a measure of central tendency.
3. With ordinal data, we can use both the mode and the mean as a measure of central tendency.
4. When the data are interval or ratio, we can use the mean as a measure of central tendency.
5. Harmonic mean is the reciprocal of arithmetic mean.
6. Sum of absolute deviations from median is minimum.
7. The mean of a data set remains unaffected if an observation equal to mean is included in it.
8. With continuous data, the median is the most appropriate measure of central tendency.
9. Weighted mean is useful in problems relating to the construction of index numbers and standardized birth and death rates.
10. It is possible to have data with three different values for measures of central tendency.
11. The median is less affected than the mean by extreme values of observations in a distribution.
12. The sum of deviations from mean is zero.
13. If the number of observations is even, the median is in the middle of the distribution.
14. The mode is always found at the highest point of a graph of a frequency distribution.
15. For grouped data, it is possible to calculate an approximate mean by assuming that each value in a given class is equal to its mid-point.

Concepts Quiz Answers

1. F	**2.** F	**3.** F	**4.** T	**5.** F	**6.** T	**7.** T	**8.** F
9. T	**10.** T	**11.** T	**12.** T	**13.** F	**14.** T	**15.** T	

Review Self-Practice Problems

3.35 The following is the data on profit margin (in per cent) of three products and their corresponding sales (in Rs.) during a particular period.

Product	*Profit Margin (Per cent)*	*Sales (Rs. in thousand)*
A	12.5	2,000
B	10.3	6,000
C	6.4	10,000

(a) Determine the mean profit margin.
(b) Determine the weighted mean considering the rupee sales as weight for each product.
(c) Which of the means calculated in part (a) and (b) is the correct one?

3.36 The number of cars sold by each of the 10 car dealers during a particular month, arranged in ascending order, is 12, 14, 17, 20, 20, 20, 22, 22, 24, 25. Considering this scale to be the statistical population of interest, determine the mean, median, and mode for the number of cars sold.

(a) Which value calculated above best describes the 'typical' sales volume per dealer?
(b) For the given data, determine the values at the (i) quartile Q_1 and (ii) percentile P_{30} for these sales amounts.

3.37 A quality control inspector tested nine samples of each of three designs A, B and C of certain bearing for a new electrical winch. The following data are the number of hours it took for each bearing to fail when the winch motor was run continuously at maximum output, with a load on the winch equivalent to 1.9 times the intended capacity.

A : 16 16 53 15 31 17 14 30 20
B : 18 27 23 21 22 26 39 17 28
C : 31 16 42 20 18 17 16 15 19

Calculate the mean and median for each group and suggest which design is best and why?

3.38 The following are the weekly wages in rupees of 30 workers of a firm:

140 139 126 114 100 88 62 77 99
103 108 129 144 148 134 63 69 148
132 118 142 116 123 104 95 80 85
106 123 133

The firm gave bonus of Rs. 10, 15, 20, 25, 30, and 35 for individuals in the respective salary slabs: exceeding 60 but not exceeding 75; exceeding 75 but not exceeding 90; and so on up to exceeding 135 and not exceeding 150. Find the average bonus paid.

3.39 The mean monthly salaries paid to 100 employees of a company was Rs. 5,000. The mean monthly salaries paid to male and female employees were Rs. 5,200 and Rs. 4,200 respectively. Determine the percentage of males and females employed by the company.

3.40 A factory pays workers on piece rate basis and also a bonus to each worker on the basis of individual output in each quarter. The rate of bonus payable is as follows:

Output (in units)	*Bonus (Rs.)*	*Output (in units)*	*Bonus (Rs.)*
70–74	40	90–94	70
75–79	45	95–99	80
80–84	50	100–104	100
85–89	60		

The individual output of a batch of 50 workers is given below:

94 83 78 76 88 86 93 80 91 82
89 97 92 84 92 80 85 83 98 103
87 88 88 81 95 86 99 81 87 90
84 97 80 75 93 101 82 82 89 72
85 83 75 72 83 98 77 87 71 80

By suitable classification you are required to find:

(a) Average bonus per worker for the quarter

(b) Average output per worker.

3.41 An economy grows at the rate of 2 per cent in the first year, 2.5 per cent in the second year, 3 per cent in the third year, 4 per cent in the fourth year . . . and 10 per cent in the tenth year. What is the average rate of growth of the company?

3.42 A man travelled by car for 3 days. He covered 480 km each day. On the first day he drove for 10 hours at 48 km an hour, on the second day he drove for 12 hours at 40 km an hour, and on the last day he drove for 15 hours at 32 km per hour. What was his average speed?

[*Bangalore Univ., B.Com, 1996*]

3.43 The price of a certain commodity in the first week of January is 400 g per rupee; it is 600 g per rupee in the second week and 500 g per rupee in the third week. Is it correct to say that the average price is 500 g per rupee? Verify.

3.44 Find the missing information in the following table:

	A	*B*	*C*	*Combined*
Number	10	8	—	24
Mean	20	—	6	15
Geometric Mean	10	7	—	8.397

[*Delhi Univ., B.Com (Hons), 1998*]

3.45 During a period of decline in stock market prices, a stock is sold at Rs. 50 per share on one day, Rs. 40 on the next day, and Rs. 25 on the third day.

(a) If an investor bought 100, 120, and 180 shares on the respective three days, find the average price paid per share.

(b) If the investor bought Rs. 1000 worth of shares on each of the three days, find the average price paid per share.

[*Delhi Univ., BA (Hons Econ.), 1998*]

Hints and Answers

3.35 (a) $\mu = \dfrac{\Sigma x_i}{N} = \dfrac{29.2}{3} = 9.73$ per cent

(b) $\mu_w = \dfrac{\Sigma w_i x_i}{\Sigma w_i} = \dfrac{1{,}50{,}800}{18{,}000} = 8.37$ per cent

(c) The weighted mean of 8.37 per cent considering sales (in Rs.) as weights is the correct mean profit margin. Percentages should never the averaged without being weighted.

3.36 $\mu = \dfrac{\Sigma x_i}{N} = \dfrac{196}{10} = 19.6$

$$\text{Med} = \frac{\left(\frac{n}{2}\right) + \left(\frac{n}{2} + 1\right)}{2} = \frac{5\text{th} + 6\text{th}}{2} = 20.0$$

M_0 = most frequent value = 20

(a) Median is best used as the 'typical' value because of the skewness in the distribution of values

(b) $Q_1 = x_{(n/4)+(1/2)} = x_{(10/4)+(1/2)} = x_{3.0} = 17$

$P_{30} = x_{(3n/10)+(1/2)} = x_{3.5} = 17 + 0.5$

$\cdot\ (20 - 17) = 18.5$

3.37 Listing the data in ascending order:

A : 14 15 16 16 17 20 30 31 53

B : 17 18 21 22 23 26 27 28 39

C : 15 16 16 17 18 19 20 31 42

$\bar{x}_A = 212/9 = 23.56$; Med (A) = 17

$\bar{x}_B = 221/9 = 24.56$; Med (B) = 23

$\bar{x}_C = 194/9 = 21.56$; Med (C) = 18

Since medians are the fifth observation in each data set, therefore design B is best because both the mean and median are highest.

3.38 Prepare a frequency distribution as follows:

Weekly Wages (Rs.)	*Frequency (f)*	*Bonus Paid (x)*	*Weekly Wages (Rs.)*	*Frequency (f)*	*Bonus Paid (x)*
61–75	3	10	106–120	5	25
76–90	4	15	121–135	7	30
91–105	5	20	136–150	6	35

Average bonus paid $= \dfrac{\Sigma fx}{n} = \dfrac{375}{30}$ = Rs. 24.5

3.39 Given $n_1 + n_2 = 100$, $\bar{x}_{12} = 5000$, $\bar{x}_1 = 5200$ and $\bar{x}_2 = 4200$

$$\bar{x}_{12} = \frac{n_1\bar{x}_1 + n_2\bar{x}_2}{n_1 + n_2}$$

or $$5000 = \frac{n_1(5200) + n_2(4200)}{n_1 + n_2}$$

$$= \frac{n_1(5200) + (100 - n_1)(4200)}{100}$$

$1000\, n_1 = 80{,}000$ or $n_1 = 80$ and $n_2 = 100 - n_1 = 20$

3.40

Output (in units)	Frequency (f)	Bonus (Rs.)	Output (in units)	Frequency (f)	Bonus (Rs.)
70–74	3	40	90–94	7	70
75–79	5	45	95–99	6	80
80–84	15	50	100–104	2	100
85–89	12	60			

(a) Average bonus/worker for quarter,

$\bar{x} = \Sigma fx/n = 2{,}985/50 =$ Rs. 59.7

(b) Total quarterly bonus paid

= Rs. 59.7 × 50 = Rs. 2,985

(c) Average output/worker, $\bar{x} = 86.1$ units

3.41 Year : 1 2 3 4 5 6 7 8 9 10

Growth rate : 2 2.5 3 4 5 6 7 8 9 10

Value at the end of year x: 102 102.5 103 104 105 106 107 108 109 110

G.M. = Antilog ($\Sigma \log x \div n$)

= Antilog (20.237 ÷ 10) = 105.6

Average growth rate = 105.6 – 100 = 5.6 per cent

3.42 $$\text{H.M.} = n\bigg/\left(\frac{1}{x_1} + \frac{1}{x_2} + \frac{1}{x_3}\right)$$

$$= 3\bigg/\left(\frac{1}{48} + \frac{1}{40} + \frac{1}{32}\right)$$

= 38.98 km per hour

3.43 $$\text{Harmonic mean} = n\bigg/\left(\frac{1}{a} + \frac{1}{b} + \frac{1}{c}\right)$$

$$= 3\bigg/\left(\frac{1}{400} + \frac{1}{600} + \frac{1}{500}\right)$$

= 0.486

3.44 Mean : Let x be the mean of B. Then

$(20 \times 10) + (8 \times x) + (6 \times 6) = (15 \times 24)$

$8x = 124$ or $x = 15.5$

Hence mean of B = 15.5

Geometric mean: Let x be the geometric mean of C. Then

$(10)^{10} \times (7)^8 \times x^6 = (8.397)^{24}$

$10 \log 10 + 8 \log 7 + 6 \log x = 24 \log 8.397$

$10 + (8 \times 0.8451) + 6 \log x = 24\ (0.9241)$

$6 \log x = 5.4176$ or $x =$ Antilog $0.9029 = 7.997$

Hence, geometric mean of C is 7.997.

3.45 Average price paid per share

$$= \frac{\Sigma\, wx}{\Sigma\, w} = \frac{14{,}300}{400} = 35.75.$$

Glosssary of Terms

Population parameter: A numerical value used as a summary measure using data of the population.
Sample statistic: A numerical value used as a summary measure using data of the sample for estimation or hypothesis testing.
Mean: The sum of all the data values divided by their number.
Mean value: A measure of central location (tendency) for a data set such that the observations in the data set tend to cluster around it.
Weighted arithmetic mean: The mean for a data set obtained by assigning each observation a weight that reflects its importance within the data set.
Geometric mean: A value that represents nth root of the product of a set of n numbers.
Harmonic mean: A value that is the reciprocal of the mean of the reciprocals of a set of numbers.

Median: A measure of central location such that one half of the observations in the data set is less than or equal to the given value.
Quartiles: The values which divide an ordered data set into 4 equal parts. The 2nd quartile is the median.
Deciles: The values which divide an ordered data set into 10 equal parts. The 5th decile is the median.
Percentiles: The values which divide an ordered data set into 100 equal parts. The 50th percentile is the median.
Mode value: A measure of location recognised by the location of the most frequently occurring value of a set of data.
Outlier: A very small or very large value in the data set.

Measures of Dispersion

LEARNING OBJECTIVES

After studying this chapter, you should be able to

- provide the importance of the concept of variability (dispersion)
- measure the spread or dispersion, understand it, and identify its causes to provide a basis for action

4.1 INTRODUCTION

Just as central tendency can be measured by a number in the form of an average, the amount of variation (dispersion, spread, or scatter) among the values in the data set can also be measured. The measures of central tendency describe that the major part of values in the data set appears to concentrate (cluster) around a central value called *average* with the remaining values scattered (spread or distributed) on either sides of that value. But these measures do not reveal how these values are dispersed (spread or scattered) on each side of the central value. *The dispersion of values is indicated by the extent to which these values tend to spread over an interval rather than cluster closely around an average.*

The statistical techniques to measure such dispersion are of two types:

(i) Techniques that are used to measure the extent of variation or the deviation (also called degree of variation) of each value in the data set from a measure of central tendency, usually the mean or median. Such statistical techniques are called *measures of dispersion* (or *variation*).

(ii) Techniques that are used to measure the direction (away from uniformity or symmetry) of variation in the distribution of values in the data set. Such statistical techniques are called *measures of skewness*, discussed in Chapter 5.

A small dispersion among values in the data set indicates that data are clustered closely around the mean. The mean is therefore considered representative of the data, i.e. mean is a reliable average. Conversely, a large dispersion among values in the data set indicates that the mean is not reliable, i.e. it is not representative of the data.

Illustration Suppose over the six-year period the net profits (in percentage) of two firms are as follows:

Firm 1	:	5.2,	4.5,	3.9,	4.7,	5.1,	5.4
Firm 2	:	7.8,	7.1,	5.3,	14.3,	11.0,	16.1

Since average amount of profit is 4.8 per cent for both firms, therefore operating results of both the firms are equally good and that a choice between them for investment purposes must depend on other considerations. However, the difference among the values is greater in Firm, 2, that is, profit is varying from 5.3 to 16.1 per cent, while the net profit values of Firm 1 were varying from 3.9 to 5.4 per cent. This shows that the values in data set 2 are spread more than those in data set 1. This implies that Firm 1 has a consistent performance while Firm 2 has a highly inconsistent performance. Thus for investment purposes, a comparison of the average (mean) profit values alone should not be sufficient.

4.2 SIGNIFICANCE OF MEASURING DISPERSION

Following are some of the purposes for which measures of variation are needed.

(i) ***Test the reliability of an average:*** Measures of variation are used to test to what extent an average represents the characteristic of a data set. If the variation is small, that is, extent of dispersion or scatter is less on each side of an average, then it indicates high unformity of values in the distribution and the average represents an individual value in the data set. On the other hand, if the variation is large, then it indicates a lower degree of uniformity in values in the data set, and the average may be unreliable. No variation indicates perfect uniformity and, therefore, values in the data set are identical.

(ii) ***Control the variability:*** Measuring variation helps to identify the nature and causes of variation. Such information is useful in controlling the variations. According to Spurr and Bonini, '*In matters of health, variations in, body temperature, pulse beat and blood pressure are the basic guides to diagnosis. Prescribed treatment is designed to control their variation. In industrial production, efficient operation requires control of quality variation, the causes of which are sought through inspection and quality control programmes.*' In social science, the measurement of 'inequality' of distribution of income and wealth requires the measurement of variability.

(iii) ***Compare two or more sets of data with respect to their variability:*** Measures of variation help in the comparison of the spread in two or more sets of data with respect to their uniformity or consistency. For example, (i) the measurement of variation in share prices and their comparison with respect to different companies over a period of time requires the measurement of variation, (ii) the measurement of variation in the length of stay of patients in a hospital every month may be used to set staffing levels, number of beds, number of doctors, and other trained staff, patient admission rates, and so on.

(iv) ***Facilitate the use of other statistical techniques:*** Measures of variation facilitate the use of other statistical techniques such as correlation and regression analysis, hypothesis testing, forecasting, quality control, and so on.

4.2.1 Essential Requisites for a Measure of Variation

The essential requisites for a good measure of variation are listed below. These requisites help in identifying the merits and demerits of individual measures of variation.

(i) It should be rigidly defined.
(ii) It should be based on all the values (elements) in the data set.
(iii) It should be calculated easily, quickly, and accurately.
(iv) It should not be unduly affected by the fluctuations of sampling and also by extreme observations.
(v) It should be amenable to further mathematical or algebraic manipulations.

4.3 CLASSIFICATION OF MEASURES OF DISPERSION

The various measures of dispersion (variation) can be classified into two categories:

(i) Absolute measures, and
(ii) Relative measures

Absolute measures are described by a number or value to represent the amount of variation or differences among values in a data set. Such a number or value is expressed in the same unit of measurement as the set of values in the data such as rupees, inches, feet, kilograms, or tonnes. Such measures help in comparing two or more sets of data in terms of absolute magnitude of variation, provided the variable values are expressed in the same unit of measurement and have almost the same average value.

The *relative measures* are described as the ratio of a measure of absolute variation to an average and is termed as *coefficient of variation*. The word 'coefficient' means a number that is independent of any unit of measurement. While computing the relative variation, the average value used as base should be the same from which the absolute deviations were calculated.

Another classification of the measures of variation is based on the method employed for their calculations:

(i) Distance measures, and
(ii) Average deviation measures

The *distance measures* describe the spread or dispersion of values of a variable in terms of difference among values in the data set. The *average deviation measures* describe the average deviation for a given measure of central tendency.

The above-mentioned classification of various measures of dispersion (variation) may be summarized as shown below:

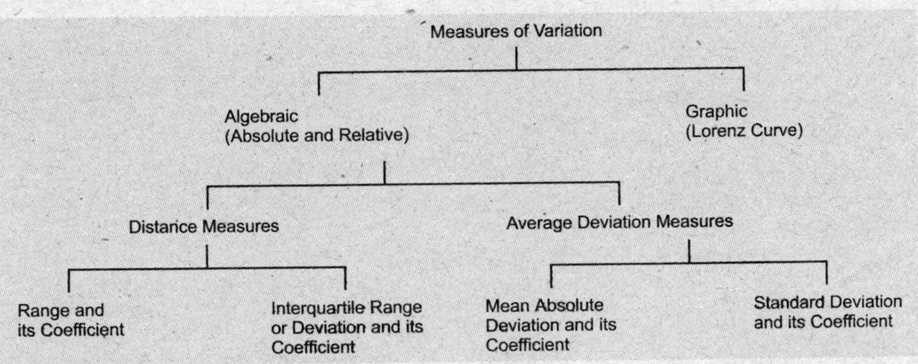

4.4 DISTANCE MEASURES

As mentioned above, two distance measures discussed in this section are namely:

(i) Range, and
(ii) Interquartile deviation

4.4.1 Range

The range is the most simple measure of dispersion and is based on the location of the largest and the smallest values in the data. Thus, the **range** *is defined to be the difference between the largest and lowest observed values in a data set*. In other words, it is the length of an interval which covers the highest and lowest observed values in a data set and thus measures the dispersion or spread within the interval in the most direct possible way.

$$\text{Range (R)} = \text{Highest value of an observation} - \text{Lowest value of an observation}$$
$$= \text{H} - \text{L} \qquad (4\text{-}1)$$

For example, if the smallest value of an observation in the data set is 160 and largest value is 250, then the range is 250 – 160 = 90.

For grouped frequency distributions of values in the data set, the range is the difference between the upper class limit of the last class and the lower class limit of first class. In this case, the range obtained may be higher than as compared to ungrouped data because of the fact that the class limits are extended slightly beyond the extreme values in the data set.

Coefficient of Range

The relative measure of range, called the coefficient of range is obtained by applying the following formula:

$$\text{Coefficient of range} = \frac{\text{H} - \text{L}}{\text{H} + \text{L}} \qquad (4\text{-}2)$$

Example 4.1: The following are the sales figures of a firm for the last 12 months.

Months :	1	2	3	4	5	6	7	8	9	10	11	12
Sales (Rs. '000) :	80	82	82	84	84	86	86	88	88	90	90	92

Calculate the range and coefficient of range for sales.

Solution: Given that H = 92 and L = 80. Therefore

$$\text{Range} = \text{H} - \text{L} = 92 - 80 = 12$$

and
$$\text{Coefficient of range} = \frac{\text{H} - \text{L}}{\text{H} + \text{L}} = \frac{92 - 80}{92 + 80} = \frac{12}{172} = 0.069$$

Example 4.2: The following data show the waiting time (to the nearest 100th of a minute) of telephone calls to be matured:

Waiting Time	*Frequency (Minutes)*	*Waiting Time*	*Frequency (Minutes)*
0.10–0.35	6	0.88–1.13	8
0.36–0.61	10	1.14–1.39	4
0.62–0.87	8		

Calculate the range and coefficient of range.

Solution: Given that, H = 1.39 and L = 0.10. Therefore

$$\text{Range} = H - L = 1.39 - 0.10 = 1.29 \text{ minutes}$$

and $$\text{Coefficient of Range} = \frac{H-L}{H+L} = \frac{1.39-0.10}{1.39+0.10} = \frac{1.29}{1.49} = 0.865$$

Advantages, Disadvantages and Applications of Range The major advantages and disadvantages of range may be summarized as follows:

Advantages

(i) It is independent of the measure of central tendency and easy to calculate and understand.

(ii) It is quite useful in cases where the purpose is only to find out the extent of extreme variation, such as industrial quality control, temperature, rainfall, and so on.

Disadvantages

(i) The calculation of range is based on only two values—largest and smallest in the data set and fail to take account of any other observations.

(ii) It is largely influenced by two extreme values and completely independent of the other values. For example, range of two data sets {1, 2, 3, 7, 12} and {1, 1, 1, 12, 12} is 11, but the two data sets differ in terms of overall dispersion of values

(iii) Its value is sensitive to changes in sampling, that is, different samples of the same size from the same population may have widely different ranges.

(iv) It cannot be computed in case of open-ended frequency distributions because no highest or lowest value exists in open-ended class.

(v) It does not describe the variation among values in the data between two extremes. For example, each of the following set of data

Set 1 :	9	21	21	21	21	21	21	21
Set 2 :	9	9	9	9	21	21	21	21
Set 3 :	9	10	12	14	15	19	20	21

has a range of 21 – 9 = 12, but the variation of values is quite different in each case between the hightest and lowest values.

Applications of Range

(i) *Fluctuation in share prices:* The range is useful in the study of small variations among values in a data set, such as variation in share prices and other commodities that are very sensitive to price changes from one period to another.

(ii) *Quality control:* It is widely used in industrial quality control. Quality control is exercised by preparing suitable *control charts*. These charts are based on setting an upper control limit (range) and a lower control limit (range) within which produced items shall be accepted. The variation in the quality beyond these ranges requires necessary correction in the production process or system.

(iii) *Weather forecasts:* The concept of range is used to determine the difference between maximum and minimum temperature or rainfall by meteorological departments to announce for the knowledge of the general public.

4.4.2 Interquartile Range or Deviation

The limitations or disadvantages of the range can partially be overcome by using another measure of variation which measures the spread over the middle half of the values in the data set so as to minimise the influence of outliers (extreme values) in the calculation of range. Since a large number of values in the data set lie in the central part of the frequency distribution, therefore it is necessary to study the **Interquartile Range** (also called midspread). To compute this value, the entire data set is divided into four parts each of which contains 25 per cent of the observed values. The quartiles are the highest values in each of these four parts. The *interquartile range* is *a measure of dispersion or spread of values in the data set between the third quartile, Q_3 and the first quartile, Q_1*. In other words, the *interquartile range or deviation* (IQR) is the range for the middle 50 per cent of the data. The concept of IQR is shown in Fig. 4.1:

$$\text{Interquartile range (IQR)} = Q_3 - Q_1 \tag{4-3}$$

Half the distance between Q_1 and Q_3 is called the *semi-interquartile range* or the *quartile deviation* (QD).

$$\text{Quartile deviation (QD)} = \frac{Q_3 - Q_1}{2} \tag{4-4}$$

The median is not necessarily midway between Q_1 and Q_3, although this will be so for a symmetrical distribution. The median and quartiles divide the data into equal numbers of values but do not necessarily divide the data into equally wide intervals.

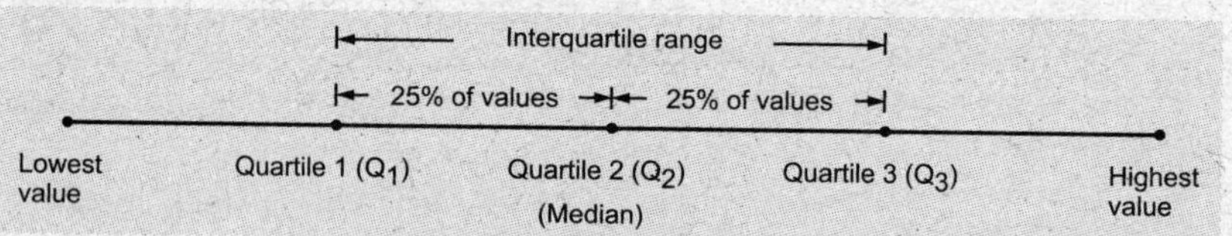

Figure 4.1 Interquartile Range

In a non-symmetrical distribution, the two quartiles Q_1 and Q_3 are at equal distance from the median, that is, Median – Q_1 = Q_3 – Median. Thus, Median ± Quartile Deviation covers exactly 50 per cent of the observed values in the data set.

A smaller value of quartile deviation indicates high uniformity or less variation among the middle 50 per cent observed values around the median value. On the other hand, a high value of quartile deviation indicates large variation among the middle 50 per cent observed values.

Coefficient of Quartile Deviation

Since quartile deviation is an absolute measure of variation, therefore its value gets affected by the size and number of observed values in the data set. Thus, the Q.D. of two or more than two sets of data may differ. Due to this reason, to compare the degree of variation in different sets of data, we compute the relative measure corresponding to Q.D., called the *coefficient of Q.D.*, and it is calculated as follows:

$$\text{Coefficient of QD} = \frac{Q_3 - Q_1}{Q_3 + Q_1} \tag{4-5}$$

Example 4.3: Use an appropriate measure to evaluate the variation in the following data:

Farm Size (acre)	*No. of Farms*	*Farm Size (acre)*	*No. of Farms*
below 40	394	161–200	169
41–80	461	201–240	113
81–120	391	241 and above	148
121–160	334		

Solution: Since the frequency distribution has open-end class intervals on the two extreme sides, therefore Q.D. would be an appropriate measure of variation. The computation of Q.D. is shown in Table 4.1.

Table 4.1 Calculations of Quartile Deviation

Farm Size (acre)	*No. of Farms*	*Cumulative Frequency (cf) (less than)*
below 40	394	394
41–80	461	855 ← Q_1 class
81–120	391	1246
121–160	334	1580 ← Q_3 class
161–200	169	1749
201–240	113	1862
241 and above	148	2010
	2010	

Q_1 = Value of $(n/4)$th observation = $2010 \div 4$ or 502.5th observation

This observation lies in the class 41–80. Therefore

$$Q_1 = l + \frac{(n/4) - cf}{f} \times h$$

$$= 41 + \frac{502.5 - 394}{461} \times 40 = 41 + 9.41 = 50.41 \text{ acres}$$

Q_3 = Value of $(3n/4)$th observation = $(3 \times 2010) \div 4$ or 1507.5th observation

This observation lies in the class 121–160. Therefore

$$Q_3 = l + \frac{(3n/4) - cf}{f} \times h$$

$$= 121 + \frac{1507.5 - 1246}{334} \times 40 = 121 + 31.31 = 152.31 \text{ acres}$$

Thus, the quartile deviation is given by

$$\text{Q.D.} = \frac{Q_3 - Q_1}{2} = \frac{152.31 - 50.41}{2} = 50.95 \text{ acres}$$

and $$\text{Coefficient of Q.D.} = \frac{Q_3 - Q_1}{Q_3 + Q_1} = \frac{50.95}{202.72} = 0.251$$

Example 4.4: The mean and S.D. of a normal distribution are Rs. 60 and Rs. 5 respectively. Find interquartile range and mean deviation of the distribution. *[Delhi Univ., BCom (Hons), 1991]*

Solution: Given $\bar{x} = 60$, $\sigma = 5$. Thus

$$\text{Mean deviation (M.D.)} = \frac{4}{5}\,\sigma = \frac{4}{5} \times 5 = 4$$

Also $$\text{Quartile deviation } (Q.D.) = \frac{2}{3}\,\sigma = \frac{2}{3} \times 5 = \frac{10}{3}. \text{ Thus}$$

$$Q.D = \frac{Q_3 - Q_1}{2} = \frac{10}{3} \quad \text{or} \quad Q_3 - Q_1 = \frac{20}{3}$$

Interquartile Range = $Q_3 - Q_1 = 20/3$.

Advantages and Disadvantages of Quartile Deviation The major advantages and disadvantages of quartile deviation are summarized as follows:

Advantages

(i) It is not difficult to calculate but can only be used to evaluate variation among observed values within the middle of the data set. Its value is not affected by the extreme (highest and lowest) values in the data set.
(ii) It is an appropriate measure of variation for a data set summarized in open-ended class intervals.
(iii) Since it is a positional measure of variation, therefore it is useful in case of erratic or highly skewed distributions, where other measures of variation get affected by extreme values in the data set.

Disadvantages

(i) The value of Q.D. is based on the middle 50 per cent observed values in the data set, therefore it cannot be considered as a good measure of variation as it is not based on all the observations.
(ii) The value of Q.D. is very much affected by sampling fluctuations.
(iii) The Q.D. has no relationship with any particular value or an average in the data set for measuring the variation. Its value is not affected by the distribution of the individual values within the interval of the middle 50 per cent observed values.

Conceptual Questions 4A

1. Explain the term variation. What does a measure of variation serve? In the light of these, comment on some of the well-known measures of variation.
2. What are the requisites of a good measure of variation?
3. Explain how measures of central tendency and measures of variation are complementary to each other in the context of analysis of data.
4. Distinguish between absolute and relative measures of variation. Give a broad classification of the measures of variation.
5. (a) Critically examine the different methods of measuring variation.
   (b) Explain with suitable examples the term 'variation'. Mention some common measures of variation and describe the one which you think is the most important.
6. What do you understand by 'coefficient of variation'? Discuss its importance in business problems.

Self-Practice Problems 4A

4.1 The following are the prices of shares of a company from Monday to Saturday:

Days	*Price (Rs.)*	*Days*	*Price (Rs.)*
Monday	200	Thursday	160
Tuesday	210	Friday	220
Wednesday	208	Saturday	250

Calculate the range and its coefficient.

4.2 The day's sales figures (in Rs.) for the last 15 days at Nirula's ice-cream counter, arranged in ascending order of magnitude, are recorded as follows: 2000, 2000, 2500, 2500, 2500, 3500, 4000, 5300, 9000, 12,500, 13,500, 24,500, 27,100, 30,900, and 41,000. Determine the range and middle 50 per cent range for this sample data.

4.3 The following distribution shows the sales of the fifty largest companies for a recent year:

Sales (Million of rupees)	*Number of Companies*
0–9	18
10–19	19
20–29	6
30–39	2
40–49	5

Calculate the coefficient of range.

4.4 You are given the frequency distribution of 292 workers of a factory according to their average weekly income.

Weekly Income (Rs.)	*No. of Workers*	*Weekly Income (Rs.)*	*No. of Workers*
Below 1350	8	1450–1470	22
1350–1370	16	1470–1490	15
1370–1390	39	1490–1510	15
1390–1410	58	1510–1530	9
1410–1430	60	1530 and above	10
1430–1450	40		

Calculate the quartile deviation and its coefficient from the above mentioned data.

4.5 You are given the data pertaining to kilowatt hours of electricity consumed by 100 persons in a city.

Consumption (kilowatt hour)	*No. of Users*
0–10	6
10–20	25
20–30	36
30–40	20
40–50	13

Calculate the range within which the middle 50 per cent of the consumers fall.

4.6 The following sample shows the weekly number of road accidents in a city during a two-year period:

Number of Accidents	*Frequency*	*Number of Accidents*	*Frequency*
0–4	5	25–29	9
5–9	12	30–34	4
10–14	32	35–39	3
15–19	27	40–44	1
20–24	11		

Find the interquartile range and coefficient of quartile deviation.

4.7 A City Development Authority subdivided the available land for housing into the following building lot sizes:

Lot Size (Square meters)	*Frequency*
Below 69.44	19
69.44–104.15	25
104.16–208.32	42
208.33–312.49	12
312.50–416.65	5
416.66 and above	17

Find the interquartile range and quartile deviation.

4.8 The cholera cases reported in different hospitals of a city in a rainy season are given below: Calculate the quartile deviation for the given distribution and comment upon the meaning of your result.

Age Group (Years)	*Frequency*	*Age Group (Years)*	*Frequency*
Less than 1	15	25–35	132
1–5	113	35–45	65
5–10	122	45–65	46
10–15	91	65 and above	15
15–25	229		

Hints and Answers

4.1 Range = Rs. 90, Coefficient of range = 0.219

4.2 Range = Rs. 39,000;

Middle 50%, R = $P_{75} - P_{25}$

$$= x_{(75n/100)+(1/2)} - x_{(25n/100)+(1/2)}$$
$$= x_{(11.25+0.50)} - x_{(3.75+0.50)}$$
$$= x_{11.75} - x_{4.25}$$
$$= (13{,}500 + 8250) - (2500 + 00)$$
$$= 19{,}250$$

Here $x_{11.75}$ is the interpolated value for the 75% of the distance between 11th and 12th ordered sales amount. Similarly, $x_{4.25}$ is the interpolated value for the 25% of the distance between 4th and 5th order sales amount.

4.3 Coefficient of range = 1

4.4 Quartile deviation = 27.76; Coeff. of Q.D. = 0.020; Q_1 = 1393.48; Q_3 = 1449

4.5 $Q_3 - Q_1 = 34 - 17.6 = 16.4$

4.6 $Q_3 - Q_1$ = 30.06; Coefficient of Q.D. = 0.561

4.7 $Q_3 - Q_1$ = 540.26; Q.D. = 270.13

4.8 Q.D. = 10 years

4.5 AVERAGE DEVIATION MEASURES

The range and quartile deviation indicate overall variation in a data set, but do not indicate spread or scatteredness around the centrilier (i.e. mean, median or mode). However, to understand the nature of distribution of values in the data set, we need to measure the 'spread' of values around the mean to indicate how representative the mean is.

In this section, we shall discuss two more measures of dispersion to measure the mean (or average) amount by which all values in a data set (population or sample) vary from their mean. These measures deal with the average deviation from some measure of central tendency—usually mean or median. These measures are:

(a) Mean Absolute Deviation or Average Deviation

(b) Variance and Standard Deviation

4.5.1 Mean Absolute Deviation

Since two measures of variation, range and quartile deviation, discussed earlier do not show how values in a data set are scattered about a central value or disperse themselves throughout the range, therefore it is quite reasonable to measure the variation as a degree (amount) to which values within a data set deviate from either mean or median.

The mean of deviations of individual values in the data set from their actual mean is always zero so such a measure (zero) would be useless as an indicator of variation. This problem can be solved in two ways:

(i) Ignore the signs of the deviations by taking their absolute value, or

(ii) Square the deviations because the square of a negative number is positive.

Since the absolute difference between a value x_i of an observation from A.M. is always a positive number, whether it is less than or more than the A.M., therefore we take the absolute value of each such deviation from the A.M. (or median). Taking the average of these deviations from the A.M., we get a measure of variation called the *mean absolute deviation* (MAD). In general, the mean absolute deviation is given by

$$\text{MAD} = \frac{1}{N}\sum_{i=1}^{N} |x - \mu|, \quad \text{for a population} \tag{4-6}$$

$$\text{MAD} = \frac{1}{n}\sum_{i=1}^{n} |x - \bar{x}|, \quad \text{for a sample}$$

where $|\,|$ indicates the absolute value. That is, the signs of deviations from the mean are disregarded.

For a grouped frequency distribution, MAD is given by

$$\text{MAD} = \frac{\sum_{i=1}^{n} f_i |x_i - \bar{x}|}{\sum f_i} \tag{4-7}$$

Formulae (4-6) and (4-7), in different contexts, indicate that the MAD provides a useful method of comparing the relative tendency of values in the distribution to scatter around a central value or to disperse themselves throughout the range.

While calculating the mean absolute deviation, the median is also considered for computing because the sum of the absolute values of the deviations from the median is smaller than that from any other value. However, in general, arithmetic mean is used for this purpose.

If a frequency distribution is symmetrical, then A.M. and median values concide and the same MAD value is obtained. In such a case $\bar{x} \pm$ MAD provides a range in which 57.5 per cent of the observations are included. Even if the frequency distribution is moderately skewed, the interval $\bar{x} \pm$ MAD includes the same percentage of observations. This shows that more than half of the observations are scattered within one unit of the MAD around the arithmetic mean.

The MAD is useful in situations where occasional large and erratic deviations are likely to occur. The standard deviation, which uses the squares of these large deviations, tends to over-emphasize them.

Coefficient of MAD

The relative measure of mean absolute deviation (MAD) called the *coefficient of MAD* is obtained by dividing the MAD by a measure of central tendency (arithmetic mean or median) used for calculating the MAD. Thus

$$\text{Coefficient of MAD} = \frac{\text{Mean absolute deviation}}{\bar{x} \text{ or Me}} \tag{4-8}$$

If the value of relative measure is desired in percentage, then

$$\text{Coefficient of MAD} = \frac{\text{MAD}}{\bar{x} \text{ or Me}} \times 100$$

Example 4.5: The number of patients seen in the emergency ward of a hospital for a sample of 5 days in the last month were: 153, 147, 151, 156 and 153. Determine the mean deviation and interpret.

Solution: The mean number of patients is, $\bar{x}$ = (153 + 147 + 151 + 156 + 153)/5 = 152. Below are the details of the calculations of MAD using formula (4-6).

Number of Patients (x)	$x - \bar{x}$	*Absolute Deviation* $\lvert x - \bar{x} \rvert$
153	153 – 152 = 1	1
147	147 – 152 = –5	5
151	151 – 152 = –1	1
156	156 – 152 = 4	4
153	153 – 152 = 1	1
		12

$$\text{MAD} = \frac{1}{n}\Sigma\lvert x - \bar{x}\rvert = \frac{12}{5} = 2.4 \cong 3 \text{ patients (approx)}$$

The mean absolute deviation is 3 patients per day. The number of patients deviate on the average by 3 patients from the mean of 152 patients per day.

Example 4.6: Calculate mean deviation from median from the data given below:

Wages (Rs.) (mid Point)	:	125	175	225	275
No. of persons	:	3	8	21	6

Solution: Calculations for mean deviation are shown below:

Mid Point	*Class Interval*	*Frequency*	*Cumulative Frequency (cf)*	$\lvert d\rvert = \lvert x - Med\rvert = \lvert x - 221.43\rvert$	$f\lvert d\rvert$
125	100 — 150	3	3	96.43	289.29
175	150 — 200	8	11	46.43	371.44
225	200 — 250	21	32	3.57	74.97
275	250 – 300	6	38	53.57	321.42
325	300 — 350	2	40	103.57	207.14
		$N = 40$			$\Sigma f\lvert d\rvert$ = 1264.26

Median = Size of $\left(\frac{n}{2}\right)^{\text{th}} = \frac{40}{2}$ = 20th item. Thus Median class is 200 – 250.

$$\text{Med} = l + \frac{\frac{n}{2} - cf}{f} \times h = 200 + \frac{20 - 11}{21} \times 50 = 221.43$$

$$\text{Mean Deviation (M.D.)} = \frac{\Sigma f\lvert d\rvert}{\Sigma f} = \frac{1264.26}{40} = 31.6.$$

Example 4.7: The income of a person in a particular week is Rs. 20 per day. Find the mean deviation of his income for 5 days.

Solution: The income for 7 days is as follows:

Days	*Income*	$\lvert d\rvert = \lvert x - 20\rvert$
Monday	20	0
Tuesday	20	0
Wednesday	20	0
Thursday	20	0
Friday	20	0
Saturday	20	0
Sunday	20	0

Since number of observations are odd, median is 4th observation, i.e. = 20. Hence

$$\text{Mean deviation (M.D.)} = \frac{\Sigma\lvert d\rvert}{n} = 0.$$

Example 4.8: Mean and S.D. of the following continuous series are 31 and 15.9 respectively. The distribution after taking step deviation is as follows:

dx :	– 3	– 2	– 1	0	1	2	3
f :	10	15	25	25	10	10	5

Determine the actual class intervals.

Solution: Calculations to determine actual class intervals are shown below:

d	f	fd	fd^2
– 3	10	– 30	90
– 2	15	– 30	60
– 1	25	– 25	25
0	25	0	0
1	10	10	10
2	10	20	40
3	5	15	45
	$N = 100$	$\Sigma fd = -40$	$\Sigma fd^2 = 270$

$$\text{Mean} = A + \frac{\Sigma fd}{N}\times h \quad \text{or} \quad 31 = A + \frac{40}{100}\times h = A - 0.40\,h$$

Also
$$\text{S.D. } (\sigma) = \sqrt{\frac{\Sigma fd^2}{n} - \left(\frac{\Sigma fd}{n}\right)^2} \times h$$

$$15.9 = \sqrt{\frac{270}{100} - \left(\frac{-40}{100}\right)^2} \times h = \sqrt{2.7 - 0.16} \times h = \sqrt{2.54} \times h$$

i.e.
$$h = \frac{15.9}{\sqrt{2.54}} = \frac{15.9}{1.59} = 10$$

Now for $i = 10$ we get $31 = A - 0.4 \times 10 = A - 4$, i.e. $A = 35$

Since, know that
$$d = \frac{m - A}{h} \quad \text{or} \quad -30 = m - 35, \text{ i.e. } m = 5$$

Similarly, we can find other mid-values as: 5, 15, 25, 35, 45, 55, 65. Since class size $h = 10$. Thus class interval corresponding to $m = 5$ is 0–10.

Similarly the other class intervals are: 0–10, 10–20, 20–30, 30–40, 40–50, 50–60, 60–70.

Example 4.9: Calculate the mean absolute deviation and its coefficient from median for the following data

Year	*Sales (Rs thousand)*	
	Product A	*Product B*
1996	23	36
1997	41	39
1998	29	36
1999	53	31
2000	38	47

Solution: The median sales (Me) of the two products A and B is Me = 38 and Me = 36, respectively. The calculations of MAD in both the cases are shown in Table 4.2.

Table 4.2 Calculations of MAD

Product A		*Product B*	
Sales (x)	$\lvert x - Me \rvert = \lvert x - 38 \rvert$	*Sales (x)*	$\lvert x - Me \rvert = \lvert x - 36 \rvert$
23	15	31	05
29	09	36	00
38	00	36	00
41	03	39	03
53	15	47	11
$n = 5$	$\sum \lvert x - \text{Me} \rvert = 42$	$n = 5$	$\sum \lvert x - \text{Me} \rvert = 19$

Product A:

$$\text{MAD} = \frac{1}{n}\sum \lvert x - \text{Me} \rvert = \frac{42}{5} = 8.4$$

$$\text{Coefficient of MAD} = \frac{\text{MAD}}{\text{Me}} = \frac{8.4}{38} = 0.221$$

Product B:

$$\text{MAD} = \frac{1}{n}\sum \lvert x - \text{Me} \rvert = \frac{19}{5} = 3.8$$

$$\text{Coefficient of MAD} = \frac{\text{MAD}}{\text{Me}} = \frac{3.8}{36} = 0.106$$

Example 4.10: Find the mean absolute deviation from mean for the following frequency distribution of sales (Rs. in thousand) in a co-operative store.

Sales :	50–100	100–150	150–200	200–250	250–300	300–350
Number of days :	11	23	44	19	8	7

Solution: The mean absolute deviation can be calculated by using the formula (4-6) for mean. The calculations for MAD are shown in Table 4.3. Let the assumed mean be, A = 175.

Table 4.3 Calculations for MAD

Sales (Rs)	*Mid-Value (m)*	*Frequency (f)*	*(m – 175)/50 (= d)*	*fd*	$\lvert x-\bar{x}\rvert = \lvert x-\bar{x}\rvert$	$f\lvert x-\bar{x}\rvert$
50–100	75	11	– 2	– 22	104.91	1154.01
100–150	125	23	– 1	– 23	54.91	1262.93
150–200	(175) ← A	44	0	0	4.91	216.04
200–250	225	19	1	19	45.09	856.71
250–300	275	8	2	16	95.09	760.72
300–350	325	7	3	21	145.09	1015.63
		112		11		5266.04

$$\bar{x} = A + \frac{\sum fd}{\sum f} \times h = 175 + \frac{11}{112} \times 50 = \text{Rs. } 179.91 \text{ per day}$$

$$\text{MAD} = \frac{\sum f\lvert x-\bar{x}\rvert}{\sum f} = \frac{5266.04}{112} = \text{Rs. } 47.01$$

Thus, the average sales is Rs. 179.91 thousand per day and the mean absolute deviation of sales is Rs. 47.01 thousand per day.

Example 4.11: A welfare organization introduced an education scholarship scheme for school going children of a backward village. The rates of scholarship were fixed as given below:

Age Group (Years)	*Amount of Scholarship per Month (Rs)*
5–7	300
8–10	400
11–13	500
14–16	600
17–19	700

The ages of 30 school children are noted as; 11, 8, 10, 5, 7, 12, 7, 17, 5, 13, 9, 8, 10, 15, 7, 12, 6, 7, 8, 11, 14, 18, 6, 13, 9, 10, 6, 15, 3, 5 years respectively. Calculate mean and standard deviation of monthly scholarship. Find out the total monthly scholarship amount being paid to the students.

Solution: The number of students in the age group from 5–7 to 17–19 are calculated as shown in Table 4.4:

Table 4.4

Age Group (Years)	*Tally Bars*	*Number of Students*
5–7	~~IIII~~ ~~IIII~~	10
8–10	~~IIII~~ III	8
11–13	~~IIII~~ II	7
14–16	III	3
17–19	II	2
		30

The calculations for mean and standard deviation are shown in Table 4.5.

Table 4.5 Calculations for Mean and Standard Deviation

Age Group (Years)	*Number of Students (f)*	*Mid-value (m)*	$d = \frac{m-A}{h} = \frac{m-12}{3}$	*fd*	*fd*^{2}
5–7	10	6	–2	–20	40
8–10	8	9	–1	–8	8
11–13	7	A →(12)	0	0	0
14–16	3	15	1	3	3
17–19	2	18	2	4	8
	30			–21	59

$$\text{Mean, } \bar{x} = A + \frac{\Sigma fd}{\Sigma f} \times h = 12 - \frac{21}{30} \times 3 = 12 - 2.1 = 9.9$$

$$\text{Standard deviation, } \sigma = \sqrt{\frac{\Sigma fd^2}{N} - \left(\frac{\Sigma fd}{N}\right)^2} \times h = \sqrt{\frac{59}{30} - \left(\frac{-21}{30}\right)^2} \times 3$$

$$= \sqrt{1.967 - 0.49} \times 3 = 1.2153 \times 3 = 3.6459$$

Calculations for monthly scholarship paid to 30 students are shown in Table 4.6.

Table 4.6 Calculations for Monthly Scholarship

Number of Students	*Amount of Scholarship per Month (Rs)*	*Total Monthly Scholarship (Rs)*
10	300	3000
8	400	3200
7	500	3500
3	600	1800
2	700	1400
		12,900

Advantages and Disadvantages of MAD The advantages and disadvantages of MAD are summarized below:

Advantages

(i) The calculation of MAD is based on all observations in the distribution and shows the dispersion of values around the measure of central tendency.

(ii) The value of MAD is easy to compute and therefore makes it popular among those users who are not even familiar with statistical methods.

(iii) While calculating MAD, equal weightage is given to each observed value and thus it indicates how far each observation lies from either the mean or median.

(iv) Average deviation from mean is always zero in any data set. The MAD avoids this problem by using absolute values to eliminate the negative signs.

Disadvantages

(i) The algebraic signs are ignored while calculating MAD. If the signs are not ignored, then the sum of the deviations taken from arithmetic mean will be zero and close to zero when deviations are taken from median.

(ii) The value of MAD is considered to be best when deviations are taken from median. However, median does not provide a satisfactory result in case of a high degree of variability in a data set.

Moreover, the sum of the deviations from mean (ignoring signs) is greater than the sum of the deviations from median (ignoring signs). In such a situation, computations of MAD by taking deviations from mean is also not desirable.

(iii) The MAD is generally unwieldy in mathematical discussions.

Inspite of all these demerits, the knowledge of MAD would help the reader to understand another important measure of dispersion called the *standard deviation*.

4.5.2 Variance and Standard Deviation

Another way to disregard the signs of negative deviations from mean is to square them. Instead of computing the absolute value of each deviation from mean, we square the deviations from mean. Then the sum of all such squared deviations is divided by the number of observations in the data set. This value is a measure called **population variance** and is denoted by σ^2 (a lower-case Greek letter sigma). It is usually referred to as 'sigma squared'. Symbolically, it is written as:

$$\text{Population variance, } \sigma^2 = \frac{1}{N}\sum_{i=1}^{N}(x_i - \mu)^2 \qquad (4\text{-}9)$$

$$= \frac{1}{N}\sum_{i=1}^{N}x_i^2 - (\mu)^2 \quad \text{(Deviation is taken from actual population A.M.)}$$

$$= \frac{\Sigma d^2}{N} - \left(\frac{\Sigma d}{N}\right)^2 \quad \text{(Deviation is taken from assumed A.M.)}$$

where $d = x - A$ and A is any constant (also called assumed A.M.)

Since σ^2 is the average or mean of squared deviations from arithmetic mean, it is also called the *mean square average*.

The population variance is basically used to measure variation among the values of observations in a population. Thus for a population of N observations (elements) and with μ denoting the population mean, the formula for population variance is shown in Eqn. (4-9). However, in almost all applications of statistics, the data being analyzed is a sample data. As a result, population variance is rarely determined. Instead, we compute a sample variance to estimate population variance, σ^2.

It was shown that if the *sum of the squared* deviations about a sample mean $\bar{x}$ in Eqn. (4-9) is divided by n (sample size), then it invariably tends to cause the resulting estimate of σ^2 to be lower than its actual value. This undesirable condition is called *bias*. However, this *bias* in the estimation of population variance from a sample can be removed by dividing the sum of the squared deviations between the sample mean and each element in the population by $n - 1$ rather than by n. Thus, the *unbiased* sample variance denoted by s^2 is defined as follows:

$$\text{Sample variance, } s^2 = \frac{\Sigma(x - \bar{x})^2}{n-1} = \frac{\Sigma x^2}{n-1} - \frac{n\bar{x}^2}{n-1} = \frac{\Sigma x^2}{n-1} - \frac{(\Sigma x)^2}{n(n-1)} \qquad (4\text{-}10)$$

The numerator $\sum(x-\bar{x})^2$ in Eqn. (4-10) is called the *total sum of squares*. This quantity measures the total variation among values in a data set (whereas the variance measures only the *average variation*). The larger the value of $\Sigma(x - \bar{x})^2$, the greater the variation among the values in a data set.

Standard Deviation

The numerical value of population or a sample variance is difficult to interpret because it is expressed in square units. To reach a interpretable measure of variance expressed in the units of original data, we take a positive square root of the variance, which is known as the **standard deviation** or *root-mean square deviation*. The standard deviation of population and sample is denoted by σ and s, respectively. We can think of the standard deviation as roughly the *average distance values fall from the mean*.

(a) *Ungrouped Data*

Population standard deviation,

$$\sigma = \sqrt{\sigma^2} = \sqrt{\frac{1}{N}\Sigma\,(x-\mu)^2} = \sqrt{\frac{1}{N}\Sigma x^2-(\mu)^2} = \sqrt{\frac{\Sigma d^2}{N}-\left(\frac{\Sigma d}{N}\right)^2}$$

Sample standard deviation, $s = \sqrt{\dfrac{\Sigma x^2}{n-1}-\dfrac{n\bar{x}^2}{n-1}}$; where n = sample size

(b) *Grouped Data*

$$\text{Population standard deviation, } \sigma = \sqrt{\frac{\Sigma fd^2}{N}-\left(\frac{\Sigma fd}{N}\right)^2}\times h$$

where f = frequency of each class interval

$N = \Sigma f$ = total number of observations (or elements) in the population

h = width of class interval

m = mid-value of each class interval

$d = \dfrac{m-A}{h}$, where A is any constant (also called assumed A.M.)

$$\text{Sample standard deviation, } s = \sqrt{s^2} = \sqrt{\frac{\Sigma f(x-\bar{x})^2}{n-1}} = \sqrt{\frac{\Sigma fx^2}{n-1}-\frac{(\Sigma fx)^2}{n(n-1)}} \qquad (4\text{-}11)$$

Remarks: 1. For any data set, MAD is always less than the σ because MAD is less sensitive to the extreme observations. Thus, when a data contains few very large observations, the MAD provides a more realistic measure of variation than σ. However σ is often used in statistical applications because it is amenable to mathematical development.

2. When sample size (n) becomes very large, (n – 1) becomes indistinguishable and irrelevant.

Advantages and Disadvantages of Standard Deviation The advantages and disadvantages of the standard deviation are summarized below:

Advantages

(i) The value of standard deviation is based on every observation in a set of data. It is the only measure of variation capable of algebraic treatment and less affected by fluctuations of sampling as compared to other measures of variation.

(ii) It is possible to calculate the combined standard deviation of two or more sets of data.

(iii) Standard deviation has a definite relationship with the area under the symmetric curve of a frequency distribution. Due to this reason, standard deviation is called a *standard* measure of variation.

(iv) Standard deviation is useful in further statistical investigations. For example, standard deviation plays a vital role in comparing skewness, correlation, and so on, and also widely used in sampling theory.

Disadvantages

(i) As compared to other measures of variation, calculations of standard deviation are difficult.

(ii) While calculating standard deviation, more weight is given to extreme values and less to those near mean. Since for calculating S.D., the deviations from the mean are squared, therefore large deviations when squared are proportionately more than small deviations. For example, the deviations 2 and 10 are in the ratio of 1 : 5 but their squares 4 and 100 are in the ratio of 1 : 25.

Example 4.12: The wholesale prices of a commodity for seven consecutive days in a month is as follows:

Days	:	1	2	3	4	5	6	7
Commodity price/quintal	:	240	260	270	245	255	286	264

Calculate the variance and standard deviation.

Solution: The computations for variance and standard deviation are shown in Table 4.7.

Table 4.7 Computations of Variance and Standard Deviation by Actual Mean Method

Observation (x)	$x - \bar{x} = x - 260$	$(x-\bar{x})^2$
240	– 20	400
260	0	0
270	10	100
245	– 15	225
255	– 5	25
286	26	676
264	4	16
1820		1442

$$\bar{x} = \frac{\Sigma x}{N} = \frac{1820}{7} = 260$$

$$\text{Variance } \sigma^2 = \frac{\Sigma(x-\bar{x})}{N} = \frac{1442}{7} = 206$$

$$\text{Standard deviation } \sigma = \sqrt{\sigma^2} = \sqrt{206} = 14.352$$

In this question, if we take deviation from an assumed A.M. = 255 instead of actual A.M. = 260. The calculations then for standard deviation will be as shown in Table 4.8.

Table 4.8 Computation of Standard Deviation by Assumed Mean Method

Observation (x)	$d = x - A = x - 255$	d^2
240	−15	225
260	5	25
270	15	225
245	−10	100
(255) ← A	0	0
286	31	961
264	9	81
	35	1617

$$\text{Standard deviation } \sigma = \sqrt{\frac{\Sigma d^2}{N} - \left(\frac{\Sigma d}{N}\right)^2} = \sqrt{\frac{1617}{7} - \left(\frac{35}{7}\right)^2}$$

$$= \sqrt{231 - 25} = \sqrt{206} = 14.352$$

This result is same as obtained earlier in Table 4.7.

Remark: When actual A.M. is not a whole number, assumed A.M. method should be used to reduce the computation time.

Example 4.13: A study of 100 engineering companies gives the following information:

Profit (Rs. in crore) :	0–10	10–20	20–30	30–40	40–50	50–60
Number of companies :	8	12	20	30	20	10

Calculate the standard deviation of the profit earned.

Solution: Let assumed mean, A be 35 and the value of h be 10. Calculations for standard deviation are shown in Table 4.9.

Table 4.9 Calculations of Standard Deviation

Profit (*Rs in crore*)	*Mid-value* (m)	$d = \frac{m-A}{h} = \frac{m-35}{10}$	f	fd	fd^2
0–10	5	−3	8	−24	72
10–20	15	−2	12	−24	48
20–30	25	−1	20	−20	20
30–40	(35) ← A	0	30	0	0
40–50	45	1	20	20	20
50–60	55	2	10	20	40
				−28	200

$$\text{Standard deviation, } \sigma = \sqrt{\frac{\Sigma fd^2}{N} - \left(\frac{\Sigma fd}{N}\right)^2} \times h$$

$$= \sqrt{\frac{200}{100} - \left(\frac{-28}{100}\right)^2} \times 10 = \sqrt{2 - 0.078} \times 10 = 13.863$$

Example 4.14: Mr. Gupta, a retired government servant is considering investing his money in two proposals. He wants to choose the one that has higher average net present value and lower standard deviation. The relevant data are given below. Can you help him in choosing the proposal?

Proposal A:

Net Present Value (NPV)	*Chance of the Possible Outcome of NPV*
1559	0.30
5662	0.40
9175	0.30

Proposal B:

Net Present Value (NPV)	*Chance of the Possible Outcome of NPV*
– 10,050	0.30
5,812	0.40
20,584	0.30

Solution: To suggest to Mr. Gupta a proposal for high average net present value, first calculate the expected (average) net present value for both the proposals.

Proposal A: Expected NPV $= 1559 \times 0.30 + 5662 \times 0.40 + 9175 \times 0.30$
$= 467.7 + 2264.8 + 2752.5 =$ Rs. 5485

Proposal B: Expected NPV $= -10{,}050 \times 0.30 + 5812 \times 0.40 + 20{,}584 \times 0.30$
$= -3015 + 2324.8 + 6175.2 =$ Rs. 5485

Since the expected NPV in both the cases is same, he would like to choose the less risky proposal. For this we have to calculate the standard deviation in both the cases.

Standard deviation for proposal A:

$NPV(x_i)$	*Expected NPV* $(\bar{x})$	$x - \bar{x}$	f	$f(x - \bar{x})^2$
1559	5485	– 3926	0.30	46,24,042.8
5662	5485	177	0.40	12,531.6
9175	5485	3690	0.30	40,84,830.0
			1.00	87,21;404.4

$$s_A = \sqrt{\frac{\Sigma f(x-x)^2}{\Sigma f}} = \sqrt{87,21,404.4} = \text{Rs. } 2953.20$$

Standard deviation for proposal B:

NPV (x_i)	*Expected NPV* ($\bar{x}$)	$x - \bar{x}$	f	$f(x-\bar{x})^2$
– 10,050	5485	– 15,535	0.30	7,24,00,867.5
5812	5485	327	0.40	42,771.6
20,584	5485	15,099	0.30	6,83,93,940
			1.00	14,08,37,579

$$s_B = \sqrt{\frac{\Sigma f(x-\bar{x})^2}{\Sigma f}} = \sqrt{14,08,37,579} = \text{Rs. } 11,867.50$$

The $s_A < s_B$ indicates uniform net profit for proposal A. Thus proposal A may be chosen.

Example 4.15: The number of employees, wages per employee and the variance of the wages of employees for two factories are given below :

No. of employees	Factory *A*	Factory *B*
Average wages per employee per month	1.200	100
Variance of the wages (Rs.)	81	256

(*a*) In which factory is there greater variation in the distribution of wages per employee?

(*b*) Suppose in factory B, the wages of an employee were wrongly noted as Rs. 900 instead of Rs. 910.

Solution: (*a*) Coefficient of variation, CV $= \frac{\sigma}{\bar{x}} \times 100$. Thus

$$\text{C.V. for factory, } A = \frac{9}{1200} \times 100 = 0.75\%$$

$$\text{C.V. for factory, } B = \frac{16}{850} \times 100 = 1.88\%$$

Since co-efficient of variation is more for firm *B*, it shows greater variation in the distribution of wages per employee in the firm *B*.

(*ii*) For factory *B*, $\Sigma x = 850 \times 100 = 85000$

$$\text{Correct } \Sigma x = 85000 - 900 + 910 = 85,010$$

$$\text{Correct, } \bar{x} = \frac{85010}{100} = 850.10$$

$$\text{Correct variance} = \frac{\Sigma x^2}{N} - (\bar{x})^2$$

$$256 = \frac{\Sigma x^2}{100} - (850)^2 \quad \text{or} \quad 25600 = \Sigma x^2 - 7,22,50,000$$

$$\Sigma x^2 = 7,22,50,000 + 25,600 = 7,22,75,600$$

Correct $\Sigma x^2 = 7{,}22{,}75{,}600 - (900)^2 + (910)^2 = 7{,}22{,}75{,}600 - 8{,}10{,}000 + 8{,}28{,}100 = 7{,}22{,}93{,}700$

$$\text{Correct variance} = \frac{\text{Correct } \Sigma x^2}{N} - (\text{Correct } (\bar{x})^2 = \frac{7{,}22{,}93{,}700}{100} - (850.10)^2$$

Example 4.16: In a series of 5 observations, the means and variance are 4.4 and 8.24. If three observations are 1, 2, 6, find other two. *[Delhi Univ., B.Com (Hons), 1993]*

Solution: Let the other two observations be x, y. Then

$$\frac{x+y+1+2+6}{5} = 4.4 \quad \text{or} \quad x + y + 9 = 4.4 \times 5 = 22$$

$$x + y = 13, \text{ i.e. } y = 13 - x$$

$$\text{Var}(\sigma^2) = \frac{\Sigma x^2}{n} - (\bar{x})^2$$

$$8.24 = \frac{\Sigma x^2}{5} - (4.4)^2 = \frac{\Sigma x^2}{5} - 19.36$$

$$8.24 + 19.36 = \frac{\Sigma x^2}{5}, \text{ i.e. } \Sigma x^2 = 138$$

or
$$x^2 + y^2 + 1 + 4 + 36 = 138$$

$$x^2 + y^2 + 41 = 138$$

$$x^2 + y^2 = 97$$

$$x^2 + (13 - x)^2 = 97 \quad (\text{since } y = 13 - x)$$

$$x^2 + 169 + x^2 - 26x = 97$$

$$2x^2 - 26x + 72 = 0$$

$$x^2 - 13x + 36 = 0$$

$$(x - 9)(x - 4) = 0 \quad \text{or} \quad x = 9, 4 \quad \text{and} \quad y = 4, 9$$

Hence, two numbers are 4, 9.

Example 4.17: Mean and S.D. of 100 items are found by a student as 50 and 0.1. If at the time of calculation, two items are wrongly taken as 40 and 50 instead of 60 and 30. find correct mean and S.D. *[Delhi Univ., B.Com, 1996]*

Solution: Given $\bar{x} = 50$, $N = 100$, $\sigma = 0.1$. Thus,

$$\bar{x} = \frac{\Sigma x}{n} \quad \text{or} \quad \Sigma x = n \times \bar{x} = 100 \times 50 = 5000$$

$$\text{Correct } \Sigma x = 5000 - \text{wrong items} + \text{correct items}$$
$$= 5000 - 40 - 50 + 60 + 30 = 5000$$

$$\text{Correct Mean, } \bar{x} = \frac{5000}{100} = 50$$

Now
$$\sigma = \sqrt{\frac{\Sigma x}{n} - (\bar{x})^2} \quad \text{or} \quad \sigma^2 = \frac{\Sigma x^2}{n} - (\bar{x})^2$$

Substituting the values as: $\sigma = 0.1$, $\bar{x} = 50$, $N = 100$, we get

$$(0.1)^2 = \frac{\Sigma x^2}{100} - (50)^2$$

$$0.01 = \frac{\Sigma x^2}{100} - 2500 \quad \text{or} \quad \Sigma x^2 = 250001$$

$$\text{Correct } \Sigma x^2 = 250001 - (40)^2 - (50)^2 + (60)^2 + (30)^2$$

$$= 250001 - 1600 - 32500 + 3600 + 900$$

$$\text{Correct, S.D.} = \sqrt{\frac{\Sigma x^2}{n} - (\bar{x})} = \sqrt{\frac{250401}{100} - (50)^2} = 2.0025.$$

Example 4.18: A charitable organization decided to give old age pension to people over sixty years of age. The scales of pension were fixed as follows:

Age Group (years)	*Amount of Pension (Rs. per month)*
60–65	20
65–70	25
70–75	30
75–80	35
80–85	40

The ages of 25 workers who secured the pension right are given as: 74, 62, 84, 72, 61, 83, 72, 81, 64, 71, 63, 61, 67, 74, 64, 79, 73, 75, 76, 69, 68, 78, 66, 67.

Calculate the monthly average pension payable per pensioner and the S.D.?

[*Delhi Univ., B.Com (Hons), 2005*]

Solution: The calculation for monthly average person and S.D. are shown below in the table:

Age Group (Years)	*No. of Workers* (f)	*Amount of Pension (Rs.)* (x)	fx	fx^2
60 – 65	7	20	140	2800
65 – 70	5	25	125	3125
70 – 75	6	30	180	5400
75 – 80	4	35	140	4900
80 – 85	3	40	120	4800

$$\text{Mean} = \frac{\Sigma fx}{\Sigma f} = \frac{705}{25} = \text{Rs. } 28.20$$

$$\text{S.D.} = \sqrt{\frac{\Sigma fx^2}{n} - (\bar{x})^2} = \sqrt{\frac{21025}{25} - (28.20)^2} = \sqrt{45.76}.$$

4.5.3 Mathematical Properties of Standard Deviation

1. **Combined standard deviation:** The combined standard deviation of two sets of data containing n_1 and n_2 observations with means $\bar{x}_1$ and $\bar{x}_2$ and standard deviations σ_1 and σ_2 respectively is given by

$$\sigma_{12} = \sqrt{\frac{n_1\left(\sigma_1^2 + d_1^2\right) + n_2\left(\sigma_2^2 + d_2^2\right)}{n_1 + n_2}}$$

where σ_{12} = combined standard deviation; $d_1 = \bar{x}_{12} - \bar{x}_1$; $d_2 = \bar{x}_{12} - \bar{x}_2$

and $$\bar{x}_{12} = \frac{n_1\bar{x}_1 + n_2\bar{x}_2}{n_1 + n_2} \text{ (combined arithmetic mean)}$$

This formula for combined standard deviation of two sets of data can be extended to compute the standard deviation of more than two sets of data on the same lines.

2. Standard deviation of natural numbers: The standard deviation of the first n natural numbers is given by

$$\sigma = \sqrt{\frac{1}{12}(n^2 - 1)}$$

For example, the standard deviation of the first 100 (i.e., from 1 to 100) natural numbers will be

$$\sigma = \sqrt{\frac{1}{12}(100^2 - 1)} = \sqrt{\frac{1}{12}(9999)} = \sqrt{833.25} = 28.86$$

3. Standard deviation is independent of change of origin but not of scale.

Example 4.19: For a group of 50 male workers, the mean and standard deviation of their monthly wages are Rs. 6300 and Rs. 900 respectively. For a group of 40 female workers, these are Rs. 5400 and Rs. 600 respectively. Find the standard deviation of monthly wages for the combined group of workers.

Solution: Given that $n_1 = 50,\ \bar{x}_1 = 6300,\ \sigma_1 = 900$

$n_2 = 40,\ \bar{x}_2 = 5400,\ \sigma_2 = 600$

Then, combined mean, $$\bar{x}_{12} = \frac{n_1\bar{x}_1 + n_2\bar{x}_2}{n_1 + n_2} = \frac{50 \times 6300 + 40 \times 5400}{50 + 40} = 5{,}900$$

and combined standard deviation

$$\sigma_{12} = \sqrt{\frac{n_1\left(\sigma_1^2 + d_1^2\right) + n_2\left(\sigma_2^2 + d_2^2\right)}{n_1 + n_2}}$$

$$= \sqrt{\frac{50(8{,}10{,}000 + 1{,}60{,}000) + 40(3{,}60{,}000 + 2{,}50{,}000)}{50 + 40}} = \text{Rs. } 900$$

where $d_1 = \bar{x}_{12} - \bar{x}_1 = 5900 - 6300 = -400$

$d_2 = \bar{x}_{12} - \bar{x}_2 = 5900 - 5400 = 500$

Example 4.20: A study of the age of 100 persons grouped into intervals 20–22, 22–24, 24–26,... revealed the mean age and standard deviation to be 32.02 and 13.18 respectively. While checking, it was discovered that the observation 57 was misread as 27. Calculate the correct mean age and standard deviation.

Solution: From the data given in the problem, we have $\bar{x} = 32.02$, $\sigma = 13.18$ and N = 100. We know that

$$\bar{x} = \frac{\Sigma fx}{N} \text{ or } \Sigma fx = N \times \bar{x} = 100 \times 32.02 = 3202$$

and $\sigma^2 = \dfrac{\Sigma f x^2}{N} - (\bar{x})^2$ or $\Sigma fx^2 = N[\sigma^2 + (\bar{x})^2] = 100[(13.18)^2 + (32.02)^2]$

$= 100[173.71 + 1025.28] = 100 \times 1198.99$

$= 1,19,899$

On re-placing the correct observation, we get

$\Sigma fx = 3202 - 27 + 57 = 3232.$

Also $\Sigma fx^2 = 1,19,899 - (27)^2 + (57)^2 = 1,19,899 - 729 + 3248 = 1,22,419$

Thus, correct A.M. is, $\bar{x} = \dfrac{\Sigma fx}{N} = \dfrac{3232}{100} = 32.32.$

and correct variance is, $\sigma^2 = \dfrac{\Sigma fx^2}{N} - (\bar{x})^2 = \dfrac{1,22,419}{100} - (32.32)^2$

$= 1224.19 - 1044.58 = 179.61$

or correct standard deviation is, $\sigma = \sqrt{\sigma^2} = \sqrt{179.61} = 13.402.$

Example 4.21: For a group containing 100 items, the A.M. and S.D. are 8 and $\sqrt{105}$. For 50 observations selected from these 100 observations, mean and S.D. are 10 and 2 respectively. Find mean and S.D. of the remaining 50 observations. *[Delhi Univ., B.Com (Hons), 1994]*

Solution: Let the two subgroups be denoted by 1 and 2. Then given

Group 1 : $n_1 = 50, \quad \bar{x}_1 = 10, \quad \sigma_1 = 2, \quad \bar{x}_{12} = 8$

Group 2 : $n_2 = 50, \quad \bar{x}_2 = ?, \quad \sigma_2 = ?, \quad \sigma_{12} = \sqrt{105}$

Combining A.M. of both groups, we get

$$\bar{x}_{12} = \frac{n_1\bar{x}_1 + n_2\bar{x}_2}{n_1 + n_2}$$

$$8 = \frac{50 \times 10 + 50\bar{x}_2}{100}, \text{ i.e. } 800 = 500 + 50\,\bar{x}_2 \quad \text{or} \quad \bar{x}_2 = 6$$

Further $d_1 = |\bar{x}_{12} - \bar{x}_1| = |8 - 10| = 2$ and $d_2 = |\bar{x}_{12} - \bar{x}_2| = |8 - 6| = 2$

$$\text{Combined, } \sigma_{12} = \sqrt{\frac{n_1\sigma_1^2 + n_2\sigma_2^2 + n_1d_1^2 + n_2d_2^2}{n_1 + n_2}}$$

$$\sqrt{105} = \sqrt{\frac{50 \times 4 + 50\sigma_2^2 + 50 \times 4 + 50 \times 4}{100}}$$

$$10.5 = \frac{200 + 50s_2^2 + 200 + 200}{100}$$

$$10.5 \times 100 = 600 + 50\,\sigma_2^2, \text{ i.e. } \sigma_2^2 = 9 \quad \text{or} \quad \sigma_2 = 3$$

Example 4.22 : The mean of two samples of sizes 50 and 100 are 54.4 and 50.3 and their S.D. are 8 and 7 respectively. Obtain the combined S. D. of 150 items. *[Delhi Univ., BCom (Hons), 2005]*

Solution: Given, $\bar{x}_1 = 54.4, \quad \bar{x}_2 = 50.3; \quad n_1 = 50, \quad n_2 = 100; \quad \sigma_1 = 8, \quad \sigma^2 = 7$. Thus

$$\text{Combined, } \bar{x}_{12} = \frac{n_1\,\bar{x}_1 + n_2\,\bar{x}_2}{n_1 + n_2} = \frac{50(54.4) + 100(50.3)}{50 + 100} = \frac{2720 + 5030}{150} = 51.67$$

Also $d_1 = |\bar{x}_{12} - \bar{x}_1| = |51.67 - 54.4| = 2.73$; $d_2 = |\bar{x}_{12} - \bar{x}_2| = |51.67 - 50.3| = 1.37$

$$\text{Combined, } \sigma = \sqrt{\frac{n_1\sigma_1^2 + n_2\sigma_2^2 + n_1 d_1^2 + n_1 d_2^2}{n_1 + n_2}}$$

$$= \sqrt{\frac{50(8)^2 + 100(7)^2 + 50(2.73)^2 + 100(1.37)^2}{50 + 100}}$$

$$= \sqrt{\frac{50 \times 64\, 100 \times 49\, 50(7.4529) + 100(1.8769)}{150}}$$

$$= \sqrt{\frac{3200 + 4900 + 372.645 + 187.69}{150}} = \sqrt{57.736} = 7.598.$$

Example 4.23: For two groups of observations, the following results are available:

Group I : $\Sigma (x - 5) = 8$, $\Sigma (x - 5)^2 = 40$, $n_1 = 20$

Group II : $\Sigma (x - 8) = -10$, $\Sigma (x - 8)^2 = 70$ $n_2 = 25$

Find mean and S.D. of both groups taken together. *[Delhi Univ., B.Com (Hons), 2006]*

Solution: From the data of the problem, we have

$$\bar{x}_1 = A + \frac{\Sigma d}{n} = 5 + \frac{8}{20} = 5 + 0.4 = 5.4$$

$$\bar{x}_2 = A + \frac{\Sigma d}{n} = 8 + \frac{(-10)}{25} = 8 - 0.4 = 7.6$$

$$\text{Combined mean, } \bar{x}_{12} = \frac{n_1\bar{x}_1 + n_2\bar{x}_2}{n_1 + n_2} = \frac{(20)(5.4) + (25)(7.6)}{20 + 25} = 6.6$$

$$\text{S.D. } (\sigma_1) = \sqrt{\frac{\Sigma d^2}{n} - \left(\frac{\Sigma d}{n}\right)^2} = \sqrt{\frac{40}{20} - \left(\frac{8}{20}\right)^2} = \sqrt{2 - 0.16} = \sqrt{1.84} = 1.4 \text{ (approx.)}$$

$$\text{S.D. } (\sigma_2) = \sqrt{\frac{\Sigma d^2}{n} - \left(\frac{\Sigma d}{n}\right)^2} = \sqrt{\frac{70}{25} - \left(\frac{-10}{25}\right)^2} = \sqrt{2.8 - 0.16} = \sqrt{2.64} = 1.6$$

$$\text{Combined S.D. } (\sigma) = \sqrt{\frac{n_1\sigma_1^2 + n_2\sigma_2^2 + n_1 d_1^2 + n_2 d_2^2}{N_1 + N_2}}$$

$$= \sqrt{\frac{20(1.4)^2 + 25(1.6)^2 + 20(1.2)^2 + 25(1.0)^2}{20 + 25}}$$

$$= \sqrt{\frac{39.2 + 64 + 28.8 + 25}{45}} = \sqrt{3.489} = 1.868.$$

where $d_1 = |\bar{x}_{12} - \bar{x}_1| = |6.6 - 5.4| = 1.2$; $d_2 = |\bar{x}_{12} - \bar{x}_2| = |6.6 - 7.6| = 1.0$

Example 4.24: The mean of 5 observations is 15 and the variance is 9. If two more observations having values – 3 and 10 are combined with these 5 observations, what will be the new mean and variance of 7 observations?

Solution: From the data of the problem, we have $\bar{x} = 15$, $\sigma^2 = 9$ and $n = 5$. We know that

$$\bar{x} = \frac{\sum x}{n} \quad \text{or} \quad \sum x = n \times \bar{x} = 5 \times 15 = 75$$

If two more observations having values – 3 and 10 are added to the existing 5 observations, then after adding these 6th and 7th observations, we get

$$\sum x = 75 - 3 + 10 = 82$$

Thus, the new A.M. is, $\bar{x} = \frac{\sum x}{n} = \frac{82}{7} = 11.71$

$$\text{Variance, } \sigma^2 = \frac{\sum x^2}{n} - (\bar{x})^2$$

$$9 = \frac{\sum x^2}{n} - (15)^2 \quad \text{or} \quad \sum x^2 = 1170$$

On adding two more observations, i.e., – 3 and 10, we get

$$\sum x^2 = 1170 + (-3)^2 + (10)^2 = 1279$$

$$\text{Variance, } \sigma^2 = \frac{\sum x^2}{n} - (\bar{x})^2 = \frac{1279}{7} - (11.71)^2 = 45.59$$

Hence, the new mean and variance of 7 observations is 11.71 and 45.59 respectively.

Relationship between Different Measures of Variation

(a) Quartile deviation (Q.D.) $= \frac{2}{3}\sigma$

Mean absolute deviation (MAD) $= \frac{4}{5}\sigma$

(b) Quartile deviation $= \frac{5}{6}$ MAD

Standard deviation $= \frac{5}{4}$ MAD or $\frac{3}{2}$ QD

(c) Mean absolute deviation $= \frac{6}{5}$ QD

These relationships are applicable only to symmetrical distributions.

Example 4.25: If S.D. is 18.5, calculate QD and MD [*Delhi Univ., B.Com(Hons), 1996*]

Solution: Since $\sigma = 18.5$, Q.D. $= \frac{2}{3} \times \sigma = \frac{2}{3} \times 18.5 = 12.33$

Also M.D. $= \frac{4}{5}\sigma = \frac{4}{5} \times 1835 = 14.8$

Example 4.26: Suppose you are in-charge of rationing in a state affected by food shortage. The following reports arrive from a local investigator. Daily caloric value of food available per adult during current period:

Area	*Mean*	*Standard Deviation*
A	2500	400
B	2000	200

The estimated requirement of an adult is taken as 2800 calories daily and the absolute minimum is 1350. Comment on the reported figures and determine which area, in your opinion, need more urgent attention.

Solution: Taking into consideration the entire population of the two areas, we have

Area A: $\mu + 3\sigma = 2500 + 3 \times 400 = 3700$ calories

$\mu - 3\sigma = 2500 - 3 \times 400 = 1300$ calories

This shows that there are adults who are taking even less amount of calories, that is, 1300 calories as compared to the absolute minimum requirement of 1350 calories.

Area B: $\mu + 3\sigma = 2000 + 3 \times 200 = 2600$ calories

$\mu - 3\sigma = 2000 - 3 \times 200 = 1400$ calories

These figures are satisfying the requirement of daily calorific need. Hence, area A needs more urgent attention.

Example 4.27: The following data give the number of passengers travelling by airplane from one city to another in one week.

115, 122, 129, 113, 119, 124, 132, 120, 110, 116,

Calculate the mean and standard deviation and determine the percentage of class that lie between (i) $\mu \pm \sigma$, (ii) $\mu \pm 2\sigma$, and (iii) $\mu \pm 3\sigma$. What percentage of cases lie outside these limits?

Solution: The calculations for mean and standard deviation are shown in Table 4.10.

Table 4.10 Calculations of Mean and Standard Deviation

x	$x - \bar{x}$	$(x - \bar{x})^2$
115	−5	25
122	2	4
129	9	81
113	−7	49
119	−1	1
124	4	16
132	12	144
120	0	0
110	−10	100
116	−4	16
1200	0	436

$$\mu = \frac{\sum x}{n} = \frac{1200}{10} = 120 \quad \text{and} \quad \sigma^2 = \frac{\sum (x - \bar{x})^2}{n} = \frac{436}{10} = 43.6$$

Therefore $\sigma = \sqrt{\sigma^2} = \sqrt{43.6} = 6.60$

The percentage of cases that lie between a given limit are as follows: .

Interval	*Values Within Interval*	*Percentage of Population*	*Percentage Falling Outside*
$\mu \pm \sigma = 120 \pm 6.60$	113, 115, 116, 119	70%	30%
$= 113.4$ and 126.6	120, 122, 124		
$\mu \pm 2\sigma = 120 \pm 2(6.60)$	110, 113, 115, 116, 119	100%	nil
$= 106.80$ and 133.20	120, 122, 124, 129, 132		

Example 4.28: A collar manufacturer is considering the production of a new collar to attract young men. Thus following statistics of neck circumference are available based on measurement of a typical group of the college students:

Mid value (in inches) :	12.0	12.5	13.0	13.5	14.0	14.5	15.0	15.5	16.0
Number of students :	2	16	36	60	76	37	18	3	2

Compute the standard deviation and use the criterion $\bar{x} \pm 3\sigma$, where σ is the standard deviation and $\bar{x}$ is the arithmetic mean to determine the largest and smallest size of the collar he should make in order to meet the needs of practically all the customers bearing in mind that collar are worn on average half inch longer than neck size.

Solution: Calculations for mean and standard deviation in order to determine the range of collar size to meet the needs of customers are shown in Table 4.11.

Table 4.11 Calculations for Mean and Standard Deviation

Mid-value (in inches)	*Number of students*	$\frac{x-A}{h} = \frac{x-14}{0.5}$	*fd*	fd^2
12.0	2	– 4	– 8	32
12.5	16	– 3	– 48	144
13.0	36	– 2	– 72	144
13.5	60	– 1	– 60	60
(14.0) ← A	76	0	0	0
14.5	37	1	37	37
15.0	18	2	36	72
15.5	3	3	9	27
16.0	2	4	8	32
	N = 250		– 98	548

$$\text{Mean}, \bar{x} = A + \frac{\Sigma fd}{N} \times h = 14.0 - \frac{98}{250} \times 0.5 = 14.0 - 0.195 = 13.805$$

$$\text{Standard deviation}, \sigma = \sqrt{\frac{\Sigma fd^2}{N} - \left(\frac{\Sigma fd}{N}\right)^2} \times h = \sqrt{\frac{548}{250} - \left(\frac{-98}{250}\right)^2} \times 0.5$$

$$= \sqrt{2.192 - 0.153} \times 0.5 = 1.427 \times 0.5 = 0.7135$$

Largest and smallest neck size = $\bar{x} \pm 3\sigma$ = 13.805 ± 3 × 0.173 = 11.666 and 15.944.

Since all the customers are to wear collar half inch longer than their neck size, 0.5 is to be added to the neck size range given above. The new range then becomes:

(11.666 + 0.5) and (15.944 + 0.5) or 12.165 and 16.444, i.e. 12.2 and 16.4 inches.

Example 4.29: The breaking strength of 80 'test pieces' of a certain alloy is given in the following table, the unit being given to the nearest thousand grams per square inch;

Breaking Strength	*Number of Pieces*
44–46	3
46–48	24
48–50	27
50–52	21
52–54	5

Calculate the average breaking strength of the alloy and the standard deviation. Calculate the percentage of observations lying between $\bar{x} \pm 2\sigma$.

Solution: The calculations for mean and standard deviation are shown in in Table 4.12.

Table 4.12 Calculations for Mean and Standard Deviation

Breaking Strength	*Number of Pieces(f)*	*Mid-value (m)*	$d = (m - A)/h$ $= (m - 49)/2$	*fd*	fd^2
44–46	3	45	−2	−6	12
46–48	24	47	−1	−24	24
48–50	27	A → (49)	0	0	0
50–52	21	51	1	21	21
52–54	5	53	2	10	20
	80			1	77

$$\text{Mean}, \bar{x} = A + \frac{\Sigma fd}{N} \times h = 49 + \frac{1}{80} \times 2 = 49.025$$

$$\text{Standard deviation,} \quad \sigma = \sqrt{\frac{\Sigma fd^2}{N} - \left(\frac{\Sigma fd}{N}\right)^2} \times h = \sqrt{\frac{77}{80} - \left(\frac{1}{80}\right)^2} \times 2$$

$$= \sqrt{0.9625 - 0.000} \times 2 = 0.9810 \times 2 = 1.962$$

Breaking strength of pieces in the range, $\bar{x} \pm 2\sigma$ is

$$\bar{x} \pm 2\sigma = 49.025 \pm 2 \times 1.962 = 45.103 \text{ and } 52.949 = 45 \text{ and } 53 \text{ (approx.)}$$

To calculate the percentage of observations lying between $\bar{x} \pm 2\sigma$, we assume that the number of observations (pieces) are equally spread within lower and upper boundary of each class interval (breaking strength). Since 45 is the mid-point of the class interval 44–46 with the frequency 3, therefore there are 1.5 frequencies at 45. Similarly, at 53 the frequency would be 2.5. Hence the total number of observations (frequencies) between 45 and 53 are = 1.5 + 24 + 27 + 21 + 2.5 = 76. So the percentage of observations lying within $\bar{x} \pm 2\sigma$ would be (76/80) × 100 = 95 per cent.

4.5.4 Coefficient of Variation

Standard deviation is an absolute measure of variation and expresses variation in the same unit of measurement as the arithmetic mean or the original data. A relative measure called the **coefficient of variation** (CV), developed by Karl Pearson is very useful measure for (i) comparing two or more data sets expressed in different units of measurement (ii) comparing data sets that are in same unit of measurement but the mean values of data sets in a comparable field are widely dissimilar (such as mean wages received per month by the top management personnel and labour class personnel of a large organization).

Thus, in view of this limitation we need to convert absolute measure of variation, that is, S.D. into a relative measure, which can be helpful in comparing the variability of two or more sets of data. The new measure, coefficient of variation (CV), measures the standard deviation relative to the mean in percentages. In other words, CV indicates how large the standard deviation is in relation to the mean and is computed as follows:

$$\text{Coefficient of variation (CV)} = \frac{\text{Standard deviation}}{\text{Mean}} \times 100 = \frac{\sigma}{\bar{x}} \times 100$$

Multiplying by 100 converts the decimal to a percent.

The set of data for which the coefficient of variation is low is said to be more uniform (consistent) or more homogeneous (stable).

Example 4.30: The weekly sales of two products A and B were recorded as given below:

Product A :	59	75	27	63	27	28	56
Product B :	150	200	125	310	330	250	225

Find out which of the two shows greater fluctuation in sales.

Solution: For comparing the fluctuation in sales of two products, we will prefer to calculate coefficient of variation for both the products (Table 4.13).

Product A: Let A = 56 be the assumed mean of sales for product A.

Table 4.13 Calculations of the Mean and Standard Deviation

Sales (x)	*Frequency (f)*	$d = x - A$	fd	fd^2
27	2	– 29	– 58	1682
28	1	– 28	– 28	784
(56) ← A	1	0	0	0
59	1	3	3	9
63	1	7	7	49
75	1	19	19	361
	7		– 57	2885

$$\bar{x} = A + \frac{\Sigma fd}{\Sigma f} = 56 - \frac{57}{7} = 47.86$$

$$s_A^2 = \frac{\Sigma fd^2}{\Sigma f} - \left(\frac{\Sigma fd}{\Sigma f}\right)^2 = \frac{2885}{7} - \left(-\frac{57}{7}\right)^2 = 412.14 - 66.30 = 345.84$$

$$= 412.14 - 66.30 = 345.84$$

$$s_A = \sqrt{345.84} = 18.59$$

Then $$\text{CV (A)} = \frac{s_A}{\bar{x}} \times 100 = \frac{18.59}{47.86} \times 100 = 38.84 \text{ per cent}$$

Product B: Let A = 225 be the assumed mean of sales for product B (Table 4.14).

Table 4.14 Calculations of Mean and Standard Deviation

Sales (x)	*Frequency (f)*	$d = x - A$	fd	fd^2
125	1	– 100	– 100	10,000
150	1	– 75	– 75	5625
200	1	– 25	– 25	625
225	1	0	0	0
250	1	25	25	625
310	1	85	85	7225
330	1	105	105	11,025
	7		15	35,125

$$\bar{x} = A + \frac{\Sigma fd}{\Sigma f} = 225 + \frac{15}{7} = 227.14$$

$$s_B^2 = \frac{\Sigma fd^2}{\Sigma f} - \left(\frac{\Sigma fd}{\Sigma f}\right)^2 = \frac{35{,}125}{7} - \left(\frac{15}{7}\right)^2$$

$$= 5017.85 - 4.59 = 5013.26$$

or $$s_B = \sqrt{5013.26} = 70.80$$

Then $$\text{CV(B)} = \frac{s_B}{\bar{x}} \times 100 = \frac{70.80}{227.14} \times 100 = 31.17 \text{ per cent}$$

Since the coefficient variation for product A is more than that of product B, therefore the sales fluctuation in case of product A is higher.

Example 4.31: Verify the correctness of the following statement: A batsman scored at an average of 60 runs in an inning against Pakistan. The S.D. of the scores by him was 12. A your later against Australia, his average came down to 50 runs an inning and the S.D. of the runs scored fell down to 9. Therefore, it is correct to say that his performance was worse against Australia and that there was lesser consistency in his batting against Australia.

Solution: Against Pakistan: $\bar{x}_p = 60 \quad \sigma_p = 12$

$$\text{CV} = \frac{\sigma_p}{\bar{x}_p} \times 100 = \frac{12}{60} \times 100 = 20\%$$

Against Australia: $\bar{x}_A = 50 \quad \sigma_A = 9$

$$\text{CV} = \frac{\sigma_A}{\bar{x}_A} \times 100 = \frac{9}{50} \times 100 = 18\%$$

Since CV for Australia is less than that of Pakistan, there is more consistency in his batting against Australia. Hence the statement is incorrect. However, the average runs scored by him were more against Pakistan.

Example 4.32: After settlement the average weekly wages in a factory has increased from Rs. 8000 to Rs. 12000 and the S.D. has increased from Rs. 100 to Rs. 150. After settlement, the wages has become higher and more uniform. Do you agree? *[Delhi Univ., B.Com (Hons), 2005]*

Solution: Before settlement, $CV = \frac{S.D.}{Mean} \times 100 = \frac{100}{8000} \times 100 = 1.25\%$

After settlement, $CV = \frac{150}{12000} \times 100 = 1.25\%$

Since there is no change in CV, there is no improvement in uniformity.

Example 4.33: The following is the record of goals scored by team *A* in a football session :

No. of goals scored : 0, 1, 2, 3, 4

No. of matches : 1, 9, 7,5, 3

From team *B*, the average number of goals scored per match are 2.5 with a standard deviation of 1.25 goals. Find which team may be considered as more consistent. *[Delhi Univ., B.Com (Pass), 2006]*

Solution: Calculating coefficient of variation of two teams to comment on consistancy as follows:

No. of goals x	*No. of Matches* f	$d = x - A$ $= x - 2$	*fd*	*fd2*
0	1	– 2	– 2	4
1	9	– 1	– 9	9
2	7	0	0	0
3	5	1	5	5
4	3	2	6	12
	$n = 25$		= 0	30

$$\overline{x} = A + \frac{\Sigma fd}{n} = 2 + \frac{0}{25} = 2$$

$$\sigma = \sqrt{\frac{\Sigma fd^2}{n} - \left(\frac{\Sigma fd}{n}\right)^2} = \sqrt{\frac{30}{25} - \left(\frac{0}{25}\right)^2} = 1.09$$

$$\text{CV for team } A = \frac{\sigma_A}{\overline{x}_A} \times 100 = \frac{1.09}{2} \times 100$$

$$\text{CV for team } B = \frac{1.25}{2.5} \times 100 = 50\%.$$

Since CV of team *B* is lesser than that of *A*, team *B* is more consistent.

Example 4.34: From the analysis of monthly wages paid to employees in two service organizations X and Y, the following results were obtained:

	Organization X	*Organization Y*
Number of wage-earners	550	650
Average monthly wages	5000	4500
Variance of the distribution of wages	900	1600

(a) Which organization pays a larger amount as monthly wages?

(b) In which organization is there greater variability in individual wages of all the wage earners taken together?

Solution: (a) For finding out which organization X or Y pays larger amount of monthly wages, we have to compare the total wages:

Total wage bill paid monthly by X and Y is

$$X \;:\; n_1 \times \bar{x}_1 = 550 \times 5000 = \text{Rs. } 27{,}50{,}000$$

$$Y \;:\; n_2 \times \bar{x}_2 = 650 \times 4500 = \text{Rs. } 29{,}25{,}000$$

Organization Y pays a larger amount as monthly wages as compared to organization X.

(b) For calculating the combined variation, we will first calculate the combined mean as follows:

$$\bar{x}_{12} = \frac{n_1\bar{x}_1 + n_2\bar{x}_2}{n_1 + n_2} = \frac{27{,}50{,}000 + 29{,}25{,}000}{1200} = \text{Rs. } 4729.166$$

$$\sigma_{12} = \sqrt{\frac{n_1\left(\sigma_1^2 + d_1^2\right) + n_2\left(\sigma_2^2 + d_1^2\right)}{n_1 + n_2}}$$

$$= \sqrt{\frac{550(900 + 73{,}351.05) + 650(1600 + 52{,}517.05)}{550 + 650}}$$

$$= \sqrt{\frac{4{,}08{,}38{,}080.55 + 3{,}51{,}76{,}082.50}{1200}} = \sqrt{63345.13} = 251.68$$

where $d_1 = |\bar{x}_{12} - \bar{x}_1| = 4729.166 - 5000 = 270.834$

$d_2 = |\bar{x}_{12} - \bar{x}_2| = 4729.166 - 4500 = 229.166$

Calculating coefficient of variance of both organization to comment on variability in wages as follows:

$$\text{CV}(x) = \frac{\sigma}{\bar{x}} \times 100 = \frac{30}{5000} \times 100 = 0.60$$

$$\text{CV}(y) = \frac{40}{4500} \times 100 = 0.88$$

Since CV(y) > CV(x), these in greater variability in individual wages of organization y.

Conceptual Questions 4B

7. What purpose does a measure of variation serve? In the light of these, comment on some of the well-known measures of variation.
8. What do you understand by 'coefficient of variation'? Discuss its importance in business problems.
9. Explain and illustrate how the measures of variation afford a supplement to the information about frequency distribution furnished by averages.
10. Explain the advantages of standard deviation as a measure of variation over range and the average deviation. Under what circumstances will the variance of a variable be zero?
11. Comment on the comparative merits and demerits of measures of variation.
12. Describe the various methods of measuring variation along with their respective merits and demerits.
13. It has been said that the lesser the variability that exists, the more an average is representative of a set of data. Comment.
14. What information is provided by variance or standard deviation?
15. What advantages are associated with variance and standard deviation relative to range as the measure of variability?

Self-Practice Problems 4B

4.9 Find the average deviation from mean for the following distribution:

Quantity demanded (in units) :
60 61 62 63 64 65 66 67 68
Frequency :
2 0 15 29 25 12 10 4 3

4.10 Find the average deviation from mean for the following distribution:

Dividend yield :
0–3 3–6 6–9 9–12 12–15 15–18 18–21
Number of companies :
2 7 10 12 9 6 4

4.11 Find the average deviation from median for the following distribution:

Sales (Rs. '000) :
1–3 3–5 5–7 7–9 9–11 11–13 13–15 15–17
Number of shops :
6 53 85 56 21 26 4 4

4.12 In a survey of 48 engineering companies, following data was collected:

Level of profit (Rs. in lakh) : 10 11 12 13 14
Number of companies : 3 12 18 12 3

Calculate the variance and standard deviation for the distribution.

4.13 A manufacturer of T-shirts approaches you with the following information

Length of shoulder (in inches) :
12.0 12.5 13.0 13.5 14 14.5 15 15.5 16
Frequency:
5 20 30 43 60 56 37 16 3

Calculate the standard deviation and advice the manufacturer as to the largest and the smallest shoulder size T-shirts he should make in order to meet the needs of his customers.

4.14 A charitable organization decided to give old-age pension to people over sixty years of age. The scales of pension were fixed as follows:

Age Group	*Pension/month (Rs.)*
60–65	200
65–70	250
70–75	300
75–80	350
80–85	400

The ages of 25 persons who secured the pension are as given below:

74 62 84 72 61 83 72 81 64
71 63 61 60 67 74 64 79 73
75 76 69 68 78 66 67

Calculate the monthly average pension payable per person and the standard deviation.

4.15 Two automatic filling machines A and B are used to fill tea in 500 g cartons. A random sample of 100 cartons on each machine showed the following:

Tea Contents (in g)	*Machine A*	*Machine B*
485–490	12	10
490–495	18	15
495–500	20	24
500–505	22	20
505–510	24	18
510–515	4	13

Comment on the performance of the two machines on the basis of average filling and dispersion.

4.16 An analysis of production rejects resulted in the following observations

No. of Rejects per Operator	*No. of Operators*	*No. of Rejects per Operator*	*No. of Operators*
21–25	5	41–45	15
26–30	15	46–50	12
31–35	28	51–55	3
36–40	42		

Calculate the mean and standard deviation.

4.17 Blood serum cholestrerol levels of 10 persons are as under:

240 260 290 245 255 288 272 263 277 250

Calculate the standard deviation with the help of assumed mean

4.18 32 trials of a process to finish a certain job revealed the following information:

Mean time taken to complete the job = 80 minutes
Standard deviation = 16 minutes

Another set of 8 trials gave mean time as 100 minutes and standard deviation equalled to 25 minutes.

Find the combined mean and standard deviation.

4.19 From the analysis of monthly wages paid to workers in two organizations X and Y, the following results were obtained:

		X	Y
Number of wage-earners	:	550	600
Average monthly wages (Rs.)	:	1260	1348.5
Variance of distribution of wages (Rs.)	:	100	841

Obtain the average wages and the variability in individual wages of all the workers in the two organizations taken together.

4.20 An analysis of the results of a budget survey of 150 families showed an average monthly expenditure of Rs. 120 on food items with a standard deviation of Rs. 15. After the analysis was completed it was noted that the figure recorded for one household was wrongly taken as Rs. 15 instead of Rs. 105. Determine the correct value of the average expenditure and its standard deviation.

4.21 The standard deviation of a distribution of 100 values was Rs. 2. If the sum of the squares of the actual values was Rs. 3,600, what was the mean of this distribution?

4.22 The hourly output of a new machine is four times that of the old machine. If the variance of the hourly output of the old machine in a period of n hours is 16, what is the variance of the hourly output of the new machine in the same period of n hours.

Coefficient of Variance

4.23 Two salesmen selling the same product show the following results over a long period of time:

	Salesman X	*Salesman Y*
Average sales volume per month (Rs.)	30,000	35,000
Standard deviation	2,500	3,600

Which salesman seems to be more consistent in the volume of sales?

4.24 Suppose that samples of polythene bags from two manufacturers A and B are tested by a buyer for bursting pressure, giving the following results:

Bursting Pressure	*Number of Bags*	
	A	*B*
5.0–9.9	2	9
10.0–14.9	9	11
15.0–19.9	29	18
20.0–24.9	54	32
25.0–29.9	11	27
30.0–34.9	5	13

(a) Which set of bags has the highest bursting pressure?

(b) Which has more uniform pressure? If prices are the same, which manufacturer's bags would be preferred by the buyer? Why?

4.25 The number of employees, average daily wages per employee, and the variance of daily wages per employee for two factories are given below:

		Factory A	*Factory B*
Number of employees	:	50	100
Average daily wages (Rs.)	:	120	85
Variance of daily wages (Rs.)	:	9	16

(a) In which factory is there greater variation in the distribution of daily wages per employee?

(b) Suppose in factory B, the wages of an employee were wrongly noted as Rs. 120 instead of Rs. 100. What would be the correct variance for factory B?

4.26 The share prices of a company in Mumbai and Kolkata markets during the last ten months are recorded below:

Month	*Mumbai*	*Kolkata*
January	105	108
February	120	117
March	115	120
April	118	130
May	130	100
June	127	125
July	109	125
August	110	120
September	104	110
October	112	135

Determine the arithmetic mean and standard deviation of prices of shares. In which market are the share prices more stable?

4.27 A person owns two petrol filling stations A and B. At station A, a representative sample of 200 consumers who purchase petrol was taken. The results were as follows:

Number of Litres of Petrol Purchased	*Number of Consumers*
0 and < 2	15
2 and < 4	40
4 and < 6	65
6 and < 8	40
8 and < 10	30
10 and over	10

A similar sample at station B users showed a mean of 4 litres with a standard deviation of 2.2 litres. At which station is the purchase of petrol relatively more variable?

Hints and Answers

4.9 MAD = 1.239; $\bar{x}$ = 63.89

4.10 $\bar{x}$ = 10.68; MAD = 3.823

4.11 Med = 6.612; MAD = 2.252

4.12 $\sigma^2 = 1$ and $\sigma = 1$

4.13 $\bar{x}$ = 14.013 inches; σ = 0.8706 inches;
$\bar{x} + 3\sigma$ = 14.884 (largest size);
$\bar{x} - 3\sigma$ = 13.142 (smallest size)

4.14 $\bar{x}$ = Rs. 280.2; σ = Rs. 60.765

4.15 Machine A: $\bar{x}_1 = 499.5$; $\sigma_1 = 7.14$;
Machine B : $\bar{x}_2 = 500.5$; $\sigma_2 = 7.40$

4.16 $\bar{x}$ = 36.96; σ = 6.375

4.17 σ = 16.48

4.18 $\bar{x}_{12}$ = 84 minutes; σ_{12} = 19.84

4.19 $\bar{x}_{12}$ = Rs. 1306; σ_{12} = Rs. 53.14

4.20 Corrected $\bar{x}$ = Rs. 120.6 and corrected σ = Rs. 12.4

4.21 $\bar{x}$ = 5.66

4.22 Variance (new machine) = 256 hours

4.23 Salesman X

4.24 Manufacture A: $\bar{x}_1 = 21$, $\sigma_1 = 4.875$ and C.V. = 23.32%

Manufacturer B : $\bar{x}_2 = 21.81$, $\sigma_2 = 7.074$ and C.V. = 32.44%; (a) Bags of manufacturer B have higher bursting pressure; (b) Bags of manufacturer A have more uniform pressure; (c) Bags of manufacturer A should be preferred by buyer as they have uniform pressure.

4.25 (a) CV(A) = 2.5 ;

CV(B) = 4.7. Variation in the distribution of daily wages per employee in factory B is more.

(b) Correct $\Sigma x = 100 \times 85 - 120 + 100 = 8{,}480$

Correct mean $\bar{x}$ = 8480/100 = 84.8

Since $\sigma^2 = (\Sigma x^2/N) - (\bar{x})^2$

or $16 = (\Sigma x^2/100) - (85)^2$

$= \Sigma x^2 - 7{,}22{,}500$

or $\Sigma x^2 = 7{,}24{,}100$

Correct $\Sigma x^2 = 7{,}24{,}100 - (120)^2 + (100)^2$

$= 7{,}19{,}700$

Correct $\sigma^2 = (7{,}19{,}700/100) - (84.8)^2$

$= 5.96$

4.26 CV(Mumbai) = 7.24% ; CV (Kolkata) = 8.48%. This shows more stability in Mumbai stock market.

4.27 CV(A) = 46.02% ; CV(B) = 55%. The purchase of petrol is relatively more variable at station B.

Formulae Used

1. Range, R
   Value of highest observation – Value of lowest observation = H – L

   Coefficient of range = $\dfrac{H-L}{H+L}$

2. Interquartile range = $Q_3 - Q_1$

   Quartile deviation, QD = $\dfrac{Q_3 - Q_1}{2}$

   Coefficient of QD = $\dfrac{Q_3 - Q_1}{Q_3 + Q_1}$

3. Mean average deviation
   For ungrouped data

   (i) MAD = $\dfrac{\Sigma\,|x-\bar{x}|}{n}$, for sample

   (ii) MAD = $\dfrac{\Sigma\,|x-\mu|}{N}$, for population

   (iii) MAD = $\dfrac{\Sigma\,|x-Me|}{n}$, from median

   For grouped data MAD = $\dfrac{\Sigma\, f|x-\bar{x}|}{\Sigma f}$

4. Coefficient of MAD = $\dfrac{MAD}{\bar{x} \text{ or } Me} \times 100$

5. Variance
   Ungrouped data

   $$\sigma^2 = \frac{\Sigma\,(x-\bar{x})^2}{N} = \frac{\Sigma\, x^2}{N} - \left(\frac{\Sigma\, x}{N}\right)^2$$

   $$= \frac{\Sigma\, d^2}{N} - \left(\frac{\Sigma\, d}{N}\right)^2$$

   where $d = x - A$; A is any assumed A.M. value

   Grouped data, $\sigma^2 = \left[\dfrac{\Sigma\, fd^2}{N} - \left(\dfrac{\Sigma\, fd}{N}\right)^2\right] h$

   where $d = (m - A)/h$; h is the class interval and m is the mid-value of class intervals.

6. Standard deviation

   Ungrouped data $\sigma = \sqrt{\sigma^2}$

   Grouped data $\sigma = \sqrt{\dfrac{\Sigma\, fd^2}{N} - \left(\dfrac{\Sigma\, fd}{N}\right)^2} \times h$

7. Coefficient of variation (CV) = $\dfrac{\sigma}{\bar{x}} \times 100$

Chapter Concepts Quiz

True and False

1. Range is a measure of variation which gives us information about scatter of values around a measure of central tendency.
2. When a distribution consists of different observations, s or σ are relatively large.
3. The interquartile range is based upon only two values in the data set.
4. Absolute measures of variation are used for comparing variability among observations in a data set.
5. The semi-interquartile range is inappropriate to use with skewed distributions.
6. Mean absolute deviation taken from median is least.
7. The standard deviation is measured in the same unit as the observations in the data set.
8. In a symmetrical distribution, semi-interquartile range is one-fourth of the range.
9. The coefficient of variation is a relative measure of dispersion.
10. The inter-quartile range measures the average range of the lower fourth of a distribution.
11. For a symmetrical distribution, mean absolute deviation equals 4/5 of standard deviation.
12. Variance indicates the average distance of any observation in the data set from the mean.
13. Sample standard deviation provides an accurate estimate of the population standard deviation.
14. Variance is the square of the standard deviation.
15. Standard deviation can be calculated by taking deviation from any measure of central tendency.

Concepts Quiz Answers

1. F	2. T	3. T	4. F	5. T	6. T	7. T	8. T	9. T
10. F	11. T	12. T	13. F	14. F	15. F			

Review Self-Practice Problems

4.28 A petrol filling station has recorded the following data for litres of petrol sold per automobile in a sample of 680 automobiles:

Petrol Sold (Litres)	*Frequency*
0– 4	74
5– 9	192
10–14	280
15–19	105
20–24	23
25–29	6

Compute the mean and standard deviation for the data.

4.29 A work-standards expert observes the amount of time (in minutes) required to prepare a sample of 10 business letters in the office with observations in ascending order: 5, 5, 5, 7, 9, 14, 15, 15, 16, 18.

(a) Determine the range and middle 70 per cent range for the sample.

(b) If the sample mean of the data is 10.9, then calculate the mean absolute deviation and variance.

4.30 ABC Stereos, a wholesaler, was contemplating becoming the supplier to three retailers, but inventory shortages have forced him to select only one. ABC's credit manager is evaluating the credit record of these three retailers. Over the past 5 years these retailers' accounts receivable have been outstanding for the following average number of days. The credit manager feels that consistency, in addition to lowest average, is important. Based on relative dispersion, which retailer would make the best customer?

Lee :	62.20	61.80	63.40	63.00	61.70
Forest :	62.50	61.90	63.80	63.00	61.70
Davis :	62.00	61.90	63.00	63.90	61.50

4.31 A purchasing agent obtained samples of 60 watt bulbs from two companies. He had the samples tested in his own laboratory for length of life with the following results:

Length of Life (in hours)	*Samples from*	
	Company A	*Company B*
1700–1900	10	3
1900–2100	16	40
2100–2300	20	12
2300–2500	8	3
2500–2700	6	2

(a) Which company's bulbs do you think are better in terms of average life?

(b) If prices of both the companies are same, which company's bulbs would you buy and why?

4.32 The Chief Medical Officer of a hospital conducted a survey of the number of days 200 randomly chosen patients stayed in the hospital following an operation. The data are given below

Hospital stay (in days) :	1–3	4–6	7–9	10–12	13–15	16–18	19–21	22–24
Number of patients:	18	90	44	21	9	9	4	5

(a) Calculate the mean number of days patients stay in the hospital along with standard deviation of the same.

(b) How many patients are expected to stay between 0 and 17 days.

4.33 There are a number of possible measures of sales performance, including how consistent a sales person is, in meeting established sales goals. The following data represent the percentage of goal met by each of three sales persons over the last five years

Raman :	88	68	89	92	103
Sindhu :	76	88	90	86	79
Prasad :	104	88	118	88	123

Which salesman is most consistent. Suggest an alternative measure of consistency (if possible).

4.34 Gupta Machine Company has a contract with one of its customers to supply machined pump gears. One requirement is that the diameter of its gears be within specific limits. The following data is of diameters (in inches) of a sample of 20 gears:

4.01 4.00 4.02 4.03 4.00 3.98 3.99 3.99
4.01 4.02 3.99 3.98 3.97 4.00 4.02 4.01
4.02 4.00 4.01 3.99

What can Gupta say to his customers about the diameters of 95 per cent of the gears they are receiving?

4.35 Public transportation and the automobiles are two options an employee can use to get to work each day. Samples of time (in minutes) recorded for each option are shown below:

Public transportation :

28 29 32 37 33 25 29 32 41 34

Automobile :

29 31 33 32 34 30 31 32 35 33

(a) Compute the sample mean time to get to work for each option.

(b) Compute the sample standard deviation for each option.

(c) On the basis of your results from parts (a) and (b), which method of transportation should be preferred? Explain.

4.36 The mean and standard deviation of a set of 100 observations were worked out as 40 and 5 respectively by a computer which, by mistake, took the value 50 in place of 40 for one observation. Find the correct mean and variance.

4.37 The number of employees, wages per employee and the variance of the wages per employee for two factories is given below:

	Factory A	Factory B
Number of employees :	100	150
Average wage per employee per month (Rs.) :	3200	2800
Variance of the wages per employee per month (Rs.) :	625	729

(a) In which factory is there greater variation in the distribution of wages per employee?

(b) Suppose in factory B, the wages of an employee were wrongly noted as Rs. 3050 instead of Rs. 3650, what would be the correct variance for factory B?

4.38 In two factories A and B engaged in the same industry, the average weekly wages and standard deviations are as follows:

Factory	*Average Weekly Wages (Rs.)*	*S.D. of Wages (Rs.)*	*No. of Wage Earners*
A	460	50	100
B	490	40	80

(a) Which factory, A or B, pays a higher amount as weekly wages?

(b) Which factory shows greater variability in the distribution of wages?

(c) What is the mean and standard deviation of all the workers in two factories taken together?

4.39 The mean of 5 observations is 4.4 and the variance is 8.24. If three of the five observations are 1, 2 and 6, find the other two.

4.40 The mean and standard deviation of normal distribution are 60 and 5 respectively. Find the inter-quartile range and the mean deviation of the distribution.

4.41 The value of the arithmetic mean and standard deviation of the following frequency distribution of a continuous variable derived from the use of working origin and scale are Rs. 107 and 13.1 respectively. Determine the actual classes.

Step deviation, d :	-3	-2	-1	0	$+1$	$+2$
Frequency, f :	1	3	4	7	3	2

4.42 The mean and standard deviation of a set of 100 observations were found to be 40 and 5 respectively. But by mistake a value 50 was taken in place of 40 for one observation. Re-calculate the correct mean and standard deviation.

4.43 The mean and the standard deviation of a sample of 10 sizes were found to be 9.5 and 2.5 respectively. Later on, an additional observation became available. This was 15.0 and was included in the original sample. Find the mean and the standard deviation of 11 observations.

4.44 The Shareholders Research Centre of India has recently conducted a research-study on price behaviour of three leading industrial shares, A, B, and C for the period 1979 to 1985, the results of which are published as follows in its Quarterly Journal:

Share	*Average Price (Rs.)*	*Standard Deviation*	*Current Selling Price (Rs.)*
A	18.2	5.4	36.00
B	22.5	4.5	34.75
C	24.0	6.0	39.00

(a) Which share, in your opinion, appears to be more stable in value?

(b) If you are the holder of all the three shares, which one would you like to dispose of at present, and why?

4.45 An analysis of the weekly wages paid to workers in two firms A and B belonging to the same industry, gives the following results:

	Firm A	*Firm B*
Number of wage-earners	550	650
Average daily wages	50	45
Standard deviation of the distribution of wages	$\sqrt{90}$	$\sqrt{120}$

(a) Which firm, A or B, pays out a larger amount as daily wages?

(b) In which firm, A or B, is there greater variability in individual wages?

(c) What are the measures of (i) average daily wages and (ii) standard deviation in the distribution of individual wages of all workers in the two firms taken together?

Hints and Answers

4.28 $\bar{x}$ = 10.74 litres per automobile, σ = 5.00 litres

4.29 (a) Range = H – L = 18 – 5 = 15 minutes

Middle 70% of R = $P_{85} - P_{15}$

$= x_{(85/100)+(1/2)} - x_{(15/100)+(1/2)}$

$= x_{(8.5+0.5)} - x_{(1.5+0.5)} = x_9 - x_2$

= 16 – 5 = 11 minutes

(b) MAD $= \dfrac{\Sigma|x-\bar{x}|}{n} = \dfrac{47}{10}$ = 4.7 minutes

$$s^2 = \frac{\Sigma x^2 - n\bar{x}^2}{n-1}$$

$$= \frac{1{,}431 - 10(10.9)^2}{10-1} = 26.99 \text{ minutes}$$

4.30 Lee : $\bar{x}$ = 62.42, s = 0.7497,

CV = $(s/\bar{x}) \times 100$ = 1.20%

Forest: $\bar{x}$ = 62.18, s = 0.9257,

CV = $(s/\bar{x}) \times 100$ = 1.49%

Davis : $\bar{x}$ = 62.46, s = 0.9762,

CV = $(s/\bar{x}) \times 100$ = 1.56%

Based on CV, Lee would be the best customer.

4.31 For company A:

$$\bar{x} = A + \frac{\Sigma fd}{N} \times h = 2200 - \frac{16}{60} \times 200$$

= 2146.67;

$$\sigma = \sqrt{\frac{\Sigma fd^2}{N} - \left(\frac{\Sigma fd}{N}\right)^2} \times h$$

$$= \sqrt{\frac{88}{60} - \left(\frac{-16}{60}\right)^2} \times 200 = 236.4$$

CV = $(\sigma/\bar{x}) \times 100$ = 11%

For company B: $\bar{x}$ = 2070 ; σ = 158.8 and CV = 7.67%.

(a) Bulbs of company A are better.

(b) CV(B) < CV(A): Buy company B bulbs as their burning hours are more uniform.

4.32 $\bar{x} = \dfrac{\Sigma fm}{n} = \dfrac{1543}{200} = 7.715$ days;

$$s^2 = \frac{\Sigma(x-\bar{x})^2}{n-1} = \frac{4384.755}{199} = 22.033$$

$s = \sqrt{22.033}$ = 4.69 days

4.33

Sales Person	$\bar{x}$	*s*	*CV* = $(s/\bar{x}) \times 100$
Raman	88	12.67	14.4%
Sindhu	83.8	6.02	7.2%
Prasad	104.2	16.35	15.7%

Sindhu is most consistent both in terms of *s* and CV.

4.34 Diameter : 3.97 3.98 3.99 4.00 4.01 4.02 4.03

Frequency : 1 2 4 4 4 4 1

$$\bar{x} = \frac{\sum x}{n} = 80.04 \div 20 = 4.002 \text{ inches}$$

$$s = \sqrt{\frac{\sum x^2 - n(\bar{x})^2}{n-1}}$$

$$= \sqrt{\frac{320.325 - 20(4.002)^2}{19}}$$

$= 0.016$ inches

If distribution is bell-shaped, then 95% of the gears will have diameters in the interval:

$\bar{x} \pm 2s = 4.002 \pm 2\,(0.016) = (3.970, 4.034)$ inches.

4.35 (a) Public : 32; Auto : 32 (b) Public : 4.64; Auto : 1.83 (c) Auto has less variability.

4.36 (i) $\bar{x} = \dfrac{\sum x}{n}$ or $\sum x = \bar{x}\,\text{N} = 40 \times 100$

$= 4{,}000$

Correct $\sum x = 4000 - 50 + 40 = 3990$.

Thus Correct, $\bar{x} = 3990 \div 100 = 39.9$

(ii) $\sigma^2 = \dfrac{\sum x^2}{\text{N}} - (\bar{x})^2$ or $25 = \dfrac{\sum x^2}{100} - (40)^2$

or $\sum x^2 = 1{,}62{,}500$

Correct $\sum x^2 = 1{,}62{,}500 - (50)^2 + (40)^2$

$= 1{,}62{,}500 - 2500 + 1600$

$= 1{,}61{,}600$

$$\text{Correct } \sigma^2 = \frac{\text{Correct} \sum x^2}{\text{N}} - (\text{Correct } \bar{x})^2$$

$$= \frac{1{,}61{,}600}{100} - (39.9)^2 = 23.99$$

4.37 (a) $\text{CV (A)} = \dfrac{\sigma}{\bar{x}} \times 100 = \dfrac{\sqrt{625}}{3200} \times 100$

$= 0.781$;

$\text{CV(B)} = \dfrac{\sqrt{729}}{2800} \times 100 = 0.964$

There is greater variation in the distribution of wages per employee in factory B.

(b) $\bar{x} = \dfrac{\sum x}{\text{N}}$ or $\sum x = \text{N}\,\bar{x} = 150 \times 2800$

$= 4{,}20{,}000$

Correct $\sum x = 4{,}20{,}000 - 3050 + 3650$

$= 4{,}20{,}600$;

Correct, $\bar{x} = \dfrac{4{,}20{,}600}{150} = 2{,}804$

Variance, $\sigma^2 = \dfrac{\sum x^2}{\text{N}} - (\bar{x})^2$

or $729 = \dfrac{\sum x^2}{150} - (2800)^2$

or $\sum x^2 = 1{,}17{,}61{,}09{,}350$

Correct $\sum x^2 = 1{,}17{,}61{,}09{,}350 - (3050)^2 + (3650)^2 = 1{,}18{,}01{,}29{,}350$

$$\text{Correct } \sigma^2 = \frac{\text{Correct} \sum x^2}{\text{N}} - (\text{Correct } \bar{x})^2$$

$$= \frac{1{,}18{,}01{,}29{,}350}{150} - (2804)^2 = 5113$$

4.38 (a) Total weekly wages: Factory A = 460 × 100 = Rs. 46,000; Factory B = 490 × 80 = Rs. 39,200.

Factory *A* pays a larger amount.

(b) $\text{CV (Factory } A) = \dfrac{\sigma}{\bar{x}} \times 100 = \dfrac{50}{460} \times 100$

$= 10.87\%$;

$\text{CV (Factory } B) = \dfrac{40}{490} \times 100 = 8.16\%$

Since CV (A) × CV (B), factory A shows greater variability in wages.

(c) $\bar{x}_{12} = \dfrac{\text{N}_1\bar{x}_1 + \text{N}_2\bar{x}_2}{\text{N}_1 + \text{N}_2}$

$$= \frac{100 \times 460 + 80 \times 490}{100 + 80} = \text{Rs. } 473.33$$

$$\sigma_{12}^2 = \frac{\text{N}_1(\sigma_1^2 + d_1^2) + \text{N}_2(\sigma_2^2 + d_2^2)}{\text{N}_1 + \text{N}_2};$$

$$= \frac{100\{(50)^2 + (13.33)^2\} + 80\{(40)^2 + (16.67)^2\}}{100 + 80}$$

$= 48.19$

$d_1 = |\bar{x}_1 - \bar{x}_{12}| = |460 - 473.33| = 13.33$

$d_2 = |\bar{x}_2 - \bar{x}_{12}| = |490 - 473.33| = 16.67$

4.39 $\bar{x} = \frac{\sum x}{N}$ or $\sum x = N\bar{x} = 5 \times 4.4 = 22$

Let two terms x_1 and x_2 are missing. Then $x_1 + x_2 + 1 + 2 + 6 = 22$ or $x_1 + x_2 = 13$

Also $\sigma^2 = \frac{\sum x^2}{N} - (\bar{x}^2)$ or 8.24

$= \frac{\sum x^2}{5} - (4.4)^2$

or $\sum x^2 = 138$

$\therefore \sum x^2 = x_1^2 + x_2^2 + (1)^2 + (2)^2 + (6)^2$

$= 138$ or $x_1^2 + x_2^2 = 97$

Now $x_1^2 + x_2^2 = (x_1 + x_2)^2 - 2x_1x_2$

or $97 = (13)^2 - 2x_1x_2$ or $x_1x_2 = 36$

$(x_1 - x_2)^2 = x_1^2 + x_2^2 - 2x_1x_2 = 97 - 2\,(36)$
$= 25,$

or $x_1 - x_2 = 5$

Solving two equations $x_1 + x_2 = 13$ and $x_1 - x_2 = 5$, we have $x_1 = 9$ and $x_2 = 4$.

4.40 $QD = \frac{2}{3}\sigma = \frac{2}{3} \times 5 = \frac{10}{3}$;

$QD = \frac{Q_3 - Q_2}{2} = \frac{10}{3}$ or

$Q_3 - Q_1 = \frac{20}{3} = 6.67$

Thus interquartile range is 6.67.

4.41 $\sigma = \sqrt{\frac{\sum fd^2}{N} - \left(\frac{\sum fd}{N}\right)^2} \times h$

or $13.1 = \sqrt{\frac{36}{20} - \left(\frac{-6}{20}\right)^2} \times h$ or $h = 10$

$\bar{x} = A + \frac{\sum fd}{N} \times h$

or $107 = A - \frac{6}{20} \times 10$, i.e., $A = 110$ (assumed mean)

Since deviations are taken from $A = 110$ and class interval is, $h = 10$, therefore the class corresponding to $d = 0$ will be 105–115. Other classes will be:

Class:	75–85	85–95	95–105	105–115	115–125	125–135
Frequency:	1	3	4	7	3	2

4.42 Correct $\bar{x} = 39.9$ and $\sigma = 4.9$

4.43 $\bar{x} = \frac{\sum x}{N}$ or $\sum x = N\bar{x} = 10 \times 9.5 = 95$

Adding the 11th observation,

We get $\sum x = 95 + 15 = 110$.

Then $\bar{x} = \frac{\sum x}{N} = 110 \div 11 = 10$

Also, $\sigma^2 = \frac{\sum x^2}{N} - (\bar{x})^2$ or $(2.5)^2$

$= \frac{\sum x^2}{10} - (9.5)^2$

or $\sum x^2 = 965$

Now value of $\sum x^2 = 965 + (15)^2 = 1190$. Then

$\sigma^2 = \frac{\sum x^2}{N} - (\bar{x})^2 = \frac{1190}{11} - (10)^2 = 2.86$

4.44 (a) CV(A) = 30, CV(B) = 20 and CV(C) = 25; Share B is more stable.

(b) Dispose share A because of high variability in its price.

4.45 (a) Firm B pays more wages;

(b) Firm B has greater variability in individual wages

(c) $\bar{x}_{12} = 47.29$ and $\sigma_{12} = 10.605$

Glossary of Terms

Range: A measure of variability, defined to be the difference between the largest and lowest values in the data set.

Interquartile range: A measure of variability, defined to be the difference between the quartiles Q_3 and Q_1.

Variance: A measure of variability based on the squared deviations of the observed values in the data set about the mean value.

Standard deviation: A measure of variability computed by taking the positive square root of the variance.

Coefficient of variation: A measure of relative variability computed by dividing the standard deviation by the mean, then multiplying by 100.

Chapter 5

Skewness and Kurtosis

LEARNING OBJECTIVES

After studying this chapter, you should be able to

- know the complementary relationship of skewness with measures of central tendency and dispersion in describing a set of data
- understand 'moments' as a convenient and unifying method for summarizing several descriptive statistical measures

5.1 INTRODUCTION

In Chapter 4 we discussed measures of variation (or disperson) to describe the spread of individual values in a data set around a central value. Such descriptive analysis of a frequency distribution remains incomplete until we measure the degree to which these individual values in the data set deviate from symmetry on both sides of the central value and the direction in which these are distributed. This analysis is important due to the fact that data sets may have the same mean and standard deviation but the frequency curves may differ in their shape. A frequency distribution of the set of values that is not 'symmetrical (normal)' is called *asymmetrical* or *skewed*. In a skewed distribution, extreme values in a data set move towards one side or tail of a distribution, thereby lengthening that tail. When extreme values move towards the upper or right tail, the distribution is positively skewed. When such values move towards the lower or left tail, the distribution is negatively skewed. As discussed, the mean, median, and mode are affected by the high-valued observations in any data set. Among these measures of central tendency, the mean value gets affected largely due to the presence of high-valued observations in one tail of a distribution. The mean value shifted substantially in the direction of high-values. The mode value is unaffected, while the median value, which is affected by the numbers but not the values of such observations, is also shifted in the direction of high-valued observations, but not as far as the mean. The median value changes about 2/3 as far as the mean value in the direction of high-valued observations (called extremes). Symmetrical and skewed distributions are shown in Fig. 5.1.

For a positively skewed distribution A.M. > Median > Mode, and for a negatively skewed distribution A.M. < Median < Mode. The relationship between these measures of central tendency is used to develop a **measure of skewness** called the *coefficient of skewness* to understand the degree to which these three measures differ.

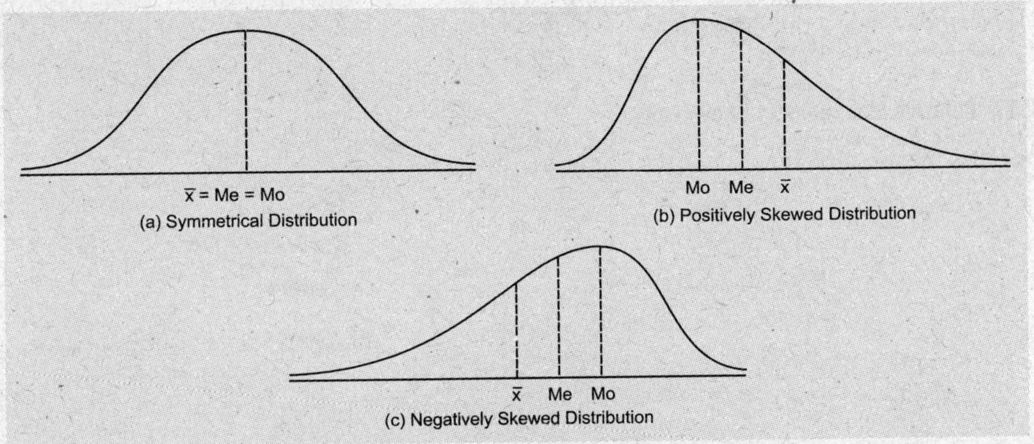

Figure 5.1 Comparison of Three Data Sets Differing in Shape

From the above discussion, two points of difference emerge between variation and skewness:

(i) Variation indicates the amount of spread or dispersion of individual values in a data set around a central value, while skewness indicates the direction of dispersion, that is, away from symmetry.

(ii) Variation is helpful in finding out the extent of variation among individual values in a data set, while skewness gives an understanding about the concentration of higher or lower values around the mean value.

5.2 MEASURES OF SKEWNESS

The degree of skewness in a distribution can be measured both in the *absolute* and *relative* sense. For an asymmetrical distribution, the distance between mean and mode may be used to measure the degree of skewness because the mean is equal to mode in a symmetrical distribution. Thus,

$$\text{Absolute } S_k = \text{Mean} - \text{Mode}$$
$$= Q_3 + Q_1 - 2\text{ Median (if measured in terms of quartiles).}$$

For a positively skewed distribution, Mean > Mode and therefore S_k is a positive value, otherwise it is a negative value. This difference is taken to measure the degree of skewness because in an asymmetrical distribution, mean moves away from the mode. Larger the difference between mean and mode, whether positive or negative, more is the asymmetrical distribution or skewness. This difference, however, may not be desirable for the following reasons:

(i) The difference between mean and mode is expressed in the same units as the distribution and therefore cannot be used for comparing skewness of two or more distributions having different units of measurement.

(ii) The difference between mean and mode may be large in one distribution and small in another, although the shape of their frequency curves is the same.

In order to overcome these two shortcomings and to make valid comparisons between skewness of two or more distributions, the absolute difference has to be expressed in relation to the standard deviation— a measure of dispersion. Since we want to express any measure of skewness as a pure (relative) number, therefore this distance is expressed in terms of the unit of measurement in units of the standard deviation.

5.2.1 Relative Measures of Skewness

The following are three important relative measures of skewness.

Karl Pearson's Coefficient of Skewness

The measure suggested by Karl Pearson for measuring coefficient of skewness is given by:

$$Sk_p = \frac{\text{Mean} - \text{Mode}}{\text{Standard deviation}} = \frac{\bar{x} - \text{Mo}}{\sigma} \tag{5-1}$$

where Sk_p = Karl Pearson's coefficient of skewness.

Since a mode does not always exist uniquely in a distribution, therefore it is convenient to define this measure using median. For a moderately skewed distribution the following relationship holds:

$$\text{Mean} - \text{Mode} = 3(\text{Mean} - \text{Median}) \quad \text{or} \quad \text{Mode} = 3\ \text{Median} - 2\ \text{Mean}$$

When this value of mode is substituted in the Eqn. (5-1) we get

$$Sk_p = \frac{3(\bar{x} - \text{Med})}{\sigma} \tag{5-2}$$

Theoretically, the value of Sk_p varies between ± 3. But for a moderately skewed distribution, value of Sk_p = ± 1. Karl Pearson's method of determining coefficient of skewness is particularly useful in open-end distributions.

Bowley's Coefficients of Skewness

The method suggested by Prof. Bowley is based on the relative positions of the median and the quartiles in a distribution. If a distribution is symmetrical, then Q_1 and Q_3 would be at equal distances from the value of the median, that is,

$$\text{Median} - Q_1 = Q_3 - \text{Median}$$

or

$$Q_3 + Q_1 - 2\ \text{Median} = 0 \quad \text{or} \quad \text{Median} = \frac{Q_3 + Q_1}{2}$$

This shows that the value of median is the mean value of Q_1 and Q_3. Obviously in such a case, the absolute value of the coefficient of skewness will be zero.

When a distribution is asymmetrical, quartiles are not at equal distance from the median. The distribution is positively skewed, if $Q_1 - \text{Me} > Q_3 - \text{Me}$, otherwise negatively skewed.

The absolute measure of skewness is converted into a relative measure for comparing distributions expressed in different units of measurement. For this, absolute measure is divided by the inter-quartile range. That is,

$$\text{Relative } Sk_b = \frac{Q_3 + Q_1 - 2\text{Med}}{Q_3 - Q_1} = \frac{(Q_3 - \text{Med}) - (\text{Med} - Q_1)}{(Q_3 - \text{Med}) + (\text{Med} - Q_1)} \tag{5-3}$$

In a distribution, if Med = Q_1, then $Sk_b = \pm 1$, but of Med = Q_3 then $Sk_b = -1$. This shows that the value of Sk_b varies between $\pm$ 1 for moderately skewed distribution. This method of measuring skewness is quite useful in those cases where (*i*) mode is ill-defined and extreme observations are present in the data, (*ii*) the distribution has open-ended classes. These two advantages of Bowley's coefficient of skewness indicate that it is not affected by extreme observations in the data set.

Remark: The values of Sk_b obtained by Karl Pearson's and Bowley's methods cannot be compared. On certain occasions it is possible that one of them gives a positive value while the other gives a negative value.

Kelly's Coefficient of Skewness

The relative measure of skewness suggested by Prof. Kelly is based on percentiles and deciles:

$$Sk_k = \frac{P_{10} + P_{90} - 2P_{50}}{P_{90} - P_{10}} \quad \text{or} \quad \frac{D_1 + D_9 - 2D_5}{D_9 - D_1} \tag{5-4}$$

This method is an extension of Bowley's method in the sense that Bowley's method is based on the middle 50 per cent of the observations while this method is based on the observations between the 10th and 90th percentiles (or first and nineth deciles).

Example 5.1: Data of rejected items during a production process is as follows:

No of rejects (per operator)	: 21–25	26–30	31–35	36–40	41–45	46–50	51–55
No. of operaters :	5	15	28	42	15	12	3

Calculate the mean, standard deviation, and coefficient of skewness and comment on the results.

Solution: The calculations for mean, mode, and standard deviation are shown in Table 5.1

Table 5.1 Calculations for Mean, Mode and Standard Deviation

Class	*Mid-value* (m)	*Frequency* (f)	$d = \frac{m - A}{h} = \frac{m - 38}{5}$	fd	fd^2
21–25	23	5	−3	−15	45
26–30	28	15	−2	−30	60
31–35	33	28 $\leftarrow f_{m-1}$	−1	−28	28
36–40	38	42 $\leftarrow f_m$	0	0	0
41–45	43	15 $\leftarrow f_{m+1}$	1	15	15
46–50	48	12	2	24	48
51–55	53	3	3	9	27
		N = 120		−25	223

Let assumed mean, A = 38. Then

$$\bar{x} = A + \frac{\Sigma fd}{N} \times h = 38 - \frac{25}{120} \times 5 = 36.96 \text{ rejects per operator}$$

$$\sigma = \sqrt{\frac{\Sigma fd^2}{N} - \left(\frac{\Sigma fd}{N}\right)^2} \times h$$

$$= \sqrt{\frac{223}{120} - \left(\frac{-25}{120}\right)^2} \times 5 = 6.736 \text{ rejects per operator}$$

By inspection, mode lies in the class 36–40. Thus

$$\text{Mo} = l + \frac{f_m - f_{m-1}}{2f_m - f_{m-1} - f_{m+1}} \times h$$

$$= 36 + \frac{42 - 28}{2 \times 42 - 28 - 15} = 36 + \frac{16}{41} \times 5 = 37.70$$

$$\text{Sk}_p = \frac{\text{Mean} - \text{Mode}}{\text{Standard deviation}} = \frac{\bar{x} - \text{Mo}}{\sigma}$$

$$= \frac{36.96 - 37.70}{6.73} = \frac{-0.74}{6.736} = -0.109$$

Since the coefficient of skewness, $S_k = -0.109$, the distribution is skewed to the left (negatively skewed). Thus, the concentration of the rejects per operator is more on the lower values of the distribution to the extent of 10.9 per cent.

Example 5.2: From the following data on age of employees, calculate the coefficient of skewness and comment on the result

Age below (years) :	25	30	35	40	45	50	55
Number of employees :	8	20	40	65	80	92	100

Solution: The data are given in a cumulative frequency distribution form. So, to calculate the coefficient of skewness, convert this data into a simple frequency distribution as shown in Table 5.2.

Table 5.2 Calculations for Coefficient of Skewness

Age (years)	*Mid-value (m)*	*Number of Employees (f)*	*d = (m – A)/h = (m – 37.5)*	*fd*	*fd²*
20–25	22.5	8	– 3	– 24	72
25–30	27.5	12	– 2	– 24	48
30–35	32.5	20 ← f_{m-1}	– 1	– 20	20
35–40	37.5	25 ← f_m	0	0	0
40–45	42.5	1 ← f_{m+1}	1	15	15
45–50	47.5	12	2	24	48
50–55	52.5	8	3	24	72
		N = 100		– 5	275

$$\text{Mean, } \bar{x} = \text{A} + \frac{\Sigma fd}{\text{N}} \times h = 37.5 - \frac{5}{100} \times 5 = 37.25$$

Mode value lies in the class interval 35–40. Thus

$$\text{Mo} = l + \frac{f_m - f_{m-1}}{2f_m - f_{m-1} - f_{m+1}} \times h$$

$$= 35 + \frac{25 - 20}{2 \times 25 - 20 - 15} \times 5 = 35 + \frac{5}{15} \times 5 = 36.67$$

$$\text{Standard deviation, } \sigma = \sqrt{\frac{\Sigma fd^2}{N} - \left(\frac{\Sigma fd}{N}\right)^2} \times h$$

$$= \sqrt{\frac{275}{100} - \left(\frac{-5}{100}\right)^2} \times 5 = \sqrt{2.75 - 0.0025} \times 5 = 8.29$$

Karl Pearson's coefficient of skewness:

$$Sk_p = \frac{\text{Mean} - \text{Mode}}{\sigma} = \frac{37.25 - 36.67}{8.29} = \frac{0.58}{8.29} = 0.07$$

The positive value of Sk_p indicates that the distribution is slightly positively skewed.

Example 5.3: (a) The sum of 50 observations is 500, its sum of squares is 6000 and median 12. Find the coefficient of variation and coefficient of skewness.

(b) For a moderately skewed distribution, the arithmetic mean is 100 and coefficient of variation 35, and Pearson's coefficient of skewness is 0.2. Find the mode and the median.

Solution: (a) Given that N = 50, $\Sigma x = 500$, $\Sigma x^2 = 6000$ and Me = 12.

$$\text{Mean, } \bar{x} = \frac{\Sigma x}{N} = \frac{500}{50} = 10$$

$$\text{Standard deviation, } \sigma = \sqrt{\frac{\Sigma x^2}{N} - (\bar{x})^2} = \sqrt{\frac{600}{50} - (10)^2} = \sqrt{120 - 100} = 4.472$$

$$\text{Coefficient of variation, CV} = \frac{\sigma}{\bar{x}} \times 100 = \frac{4.472}{10} \times 100 = 44.7 \text{ per cent}$$

Mode = 3 Median – 2 Mean = 3 × 12 – 2 × 10 = 16

$$\text{Coefficient of skewness, } Sk_p = \frac{\bar{x} - Mo}{\sigma} = \frac{10 - 16}{4.472} = -1.341$$

(b) Given that $\bar{x} = 100$, CV = 35, $Sk_p = 0.2$.

$$CV = \frac{\sigma}{\bar{x}} \times 100 \quad \text{or} \quad 35 = \frac{\sigma}{100} \times 100 \text{ or } \sigma = 35$$

$$\text{Also } Sk_p = \frac{\bar{x} - Mo}{\sigma} \text{ or } 0.2 = \frac{100 - Mo}{35} \text{ or } Mo = 93$$

Mode = 3Med – $2\bar{x}$ or 93 = 3Med – 2 × 100 or Med = 97.7

Hence, Mode is 93 and median is 97.7.

Example 5.4: The daily expenditure of 100 families is given below :

Daily Expenditure :	0–20	20–40	40–60	60–80	80–100
No. of Families :	13	?	27	?	16

If the mode of the distribution is 44, calculate the Karl Pearson coefficient of skewness.

Solution: Calculations for missing for quencies are shown below:

Daily Expenditure	*Mid Value* m	*No. of Families* f
0–20	10	13
20–40	30	x
40–60	50	27
60–80	70	y
80–100	90	16

Since mode is 44, modal class is 40–60. Thus

$$\text{Mode}, M_0 = l + \frac{f_m - f_{m-1}}{2f_m - f_{m-1} - f_{m+1}}$$

$$\therefore \quad 44 = 40 + \frac{27 - x}{54 - x - y} \times 20$$

$$\frac{44 - 40}{20} = \frac{(27 - x)}{54 - x - y)}$$

$$\frac{1}{5} = \frac{27 - x}{54 - x - y}$$

or $\quad 54 - x - y = 135 - 5x$

$4x - y = 81$

Also $\quad 13 + x + 27 + y + 16 = 100$

or $\quad x + y = 44$

Solving these two equations, we get $x = 25$, $y = 19$. Now, the calculations for mean and standard deviation are as follows:

Class Interval	*Mid-value m*	f	$d = (m - 50)/20$	fd	fd^2
0–20	10	13	– 2	– 26	52
20–40	30	25	– 1	– 25	25
40–60	50	27	0	0	0
60–80	70	19	1	19	19
80–100	90	16	2	32	64
		$N = 100$		0	160

$$\text{Mean}, \bar{x} = A + \frac{\Sigma fd}{N} \times h = 50 + \frac{0}{100} \times 20 = 50$$

$$\text{S.D.}, \sigma = \sqrt{\frac{\Sigma fd^2}{N} - \left(\frac{\Sigma fd}{N}\right)^2} \times h = \sqrt{\frac{160}{100} - \left(\frac{0}{100}\right)^2} \times 20 = \sqrt{1.6} \times 20 = 12.6 \times 20 = 25.2$$

Hence, $\quad Sk_p = \dfrac{\bar{x} - \text{Mode}}{\sigma} = \dfrac{50 - 40}{25.2} = 0.238$

Example 5.5: Pearson's coefficient of skewness for a data distribution is 0.5 and coefficient of variation is 40%. Its mode is 80. Find the mean and median of the distribution.

[*Delhi Univ., B.Com(Hons), 2004*]

Solution: Given, $Sk_p = 0.5$, CV = 0.4, and Mode = 80. Thus

$$\text{CV} = \frac{\sigma}{\bar{x}} \times 100 \quad \text{or} \quad 40 = \frac{\sigma}{\bar{x}} \times 100 \quad \text{or} \quad \sigma = 0.4\bar{x}$$

Also $\quad Sk_p = \dfrac{\text{Mean} - \text{Mode}}{\text{S.D.}} \quad \text{or} \quad 0.5 = \dfrac{\bar{x} - 80}{0.4\bar{x}}$

$$0.5 \times 0.4\bar{x} = \bar{x} - 80 \text{ i.e. } \bar{x} = 100$$

Now $\quad \text{Mode} = 3\text{ Med} - 2\text{ Mean}$

$$80 = 3\text{ Med} - 2\,(100) \quad \text{or} \quad \text{Med} = \frac{280}{3}.$$

Example 5.6: The data on the profits (in Rs. lakh) earned by 60 companies is as follows:

Profits :	Below 10	10–20	20–30	30–40	40–50	50 and above
No. of Companies :	5	12	20	16	5	2

(a) Obtain the limits of profits of the central 50 per cent companies.
(b) Calculate Bowley's coefficient of skewness.

Solution: (a) Calculations for different quartiles are shown in Table 5.3.

Table 5.3 Computation of Quartiles

Profits (in Rs lakh)	*Frequency (f)*	*Cumulative Frequency (c.f.)*
Below 10	5	5
10–20	12	17 ← Q_1 Class
20–30	20	37
30–40	16	53 ← Q_3 Class
40–50	5	58
50 and above	2	60
	N = 60	

Q_1 = size of (N/4)th observation = (60 ÷ 4)th = 15th observation. Thus, Q_1 lies in the class 10–20, and

$$Q_1 = l + \left[\frac{(N/4) - cf}{f}\right] \times h$$

$$= 10 + \left[\frac{15 - 5}{12}\right] \times 10 = 10 + 8.33 = 18.33 \text{ lakh}$$

Q_3 = size of (3N/4)th observation = 45th observation. Thus, Q_3 lies in the class 30–40, and

$$Q_3 = l + \left[\frac{(3N/4) - cf}{f}\right] \times h$$

$$= 30 + \left[\frac{45 - 37}{16}\right] \times 10 = 30 + 5 = 35 \text{ lakh}$$

Hence, the profit of central 50 per cent companies lies between Rs. 35 lakhs and Rs. 10.83 lakh

$$\text{Coefficient of quartile deviation, Q.D.} = \frac{Q_3 - Q_1}{Q_3 + Q_1} = \frac{35 - 18.33}{35 + 18.33} = 0.313$$

(b) **Median** = size of (N/2)th observation = 30th observation. Thus, median lies in the class 20–30, and

$$\text{Me} = l + \left[\frac{(N/2) - cf}{f}\right] \times h = 20 + \left(\frac{30 - 17}{20}\right) \times 10 = 20 + 6.5 = 26.5 \text{ lakh}$$

$$\text{Coefficient of skewness, } Sk_b = \frac{Q_3 + Q_1 - 2\text{Med}}{Q_3 - Q_1} = \frac{35 + 18.33 - 2(26.5)}{35 - 18.33} = 0.02$$

The positive value of Sk_b indicates that the distribution is positively skewed and therefore, there is a concentration of larger values on the right side of the distribution.

Example 5.7: Apply an appropriate measure of skewness to describe the following frequency distribution.

Age (yrs)	*Number of Employees*	*Age (yrs)*	*Number of Employees*
Below 20	13	35–40	112
20–25	29	40–45	94
25–30	46	45–50	45
30–35	60	50 and above	21

Solution: Since given frequency distribution is an open-ended distribution, Bowley's method of calculating skewness should be more appropriate. Calculations are shown in Table 5.4.

Table 5.4 Calculations for Bowley's Coefficient of Skewness

Age (yrs)	*Number of Employees (f)*	*Cumulative Frequency (cf)*
Below 20	13	13
20–25	29	42
25–30	46	88
30–35	60	148 ← Q_1 class
35–40	112	260
40–45	94	354 ← Q_3 class
45–50	45	399
50 and above	21	420
	N = 420	

Q_1 = size of (N/4)th observation = (420/4) = 105th observation. Thus, Q_1 lies in the class 30–35, and

$$Q_1 = l + \frac{(N/4) - cf}{f} \times h = 30 + \frac{105 - 88}{60} \times 5 = 30 + 1.42 = 31.42 \text{ years}$$

Q_3 = size of (3N/4)th observation = (3 × 420/4) = 315th observation. Thus, Q_3 lies in the class 40–45, and

$$Q_3 = l + \frac{(3N/4) - cf}{f} \times h = 40 + \frac{315 - 260}{94} \times 5 = 40 + 2.93 = 42.93 \text{ years}$$

Median = size of (N/2)th = (420/2) = 210th observation. Thus, median lies in the class 35–40, and

$$Me = l + \frac{(N/2) - cf}{f} \times h = 35 + \frac{210 - 148}{112} \times 5 = 35 + 2.77 = 37.77 \text{ years}$$

$$\text{Coefficient of skewness, } Sk_b = \frac{Q_3 + Q_1 - 2\text{Med}}{Q_3 - Q_1} = \frac{42.93 + 31.42 - 2 \times 37.77}{42.93 - 31.42}$$

$$= -\frac{1.19}{11.51} = -0.103$$

The negative value of Sk_b indicates that the distribution is negatively skewed.

Example 5.8: In a frequency distribution, coefficient of skewness based on quartiles is 0.6. If the sum of upper and lower quartile is 100 and median is 38, find the values of lower and upper quartiles.

[Delhi Unit., BCom(Hons), 1993]

Solution: Given $Sk_b = 0.6$; $Q_3 + Q_1 = 100$, and Med = 38

We have $$Sk_b = \frac{Q_3 + Q_1 - 2\text{ Med}}{Q_3 - Q_1} \quad \text{or} \quad 0.6 = \frac{100 - 2(38)}{Q_3 - Q_1}$$

$$Q_3 - Q_1 = \frac{100 - 76}{0.6} = 40$$

Since $Q_3 + Q_1 = 100$, and $Q_3 - Q_1 = 40$, solving these equations, we get $Q_3 = 70$ and $Q_1 = 30$

Example 5.9: Pearson's coefficient of skewness is 0.4, coefficient of variation is 30% and the mode = 88. Find mean.

[Delhi Univ., BCom(Hons), 1997]

Solution: Given $Sk_p = 0.4$, $CV = \sigma/\bar{x} = 0.30$, Mode = 88

$$Sk_p = \frac{\bar{x} - M_0}{\sigma} = \frac{\bar{x} - M_0}{CV \times \bar{x}} = \frac{1 - (M_0/\bar{x})}{CV}$$

or $$0.40 = \frac{1 - (88/\bar{x})}{0.30} \quad \text{or} \quad 1 - \left(\frac{88}{\bar{x}}\right) = 0.12, \text{ i.e. } \bar{x} = 100$$

Example 5.10: The mean, mode and *Q.D.* of a distribution are 42, 36 and 15 respectively. If its Bowley's coefficient of skewness is 1/3, find the values of the two quartiles.

[Delhi Univ., BCom(Hons), 2005]

Solution: Given $\bar{x} = 42$, Mode = 36, $Q.D. = 15$, and $Sk_b = 1/3$

Since $$Q.D. = \frac{Q_3 - Q_1}{2} = 15 \quad \text{or} \quad Q_3 - Q_1 = 30 \qquad \text{(i)}$$

Also $$\text{Mode} = 3\text{ Med} - 2\text{ Mean}$$
$$36 = 3\text{ Med} - 2(42), \text{ i.e. Med} = 40$$

Now $$Sk_b = \frac{Q_3 + Q_1 - 2\text{ Med}}{30} \quad \text{or} \quad Q_3 + Q_1 = 90 \qquad \text{...(ii)}$$

Since $Q_3 + Q_1 = 90$ and $Q_3 - Q_1 = 30$, solving these equations we get $Q_3 = 60$ and $Q_1 = 30$.

Conceptual Questions 5A

1. Explain the meaning of skewness using sketches of frequency curves. State the different measures of skewness that are commonly used. How does skewness differ from dispersion?
2. Measures of central tendency, dispersion, and skewness are complementary to each other in describing a frequency distribution. Elucidate.
3. Distinguish between Karl Pearson's and Bowley's measure of skewness. Which one of these would you prefer and why?
4. Explain brieflty the different methods of measuring skewness.
5. Distinguish between variation and skewness and point out the various methods of measuring skewness.
6. Briefly mention the tests which can be applied to determine the presence of skewness.
7. Explain the term 'skewness'. What purpose does a measure of skewness serve? Comment on some of the well known measures of skewness.

Self-Practice Problems 5A

5.1 The following data relate to the profits (in Rs. '000) of 1,000 companies:

Profits : 100–120 120–140 140–160 160–180 180–200 200–220 220–240

No. of companies : 17 53 199 194 327 208 2

Calculate the coefficient of skewness and comment on its value.

5.2 A survey was conducted by a manufacturing company to find out the maximum price at which people would be willing to buy its product. The following table gives the stated price (in rupees) by 100 persons:

Price : 2.80–2.90 2.90–3.00 3.00–3.10 3.10–3.20 3.20–3.30

No. of persons: 11 29 18 27 15

Calculate the coefficient of skewness and interpret its value.

5.3 Calculate coefficient of variation and Karl Pearson's coefficient of skewness from the data given below:

Marks (less than) : 20 40 60 80 100

No. of students : 18 40 70 90 100

5.4 The following table gives the length of the life (in hours) of 400 TV picture tubes:

Length of Life (in hours)	*No. of Picture Tubes*	*Length of Life (in hours)*	*No. of Picture Tubes*
4000–4199	12	5000–5199	55
4200–4399	30	5200–5399	36
4400–4599	65	5400–5599	25
4600–4799	78	5600–5799	9
4800–4999	90		

Compute the mean, standard deviation, and coefficient of skewness.

5.5 Calculate Karl Pearson's coefficient of skewness from the following data:

Profit (in Rs. lakh) : Below 20 40 60 80 100

No. of companies : 8 20 50 64 70

5.6 From the following information, calculate Karl Pearson's coefficient of skewness.

Measure	*Place A*	*Place B*
Mean	256.5	240.8
Median	201.0	201.6
S.D.	215.0	181.0

5.7 From the following data, calculate Karl Pearson's coefficient of skewness:

Marks (more than) : 0 10 20 30 40 50 60 70 80

No. of students : 150 140 100 80 80 70 30 14 0

5.8 Calculate Bowley's coefficient of skewness from the following data

Sales (in Rs. lakh) : Below 50 60 70 80 90

No. of companies : 8 20 40 65 80

5.9 The following table gives the distribution of weekly wages of 500 workers in a factory:

Weekly Wages (Rs.)	*No. of Workers*
Below 200	10
200–250	25
250–300	145
300–350	220
350–400	70
400 and above	30

(a) Obtain the limits of income of the central 50 per cent of the observed workers.

(b) Calculate Bowley's coefficient of skewness.

5.10 Find Bowley's coefficient of skewness for the following frequency distribution

No. of children per family : 0 1 2 3 4

No. of families : 7 10 16 25 18

5.11 In a frequency distribution, the coefficient of skewness based on quartiles is 0.6. If the sum of the upper and the lower quartiles is 100 and the median is 38, find the value of the upper quartile.

5.12 Calculate Bowley's measure of skewness from the following data:

Payment of Commission	*No. of Salesmen*	*Payment of Commission*	*No. of Salesmen*
100–120	4	200–220	80
120–140	10	220–240	32
140–160	16	240–260	23
160–180	29	260–280	17
180–200	52	280–300	7

Hints and Answers

5.1 $\bar{x} = A + \dfrac{\sum fd}{N} \times h = 170 + \dfrac{393}{1000} \times 20 = 177.86$

$$\text{Mo} = \frac{f_m - f_{m-1}}{2f_m - f_{m-1} - f_{m+1}} \times h$$

$$= 180 + \frac{233}{252} \times 20 = 190.55$$

$$\sigma = h\sqrt{\frac{\sum fd^2}{N} - \left(\frac{\sum fd}{N}\right)^2}$$

$$= 20\sqrt{\frac{1741}{1000} - \left(\frac{393}{1000}\right)^2} = 25.2$$

$$\text{Sk}_p = \frac{\bar{x} - \text{Mo}}{\sigma} = \frac{177.86 - 190.55}{25.2} = -0.5035$$

5.2 $\bar{x} = A + \dfrac{\sum fd}{N} \times h = 3.05 + \dfrac{6}{100} \times 0.1 = 3.056$

$$\text{Mo} = l + \frac{f_m - f_{m-1}}{2f_m - f_{m-1} - f_{m+1}} \times h$$

$$= 2.9 + \frac{29 - 11}{2 \times 29 - 11 - 18} \times 0.1 = 2.962$$

$$\sigma = h\sqrt{\frac{\sum fd^2}{N} - \left(\frac{\sum fd}{N}\right)^2}$$

$$= 0.1\sqrt{\frac{160}{100} - \left(\frac{6}{100}\right)^2} = 0.1264$$

$$\text{Sk}_p = \frac{\bar{x} - \text{Mo}}{\sigma} = \frac{3.056 - 2.962}{0.1264} = 0.744$$

5.3 $\bar{x} = A + \dfrac{\sum fd}{N} \times h = 50 - \dfrac{18}{100} \times 20 = 46.4$

$$\sigma = h\sqrt{\frac{\sum fd^2}{N} - \left(\frac{\sum fd}{N}\right)^2}$$

$$= 20\sqrt{\frac{154}{100} - \left(\frac{-18}{100}\right)^2} = 24.56$$

$$\text{C.V.} = \frac{\sigma}{\bar{x}} \times 100 = \frac{24.56}{46.4} \times 100 = 52.93$$

$$\text{Mo} = l + \frac{f_m - f_{m-1}}{2f_m - f_{m-1} - f_{m+1}} \times h = 39.52;$$

$\text{Sk}_p = 0.280$

5.4 $\bar{x} = A + \dfrac{\sum fd}{N} \times h = 4899.5 - \dfrac{108}{400} \times 200 = 4845.5$

$$\sigma = h\sqrt{\frac{\sum fd^2}{N} - \left(\frac{\sum fd}{N}\right)^2}$$

$$= 200\sqrt{\frac{1368}{400} - \left(\frac{-108}{400}\right)^2} = 365.9$$

Mo = Mode lies in the class 4800–4999 ; but real class interval is 4799.5–4999.5

$$= l + \frac{f_m - f_{m-1}}{2f_m - f_{m-1} - f_{m+1}} \times h$$

$$= 4799.5 + \frac{12}{180 - 78 - 55} \times 200 = 4850.56;$$

$\text{Sk}_p = -0.014$

5.5 $\bar{x} = A + \dfrac{\sum fd}{N} \times h = 50 - \dfrac{2}{70} \times 20 = 49.43$

$$\text{Mo} = l + \frac{f_m - f_{m-1}}{2f_m - f_{m-1} - f_{m+1}} \times h$$

$$= 40 + \frac{14}{12 + 14} \times 20 = 50.76$$

$$\sigma = h\sqrt{\frac{\sum fd^2}{N} - \left(\frac{\sum fd}{N}\right)^2}$$

$$= 20\sqrt{\frac{80}{70} - \left(\frac{-2}{70}\right)^2} = 21.64;$$

$\text{Sk}_p = -0.061$

5.6 $a \cong \bar{x}$ and $z \cong \text{Mo}$;

Place A : Mode = 3Med – 2$\bar{x}$ = 90;

$$\text{Sk}_p = \frac{266.5 - 90}{215} = 0.823$$

Place B : Mode = 3Med – 2$\bar{x}$ = 123.2;

$$\text{Sk}_p = \frac{240.8 - 123.2}{181} = 0.649$$

5.7

Marks	*No. of Students*
0–10	10
10–20	40
20–30	20
30–40	0
40–50	10
50–60	40
60–70	16
70–80	14

$\bar{x} = 39.27$; $\sigma = 22.81$;

$$Sk_p = \frac{3(\bar{x} - \text{Med})}{\sigma} = \frac{3(39.27 - 45)}{22.81}$$

$= -0.754.$

5.8 Q_1 lies in the class 50–60; $Q_1 = 60$; Q_3 lies in the class 70–80; $Q_3 = 78$

Median ($= Q_2$) lies in the class 60–70; Med = 70

$$\text{Bowley's coeff. of } Sk_b = \frac{Q_3 + Q_1 - 2\text{Med}}{Q_3 - Q_1}$$

$= -0.111$

5.9 $Q_1 = (80/4) = 20$th observation lies in the class 250–300; $Q_1 = 281.03$; $Q_3 = (3 \times 80)/4 = 60$th observation lies in the class 300–350;

$Q_3 = 344.32$

Median lies in the class 300–350, Me = 315.9

Bowley's coeff. of $Sk_b = -0.111$ (negatively skewed distribution)

5.10 $Q_1 = \text{size of } \left(\frac{n+1}{4}\right)$th observation = 24th observation = 2

$Q_3 = \text{size of } \frac{3(n+1)}{4}$th observation = 72th observation = 4

$\text{Me} = \text{size of } \left(\frac{n+1}{2}\right)$th observation = 48th observation; $Sk_b = \frac{4 + 2 - 2(3)}{4 - 2} = 0$

5.11 Given $Sk_b = 0.6$; $Q_1 + Q_3 = 100$; Me = 38; $Q_3 = ?$

$$Sk_b = \frac{Q_3 + Q_1 - 2\text{Me}}{Q_3 - Q_1} \text{ or}$$

$$0.6 = \frac{100 - 2(38)}{Q_3 - (100 - Q_3)} \text{ or } Q_3 = 70$$

5.12 $Q_1 = (n/4)$th observation = 67.5th observation lies in class 180–200;

$Q_1 = 183.26$

$Q_3 = \left(\frac{3n}{4}\right)$th observation = 202.5th observation lies in class 220–240;

$Q_3 = 227.187$

Me = $(n/2)$th observation = 135th observation lies in class 200–220;

Me = 206

$$Sk_b = \frac{Q_3 + Q_1 - 2\text{Me}}{Q_3 - Q_1} = -0.035$$

5.3 KURTOSIS

The measure of kurtosis, describes the degree of concentration of frequencies (observations) in a given distribution. That is, whether the observed values are concentrated more around the mode (a peaked curve) or away from the mode towards both tails of the frequency curve.

The word '**kurtosis**' comes from a Greek word meaning 'humped'. In statistics, it refers to the degree of flatness or peakedness in the region about the mode of a frequency curve. A few definitions of kurtosis are as follows:

- *The degree of kurtosis of a distribution is measured relative to the peakedness of a normal curve.* —Simpson and Kafka
- *A measure of kurtosis indicates the degree to which a curve of a frequency distribution is peaked or flat-topped.* —Croxten and Cowden
- *Kurtosis refers to the degree of peakedness of hump of the distribution.* —C. H. Meyers

Two or more distributions may have identical average, variation, and skewness, but they may show different degrees of concentration of values of observations around the mode, and hence may show different degrees of peakedness of the hump of the distributions as shown in Fig. 5.2.

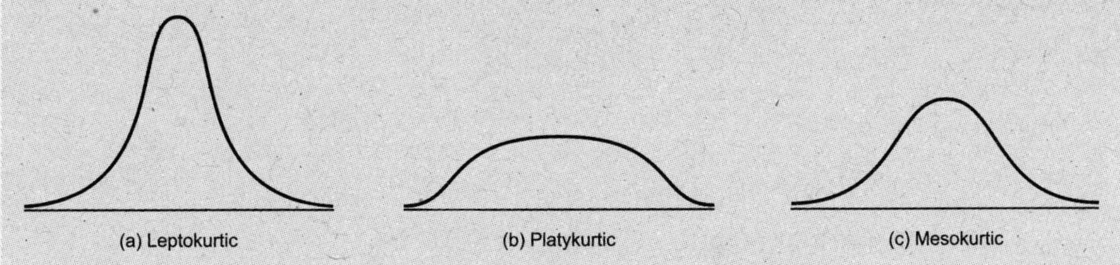

Figure 5.2 Shape of Three Different Curves Introduced by Karl Pearson

5.3.1 Measures of Kurtosis

The fourth standardized moment α_4 (or β_2) is a measure of *flatness or peakedness* of a single *humped* distribution (also called *Kurtosis*). For a normal distribution $\alpha_4 = \beta_2 = 3$ so that $\gamma_2 = 0$ and hence any distribution having $\beta_2 > 3$ will be peaked more sharply than the normal curve known as ***leptokurtic*** (narrow) while if $\beta_2 < 3$, the distribution is termed as ***platykurtic*** (broad).

The value of β_2 is helpful in selecting an appropriate measure of central tendency and variation to describe a frequency distribution. For example, if $\beta_2 = 3$, mean is preferred; if $\beta_2 > 3$ (leptokurtic distribution), median is preferred; while for $\beta_2 < 3$ (platykurtic distribution), quartile range is suitable.

Remark: W. S. Gosset, explained different shapes of frequency curves as: Platykurtic curves, like the platypas, are squat with short tails; leptokurtic curves are high with long tails like the Kangaroos noted for leaping.

Example 5.11: The first four moments of a distribution about the value 5 of the variable are 2, 20, 40, and 50. Show that the mean is 7. Also find the other moments, β_1 and β_2, and comment upon the nature of the distribution.

Solution: From the data of the problem, we have

$$\mu_1' = 2,\ \mu_2' = 20,\ \mu_3' = 40,\ \mu_4' = 40 \text{ and } A = 5$$

Now the moments about the arbitrary point 5 are calculated as follows:

$$\text{Mean, } \bar{x} = \mu_1' + A = 2 + 5 = 7$$

$$\text{Variance, } \mu_2 = \mu_2' - (\mu_1')^2 = 20 - (2)^2 = 16$$

$$\mu_3 = \mu_3' - 3\mu_1'\mu_2' + 2(\mu_1')^3 = 40 - 3(2)(20) + 2(2)^3 = -64$$

$$\mu_4 = \mu_4' - 4\mu_1'\mu_3' + 6\mu_2'(\mu_1')^2 - 3(\mu_1')^4$$
$$= 50 - 4(2)(40) + 6(20)(2)^2 - 3(2)^4 = 162$$

The two constants, β_1 and β_2, calculated from central moments are as follows:

$$\beta_1 = \frac{\mu_3^2}{\mu_2^3} = \frac{(-64)^2}{(16)^3} = \frac{4096}{4096} = 1$$

$$\beta_2 = \frac{\mu_4}{\mu_2^2} = \frac{162}{(16)^2} = \frac{162}{256} = 0.63$$

$$\gamma_1 = \frac{\mu_3}{\mu_2^{3/2}} = \frac{-64}{(16)^{3/2}} = -1\ (< 0), \text{ distribution is negatively skewed.}$$

$$\gamma_2 = \beta_2 - 3 = 0.63 - 3 = -2.37\ (< 0), \text{ distribution is platykurtic.}$$

Example 5.12: Find the standard deviation and kurtosis of the following set of data pertaining to kilowatt hours (kwh) of electricity consumed by 100 persons in a city.

Consumption (in kwh)	:	0–10	10–20	20–30	30–40	40–50
Number of users	:	10	20	40	20	10

Solution: The calculations for standard deviation and kurtosis are shown in Table 5.5.

Table 5.5 Calculations of Standard Deviation and Kurtosis

Consumption (in kwh)	*Number of Users* (f)	*Mid-Value* (m)	$d = (m - A)/10$ $= (m - 25)/10$	$-fd$	fd^2
0–10	10	5	–2	–20	40
10–20	20	15	–1	–20	20
20–30	40	(25) ← A	0	0	0
30–40	20	35	1	20	20
40–50	10	45	2	20	40
	100			0	120

$$\bar{x} = A + \frac{\Sigma fd}{N} \times h = 25 + \frac{0}{100} \times 10 = 25$$

Since $\bar{x} = 25$ is an integer value, therefore we may calculate moments about the actual mean

$$\mu_r = \frac{1}{n}\Sigma f(x - \bar{x})^r = \frac{1}{n}\Sigma f(m - \bar{x})^r$$

Let $d = \dfrac{m - \bar{x}}{h}$ or $(m - \bar{x}) = hd$. Therefore

$$\mu_r = h^r \frac{1}{n}\Sigma fd^r\ ; \quad h = \text{width of class intervals}$$

The calculations for moments are shown in Table 5.6.

Table 5.6 Calculations for Moments

Mid-value (m)	*Frequency* (f)	$d = \dfrac{m-25}{10}$	fd	fd^2	fd^3	fd^4
5	10	–2	–20	40	–80	160
15	20	–1	–20	20	–20	20
(25) ← A	40	0	0	0	0	0
35	20	1	20	20	20	20
45	10	2	20	40	80	160
	100		0	120	0	360

Moments about the origin A = 25 are:

$$\mu_1 = h\frac{1}{N}\Sigma fd = 10 \times \frac{1}{100} = 0$$

$$\mu_2 = h^2\frac{1}{N}\Sigma fd^2 = (10)^2\frac{1}{100}\times 120 = 120$$

$$\mu_3 = h^3\frac{1}{N}\Sigma fd^3 = (10)^3\frac{1}{100}\times 0 = 0$$

$$\mu_4 = h^4\frac{1}{N}\Sigma fd^4 = (10)^4\frac{1}{100}\times 360 = 36{,}000$$

$$\text{S.D. } (\sigma) = \sqrt{\mu_2} = \sqrt{120} = 10.95$$

Karl Pearson's measure of kurtosis is given by

$$\beta_2 = \frac{\mu_4}{\mu_2^2} = \frac{36{,}000}{(120)^2} = 2.5$$

and therefore $\gamma_2 = \beta_2 - 3 = 2.5 - 3 = -0.50$

Since $\beta_2 < 3$ (or $\gamma_2 < 0$), distribution curve is platykurtic.

Example 5.13: Calculate the first four moments about the mean from the following data. Also calculate the value of β_1 and β_2 :

Marks :	0–10	10–20	20–30	30–40	40–50	50–60	60–70
No. of Students :	5	12	18	40	15	7	3

[*Delhi Unit., BCom(Hons), 1997*]

Solution: Calculations for first moments are shown below:

Marks X	*Mid Value*	*No. of Students* f	$d = X - 35$	$d' = d/10$	fd'	fd'^2	fd'^3	fd'^4
0–10	5	5	– 30	– 3	– 15	45	– 135	405
10–20	15	12	– 20	– 2	– 24	48	– 96	192
20–30	25	18	– 10	– 1	– 18	18	– 18	18
30–40	35	40	0	0	0	0	0	0
40–50	45	45	10	1	15	15	15	15
50–60	55	7	20	2	14	28	56	112
60–70	65	3	30	3	9	27	81	243
		100			– 19	181	– 97	985

$$\mu_1' = \text{First moment about } 35 = \frac{\Sigma fd'}{\Sigma V}\times 10 = \frac{-19}{100}\times 10 = -1.9$$

$$\mu_2' = \text{Second moment about } 35 = \frac{\Sigma fd'^2}{\Sigma f}\times (10)^2 = \frac{181}{100}\times 100 = 181$$

$$\mu'_3 = \frac{\Sigma fd'^4}{\Sigma f} \times (10)^4 = \frac{985}{100} \times 10000 = 98500$$

Now the moments about the arbitrary point are calculated as follows:

$$\mu_1 = 0$$

$$\mu_2 = \mu'_2 - \mu'^2_1 = 181 - (-1.9)^2 = 177.39$$

$$\mu_3 = \mu'_3 - 3\mu'_2\,\mu'_1 + (2\mu'_1)^3$$

$$= -970 - 3 \times 181 \times (-1.9) + 2(-1.9)3 = 47.982$$

$$\mu_4 = \mu'_4 - 4\mu'_1\,\mu'_3, + 6\mu'_2\,(\mu'_1)^2 - 3\mu'_1)^4$$

$$= 98500 - 4(-970)(-1.9) + 6(181)\,(-1.9)^2 - 3(-1.9)^4$$

$$= 98500 - 7372 + 3920.46 - 39.096 = 95009.364$$

$$\beta_1 = \frac{\mu_3^2}{\mu_2^3} = \frac{(47.982)^2}{(177.39)^3} = 0.0203$$

$$\beta_2 = \frac{\mu_4}{\mu_2^2} = \frac{95009.364}{(177.39)^2} = 3.019$$

Example 5.14: From the following data, calculate moments about assumed mean 25 and convert them into central moments :

x :	0–10	10–20	20–30	30–40
f :	1	3	4	2

[*Delhi Univ., BCom(Hons), 2000*]

Solution: Calculations for moments about assumed mean, A = 25, are shown below:

x	*Mid – value(m)*	f	$x - 25 = d$	$(x-25)^2 = d^2$	$(x-25)^3 = d^3$	$f(x-25) = fd$	$f(x-25)^2 = fd^2$	$f(x-25)^3 = fd^3$	$f(x-25)^4 = fd^4$
0–10	5	1	– 20	400	– 8.000	– 20	400	– 8000	1,60.000
10–20	15	3	– 10	100	– 1.000	– 30	300	– 3000	30,000
20–30	25	4	0	0	0	0	0	0	0
30–40	35	2	10	100	1,000	20	200	2000	20,000
		10				– 30	900	– 9000	2,10.000

$$\mu'_1 = \text{First moment about 25} = \frac{\Sigma fd}{\Sigma f} = \frac{-30}{10} = -3$$

$$\mu'_2 = \text{Second moment about 25} = \frac{\Sigma fd^2}{\Sigma f} = \frac{900}{10} = 90$$

$$\mu'_3 = \text{Third moment about 25} = \frac{\Sigma fd^3}{\Sigma f} = \frac{-9000}{10} = -900$$

$$\mu'_4 = \text{Fourth moment about 25} = \frac{\Sigma fd^4}{\Sigma f} = \frac{2{,}10{,}000}{10} = 21{,}000$$

$\mu_1 = 0$

$\mu_2 = \mu'_2 - \mu'^2_1 = 90 - 9 = 81$

$\mu_3 = \mu'_3 - 2\mu'_2\,\mu'_1 + 2(\mu'_1)^3$

$= -900 - 3 \times 90 \times -3 + 2 \times (-3)^3 = -900 + 810 - 54 = -144$

$\mu_4 = \mu'_4 - 4\mu'_3\,\mu'_1 + 6\mu'_2\,(\mu'_1)^2 - 3(\mu'_1)^4$

$= 21{,}000 - 4(-900)(-3) + 6 \times 90\,(-3)^2 - 3(-3)^4$

$= 21{,}000 - 10{,}800 + 4860 - 243 = 14{,}817.$

Example 5.15: The first four moments of a distribution about value 2 are 1, 2.5, 5.5 and 16 respectively. Calculate the four moments about mean and comment on the nature of the distribution.

[*Delhi Univ., BCom(Hons), 2002*]

Solution: The moments about the arbitrary value 2 are : $\mu'_1 = 1$, $\mu'_2 = 2.5$, $\mu'_3 = 5.5$ and $\mu'_4 = 16$

The calculations for moments about mean from the given moments are shown below :

$\mu_1 = 0$

$\mu_2 = \mu'_2 - (\mu'_1)^2 = 2.5 - (1)2 = 1.5$

$\mu_3 = \mu'_3 - 3\mu'_1\,\mu'_2 + 2(\mu'_1)^3 = 5.5 - 3(1)(2.5) + 2(1)^3 = 5.5 - 7.5 + 2 = 0$

$\mu_4 = \mu'_4 - 4\mu'_1\,\mu'_3 + 6(\mu_1')^2\,\mu'_2 - 3(\mu'_1)^4 = 16 - 4(1)(5.5) + 6(2.5)(1)^2 - 3(1)^4$

$= 16 - 22 + 15 - 3 = 6$

The values of β_1 and β_2 to comment upon the nature of distribution are:

$$\beta_1 = \frac{\mu_3^2}{\mu_2^3} = \frac{0}{(1.5)^3} = 0$$

Since $\beta_1 = 0$, the distribution is symmetrical.

$$\beta_2 = \frac{\mu_4}{\mu_2^2} = \frac{6}{(1.5)^2} = \frac{6}{2.25} = 2.6$$

Since $\beta_2 < 3$, the distribution curve is platykurtic.

Example 5.16: Find the four moments about mean from the following data. Also decide whether it is a platykurtic distribution.

Central size of item :	1	2	3	4	5
Frequency :	2	3	5	4	1

[*Delhi Univ., BCom(Hons) 1996*]

Solution: The calculations for first four moments about the value 3 are shown below:

x	f	$d = x - 3$	fd	fd^2	fd^3	fd^4
1	2	– 2	– 4	8	– 16	32
2	3	– 1	– 3	3	– 3	3
3	5	0	0	0	0	0
4	4	1	4	4	4	4
5	1	2	2	4	8	16
	15		– 1	19	– 7	55

Let $A = 3$. Then $d = x - 3$. Thus

$$\mu'_1 = \frac{\Sigma fd}{N} = \frac{-1}{15} = -0.07; \quad \mu'_2 = \frac{\Sigma fd^2}{N} = \frac{19}{15} = 1.27$$

$$\mu_3' = \frac{\Sigma fd^3}{N} = \frac{-7}{15} = -0.47; \quad \mu_4' = \frac{\Sigma fd^4}{N} = \frac{55}{15} = 3.67$$

Central moments or moments about mean are given by

$$\mu_1 = 0,$$

$$\mu_2 = \mu_2' - \mu_1'^2 = 1.27 - (-0.07)^2 = 1.27 - 0.0049 = 1.2651$$

$$\mu_3 = \mu_3' - 3\mu'_2\,\mu_1' + 2\mu_1'^3$$

$$= -0.47 - 3(1.2651)(-0.07) + 2(-0.07)^3 = -0.205015$$

$$\mu_4 = \mu_4' - 4\mu_3'\,\mu_1' + 6\mu'_2(\mu'_1)^2 - 3(\mu'_1)^4$$

$$= 3.67 - 4(-0.21)(-0.07) + 6(1.27)(-0.07)^2 - 3(-0.07)^4 = 3.648466$$

$$\beta_2 = \frac{\mu_4}{\mu_2^2} = \frac{3.6}{(1.2651)^2} = \frac{3.6}{1.6} = 2.25$$

Since $\beta_2 < 3$, therefore distribution is platykurtic.

Example 5.17: If $\beta_1 = 1$ and $\beta_2 = 4$ and variance = 9, find the values of μ_3 and μ_4. Comment upon the nature of the distribution. *[Delhi Univ., BCom(Hons), 1995]*

Solution: Givne $\beta_1 = 1$, $\beta_2 = 4$, and $\sigma^2 = 9$. We know that

$$\beta_1 = \frac{\mu_3^2}{\mu_2^3}$$

or

$$1 = \frac{\mu_3^2}{(9)^3} \text{ [since } \mu_2 = \sigma^2 = 9]$$

$$\mu_3^2 = 729, \text{ i.e. } \mu_3 = \sqrt{729} = 27$$

Also

$$\beta_2 = \frac{\mu_4}{\mu_2^2} \text{ or } 4 = \frac{\mu_4}{(9)^2}, \text{ i.e. } \mu_4 = 324.$$

Example 5.18: In a certain distribution, the first four moments about 5 are 2, 20, 40, 50. Calculate β_1 and β_2. State whether the distribution is leptokurtic or platykurtic.

[Delhi Univ., B.Com (Hons), 2006]

Solution: Given, $A = 5$, $\mu_1' = 2$, $\mu_2' = 20$, $\mu_3' = 40$, $\mu_4' = 50$. Values of central moments are calculated as follows:

$$\mu_1 = 0$$

$$\mu_2 = \mu'_2 - \mu'^2_1 = 20 - (2)^2 = 16$$

$$\mu_3 = \mu'_3 - 3\mu'_2\,\mu'_1 + (2\mu'_1)^3 = 40 - 3(20)(2) + 2(2)^3$$

$$= 40 - 120 + 16 = -64$$

$$\mu_4 = \mu'_4 - 4\mu'_1\mu'_3 + 6\mu'_2(\mu'_1)^2 - 3(\mu'_1)^4 = 50 - 4(2)(40) + 6(20)(2)^2 - 3(2)^4$$

$$= 50 - 320 + 480 - 48 = 162$$

$$\beta_1 = \frac{\mu_3^2}{\mu_2^3} = \frac{(-64)^2}{(16)^3} = 1$$

$$\beta_2 = \frac{\mu_4}{\mu_2^2} = \frac{162}{(16)^2} = 0.633$$

Since $\beta_2 < 3$, distribution is platykurtic.

Example 5.19: For a distribution the mean is 10, standard deviation is 4, $\sqrt{\beta_1} = 1$ and $\beta_2 = 4$. Obtain the first four moments about the origin, i.e., zero. *[Delhi Univ., BCom(Hons), 1992]*

Solution: Givne $\mu_2 = \sigma^2 = (4)^2 = 16$. Also $\sqrt{\beta_1} = 1$ or $\beta_1 = 1$. Thus

$$\beta_2 = \frac{\mu_4}{(\mu_2)^2} \quad \text{or} \quad 4 = \frac{\mu_4}{(16)^2}, \text{ i.e. } \mu_4 = 4 \times (16)^2 = 4 \times 256 = 1024$$

Also $$\beta_1 = \frac{(\mu_3)^2}{(\mu_2)^3} \quad \text{or} \quad 1 = \frac{(\mu_3)^2}{(16)^3}, \text{ i.e. } \mu_3^2 = (16)^3 = 4096 \quad \text{or} \quad \mu_3 = \sqrt{4096} = 64$$

Now moments about zero (i.e. original):

$$v_1 = \bar{x} = 10$$
$$v_2 = \mu_2 + (v_1)^2 = 16 + (10)^2 = 116$$
$$v_3 = \mu_3 + 3v_2v_1 - 2(v_1)^3 = 64 + 3(116)(10) - 2(10)^3$$
$$= 64 + 3480 - 2000 = 1544$$
$$v_4 = \mu_4 + 4v_3v_1 - 6V_2(v_1)^2 + 3(v_1)^4$$
$$= 1024 + 4(1544)(10) - 6(116)(10)^2 + 3(10)^4$$
$$= 1024 + 61760 - 69600 + 30000 = 23184$$

Example 5.20: Given the following information: $N = 100$, $\Sigma(x - 98) = 50$, $\Sigma(x - 98)^2 = 1970$; $\Sigma(x - 98)^3 = 2948$, $\Sigma(x - 98)^4 = 86752$. Do you think that the distribution is platykurtic?

[Delhi Univ., BCom(Hons),1993]

Solution: The most important measure of Kurtosis is the value of coefficient β_2. It is defined as

$$\beta_2 = \mu_2/(\mu_2)^2$$

where μ_4 = 4th moment and μ_2 = 2nd moment

The greater the value of β_2, more peaked the distribution will be. Let $d = \Sigma(x - 98)$. Then

$$\beta'_1 = \frac{\Sigma d}{n} = \frac{50}{100} = 0.5$$

$$\beta'_2 = \frac{\Sigma d^2}{n} = \frac{1970}{100} = 19.70$$

$$\beta'_3 = \frac{\Sigma d^3}{n} = \frac{2948}{100} = 29.48,$$

$$\beta'_4 = \frac{\Sigma d^4}{n} = \frac{86752}{100} = 867.52$$

$$\mu_2 = \beta'_2 - (\beta'_1)^2 = 19.70 - (0.5)^2 = 19.70 - 0.25 = 19.45$$
$$\mu_3 = \beta'_3 - 3\beta'_1\,\beta'_2 + 2\beta'^3_1 = 29.48 - 3(0.5)(19.70) + 2(0.5)^3 = 0.18$$
$$\mu_4 = \beta'_4 - 4\beta'_1\,\beta'_3 + 6\beta'_2\,(\beta'_1)^2 - 3(\beta'_1)$$
$$\mu_4 = 867.52 - 4(0.5)\,(29.48) + 6(19.70)\,(0.5)^2 - 3(0.5)^4 = 837.92$$

$$\beta_2 = \frac{\mu_4}{\mu_2^2} = \frac{837.9225}{378.3025} = 2.215$$

Since the value of β_2 is less than 3, the distribution is platykurtic.

Example 5.21: The first four moments from mean of a distribution are 0, 2.5, 0.7 and 18.75. The mean value is 11. Comment on the skewness and kurtosis of the distribution.

Solution: The measure of Skewness, β_1 is given by

and $$\beta_1 = \frac{\mu_3^2}{\mu_2^3} = \frac{0.7^2}{2.5^3} = \frac{0.49}{15.62} = 0.031(\text{Given})$$

Since $\beta_1 \neq 0$, distribution is not perfectly symmetrical, it is skewed. Further β_2 is the measure of Kurtosis,

$$\beta_2 = \frac{\mu_4}{\mu_2^2} = \frac{18.75}{(2.5)^2} = \frac{18.75}{6.25} = 3$$

Since $\beta_2 = 3$, distribution is mesokurtic.

Example 5.22: The first four moments of the distribution about $x = 4$ are 1, 4, 10, 45. Obtain the various characteristics of the distribution on the basis of information given. Comment on the nature of distribution. *[Delhi Univ., BCom(Hons), 2003]*

Solution: Given: $A = 4$, $\mu'_1 = 1$, $\mu'_2 = 4$, $\mu'_3 = 10$ and $\mu'_4 = 45$. Calculating central moments to obtain the various characteristics of the distribution as follows:

$$\mu_1 = 0$$
$$\mu_2 = \mu'_2 - (\mu'_1)^2 = 4 - (1)^2 = 4 - 1 = 3$$
$$\mu_2 = \mu'_3 - 3\mu'_2\,\mu'_1 + 2(\mu'_1)^3 = 10 - 3(4)(1) + 2(1)^3 = 0$$
$$\mu_4 = \mu'_4 - 4\mu'_3\,\mu'_1 + 6\mu'_2\,\mu'^2_1 - 3(\mu'_1)^4$$
$$= 45 - 4(10)(1) + 6(4)(1)^2 - 3(1)^4 = 26$$

Since $\mu_2 = \sigma^2 = 3$, therefore $\sigma = \sqrt{3} = 1.732$. Also $v_1 = A + \mu_1{}' = 4 + 1 = 5$, therefore Mean = 5 and coefficient of Skewness based on moments

$\beta_1 = \frac{\mu_3^2}{\mu_2^3} = \frac{0^2}{3^3} = 0$. This implies that the distribution is symmetrical. The measure of kurtosis β_2 is:

$\beta_2 = \frac{\mu_4}{\mu_2^2} = \frac{26}{(3)^2} = \frac{26}{9} = 2.89\ (< 3)$, distribution is platykurtik.

Example 5.23: Examine whether the following results of a piece of computation for obtaining the second central moments are consistent or not : $N = 120$, $\Sigma fx = -125$, $\Sigma fx^2 = 128$ *[Delhi Univ., BCom(Hons), 2005]*

Solution: Second central moment, $\mu_2\ (= \sigma^2) = \frac{\Sigma fx^2}{N} - \left(\frac{\Sigma fx}{N}\right)^2 = \frac{128}{120} - \left(\frac{-125}{120}\right)^2$

$$= 1.066 - 1.085 = -0.019, \text{ which is negative}$$

Since μ_2 being variance can never be negative, information is not consistent.

Example 5.24: For a distribution, mean = 10, variance = 16, $\gamma_1 = 1$, $\beta_2 = 4$. Obtain the first four moments about origin, i.e. zero. Comment upon the nature of distribution. *[Delhi Univ., BCom(Hons), 2005]*

Solution: Given, Mean $\bar{x} = 10$, Var, $\sigma^2 = 16$, $\gamma_1 = 2$, $\beta_2 = 4$. Thus

First moment about zero, $v_1\ (= \bar{x}) = 10$

Var $\sigma_2 = \mu_2 =$ second moment about mean = 16

Second moment about zero, $v_2 = \mu_2 + v_1^2 = 16 + (10)^2 = 116$

Now $\gamma_1 = \sqrt{\beta_1}$ or $\gamma_1^2 = \beta_1$, i.e. $\beta_1 = 1$

We know that $\beta_1 = \dfrac{\mu_3^2}{\mu_2^3}$ or $1 = \dfrac{\mu_3^2}{(16)^3}$, i.e. $\mu_3 = 64$.

Third moment about zero, $v_3 = \mu_3 + 3\,v_2\,v_1 - 2v_1^3$

$= 64 + 3(116)\,(10) - 2(10)^3 = 64 + 3480 - 2000 = 1544$

We are given that $\beta_2 = 4$, so $\beta_2 = \dfrac{\mu_4}{\mu_2^2} = 4$ or $\mu_4 = 4\mu_2^2 = 4(16)^2 = 1024$

Fourth Moment about zero, $v_4 = \mu_4 + 4v_3v_1 - 6v_2v_1^{\,2} + 3v_1^{\,4}$

$= 1024 + 4(1544)\,(10) - 6(116)(10)^2 + (10)^4$

$= 1024 + 61760 - 69600 + 30000 = 23184.$

Conceptual Questions 5B

8. What do you understand by the terms skewness and kurtosis? Point out their role in analysing a frequency distribution.

9. Averages, dispersion, skewness, and kurtosis are complementary to one another in understanding a frequency distribution? Elucidate.

10. Explain how the measure of skewness and kurtosis can be used in describing a frequency distribution.

11. Explain the terms 'skewness' and 'kurtosis' used in connection with the frequency distribution of a continuous variable. Give the different measures of skewness (any two of the measures to be given) and kurtosis.

12. What do you mean by 'kurtosis' in statistics? Explain one of the methods of measuring it.

Self-Practice Problems 5B

5.13 Explain whether the following results of a piece of computation for obtaining the second central moment are consistent or not;

$n = 120,\ \Sigma f x = -125,\ \Sigma f x^2 = 128.$

5.14 The first four central moments are 0, 4, 8, and 144. Examine the skewness and kurtosis.

5.15 Compute the first four moments about the mean from the following data:

Mid-value of variate :	5	10	15	20	25	30	35
Frequency :	8	15	20	32	23	17	5

Comment upon the nature of the distribution.

5.16 A record was kept over a period of 6 months by a sales manager to determine the average number of calls made per day by his six salesmen. The results are shown below:

Salesmen :	A	B	C	D	E	F
Average number of calls per day :	8	10	12	15	7	5

(a) Compute a measure of skewness. Is the distribution symmetrical?

(b) Compute a measure of kurtosis. What does this measure mean?

5.17 Find the second, third, and fourth central moments of the frequency distribution given below. Hence find the measure of skewness and a measure of kurtosis of the following distribution:

Class limits	Frequency
100–104.9	7
105–109.9	13
110–114.9	25
115–119.9	25
120–124.9	30

5.18 Find the first four moments about the mean for the following distribution:

Class Interval :	60–62	63–65	66–68	69–71	72–74
Frequency :	5	18	42	27	8

5.19 Find the variance, skewness, and kurtosis of the following frequency distribution by the method of moments:

Class interval :	0–10	10–20	20–30	30–40
Frequency :	1	4	3	2

5.20 Find the kurtosis for the following distribution

Class interval :	0–10	10–20	20–30	30–40
Frequency :	1	3	4	2

Comment on the nature of the distribution.

Hints and Answers

5.13 $\mu_2 = \sum fx^2/N - (\sum fx/N)^2$
$= 128/120 - (-125/120)^2 = -0.0146$
since σ^2 cannot be negative, therefore the data is inconsistent.

5.14 $\beta_1 = \mu_3^2/\mu_2^3 = 2/(4)^3 = 1; \quad \gamma_1 = +\sqrt{\beta_1} = 1$
$\beta_2 = \mu_4/\mu_2^2 = 144/(4)^2 = 9; \quad \gamma_2 = \beta_2 - 3 = 6$

5.16 $\beta_1 = 0.11; \quad \beta_2 = 1.97$

5.17 $\mu_2 = 54; \quad \mu_3 = 100.5, \mu_4 = 7827;$
$\gamma_1 = +\sqrt{\beta_1} = 0.2533; \quad \gamma_2 = \beta_2 - 3 = -0.3158$

5.18 $\mu_1 = 0, \quad \mu_2 = 8.527, \quad \mu_3 = -2.693,$
$\mu_4 = 199.375$

5.19 $\sigma^2 = \mu_2 = 84, \quad \gamma_1 = +\sqrt{\beta_1} = 0.0935;$
$\beta_2 = 2.102$

5.20 $\mu_2 = 81, \quad \mu_2 = 14817; \quad \beta_2 = \mu_4/\mu_2^2 = 2.26$

Formulae Used

1. Absolute measure of skewness
   $Sk = \bar{x} - \text{Mode or } Q_3 + Q_1 - 2\text{ Med}$
2. Coefficient of skewness
   Karl Pearson's
   $$Sk_p = \frac{\bar{x} - \text{Mo}}{\sigma} \quad \text{or} \quad \frac{3(\bar{x} - \text{Med})}{\sigma}$$
   $$\text{Bowley's, } Sk_b = \frac{Q_3 + Q_1 - 2\text{Med}}{Q_3 - Q_1}$$
   $$\text{Kelly's, } Sk_k = \frac{P_{90} + P_{10} - 2P_{50}}{P_{90} - P_{10}}$$
   $$\text{or} \quad \frac{D_9 + D_1 - 2D_5}{D_9 - D_1}$$
5. Kurtosis $\quad \gamma_1 = \sqrt{\beta_1} = \dfrac{\mu_3}{\mu_2^{3/2}}$
   $$\gamma_2 = \beta_2 - 3 = \frac{\mu_4}{\mu_2^2} - 3$$
6. For a normal curve, $\beta_2 = 3$ or $\gamma_2 = 0$; for a leptokurtic curve, $\beta_2 > 3$ or $\gamma_2 > 0$ and for a platykurtic curve, $\beta_2 < 3$ or $\gamma_2 < 0$.

Review Self-Practice Problems

5.21 Find the coefficient of skewness from the following information:

Difference of two quartiles = 8; Mode = 1;

Sum of two quartiles = 22; Mean = 8.

[Delhi Univ., BCom (H), 1997]

5.22 From the data given below calculate the coefficient of variation:

Karl pearson's coefficient of skewness = 0.42

Arithmetic mean = 86

Median = 80

[Osmania Univ., BCom, 1998]

5.23 In a frequency distribution, the coefficient of skewness based on quartiles is 0.6. If the sum of upper and lower quartiles is 100 and the median is 38, find the value of the upper quartile.

5.24 The daily expenditure (in Rs.) of 100 families is given below

Daily expenditure :	0–20	20–40	40–60	60–80	80–100
Number of families :	13	f_2	27	f_4	16

If mode of the distribution is 44, calculate Karl Pearson's coefficient of skewness.

5.25 Pearson's coefficient of skewness for a distribution is 0.4 and coefficient of variance is 30 per cent. Its mode is 88. Find the mean and median.

5.26 The following table gives the distribution of monthly wages of 500 workers in a factory:

Monthly Wages (Rs. hundred)	*Number of Workers*	*Monthly Wages (Rs. hundred)*	*Number of Workers*
15–20	10	30–35	220
20–25	25	35–40	70
25–30	145	40–45	30

Compute Karl Pearson's and Bowley's coefficient of skewness. Interpret your answer.

Hints and Answers

5.21 Mode = 3 Median – 2 Mean

or 11 = 3 Med – 2 × 8 or Med = 9

$Q_3 + Q_1 = 22$ and $Q_3 - Q_1 = 8$, i.e.,

$Q_3 = 15, Q_1 = 7$

$$\text{Coefficient of skewness} = \frac{Q_3 + Q_1 - 2\text{Med}}{Q_3 - Q_1}$$

$$= \frac{15 + 7 - 2(9)}{8} = 0.5$$

5.22 Mode = 3 Median – 2 Mean = 3 (80) – 2 (86) = 68

$$\text{Coefficient of skewness} = \frac{\bar{x} - \text{Mode}}{\sigma}$$

$$\text{or} \quad 0.42 = \frac{86 - 68}{\sigma} \quad \text{or} \quad \sigma = 42.86$$

Coefficient of variation (CV)

$$= \frac{\sigma}{\bar{x}} \times 100 = \frac{42.86}{68} \times 100 = 49.84 \text{ per cent.}$$

5.23 Given Sk = 0.6, $Q_1 + Q_3 = 100$, Med = 38

$$Sk_b = \frac{Q_3 + Q_1 - 2\text{Med}}{Q_3 - Q_1}$$

$$\text{or } 0.6 = \frac{100 - 2 \times 38}{Q_3 - Q_1}$$

$$= \frac{100 - 76}{Q_3 - (100 - Q_3)} \text{ or } Q_3 = 70$$

5.24 Let the frequency for the class 20–40 be f_2. Then frequency for the class 60–80 will be

$$f_4 = 100\,(13 + f_2 + 27 + 16) = 44 - f_2$$

Expenditure	*Number of Families (f)*	*Cumulative Frequency (cf)*
0–20	13	13
20–40	f_2	$13 - f_2$
40–60	27	$40 - f_2$
60–80	$44 - f_2$	84
80–100	16	100

$$\text{Mode} = l + \frac{f_m - f_{m-1}}{2f_m - f_{m-1} - f_{m+1}} \times h$$

$$= 40 + \frac{27 - f_2}{54 - f_2 - 44 + f_2} \times 20$$

or $f_2 = 25$

Thus frequency for the class 20–40 is 25 and for the class 60–80 is 44 – 25 = 19

Apply the formula, $Sk_p = \frac{\bar{x} - Mo}{\sigma} = \frac{50 - 44}{25.3}$

$= 0.237$

5.25 Given $Sk_p = 0.4$, $CV = 0.30$, Mode = 88

$$Sk_p = \frac{\bar{x} - Mo}{\sigma} = \frac{1 - (M_0/\bar{x})}{(\sigma/\bar{x})} = \frac{1 - (88/\bar{x})}{0.30};$$

$CV = \sigma/\bar{x}$ or $0.30 = \sigma/\bar{x}$

$\frac{88}{\bar{x}} = 1 - 0.4 \times 0.3 = 0.88$ or $\bar{x} = 100$

Also, Mode = 3 Med – 2 $\bar{x}$

or 88 = 3 Med – 2 (100) or Med = 96

Glossary of Terms

Measure of skewness: The statistical technique to indicate the direction and extent of skewness in the distribution of numerical values in the data set.

Moments: Represent a convenient and unifying method for summarizing certain descriptive statistical measures.

Kurtosis: The degree of flatness or peakedness in the region around the mode of a frequency curve.

Leptokurtic: A frequency curve that is more peaked than the normal curve.

Platykurtic: A frequency curve that is flat-topped than the normal curve.

Mesokurtic: A frequency curve that is a normal (symmetrical) curve.

Chapter 6

Probability and Probability Distributions

LEARNING OBJECTIVES

After studying this chapter, you should be able to

- help yourself to understand the amount of uncertainty that is involved before making important decisions
- understand fundamentals of probability and various probability rules that help you to measure uncertainty involving uncertainty
- distinguish between discrete and continuous probability distributions
- computer expected value and variance of a random variable.

6.1 INTRODUCTION

Decision-makers always face some degree of risk while selecting a particular course of action or strategy to solve a decision problem involving uncertainty. It is because each strategy can lead to a number of different possible outcomes (or results). Thus, it is necessary for the decision-makers to enhance their capability of grasping the probabilistic situation so as to gain a deeper understanding of the decision problem and base their decisions on rational considerations.

6.2 CONCEPTS OF PROBABILITY

In order to obtain a deeper understanding of probability, it is necessary to use certain terms and definitions more precisely. A special type of phenomenon known as *randomness* or *random variation* is of fundamental importance in probability theory. Based upon situations where randomness is present, we can define particular types of occurrences or *events*.

6.2.1 Random Experiment

Random experiment (also called *act, trial, operation* or *process*) is an activity that leads to the occurrence of one and only one of several possible outcomes which is not likely to be known until its completion, that is, the outcome is not perfectly predictable. This process has the properties that (i) all possible outcomes can be specified in advance, (ii) it can be repeated, and (iii) the same outcome may not occur on various repetitions so that the actual outcome is not known in advance. The variation among experimental outcomes caused by the effects of uncontrolled factors is called *random variation*. It is assumed that these effects vary randomly and unpredictably from one repetition of an experiment to the next.

The outcome (observation or measurement) generated by an experiment may or may not produce a numerical value. Few examples of experiments are as follows:

(i) Measuring blood pressure of a group of individuals.
(ii) checking an automobile's petrol mileage.
(iii) Tossing a coin and observing the face that appears.
(iv) Testing a product to determine whether it is defective or an acceptable product.
(v) Measuring daily rainfall, and so on.

In all such cases, there is uncertainty surrounding the outcome until an outcome is observed. For example, if we toss a coin, the outcome will not be known with certainty until either the head or the tail is observed. The number of outcomes may be finite or infinite depending on the nature of the experiment. For example, in the experiment of tossing a coin, the outcomes are finite and are represented by the head and tail, whereas in the experiment of measuring the time between successive failures of an electronic device, the outcomes are infinite and are represented by the time of failure.

Although an individual outcome associated with a random experiment cannot be predicted exactly, the frequency of occurrence of such an outcome can be noted in a large number of repetitions and thus becomes the basis for resolving problems dealing with uncertainty.

Each experiment may result in one or more outcomes, which are called **events** and denoted by capital letters.

6.2.2 Sample Space

The set of all possible distinct outcomes (events) for a random experiment is called the **sample space** (or *event space*) provided.

(i) no two or more of these outcomes can occur simultaneously;
(ii) exactly one of the outcomes must occur, whenever the experiment is performed.

Sample space is denoted by the capital letter S.

Illustrations

1. Consider the experiment of recording a person's blood type. The four possible outcomes are the following simple events:

   E_1 : Blood type A $\quad$ E_2 : Blood type B

   E_3 : Blood type AB $\quad$ E_4 : Blood type O

   The sample space is $S = \{E_1, E_2, E_3, E_4\}$.

2. Consider the experiment of tossing two coins. The four possible outcomes are the following sample events

   E_1 : HH $\quad$ E_2 = HT $\quad$ E_3 : TH $\quad$ E_4 : T T

   The sample space is $S = \{E_1, E_2, E_3, E_4\}$.

6.2.3 Event Types

A single possible outcome (or result) of an experiment is called a simple (or elementary) event. An **event** is the set (or collection) of one or more simple events of an experiment in the sample space and having a specific common characteristic. For example, for the above-defined sample space S, the collection (H, T), (T, H) is the event containing simple event as: H or T. Other examples of events are:

- More than 5 customers at a service facility in one hour
- Telephone calls lasting no more than 10 minutes
- 75 per cent marks or better in an examination
- Sales volume of a retail store more than Rs. 2,000 on a given day

Mutually Exclusive Events If two or more events cannot occur simultaneously in a single trial of an experiment, then such events are called mutually exclusive events or disjoint events. In other words, two events are mutually exclusive if the occurrence of one of them prevents or rules out the occurrence of the other. For example, the numbers 2 and 3 cannot occur simultaneously on the roll of a dice.

Symbolically, a set of events $\{A_1, A_2, \ldots, A_n\}$ is mutually exclusive if $A_i \cap A_j = \varnothing \ (i \neq j)$. This means the intersection of two events is a null set ($\varnothing$); it is impossible to observe an event that is common in both A_i and A_j.

Collectively Exhaustive Events A list of events is said to be collectively exhaustive when all possible events that can occur from an experiment includes every possible outcome. That is, two or more events are said to be collectively exhaustive if one of the events must occur. Symbolically, a set of events $\{A_1, A_2, \ldots, A_n\}$ is collectively exhaustive if the union of these events is identical with the sample space S. That is,

$$S = \{A_1 \cup A_2 \cup \ldots \cup A_n\}$$

For example, being a male and female are mutually exclusive and collectively exhaustive events. Similarly, the number 7 cannot come upon the uppermost face during the experiment of rolling a dice because the number of faces uppermost has the sample space S = {1, 2, 3, 4, 5, 6}.

Independent and Dependent Events Two events are said to be *independent* if information about one tells nothing about the occurrence of the other. In other words, outcome of one event does not affect, and is not affected by, the other event. The outcomes of successive tosses of a coin are independent of its preceding toss. Increase in the population (in per cent) per year in India is independent of increase in wheat production (in per cent) per year in the USA.

However, two or more events are said to be dependent if information about one tells something about the other. That is, dependence between characteristics implies that a relationship exists, and therefore, knowledge of one characteristic is useful in assessing the occurrence of the other. For example, drawing of a card (say a queen) from a pack of playing cards without replacement reduces the chances of drawing a queen in the subsequent draws.

Compound Events When two or more events occur in connection with each other, then their simultaneous occurrence is called a compound event. These event may be (i) independent, or (ii) dependent.

Equally Likely Events Two or more events are said to be equally likely if each has an equal chance to occur. That is, one of them cannot be expected to occur in preference to the other. For example, each number may be expected to occur on the uppermost face of a rolling die the same number of times in the long run.

Complementary Events If E is any subset of the sample space, then its complement denoted by (read as E-bar) contains all the elements of the sample space that are not part of E. If S denotes the sample space then

$$\overline{E} = S - E = \{\text{All sample elements not in E}\}$$

For example, if E represents companies with sales less than or equal to Rs. 25 lakh, written as E = $\{x : x \leq 25\}$, then this set is a complement of the set, $\overline{E} = \{x : x > 25\}$. Obviously such events must be mutually exclusive and collective exhaustive.

6.3 DEFINITION OF PROBABILITY

A general definition of probability states that *probability is a numerical measure (between 0 and 1 inclusively) of the likelihood or chance of occurrence of an uncertain event*. However, it does not tell us how to compute the probability.

6.3.1 Classical Approach

This approach of defining the probability is based on the assumption that all the possible outcomes (finite in number) of an experiment are mutually exclusive and equally likely. It states that, during a random experiment, if there are 'a' possible outcomes where the favouable event A occurs and 'b' possible outcomes where the event A does not occur, and all these possible outcomes are mutually exclusive, exhaustive, and equiprobable, then the probability that event A will occur is defined as

$$P(A) = \frac{a}{a+b} = \frac{\text{Number of favourable outcomes}}{\text{Total number of possible outcomes}} = \frac{c(A)}{c(S)}$$

For example, if a fair die is rolled, then on any trial, each event (face or number) is equally likely to occur since there are six equally likely exhaustive events, each will occur 1/6 of the time, and therefore the probability of any one event occurring is 1/6. Similarly for the process of selecting a card at random, each event or card is mutually exclusive, exhaustive, and equiprobable. The probability of selecting any one card on a trial is equal to 1/52, since there are 52 cards. Hence, in general, for a random experiment with n mutually exclusive, exhaustive, equiprobable events, the probability of any of the events is equal to $1/n$.

Since the probability of occurrence of an event is based on prior knowledge of the process involved, therefore this approach is often called *a priori classical probability approach*. This means, we do not have to perform random experiments to find the probability of occurrence of an event. This also implies that no experimental data are required for computation of probability. Since the assumption of equally likely simple events can rarely be verified with certainty, therefore this approach is not used often other than in games of chance.

The assumption that all possible outcomes are equally likely may lead to a wrong calculation of probability in case some outcomes are more or less frequent in occurrence. For example, if we classify two children in a family according to their sex, then the possible outcomes in terms of number of boys in the family are 0, 1, 2. Thus, according to the **classical approach**, the probability for each of the outcomes should be 1/3. However, it has been calculated that the probabilities are approximately 1/4, 1/2, and 1/4 for 0, 1, 2 boys respectively. Similarly, we cannot apply this approach to find the probability of a defective unit being produced by a stable manufacturing process as there are only two possible outcomes, defective or non-defective.

6.3.2 Relative Frequency Approach

This approach of computing probability is based on the assumption that a random experiment can be repeated a large number of times under identical conditions where trials are independent to each other. While conducting a random experiment, we may or may not observe the desired event. But as the experiment is repeated many times, that event may occur some proportion of time. Thus, the approach calculates *the proportion of the time (i.e. the* ***relative frequency****) with which the event occurs over an infinite number of repetitions of the experiment under identical conditions.* Since no experiment can be repeated an infinite number of times, therefore a probability can never be exactly determined. However, we can approximate the probability of an event by recording the relative frequency with which the event has occurred over a finite number of repetitions of the experiment under identical conditions. For example, if a die is tossed n times and s denotes the number of times the event A (i.e., number 4, 5, or 6) occurs, then the ratio $P(A) = c(s)/n$ gives the proportion of times the event A occurs in n trials, and are also called relative frequencies of the event in n trials. Although our estimate about P(A) may change after every trial, yet we will find that the proportion $c(s)/n$ tends to cluster around a unique central value as the number of trials n becomes even larger. This unique central value (also called probability of event A) is defined as:

$$P(A) = \lim_{n \to \infty} \left\{ \frac{c(s)}{n} \right\}$$

where $c(s)$ represents the number of times that an event s occurs in n trials of an experiment.

Since the probability of an event is determined objectively by repetitive empirical observations of experimental outcomes, it is also known as *empirical probability*. Few situations to which this approach can be applied are follows:

(i) Buying lottery tickets regularly and observing how often you win.
(ii) Commuting to work daily and observing whether or not a certain traffic signal is red when you cross it.
(iii) Observing births and noting how often the baby is a female.
(iv) Surveying many adults and determing what proportion smokes.

6.3.3 Subjective Approach

The **subjective approach** of calculating probability is always based on the degree of beliefs, convictions, and experience concerning the likelihood of occurrence of a random event. It is thus a way to quantify an individual's beliefs, assessment, and judgment about a random phenomenon. Probability assigned for the occurrence of an event may be based on just guess or on having some idea about the relative frequency of past occurrences of the event. This approach must be used when either sufficient data are not available or sources of information giving different results are not known.

6.3.4 Fundamental Rules of Probability

No matter which approach is used to define probability, the following fundamental rules must be satisfied. Let S be the sample space of an experiment that is partitioned into mutually exclusive and exhaustive events $A_1, A_2, \ldots, A_n$ which may be elementary or compound. The probability of any event A in S is governed by the following rules:

(i) Each probability should fall between 0 and 1, i.e. $0 \leq P(A_i) \leq 1$, for all i, where $P(A_i)$ is read as: 'probability of event A_i'. In other words, the probability of an event is restricted to the range *zero* to *one* inclusive, where zero represents an impossible event and one represents a certain event.

For example, probability of the number seven occurring, on rolling a dice, P(7) = 0, because this number is an impossible event for this experiment.

(ii) $P(S) = P(A_1) + P(A_2) + \ldots + P(A_n) = 1$, where P(S) is read as: 'probability of the certain event'. This rule states that the sum of probabilities of all simple events constituting the sample space is equal to one. This also implies that if a random experiment is conducted, one of its outcomes in its sample space is certain to occur.

Similarly, the probability of an impossible event or an empty set is zero. That is $P(\Phi) = 0$.

(iii) If events A_1 and A_2 are two elements in S and if occurrence of A_1 implies that A_2 occurs, that is, if A_1 is a subset of A_2, then the probability of A_1 is less than or equal to the probability of A_2. That is, $P(A_1) \le P(A_2)$.

(iv) $P(\overline{A}) = 1 - P(A)$, that is, the probability of an event that does not occur is equal to one minus the probability of the event that does occur (the probability rule for complementary events).

6.3.5 Glossary of Probability Terms

If A and B are two events, then

$A \cup B$ = an event which represents the occurrence of either A or B or both.

$A \cap B$ = an event which represents the simultaneous occurrence of A and B.

$\overline{A}$ = complement of event A and represents non-occurrence of A.

$\overline{A} \cap \overline{B}$ = both A and B do not occur.

$\overline{A} \cap B$ = event A does not occur but event B occurs.

$A \cap \overline{B}$ = event A occurs but event B does not occur.

$(A \cap \overline{B}) \cup (\overline{A} \cap B)$ = exactly one of the two events A and B occurs.

6.4 COMBINATIONS AND PERMUTATIONS

Combinations sometimes the ordering or arrangement of objects is not important, but only the objects that are chosen. For example, (i) you may not care in what order the books are placed on the shelf, but only which books you are able to shelve. (ii) When a five-person committee is chosen from a group of 10 students, the order of choice is not important because all 5 students will be equal members of committe.

This counting rule for combinations allows us to select r (say) number of outcomes from a collection of n distinct outcomes without caring in what order they are arranged. This rule is denoted by

$$C(n, r) = {}^nC_r = \frac{n!}{r!\,(n-r)!}$$

where $n! = n(n-1)(n-2)\ldots3.2.1$ and $0! = 1$.

The notation ! means *factorial*, for example, $4! = 4 \times 3 \times 2 \times 1 = 24$.

Important Results

1. ${}^nC_r = {}^nC_{n-r}$ and ${}^nC_n = 1$.
2. If n objects consist of all n_1 of one type, all n_2 of another type, and so on upto n_k of the kth type, then the total number of selections that can be made of 1, 2, 3 upto n objects is $(n_1 + 1)(n_2 + 1)\ldots(n_k + 1) - 1$.
3. The total number of selections from n objects all different is $2^n - 1$.

Permutations This rule of counting involves ordering or permutations. This rule helps us to compute the number of ways in which n distinct objects can be arranged, taking r of them at a time.

The total number of permutations of n objects taken r at a time is given by

$$P(n, r) = {}^{n}P_{r} = \frac{n!}{(n-r)!}$$

By permuting each combination of r objects among themselves, we shall obtain all possible permutations of n objects, r at a time. Each combination gives rise to $r!$ permutations, so that $r!\,C(n, r) = P(n, r) = n!/(n-r)!$.

Example 6.1: Of ten electric bulbs, three are defective but it is not known which are defective. In how many ways can three bulbs be selected? How many of these selections will include at least one defective bulb?

Solution: Three bulbs out of 10 bulbs can be selected in ${}^{10}C_3 = 120$ ways. The number of selections which include exactly one defective bulb will be ${}^{7}C_2 \times {}^{3}C_1 = 63$.

Similarly, the number of selections which include exactly two and three defective bulbs will be ${}^{7}C_1 \times {}^{3}C_2 = 21$ and ${}^{3}C_3 = 1$, respectively. Thus, the total number of selections including at least one defective bulb is $63 + 21 + 1 = 85$.

Example 6.2: A bag contains 6 red and 8 green balls.

(a) If one ball is drawn at random, then what is the probability of the ball being green?

(b) If two balls are drawn at random, then what is the probability that one is red and the other green?

Solution: (a) Since the bag contains 6 red and 8 green balls, therefore it contains $6 + 8 = 14$ equally likely outcomes, that is, $S = \{r, g\}$. But one ball out of 14 balls can be drawn in ways, that is,

$$^{14}C_1 = \frac{14!}{1!\,(14-1)!} = 14 \text{ ways}$$

Let A be the event of drawing a green ball. Then, out of these 8 green balls, one green ball can be drawn in ${}^{8}C_1$ ways:

$$^{8}C_1 = \frac{8!}{1!\,(8-1)!} = 8$$

Hence, $$P(A) = \frac{c(A)}{c(S)} = \frac{8}{14}$$

(b) All exhaustive number of cases, $c(S) = {}^{14}C_2 = \dfrac{14!}{2!\,(14-2)!} = 91.$

Also, out of 6 red balls, one red ball can be drawn in ${}^{6}C_1$ ways and out of 8 green balls, one green ball can be drawn in ${}^{8}C_1$ ways. Thus, the total number of favourable cases is:

$$c\,(B) = {}^{6}C_1 \times {}^{8}C_1 = 6 \times 8 = 48$$

Thus, $$P(B) = \frac{c(B)}{c(S)} = \frac{48}{91}$$

Example 6.3. A bag contains 2 white balls and 3 black balls. Four persons A, B, C and D in the order named, each draw one ball and do not replace it. The first to draw a white ball receives Rs. 20. Determine their expectation. *[Delhi Univ., BA Eco(Hons), 1995]*

Solution: Thus draw the balls successively without replacement and the one who first draw the white balls wins.

$$P(A \text{ wins}) = P(A \text{ draw white ball in first draw}) = 2/5 = 0.4$$

$P(B \text{ wins})$ = P(A fails and B draw white ball)

$$= \left(1-\frac{2}{5}\right)\left(\frac{2}{4}\right) = \frac{3}{5}\times\frac{2}{4} = 0.3$$

$P(C \text{ wins}) = P(A$ and B both fails in first two draws and C gets the white ball)

$$= \left(1-\frac{2}{5}\right)\times\left(1-\frac{2}{4}\right)\times\frac{2}{3} = 0.2$$

$P(D \text{ wins}) = P(A, B, C$ all fails in first three draws and then D wins)

$$= \left(1-\frac{2}{5}\right)\times\left(1-\frac{2}{4}\right)\left(1-\frac{2}{3}\right)\left(\frac{2}{3}\right) = 0.1$$

Expectations of A, B, C and D

A's Expectation = 20 × 0.4 = Rs.8; B's Expectation = 20 × 0.3 = Rs. 6

C's Expectation = 20 × 0.2 = Rs. 4; D's Expectation = 20 × 0.1 = Rs. 2

Example 6.4. If n biscuits are distributed among N beggars, find the probability a particular beggar receives $r(< n)$ biscuits.

Solution: n biscuits can be distributed among N beggars in N^n ways. Moreover, r biscuits can be given to any particular beggar in ${}^nC_r$ ways. The remaining $(n - r)$ biscuits will be distributed among the remaining $(N - 1)$ beggars in $(N - 1)^{n-r}$ ways. Thus, the total number of favourable ways $= {}^nC_r(N - 1)^{n-r}$

$$\text{Hence required probability} = \frac{{}^nC_r(N-1)^{n-r}}{N^n}.$$

Example 6.5: Cards are dealt one by one from a well shuffled pack until an ace appears. Show that the probability that exactly n cards are dealt before the first ace appears is $\dfrac{4(51-n)(50-n)(49-n)}{52.51.50.49}$.

[*Delhi Univ., B.Sc, 1994, 96, Phy(Hons) 1997*]

Solution: Probability that an ace does not appear in first draw $= 1 - \dfrac{4}{52} = \dfrac{48}{52}$

Probability that ace does not appear in $(n - 1)^{\text{th}}$ draw $= 1 - \dfrac{4}{52-(n-2)} = \dfrac{50-n}{52-(n-2)}$

Probability that ace does not appear in n^{th} draw $= 1 - \dfrac{4}{52-(n-1)} = \dfrac{50-n}{52-(n-1)}$

Probability that first ace appears in $(n + 1)$th draw $= \dfrac{4}{52-n}$

Hence, the required probability becomes

$$= \left(\frac{48}{52}\times\frac{47}{51}\times\frac{46}{50}\times\frac{45}{49}\times\frac{44}{48}\times\ldots\times\frac{52-n}{52-(n-4)}\times\frac{51-n}{52-(n-3)}\times\frac{50-n}{52-(n-2)}\times\frac{49-n}{52-(n-1)}\times\frac{4}{52-n}\right)$$

$$= \frac{(51-n)(50-n)(49-n)(4)}{52\times51\times50\times49}$$

Example 6.6: Tickets are numbered from 1 to 100. They are well shuffled and a ticket is drawn at random. What is the probability that the drawn ticket has

(a) an even number?

(*b*) the number 5 or a multiple of 5?

(c) a number which is greater than 75?

(*d*) a number which is a square?

Solution: Since any of the 100 tickets can be drawn, therefore exhaustive number of cases are $c(S) = 100$.

(a) Let A be the event of getting an even numbered tickets. Then, $c(A) = 50$, and hence

$$P(A) = 50/100 = 1/2$$

(b) Let B be the event of getting a ticket bearing the number 5 or a multiple of 5, that is,

$$B = [5, 10, 15, 20, \ldots, 95, 100]$$

which are 20 in number, $c(B) = 20$. Thus, $P(B) = 20/100 = 1/5$.

(c) Let C be the event of getting a ticket bearing a number greater than 75, that is,

$$C = \{76, 77, \ldots, 100\}$$

which are 25 in number, $c(C) = 25$. Thus, $P(C) = 25/100 = 1/4$.

(*d*) Let D be the event of getting a ticket bearing a number which is a square, that is,

$$D = \{1, 4, 9, 16, 25, 36, 49, 64, 81, 100\}$$

which are 10 in number, $c(D) = 10$. Thus, $P(D) = 10/100 = 1/10$.

Conceptual Questions 6A

1. (a) Discuss the different schools of thought on the interpretation of probability. How does each school define probability?

(b) Describe briefly the various schools of thought on probability. Discuss its importance in business decision-making.

2. Explain what you understand by the term probability. Discuss its importance in busines decision-making.

3. Define independent and mutually exclusive events. Can two events be mutually exclusive and independent simultaneously? Support your answer with an example.

4. Explain the meaning of each of the following terms:
(a) Random phenomenon
(b) Statistical experiment
(c) Random event
(d) Sample space

5. What do you mean by probability? Explain the importance of probability.

6. Distinguish between the two concepts in each of the following pairs:
(a) Elementary event and compound events
(b) Mutually exclusive events and overlapping events
(c) Sample space and sample point

Self-Practice Problems 6A

6.1 Three unbiased coins are tossed. What is the probability of obtaining:
(a) all heads (b) two heads
(c) one head (d) at least one head
(e) at least two heads (f) all tails

6.2 A card is drawn from a well-shuffled of 52 cards. Find the probability of drawing a card which is neither a heart nor a king.

6.3 In a single throw of two dice, find the probability of getting (a) a total of 11, (b) a total of 8 or 11, and (c) same number on both the dice.

6.4 Five men in a company of 20 are graduates. If 3 men are picked out of the 20 at random, what is the probability that they are all graduates? What is the probability of at least one graduate?

6.5 A bag contains 25 balls numbered 1 through 25. Suppose an odd number is considered a 'success'. Two balls are drawn from the bag with replacement. Find the probability of getting
(a) two successes (b) exactly one success
(c) at least one success (d) no success

6.6 A bag contains 5 white and 8 red balls. Two drawings of 3 balls are made such that (a) the balls are replaced before the second trial, and (b) the balls are not replaced before the second trial. Find the probability that the first drawing will give 3 white and the second, 3 red balls in each case.

6.7 Three groups of workers contain 3 men and one woman, 2 men and 2 women, and 1 man and 3 women respectively. One worker is selected at random from each group. What is the probability that the group selected consists of 1 man and 2 women?

6.8 What is the probability that a leap year, selected at random, will contain 53 Sundays?

6.9 A university has to select an examiner from a list of 50 persons, 20 of them women and 30 men, 10 of them knowing Hindi and 40 not, 15 of them being teachers and the remaining 35 not. What is the probability of the university selecting a Hindi-knowing woman teacher?

Hints and Answers

6.1 (a) P(all heads) = 1/8
(b) P(two heads) = 3/8
(c) P(one head) = 3/8
(d) P(at least one head) = 7/8
(e) P(at least two heads) = 4/8 = 1/2
(f) P(all tails) = 1/8.

6.2 P(neither a heart nor a king) $= \frac{^{36}C_1}{^{52}C_1} = \frac{36}{52}$

6.3 c(S) = 36; P(total of 11) = 2/36 P(total of 9 or 11) = 7/36

6.4 P(all graduate) $= \frac{^5C_3 \times {^{15}C_0}}{^{20}C_3} = \frac{10 \times 1}{1140} = \frac{1}{114}$

P(no graduate) $= \frac{^{15}C_3 \times {^5C_0}}{^{20}C_2} = \frac{455 \times 1}{1140} = \frac{91}{28}$

P(at least one graduate) $= 1 - \frac{91}{228} = \frac{137}{228}$

6.5 (a) P(two successes) $= \frac{13}{25} \times \frac{13}{25} = \frac{169}{625}$

(b) P(exactly one success)

$$= \frac{13}{25} \times \frac{12}{25} + \frac{13}{25} \times \frac{12}{25} = \frac{312}{625}$$

(c) P(at least one success) = P(exactly one success) + P(two successes)

$$= \frac{312}{625} + \frac{169}{625} = \frac{481}{625}$$

(d) P(no successes) $= \frac{12}{25} \times \frac{12}{25} = \frac{144}{625}$

6.6 (a) *When balls are replaced:*

Total number of balls in the bag

$$= 5 + 8 = 13.$$

3 balls can be drawn from 13 in $^{13}C_3$ ways;
3 white balls can be drawn from 5 in $^5C_3$ ways;
3 red balls can be drawn from 8 in $^8C_3$ ways.
The probability of 3 red balls in the second trial

$$= \frac{^5C_3}{^{13}C_3} = \frac{5}{143}$$

Probability of 3 red balls in the second trial

$$= \frac{^4C_2}{^{12}C_2} = \frac{28}{143}$$

The probability of the compound event

$$\frac{5}{143} \times \frac{28}{143} = \frac{140}{20449} = 0.007$$

(b) *When balls are not replaced:*

At the first trial, 3 white balls can be drawn in $^5C_3$ ways.

The probability of drawing three white balls at the first trial $= \frac{^5C_3}{^{13}C_3} = \frac{5}{143}$

When the white balls have been drawn and not replaced, the bag contains 2 white and 8 red balls. Therefore, at the second trial, 3 balls can be drawn from 10 in ${}^{10}C_3$ ways and 3 red balls can be drawn from 8 in ${}^{8}C_3$ ways.

The probability of 3 red balls in the second trial

$$= \frac{{}^{8}C_3}{{}^{10}C_3} = \frac{7}{15}$$

The probability of the compound event

$$= \frac{5}{142} \times \frac{7}{15} = \frac{7}{429} = 0.016.$$

6.7 There are three possibilities in this case:

(i) Man is selected from the 1st group and women from 2nd and 3rd groups; or

(ii) Man is selected from the 2nd group and women from the 1st and 3rd groups; or

(iii) Man is selected from the 3rd group and women from 1st and 2nd groups.

The probability of selecting a group of 1 man and 2 women is:

$$\left(\frac{3}{4} \times \frac{2}{4} \times \frac{3}{4}\right) + \left(\frac{2}{4} \times \frac{1}{4} \times \frac{3}{4}\right) + \left(\frac{1}{4} \times \frac{1}{4} \times \frac{2}{4}\right)$$

$$= \frac{9}{32} + \frac{3}{32} + \frac{1}{32} = \frac{13}{32}.$$

6.8 A leap year consists of 366 days, therefore it contains 52 complete weeks and 2 extra days. These 2 days may make the following 7 combinations:

(i) Monday and Tuesday

(ii) Tuesday and Wednesday

(iii) Wednesday and Thursday

(iv) Thursday and Friday

(v) Friday and Saturday

(vi) Saturday and Sunday

(vii) Sunday and Monday

Of these seven equally likely cases, only the last two are favourable. Hence the required probability is 2/7.

6.9 Probability of selecting a woman = 20/50;

Probability of selecting a teacher = 15/50;

Probability of selecting a Hindi-knowing candidate = 10/50.

Since the events are independent, the probability of the university selecting a Hindi knowing woman teacher = (20/50) × (15/50) × (10/50) = 3/125.

6.5 RULES OF PROBABILITY AND ALGEBRA OF EVENTS

In probability, we use set theory notations to simplify the presentation of ideas. As discussed earlier in this chapter, the probability of the occurrence of an event A is expressed as:

$$P(A) = \text{probability of event A occurrence}$$

Such single probabilities are called **marginal** (or unconditional) **probabilities** because it is the probability of a single event occurring. In the coin tossing example, the marginal probability of a tail or head in a toss can be stated as P(T) or P(H).

6.5.1 Rules of Addition

The addition rules are helpful when we have two events and are interested in knowing the probability that at least one of the events occurs.

Mutually Exclusive Events The rule of addition for mutually exclusive (disjoint), exhaustive, and equally likely events states that

If two events A and B are mutually exclusive, exhaustive, and equiprobable, then the probability of either event A or B or both occurring is equal to the sum of their individual probabilities.

This rule is expressed in the following formula:

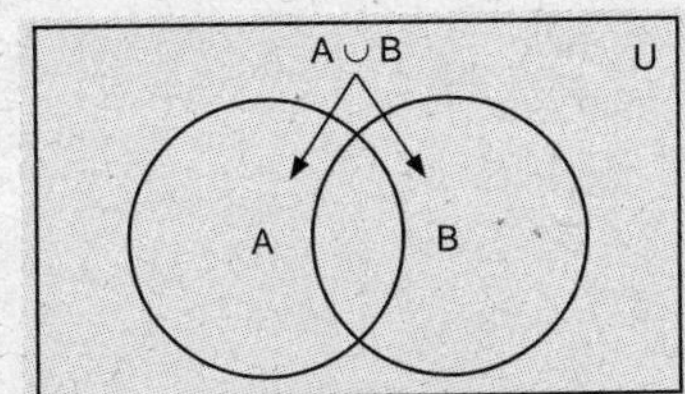

Figure 6.1 Union of Two Events

$$P(A \text{ or } B) = P(A \cup B) = \frac{n(A \cup B)}{n(S)} = \frac{n(A) + n(B)}{n(S)}$$

$$= \frac{n(A)}{n(S)} + \frac{n(B)}{n(S)} = P(A) + P(B) \qquad (6\text{-}1)$$

where $A \cup B$ (read as 'A *union* B') denotes the union of two events A and B and it is the set of all sample points belonging to A or B or both. This rule can also be illustrated by the **Venn diagram** shown in Fig. 6.1. Here two circles contain all the sample points in events A and B. The overlap of the circles indicates that some sample points are contained in both A and B.

Illustration: Consider the pattern of arrival of customers at a service counter during the first hour it is open along with its probability:

No. of persons	:	0	1	2	3	4 or more
Probability	:	0.1	0.2	0.3	0.3	0.1

To understand the probability that either 2 or 3 persons will be there during the first hour, we have

$$P(2 \text{ or } 3) = P(2) + P(3) = 0.3 + 0.3 = 0.6$$

The formula (6-1) can be expanded to include more than two events. In particular, if there are n events in a sample space that are mutually exclusive, then the probability of the union of these events is given by

$$P(A_1 \cup A_2 \cup \ldots \cup A_n) = P(A_1) + P(A_2) + \ldots + P(A_n) \qquad (6\text{-}2)$$

For example, if we are interested in knowing the probability that there will be two or more persons during the first hour, then using formula (6-2), we have

$$P(2 \text{ or more}) = P(2, 3, 4 \text{ or more}) = P(2) + P(3) + P(4)$$
$$= 0.3 + 0.3 + 0.1 = 0.7$$

An important special case of formula (6-1) is for complementary events. Let A be any event and $\overline{A}$ be the complement of A. Obviously A and $\overline{A}$ are mutually exclusive and exhaustive events. Thus, either A occurs or it does not, is given by

$$P(A \text{ or } \overline{A}) = P(A) + P(\overline{A}) = P(A) + \{1 - P(A)\} = 1$$

or $$P(A) = 1 - P(\overline{A}) \qquad (6\text{-}3)$$

For example, if a dice is rolled, then the probability whether an odd number of spots occurs or does not.

Partially Overlapping (or Joint) Events If events A and B are not mutually exclusive, it is possible for both events to occur simultaneously? This means these events have some sample points in common. Such events are also called *joint* (or *overlapping*) *events*. The sample points in common (belong to both events) represent the joint event $A \cap B$ (read as: A intersection B). The addition rule in this case is stated as:

> *If two events A and B are not mutually exclusive, then the probability of either A or B or both occurring is equal to the sum of their individual probabilities minus the probability of A and B occurring together.*

This rule is expressed in the following formula:

$$P(A \text{ or } B) = P(A) + P(B) - P(A \text{ and } B)$$

or $$P(A \cup B) = P(A) + P(B) - P(A \cap B) \qquad (6\text{-}4)$$

This addition rule can also be illustrated by the Venn-diagram shown in Fig. 6.2.

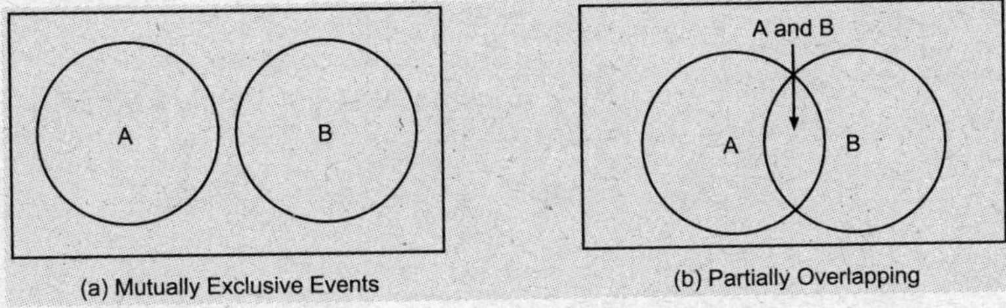

Figure 6.2 Partially Overlapping Events

Illustration: Suppose 70 per cent of all tourists who come to India will visit Agra while 60 per cent will visit Goa and 50 per cent of them will visit both Agra and Goa. The probability that a tourist will visit either Goa or Agra or both is obtained by applying formula (6-4) as follows:

$$\begin{aligned} P(\text{Agra or Goa}) &= P(\text{Agra}) + P(\text{Goa}) - P(\text{both Agra and Goa}) \\ &= 0.70 + 0.60 - 0.50 = 0.8 \end{aligned}$$

Consequently, the probability that a tourist will visit neither Agra nor Goa is calculated by

$$P(\text{neither Agra nor Goa}) = 1 - P(\text{Agra or Goa}) = 1 - 0.80 = 0.20$$

The formula (6-4) can be expanded to include more than two events. In particular, if there are three events that are not mutually exclusive, then the probability of the union of these events is given by

$$\begin{aligned} P(A \cup B \cup C) &= P(A) + P(B) + P(C) - P(A \cap B) - P(B \cap C) \\ &\quad - P(C \cap A) + P(A \cap B \cap C) \end{aligned} \tag{6-5}$$

Remark: The rules of addition are applicable for calculating probability of events in case of simultaneous trails.

Example 6.7: What is the probability that a randomly chosen card from a deck of cards will be either a king or a heart.

Solution: Let event A and B be the king and heart in a deck of 52 cards, respectively. Then, it is given that

Card	*Probability*	*Reason*
King	P(A) = 4/52	4 kings in a deck of 52 cards
Heart	P(B) = 13/52	13 hearts in a deck of 52 cards
King of heart	P(A and (B) = 1/52	1 King of heart in a deck of 52 cards

Using the formula (6-4), we get

$$P(A \text{ or } B) = P(A) + P(B) - P(A \text{ and } B) = \frac{4}{52} + \frac{13}{52} - \frac{1}{52} = \frac{16}{52} = 0.3077$$

Example 6.8: Of 1000 assembled components, 10 have a working defect and 20 have a structural defect. There is a good reason to assume that no component has both defects. What is the probability that randomly chosen component will have either type of defect?

Solution: Let the event A and B be the component which has working defect and has structural defect, respectively. Then it is given that

$$P(A) = 10/1000 = 0.01,\ P(B) = 20/1000 = 0.02 \text{ and } P(A \text{ and } B) = 0$$

The probability that a randomly chosen component will have either type of defect is given by

$$P(A \text{ or } B) = P(A) + P(B) - P(A \text{ and } B) = 0.01 + 0.02 - 0.0 = 0.03$$

Example 6.9: A survey of 200 retail grocery shops revealed following monthly income pattern:

Monthly Income (Rs.)	*Number of Shops*
Under Rs. 20,000	102
20,000 to 30,000	61
30,000 and above	37

(a) What is the probability that a particular shop has monthly income under Rs. 20,000

(b) What is the probability that a shop selected at random has either an income between Rs. 20,000 and Rs. 30,000 or an income of Rs. 30,000 and more?

Solution: Let the events A, B and C represent the income under three categories, respectively.

(a) Probability that a particular shop has monthly income under Rs. 20,000 is $P(A) = 102/200 = 0.51$.

(b) Probability that shop selected at random has income between Rs. 20,000 and Rs. 30,000 or Rs. 30,000 and more is given by

$$P(A \text{ or } B) = P(A) + P(B) = \frac{61}{200} + \frac{37}{200} = 0.305 + 0.185 = 0.49$$

Example 6.10: From a sales force of 150 persons, one will be selected to attend a special sales meeting. If 52 of them are unmarried, 72 are college graduates, and 3/4 of the 52 that are unmarried are college graduates, find the probability that the sales person selected at random will be neither single nor a college graduate.

Solution: Let A and B be the events that a sales person selected is married and that he is a college graduate, respectively. Then, it is given that

$$P(A) = 52/150, \; P(B) = 72/150; \; P(A \text{ and } B) = (3/4)\,(52/150) = 39/150$$

The probability that a salesperson selected at random will be neither single nor a college graduate is:

$$P(\bar{A} \cap \bar{B}) = 1 - P(A \cup B) = 1 - \{P(A) + P(B) - P(A \cap B)\}$$

$$= 1 - \left\{\frac{52}{150} + \frac{72}{150} - \frac{39}{150}\right\} = \frac{13}{30}$$

Example 6.11: The probability that a contractor will get a plumbing contract is 2/3 and the probability that he will not get an electrical contract is 5/9. If the probability of getting at least one contract is 4/5, what is the probability that he will get both?

Solution: Let A and B denote the events that the contractor will get a plumbing and electrical contract, respectively. Given that

$$P(A) = 2/3; \quad P(B) = 1 - (5/9) = 4/9; \quad P(A \cup B) = 4/5$$

$$P(A \cap B) = P(A) + P(B) - P(A \cup B) = \frac{2}{3} + \frac{4}{9} - \frac{4}{5} = \frac{14}{45} = 0.31$$

Thus, the probability that the contractor will get both the contracts is 0.31.

Example 6.12: The probability that X passed in maths is 2/3. The probability that he passed in statistics is 4/9. The probability that he passed in atleast one subject is 4/5. What is the probability that he passed in both subjects ? *[GJ Univ., BBA, 2004]*

Solution: Let A be the event that Mr. X passed in maths, i.e.. $P(A) = 2/3$ and B be the event that Mr. X passed in statistics, i.e. $P(B) = 4/9$. Then $P(A \cup B) = 4/5$. The probability that he passed in at least one subject is given by

$$P(A \cup B) = P(A) + P(B) - P(A \cap B)$$

$$\frac{4}{5} = \frac{2}{3} + \frac{4}{9} - P(A \cap B)$$

$$P(A \cap B) = \frac{2}{3} + \frac{4}{9} - \frac{4}{5} = \frac{30 + 20 - 36}{45} = \frac{14}{45}.$$

6.5.2 Rules of Multiplication

Statistically Independent Events When the occurrence of an event does not affect and is not affected by the probability of occurrence of any other event, the event is said to be a *statistically independent event*. There are three types of probabilities under statistical independence: *marginal*, *joint*, and *conditional*.

- *Marginal Probability:* A marginal or unconditional probability is the simple probability of the occurrence of an event. For example, in a fair coin toss, the outcome of each toss is an event that is statistically independent of the outcomes of every other toss of the coin.
- *Joint Probability:* The probability of two or more independent events occurring together or in succession is called the **joint probability**. The joint probability of two or more independent events is equal to the product of their marginal probabilities. In particular, if A and B are independent events, the probability that both A and B will occur is given by

$$P(AB) = P(A \cap B) = P(A) \times P(B) \tag{6-6}$$

  Suppose we toss a coin twice. The probability that in both the cases the coin will turn up head is given by

$$P(H_1H_2) = P(H_1) \times P(H_2) = \frac{1}{2} \times \frac{1}{2} = \frac{1}{4},$$

  The formula (6-6) is applied here because the probability of any outcome is not affected by any preceding outcome, in other words, outcomes are independent.
- *Conditional Probability:* It is the probability of a particular event occuring, given that another event has occurred. The **conditional probability** of event A, given that event B has already occurred is written as: P (A|B). Similarly, we may write P (B|A). The vertical bar is read as 'given' and events appearing to the right of the bar are those that you know have occurred. Two events A and B are said to be independent if and only $P(A|B) = P(A)$ or $P(B|A) = P(B)$. Otherwise, events are said to be dependent.

Since, in the case of independent events the probability of occurrence of either of the events does not depend or affect the occurrence of the other, therefore in the coin tossing example, the probability of a head occurrence in the second toss, given that head resulted in the first toss, is still 0.5. That is, $P(H_2 \mid H_1) = 0.5 = P(H_2)$. It is because of the fact that the probabilities of heads and tails are the same for every toss and in no way influenced by whether it was a head or tail which occurred in the previous toss.

Statistically Dependent Events When the probability of an event is dependent upon or affected by the occurrence of any other event, the events are said to be **statistically dependent**. There are three types of probabilities under statistical dependence: *joint*, *conditional*, and *marginal*.

- *Joint Probability*: If A and B are dependent events, then the joint probability as discussed under statistical dependence case is no longer equal to the product of their respective probabilites. That is, for dependent events

$$P(A \text{ and } B) = P(A \cap B) \neq P(A) \times P(B)$$

Accordingly, $P(A) \neq P(A \mid B)$ and $P(B) \neq P(B \mid A)$

The joint probability of events A and B occurring together or in succession under statistical dependences is given by

$$P(A \cap B) = P(A) \times P(B \mid A)$$

or $$P(A \cap B) = P(B) \times P(A \mid B)$$

- *Conditional Probability:* Under statistical dependence, the conditional probability of event B, given that event A has already occurred, is given by

$$P(B \mid A) = \frac{P(A \cap B)}{P(A)}$$

Similarly, the conditional probability of A, given that event B has occurred, is

$$P(A \mid B) = \frac{P(A \cap B)}{P(B)}$$

- *Marginal Probability*: The marginal probability of an event under statistical dependence is the same as the marginal probability of an event under statistical independence.

The marginal probability of events A and B can be written as:

$$P(A) = P(A \cap B) + P(A \cap \bar{B})$$

and $$P(B) = P(A \cap B) + P(\bar{A} \cap B)$$

Example 6.13: The odds against student X solving a Business Statistics problem are 8 to 6, and odds in favour of student Y solving the problem are 14 to 16.

(a) What is the chance that the problem will be solved if they both try independently of each other?

(b) What is the probability that none of them is able to solve the problem?

Solution: Let A = The event that the first student solves the problem,

B = The event that the second student solves the problem.

$$P(A) = \frac{6}{8+6} = \frac{6}{14} \text{ and } P(B) = \frac{14}{14+16} = \frac{14}{30}$$

(a) Probability that the problem will be solved

$$= P\text{ (at least one of them solves the problem)}$$
$$= P(A \text{ or } B) = P(A) + P(B) - P(A \text{ and } B)$$
$$= P(A) + P(B) - P(A) \times P(B) \text{ [because the events are independent]}$$
$$= \frac{6}{14} + \frac{14}{30} - \frac{6}{14} \times \frac{14}{30} = \frac{73}{105} = 0.695$$

(b) Probability that neither A nor B solves the problem

$$P(\bar{A} \text{ and } \bar{B}) = P(\bar{A}) \times P(\bar{B})$$
$$= [1 - P(A)] \times [1 - P(B)] = \frac{8}{14} \times \frac{16}{30} = \frac{32}{105} = 0.305$$

Example 6.14: The probability that a new marketing approach will be successful is 0.6. The probability that the expenditure for developing the approach can be kept within the original budget is 0.50. The probability that both of these objectives will be achieved is 0.30. What is the probability that at least one of these objectives will be achieved. For the two events described above, determine whether the events are independent or dependent.

Solution: Let A = The event that the new marketing approach will be successful

B = The event that the expenditure for developing the approach can be kept within the original budget

Given that P(A) = 0.60, P(B) = 0.50 and $P(A \cap B) = 0.30$

Probability that both events A and B will be achieved is given by

$$P(A \cup B) = P(A) + P(B) - P(A \cap B)$$
$$= 0.60 + 0.50 - 0.30 = 0.80$$

If events A and B are independent, then their joint probability is given by

$$P(A \cap B) = P(A) \times P(B) = 0.60 \times 0.50 = 0.30$$

Since this value is same as given in the problem, events are independent.

Example 6.15: A piece of equipment will function only when the three components A, B, and C are working. The probability of A failing during one year is 0.15, that of B failing is 0.05, and that of C failing is 0.10. What is the probability that the equipment will fail before the end of the year?

Solution: Given that

$$P(\text{A failing}) = 0.15;\ P(\text{A not failing}) = 1 - P(A) = 0.85$$
$$P(\text{B failing}) = 0.05;\ P(\text{B not failing}) = 1 - P(B) = 0.95$$
$$P(\text{C failing}) = 0.10;\ P(\text{C not failing}) = 1 - P(C) = 0.90$$

Since all the three events are independent, therefore the probability that the equipment will work is given by

$$P(\bar{A} \cap \bar{B} \cap \bar{B}) = P(\bar{A}) \times P(\bar{B}) \times P(\bar{C}) = 0.85 \times 0.95 \times 0.90 = 0.726$$

Probability that the equipment will fail before the end of the year is given by

$$P(A \cup B \cup C) = 1 - P(\bar{A} \cap \bar{B} \cap \bar{C})$$
$$= 1 - P(\bar{A}).\ P(\bar{B}).\ P(\bar{C})$$
$$= 1 - \{0.85 \times 0.95 \times 0.90\} = 1 - 0.726 = 0.274$$

Example 6.16: A company has two plants to manufacture scooters. Plant I manufactures 80 per cent of the scooters and plant II manufactures 20 per cent. In plant I, only 85 out of 100 scooters are considered to be of standard quality. In plant II, only 65 out of 100 scooters are considered to be of standard quality. What is the probability that a scooter selected at random came from plant I, if it is known that it is of standard quality? *[Madras Univ., MCom, 1996]*

Solution: Let A = The scooter purchased is of standard quality

B = The scooter is of standard quality and came from plant I

C = The scooter is of standard quality and came from plant II

D = The scooter came from plant I

The percentage of scooters manufactured in plant I that are of standard quality is 85 per cent of 80 per cent, that is, $0.85 \times (80 \div 100) = 68$ per cent or P(B) = 0.68.

The percentage of scooters manufactured in plant II that are of standard quality is 65 per cent of 20 per cent, that is, $0.65 \times (20 \div 100) = 13$ per cent or P(C) = 0.13.

The probability that a customer obtains a standard quality scooter from the company is, 0.68 + 0.13 = 0.81.

The probability that the scooters selected at random came from plant I, if it is known that it is of standard quality, is given by

$$P(D|A) = \frac{P(D \text{ and } A)}{P(A)} = \frac{0.68}{0.81} = 0.84$$

Example 6.17: In a railway reservation office, two clerks are engaged in checking reservation forms. On an average, the first clerk checks 55% of the forms, while the second does the remaining. The first clerk has an error rate of 0.03 and second has an error rate of 0.02. A reservation for m is selected at random from the total number of forms checked during a day, and is found to have an error. Find the probability that it was checked (*a*) by the first (*b*) by the second clerk.

Solution: Let us define the following events :

A : The selected form is checked by clerk 1

B : The selected form is checked by clerk 2

E : The selected form has an error.

Given, $P(A) = 0.55,\quad P(B) = 0.45,\quad P(E|A) = 0.03,\quad P(E|B) = 0.02.$

We find $P(A|E)$ and $P(B|E)$

$$P(E) = P(A)\,P(E|A) + P(B)\,P(E|B) = 0.55 \times 0.03 + 0.45 \times 0.02$$
$$= 0.0165 + 0.009 = 0.0255$$

Now,
$$P(A|E) = \frac{P(A \cap E)}{P(E)} = \frac{P(A)\,P(E|A)}{P(E)}$$
$$= \frac{055 \times 0.03}{0.0255} = 0.647$$

Similarly,
$$P(B|E) = \frac{P(B \cap E)}{P(E)} = \frac{P(E\,|\,B).P(B)}{P(E)}$$
$$= \frac{0.02 \times 0.45}{0.0255} = 0.053.$$

Example 6.18: A husband and wife appear in an interview for two vacancies in the same post. The probability of husband's selection is 1/7 and that of wife's selection is 1/5. What is the probability that

(a) both of them will be selected,

(b) only one of them will be selected, and

(c) none of them will be selected. [*Bharthidasan Univ., MCom, 1996*]

Solution: Let A and B be the events of the husband's and wife's selection, respectively. Given that P(A) = 1/7 and P(B) = 1/5.

(a) The probability that both of them will be selected is:

$$P(A \text{ and } B) = P(A)\,P(B) = (1/7) \times (1/5) = 1/35 = 0.029$$

(b) The probability that only one of them will be selected is:

$$P[(A \text{ and } \bar{B}) \text{ or } (B \text{ and } \bar{A}) = P(A \text{ and } \bar{B}) + P(B \text{ and } \bar{A}) = P(A)\,P(\bar{B}) + P(B)\,P(\bar{A})$$
$$= P(A)\,[1 - P(B)] + P(B)\,[1 - P(A)]$$
$$= \frac{1}{7}\left(1 - \frac{1}{5}\right) + \frac{1}{5}\left(1 - \frac{1}{7}\right) = \left(\frac{1}{7} \times \frac{4}{5}\right) + \left(\frac{1}{5} \times \frac{6}{7}\right)$$
$$= \frac{10}{35} = 0.286$$

(c) The probability that none of them will be selected is:

$$P(\bar{A}) \times P(\bar{B}) = (6/7)\times(4/5) = 24/35 = 0.686$$

Example 6.19: The odds that A speaks the truth is 3 : 2 and the odds that B speaks the truth is 5 : 3. In what percentage of cases are they likely to contradict each other on an identical point?

Solution: Let X and Y denote the events that A and B speak truth, respectively. Given that

$$P(X) = 3/5;\quad P(\bar{X}) = 2/5;\quad P(Y) = 5/8;\quad P(\bar{Y}) = 3/8$$

The probability that A speaks the truth and B speaks a lie is: (3/5) (3/8) = 9/40

The probability that B speaks the truth and A speaks a lie is: (5/8) (2/5) = 10/40

So the compound probability is: $\frac{9}{40} + \frac{10}{40} = \frac{19}{40}$

Hence, percentage of cases in which they contradict each other is (19/40) × 100 = 47.5 per cent.

Example 6.20: A market survey was conducted in four cities to find out the preference for brand A soap. The responses are shown below:

	Delhi	*Kolkata*	*Chennai*	*Mumbai*
Yes	45	55	60	50
No	35	45	35	45
No opinion	5	5	5	5

(a) What is the probability that a consumer selected at random, preferred brand A?
(b) What is the probability that a consumer preferred brand A and was from Chennai?
(c) What is the probability that a consumer preferred brand A, given that he was from Chennai?
(d) Given that a consumer preferred brand A, what is the probability that he was from Mumbai?

Solution: The information from responses during market survey is as follows:

	Delhi	*Kolkata*	*Chennai*	*Mumbai*	*Total*
Yes	45	55	60	50	210
No	35	45	35	45	160
No opinion	5	5	5	5	20
Total	85	105	100	100	390

Let X denote the event that a consumer selected at random preferred brand A. Then

(a) The probability that a consumer selected at random preferred brand A is:

$$P(X) = 210/390 = 0.5398$$

(b) The probability that a consumer preferred brand A and was from Chennai (C) is:

$$P(X \cap C) = 60/390 = 0.1538$$

(c) The probability that a consumer preferred brand A, given that he was from Chennai:

$$P(X|C) = \frac{P(A \cap C)}{P(C)} = \frac{60/390}{100/390} = \frac{0.153}{0.256} = 0.597$$

(d) The probability that the consumer belongs to Mumbai, given that he preferred brand A

$$P(M|X) = \frac{P(M \cap X)}{P(X)} = \frac{50/390}{210/390} = \frac{0.128}{0.538} = 0.237$$

Self-Practice Problems 6B

6.10 Mr. X has 2 shares in a lottery in which there are 2 prizes and 5 blanks. Mr. Y has 1 share in a lottery in which there is 1 prize and 2 blanks. Show that the chance of Mr. X's success to that of Mr. Y's is 15 : 7.

6.11 Explain whether or not each of the following claims could be correct:

(a) A businessman claims that the probability that he will get contract A is 0.15 and that he will get contract B is 0.20. Furthermore, he claims that the probability of getting A or B is 0.50.

(b) A market analyst claims that the probability of selling ten million rupees of plastic A or five million rupees of plastic B is 0.60. He also claims that the probability of selling ten million rupees of A and five million rupees of B is 0.45.

6.12 The probability that an applicant for a Management Accountant's job has a postgraduate degree is 0.3, he has had some work experience as a chief Financial Accountant is 0.7, and that he has both is 0.2. Out of 300 applicants, approximately, what number would have either a postgraduate degree or some professional work experience?

6.13 A can hit a target 3 times in 5 shots; B, 2 times in 5 shots; C, 3 times in 4 shots. They fire a volley. What is the probability that 2 shots hit?

6.14 A problem in business statistics is given to five students, A, B, C, D, and E. Their chances of solving it are 1/2, 1/3, 1/4, 1/5, and 1/6 respectively. What is the probability that the problem will be solved?

[*Madras Univ., BCom, 1996*]

6.15 A husband and wife appear in an interview for two vacancies for the same post. The probability of husband's selection is 1/7 and that of wife's selection is 1/5. What is the probability that

(a) only one of them will be selected?

(b) both of them will be selected?

(c) none of them will be selected?

6.16 There is 50-50 chance that a contractor's firm, A, will bid for the construction of a multi-storeyed building. Another firm, B, submits a bid and the probability is 3/5 that it will get the job, provided that firm A does not submit a bid. If firm A submits a bid, the probability that firm B will get the job is only 2/3. What is the probability that firm B will get the job?

6.17 Plant I of XYZ manufacturing organization employs 5 production and 3 maintenance foremen, plant II of same organization employs 4 production and 5 maintenance foremen. From any one of these plants, a single selection of two foremen is made. Find the probability that one of them would be a production and the other a maintenance foreman.

6.18 If a machine is correctly set up, it will produce 90 per cent acceptable items. If it is incorrectly setup, it will produce 40 per cent acceptable items. Past experience shows that 80 per cent of the setups are correctly done. If after a certain setup, the machine produces 2 acceptable items as the first 2 pieces, find the probability that the machine is correctly set up.

[*Delhi Univ., BCom, (Hons), 1998*]

6.19 A firm plans to bid Rs. 300 per tonne for a contract to supply 1,000 tonnes of a metal. It has two competitors A and B. It assumes the probability of A bidding less than Rs. 300 per tonne to be 0.3 and B's bid to be less than Rs. 300 per tonne to be 0.7. If the lowest bidder gets all the business and the firms bid independently, what is the expected value of the contract to the firm?

6.20 An investment consultant predicts that the odds against the price of a certain stock going up during the next week are 2 : 1 and odds in favour of the price remaining the same are 1 : 3. What is the probability that the price of the stock will go down during the next week?

6.21 An article manufactured by a company consists of two parts A and B. In the process of manufacture of part A, 9 out of 100 are likely to be defective. Similarly, 5 out of 100 are likely to be defective in the manufacture of part B. Calculate the probability that the assembled part will not be defective.

6.22 A product is assembled from three components X, Y, and Z, the probability of these components being defective is 0.01, 0.02, and 0.05, respectively. What is the probability that the assembled product will not be defective?

6.23 The daily production of a machine producing a very complicated item gives the following probabilities for the number of items produced: P(1) = 0.20, P(2) = 0.35, and P(3) = 0.45. Furthermore, the probability of defective items being produced is 0.02. Defective items are assumed to occur independently. Determine the probability of no defectives during a day's production.

6.24 You note that your officer is happy in 60 per cent cases of your calls. You have also noticed that if he is happy, he accedes to your requests with a probability of 0.4, whereas if he is not happy, he accedes to your requests with a probability of 0.1. You call on him one day and he accedes to your request. What is the probability of his being happy?

6.25 In a colour preference experiment, eight toys are placed in a container. The toys are identical except for colour — two are red, and six are green. A child is asked to choose two toys at random. What is the probability that the child chooses the two red toys?

Hints and Answers

6.10 Considering Mr. X's chances of success.

A = event that 1 share brings a prize and 1 share goes blank.

B = event that both the shares bring prizes.

C = event that X succeeds in getting atleast one prize

$= A \cup B$.

Since A and B are mutually exclusive, therefore

$$P(C) = P(A \cup B) = P(A) + P(B)$$

$$= \frac{{}^2C_1 \times {}^5C_1}{{}^7C_2} + \frac{{}^2C_2 \times {}^5C_0}{{}^7C_2}$$

Similarly, if D denotes the event that Y succeeds in getting a prize, then we have

$$P(D) = \frac{{}^1C_1}{{}^3C_1} = \frac{1}{3}$$

X's chance of success: Y's chance of success

$$= : \frac{1}{3} = 15 : 7.$$

6.11 (a) $P(A \cap B) = -0.15$

(b) $P(A) + P(B) = 1.05$

6.12 Let A = Applicant has P.G degree; B = Applicant has work experience;

Given, $P(A) = 0.3$, $P(B) = 0.7$, and $P(A \cap B) = 0.2$. Therefore

$300 \times P(A \cup B) = 300[P(A) + P(B) - P(A \cap B)] = 240$

6.13 The required event that two shots may hit the target, can happen in the following mutually exclusive cases:

(i) A and B hit and C fails to hit the target

(ii) A and C hit and B fails to hit the target

(iii) B and C hit and A fails to hit the target

Hence, the required probability that any two shots hit is given by, P = P(i) + P(ii) + P(iii).

Let E_1, E_2, and E_3 be the event of hitting the target by A, B, and C respectively. Therefore

$$P(i) = P(E_1 \cap E_2 \cap \bar{E}_3)$$

$$= P(E_1) \cdot P(E_2) \cdot P(\bar{E}_3)$$

$$= \left(\frac{3}{5}\right)\cdot\left(\frac{2}{5}\right)\cdot\left(1 - \frac{3}{4}\right) = \frac{6}{100}$$

$$P(ii) = P(E_1 \cap \bar{E}_2 \cap E_3) = \left(\frac{3}{5}\right)\left(1 - \frac{2}{5}\right)\left(\frac{3}{4}\right)$$

$$= \frac{27}{100}$$

$$P(iii) = P(\bar{E}_1 \cap E_2 \cap E_3) = \left(1 - \frac{3}{5}\right)\left(\frac{2}{5}\right)\left(\frac{3}{4}\right)$$

$$= \frac{12}{100}$$

Since all the three events are mutually exclusive events, hence the required probability is given by

$$P(i) + P(ii) + P(iii) = \frac{6}{100} + \frac{27}{100} + \frac{12}{100} = \frac{9}{20}$$

6.14 P(problem will be solved)

= 1 – P(problem is not solved)

= 1 – P(all students fail to solve the problem)

$= 1 - P(\bar{A} \cap \bar{B} \cap \bar{C} \cap \bar{D} \cap \bar{E})$

$= 1 - P(\bar{A})\, P(\bar{B})\, P(\bar{C})\, P(\bar{D})\, P(\bar{E})$

$$= 1-\left(1-\frac{1}{2}\right)\left(1-\frac{1}{3}\right)\left(1-\frac{1}{4}\right)\left(1-\frac{1}{5}\right)\left(1-\frac{1}{6}\right)$$

$$= 1-\frac{1}{6} = \frac{5}{6}$$

6.15 P(only one of them will be selected)

$$= P(H \cap \bar{W}) \cup (\bar{H} \cap W)$$

$$= P(H \cap \bar{W}) + (\bar{H} \cap W)$$

$$= P(H)\,P(\bar{W}) + P(\bar{H})\,P(W)$$

$$= \frac{1}{7}\left(1-\frac{1}{5}\right)+\left(1-\frac{1}{7}\right)\frac{1}{5} = \frac{2}{7}$$

(b) P(both of them will be selected)

$$P(H \cap W) = P(H)\cdot P(W) = \frac{1}{35}$$

(c) P(none of them will be selected)

$$P(\bar{H} \cap \bar{W}) = P(\bar{H})\cdot P(\bar{W}) = \frac{24}{35}$$

6.16 $P(A) = 1/2$, $P(B \mid A) = 2/3$. and $P(B \mid \bar{A}) = 3/5$.

$$P(B) = P(A \cap B) + P(\bar{A} \cap B)$$

$$= P(A)\cdot P(B|A) + P(\bar{A})\cdot P(B \mid \bar{A})$$

$$= \frac{1}{2}\cdot\frac{2}{3}+\frac{1}{2}\cdot\frac{3}{5} = \frac{19}{30}.$$

6.17 Let E_1 and E_2 be the events that Plant I and II is selected respectively. Then, the probability of the event E that in a batch of 2, one is the production and the other is the maintenance man is

$$P(E) = P(E_1 \cap E) + P(E_2 \cap E)$$

$$= P(E_1)\cdot P(E|E_1) + P(E_2)\cdot P(E|E_2)$$

$$= \frac{1}{2}\cdot\frac{{}^5C_1\cdot{}^3C_1}{{}^8C_2}+\frac{1}{2}\cdot\frac{{}^4C_1\cdot{}^5C_1}{{}^9C_2}$$

$$= \frac{1}{2}\cdot\frac{15}{28}+\frac{1}{2}\cdot\frac{5}{9} = \frac{275}{504}$$

6.18 Let A = event that the item is acceptable;

B_1 and B_2 = events that machine is correctly and incorrectly setup, respectively.

Given, $P(A|B_1) = 0.9$; $P(A \mid B_2) = 0.4$; $P(B_1) = 0.8$ and $P(B_2) = 0.2$. Then $P(B_1 \mid A) = 0.9$.

6.19 There are two competitors A and B and the lowest bidder gets the contract.

Value of plan = 300 × 1,000 = 3,00,000

Contractor A: P(Bid < 300) = 0.3;

P(Bid ≥ 300) = 0.7

Contractor B: P(Bid < 300) = 0.7;

P(Bid ≥ 300) = 0.3

(i) If both bids are less than Rs. 300, probability is 0.3 × 0.7 = 0.21. Therefore plan value is:

3,00,000 × 0.21 = 63,000.

(ii) If A bids less than 300 and B bids more than 300, probability is 0.3 × 0.3 = 0.9. Therefore, plan value is: 3,00,000 × 0.09 = 27,000.

(iii) B bids less than 300 while A bids more than 300, probability is: 0.7 × 0.7 = 0.49. Therefore plan value is: 3,00,000 × 0.49 = 1,47,000.

Therefore, expected value of plan is

63,000 + 27,000 + 1,47,000 = 2,37,000.

6.20. P(price of a certain stock not going up) = 2/3

P(price of a certain stock remaining same) = 1/4

The probability that the price of the stock will go down during the next week

= P(price of the stock not going up and not remaining same)

= P(price of the stock not going up × P(price of the stock not remaining same)

$$= \left(\frac{2}{3}\right)\times\left(1-\frac{1}{4}\right) = \left(\frac{2}{3}\right)\times\left(\frac{3}{4}\right) = \frac{1}{2} = 0.5$$

6.21 The assembled part will be defective if any of the parts is defective.

The probability of the assembled part being defective:

= P[Any of the part is defective]

$$= P[A \cup B] = P(A) + P(B) - P(AB)$$

$$= \frac{9}{100}+\frac{5}{100}-\left(\frac{9}{100}\right)\times\left(\frac{5}{100}\right)$$

$$= 0.1355$$

The probability that assembled part is not defective

$$= 1 - 0.1355 = 0.8645.$$

6.22 Let A, B, and C denote the respective probabilities of components X, Y, and Z being defective.

$$P(A) = 0.01,\; P(B) = 0.02,$$

$$P(C) = 0.05$$

$$P(A \text{ or } B \text{ or } C) = P(A) + P(B) + P(C) - P(AB) - P(BC) - P(AC) + P(ABC)$$

$= 0.01 + 0.02 + 0.05 - 0.0002$
$- 0.0010 - 0.0005 + 0.00001$
$= 0.0784$

Hence the probability that the assembled product will not be defective = 1 – 0.0784 or 0.9216.

6.23 Let A be the event that no defective item is produced during a day. Then

$$P(A) = P(I) \cdot P(A|I) + P(2) \cdot P(A|2) + P(3) \cdot P(A|3)$$

The probability that a defective item is produced = 0.02. Probability that a non-defective item is produced = 1 – 0.02 = 0.98. Also defectives are assumed to occur independently, therefore:

$P(A \mid I) = 0.98$, $P(A \mid 2) = (0.98)(0.98)$ and

$P(A \mid 3) = (0.98)(0.98)(0.98)$

$$P(A) = (0.20)(0.98) + (0.35)(0.98)^2 + (0.45)(0.98)^3$$

$$= 0.1960 + 0.3361 + 0.4322$$
$$= 0.9643$$

Hence the probability of no defectives during a day's production is 0.9643.

6.24 The probability that the officer is happy and accedes to requests = 0.6 × 0.4.

The probability that the officer is unhappy and accedes to requests = 0.4 × 0.1 = 0.04.

Total probability of acceding to requests = 0.24 + 0.04 = 0.28.

The probability of his being happy if he accedes to requests = 0.24/0.28 = 0.875.

6.25 Let R = Red toy is chosen and G = Green toy is chosen.

P(Both toys are R) = P(R on first choice ∩ R on second choice)
= P(R on first choice). P(R on second choice | R on first choice)
= (2/8) (1/7) = 1/28.

6.6 BAYES' THEOREM

In the 18th century, reverend Thomas Bayes, an English Presbyterian minister, raised a question: Does God really exist? To answer this question, he attempted to develop a formula to determine the probability that God does exist, based on evidence that was available to him on earth. Later, Laplace refined Bayes' work and gave it the name *Bayes' Theorem*.

The **Bayes' theorem** is useful in revising the original probability estimates of known outcomes as we gain additional information about these outcomes. The prior probabilities, when changed in the light of new information, are called *revised* or *posterior probabilities*.

Suppose $A_1, A_2, \ldots, A_n$ represent n mutually exclusive and collectively exhaustive events with prior marginal probabilities $P(A_1), P(A_2), \ldots, P(A_n)$. Let B be an arbitrary event with $P(B) \neq 0$ for which conditional probabilities $P(B|A_1), P(B|A_2), \ldots, P(B|A_n)$ are also known. Given the information that outcome B has occured, the revised (or posterior) probabilities $P(A_i|B)$ are determined with the help of Bayes' theorem using the formula:

$$P(A_i|B) = \frac{P(A_i \cap B)}{P(B)} \quad (6\text{-}7)$$

where the posterior probability of events A_i given event B is the conditional probability $P(A_i|B)$.

Since events $A_1, A_2, \ldots, A_n$ are mutually exclusive and collectively exhaustive, the event B is bound to occur with either $A_1, A_2, \ldots, A_n$. That is,

$$B = (A_1 \cap B) \cup (A_2 \cap B) \cup \ldots \cup (A_n \cap B)$$

where the **posterior probability** of A_i given B is the conditonal probability $P(A_i|B)$.

Example 6.21: Suppose an item is manufactured by three machines X, Y, and Z. All the three machines have equal capacity and are operated at the same rate. It is known that the percentages of defective items produced by X, Y, and Z are 2, 7, and 12 per cent, respectively. All the items produced by X, Y, and Z are put into one bin. From this bin, one item is drawn at random and is found to be defective. What is the probability that this item was produced on Y?

Solution: Let A be the defective item. We know the prior probability of defective items produced on X, Y, and Z, that is, P(X) = 1/3; P(Y) = 1/3 and P(Z) = 1/3. We also know that

$$P(A|X) = 0.02, \quad P(A|Y) = 0.07, \quad P(A|Z) = 0.12$$

Now, having known that the item drawn is defective, we want to know the probability that it was produced by Y. That is

$$P(Y|A) = \frac{P(A|Y).P(Y)}{P(X).P(A|X) + P(Y).P(A|Y) + P(Z).P(A|Z)}$$

$$= \frac{(0.07).(1/3)}{(1/3)(0.02) + (1/3)(0.07) + (1/3)(0.12)} = 0.33$$

Example 6.22: In class of 75 students, 15 were considered to be very intelligent, 45 as medium and rest below average the probability that a very intelligent student fails in a viva-voice examination is 0.005. The medium student failing has a probability 0.05 and the corresponding probability for a below average student is 0.15. If student is known to have passed the viva-voice examination, what is the probability that he is below average ?

Solution: Let us define the events :

A : students is very intelligent, *B* : student is medium
C : student is below average, *E* : student passed in viva-voice examination.

Given, $P(A) = 15/75 = 0.2$, $P(B) = 45/75 = 0.6$, $P(C) = 15/75 = 0.2$ and the need to find $P(C \mid E)$

$P(E|A) = 1 - 0.005 = 0.995$; $P(E|B) = 1 - 0.05 = 0.95$; $P(E|C) = 1 - 0.15 = 0.85$

$$P(C|E) = \frac{P(C \cap E)}{P(E)} = \frac{P(C)P(E|V)}{P(A)P(E|A) + P(B)P(E|B) + P(C)P(E|C)} \quad \text{(By Baye's Rule)}$$

$$= \frac{0.2 \times 0.85}{0.2 \times 0.995 + 0.6 \times 0.95 + 0.2 \times 0.85}$$

$$= \frac{0.170}{0.199 + 0.57 + 0.17} = \frac{0.17}{0.939} = 0.181.$$

Self-Practice Problems 6C

6.26 In a post office, three clerks are assigned to process incoming mail. The first clerk, A, processes 40 per cent; the second clerk, B, processes 35 per cent; and the third clerk, C, processes 25 per cent of the mail. The first clerk has an error rate of 0.04, the second has an error rate of 0.06, and the third has an error rate of 0.03. A mail selected at random from a day's output is found to have an error. The postmaster wishes to know the probability that it was processed by clerk A or clerk B or clerk C.

6.27 A certain production process produces items 10 per cent of which defective. Each item is inspected before supplying to customers but 10 per cent of the time the inspector incorrectly classifies an item. Only items classified as good are supplied. If 820 items have been supplied in all, how many of them are expected to be defective?

6.28 A factory produces certain types of output by three machines. The respective daily production figures are: Machine A = 3000 units; Machine B = 2500 units; and Machine C = 4500 units. Past experience shows that 1 per cent of the output produced by machine A is defective. The corresponding fractions of defectives for the other two machines are 1.2 and 2 per cent respectively. An item is drawn at random from the day's production and is found to be defective. What is probability that it comes from the output of (a) Machine A; (b) Machine B; (c) Machine C?

6.29 In a bolt factory machines A, B, and C manufacture 25 per cent, 30 per cent and 40 per cent of the total output respectively. Of the total of their output 5, 4, and 2 per cent are defective bolts. A bolt is drawn at random from the lot and is found to be defective. What are the probabilities that it was manufactured by machines A, B, or C?

6.30 In a factory manufacturing pens, machines X, Y, and Z manufacture 30, 30, and 40 per cent of the total production of pens, respectively. Of their output 4, 5, and 10 per cent of the pens are defective. If one pen is selected at random, and it is found to be defective, what is the probability that it is manufactured by machine Z?

6.31 A worker-operated machine produces a defective item with probability 0.01, if the worker follows the machine's operating instruction exactly, and with probability 0.03 if he does not. If the worker follows the instructions 90 per cent of the time, what proportion of all items produced by the machine will be defective?

6.32 Medical case histories indicate that different illnesses may produce identical symptoms. Suppose a particular set of symptoms, 'H' occurs only when one of three illnesses: A, B or C occurs, with probabilities 0.01, 0.005 and 0.02 respectively. The probability of developing the symptoms H, given a illness A, B and C are 0.90, 0.95 and 0.75 respectively. Assuming that an ill person shows the symptoms H, what is the probability that a person has illness A?

Hints and Answers

6.26 Let A, B, and C = mail processed by first, second, and third clerk, respectively

E = mail containing error

Given P(A) = 0.40, P(B) = 0.35, and P(C) = 0.25

P(E | A) = 0.04, P(E | B) = 0.06, and P(E | C) = 0.03

$$\therefore\ P(A \mid E) = \frac{P(A)\,P(E|A)}{P(E)}$$

$$= \frac{P(A)\,P(E|A)}{P(A)\,P(E|A) + P(B)\,P(E|B) + P(C)\,P(E|C)}$$

$$= \frac{0.40 \times 0.04}{0.40\,(0.04) + 0.35\,(0.06) + 0.25\,(0.03)}$$

= 0.36

Similarly $P(B|E) = [P(B)\,P(E|B)]/P(E) = 0.47$

$P(C|E) = [P(C)\,P(E|C)]/P(E) = 0.17$

6.27 P(D) = Probability of defective item = 0.1; P(classified as good | defective) = 0.1

∴ P(G) = Probability of good item = 1 – P(D) = 1 – 0.1 = 0.9

P(classified as good | good) = 1 – P(classified as good | defective) = 1 – 0.1 = 0.9

∴ P(defective | classified as good)

$$= \frac{P(D)\cdot P(\text{classified as good} \mid \text{defective})}{[P(D)\cdot P(\text{classified as good} \mid D) + P(G)\,P(\text{classified as good} \mid G)]}$$

$$= \frac{0.1\times 0.1}{0.1\times 0.1 + 0.9\times 0.9} = \frac{0.01}{0.82} = 0.012.$$

6.28 (a) 0.20 (b) 0.20 (c) 0.60

6.29 P(A) = 0.37, P(B) = 0.40, P(C) = 0.23

6.30 P(Z) = 0.6639

6.31 P(A) = 0.012

6.32 P(A | H) = 0.3130

6.7 PROBABILITY DISTRIBUTIONS

In any probabilistic situation each strategy (course of action) may lead to a number of different possible outcomes. For example, a product whose sale is estimated around 100 units, may be equal to 100, less, or more. Here the sale (i.e., an outcome) of the product is measured in real numbers but the volume of the sales is uncertain. The volume of sale which is an uncertain quantity and whose definite value is determined by chance is termed as *random (chance* or *stochastic) variable*. A listing of all the possible outcomes of a random variable with each outcome's associated probability of occurrence is called *probability distribution*. The numerical value of a random variable depends upon the outcome of an experiment and may be different for different trials of the same experiment. The set of all such values so obtained is called the *range space* of the random variable.

Illustration: If a coin is tossed twice, then the sample space of events, for this random experiment is

$$S = \{H\,H, T\,H, H\,T, T\,T\}$$

In this case, if the decision-maker is interested to know the probability distribution for the number of heads on two tosses of the coin, then a random variable (x) may be defined as:

$$x = \text{number of H's occurred}$$

The values of x will depend on chance and may take the values: H H = 2, H T = 1, T H = 1, T T = 0. Thus the range space of x is $\{0, 1, 2\}$.

When a random variable x is defined, a value is given to each simple event in the sample space. The probability of any particular value of x can then be found by adding the probabilities for all the simple events that have that value of x. For example, the probabilities of occurrence of 'heads' can be associated with each of the random variable values. Supposing $P(x = r)$ represents the probability of the random variable taking the value r (here r represents the number of heads occurred). Then probabilities of occurrence of different number of heads are computed as:

Number of Heads (x)	*Probability of Outcome P(x)*
0	$P(x = 0) = P(T\,T) = P(T) \times P(T) = 0.5 \times 0.5 = 0.25$
1	$P(x = 1) = P(H\,T) + P(T\,H) = P(H) \times P(T) + P(T) \times P(H)$
	$= 0.5 \times 0.5 + 0.5 \times 0.5 = 0.25 + 0.25 = 0.50$
2	$P(x = 2) = P(H\,H) = P(H) \times P(H) = 0.5 \times 0.5 = 0.25$

Broad Classes of Random Variable A random variable may be either discrete or continuous. A **discrete random variable** can take on only a finite or countably infinite number of distinct values such as 0, 1, 2, . . ., A discrete random variable is usually the result of counting. The number of letters received by a post office during a particular time period, the number of machines breaking down on a given day, the number of vehicles arriving at a toll bridge, and so on, are a few examples of discrete random variables.

A **continuous random variable** can take any numerical value in an interval or collection of intervals. A continuous random variable is usually the result of experimental outcomes that are based on measurement scales. For instance, measurement of time, weight, distance, temperature, and so on are all treated as continuous random variables. Tonnage produced by a steel blast furnace, amount of rainfall in a rainy season, height of individuals, time between arrival of customers at a service system in minutes, are also few examples of continuous random variables.

6.8 EXPECTED VALUE AND VARIANCE OF A RANDOM VARIABLE

Expected Value The mean (also referred as **expected value) of a random variable** is a typical value used to summarize a probability distribution. It is the weighted average, where the possible values of random variable are weighted by the corresponding probabilities of occurrence. If x is a random variable with possible values x_1, $x_2,\ldots, x_n$ occuring with probabilities $P(x_1)$, $P(x_2),\ldots, P(x_n)$, then the expected value of x denoted by $E(x)$ or μ is the sum of the values of the random variable weighted by the probability that the random variable takes on that value.

$$E(x) = \sum_{j=1}^{n} x_j P(x_j), \text{ provided } \sum_{j=1}^{n} P(x_j) = 1$$

Similarly, for the continuous random variable, the expected value is given by:

$$E(x) = \int_{-\infty}^{\infty} x f(x)\, dx$$

where $f(x)$ is the probability distribution function.

If $E(x)$ is calculated in terms of rupees, then it is known as *expected monetary value* (EMV). For example, consider the price range of an item along with the probabilities as below:

Price, x :	50	60	70	80
Probability, $P(x)$:	0.2	0.5	0.2	0.1

Thus the expected monetary value of the item is given by

$$\text{EMV}(x) = \sum_{j=1}^{n} x_j P(x_j) = 50\times 0.2 + 60\times 0.5 + 70\times 0.2 + 80\times 0.1 = \text{Rs. } 62.$$

Variance and Standard Deviation The expected value measures the *central tendency* of a probability distribution, while variance determines the *dispersion* or *variability* to which the possible random values differ among themselves.

The variance, denoted by $\text{Var}(x)$ or σ^2 of a random variable x is the squared deviation of the individual values from their expected value or mean. That is

$$\begin{aligned}\text{Var}(x) &= E[(x-\mu)^2] = E(x_j - \mu)^2\, P(x_j), \text{ for all } j\\ &= E[(x^2 - 2x\mu + \mu^2)]\\ &= E(x^2) - 2\mu E(x) + \mu^2 = E(x^2) - \mu^2\end{aligned}$$

where $E(x^2) = \sum_{j=1}^{n} x_j^2 P(x_j)$ and $\mu = \sum_{j=1}^{n} x_j P(x_j)$

The variance has the disadvantage of squaring the unit of measurement. Thus, if a random variable is measured in rupees, the variance will be measured in rupee squared. This shortcoming can be avoided by using *standard deviation* (σ_x) as a measure of dispersion so as to have the same unit of measurement. That is

$$\sigma_x = \sqrt{\text{Var}(x)} = \sqrt{\sum_{j=1}^{n} (x_j - \mu)^2 P(x_j)}$$

6.8.1 Properties of Expected Value and Variance

The following are the important properties of an expected value of a random variable:

1. The expected value of a constant c is constant. That is, $E(c) = c$, for every constant c.
2. The expected value of the product of a constant c and a random variable x is equal to constant c times the expected value of the random variable. That is, $E(cx) = cE(x)$.
3. The expected value of a linear function of a random variable is same as the linear function of its expectation. That is, $E(a + bx) = a + bE(x)$.
4. The expected value of the product of two independent random variables is equal to the product of their individual expected values. That is, $E(xy) = E(x)\,E(y)$.
5. The expected value of the sum of the two independent random variables is equal to the sum of their individual expected values. That is, $E(x + y) = E(x) + E(y)$.
6. The variance of the product of a constant and a random variable X is equal to the constant squared times the variance of the random variable X. That is, $\text{Var}(cx) = c^2\,\text{Var}(x)$.
7. The variance of the sum (or difference) of two independent random variables equals the sum of their individual variances. That is, $\text{Var}(x \pm y) = \text{Var}(x) \pm \text{Var}(y)$.

Example 6.23: From a bag containing 3 red balls and 2 white balls, a man is to draw two balls at random without replacement. He gains Rs. 20 for each red ball and Rs. 10 for each white one. What is the expectation of his draw?

Solution: Let x be the random variable denoting the number of red and white balls in a draw. Then x can take up the following values.

$$P(x = 2 \text{ red balls}) = \frac{{}^3C_2}{{}^5C_2} = \frac{3}{10}$$

$$P(x = 1 \text{ red and 1 white ball}) = \frac{{}^3C_1 \times {}^2C_1}{{}^5C_2} = \frac{3}{5}$$

$$P(x = 2 \text{ white balls}) = \frac{{}^2C_2}{{}^5C_2} = \frac{1}{10}$$

Thus, the probability distribution of x is:

Variable :	2R	1R and 1W	2W
Gain, x :	40	30	20
Probability, $P(x)$:	3/10	3/5	1/10

Hence, expected gain is, $E(x) = 40\times(3/10) + 30\times(3/5) + 20\times(1/10) = \text{Rs. } 32.$

Example 6.24: In a cricket match played to benefit an ex-player, 10,000 tickets are to be sold at Rs. 500. The prize is a Rs. 12,000 fridge by lottery. If a person purchases two tickets, what is his expected gain?

Solution: The gain, say x may take one of two values: he will either lose Rs. 1,000 (i.e. gain will be – Rs. 1,000) or win Rs. (12,000–1,000) = Rs. 11,000, with probabilities 9,998/10,000 and 2/10,000, respectively. The probability distribution for the gain x is given below:

x	$P(x)$
– Rs. 1000	9,998/10,000
Rs. 11000	2/10,000

The expected gain will be

$$\mu = E(x) = \Sigma x\ P(x)$$
$$= -1000 \times (9{,}998/10{,}000) + 11000 \times (2/10{,}000) = -\text{Rs. } 997.6$$

The result implies that if the lottery were repeated an infinitely large number of times, average or expected loss will be Rs. 997.6.

Example 6.25: A market researcher at a major automobile company classified house-holds by car ownership. The relative frequencies of households for each category of ownership are shown below:

Number of Cars Per House hold	*Relative Frequency*
0	0.10
1	0.30
2	0.40
3	0.12
4	0.06
5	0.02

Calculate the expected value and standard deviation of the random variable and interpret the result.

Solution: The necessary calculations required to calculate expected and standard deviation of a random variable, say x are shown is Table 6.1.

Table 6.1 Calculations of Expected Value and Standard Deviation

Number of Cars Per Households x	*Relative Frequency, P(x)*	$x \times P(x)$	$x^2 \times P(x)$
0	0.10	0.10	0.00
1	0.30	0.30	0.30
2	0.40	0.80	1.60
3	0.12	0.36	1.08
4	0.06	0.24	0.96
5	0.02	0.10	0.50
		1.80	4.44

Expected value, $\mu = E(x) = \Sigma x\ P(x) = 1.80$. This value indicates that there are on an average 1.8 cars per household.

Variance, $\sigma^2 = \Sigma x^2\ P(x) - [E(x)]^2 = 4.44 - (1.80)^2 = 4.44 - 3.24 = 1.20$

Standard deviation $\sigma = \sqrt{\sigma^2} = \sqrt{1.20} = 1.095$ cars.

Conceptual Questions 6B

7. Define 'random variable'. How do you distinguish between discrete and continuous random variables? Illustrate your answer with suitable examples.

8. What do you understand by the expected value of a random variable?

9. What are the properties of expected value and variance of a random variable?

Self-Practice Problems 6D

6.33 Anil company estimates the net profit on a new product it is launching to be Rs. 30,00,000 during the first year if it is 'successful' Rs. 10,00,000 if it is 'moderately successful'; and a loss of Rs. 10,00,000 if it is 'unsuccessful'. The firm assigns the following probabilities to its first year prospects for the product: Successful : 0.15, moderately successful : 0.25. What are the expected value and standard deviation of first year net profit for this product?

6.34 A box contains 12 items of which 3 are defective. A sample of 3 items is selected at random from this box. If x represents the number of defective items of 3 selected items, describe the random variable x completely and obtain its expectation.

6.35 Fifty per cent of all automobile accidents lead to property damage of Rs. 100, forty per cent lead to damage of Rs. 500, and ten per cent lead to total loss, that is, damage of Rs. 1800. If a car has a 5 per cent chance of being in an accident in a year, what is the expected value of the property damage due to that possible accident?

6.36 The probability that there is atleast one error in an account statement prepared by A is 0.2 and for B and C it is 0.25 and 0.4 respectively. A, B, and C prepared 10, 16, and 20 statements respectively. Find the expected number of correct statements in all.

6.37 A lottery sells 10,000 tickets at Re 1 per ticket, and the prize of Rs. 5000 will be given to the winner of the first draw. Suppose you have bought a ticket, how much should you expect to win?

6.38 The monthly demand for transistors is known to have the following probability distribution:

Demand (n)	:	1	2	3	4	5	6
Probability (P)	:	0.10	0.15	0.20	0.25	0.18	0.12

Determine the expected demand for transistors. Also obtain the variance. Suppose the cost (C) of producing 'n' transistors is given by the relationship, $C = 10{,}000 + 500n$. Determine the expected cost.

6.39 A consignment of machine parts is offered to two firms, A and B, for Rs. 75,000. The following table shows the probabilities at which firms A and B will be able to sell the consignment at different prices.

Probability	*Price (in Rs.) at which the Consignment Can be Sold*			
	60,000	70,000	80,000	90,000
A	0.40	0.30	0.20	0.10
B	0.10	0.20	0.50	0.20

Which firm, A or B, will be more inclined towards this offer?

6.40 A survey conducted over the last 25 years indicated that in 10 years the winter was mild, in 8 years it was cold, and in the remaining 7 it was very cold. A company sells 1000 woollen coats in a mild year, 1300 in a cold year, and 2000 in a very cold year. You are required to find the yearly expected profit of the company if a woollen coat costs Rs. 173 and it is sold to stores for Rs. 248.

Hints and Answers

6.33

x	:	3	1	−1
P(x)	:	0.15	0.25	1 − 0.15 − 0.25 = 0.60

E(x) = Rs. 0.10 million, Var (x) = Rs. 2.19 million, and σ_x = Rs. 1.48 million.

6.34

x	:	0	1	2	3
P(x)	:	27/64	27/64	9/64	1/64;

E(x) = 0.75

6.35

x	:	100	500	1,800
P(x)	:	0.50	0.40	0.10

E(x) = Rs. 430; 0.5 E(x) = Rs. 215

6.36 P(A) = 0.2; P(B) = 0.25; P(C) = 0.4; and $P(\bar{A}) = 0.8$; $P(\bar{B}) = 0.75$; $P(\bar{C}) = 0.6$

$E(x) = x_1 P(\bar{A}) + x_2 P(\bar{B}) + x_3 P(\bar{C}) = 32$

7.37 P(Win) = $\frac{9999}{10,000}$ and $\frac{1}{1000}$

$$E(x) = -1 \times \frac{9999}{10,000} + 4999 \times \frac{1}{1000}$$

= Rs. 3.9991

7.38 Expected demand for transistors, $E(n) = \Sigma\, np$ = 3.62

$$E(C) = (10,000 + 500n) = 10,000 + 50\,E(n)$$

= Rs. 11,810.

7.39 $EMV(A) = 6 \times 0.4 + 7 \times 0.3 + 8 \times 0.2 + 9 \times 0.1$

= Rs. 70,000.

$EMV(B) = 6 \times 0.1 + 7 \times 0.2 + 8 \times 0.5 + 9 \times 0.2$

= Rs. 78,000.

Firm B will be more inclined towards the offer.

7.40

State of Nature	*Mild*	*Cold*	*Very Cold*
Prob. P(x)	0.40	0.32	0.28
Sale of coat	1000	1300	2000
Profit, x	1000× (248 – 173)	1300× (248 – 173)	2000× (248 – 173)

E(Profit) = Rs. 1,03,200

6.9 DISCRETE PROBABILITY DISTRIBUTIONS

6.9.1 Binomial Probability Distribution

Binomial probability distribution is a widely used probability distribution for a discrete random variable. This distribution describes discrete data resulting from an experiment called a *Bernoulli process* (named after Jacob Bernoulli, 1654–1705, the first of the Bernoulli family of Swiss mathematicians). For each trial of an experiment, *there are only two possible complementary (mutually exclusive)* outcomes such as, defective or good, head or tail, zero or one, boy or girl. In such cases the outcome of interest is referred to as a '*success*' and the other as a '*failure*'. The term 'binomial' literally means two names.

Bernoulli process: *It is a process wherein an experiment is performed repeatedly, yielding either a success or a failure in each trial and where there is absolutely no pattern in the occurrence of successes and failures. That is, the occurrence of a success or a failure in a particular trial does not affect, and is not affected by, the outcomes in any previous or subsequent trials. The trials are independent.*

Conditions for Binomial Experiment The Bernoulli process involving a series of independent trials, is based on certain conditions as under:

(i) There are only two mutually exclusive and collective exhaustive outcomes of the random variable and one of them is referred to as a *success* and the other as a *failure*.

(ii) The random experiment is performed under the same conditions for a fixed and finite (also discrete) number of times, say n. Each observation of the random variable in an random experiment is called a *trial*. Each trial generates either a *success* denoted by p or *a failure* denoted by q.

(iii) The outcome (i.e., success or failure) of any trial is not affected by the outcome of any other trial.

(iv) All the observations are assumed to be independent of each of each other. This means that the probability of outcomes remains constant throughout the process. Thus, the probability of a success, denoted by p, remains constant from trial to trial. The probability of a failure is $q = 1 - p$.

To understand the Bernoulli process, consider the coin tossing problem where 3 coins are tossed. Suppose we are interested to know the probability of two heads. The possible sequence of outcomes involving two heads can be obtained in the following three ways: HHT, HTH, THH.

The probability of each of the above sequences can be found by using the multiplication rule for independent events. Let the probability of a head be p and the probability of tail be q. The probability of each sequence can be written as:

$$ppq \quad pqp \quad qpp$$

Each of these probabilities can be written as p^2q, they are all equal.

Since three sequences correspond to the same event '2 heads', therefore the probability of 2 heads in 3 tosses is obtained by using the addition rule of probabilities for mutually exclusive events. Since the probability of each sequence is same, we can multiply p^2q (probability of one sequence) by 3 (number of possible sequences or orderings of 2 heads). Hence

$$\text{P(2 heads)} = 3p^2q = {}^3C_2\, p^2q$$

Here it may be noted that the possible sequences equals the binomial coefficient ${}^3C_2 = 3$. This coefficient represents the number of ways that three symbols, of which two are alike (i.e., 2H and one T), can be ordered (or arranged). In general, the binomial coefficient ${}^nC_r$ represents the number of ways that n symbols, of which r are alike, can be ordered.

Since events H and T are equally likely and mutually exclusive, therefore $p = 0.5$ and $q = 0.5$ for a toss of the coin. Thus the probability of 2 heads in 3 tosses, is

$$P(x = 2 \text{ heads}) = {}^3C_2\,(0.5)^2\,(0.5) = 3\,(0.25)\,(0.5) = 0.375$$

Binomial Probability Function In general, for a binomial random variable, x the probability of success (occurrence of desired outcome) r number of times in n independent trials, regardless of their order of occurrence is given by the formula:

$$P\,(x = r \text{ successes}) = {}^nC_r\, p^r q^{n-r} = \frac{n!}{r!\,(n-r)!}\, p^r\, q^{n-r},\; r = 0, 1, 2, ..., n \qquad (6\text{-}8)$$

where n = number of trials (specified in advance) or sample size

p = probability of success

q = $(1 - p)$, probability of failure

x = discrete binomial random variable

r = number of successes in n trials

In formula (6-8), the term $p^r\, q^{n-r}$ represents the probability of one sequence where r number of events (called successes) occur in n trials in a particular sequence, while the term ${}^nC_r$ represents the number of possible sequences (combinations) of r successes that are possible out of n trials.

The expression (6-8) is known as **binomial distribution** with parameters n and p. Different values of n and p identify different binomial distributions which lead to different probabilities of r-values. The *mean* and *standard deviation* of a binomial distribution are computed in a shortcut manner as follows:

Mean, $\mu = np$,

Standard deviation, $\sigma = \sqrt{n\,p\,q}$

Example 6.26: In a binomial distribution with 6 independent trials, the probability of 3 and 4 success is found to be 0.2457 and 0.0819 respectively. Find the parameters p and q of the binomial distribution.

[*Delhi Univ., B.Com(Hons), 1998, 2002*]

Solution: Given, $n = 6$, $P(3) = 0.2457$, $P(4) = 0.0819$. Applying the formula of binomial distribution, we get

$$P(x = r)\, {}^nC_r\, p^r\, q^{n-r};\quad r = 0, 1, ..., 6$$

For $r = 3$, $P(x = 3) = {}^6C_3\, p^3\, q^3$ or $0.2457 = 20\, p^3\, q^3$

For $r = 4$, $P(x = 4) = {}^6C_4\, p^4\, q^2$ or $0.0819 = 15\, p^4\, q^2$

Divide $P(x = 4)$ by $P(x = 3)$, we get, $\frac{0.0819}{0.2457} = \frac{15p^4q^2}{20p^3q^3}$ or $\frac{1}{3} = \frac{3p}{4q}$

$$p = \frac{4}{9}q = \frac{4}{9}(1-p) \qquad \text{[because } q = 1 - p\text{]}$$

$$p + \frac{4}{9}p = \frac{4}{9}$$

$$13p = 4, \text{ i.e. } p = \frac{4}{13} \quad \text{and} \quad q = 1 - p = 1 - \frac{4}{13} = \frac{9}{13}.$$

Example 6.27: A salesman makes a sale on the average to 40 per cent of the customers he contacts. If 4 customers are contacted today, what is the probability that he makes sales to exactly two?

[Delhi Univ., BA Eco(Hons), 1998]

Solution: Let x be the random variable showing the number of sales. Given that

p = probability of making sale = 0.4, and $q = 1 - p = 0.6$

Apply binomial distribution formula:

$$P(x = r) = {}^nC_r p^r q^{n-r} = {}^4C_r (0.4)^r (0.6)^{4-r}$$

When $r = 2$, $P(x = 2) = {}^4C_2 (0.4)^2(0.6)^2 = 6(0.16)(0.36) = 0.3456$

Hence, probability of making sales to exactly two customers is: 0.3456.

Example 6.28: Suppose that the probability is (0.50) that a car stolen in Delhi will be recovered. Find the probability that atleast one out of 20 cars stolen in the city on a particular day will be recovered. *[Delhi Univ., B.A Eco(Hons), 2002]*

Solution: Probability that a stolen car is recovered = (0.50) and probability that a stolen car is not recovered = 1 – (0.05) = (0.05). Thus

P(atleast one car is recovered) = 1 – P(none of the stolen car is recovered)

$= 1 - (0.05)^{20}$ [since there are 20 cars in all]

Example 6.29: A brokerage survey reports that 30 per cent of individual investors have used a discount broker, i.e. one which does not charge the full commission. In a random sample of 9 individuals, what is the probability that

(a) exactly two of the sampled individuals have used a discount broker?

(b) not more than three have used a discount broker

(c) at least three of them have used a discount broker

Solution: The probability that individual investors have used a discount broker is, $p = 0.30$, and therefore $q = 1 - p = 0.70$

(a) Probability that exactly 2 of the 9 individual have used a discount broker is given by

$$P(x = 2) = {}^9C_2 (0.30)^2 (0.70)^7 = \frac{9!}{(9-2)!\,2!}(0.30)^2 (0.70)^7$$

$$= \frac{9 \times 8}{2} \times 0.09 \times 0.082 = 0.2656$$

(b) Probability that out of 9 randomly selected individuals not more than three have used a discount broker is given by

$$P(x \le 3) = P(x=0) + P(x=1) + P(x=2) + P(x=3)$$

$$= {}^9C_0 (0.30)^0 (0.70)^9 + {}^9C_1 (0.30)(0.70)^8 + {}^9C_2 (0.30)^2 (0.70)^7 + {}^9C_3 (0.30)^3 (0.70)^6$$

$$= 0.040 + 9 \times 0.30 \times 0.058 + 36 \times 0.09 \times 0.082 + 84 \times 0.027 \times 0.118$$
$$= 0.040 + 0.157 + 0.266 + 0.268 = 0.731$$

(c) Probability that out of 9 randomly selected individuals, at least three have used a discount broker is given by

$$P(x \geq 3) = 1 - P(x < 3) = 1 - [P(x=0) + P(x=1) + P(x=2)]$$
$$= 1 - [0.040 + 0.157 + 0.266] = 0.537$$

Example 6.30: Mr Gupta applies for a personal loan of Rs. 1,50,000 from a nationalised bank to repair his house. The loan offer informed him that over the years, bank has received about 2920 loan applications per year and that the probability of approval was, on average, above 0.85

(a) Mr Gupta wants to know the average and standard deviation of the number of loans approved per year.

(b) Suppose bank actually received 2654 loan applications per year with an approval probability of 0.82. What are the mean and standard deviation now?

Solution: (a) Assuming that approvals are independent from loan to loan, and that all loans have the same 0.85 probability of approval. Then

Mean, $\mu = np = 2920 \times 0.85 = 2482$

Standard deviation, $\sigma = \sqrt{npq} = \sqrt{2920 \times 0.85 \times 0.15} = 19.295$

(b) Mean, $\mu = np = 2654 \times 0.82 = 2176.28$

Standard deviation, $\sigma = \sqrt{npq} = \sqrt{2654 \times 0.82 \times 0.18} = 19.792$

Example 6.31: Suppose 10 per cent of new scooters will require warranty service within the first month of its sale. A scooter manufacturing company sells 1000 scooters in a month,

(a) Find the mean and standard deviation of scooters that require warranty service.

(b) Calculate the moment coefficient of skewness and kurtosis of the distribution.

Solution: Given that $p = 0.10$, $q = 1 - p = 0.90$ and $n = 1000$

(a) Mean, $\mu = np = 1000 \times 0.10 = 100$ scooters

Standard deviation, $\sigma = \sqrt{npq} = \sqrt{1000 \times 0.10 \times 0.90} = 10$ scootors (approx.)

(b) Moment coefficient of skewness

$$\gamma_1 = \sqrt{\beta_1} = \frac{q-p}{\sqrt{npq}} = \frac{0.90 - 0.10}{9.48} = 0.084$$

Since γ_1 is more than zero, the distribution is positively skewed.

Moment coefficient of kurtosis, $\gamma_2 = \beta_2 - 3$

$$= \frac{1-6pq}{npq} = \frac{1-6(0.10)(0.90)}{90} = \frac{0.46}{90} = 0.0051$$

Since γ_2 is positive, the distribution is platykurtic.

Example 6.32: The incidence of occupational disease in an industry is such that the workers have 20 per cent chance of suffering from it. What is the probability that out of six workers 4 or more will come in contact of the disease?

Solution: The probability of a worker suffering from the disease is, $p = 20/100 = 1/5$. Therefore $q = 1 - p = 1 - (1/5) = 4/5$.

The probability of 4 or more, that is, 4, 5, or 6 coming in contact of the disease is given by

$$P(x \geq 4) = P(x = 4) + P(x = 5) + P(x = 6)$$

$$= {}^6C_4\left(\frac{1}{5}\right)^4\left(\frac{4}{5}\right)^2 + {}^6C_5\left(\frac{1}{5}\right)^5\left(\frac{4}{5}\right) + {}^6C_4\left(\frac{1}{5}\right)^6$$

$$= \frac{15 \times 16}{15625} + \frac{6 \times 4}{15625} + \frac{1}{15625} = \frac{1}{15625}(240 + 24 + 1)$$

$$= \frac{265}{15625} = 0.01695$$

Hence the probability that out of 6 workers 4 or more will come in contact of the disease is 0.01695.

Example 6.33: A multiple-choice test contains 8 questions with 3 answers to each question (of which only one is correct). A student answers each question by rolling a balanced dice and checking the first answer if he gets 1 or 2, the second answer if he gets 3 or 4, and the third answer if he gets 5 or 6. To get a distinction, the student must secure at least 75 per cent correct answers. If there is no negative marking, what is the probability that the student secures a distinction?

Solution: Probability of a correct answer, p is one in three so that $p = 1/3$ and probability of wrong answer $q = 2/3$.

The required probability of securing a distinction (i.e., of getting the correct answer of at least 6 of the 8 questions) is given by:

$$P(x \geq 6) = P(x = 6) + P(x = 7) + P(x = 8)$$

$$= {}^8C_6\left(\frac{1}{3}\right)^6\left(\frac{2}{3}\right)^2 + {}^8C_7\left(\frac{1}{3}\right)^7\left(\frac{2}{3}\right) + {}^8C_8\left(\frac{1}{3}\right)^8$$

$$= \left(\frac{1}{3}\right)^6\left[{}^8C_6\left(\frac{2}{3}\right)^2 + {}^8C_7\left(\frac{1}{3}\right)\left(\frac{2}{3}\right) + {}^8C_8\left(\frac{1}{3}\right)^2\right]$$

$$= \frac{1}{729}\left[28 \times \frac{4}{9} + 8 \times \frac{2}{9} + \frac{1}{9}\right] = \frac{1}{729}(12.45 + 0.178 + 0.12) = 0.0196$$

Conceptual Questions 6C

10. (a) Define binomial distribution stating its parameters, mean, and standard deviation, and give two examples where such a distribution is ideally suited.

    (b) Define binomial distribution. Point out its chief characteristics and uses. Under what conditions does it tend to Poisson distribution?

11. For a binomial distribution, is it true that the mean is the most likely value? Explain.

12. Demonstrate that the binomial coefficient ${}^nC_r$ equals ${}^nC_{n-r}$ and illustrate this with a specific numerical example.

13. What assumptions must be met for a binomial distribution to be applied to a real life situation?

14. What is meant by the term parameter of a probability distribution? Relate the concept to the binomial distribution?

15. What is a binomial coefficient and illustrate this with a specific numerical example.

Self-Practice Problems 6E

6.41 The normal rate of infection of a certain disease in animals is known to be 25 per cent. In an experiment with 6 animals injected with a new vaccine it was observed that none of the animals caught the infection. Calculate the probability of the observed result.

6.42 Out of 320 families with 5 children each, what percentage would be expected to have (i) 2 boys and 3 girls, (ii) at least one boy? Assume equal probability for boys and girls.

6.43 The mean of a binomial distribution is 40 and standard deviation 6. Calculate n, p, and q.

6.44 A student obtained answers with mean $\mu = 2.4$ and variance $\sigma^2 = 3.2$ for a certain problem given to him using binomial distribution. Comment on the result.

6.45 The probability that an evening college student will graduate is 0.4. Determine the probability that out of 5 students (a) none, (b) one, and (c) at least one will graduate.

6.46 The normal rate of infection of a certain disease in animals is known to be 25 per cent. In an experiment with 6 animals injected with a new vaccine it was observed that none of the animals caught infection. Calculate the probability of the observed result.

6.47 Is there any inconsistency in the statement that the mean of a binomial distribution is 20 and its standard deviation is 4? If no inconsistency is found what shall be the values of p, q, and n.

6.48 Find the probability that in a family of 5 children there will be (i) at least one boy (ii) at least one boy and one girl (Assume that the probability of a female birth is 0.5).

Hints and Answers

6.41 Let P denote infection of the disease. Then $p = 25/100 = 1/4$ and $q = 3/4$.

$$P(x = 0) = {}^6C_0 \left(\frac{1}{4}\right)^0 \left(\frac{3}{4}\right)^6 = \frac{729}{4096}$$

6.42 (i) Given $p = q = 1/2$

$$P(\text{boy} = 2) = {}^5C_2 p^2 q^3 = {}^5C_2 \left(\frac{1}{2}\right)^2 \left(\frac{1}{2}\right)^3 = \frac{5}{16} \text{ or } 31.25\%$$

(ii) $P(\text{boy} \geq 1) = 1 - {}^5C_0 q^5 = 1 - \frac{1}{32} = \frac{31}{32}$ or 97 per cent.

6.43 Given $\mu = np = 40$ and $\sigma = \sqrt{npq} = 6$. Squaring σ, we get $npq = 36$ or $40q = 36$ or $q = 0.9$. Then $p = 1 - q = 0.28$.
Since $np = 40$ or $n = 40/p = 40/0.1 = 400$.

6.44 Given $\sigma^2 = npq = 3.2$ and $\mu = np = 2.4$. Then $2.4q = 3.2$ or $q = 3.2/2.4 = 1.33$ (inconsistent result)

6.45 Given $p = 0.4$ and $q = 0.6$

(a) $P(x = \text{no graduate}) = {}^5C_0 (0.4) (0.6)^5 = 1 \times 1 \times 0.0777 = 0.0777$

(b) $P(x = 1) = {}^5C_1 (0.4)^1 (0.6)^4 = 0.2592$

(c) $P(x \geq 1) = 1 - P(x = 0) = 1 - 0.0777 = 0.9223$

6.46 Probability of infection of disease $= 25/100 = 0.25$; $q = 1 - p = 0.75$.
The first term in the expansion of $(q + p)^n = \left(\frac{3}{4} + \frac{1}{4}\right)^6$ is ${}^6C_0 \left(\frac{3}{4}\right)^6 = 0.177$, which is also the required probability.

6.47 Given $\mu = np = 20$ and $\sigma = \sqrt{npq} = 4$ or $npq = 16$ or $20q = 16$ or $q = 16/20 = 0.80$ and then $p = 1 - q = 0.20$. Hence $npq = 16$ gives $n = 16/pq = 16/(0.20 \times 0.80) = 100$.

6.48 Since $p = q = 0.5$, therefore

(i) $P(\text{boy} = 0) = {}^5C_0 (0.5)^0 (0.5)^5 = 0.031$
P(at least one boy) $= 1 - 0.031 = 0.969$

(ii) $P(\text{at least 1B and 1G}) = {}^5C_1 (0.5)^1 (0.5)^4 + {}^5C_2 (0.5)^2 (0.5)^3 + {}^5C_3 (0.5)^3 (0.5)^2 + {}^5C_4 (0.5)^4 (0.5) = 30/32$

6.9.2 Poisson Probability Distribution

Poisson distribution is named after the French mathematician S. Poisson (1781–1840), The Poisson process measures the number of occurrences of a particular outcome of a discrete random variable in a *predetermined time interval, space, or volume*, for which an *average number* of occurrences of the outcome is known or can be determined. In the Poisson process, the random variable values need counting. Such a count might be (i) number of telephone calls per hour coming into the switchboard, (ii) number of fatal traffic accidents per week in a city/state, (iii) number of patients arriving at a health centre every hour, (iv) number of organisms per unit volume of some fluid, (v) number of cars waiting for service in a workshop, (vi) number of flaws per unit length of some wire, and so on. The Poisson probability distribution provides a simple, easy-to compute and accurate approximation to a binomial distribution when the probability of success, p is very small and n is large, so that $\mu = np$ is small, preferably $np > 7$. It is often called the '*law of improbable*' events meaning that the probability, p, of a particular event's happening is very small. As mentioned above **Poisson distribution** occurs in business situations in which there are a few successes against a large number of failures or vice-versa (i.e. few successes in an interval) and has single independent events that are mutually exclusive. Because of this, the probability of success, p is very small in relation to the number of trials n, so we consider only the probability of success.

Conditions for Poisson Process The use of Poisson distribution to compute the probability of the occurrence of an outcome during a specific time period is based on the following conditions:

(i) The outcomes within any interval occur randomly and independently of one another.
(ii) The probability of one occurrence in a small time interval is proportional to the length of the interval and independent of the specific time interval.
(iii) The probability of more than one occurrence in a small time interval is negligible when compared to the probability of just one occurrence in the same time interval.
(iv) The average number of occurrences is constant for all time intervals of the same size.

Poisson Probability Function If the probability, p of occurrence of an outcome of interest (i.e., success) in each trial is very small, but the number of independent trials n is sufficiently large, then the average number of times that an event occurs in a certain period of time or space, $\lambda = np$ is also small. Under these conditions the binomial probability function

$$P(x = r) = {}^nC_r\, p^r q^{n-r} = \frac{n(n-1)(n-2)\ldots(n-r+1)}{r!}\, p^r q^{n-r}$$

$$= \left(1-\frac{1}{n}\right)\left(1-\frac{2}{n}\right)\ldots\left(1-\frac{r-1}{n}\right)\frac{\lambda^r}{r!}\left(1-\frac{\lambda}{n}\right)^{n-r} ;\ np = \lambda \text{ or } p = \lambda/n$$

tends to $\frac{\lambda^r}{r!}e^{-\lambda}$ for a fixed r. Thus the Poisson probability distribution which approximates the binomial distribution is defined by the following probability function:

$$P(x = r) = \frac{\lambda^r e^{-\lambda}}{r!},\ r = 0, 1, 2, \ldots \tag{6-9}$$

where $e = 2.7183$.

Characteristics of Poisson Distribution Since Poisson probability distribution is specified by a process rate λ and the time period t, its mean and variance are identical and are expressed in terms of the parameters: n and p as shown below:

- The *arithmetic mean*, $\mu = E(x)$ of Poisson distribution is given by

$$\mu = \sum xP(x) = \sum x \frac{e^{-\lambda}\lambda^x}{x!}, \quad x = 1, 2, 3, \ldots \text{ and } x\,P(x) = 0 \text{ for } x = 0$$

$$= \lambda e^{-\lambda} + \lambda^2 e^{-\lambda} + \frac{\lambda^3 e^{-\lambda}}{2!} + \ldots + \frac{\lambda^r e^{-\lambda}}{(x-1)!} + \ldots$$

$$= \lambda e^{-\lambda}\left[1 + \lambda + \frac{\lambda^2}{2!} + \ldots + \frac{\lambda^{r-1}}{(x-1)!} + \ldots\right] = \lambda e^{-\lambda} e^{\lambda} = \lambda$$

Thus the mean of the distribution is $\mu = \lambda = np$.

- *The variance* σ^2 of Poisson distribution is given by

$$\sigma^2 = E(x^2) - [E(x)]^2 = E(x^2) - \lambda^2$$

$$= \sum x^2 \frac{e^{-\lambda}\lambda^x}{x!} - \lambda^2 = e^{-\lambda}\sum \frac{x(x-1)+x}{x!}\lambda^x - \lambda^2$$

$$= \lambda^2 e^{-\lambda}\sum \frac{\lambda^{x-2}}{(x-2)!} + \lambda e^{-\lambda}\sum \frac{\lambda^{x-1}}{(x-1)!} - \lambda^2$$

$$= \lambda^2 e^{-\lambda} e^{\lambda} + \lambda e^{-\lambda} e^{\lambda} - \lambda^2 = \lambda^2 + \lambda - \lambda^2 = \lambda$$

Thus the variance of the distribution is $\sigma^2 = \lambda = np$.

It is very *rare for more than one event to occur* during a short interval of time. The shorter the duration of interval, the occurrence of two or more events also becomes rare. The probability that exactly one event will occur in such an interval is approximately λ times its duration.

The typical application of Poisson distribution is for analysing queuing (or waiting line) problems in which arriving customers during an interval of time arrive independently and the number of arrivals depends on the length of the time interval. While applying Poisson distribution if we consider a time period of different length, the distribution of number of events remains Poisson with the mean proportional to the length of the time period.

Example 6.34: What probability model is appropriate to describe a situation where 100 misprints are distributed randomly throughout the 100 pages of a book? For this model, what is the probability that a page observed at random will contain at least three misprints?

Solution: Since 100 misprints are distributed randomly throughout the 100 pages of a book, therefore on an average there is only one mistake on a page. This means, the probability of there being a misprint, $p = 1/100$, is very small and the number of words, n, in 100 pages are vary large. Hence, Poisson distribution is best suited in this case.

Average number of misprints in one page, $\lambda = np = 100 \times (1/100) = 1$. Therefore $e^{-\lambda} = e^{-1} = 0.3679$.

Probability of at least three misprints in a page is

$$P(x \geq 3) = 1 - P(x < 3) = 1 - \{P(x = 0) + P(x = 1) + P(x = 2)\}$$

$$= 1 - [e^{-\lambda} + \lambda e^{-\lambda} + \frac{1}{2!}\lambda^2 e^{-\lambda}]$$

$$= 1 - \left\{e^{-1} + e^{-1} + \frac{e^{-1}}{2!}\right\} = 1 - 2.5\,e^{-1} = 1 - 2.5\,(0.3679) = 0.0802$$

Example 6.35: A new automated production process has had an average of 1.5 breakdowns per day. Because of the cost associated with a breakdown, management is concerned about the possibility of having three or more breakdowns during a day. Assume that breakdowns occur randomly, that the probability of a breakdown is the same for any two time intervals of equal length, and that breakdowns in one period are independent of breakdowns in other periods. What is the probability of having three or more breakdowns during a day?

Solution: Given that, $\lambda = np = 1.5$ breakdowns per day. Thus probability of having three or more breakdowns during a day is given by

$$P(x \geq 3) = 1 - P(x < 3) = 1 - [P(x=0) + P(x=1) + P(x=2)]$$

$$= 1 - \left[\frac{\lambda^0 e^{-\lambda}}{0!} + \frac{\lambda e^{-\lambda}}{1!} + \frac{\lambda^2 e^{-\lambda}}{2!}\right]$$

$$= 1 - e^{-\lambda}\left[1 + \lambda + \frac{1}{2}\lambda^2\right] = 1 - 0.2231\left[1 + 1.5 + \frac{1}{2}(1.5)^2\right]$$

$$= 1 - 0.2231\ (3.625) = 1 - 0.8088 = 0.1912$$

Example 6.36: Suppose a life insurance company insures the lives of 5000 persons aged 42. If studies show the probability that any 42-years old person will die in a given year to be 0.001, find the probability that the company will have to pay at least two claims during a given year.

Solution: Given that, $n = 5000$, $p = 0.001$, so $\lambda = np = 5000 \times 0.001 = 5$. Thus the probability that the company will have to pay at least 2 claims during a given year is given by

$$P(x \geq 2) = 1 - P(x < 2) = 1 - [P(x = 0) + P(x = 1)]$$

$$= 1 - [e^{-\lambda} + \lambda e^{-\lambda}] = 1 - [e^{-5} + 5e^{-5}] = 1 - 6e^{-5}$$

$$= 1 - 6 \times 0.0067 = 0.9598$$

Example 6.37: A manufacturer who produces medicine bottles, finds that 0.1 per cent of the bottles are defective. The bottles are packed in boxes containing 500 bottles. A drug manufacturer buys 100 boxes from the producer of bottles. Using Poisson distribution, find how many boxes will contain:

(a) no defectives
(b) at least two defectives

Solution: Given that, $p = 1$ per cent $= 0.001$, $n = 500$, $\lambda = np = 500 \times 0.001 = 0.5$

(a) $P[x = 0] = e^{-\lambda} = e^{-0.5} = 0.6065$

Therefore, the required number of boxes are : $0.6065 \times 100 = 61$ (approx.)

(b) $$P(x > 2) = 1 - P(x \leq 1) = 1 - [P(x = 0) + P(x = 1)]$$

$$= 1 - [e^{\lambda} + \lambda e^{-\lambda}] = 1 - [0.6065 + 0.5(0.6065)]$$

$$= 1 - 0.6065\ (1.5) = 1 - 0.90975 = 0.09025.$$

Therefore, the required number of boxes are $100 \times 0.09025 = 10$ (approx.)

Example 6.38: The following table gives the number of days in a 50-day period during which automobile accidents occurred in a city :

No. of accidents :	0	1	2	3	4
No. of days :	21	18	7	3	1

Fit a Poisson distribution to the data.

Solution: Calculations for fitting of Poisson distribution are shown in the Table 6.2.

Table 6.2 Calculations for Poisson Distribution

Number of Accidents (x)	*Number of Days* (f)	fx
0	21	0
1	18	18
2	7	14
3	3	09
4	1	04
	$n = 50$	$\Sigma fx = 45$

Thus $$\bar{x}\,(\text{or } \lambda) = \frac{\Sigma fx}{n} = \frac{45}{50} = 0.9, \text{ and}$$

$$P(x=0) = e^{-\lambda} = e^{-0.9} = 0.4066$$

$$P(x=1) = \lambda\, P(x=0) = 0.9(0.4066) = 0.3659$$

$$P(x=2) = \frac{\lambda}{2}\; P(x=1) = \frac{0.9}{2}\;(0.3659) = 0.1647$$

$$P(x=3) = \frac{\lambda}{3}\; P(x=2) = \frac{0.9}{3}\;(0.1647) = 0.0494$$

$$P(x=4) = \frac{\lambda}{4}\; P(x=3) = \frac{0.9}{4}\;(0.0494) = 0.0111$$

In order to fit a Poisson distribution, we shall multiply each of these values by N = 50 (total frequencies). Hence the expected frequencies are:

x :	0	1	2	3	4
f :	0.4066×50 $= 20.33$	0.3659×50 $= 18.30$	0.1647×50 $= 8.23$	0.0494×50 $= 2.47$	0.0111×50 $= 0.56$

Conceptual Questions 6D

16. If x has a Poisson distribution with parameter λ, then show that E(x) and V(x) = λ. Further, show that the Poisson distribution is a limiting form of the binomial distribution.

17. What is Poisson distribution? Point out its role in business decision-making. Under what conditions will it tend to become a binomial distribution?

18. When can Poisson distribution be a reasonable approximation of the binomial?

19. Discuss the distinctive features of Poisson distribution. When does a binomial distribution tend to become a Poisson distribution?

20. Under what conditions is the Poisson probability distribution appropriate? How are its mean and variance calculated?

Self-Practice Problems 6F

6.49 In a town 10 accidents took place in a span of 50 days. Assuming that the number of accidents per day follows the Poisson distribution, find the probability that there will be three or more accidents in a day.

6.50 Find the probability that at most 5 defective bolts will be found in a box of 200 bolts if it is known that 2 per cent of such bolts are expected to be defective [you may take the distribution to be Poisson; $e^{-4} = 0.0183$].

6.51 On an average, one in 400 items is defective. If the items are packed in boxes of 100, what is the probability that any given box of items will contain: (i) no defectives; (ii) less than two defectives; (iii) one or more defectives; and (iv) more than three defectives.

6.52 It is given that 30 per cent of electric bulbs manufactured by a company are defective. Find the probability that a sample of 100 bulbs will contain (i) no defective, and (ii) exactly one defective.

6.53 One-fifth per cent of the blades produced by a blade manufacturing factory turn out to be defective. The blades are supplied in packets of 10. Use Poisson distribution to calculate the approximate number of packets containing no defective, one defective, and two defective blades respectively in a consignment of 1,00,000 packets.

6.54 A factory produces blades in packets of 10. The probability of a blade to be defective is 0.2 per cent. Find the number of packets having two defective blades in a consignment of 10,000 packets.

6.55 In a certain factory manufacturing razor blades, there is small chance 1/50 for any blade to be defective. The blades are placed in packets, each containing 10 blades. Using an appropriate probability distribution, calculate the approximate number of packets containing not more than 2 defective blades in a consignment of 10,000 packets.

6.56 Suppose that a manufactured product has 2 defects per unit of product inspected. Using Poisson distribution, calculate the probabilities of finding a product without any defect, 3 defects, and 4 defects. (Given $e^{-2} = 0.135$).

Hints and Answers

6.49 The average number of accidents per day $= 10/50 = 0.2$

$$P(x \geq 3 \text{ accidents}) = 1 - P(2 \text{ or less accidents}) = 1 - [P(0) + P(1) + P(2)]$$

$$= -\left[e^{-2} + 2e^{-2} + \frac{e^{-2} \times 0.2 \times 0.2}{2}\right]$$

$$= 1 - e^{-2}[1 + 0.2 + 0.02] = 1 - 0.8187 \times 1.22$$

(From table of $e^{-\lambda}$)

$$= 1 - 0.998 = 0.002$$

6.50 $p(\text{defective bolt}) = 2\% = 0.02$. Given $n = 200$, so $\lambda = np = 200 \times 0.02 = 4$

$$P(0) = \frac{e^{-\lambda}\lambda^0}{0!} = e^{-4} = 0{,}0183$$

$$P(x \leq 5) = P(x = 0) + P(x = 1) + P(x = 2) + P(x = 3) + P(x = 4) + P(x = 5)$$

$$= e^{-4}\left(1 + 4 + \frac{4^2}{2!} + \frac{4^3}{3!} + \frac{4^4}{4!} + \frac{5^5}{5!}\right)$$

$$= 0.0183 \times (643/15) = 0.7844.$$

6.52 $\lambda = np = 100 \times 0.30 = 3$

$P(x = 0) = e^{-\lambda} = e^{-3} = 0.05$;

$P(x = 1) = \lambda P(x = 0) = 3 \times 0.03 = 0.15$

6.53 Given $n = 10$, $p = 1/500$, $\lambda = np = 10/500 = 0.02$

(i) $P(x = 0) = e^{-\lambda} = e^{-0.02} = 0.9802$

$NP(x = 0) = 1{,}00{,}000 \times 0.9802 = 98020$ packets

(ii) $P(x = 1) = \lambda P(x = 0)$
$= \lambda e^{-\lambda} = 0.02 \times 0.9802$
$= 0.019604$
$NP(x = 1) = 1{,}00{,}000 \times 0.019604$
$= 1960$ packets

(iii) $P(x = 2) = \dfrac{\lambda^2}{2}$

$P(x = 0) = \dfrac{(0.02)^2}{2} \times 0.9802$
$= 0.00019604$
$NP(x = 2) = 1{,}00{,}000 \times 0.00019604$
$= 19.60 \cong 20$ packets

6.54 Given $n = 10, p = 0.002, \lambda = np = 10 \times 0.002 = 0.02$.

$$P(x = 2) = \frac{e^{-\lambda}\lambda^2}{2!} = \frac{e^{-0.02}(0.02)^2}{2!}$$
$$= 0.000196$$

The required number of packets having two defective blades each in a consignment of 10,000 packets $= 10{,}000 \times 0.000196 \cong 2$.

6.55 Given $N = 10{,}000$, $p = 1/50$ and $n = 10$.
Thus $\lambda = np = 0.20$ and
$NP(x = 0) = 10{,}000\, e^{-\lambda} = 10{,}000\, e^{-0.20} = 8187$;
$P(x = 1) = NP(x = 0) \times \lambda = 8187 \times 0.2 = 1637.4$.

$$NP(x = 2) = NP(x = 1) \times \frac{\lambda}{2} = 1637.4 \times \frac{0.2}{2}$$
$$= 163.74$$

The approximate number of packets containing not more than 2 defective blades in a consignment of 10,000 packets will be: $10{,}000 - (8187 + 1637.40 + 163.74)$
$= 12$ approx.

6.56 Given average number of defects, $\lambda = 2$.
$P(x = 0) = e^{-\lambda} = e^{-2} = 0.135$;
$P(x = 1) = P(x = 0) \times \lambda = 0.135 \times 2 = 0.27$

$$P(x = 2) = P(x = 1) \times \frac{\lambda}{2} = 0.27 \times \frac{2}{2} = 0.27$$

$$P(x = 3) = P(x = 2) \times \frac{\lambda}{3} = 0.27 \times \frac{2}{3} = 0.18$$

$$P(x = 4) = P(x = 3) \times \frac{\lambda}{4} = 0.18 \times \frac{2}{4} = 0.09$$

6.10 CONTINUOUS PROBABILITY DISTRIBUTIONS

If a random variable is discrete, then it is possible to assign a specific probability to each of its value and get the probability distribution for it. The sum of all the probabilities associated with the different values of the random variable is 1. However, not all experiments result in random variables that are discrete. Continuous random variables such as height, time, weight, monetary values, length of life of a particular product, etc. can take large number of obserable values corresponding to points on a line interval much like the infinite number of gains of sand on a beach. The sum of probability to each of these infinitely large values is no longer sum to 1.

Unlike discrete random variables, continuous random variables do not have probability distribution functions specifying the exact probabilities of their specified values. Instead, probability distribution is created by distributing one unit of probability along the real line, much like distributing a handful of sand along a line. The probability of measurements (e.g. gains of sand) piles up in certain places resulting into a probability distribution called *probability density function*. Such distribution is used to find probabilities that the random variable falls into a specified interval of values.

Certain characteristics of probability density function for the continuous random variable, x are follows:

(i) The area under a continuous probability distribution is equal to 1.
(ii) The probability $P(a \leq x \geq b)$ that random variable x value will fall into a particular interval from a to b is equal to the area under the density curve between the points (values) a and b.

Nature seems to follows a predictable pattern for many kinds of measurments. Most numerical values of a random variable are spread arround the center, and greater the distance a numerical value has from the centre, the fewer numerical values have that specific value. A frequency distribution of values of random variable observed in nature which follows this pattern is approximately bell shaped. A special case of distribution of measurements is called a **normal curve (or distribution).**

If a population of numerical values follows a normal curve and x is the randomly selected numerical value from the population, then x is said to be *normal random variable*, which has a normal probability distribution.

6.10.1 Normal Probability Distribution Function

The formula that generates normal probability distribution is as follows:

$$f(x) = \frac{1}{\sigma\sqrt{2\pi}} e^{(-1/2)[(x-\mu)/\sigma]^2}, \quad -\infty < x < \infty \tag{6-10}$$

where π = constant 3.1416

e = constant 2.7183

μ = mean of the normal distribution

σ = standard of normal distribution

The $f(x)$ values represent the relative frequencies (height of the curve) within which values of random variable x occur. The graph of a normal probability distribution with mean μ and standard deviation σ is shown in Fig. 8.8. The distribution is symmetric about its mean μ that locates at the centre.

Since the total area under the normal probability distribution is equal to 1, the symmetry implies that the area on either side of μ is 50 per cent or 0.5. The *shape* of the distribution is determined by μ and σ values.

In symbols, if a random variable x follows normal probability distribution with mean μ and standard deviation σ, then it is also expressed as: $x \sim N(\mu, \sigma)$.

Standard Normal Probability Distribution: To deal with problems where the normal probability distribution is applicable more simply, it is necessary that a random variable x is standardized by expressing its value as the number of standard deviations (σ) it lies to the left or right of its mean (μ). The *standardized normal random variable*, z (also called *z–statistic*, *z–score* or *normal variate*) is defined as:

$$z = \frac{x - \mu}{\sigma} \tag{6-11}$$

or equivalently $x = \mu + z\sigma$

A z–score measures the number of standard deviations that a value of the random variable x fall from the mean. From formula (6.9) we may conclude that

(i) When x is less than the mean (μ), the value of z is negative

(ii) When x is more than the mean (μ), the value of z is positive

(iii) When $x = \mu$, the value of $z = 0$.

Any normal probability distribution with a set of μ and σ value with random variable can be converted into a distribution called **standard normal probability distribution** z, as shown in Fig. 6.3, with mean $\mu_z = 0$ and standard deviation $\sigma_z = 1$ with the help of the formula (6–9).

A z-value measures the distance between a particular value of random variable x and the mean (μ) in units of the standard deviation (σ). With the value of z obtained by using the formula (6.9), we can find the area or probability of a random varible under the normal curve by referring to the standard distribution in Appendix. For example $z = \pm 2$ implies that the value of x is 2 standard deviations above or below the mean (μ).

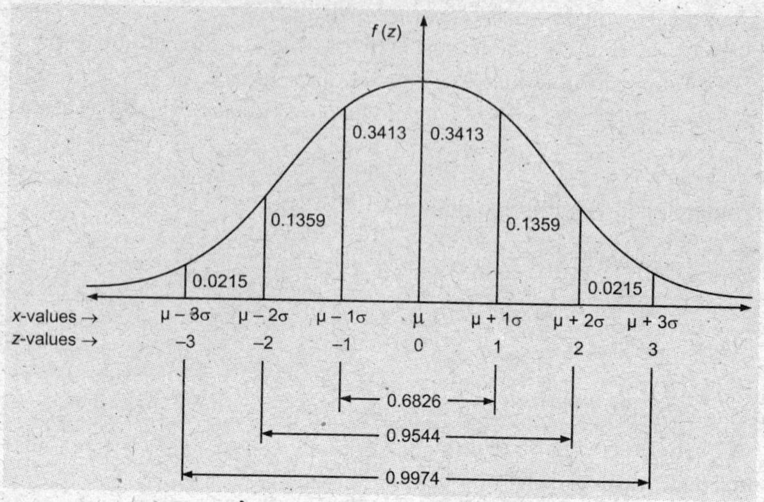

Figure 6.3 Standard Normal Distribution

Example 6.39: 1000 light bulbs with a mean life of 120 days are installed in a new factory and their length of life is normally distributed with standard deviation of 20 days.

(a) How many bulbs will expire in less than 90 days?

(b) If it is decided to replace all the bulbs together, what interval should be allowed between replacements if not more than 10% should expire before replacement?

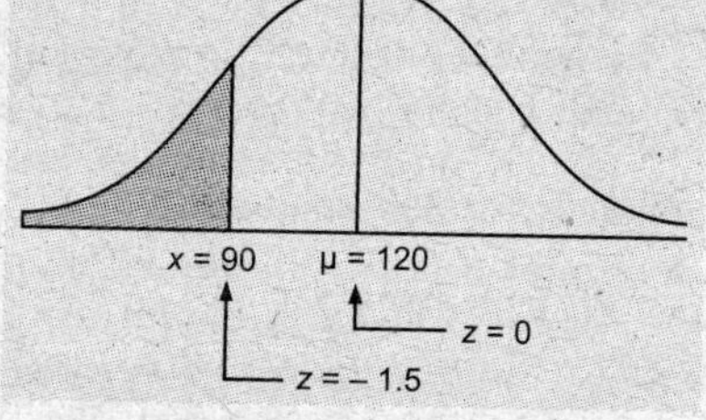

Solution: (a) Given, $\mu = 120, \sigma = 20$, and $x = 90$. Then

$$z = \frac{x-\mu}{\sigma} = \frac{90-120}{20} = -1.5$$

The area under the normal curve between $z = 0$ and $z = -1.5$ is 0.4332. Therefore area to the left of – 1.5 is 0.5 – 0.4332 = 0.0668. Thus the expected number of bulbs to expire in less than 90 days will be 0.0668 × 1000 = 67 (approx.).

(b) The value of z corresponding to an area 0.4 (0.5 – 0.10). Under the normal curve is 1.28. Therefore

$$z = \frac{x-\mu}{\sigma} \text{ or } -1.28 = \frac{x-120}{20} \text{ or } x = 120 - 20(-1.28) = 94$$

Hence, the bulbs will have to be replaced after 94 days.

Example 6.40: The lifetimes of certain kinds of electronic devices have a mean of 300 hours and standard deviation of 25 hours. Assuming that the distribution of these lifetimes, which are measured to the nearest hour, can be approximated closely with a normal curve.

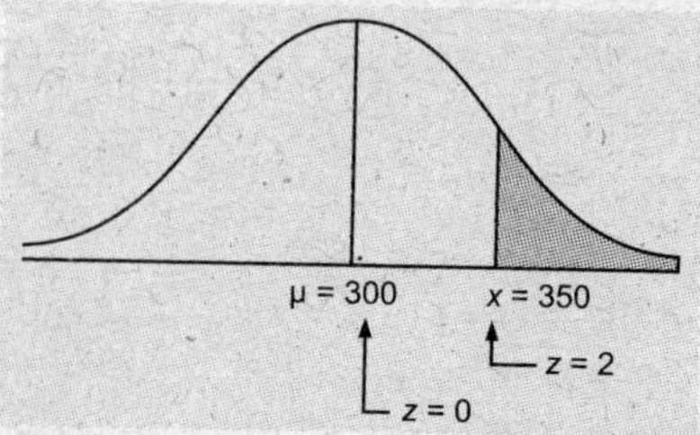

(a) Find the probability that any one of these electronic devices will have a lifetime of more than 350 hours.

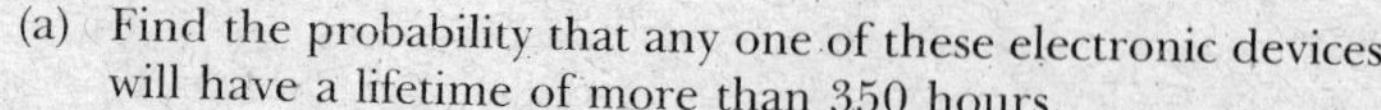

(b) What percentage will have lifetimes of 300 hours or less?

(c) What percentage will have lifetimes from 220 or 260 hours?

Solution: (a) Given, $\mu = 300$, $\sigma = 25$, and $x = 350$. Then

$$z = \frac{x-\mu}{\sigma} = \frac{350-300}{25} = 2$$

The area under the normal curve between $z = 0$ and $z = 2$ is 0.9772. Thus the required probability is, $1 - 0.9772 = 0.0228$.

(b) $z = \dfrac{x-\mu}{\sigma} = \dfrac{300-300}{25} = 0$

Therefore, the required percentage is, $0.5000 \times 100 = 50\%$.

(c) Given, $x_1 = 220$, $x_2 = 260$, $\mu = 300$ and $\sigma = 25$. Thus

$$z_1 = \frac{220-300}{25} = -3.2 \text{ and } z_2 = \frac{260-300}{25} = -1.6$$

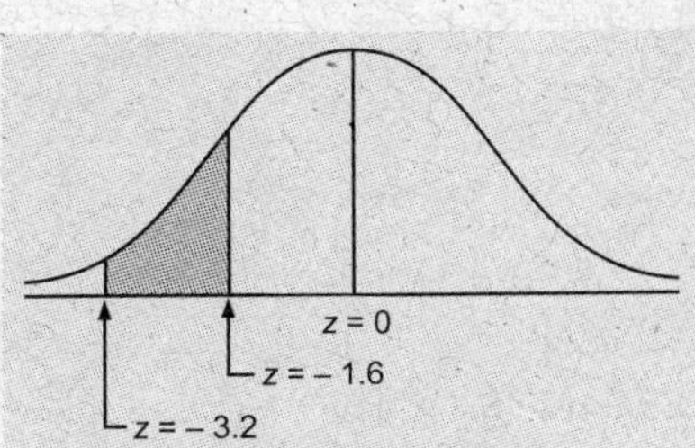

From the normal table, we have

$$P(z = -1.6) = 0.4452 \text{ and } P(z = -3.2) = 0.4903$$

Thus the required probability is

$$P(z = -3.2) - P(z = -1.6) = 0.4903 - 0.4452 = 0.0541$$

Hence the required percentage $= 0.0541 \times 100 = 5.41$ per cent.

Example 6.41: In an intelligence test given to 1500 candidates appearing in an examination carrying a maximum of 100 marks, it was found that marks were normally distributed with mean 39.5 and S.D. = 12.5. Determine the number of candidates who securred a first class for which a minimum of 60 marks is necessary.

Solution: Given, mean (μ) = 39.5, and S.D. (σ) = 12.5. Then

$$P(x \geq 60) = P\left(\frac{x-\mu}{\sigma} \geq \frac{60-\mu}{\sigma}\right) = P\left(Z \geq \frac{60-39.5}{12.5}\right)$$
$$= P(Z > 1.64) = 0.5 - P(0 < Z < 1.64)$$
$$= 0.5 - 0.4495 = 0.0505$$

Students securing first class $= 1500 \times 0.0505 = 76$ students (approx).

Example 6.42: The mean (μ) of a binomial distribution is 40 and standard deviation (σ) is 2. Find n, p, q.

Solution: Given, mean ($= np$) = 40, and σ ($= \sqrt{npq}$) = 2 or $npq = 4$. Then

$$\frac{npq}{np} = \frac{4}{40} = 0.1 \quad \text{or} \quad q = 0.1 \quad \text{and} \quad p = 1 - 0.1 = 0.9$$

$$\text{Mean, } np = 40 \quad \text{or} \quad n \times 0.9 = 40, \text{ i.e., } n = 40/0.9 = 44.4$$

Example 6.43: Time taken by a crew, of a company, to construct a small bridge is a normal variate with mean 400 labour hours and standard deviation of 100 labour hours.

(a) What is the probability that the bridge gets constructed between 350 to 450 labour hours ?

(b) If the company promises to construct the bridge in less than 450 labour hours and agrees to pay a penalty of Rs. 100 for each labour hour spent in excess of 450, what is the probability that the company pays a penalty of atleast Rs. 2000? *[Delhi Univ., BA Eco(Hons), 1998]*

Solution: Let x be the time (in labour hours) to construct the bridge. Given, mean, $\mu = 400$, and $\sigma = 100$.

(a) Probability that the bridge gets constructed between 350 and 450 labour hours

$$P(350 \leq x \leq 450) = P\left(\frac{350-\mu}{\sigma} \leq \frac{x-\mu}{\sigma} \leq \frac{450-\mu}{\sigma}\right) = P\left(\frac{350-400}{100} \leq z \leq \frac{450-400}{100}\right)$$

$$= P\left(\frac{-50}{100} \le z \le \frac{50}{100}\right) = P(-0.5 \le z \le 0.5)$$

$$= 2P(0 \le z \le 0.5) = 2 \times 0.1915 = 0.3830.$$

(b) The penalty for each labour hour in excess of 450 is Rs. 100. If the minimum penalty paid is Rs. 2000, then delay in completing the project is more than 2000/100 = 20 hours.

Company will take a minimum (450 + 20 = 470 hrs) to complete the bridge. Thus, the required probability is:

$$P(x \ge 470) = P\left(\frac{x-\mu}{\sigma} \ge \frac{470-\mu}{\sigma}\right) = P\left(z \ge \frac{470-400}{100}\right)$$

$$= P\left(z \ge \frac{10}{100}\right) = P(z \le 0.7)$$

$$= 0.5 - P(0 \le z \le 0.7) = 0.5 - 0.2580 = 0.2420.$$

Example 6.44: The marks of the students in a certain examination are normally distributed with mean marks as 40% and standard deviation marks at 20%. On this basis, 60% students failed. The result was moderated and 70% student passed. Find the pass marks before and after moderation.

[Delhi Unit., BCom (H), 2002]

Solution: Let x be the per cent of marks before and after moderation to pass the examination. Given, mean (μ) = 40 and SD(σ) = 20

Before Moderation: Let pass percentage of marks be x_1 per cent. Then 60% students failed imply that 40%, i.e. passed students.

$$P(x \ge x_1) = 0.40$$

$$P\left(\frac{x-\mu}{\sigma} \ge \frac{x-\mu}{\sigma}\right) = 0.40$$

$$P(z \ge z_1) = 0.40$$

$$0.5 - P(0 < z < z_1) = 0.40 \quad \text{or} \quad P(0 < z < z_1) = 0.10$$

or
$$z_1 = \frac{x_1-\mu}{\sigma} = 0.25$$

$$x_1 = 0.25\sigma + \mu = 0.25 \times 20 + 40 = 45$$

Hence, pass percentage is 45 per cent before moderation.

After Moderation: Let pass percentage of marks be x_2 per cent. Then

$$P(x \ge x_2) = 0.70$$

$$P\left(\frac{x-\mu}{\sigma} \ge \frac{x_2-\mu}{\sigma}\right) = 0.70$$

$\Rightarrow$
$$P(z \ge -z_2) = 0.70 \qquad \text{[because } z_2 \text{ is located to left of } z = 0\text{]}$$

$$P(z \ge -z_2) = 0.5 + P(-z_2 < z < 0)$$

$$0.70 = 0.5 + P(0 \le z \le z_2)$$

$$P(0 \le z \le z_2) = 0.2$$

From normal table, we get

$$z_2 = 0.525 \quad \text{or} \quad \frac{x_2-\mu}{\sigma} = -0.525$$

$$x_2 = -0.525\sigma + \mu = -0.525(20) + 40 = 29.5$$

Hence, pass percentage is 29.5% after moderation.

Conceptual Questions 6E

21. State the conditions under which a binomial distribution tends to (i) Poisson distribution, (ii) normal distribution. Write down the probability functions of binomial and Poisson distributions.
22. Normal distribution is symmetric with a single peak. Does this mean that all symmetric distributions are normal? Explain.
23. When finding probabilities with a normal curve we always deal with intervals; the probability of a single value of x is defined equal to zero. Why is this so?
24. What are the parameters of normal distribution? What information is provided by these parameters?
25. What are the chief properties of normal distribution? Describe briefly the importance of normal distribution in statistical analysis.
26. Discuss the distinctive features of the binomial, Poisson, and normal distributions. When does a binomial distribution tend to become a normal distribution?

Self-Practice Problems 6G

6.57 A cigarette company wants to promote the sales of X's cigarettes (brand) with a special advertising campaign. Fifty out of every thousand cigarettes are rolled up in gold foil and randomly mixed with the regular (special king-sized, mentholated) cigarettes. The company offers to trade a new pack of cigarettes for each gold cigarette a smoker finds in a pack of brand X. What is the probability that buyers of brand X will find X = 0, 1, 2, 3, . . . gold cigarettes in a single pack of 10?

6.58 You are in charge of rationing in a State affected by food shortage. The following reports were received from investigators:

Daily calories of food available per adult during current period

Area	*Mean*	*S.D.*
A	2000	350
B	1750	100

The estimated daily requirement of an adult is taken as 2500 calories and the absolute minimum is 1000. Comment on the reported figures and determine which area in your opinion needs more urgent attention.

6.59 Assume the mean height of soldiers to be 68.22 inches with a variance of 10.8 inches. How many soldiers in a regiment of 1,000 would you expect to be over six feet tall?

6.60 In an intelligence test administered to 1000 students, the average score was 42 and standard deviation 24.

Find (a) the number of students exceeding a score of 50, (b) the number of students lying between 30 and 54, (c) the value of the score exceeded by the top 100 students.

6.61 An aptitude test for selecting officers in a bank was conducted on 1000 candidates. The average score is 42 and the standard deviation of scores is 24. Assuming normal distribution for the scores, find:

(a) the number of candidates whose scores exceeds 58.

(b) the number of candidates whose scores lie between 30 and 66.

6.62 A workshop produces 2000 units of an item per day. The average weight of units is 130 kg with a standard deviation of 10 kg. Assuming normal distribution, how many units are expected to weigh less than 142 kg?

6.63 Management of a company is considering adopting a bonus system to increases production. One suggestion is to pay a bonus on the highest 5 per cent of production based on past experience. Past records indicate that, on the average, 4000 units of a small assembly are produced during a week. The distribution of the weekly production is approximately normal with a standard deviation of 60 units. If the bonus is paid on the upper 5 per cent of production, the bonus will be paid on how many units or more?

Hints and Answers

6.57 An experiment, with $n = 10$ trials, probability of finding a golden cigarette (a success) is $p = 50/100 = 0.05$. The expected number of golden cigarettes per pack is, $\lambda = np = 10(0.05)$.

Number of Golden Cigarettes per Pack	*Probability*
0	0.6065
1	0.3033
2	0.0758
3	0.0126
4	0.0016

6.58

Area A	*Area B*
Mean ± 3σ	Mean ± 3σ
= 2,000 ± (3 × 350)	= 1,750 ± (2 × 100)
or 950 and 3,050 calories	1,450 and 2,050 calories

Since the estimated requirement is minimum of 1,000 calories, area A needs more urgent attention.

6.59 Assuming that the distribution of height is normal. Given that, $x = 72$ inches, $\mu = 68.22$, $\sigma = \sqrt{10.8} = 3.286$. Therefore

$$z = \frac{x-\mu}{\sigma} = \frac{72 - 68.22}{3.286} = 1.15$$

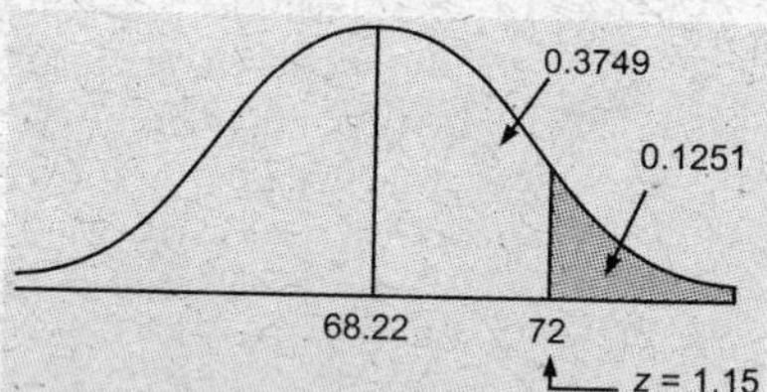

Area to the right of $z = 1.15$ from the normal table is $(0.5000 - 0.3749) = 0.1251$. Probability of getting soldiers above six feet is 0.1251 and their expected number is $0.1251 \times 1000 = 125$.

6.60 (a) Given $\mu = 42$, $x = 50$, $\sigma = 24$. Thus

$$z = \frac{x - \mu}{\sigma} = \frac{50 - 42}{24} = 0.333$$

Area to the right of $z = 0.333$ under the normal curve is $0.5 - 0.1304 = 0.3696$

Expected number of children exceeding a score of 50 are $0.3696 \times 1{,}000 = 370$.

(b) Standard normal variate for score 30

$$z = \frac{x - \mu}{\sigma} = \frac{30 - 42}{24} = -0.5$$

Standard normal variate for score 54

$$z = \frac{x - \mu}{\sigma} = \frac{54 - 42}{24} = 0.5$$

Area between $z = 0$ to $z = 0.5 = 0.1915$

Area between $z = -0.5$ to $z = 0$ is 0.1915

Area between $z = -0.5$ to $z = 0.5$ is

$0.1915 + 0.1915 = 0.3830$

6.61 (a) Number of candidates whose score exceeds 58.

$$z = \frac{x - \mu}{\sigma} = \frac{60 - 42}{24} = 0.667$$

Area to the right of $z = 0.667$ under the normal curve is $(0.5 - 0.2476) = 0.2524$

Number of candidates whose score exceeds 60 is: $100 \times 0.2524 = 252.4$ or 252

(b) Number of candidates whose score lies between 30 and 66.

Standard normal variate corresponding to 30,

$$z = \frac{30 - 42}{24} = -0.5$$

Standard normal variate corresponding to 66,

$$z = \frac{66 - 42}{24} = 1$$

Area between $z = -0.5$ and $z = 1$, is

$0.1915 + 0.3413 = 0.5328$

Number of candidates whose score lies between 30 and 66 : $1000 \times 0.5328 = 532.8$ or 533

6.62 Given $N = 2000$, $\mu = 130$, $\sigma = 10$ and $x = 142$,

$$z = \frac{x-\mu}{\sigma} = \frac{142-130}{10} = 1.2 \cong 0.3849$$

$P(x \le 142) = 0.5 + 0.3849 = 0.8849$

Expected number of units weighing less than 142 kg is $2000 \times 0.8849 = 1{,}770$ approx.

6.63 $z = \dfrac{x-\mu}{\sigma}$ or $1.65 = \dfrac{x-4000}{60}$

or $x = 4{,}099$ units.

Formulae Used

1. Counting methods for determining the number of outcomes
   - Multiplication method
     (i) $n_1 \times n_2 \times \ldots \times n_k$
     (ii) $n_1 \times n_2 \times \ldots \times n_k = n^k$
   - when the event in each trial is the same
   - Number of Permutations $^nP_r = \dfrac{n!}{(n-r)!}$
   - Number of Combinations $^nC_r = \dfrac{n!}{r!\,(n-r)!}$
2. Classical or *a priori* approach of computing probability of an event A

$$P(A) = \frac{\text{Number of favourable cases for A}}{\text{All possible cases}} = \frac{c(n)}{c(s)}$$

3. Relative frequency approach of computing probability of an event A in n trials of an experiment

$$P(A) = \lim_{n\to\infty} \frac{c(A)}{n}$$

4. Rule of addition of two events
   - When events A and B are mutually exclusive
     $P(A \text{ or } B) = P(A) + P(B)$
   - When events A and B are not mutually exclusive
     $P(A \text{ or } B) = P(A) + P(B) - P(A \text{ and } B)$
5. Conditional probability
   - For statistically independent events
     $P(A|B) = P(A);\ P(B|A) = P(B)$
   - For statistically dependent events

$$P(A|B) = \frac{P(A \text{ and } B)}{P(B)}$$

$$P(B|A) = \frac{P(A \text{ and } B)}{P(A)}$$

6. Rule of multiplication of two events
   - Joint probability of independent events
     $P(A \text{ and } B) = P(A) \times P(B)$
   - Joint probability of dependent events
     $P(A \text{ and } B) = P(A|B) \times P(B)$
     $P(A \text{ and } B) = P(B|A) \times P(A)$
7. Rule of elimination
   (i) $P(B) = \Sigma P(A_i)\, P(B|A_i)$
   (ii) $P(A) = \Sigma P(B_i)\, P(A|B_i)$
8. Baye's rule

$$P(A_i|B) = \frac{P(A_i)\, P(B|A_i)}{\Sigma\, P(A_i)\, P(B|A_i)}$$

9. Basic rules for assigning probabilities
   - The probability assigned to each experimental outcome
     $0 \le P(A_i) \le 1$, for all i
   - Sum of the probabilities for all the experimental outcomes
     $\Sigma P(A_i) = P(A_1) + P(A_2) + \ldots + P(A_n) = 1$

   Complement of an event, $P(A) = 1 - P(\bar{A})$
10. Expected value of a random variable x
    $E(x) = \Sigma\, x.P(x)$
    where x = value of the random variable
    $P(x)$ = probability that the random variable will take on the value x.
11. Binomial probability distribution
    - Probability of r success in n Bernoulli trials

$$P(x = r) = {}^nC_r p^r q^{n-r} = \frac{n!}{r!\,(n-r)!}\, p^r q^{n-r}$$

    where p = probability of success
    q = probability of failure, $q = 1 - p$
    - Mean and standard deviation of binomial distribution
      Mean $\mu = np$
      Standard deviation $\sigma = \sqrt{npq}$
12. Poisson probability distribution
    - Probability of getting exactly r occurrences of random event

$$P(x = r) = \frac{\lambda^r e^{-\lambda}}{r!}$$

    where $\lambda = np$, mean number of occurrences per interval of time
    $e = 2.71828$, a constant that represents the base of the natural logarithm system
    - Mean and standard deviation of Poisson distribution
      $\lambda = np, \sigma = np$
13. Normal distribution formula:
    Number of standard deviations σ a value of random variable x is away from the mean μ of normal distribution:

$$z = \frac{x - \mu}{\sigma}$$

Chapter Concepts Quiz

True or False

1. The classical approach to probability theory requires that the total number of possible outcomes be known or calculated and that each of the outcomes be equally likely.
2. For any two statistically independent events, P(A or B) = P(A) + P(B).
3. The marginal probability of an event can be formed by all the possible joint probabilities which include the event as one of the events.
4. The posterior probabilities help a decision-maker to update his prior probabilities by using additional experimental data.
5. The posterior probabilities are valid only when there are two elementary events and consistent outcomes.
6. When someone says that the probability of occurrence of an event is 30 per cent, he is stating a classical probability.
7. If $x = 4!/0!$, then x is not well defined.
8. Two events are mutually exclusive if their probabilities are less than one.
9. If events are mutually exclusive and collectively exhaustive, then posterior probabilities for these events can be equal to their prior probabilities.
10. *A priori* probability is estimated prior to receiving new information.
11. An event is one or more of the possible outcomes which result from conducting an experiment.
12. The condition of statistical independence arise when the occurrence of one event has no effect upon the probability of occurrence of any other event.
13. The collective exhaustive list of outcomes to an experiment contains every single outcome possible.
14. A marginal probability is also known as unconditional probability.
15. The relative frequency approach of assessing the probability of some event gives the greatest flexibility.
16. The expected value of a random variable describes the long range weighted average of its values.
17. The mean of the binomial distribution is greater than its variance.
18. A binomial distribution is positively stewed when $p > 0.5$.
19. The mean, median, and mode always coincide in the normal distribution.
20. The expected value of a random variable is always a non-negative number.
21. The binomial distribution is symmetrical for any value of p (probability of success).
22. Poisson distribution generally describes arrivals at a service facility.
23. In a Bernoulli process, the probability of success must equal the probability of failure.
24. The symmetry of the normal distribution about its mean ensure that its tails extend indefinitely in both the positive and negative directions.
25. All normal distributions are defined by two measures – the mean and the standard deviation.
26. The expected value of a discrete random variable may be determined by taking an average of the values of the random variable.
27. Within 2σ limits from mean, the area under a normal curve is 95.45 per cent.
28. Any course of action that maximizes expected gain also minimizes expected loss.
29. The value of normal variate for some value of the random variable x lying in a normal distribution is the area between x and the mean μ of the distribution.
30. For a given binomial distribution with n fixed, if $p < 0.5$, then distribution will be skewed to the right.

Concepts Quiz Answers

1. T	2. F	3. T	4. T	5. F	6. F	7. F	8. F	9. T
10. T	11. T	12. T	13. T	14. T	15. F	16. T	17. T	18. T
19. T	20. F	21. F	22. T	23. F	24. T	25. F	26. F	27. T
28. F	29. T	30. T						

Review Self-Practice Problems

6.64 The useful life of a certain brand of radial tyre has been found to follow a normal distribution with mean μ = 38,000 km and standard deviations = 3000 km. If a dealer orders 500 tyres for sale, then

(a) find the probability that a randomly chosen tyre will have a useful life of at least 35,000 km.

(b) find the approximate number of tyres that will last between 40,000 and 45,000 km.

(c) If an individual buys 2 tyres, then what is the probability that these tyres will last at least 38,000 km each?

6.65 The amount of time consumed by an individual at a bank ATM is found to be normally distributed with mean μ = 130 seconds and standard deviation σ = 45 seconds.

(a) What is the probability that a randomly selected individual will consume less than 100 seconds at the ATM?

(b) What is the probability that a randomly selected individual will spend between 2 to 3 minutes at the ATM?

(c) Within what length of time do 20 per cent of individuals complete their job at the ATM?

(d) What is the least amount of time required for individuals with top 5 per cent of required time?

6.66 An aptitude test for selecting officers in a bank was conducted on 1000 candidates. The average score is 42 and the standard deviation of scores is 24. Assuming normal distribution for the scores, find the

(a) number of candidates whose scores exceed 58.

(b) number of candidates whose scores lie between 30 and 66.

[*Karnataka Univ., BCom, 1995*]

6.67 The mean inside diameter of a sample of 500 washers produced by a machine is 5.02 mm and the standard deviation is 0.05 mm. The purpose for which these washers are intended allows a maximum tolerance in the diameter of 4.96 to 5.08 mm, otherwise the washers are considered defective. Determine the percentage of defective washers produced by the machine, assuming the diameters are normally distributed.

6.68 In a binomial distribution consisting of 5 independent trials, the probability of 1 and 2 successes are 0.4096 and 0.2048, respectively. Find the parameter p of the distribution.

6.69 The probability of a bomb hitting a target is 0.20. Two bombs are enough to destroy a bridge. If 6 bombs are aimed at the bridge, find the probability that the bridge will be destroyed.

6.70 In an Indian university, it has been found that 25 per cent of the students come from upper income families (U), 35 per cent from middle income families (M), and 40 per cent from lower income families (L). A sample of 10 students is taken at random. What is the probability that the sample will contain 5 students from U; 2 from M and 3 from L?

6.71 A firm uses a large fleet of delivery vehicles. Their record over a period of time (during which fleet size utilization may be assumed to have remained suitably constant) shows that the average number of vehicles unserviceable per day is 3. Estimate the probability on a given day when

(a) all vehicles will be serviceable.

(b) more than 2 vehicles will be unserviceable.

6.72 The director, quality control of automobile company, while conducting spot checking of automatic transmission, removed ten transmissions from the pool of components and checked for manufacturing defects. In the past, only 2 per cent of the transmissions had such flaws. (Assume that flaws occur independently in different transmissions.)

(a) What is the probability that sample contains more than two transmissions with manufacturing flaws?

(b) What is the probability that none of the selected transmission has any manufacturing flaw?

6.73 In the past 2 months, on an average, only 3 per cent of all cheques sent for clearance by a Group Housing Welfare Society (GHWS) have bounced. This month, the GHWS received 200 cheques. What is the probability that exactly ten of these cheques bounced?

6.74 Mr Tiwari is campaign manager for a candidate for Lok Sabha. General impression is that the candidate has the support of 40 per cent of registered voters. A random sample of 300 registered voters shows that 34 per cent would vote for the candidate. If 40 per cent of voters really are allied with the candidate, what is the probability that a sample of 300 voters would indicate 34 per cent or fewer on his side? Is it likely that the 40 per cent estimate is correct?

Hints and Answers

6.64 (a) $z = \dfrac{x-\mu}{\sigma} = \dfrac{35{,}000 - 38{,}000}{3{,}000} = -1.00$

$P(x \geq 35{,}000) = P(z \geq -1.00)$
$= 0.500 + 0.3413$
$= 0.8413$

(b) $z_1 = \dfrac{x_1-\mu}{\sigma} = \dfrac{40{,}000 - 38{,}000}{3{,}000} = 0.67$

$z_2 = \dfrac{x_1-\mu}{\sigma} = \dfrac{45{,}000 - 38{,}000}{3{,}000} = 2.33$

$P(40{,}000 \leq x \leq 45{,}000) = P(0.67 \leq z \leq 2.33)$
$= 0.4901 – 0.2486$
$= 0.2415$

(c) $P(x \geq 38{,}000) = P(z \geq 0) = 0.500$

P(2 tyres each will last at least 38,000 km) $= (0.5000)^2 = 0.2500$ (based on the multiplication rule for the joint occurrence of independent events).

6.65 (a) $z = \dfrac{x-\mu}{\sigma} = \dfrac{100-130}{45} = -0.67$

$P(x < 100) = P(z < -0.67)$
$= 0.5000 - 0.2486$
$= 0.2574$

(b) $z_1 = \dfrac{120-130}{45} = -0.22;$

$z_2 = \dfrac{180-130}{45} = 1.11$

$P(120 \leq x \leq 180) = P(-0.22 \leq z \leq 1.11)$
$= 0.0871 + 0.3655$
$= 0.4536$

(c) $x = \mu + z\sigma = 130 + (-0.84)\,45$
$= 92$ seconds

(d) $x = \mu + z\sigma = 130 + (1.65)\,45$
$= 204$ seconds

6.66 (a) $z = \dfrac{x-\mu}{\sigma} = \dfrac{58-42}{24} = 0.67$

$P(x > 58) = P(z > 0.67)$
$= 0.5000 - 0.2476 = 0.2524$

Expected number of candidates whose score exceeds 58 is 1000 (0.2524) = 2524

(b) $z_1 = \dfrac{30-42}{24} = -0.50;$

$z_2 = \dfrac{66-42}{24} = 1.00$

$P(30 \leq x \leq 66) = P(-0.50 \leq z \leq 1.00)$
$= 0.1915 + 0.3413$
$= 0.5328$

Expected number of candidates whose scores lie between 30 and 66 is 1000 (0.5328) = 5328.

6.67 $z_1 = \dfrac{x-\mu}{\sigma} = \dfrac{4.96-5.02}{0.05} = -1.20;$

$z_2 = \dfrac{5.08-5.02}{0.05} = 1.20$

$P(4.96 \leq x \leq 5.08) = P(-1.20 \leq z \leq 1.20)$
$= 2P(0 \leq z \leq 1.20)$
$= 2(0.3849)$
$= 7698$ or 76.98%

Percentage of defective washers = 100 – 76.98 = 23.02%.

6.68 Given $n = 5$; $f(x = 1) = {}^nC_1 p^n q^{n-1}$
$= {}^5C_1 p^1 q^4 = 5pq^4$
$= 0.4096$

$f(x = 2) = {}^nC_2 p^2 q^{n-2} = {}^5C_2 p^2 q^3$
$= 10p^2q^3 = 0.2048$

Thus $\dfrac{f(x=2)}{f(x=2)} = \dfrac{10\,p^2q^3}{5pq^4} = \dfrac{0.2048}{0.4096}$

or $\dfrac{2p}{q} = \dfrac{1}{2}$

or $4p = q\ (= 1 - p)$, i.e. $p = 1/5$

6.69 Given $p = 0.20, q = 0.80$ and $n = 6$. The bridge is destroyed if at least 2 of the bombs hit it. The required probability is

$$P(x \geq 2) = P(x = 1) + P(x = 2) + \ldots + P(x \geq 6)$$
$$= 1 - [P(x = 0) + P(x = 1)]$$
$$= 1 - [{}^6C_0\,(0.80)^6 + {}^6C_1\,(0.20)\,(0.80)^5]$$
$$= 1 - \frac{2048}{3125} = 0.345$$

6.70 Required probability

$$= \frac{10!}{5!\,3!\,2!}(0.25)^2\,(0.35)^2\,(0.40)^3$$
$$= 0.0193$$

(Based on the rule of multinomial rule of probability)

6.71 (a) $P(x = 0) = \dfrac{e^{-3}\,(3)^0}{0!} = 0.0497$

(b) $P(x > 2) = 1 - P(x \leq 2)$

$$= 1 - [P(x = 0) + P(x = 1) + P(x = 2)]$$
$$= 1 - \left[e^{-3} + 3e^{-3} + \frac{9}{2}e^{-3}\right]$$
$$= 1 - e^{-3}\left(1 + 3 + \frac{9}{2}\right)$$
$$= 1 - \frac{11}{2}(0.0497)$$
$$= 1 - 0.4224 = 0.5776$$

6.72 (a) Given, $p = 0.02, q = 0.98, n = 10$

$$P(x > 2 \text{ flaws}) = 1 - [P(x = 0) + P(x = 1) + P(x = 2)]$$
$$= 1 - [{}^{10}C_0\,(0.98)^{10} + {}^{10}C_1\,(0.02)\,(0.98)^9 + {}^{10}C_2\,(0.02)^2\,(0.98)^8]$$
$$= 1 - [0.8171 + 0.1667 + 0.0153]$$
$$= 0.0009$$

(b) $P(x = 0 \text{ flaw}) = {}^nC_0 p^0 q^n$

$$= {}^{10}C_0\,(0.02)^0 (0.98)^{10}$$
$$= 10\,(0.98)^{10} = 0.8171$$

6.73 Given $n = 200, p = 0.03, \lambda = np = 200(0.03) = 6.$

$$P(x = 10) = \frac{e^{-\lambda}\,\lambda^r}{r!} = \frac{e^{-6}\,(6)^{10}}{10!} = 0.0413$$

6.74 Given $n = 300, p = 0.40; \mu = np = 300(0.40) = 120;$

$$\sigma = \sqrt{npq} = \sqrt{120\,(06)} = 8.48$$

$$P(x \leq 0.34 \times 300 = 102)$$
$$= P\left[z < \frac{x - \mu}{\sigma}\right] = P\left[z < \frac{102 - 120}{8.48}\right]$$
$$= P\,[z \leq -2.12] = 0.5000 - 0.4830$$
$$= 0.0170$$

Since the probability that the sample would indicate 34 per cent or less is very small, it is unlikely that the 40 per cent estimate is correct.

Glossary of Terms

Random experiment: A process of obtaining information through observation or measurement of a phenomenon whose outcome is subject to chance.

A simple event: The basic possible outcome of an experiment, it cannot be broken down into simple outcomes.

Sample space: The set of all possible outcomes or simple events of an experiment.

Event: Any subset of outcomes of an experiment.

Mutually exclusive events: Events which cannot occur together or simultaneously.

Collectively exhaustive events: The list of events that represents all possible experimental outcomes.

Probability: A numerical measure of the likelihood of occurrence of an uncertain event.

Classical approach: The probability of an event A is the ratio of the number of outcomes in favour of A to the number of all possible outcomes, provided experimental outcomes are equally likely to occur.

Relative frequency approach: The probability of an event A is the ratio of the number of times that A has occurred in n trails of an experiment.

Subjective approach: The probability of an event based on the personal beliefs of an individual.

Marginal probability: The unconditional probability of an event occurring.

Venn diagram: A pictorial representation for showing the sample space and operations involving events. The sample space is represented by a rectangle and events as circles.

Joint probability: The probability of two events occurring together or in succession.

Conditional probability: The probability of an event occurring, given that another event has occurred.

Statistical dependence: The condition when the probability of occurrence of an event is dependent upon, or affected by, the occurrence of some other event.

Bayes' theorem: A method to compute posterior probabilities (conditional probabilities under statistical dependence).

Posterior probability: A revised probability of an event obtained after getting additional information.

Discrete random variable: A variable that is allowed to take on only integer values.

Continuous random variable: A variable that is allowed to take on any value within a given range.

Discrete probability distribution: A probability distribution in which the random variable is permitted to take on only integer values.

Continuous probability distribution: A probability distribution in which the random variable is permitted to take any value within a given range

Expected value of a random variable: A weighted average obtained by multiplying each possible value of the random variable with its probability of occurrence.

Bernoulli process: A process in which each trial has only two possible outcomes, the probability of the outcome at any trial remains fixed over time, and the trials are statistically independent.

Binomial distribution: A discrete probability distribution of outcomes of an experiment known as a Bernoulli process.

Poisson distribution: A discrete probability distribution in which the probability of occurrence of an outcome within a very small time period is very small, and the probability that two or more such outcomes will occur within the same small time interval is negligible. The occurrence of an outcome within one time period is independent of the other.

Sampling and Sampling Distributions

LEARNING OBJECTIVES

After studying this chapter, you should be able to

- distinguish between population parameter and sample statistics
- know various procedures of sampling that provide an attractive means of learning about a population or process
- develop the concept of a sampling distribution that helps you understand the methods and underlaying thinking of statistical inference.

7.1 INTRODUCTION

So far we introduced certain statistical methods to analyse a data set and the concepts of probability and its distributions to increase our knowledge about unknown features (characteristics) of a population or a process. In statistical inference we use random sample or samples to extract information about the population from which it is drawn. The information we extract is in the form of summary statistics: a sample mean, a sample standard deviation or other measures computed from the sample.

Sampling The process of selecting a sample from a population is called *sampling*. In sampling, a representative *sample* or *portion* of elements of a population or process is selected and then analysed. Based on sample results, called *sample statistics*, *statistical inferences* are made about the population characteristic. For instance, a political analyst selects specific or random set of people for interviews to estimate the proportion of the votes that each candidate may get from the population of voters; an auditor selects a sample of vouchers and calculates the sample mean for estimating population average amount; or a doctor examines a few drops of blood to draw conclusions about the nature of disease or blood constitution of the whole body.

7.2 REASONS OF SAMPLE SURVEY

A census is a count of all the elements in a population. Few examples of census are: population of eligible voters; census of consumer preference to a particular product, buying habits of adult Indians. Some of the reasons to prefer sample survey instead of census are given below:

1. ***Movement of Population Element*** The population of fish, birds, snakes, mosquitoes, etc. are large and are constantly moving, being born and dying. So instead of attempting to count all elements of such populations, it is desirable to make estimates using techinques such as counting birds at a place picked at random, setting nets at predetermined places, etc.

2. ***Cost and/or Time Required to Contact the Whole Population*** A census involves a complete count of every individual member of the population of interest, such as persons in a state, households in a town, shops in a city, students in a college, and so on. Apart from the cost and the large amount of resources (such as enumerators, clerical assistance, etc.) that are required, the main problem is the time required to process the data. Hence the results are known after a big gap of time.

3. ***Destructive Nature of Certain Tests*** The census becomes extremely difficult, if not impossible, when the population of interest is either infinite in terms of size (number); constantly changing; in a state of movement; or observation results required destruction. For example, sometimes it is required to test the strength of some manufactured item by applying a stress until the unit breaks. The amount of stress that results in breakage is the value of the observation that is recorded. If this procedure is applied to an entire population, there would be nothing left. This type of testing is called destructive testing and requires that a sample be used in such cases.

7.3 POPULATION PARAMETERS AND SAMPLE STATISTICS

Parameters An exact, but generally unknown measure (or value) which describes the entire population or process characteristics is called a *parameter*. For example, quantities such as mean μ, variance σ^2, standard deviation σ, median, mode, and proportion p computed from a data set (also called population) are called parameters. A parameter is usually denoted with letters of the lower case Greek alphabet, such as mean μ and standard deviation σ.

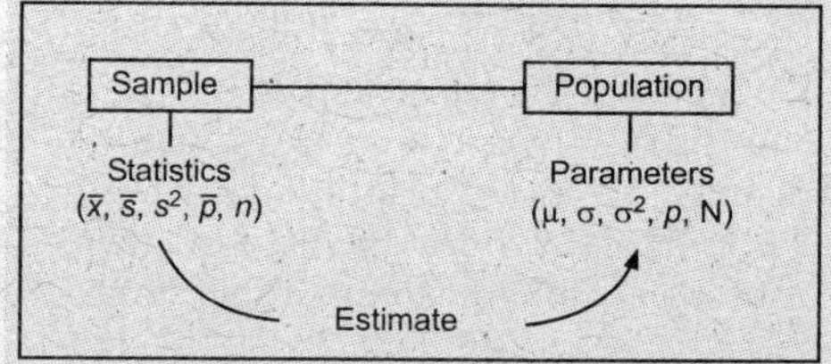

Figure 7.1 Estimation Relationship between Sample and Population Measures

Sample Statistics A measure (or value) found from analysing sample data in called a *sample statistic* or simply a *statistic*. Inferential statistical methods attempt to estimate population parameters using sample statistics. **Sample statistics** are usually denoted by Roman letters such as mean $\bar{x}$, standard deviation s, variance s^2 and proportion $\bar{p}$.

The value of every statistic varies randomly from one sample to another whereas the value of a parameter is considered as constant. The value for statistic calculated from any sample depends on the particular random sample drawn from a population. Thus probabilities are attached to possible outcomes in order to assess the reliability or sample error associated with a statistical inference about a population based on a sample. Figure 7.1 shows the estimation relationships between sample statistics and the population parameters.

7.4 SAMPLING METHODS

As mentioned above, sampling methods compared to census provides an attractive means of learning about a population or process in terms of reduced cost, time and greater accuracy. The representation basis and the element selection techniques from the given population, classify several sampling methods into two categories as shown in Tabel 7.1.

Table 7.1 Types of Sampling Methods

Element Selection	*Representation Basis*	
	Probability (Random)	*Non-probability (Non-random)*
• Unrestrieted	Simple random sampling	Convenience sampling
• Restricted	Complex random sampling	Purposive sampling
	• Stratified sampling	• Quota sampling
	• Cluster sampling	• Judgement sampling
	• Systematic sampling	
	• Multi-stage sampling	

7.4.1 Probability Sampling Methods

Several probability sampling methods for selecting samples from a population or process are as follows:

Simple Random (Unrestricted) Sampling In this method, every member (or element) of the population has an equal and independent chance of being selected again and again when a sample is drawn from the population. To draw a random sample, we need a complete list of all elements in the population of interest so that each element can be identified by a distinct number. Such a list is called *frame for experiment*. The frame for experiment allows us to draw elements from the population by randomly generating the numbers of the elements to be included in the sample.

For instance, in drawing the random sample of 50 students from a population of 3500 students in a college we make a list of all 3500 students and assign each student an identification number. This gives us a list of 3500 numbers, called frame for experiment. Then we generate by computer or by other means a set of 50 random numbers in the range of values from 1 and 3500. The procedure gives every set of 50 students in the population an equal chance of being included in the sample. Selecting a random sample is analogous to using a gambling device to generate numbers from this list.

This method is suitable for sampling, as many statistical tests assume independence of sample elements. One disadvantage with this method is that all elements of the population have to be available for selection, which many a times is not possible.

Stratified Sampling This method is useful when the population consists of a number of heterogeneous subpopulations and the elements within a given subpopulation are relatively homogeneous compared to the population as a whole. Thus, population is divided into mutually exclusive groups called *strata* that are relevent, appropriate and meaningful in the context of the study. A simple random sample, called a *sub-sample,* is then drawn from each *strata* or *group*, in proportion or a non-proportion to its size. As the name implies, a proportional sampling procedure requires that the number of elements in each stratum be in the same proportion as in the population. In non-proportional procedure, the number of elements in each stratum are disproportionate to the respective numbers in the population. The basis for forming the strata such as location, age, industry type, gross sales, or number of employees, is at the discretion of the investigator. Individual stratum samples are combined into one to obtain an overall sample for analysis.

This sampling procedure is more efficient than the simple random sampling procedure because, for the same sample size, we get more representativeness from each important segment of the population and obtain more valuable and differentiated information with respect to each strata.

Disproportionate sampling decisions are made either when strata are either too small, too large, or when there is more variability suspected within a particular stratum. For example, the educational levels in a particular strata might be expected to influence perceptions, so more people will be sampled at this level. Disproportionate sampling is done when it is easier, and less expensive to collect data from one or more strata than from others.

For this method of sampling to be more effective in terms of reliability, efficiency, and precision, any stratification should be done which ensures

(i) maximum uniformity among members of each strata,
(ii) largest degree of variability among various strata.

Cluster Sampling This method, sometimes known as *area sampling method*, has been devised to meet the problem of costs or inadequate sampling frames (a complete listing of all elements in the population so that each member can be identified by a distinct number). The entire population to be analysed is divided into smaller groups or chunks of elements and a sample of the desired number of areas selected by a simple random sampling method. Such groups are termed as *clusters*. The elements of a cluster are called *elementary units*. These clusters do not have much heterogeneity among the elements. A household where individuals live together is an example of a cluster.

If several groups with intragroup heterogeneity and intergroup homogeneity are found, then a random sampling of the clusters or groups can be done with information gathered from each of the elements in the randomly chosen clusters. Cluster samples offer more heterogeneity within groups and more homogeneity among groups—the reverse of what we find in stratified random sampling, where there is homogeneity within each group and heterogeneity across groups.

For instance, committees formed from various departments in an organization to offer inputs to make decisions on product development, budget allocations, marketing strategies, etc are examples of different clusters. Each of these clusters or groups contains a heterogeneous collection of members with different interests, orientations, values, philosophy, and vested interests. Based on individual and combined perceptions, it is possible to make final decision on strategic moves for the organization.

Multistage Sampling This method of sampling is useful when the population is very widely spread and random sampling is not possible. The researcher might stratify the population in different regions of the country, then stratify by urban and rural and then choose a random sample of communities within these strata. These communities are then divided into city areas as clusters and randomly consider some of these for study. Each element in the selected cluster may be contacted for desired information.

For example, for the purpose of a national pre-election opinion poll, the *first stage* would be to choose as a sample a specific state (region). The size of the sample, that is the number of interviews, from each region would be determined by the relative populations in each region. In the *second stage*, a limited number of towns/cities in each of the regions would be selected, and then in the *third stage*, within the selected towns/cities, a sample of respondents could be drawn from the electoral roll of the town/city selected at the second stage.

The essence of this type of sampling is that a subsample is taken from successive groups or strata. The selection of the sampling units at each stage may be achieved with or without stratification. For example, at the second stage when the sample of towns/cities is being drawn, it is customary to classify all the urban areas in the region in such a way that the elements (towns/cities) of the population in those areas are given equal chances of inclusion.

Systematic Sampling This procedure is useful when elements of the population are already physically arranged in some order, such as an alphabetized list of people with driving licenses, list of bank customers by account numbers. In these cases one element is chosen at random from first k element and then every kth element (member) is included in the sample. The value k is called the *sampling interval*. For example, suppose a sample size of 50 is desired from a population consisting of 100 accounts receivable. The sampling interval is $k = N/n = 1000/50 = 20$. Thus a sample of 50 accounts is identified by moving systematically through the population and identifying every 20th account after the first randomly selected account number.

7.4.2 Non-Random Sampling Methods

Several non-random sampling methods for selecting samples from a population or process are as follows:

Convenience Sampling In this procedure, units to be included in the sample are selected at the convenience of the investigator rather than by any prespecified or known probabilities of being selected. For example, a student for his project on 'food habits among adults' may use his own friends in the college to constitute a sample simply because they are readily available and will participate for little or no cost. Other examples are, public opinion surveys conducted by any TV channel near the railway station; bus stop, or in a market.

Convenience samples are easy for collecting data on a particular issue. However, it is not possible to evaluate its representativeness of the population and hence precautions should be taken in interpreting the results of convenient samples that are used to make inferences about a population.

Purposive Sampling Instead of obtaining information from those who are most conveniently available, it sometimes becomes necessary to obtain information from specific targets–respondents who will be able to provide the desired information either because they are the only ones who can give the desired information or because they satisfy to some criteria set by researcher.

Judgement Sampling Judgement sampling involves the selection of respondents who are in the best position to provide the desired information. The judgment sampling is used when a limited number of respondents have the information that is needed. In such cases, any type of probability sampling across a cross section of respondents is purposeless and not useful. This sampling method may curtail the generalizability of the findings due to the fact that we are using a sample of respondents who are conventiently available to us. It is the only viable sampling method for obtaining the type of information that is required from very specific section of respondents who possess the knowledge and can give the desired information.

However, the validity of the sample results depend on the proper judgment of the investigator in choosing the sample. Great precaution is needed in drawing conclusions based on judgment samples to make inferences about a population.

Quota Sampling Quota Sampling is a form of proportionate stratified sampling in which a predetermined proportion of elements are sampled from different groups in the population, but on convenience basis. In other words, in quota sampling the selection of respondents lies with the investigator, although in making such selection he/she must ensure that each respondent satisfies certain criteria which is essential for the study. For example, the investigator may choose to interview ten men and ten women in such a way that two of them have annual income of more than two lakh rupees five of them have annual income between one and two lakh rupees and thirteen whose annual income is below one lakh rupees. Furthermore, some of them should be between 25 and 35 years of age, others between 36 and 45 years of age, and the balance over 45 years. This means that the investigator's choice of respondent is partly dictated by these 'controls'.

Quota sampling has been criticized because it does not satisfy the fundamental requirement of a sample, that is, it should be random. Consequently, it is not possible to achieve precision of results on any valid basis.

7.5 SAMPLING DISTRIBUTIONS

In Chapter 3 we have discussed several statistical methods to calculate parameters such as the mean and standard deviation of the population of interest. These values were used to describe the characteristics of the population. If a population is very large and the description of its characteristics is not possible by the census method, then to arrive at the statistical inference, samples of a given size are drawn repeatedly from the population and a particular *'statistic'* is computed for each sample. The computed value of a particular statistic will differ from sample to sample. In other words, if the same statistic is computed for each of the samples, the value is likely to vary from sample to sample. Thus, theoretically it would be possible to construct a frequency table showing the values assumed by the statistic and the frequency of their occurrence. This *distribution of values of a statistic is called a* **sampling distribution**, because the values are the outcome of a process of sampling. Since the values of statistic are the result of several simple random samples, therefore these are random variables.

Suppose all possible random samples of size n are drawn from a population of size N, and the 'mean' values computed. This process will generate a set of $^{N}C_{n} = N!/n!\,(N - n)!$ sample means, which can be arranged in the form of a distribution. This distribution would have its mean denoted by $\mu_{\bar{x}}$ and standard deviation is denoted by $\sigma_{\bar{x}}$ (also called *standard error*). We may follow this procedure to compute any other statistic from all possible samples of given size drawn from a population.

Conceptual Questions 7A

1. Briefly explain
   (a) The fundamental reason for sampling
   (b) Some of the reasons why a sample is chosen instead of testing the entire population
2. Is it possible to develop a sampling distribution for other statistics besides sample mean? Explain.
3. If only one sample is selected in a sampling problem, how is it possible to have an entire distribution of the sample mean?
4. What is sampling? Explain the importance in solving business problems. Critically examine the well-known methods of probability sampling and non-probability sampling.
5. Point out the differences between a sample survey and a census survey. Under what conditions are these undertaken? Explain the law which forms the basis of sampling.
6. Why does the sampling distribution of mean follow a normal distribution for a large sample size even though the population may not be normally distributed?

7. Enumerate the various methods of sampling and describe two of them mentioning the situations where each one is to be used.

8. Is the standard deviation of sampling distribution of mean the same as the standard deviation of the population? Explain.

7.6 SAMPLING DISTRIBUTION OF SAMPLE MEAN

In general, the sampling distribution of sample means depending on the distribution of the population or process from which samples are drawn. If a population or process is normally distributed, then sampling distribution of sample means is also normally distributed regardless of the sample size. Even if the population or process in not distributed normally, the sampling distribution of sample mean tends to be distributed normally as the sample size is sufficiently large.

7.6.1 Sampling Distribution of Mean When Population Has Normal Distribution

Population Standard Deviation σ is Known As mentioned earlier that no matter what the population distribution is, for any given sample of size n taken from a population with mean μ and standard deviation σ, the sampling distribution of a sample statistic, such as mean and standard deviation are defined respectively by

- Mean of the distribution of sample means or expected value of the mean $\qquad \mu_{\bar{x}}$ or $E(\bar{x}) = \mu$
- Standard deviation (or error) of the distribution of sample means or standard error of the mean $\qquad \sigma_{\bar{x}} = \dfrac{\sigma}{\sqrt{n}}$

If all possible samples of size n are drawn *with replacement* from a population having normal distribution with mean μ and standard deviation σ, then it can be shown that the sampling distribution of mean $\bar{x}$ and standard error $\sigma_{\bar{x}}$ will also be normally distributed irrespective of the size of the sample. This result is true because any linear combination of normal random variables is also a normal random variable. In particular, if the sampling distribution of $\bar{x}$ is normal, the standard error of the mean $\sigma_{\bar{x}}$ can be used in conjunction with normal distribution to determine the probabilities of various values of sample mean. For this purpose, the value of sample mean $\bar{x}$ is first converted into a value z on the standard normal distribution to know how any single mean value deviates from the mean $\bar{x}$ of sample mean values, by using the formula

$$z = \frac{\bar{x} - \mu_{\bar{x}}}{\sigma_{\bar{x}}} = \frac{\bar{x} - \mu}{\sigma/\sqrt{n}}$$

since $\sigma_{\bar{x}}$ measures the dispersion (standard deviation) of values of sample means in the sampling distribution of the means, it can be said that

- $\bar{x} \pm \sigma_{\bar{x}}$ covers about the middle 68 per cent of the total possible sample means
- $\bar{x} \pm 1.96\,\sigma_{\bar{x}}$ covers about the middle 95 per cent of the total possible sample means

The procedure for making statistical inference using sampling distribution about the population mean μ based on mean $\bar{x}$ of sample means is summarized as follows:

- If the population standard deviation σ value is known and either

  (a) population distribution is normal, or

(b) population distribution is not normal, but the sample size n is large ($n \geq 30$), then the sampling distribution of mean $\mu_{\bar{x}} = \mu$ and standard deviation $\sigma_{\bar{x}} = \sigma/\sqrt{n}$, is very close to the standard normal distribution given by

$$z = \frac{\bar{x} - \mu_{\bar{x}}}{\sigma_{\bar{x}}} = \frac{\bar{x} - \mu}{\sigma/\sqrt{n}}$$

- If the population is finite with N elements whose mean is μ and *variance* is σ^2 and the samples of fixed size n are drawn *without replacement*, then the standard deviation (also called standard error) of sampling distribution of mean $\bar{x}$ can be modified to adjust the continued change in the size of the population N due to the several draws of samples of size n as follows:

$$\sigma_{\bar{x}} = \frac{\sigma}{\sqrt{n}}\sqrt{\frac{N-n}{N-1}}$$

The term $\sqrt{(N-n)/(N-1)}$ is called the **finite population multiplier or finite correction factor.** In general, this factor has little effect on reducing the amount of sampling error when the size of the sample is less than 5 per cent of the population size. But if N is large relative to the sample size n, $\sqrt{(N-n)/(N-1)}$ is approximately equal to 1.

Population Standard Deviation σ is Not Known While calculating standard error $\sigma_{\bar{x}}$ of normally distributed sampling distribution, so far we have assumed that the population standard deviation σ is known. However, if σ is not known, the value of the normal variate z cannot be calculated for a specific sample. In such a case, the standard deviation of population σ must be estimated using the sample standard deviation σ. Thus the standard error of the sampling distribution of mean $\bar{x}$ becomes

$$\sigma_{\bar{x}} = \frac{s}{\sqrt{n}}$$

Since the value of $\sigma_{\bar{x}}$ varies according to each sample standard deviation, therefore instead of using the conversion formula

$$z = \frac{\bar{x} - \mu}{\sigma/\sqrt{n}}$$

we use following formula, called 'Student's *t*-distribution'

$$t = \frac{\bar{x} - \mu}{s/\sqrt{n}}, \quad \text{where } s = \sqrt{\Sigma(x-\bar{x})^2/(n-1)}.$$

Example 7.1: The mean length of life of a certain cutting tool is 41.5 hours with a standard deviation of 2.5 hours. What is the probability that a simple random sample of size 50 drawn from this population will have a mean between 40.5 hours and 42 hours?

Solution: We are given the following information

$$\mu = 41.5 \text{ hours}, \ \sigma = 2.5 \text{ hours, and } n = 50$$

It is required to find the probability that the mean length of life, $\bar{x}$, of the cutting tool lies between 40.5 hours and 42 hours, that is, $P(40.5 \leq \bar{x} \leq 42)$.

Based upon the given information, the statistics of the sampling distribution are computed as:

$$\mu_{\bar{x}} = \mu = 41.5$$

and $$\sigma_{\bar{x}} = \frac{\sigma}{\sqrt{n}} = \frac{2.5}{\sqrt{50}} = \frac{2.5}{7.0711} = 0.3536$$

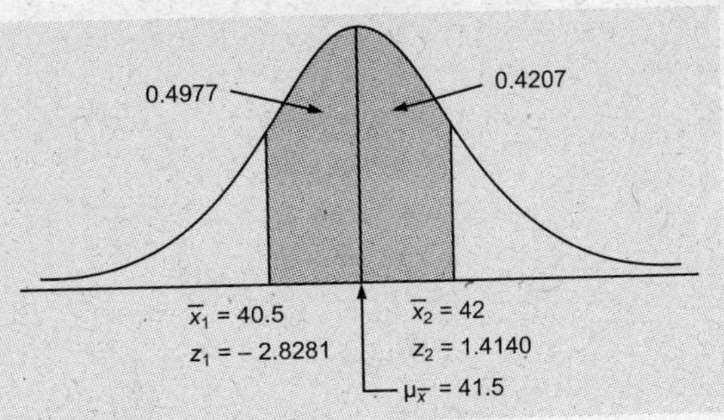

Figure 7.2 Normal curve

The population distribution is unknown, but sample size $n = 50$ is large enough to apply the central limit theorem. Hence, the normal distribution can be used to find the required probability as shown by the shaded area in Fig. 7.2.

$$P(40.5 \le \bar{x} \le 42) = P\left[\frac{\bar{x}_1 - \mu}{\sigma_{\bar{x}}} \le z \le \frac{\bar{x}_2 - \mu}{\sigma_{\bar{x}}}\right] = P\left[\frac{40.5 - 41.5}{0.3536} \le z \le \frac{42 - 41.5}{0.3536}\right]$$

$$= P[-2.8281 \le z \le 1.4140]$$

$$= P[z \ge -2.8281] + P[z \le 1.4140]$$

$$= 0.4977 + 0.4207 = 0.9184$$

Thus 0.9184 is the probability of the tool of having a mean life between the required hours.

Example 7.2: A continuous manufacturing process produces items whose weights are normally distributed with a mean weight of 800 gms and a standard deviation of 300 gms. A random sample of 16 items is to be drawn from the process.

(a) What is the probability that the arithmetic mean of the sample exceeds 900 gms? Interpret the results.

(b) Find the values of the sample arithmetic mean within which the middle 95 per cent of all sample means will fall.

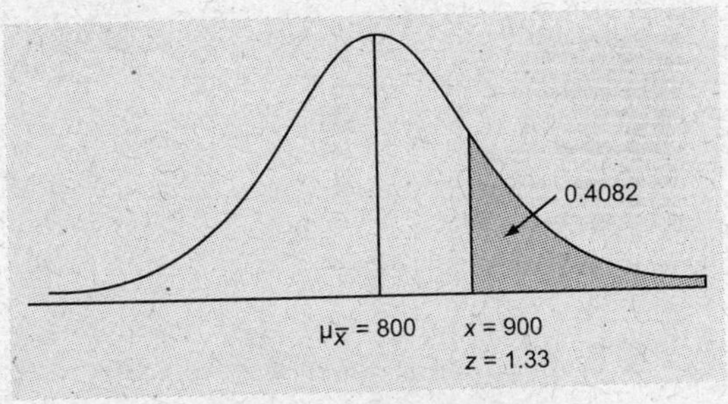

Solution: (a) We are given the following information

$\mu = 800$ g, $\sigma = 300$ g, and $n = 16$

Since population is normally distributed, the distribution of sample mean is normal with mean and standard deviation equal to

$$\mu_{\bar{x}} = \mu = 800$$

and $$\sigma_{\bar{x}} = \frac{\sigma}{\sqrt{n}} = \frac{300}{\sqrt{16}} = \frac{300}{4} = 75$$

Figure 7.3 Normal curve

The required probability, $P(\bar{x} > 900)$ is represented by the shaded area in Fig. 7.3 of a normal curve. Hence

$$P(\bar{x} > 900) = P\left[z > \frac{\bar{x} - \mu}{\sigma_{\bar{x}}} = \frac{900 - 800}{75}\right] = P[z > 1.33]$$

$$= 0.5000 - 0.4082 = 0.0918$$

Hence, 9.18 per cent of all possible samples of size n = 16 will have a sample mean value greater than 900 g.

(b) Since z = 1.96 for the middle 95 per cent area under the normal curve as shown in Fig. 7.4, therefore using the formula for z to solve for the values of $\bar{x}$ in terms of the known values are as follows:

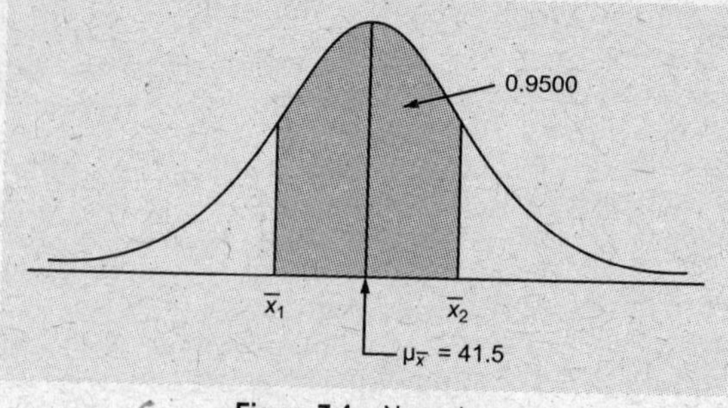

Figure 7.4 Normal curve

$$\bar{x}_1 = \mu_{\bar{x}} - z\,\sigma_{\bar{x}}$$
$$= 800 - 1.96(75) = 653 \text{ g}$$

and
$$\bar{x}_2 = \mu_{\bar{x}} + z\,\sigma_{\bar{x}}$$
$$= 800 + 1.96(75) = 947 \text{ g}$$

Example 7.3: Big Bazar, a chain of 130 shoping malls has been bought out by another larger nationwide supermarket chain. Before the deal is finalized, the larger chain wants to have some assurance that Big Bazar will be a consistent money maker. The larger chain has decided to look at the financial records of 25 of the Big Bazar outlets. Big Bazar claims that each outlet's profits have an approximately normal distribution with the same mean and a standard deviation of Rs. 40 million. If the Big Bazar management is correct, then what is the probability that the sample mean for 25 outlets will fall within Rs. 30 million of the actual mean?

Solution: Given N = 130, n = 25, σ = 40. Based upon the given information the statistics of the sampling distribution are compated as:

$$\sigma_{\bar{x}} = \frac{\sigma}{\sqrt{n}}\sqrt{\frac{N-n}{N-1}} = \frac{40}{\sqrt{25}}\sqrt{\frac{130-25}{130-1}}$$

$$= \frac{40}{5}\sqrt{\frac{105}{129}} = 8 \times 0.902 = 13.72$$

The probability that the sample mean for 25 stores will fall within Rs. 30 million is given by

$$P(\mu - 30 \le \bar{x} \le \mu + 30) = P\left[\frac{-30}{13.72} \le \frac{\bar{x}-\mu}{\sigma_{\bar{x}}} \le \frac{30}{13.72}\right]$$
$$= P(-2.18 \le z \le 2.18)$$
$$= 0.4854 + 0.4854 = 0.9708$$

Example 7.4: Chief Executive officer (CEO) of a life insurance company wants to undertake a survey of the huge number of insurance policies that the company has underwritten. The company makes an yearly profit on each policy that is distributed with mean Rs. 8000 and standard deviation Rs. 300. It is desired that the survey must be large enough to reduce the standard error to no more than 1.5 per cent of the population mean. How large should sample be?

Solution: Given μ = Rs. 8000, and σ = Rs. 300. The aim is to find sample size n be large enough so that

Standard error of estimate, $\sigma_{\bar{x}} = \frac{\sigma}{\sqrt{n}} \le 1.5$ per cent of Rs. 8000 or $\frac{300}{\sqrt{x}} \le 0.015 \times 8000 = 120$

$$300 \le 120\sqrt{n} \text{ or } \sqrt{n} \ge 25, \text{ or } n \ge 625$$

Thus, a sample size of at least 625 insurance policies is needed.

Example 7.5: Safal, a tea manufacturing company, is interested in determining the consumption rate of tea per household in Delhi. The management believes that yearly consumption per household is normally distributed with an unknown mean μ and standard deviation of 1.50 kg.

(a) If a sample of 25 household is taken to record their consumption of tea for one year, what is the probability that the sample mean is within 500 gms of the population mean?

(b) How large a sample must be in order to be 98 per cent certain that the sample mean is within 500 gms of the population mean?

Solution: Given $\mu = 500$ gms, $n = 25$ and $\sigma_{\bar{x}} = \sigma/\sqrt{n} = 1.5/\sqrt{25} = 0.25$ kg.

(a) Probability that the sample mean is within 500 gms or 0.5 kg of the population mean is calculated as follows:

$$P(\mu - 0.5 \le \bar{x} \le \mu + 0.5) = P\left[\frac{-0.5}{\sigma/\sqrt{n}} \le z \le \frac{0.5}{\sigma/\sqrt{n}}\right]$$

$$= P\left[\frac{-0.5}{0.25} \le z \le \frac{0.5}{0.25}\right] = P[-2 \le z \le 2]$$

$$= 0.4772 + 0.4772 = 0.9544$$

(b) For 98 per cent confidence, the sample size is calculated as follows:

$$P(\mu - 0.5 \le \bar{x} \le \mu + 0.5) = P\left[\frac{-0.5}{1.5/\sqrt{n}} \le z \le \frac{0.5}{1.5/\sqrt{n}}\right]$$

Since z = 2.33 for 98 per cent area under normal curve, therefore

$$2.33 = \frac{0.5}{1.5/\sqrt{n}} \quad \text{or} \quad 2.33 = 0.33\sqrt{n}$$

$$n = (2.33/0.33)^2 = 49.84$$

Hence, the management of the company should sample at least 50 households.

7.6.2 Sampling Distribution of Difference Between Two Sample Means

The concept of sampling distribution of sample mean introduced earlier in this chapter can also be used to compare a population of size N_1 having mean μ_1 and standard deviation σ_1 with another similar type of population of size N_2 having mean μ_2 and standard deviation σ_2.

Let $\bar{x}_1$ and $\bar{x}_2$ be the mean of sampling distribution of mean of two populations, respectively. Then the difference between their mean values μ_1 and μ_2 can be estimated by generalizing the formula of standard normal variable as follows:

$$z = \frac{(\bar{x}_1 - \bar{x}_2) - (\mu_{\bar{x}_1} - \mu_{\bar{x}_2})}{\sigma_{\bar{x}_1 - \bar{x}_2}} = \frac{(\bar{x}_1 - \bar{x}_2) - (\mu_1 - \mu_2)}{\sigma_{\bar{x}_1 - \bar{x}_2}}$$

where $\mu_{\bar{x}_1 - \bar{x}_2} = \mu_{\bar{x}_1} - \mu_{\bar{x}_2} = \mu_1 - \mu_2$ (mean of sampling distribution of difference of two means)

$$\sigma_{\bar{x}_1 - \bar{x}_2} = \sqrt{\sigma_{\bar{x}_1}^2 + \sigma_{\bar{x}_2}^2} = \sqrt{\frac{\sigma_1^2}{n_1} + \frac{\sigma_2^2}{n_2}}$$ (Standard error of sampling distribution of two means)

n_1, n_2 = independent random samples drawn from first and second population, respectively.

Example 7.6: Car stereos of manufacturer A have a mean lifetime of 1400 hours with a standard deviation of 200 hours, while those of manufacturer B have a mean lifetime of 1200 hours with a standard deviation of 100 hours. If a random sample of 125 stereos of each manufacturer are tested, what is the probability that manufacturer A's stereos will have a mean lifetime which is at least (a) 160 hours more than manufacturer B's stereos and (b) 250 hours more than the manufacturer B's stereos?

Solution: We are given the following information

Manufacturer A: $\mu_1 = 1400$ hours, $\sigma_1 = 200$ hours, $n_1 = 125$
Manufacturer B: $\mu_2 = 1200$ hours, $\sigma_2 = 100$ hours, $n_2 = 125$

Thus, $\mu_{\bar{x}_1 - \bar{x}_2} = \mu_{\bar{x}_1} - \mu_{\bar{x}_2} = \mu_1 - \mu_2 = 1400 - 1200 = 200$

$$\sigma_{\bar{x}_1 - \bar{x}_2} = \sqrt{\frac{\sigma_1^2}{n_1} + \frac{\sigma_2^2}{n_2}} = \sqrt{\frac{(200)^2}{125} + \frac{(100)^2}{125}}$$

$$= \sqrt{80 + 320} = \sqrt{400} = 20$$

Figure 7.5 Normal curve

(a) Let $\bar{x}_1 - \bar{x}_2$ be the difference in mean lifetime of stereo manufactured by the two manufacturers. Then we are required to find the probability that this difference is more than or equal to 160 hours, as shown in Fig. 7.5. That is,

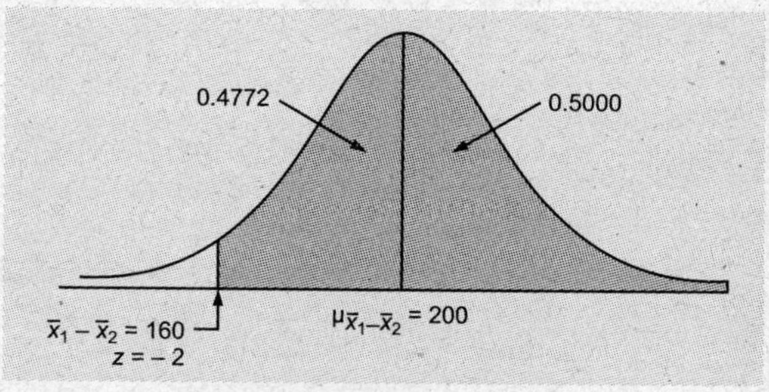

$$P[(\bar{x}_1 - \bar{x}_2) \geq 160] = P\left[z \geq \frac{(\bar{x}_1 - \bar{x}_2) - (\mu_1 - \mu_2)}{\sigma_{\bar{x}_1 - \bar{x}_2}}\right]$$

$$= P\left[z \geq \frac{160 - 200}{20}\right] = P[z \geq -2]$$

$$= 0.5000 + 0.4772$$

$$= 0.9772 \text{ (Area under normal curve)}$$

Hence, the probability is very high that the mean lifetime of the stereos of A is 160 hours more than that of B.

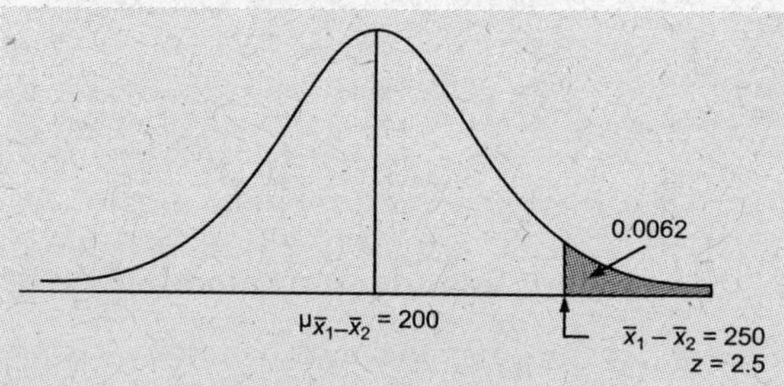

Figure 7.6 Normal curve

(b) Proceeding in the same manner as in part (a) as follows:

$$P[(\bar{x}_1 - \bar{x}_2) \geq 250] = P\left[z \geq \frac{(\bar{x}_1 - \bar{x}_2) - (\mu_1 - \mu_2)}{\sigma_{\bar{x}_1 - \bar{x}_2}}\right]$$

$$= P\left[z \geq \frac{250 - 200}{20}\right] = P[z \geq 2.5] = 0.500 - 0.4938$$

$$= 0.0062 \text{ (Area under normal curve)}$$

Hence, the probability is very less that the mean lifetime of the stereos of A is 250 hours more than that of B as shown in Fig. 7.6.

Self-Practice Problems 7A

7.1 A diameter of a component produced on a semi-automatic machine is known to be distributed normally with a mean of 10 mm and a standard deviation of 0.1 mm. If a random sample of size 5 is picked up, what is the probability that the sample mean will be between 9.95 mm and 10.05 mm?

7.2 The time between two arrivals at a queuing system is normally distributed with a mean of 2 minutes and standard deviation 0.25 minute. If a random sample of 36 is drawn, what is the probability that the sample mean will be greater than 2.1 minutes?

7.3 The strength of the wire produced by company A has a mean of 4,500 kg and a standard deviation of 200 kg. Company B has a mean of 4,000 kg and a standard deviation of 300 kg. If 50 wires of company A and 100 wires of company B are selected at random and tested for strength, what is the probability that the sample mean strength of A will be atleast 600 kg more than that of B?

7.4 For a certain aptitude test, it is known from past experience that the average score is 1000 and the standard deviation is 125. If the test is administered to 100 randomly selected individuals, what is the probability that the value of the average score for this sample will lie in the interval 970 and 1030? Assume that the population distribution is normal.

7.5 A manufacturing process produces ball bearings with mean 5 cm and standard deviation 0.005 cm. A random sample of 9 bearings is selected to measure their average diameter and find it to be 5.004 cm. What is the probability that the average diameter of 9 randomly selected bearings would be at least 5.004 cm?

7.6 A population of items has an unknown distribution but a known mean and standard deviation of 50 and 100, respectively. Based upon a randomly drawn sample of 81 items drawn from the population, what is the probability that the sample arithmetic mean does not exceed 40?

7.7 Assume that the height of 300 soldiers in an army batallion are normally distributed with mean 68 inches and standard deviation 3 inches. If 80 samples consisting of 25 soldiers each are taken, what would be the expected mean and standard deviation of the resulting sampling distribution of means if the sampling is done (a) with replacement and (b) without replacement?

Hints and Answers

7.1 Given $\mu_{\bar{x}} = \mu = 10, \sigma = 0.1$ and $n = 10$. Thus

$$\sigma_{\bar{x}} = \sigma/\sqrt{n} = 0.1/\sqrt{5} = 0.047$$

$$P[9.95 \le \bar{x} \quad \le 10.05]$$

$$= P\left[\frac{\bar{x}_1 - \mu}{\sigma_{\bar{x}_1}} \le z \le \frac{\bar{x}_2 - \mu}{\sigma_{\bar{x}_2}}\right]$$

$$= P\left[\frac{9.95 - 10}{0.047} \le z \le \frac{10.05 - 10}{0.047}\right]$$

$$= P[-1.12 \le z \le 1.12]$$

$$= P[z \ge -1.12] + P[z \le 1.12]$$

$$= 0.3686 + 0.3686 = 0.7372$$

7.2 Given $\mu_{\bar{x}} = \mu = 2, \sigma = 0.25$ and $n = 36$. Thus

$$\sigma_{\bar{x}} = \sigma/\sqrt{n} \frac{3,37,000 - 3,40,000}{20,000/\sqrt{50}}$$

$$= 0.25/\sqrt{36} = 0.042$$

$$P[\bar{x} \ge 2.1] = P\left[z \ge \frac{\bar{x} - \mu}{\sigma_{\bar{x}}}\right] = P\left[z \ge \frac{2.1 - 2}{0.042}\right]$$

$$= P[z \ge 2.38] = 0.5000 - 0.4913$$

$$= 0.0087$$

7.3 Given $\mu_1 = 4500, \sigma_1 = 200$ and $n_1 = 50$; $\mu_2 = 4000, \sigma_2 = 300$ and $n_2 = 100$.

Then

$$\mu_{\bar{x}_1 - \bar{x}_2} = \mu_1 - \mu_2 = 4500 - 4000 = 500$$

$$\sigma_{\bar{x}_1 - \bar{x}_2} = \sqrt{\frac{\sigma_1^2}{n_1} + \frac{\sigma_2^2}{n_2}}$$

$$= \sqrt{\frac{40,000}{50} + \frac{90,000}{100}}$$

$$= 41.23$$

$$P[(\bar{x}_1 - \bar{x}_2) \geq 600] = P\left[z \geq \frac{(\bar{x}_1 - \bar{x}_2) - (\mu_1 - \mu_2)}{\sigma_{\bar{x}_1 - \bar{x}_2}}\right]$$

$$= P\left[z \geq \frac{600 - 500}{41.23}\right]$$

$$= P(z \geq 2.43)$$

$$= 0.5000 - 0.4925 = 0.0075$$

7.4 Given $\mu_{\bar{x}} = \mu = 1000$, $\sigma = 125$ and $n = 100$. Thus $\sigma_{\bar{x}} = \sigma/\sqrt{n} = 125/\sqrt{100} = 12.5$

$P(970 \leq \bar{x} \leq 1030)$

$$= P\left[\frac{\bar{x}_1 - \mu}{\sigma_{\bar{x}}} \leq z \leq \frac{\bar{x}_2 - \mu}{\sigma_{\bar{x}}}\right]$$

$$= P\left[\frac{970 - 1000}{12.5} \leq z \leq \frac{1030 - 1000}{12.5}\right]$$

$$= P(-2.4 \leq z \leq 2.4)$$

$$= P(z \leq 2.4) + P(z \geq -2.4)$$

$$= 0.4918 + 0.4918 = 0.9836$$

7.5 Given $\mu_{\bar{x}} = \mu = 5$, $\sigma = 0.005$ and $n = 9$. Thus

$$\sigma_{\bar{x}} = \sigma/\sqrt{n} = 0.005/\sqrt{9} = 0.0017$$

$$P(\bar{x} \geq 5.004) = P\left[z \geq \frac{\bar{x} - \mu}{\sigma_{\bar{x}}}\right]$$

$$= P\left[z \geq \frac{5.004 - 5.000}{0.0017}\right]$$

$$= P(z \geq 2.4) = 1 - P(z \leq 2.4)$$

$$= 1 - 0.9918 = 0.0082$$

7.6 Given $\mu_{\bar{x}} = \mu = 50$, $\sigma = 100$ and $n = 81$. Thus

$$\sigma_{\bar{x}} = \sigma/\sqrt{n} = 100/\sqrt{81} = 11.1$$

$$P(\bar{x} \leq 40) = P\left[z \geq \frac{\bar{x} - \mu}{\sigma_{\bar{x}}}\right] = P\left[z \leq \frac{40 - 50}{11.1}\right]$$

$$= P(z \leq -0.90) = 0.5000 - 0.3159$$

$$= 0.1841$$

7.7 The number of possible samples of size 25 each from a group of 3000 soldiers with and without replacement are $(3000)^{25}$ and ${}^{300}C_{25}$, respectively. These numbers are much larger than 80—actually drawn samples. Thus we will get only an experimental sampling distribution of means rather than true sampling distribution. Hence mean and standard deviation would be close to those of the theoretical distribution. That is:

(a) $\mu_{\bar{x}} = \mu = 68$ and $\sigma_{\bar{x}}$

$$= \sigma/\sqrt{n} = 3/\sqrt{25} = 0.60$$

(b) $\mu_{\bar{x}} = \mu = 68$ and $\sigma_{\bar{x}} = \frac{\sigma}{\sqrt{n}}\sqrt{\frac{N-n}{N-1}}$

$$= \frac{3}{\sqrt{25}}\sqrt{\frac{3000 - 25}{3000 - 1}} = 1.19$$

7.7 SAMPLING DISTRIBUTION OF SAMPLE PROPORTION

There are many situations in which each element of the population can be classified into two mutually exclusive categories such as success or failure, accept or reject, head or tail of a coin, and so on. These and similar situations provide practical examples of binomial experiments, if the sampling procedure has been conducted in an appropriate manner. If a random sample of n elements is selected from the binomial population and x of these possess the specified characteristic, then the sample proportion $\bar{p}$ is the best statistic to use for statistical inferences about the population proportion parameter p. The sample proportion can be defined as:

$$\bar{p} = \frac{\text{Elements of sample having characteristic, } x}{\text{Sample size, } n}$$

With the same logic of sampling distribution of mean, the sampling distribution of sample proportions with mean $\mu_{\bar{p}}$ and standard deviation (also called *standard error*) $\sigma_{\bar{p}}$ is given by

$$\mu_{\bar{p}} = p \text{ and } \sigma_{\bar{p}} = \sqrt{\frac{pq}{n}} = \sqrt{\frac{p(1-p)}{n}}$$

If the sample size n is large ($n \geq 30$), the sampling distribution of $\bar{p}$ can be approximated by a normal distribution. The approximation will be adequate if

$$np \geq 5 \text{ and } n(1-p) \geq 5$$

It may be noted that the sampling distribution of the proportion would actually follow binomial distribution because population is binomially distributed.

The mean and standard deviation (error) of the sampling distribution of proportion are valid for a finite population in which sampling is with replacement. However, for finite population in which sampling is done without replacement, we have

$$\mu_{\bar{p}} = p \quad \text{and} \quad \sigma_{\bar{p}} = \sqrt{\frac{pq}{n}}\sqrt{\frac{N-n}{N-1}}$$

Under the same guidelines as mentioned in previous sections, for a large sample size n (≥ 30), the sampling distribution of proportion is closely approximated by a normal distribution with mean and standard deviation as stated above. Hence, to standardize sample proportion $\bar{p}$, the standard normal variable.

$$z = \frac{\bar{p} - \mu_{\bar{p}}}{\sigma_{\bar{p}}} = \frac{\bar{p} - p}{\sqrt{p(1-p)/n}}$$

is approximately the standard normal distribution.

7.7.1 Sampling Distribution of the Difference of Two Proportions

Suppose two populations of size N_1 and N_2 are given. For each sample of size n_1 from first population, compute sample proportion $\bar{p}_1$ and standard deviation $\sigma_{\bar{p}_1}$. Similarly, for each sample of size n_2 from second population, compute sample proportion $\bar{p}_2$ and standard deviation $\sigma_{\bar{p}_2}$.

For all combinations of these samples from these populations, we can obtain a sampling distribution of the difference $\bar{p}_1 - \bar{p}_2$ of samples proportions. Such a distribution is called *sampling distribution of difference of two proportions*. The mean and standard deviation of this distribution are given by

$$\mu_{\bar{p}_1 - \bar{p}_2} = \mu_{\bar{p}_1} - \mu_{\bar{p}_2} = p_1 - p_2$$

and $$\sigma_{\bar{p}_1 - \bar{p}_2} = \sqrt{\sigma^2_{\bar{p}_1} + \sigma^2_{\bar{p}_2}} = \sqrt{\frac{p_1(1-p_1)}{n_1} + \frac{p_2(1-p_2)}{n_2}}$$

If sample size n_1 and n_2 are large, that is, $n_1 \geq 30$ and $n_2 \geq 30$, then the sampling distribution of difference of proportions is closely approximated by a normal distribution.

Example 7.7: A manufacturer of watches has determined from experience that 3 per cent of the watches he produces are defective. If a random sample of 300 watches is examined, what is the probability that the proportion defective is between 0.02 and 0.035?

Solution: We are given the following information

$$\mu_{\bar{p}} = p = 0.03, \ \bar{p}_1 = 0.02, \ \bar{p}_2 = 0.035 \text{ and } n = 300$$

Thus standard error of proportion is given by

$$\sigma_{\bar{p}} = \sqrt{\frac{p(1-p)}{n}} = \sqrt{\frac{0.03 \times 0.97}{300}} = \sqrt{0.000097} = 0.0098$$

For calculating the desired probability, we apply the following formula (Fig. 7.7)

$$P[0.02 \le \bar{p} \le 0.035] = P\left[\frac{\bar{p}_1 - p}{\sigma_{\bar{p}}} \le z \le \frac{\bar{p}_2 - p}{\sigma_{\bar{p}}}\right]$$

$$= P\left[\frac{0.02 - 0.03}{0.0098} \le z \le \frac{0.035 - 0.03}{0.0098}\right]$$

$$= P[-1.02 \le z \le 0.51]$$

$$= P(z \ge -1.02) + P(z \le 0.51)$$

$$= 0.3461 + 0.1950 = 0.5411$$

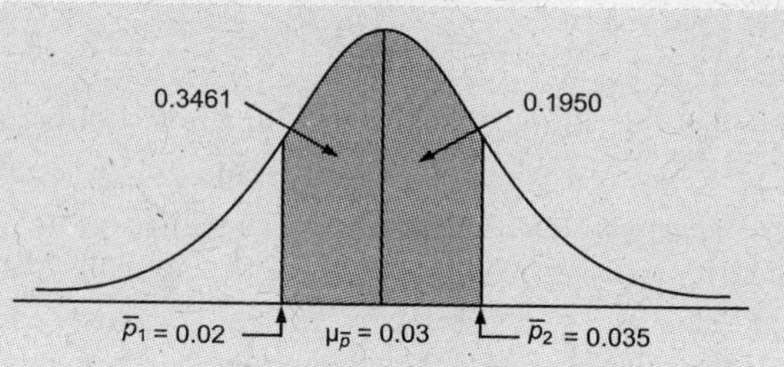

Figure 7.7 Normal curve

Hence the probability that the proportion of defectives will lie between 0.02 and 0.035 is 0.5411.

Example 7.8: Few years back, a policy was introduced to give loan to unemployed engineers to start their own business. Out of 1,00,000 unemployed engineers, 60,000 accept the policy and got the loan. A sample of 100 unemployed engineers is taken at the time of allotment of loan. What is the probability that sample proportion would have exceeded 50 per cent acceptance?

Solution: We are given the following information

$$\mu_{\bar{p}} = p = 0.60, \text{ N} = 1,00,000 \text{ and } n = 100$$

Thus the standard error of proportion in a finite population of size 1,00,000 is given by

$$\sigma_{\bar{p}} = \sqrt{\frac{p(1-p)}{n}}\sqrt{\frac{N-n}{N-1}} = \sqrt{\frac{0.60 \times 0.40}{100}}\sqrt{\frac{1,00,000-100}{1,00,000-1}}$$

$$= \sqrt{0.0024}\sqrt{0.9990} = 0.0489 \times 0.9995 = 0.0488$$

The probability that sample proportion would have exceeded 50 per cent acceptance is given by

$$P(x \ge 0.50) = P\left[z \ge \frac{\bar{p} - p}{\sigma_{\bar{p}}}\right] = P\left[z \ge \frac{0.50 - 0.60}{0.0489}\right]$$

$$= P[z \ge -2.04] = 0.5000 + 0.4793 = 0.9793$$

Example 7.9: Ten per cent of machines produced by company A are defective and five per cent of those produced by company B are defective. A random sample of 250 machines is taken from company A and a random sample of 300 machines from company B. What is the probability that the difference in sample proportion is less than or equal to 0.02?

Solution: We are given the following information

$$\mu_{\bar{p}_1 - \bar{p}_2} = \mu_{\bar{p}_1} - \mu_{\bar{p}_2} = p_1 - p_2 = 0.10 - 0.05 = 0.05; n_1 = 250 \text{ and } n_2 = 300$$

Thus standard error of the difference in a sample proportion is given by

$$\mu_{\bar{p}_1 - \bar{p}_2} = \sqrt{\frac{p_1(1-p_1)}{n_1} + \frac{p_2(1-p_2)}{n_2}} = \sqrt{\frac{0.10 \times 0.90}{250} + \frac{0.05 \times 0.95}{300}}$$

$$= \sqrt{\frac{0.90}{250} + \frac{0.0475}{300}} = \sqrt{0.00052} = 0.0228$$

The desired probability of difference in sample proportions is given by

$$P[(\bar{p}_1 - \bar{p}_2) \le 0.02] = P\left[z \le \frac{(\bar{p}_1 - \bar{p}_2) - (p_1 - p_2)}{\sigma_{\bar{p}_1 - \bar{p}_2}}\right]$$

$$= P\left[z \le \frac{0.02 - 0.05}{0.0228}\right]$$

$$= P[z \le -1.32]$$

$$= 0.5000 - 0.4066 = 0.0934$$

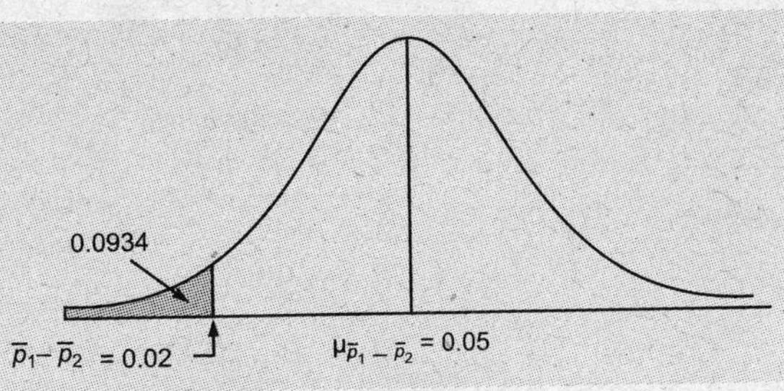

Figure 7.8 Normal curve

Hence the desired probability for the difference in sample proportions is 0.0934 (Fig. 7.8).

Self Practice Problems 7B

7.8 Assume that 2 per cent of the items produced in an assembly line operation are defective, but that the firm's production manager is not aware of this situation. What is the probability that in a lot of 400 such items, 3 per cent or more will be defective?

7.9 If a coin is tossed 20 times and the coin falls on head after any toss, it is a success. Suppose the probability of success is 0.5. What is the probability that the number of successes is less than or equal to 12?

7.10 The quality control department of a paints manufacturing company, at the time of despatch of decorative paints, discovered that 30 per cent of the containers are defective. If a random sample of 500 containers is drawn with replacement from the population, what is the probability that the sample proportion will be less than or equal to 25 per cent defective?

7.11 A manufacturer of screws has found that on an average 0.04 of the screws produced are defective. A random sample of 400 screws is examined for the proportion of defective screws. Find the probability that the proportion of defective screws in the sample is between 0.02 and 0.05.

7.12 A manager in the billing section of a mobile phone company checks on the proportion of customers who are paying their bills late. Company policy dictates that this proportion should not exceed 20 per cent. Suppose that the proportion of all invoices that were paid late is 20 per cent. In a random sample of 140 invoices, determine the probability that more than 28 per cent invoices were paid late.

Hints and Answers

7.8 $\mu_{\bar{p}} = np = 400 \times 0.02 = 8$;

$$\sigma_p = \sqrt{npq} = \sqrt{400 \times 0.02 \times 0.98} = 2.8$$

and 3% of 400 = 12 defective items. Thus

$$P(\bar{p} \ge 12) = P\left[z \ge \frac{\bar{p} - np}{\sigma_p}\right] = P\left[z \ge \frac{12-8}{2.8}\right]$$

$$= P(z \ge 1.42) = 0.5000 - 0.4222$$

$$= 0.0778$$

7.9 Given $\mu_{\bar{p}} = np = 20 \times 0.50 = 10$;

$$\sigma_{\bar{p}} = \sqrt{npq} = \sqrt{20 \times 0.50 \times 0.50} = 2.24$$

$$P(\bar{p} \le 12) = P\left[z \le \frac{\bar{p} - np}{\sigma_{\bar{p}}}\right] = P\left[z \le \frac{12-10}{2.24}\right]$$

$$= P(z \le 0.89) = 0.8133$$

7.10 Given $\mu_{\bar{p}} = p = 0.30, n = 500;$

$$\sigma_{\bar{p}} = \sqrt{\frac{p(1-p)}{n}} = \sqrt{\frac{0.30 \times 0.70}{500}} = 0.0205.$$

$$P(\bar{p} \leq 0.25) = P\left[z \leq \frac{\bar{p}-p}{\sigma_{\bar{p}}}\right] = \left[z \leq \frac{0.25-0.30}{0.0205}\right]$$

$$= P[z \leq -2.43] = 0.5000 - 0.4927$$

$$= 0.0083$$

7.11 Given $\mu_{\bar{p}} = p = 0.04, n = 400;$

$$\sigma_{\bar{p}} = \sqrt{\frac{p(1-p)}{n}} = \sqrt{\frac{0.04 \times 0.96}{400}} = 0.009$$

$$P[0.02 \leq \bar{p} \leq 0.05] = P\left[\frac{\bar{p}_1-p}{\sigma_{\bar{p}}} \leq z \leq \frac{\bar{p}_2-p}{\sigma_{\bar{p}}}\right]$$

$$= P\left[\frac{0.02-0.04}{0.009} \leq z \leq \frac{0.05-0.04}{0.009}\right]$$

$$= P[-2.22 \leq z \leq 2.22]$$

$$= P[z \geq -2.22] + P[z \leq 2.22]$$

$$= 0.4861 + 0.4861 = 0.9722$$

7.12 Given $\mu_{\bar{p}} = p = 0.20, n = 140;$

$$\sigma_{\bar{p}} = \sqrt{\frac{p(1-p)}{n}} = \sqrt{\frac{0.20 \times 0.80}{140}} = 0.033$$

$$P[\bar{p} \geq 0.28] = P\left[z \geq \frac{\bar{p}-p}{\sigma_{\bar{p}}}\right]$$

$$= P\left[z \geq \frac{0.28-0.20}{0.033}\right]$$

$$= P[z \geq 2.42]$$

$$= 0.5000 - 0.4918 = 0.0082$$

Formulae Used

1. Standard deviation (or standard error) of sampling distribution of mean, $\bar{x}$

   - Infinite Population: $\sigma_{\bar{x}} = \dfrac{\sigma}{\sqrt{n}}$

   - Finite Population: $\sigma_{\bar{x}} = \dfrac{\sigma}{\sqrt{n}}\sqrt{\dfrac{N-n}{N-1}}$

   where $n < 0.5N$; n, N = size of sample and population, respectively.

2. Estimate of $\sigma_{\bar{x}}$ when population standard deviation is not known

   - Infinite Population: $s_{\bar{x}} = \dfrac{s}{\sqrt{n}}$

   - Finite Population: $\sigma_{\bar{x}} = \dfrac{s}{\sqrt{n}}\sqrt{\dfrac{N-n}{N-1}}$

3. Standard deviation (or standard error) of sampling distribution of proportion

   - Infinite Population: $\sigma_{\bar{p}} = \sqrt{\dfrac{p(1-p)}{n}}$; $q = 1-p$

   - Finite Population: $\sigma_{\bar{p}} = \sqrt{\dfrac{p(1-p)}{n}}\sqrt{\dfrac{N-n}{N-1}}$

4. Standard deviation of sampling distribution of sample proportions

$$\sigma_{p_1-p_2} = \frac{(\bar{p}_1-\bar{p}_2)-(p_1-p_2)}{\sqrt{\dfrac{p_1q_1}{n_1}+\dfrac{p_2q_2}{n_2}}};$$

$$q_1 = 1-p_1; \quad q_2 = 1-p_2$$

Chapter Concepts Quiz

True or False

1. The sampling distribution provides the basis for statistical inference when sample results are analysed.
2. The sampling distribution of mean is the probability density function that describes the distribution of the possible values of a sample mean.
3. The expected value (mean) is equal to the population mean from which the sample is chosen.
4. As the sample size is increased, the sampling distribution of the mean approaches the normal distribution regardless of the population distribution.
5. A sample size of $n \geq 30$ is considered large enough to apply the central limit theorem.
6. Standard error of the mean is the standard deviation of the sampling distribution of the mean.
7. The finite correction factor may be omitted of $n < 0.5$ N.
8. The principles of the 'inertia of large number' and 'statistical regularity' govern random sampling.
9. Every member of the population is tested in a sample survey.
10. Simple random sampling is non-probability sampling method.
11. Expected value (mean) of samples drawn randomly from a population are always same.
12. The standard error becomes stable with an increase in sample size.
13. The principle of 'inertia of large number' is a corollary of the principle of 'statistical regularity'.
14. Cluster sampling is a non-random sampling method.
15. Quota sampling method is used when the population is widely scattered.

Concepts Quiz Answers

1. T	2. T	3. T	4. T	5. F	6. T	7. T	8. T	9. F
10. F	11. F	12. F	13. T	14. F	15. F			

Review Self-Practice Problems

7.13 An auditor takes a random sample of size $n = 36$ from a population of 1000 accounts receivable. The mean value of the accounts receivable for the population is Rs. 260 with the population standard deviation Rs. 45. What is the probability that the sample mean will be less than Rs. 250?

7.14 A marketing research analyst selects a random sample of 100 customers out of the 400 who purchased a particular item from central store. The 100 customers spent an average of Rs. 250 with a standard deviation of Rs. 70. For a middle 95 per cent customers, determine the mean purchase amount for all 400 customers.

7.15 In a particular coal mine, 5000 employees on an average are of 58 years of age with a standard deviation of 8 years. If a random sample of 50 employees is taken, what is the probability that the sample will have an average age of less than 60 years?

7.16 A simple random sample of 50 ball bearings taken from a large number being manufactured has a mean weight of 1.5 kg per bearing with a standard deviation of 0.1 kg.

(a) Estimate the value of the standard error of the mean

(b) If the sample of 50 ball bearings is taken from a particular production run that includes just 150 bearings as the total population, then estimate the standard error of the mean and compare it with the result of part (a).

7.17 A population proportion is 0.40. A simple random sample of size 200 will be taken and the sample proportion will be used to estimate the population proportion, what is the probability that the sample proportion will be within ± 0.03 of the population proportion?

7.18 A sales manager of a firm believes that 30 per cent of the firm's orders come from first time customers. A simple random sample of 100 orders will be used to estimate the proportion of first-time customers. Assume that the sales manager is correct and proportion is 0.30.

(a) Justify sampling distribution of proportion for this case.

(b) What is probability that the sample proportion will be between 0.20 and 0.40?

7.19 The diameter of a steel pipe manufactured at a large factory is expected to be approximately normally distributed with a mean of 1.30 inches and a standard deviation of 0.04 inch.

(a) If a random sample of 16 pipes is selected, then what is the probability that randomly selected pipe will have a diameter between 1.28 and 1.30 inches?

(b) Between what two values will 60 per cent of the pipes fall in terms of the diameter?

Hints and Answers

7.13 Given $\mu_{\bar{x}} = \mu = 260$; $n = 36$;

$$\sigma_{\bar{x}} = \sigma/\sqrt{n} = 45/\sqrt{36} = 7.5$$

$$P[\bar{x} \le 250] = P\left[z \le \frac{\bar{x} - \mu}{\sigma_{\bar{x}}}\right]$$

$$= P\left[z \le \frac{250 - 260}{7.5}\right]$$

$$= P[z \le -1.33]$$

$$= 0.5000 - 0.4082 = 0.0918$$

7.14 Given $s = 70$, $n = 100$, $\bar{x} = 250$, $z = 1.96$ at 95% confidence. Thus

$$s_{\bar{x}} = \frac{s}{\sqrt{n}}\sqrt{\frac{N-n}{N-1}} = \frac{70}{\sqrt{100}}\sqrt{\frac{400-100}{400-1}}$$

$$= 7(0.867) = 11.33$$

$$\bar{x} \pm z\,s_{\bar{x}} = 250 \pm 1.96(11.33)$$

$$= \text{Rs. } 227.80 \text{ to Rs. } 272.20$$

7.15 Given $n = 50$, $N = 5000$, $\mu = 58$, and $\sigma = 8$

$$\sigma_{\bar{x}} = \frac{\sigma}{\sqrt{n}}\sqrt{\frac{N-n}{N-1}} = \frac{8}{\sqrt{50}}\sqrt{\frac{5000-50}{5000-1}}$$

$$= 1.131 \times 0.995 = 1.125$$

$$P(\bar{x} \le 60) = P\left[z \le \frac{\bar{x} - \mu}{\sigma_{\bar{x}}}\right] = P\left[z \le \frac{58-60}{1.125}\right]$$

$$= P[z \le -1.77]$$

$$= 0.5000 - 0.4616 = 0.0384$$

7.16 Given $\mu_{\bar{x}} = \mu = 1.5$, $n = 50$, $N = 150$ and $s = 0.1$.

(a) $s_{\bar{x}} = s/\sqrt{n} = 0.1/\sqrt{50} = 0.014$ kg

(b) $s_{\bar{x}} = \dfrac{s}{\sqrt{n}}\sqrt{\dfrac{N-n}{N-1}}$

$$= 0.014\sqrt{\frac{150-50}{150-1}} = 0.011 \text{ kg.}$$

It is less than the value in part (a) due to finite correction factor.

7.17 Given $\mu_{\bar{p}} = \bar{p} = 0.40$, $n = 200$

$$\sigma_{\bar{p}} = \sqrt{\frac{p(1-p)}{n}} = \sqrt{\frac{0.40 \times 0.60}{200}} = 0.0346$$

$$P(-0.03 \le \bar{p} \le 0.03) = 2P\left[z \le \frac{\bar{p} - p}{\sigma_{\bar{p}}}\right]$$

$$= 2P\left[z \le \frac{0.03}{0.0346}\right] = 2P(z \le 0.87)$$

$$= 2 \times 0.3078 = 0.6156$$

7.18 Given $p = 0.30$, $n = 100$. Thus

$$\sigma_{\bar{p}} = \sqrt{\frac{p(1-p)}{n}} = \sqrt{\frac{0.30 \times 0.70}{100}} = 0.0458$$

(a) Since both $np = 100\,(0.30) = 30$ and $nq = n(1-p) = 100\,(0.70) = 70$ are greater than 5, the normal distribution is appropriate to use.

(b) $P(0.20 \leq \bar{p} \leq 0.40)$

$$= P\left[\frac{0.20 - 0.30}{0.0458} \leq z \leq \frac{0.40 - 0.30}{0.0458}\right]$$

$$= P[-2.18 \leq z \leq 2.18]$$

$$= 2P(z \leq 2.18) = 2 \times 0.4854 = 0.9708$$

7.19 Given $\mu_{\bar{x}} = \mu = 1.30$, $\sigma = 0.04$ and $n = 16$,

$$\sigma_{\bar{x}} = \sigma/\sqrt{n} = 0.04/\sqrt{16} = 0.01$$

(a) $P(1.28 \leq \bar{x} \leq 1.30)$

$$= P\left[\frac{\bar{x}_1 - \mu}{\sigma_{\bar{x}}} \leq z \leq \frac{\bar{x}_2 - \mu}{\sigma_{\bar{x}}}\right]$$

$$= P\left[\frac{1.28 - 1.30}{0.01} \leq z \leq \frac{1.30 - 1.30}{0.01}\right]$$

$$= P[2 \leq z \leq 0] = 0.5000 - 0.4772 = 0.0228$$

(b) $\bar{x} \pm z\sigma_{\bar{x}} = 1.30 \pm 0.84\,(0.01) = 1.30 \pm 0.0084 = 1.2916$ to 1.3084

Glossary of Terms

Sample statistic A sample measure, such as mean $\bar{x}$, standard deviation, s, pro-portion $\bar{p}$, and so on.

Sampling distribution A probability distribution consisting of all possible values of a sample statistic.

Finite population correction factor The term $\sqrt{(N-n)/(N-1)}$ is multiplied with for $\sigma_{\bar{x}}$ and $\sigma_{\bar{p}}$ a finite population is being sampled. In general, ignore the finite population correction factor whenever $n/N \leq 0.05$.

Degrees of freedom The number of unrestricted chances for variation in the measurement being made.

Chapter 8

Hypothesis Testing

LEARNING OBJECTIVES

After studying this chapter, you should be able to

- explain why hypothesis testing is important
- know how to establish null and alternative hypotheses about a population parameter
- develop hypothesis testing methodology for accepting or rejecting null hypothesis
- use the test statistic *z*, *t*, and *F* to test the validity of a claim or assertion about the true value of any population parameter
- understand Type I and Type II errors and its implications in making a decision
- compute and interpret p-values
- interpret the confidence level, the significance level, and the power of a test

8.1 INTRODUCTION

A *statistical hypothesis* is a claim (assertion, statement, belief or assumption) about an unknown population parameter value. For example (i) a judge assumes that a person charged with a crime is innocent and subject this assumption (hypothesis) to a verification by reviewing the evidence and hearing testimony before reaching to a verdict, (ii) a phamaceutical company claims the efficacy of a medicine against a disease that 95 per cent of all persons suffering from the said disease get cured, (iii) an investment company claims that the average return across all its investments is 20 per cent, and so on.

To test such claims or assertions statistically, sample data are collected and analysed. On the basis of sample findings the hypothesized value of the population parameter is either accepted or rejected. *The process that enables a decision maker to test the validity (or significance) of his claim by analysing the difference between the value of sample statistic and the corresponding hypothesized population parameter value, is called hypothesis testing.*

8.2 GENERAL PROCEDURE FOR HYPOTHESIS TESTING

As mentioned before, to test the validity of the claim or assumption about the population parameter, a sample is drawn from the population and analysed. The results of the analysis are used to decide whether the claim is true or not. The steps of general procedure for any hypothesis testing are summarized below:

Step 1: State the Null Hypothesis (H_0) and Alternative Hypothesis (H_1)

The **null hypothesis** H_0 (read as H_0 sub-zero) represents the claim or statement made about the value or range of values of the population parameter. The capital letter H stands for hypothesis and the subscript *'zero' implies 'no difference'* between sample statistic and the parameter value. Thus hypothesis testing requires that the null hypothesis be considered *true* (*status quo* or *no difference*) until it is proved false on the basis of results observed from the sample data. The null hypothesis is always expressed in the form of mathematical statement which includes the sign ($\leq$, $=$, $\geq$) making a claim regarding the specific value of the population parameter. That is:

$$H_0 : \mu \ (\leq, =, \geq) \ \mu_0$$

where μ is population mean and μ_0 represents a hypothesized value of μ. Only one sign out of $\leq$, $=$ and $\geq$ will appear at a time when stating the null hypothesis

An **alternative hypothesis**, H_1, is the counter claim (statement) made against the value of the particular population parameter. That is, an alternative hypothesis must be true when the null hypothesis is found to be false. In other words, the alternative hypothesis states that specific population parameter value is not equal to the value stated in the null hypothesis and is written as:

$$H_1 : \mu \neq \mu_0$$

Consequently $\quad H_1 : \mu < \mu_0 \quad$ or $\quad H_1 : \mu > \mu_0$

Each of the following statements is an example of a null hypothesis and alternative hypothesis:

• $H_0 : \mu = \mu_0$;	$H_1 : \mu \neq \mu_0$
• $H_0 : \mu \leq \mu_0$;	$H_1 : \mu > \mu_0$
• $H_0 : \mu \geq \mu_0$;	$H_1 : \mu < \mu_0$

Step 2: State the Level of Significance, α (alpha)

The level of significance, usually denoted by α (alpha), is specified before the samples are drawn, so that the results obtained should not influence the choice of the decision-maker. It is specified in terms of the probability of null hypothesis H_0 being wrong. In other words, the level of significance defines the likelihood of rejecting a null hypothesis when it is true, i.e. it is *the risk a decision-maker takes of rejecting the null hypothesis when it is really true*. The guide provided by the staistical theory is that this probability must be 'small'. Traditionally $\alpha = 0.05$ is selected for consumer research projects, $\alpha = 0.01$ for quality assurance and $\alpha = 0.10$ for political polling.

Step 3: Establish Critical or Rejection Region

The area under the sampling distribution curve of the test statistic is divided into two mutually exclusive regions (areas) as shown in Fig. 8.1. These regions are called the *acceptance region* and the *rejection* (or *critical*) *region*.

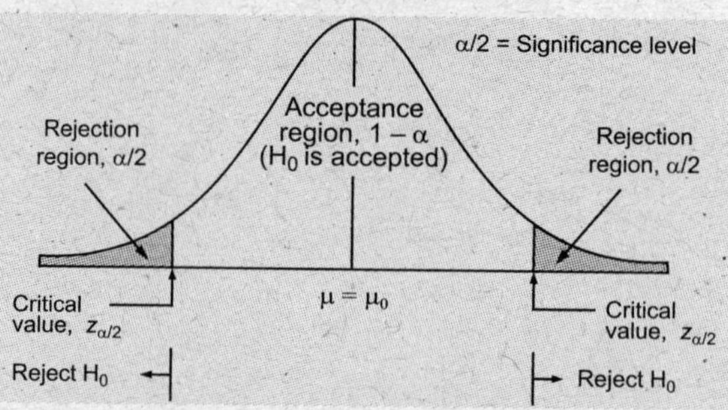

Figure 8.1 Areas of Acceptance and Rejection of H_0 (Two-Tailed Test)

The acceptance region is a *range of values* of the sample statistic spread around the *null hypothesized population parameter*. If values of the sample statistic fall within the limits of acceptance region, the null hypothesis is accepted, otherwise it is rejected.

The **rejection region** is the *range of sample statistic values* within which if values of the sample statistic falls (i.e. outside the limits of the acceptance region), then null hypothesis is rejected.

The value of the sample statistic that separates the regions of acceptance and rejection is called **critical value.**

The size of the rejection region is directly related to the level of precision to make decisions about a population parameter. Decision rules concerning null hypothesis are as follows:

- If prob (H_0 is true) $\leq \alpha$, then reject H_0
- If prob (H_0 is true) $> \alpha$, then accept H_0

In other words, if probability of H_0 being true is less than or equal to the significance level, α then reject H_0, otherwise accept H_0, i.e. the *level of significance* α *is used as the cut-off point which separates the area of acceptance from the area of rejection.*

Step 4: Select the Suitable Test of Significance or Test Statistic

For choosing a particular test of significance following three factors are considered:

(a) Whether the test involves one sample, two samples, or *k* samples?

(b) Whether two or more samples used are independent or related?

(c) Is the measurement scale nominal, ordinal, interval, or ratio?

Further, it is also important to know: (i) sample size, (ii) the number of samples, and their size, (iii) whether data have been weighted. Such questions help in selecting an appropriate test statistic.

One-sample tests are used for single sample and to test the hypothesis that it comes from a specified population. The following questions need to be answered before using one sample tests:

- Is there a difference between observed frequencies and the expected frequencies based on a statistical theory?
- Is there a difference between observed and expected proportions?
- Is it reasonable to conclude that a sample is drawn from a population with some specified distribution (normal, Poisson, and so on)?
- Is there a significant difference between some measures of central tendency and its population parameter?

The value of test statistic is calculated from the distribution of sample statistic by using the following formula

$$\text{Test statistic} = \frac{\text{Value of sample statistic} - \text{Value of hypothesized population parameter}}{\text{Standard error of the sample statistic}}$$

The choice of a probability distribution of a sample statistic is guided by the sample size n and the value of population standard deviation σ as shown in Table 8.1 and Fig. 8.2.

Table 8.1 Choice of Probability Distribution

Sample Size n	*Population Standard Deviation σ*	
	Known	*Unknown*
• $n > 30$	Normal distribution	Normal distribution
• $n \leq 30$, population being assumed normal	Normal distribution	t-distribution

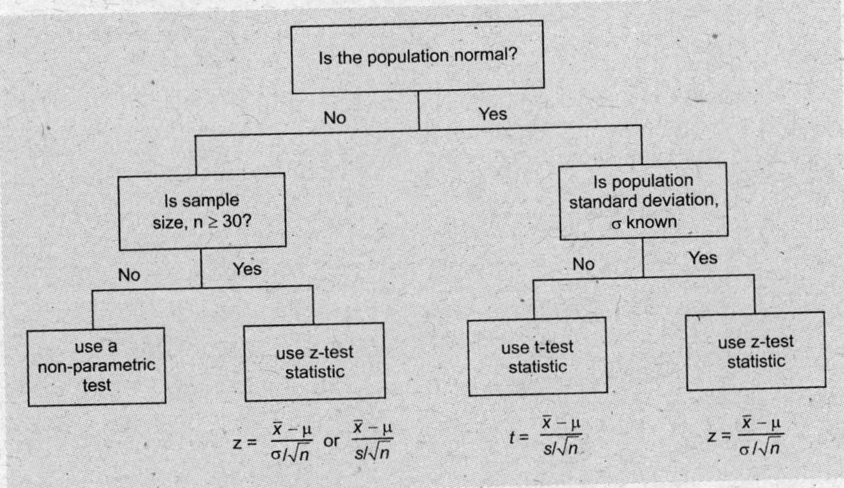

Figure 8.2 Choice of the Test Statistic

Step 5: Formulate a Decision Rule to Accept Null Hypothesis

Compare the calculated value of the test statistic with the critical value (also called *standard table value* of test statistic). The decision rules for null hypothesis are as follows:

- Accept H_0 if the test statistic value falls within the area of acceptance.
- Reject otherwise

In other words, if the calculated absolute value of a test statistic is less than or equal to its critical (or table) value, then accept the null hypothesis, otherwise reject it.

8.3 DIRECTION OF THE HYPOTHESIS TEST

The location of rejection region (or area) under the sampling distribution curve determines the direction of the hypothesis test, i.e. either lower tailed or upper tailed of the sampling distribution of relevant sample statistic being tested. It indicates the range of sample statistic values that would lead to a rejection of the null hypothesis. Figure 8.1, 8.3(a) and 8.3(b) illustrate the acceptance region and rejection region about a null hypothesized population mean, μ value for three different ways of formulating the null hypothesis..

(i) Null hypothesis and alternative hypothesis stated as

$$H_0 : \mu = \mu_0 \quad \text{and} \quad H_1 : \mu \neq \mu_0$$

imply that the sample statistic values which are either significantly smaller than or greater than the null hypothesized population mean, μ_0 value will lead to rejection of the null hypothesis. Hence, it is necessary to keep the rejection region at 'both tails' of the sampling distribution of the sample statistic. This type of test is called *two-tailed test* or *non-directional test* as shown in Fig. 8.1. If the significance level for the test is α per cent, then rejection region equal to α/2 per cent is kept in each tail of the sampling distribution.

(ii) Null hypothesis and alternative hypothesis stated as

$$H_0 : \mu \leq \mu_0 \quad \text{and} \quad H_1 : \mu > \mu_0 \text{ (Right-tailed test)}$$

or $$H_0 : \mu \geq \mu_0 \quad \text{and} \quad H_1 : \mu < \mu_0 \text{ (Left-tailed test)}$$

imply that the value of sample statistic is either 'higher than (or above)' or 'lower than (or below)' than the hypothesized population mean, μ_0 value. This lead to the rejection of null hypothesis for significant deviation from the specified value μ_0 in one direction (or tail) of the sampling distribution. Thus, the entire rejection region corresponding to the level of significance, α per cent, lies only in one tail of the sampling distribution of the sample statistic, as shown in Figs. 8.3(a) and (b). This type of test is called **one-tailed test** *or directional test.*

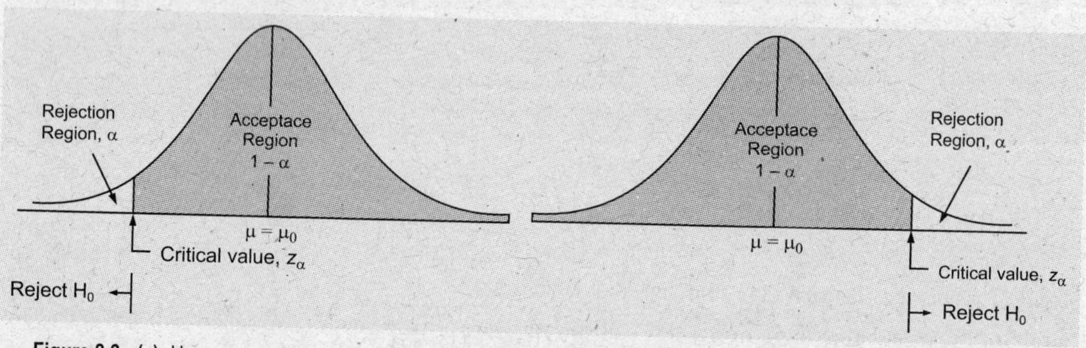

Figure 8.3: (a) $H_0 : \mu \geq \mu_0; H_1 : \mu < \mu_0$, Left-tailed Test **Figure 8.3: (b)** $H_0 : \mu \leq \mu_0; H_1 : \mu > \mu_0$, Right-tailed Test,

8.4 ERRORS IN HYPOTHESIS TESTING

A decision-maker may commit two types of errors while testing a null hypothesis. The two types of errors that can be made in any hypothesis testing are shown in Table 8.2.

Type I Error This is the *probability of rejecting the null hypothesis when it is true* and some alternative hypothesis is wrong. The probability of making a Type I error is denoted by the symbol α. It is represented by the area under the sampling distribution curve over the region of rejection.

Table 8.2 Errors in Hypothesis Testing

Decision	*State of Nature*	
	H_0 is True	*H_0 is False*
Accept H_0	Correct decision with confidence (1 – α)	Type II error (β)
Reject H_0	Type I error (α)	Correct decision (1 – β)

The probability of making a Type I error, is referred to as the **level of significance.** The probability level of this error is decided by the decision-maker before the hypothesis test is performed and is based on his tolerence in terms of risk of rejecting the true null hypothesis. The risk of making Type I error depends on the cost and/or goodwill loss. The complement (1–α) of the probability of Type I error measures the probability level of not rejecting a true null hypothesis. It is also referred to as *confidence level*.

Type II Error This is the *probability of accepting the null hypothesis when it is false* and some alternative hypothesis is true. The probability of making a Type II is denoted by the symbol β.

The probability of Type II error varies with the actual values of the population parameter being tested when null hypothesis H_0 is false. The probability of commiting a Type II error depends on five factors: (i) the actual value of the population parameter, being tested, (ii) the level of significance selected, (iii) type of test (one or two tailed test) used to evaluate the null hypothesis, (iv) the sample standard deviation (also called standard error) and (v) the size of sample.

A summary of certain critical values at various significance levels for test statistic z is given in Table 8.3.

Table 8.3 Summary of Certain Critical Values for Sample Statistic z

Rejection Region	*Level of Significance, α per cent*			
	α = 0.10	*α = 0.05*	*0.01*	*α = 0.005*
One-tailed region	± 1.285	± 1.645	± 2.33	± 2.58
Two-tailed region	± 1.645	± 1.96	± 2.58	± 2.81

Conceptual Questions 8A

1. Describe the various steps involved in testing of hypothesis. What is the role of standard error in testing of hypothesis?
2. What do you understand by null hypothesis and level of significance? Explain with the help of one example.
3. What is a test statistic? How is it used in hypothesis testing?
4. Define the term 'level of significance'. How is it related to the probability of committing a Type I error?
   (a) Explain the general steps needed to carry out a test of any hypothesis.
   (b) Explain clearly the procedure of testing hypothesis. Also point out the assumptions in hypothesis testing in large samples.
5. This is always a trade-off between Type I and Type II errors. Discuss.
6. When should a one-tailed alternative hypothesis be used? Under what circumstances is each type of test used?

7. What is meant by the terms hypothesis and a test of a hypothesis?
8. Define the terms 'decision rule' and 'critical value'. What is the relationship between these terms?
9. Write short notes on the following:
   (a) Acceptance and rejection regions
   (b) Type I and Type II errors
   (c) Null and alternative hypotheses
   (d) One-tailed and two-tailed tests

8.5 HYPOTHESIS TESTING FOR SINGLE POPULATION MEAN

Two-tailed Test Let μ_0 be the hypothesized value of the population mean to be tested. For this the null and alternative hypotheses for two-tailed test are defined as:

$$H_0 : \mu = \mu_0 \quad \text{or} \quad \mu - \mu_0 = 0$$

and

$$H_1 : \mu \neq \mu_0$$

If standard deviation σ *of the population is known*, then based on the central limit theorem, the sampling distribution of mean $\bar{x}$ would follow the standard normal distribution for a large sample size. The z-test statistic is given by

$$\text{Test-statistic: } z = \frac{\bar{x} - \mu}{\sigma_{\bar{x}}} = \frac{\bar{x} - \mu}{\sigma/\sqrt{n}}$$

In this formula, the numerator $\bar{x} - \mu$, measures how far (in an absolute sense) the observed sample mean $\bar{x}$ is from the hypothesized mean μ. The denominator $\sigma_{\bar{x}}$ is the *standard error of the mean*, so the z-test statistic represents how many standard errors $\bar{x}$ is from μ.

If the population standard deviation σ *is not known*, then a sample standard deviation s is used to estimate σ. The value of the z-test statistic is given by

$$z = \frac{\bar{x} - \mu}{s/\sqrt{n}}$$

The two rejection areas in two-tailed test are determined so that half the level of significance, $\alpha/2$ appears in each tail of the distribution of mean. Hence $z_{a/2}$ represents the standardized normal variate corresponding to $\alpha/2$ in both the tails of normal curve as shown in Fig 8.1. The decision rule based on sample mean for the two-tailed test takes the form

- Reject H_0 if $z_{cal} \leq -z_{\alpha/2}$ or $z_{cal} \geq z_{\alpha/2}$
- Accept H_0 if $-z_{\alpha/2} < z < z_{\alpha/2}$

where $z_{\alpha/2}$ is the table value (also called CV, critical value) of z at a chosen level of significance α.

Left-tailed Test Large sample ($n > 30$) hypothesis testing about a population mean for a left-tailed test is of the form

$$H_0 : \mu \geq \mu_0 \quad \text{and} \quad H_1 : \mu < \mu_0$$

$$\text{Test statistic: } z = \frac{\bar{x} - \mu}{\sigma_{\bar{x}}} = \frac{\bar{x} - \mu}{\sigma/\sqrt{n}}$$

Decision rule:
- Reject H_0 if $z_{cal} \leq -z_{\alpha}$ (Table value of z at α)
- Accept H_0 if $z_{\alpha/2}\ z > -z_{\alpha}$

Right-tailed Test Large sample ($n > 30$) hypothesis testing about a population mean for a right-tailed test is of the form

$H_0 : \mu \le \mu_0$ and $H_1 : \mu > \mu_0$ (Right-tailed test)

Test statistic: $z = \dfrac{\bar{x} - \mu}{\sigma_{\bar{x}}} = \dfrac{\bar{x} - \mu}{\sigma/\sqrt{n}}$

Decision rule: • Reject H_0 if $z_{cal} \ge z_\alpha$ (Table value of z at α)

• Accept H_0 if $z_{cal} < z_\alpha$

Example 8.1: A sample of 900 members is found to have a mean of 3.4 cm. Can it be reasonably regarded as a simple from a large population of mean 3.25 cm and standard deviation, 2.61 cm? Also obtain 95% confidence limits of mean.

Solution: Let us take the null hypothesis and alternative hypothesis defined as follows:

$$H_0 : \mu = 3.25 \text{ cm} \quad \text{and} \quad H_1 : \mu \ne 3.25 \text{ cm (Two-tailed test)}$$

Given $n = 900$, $\bar{x} = 3.4$ cm, $\sigma = 2.61$ cm and $\alpha = 5$ per cent. Thus using the z-test statistic

$$z = \frac{\bar{x} - \mu}{\sigma/\sqrt{n}} = \frac{3.40 - 3.25}{2.61/\sqrt{900}} = \frac{0.15 \times 30}{2.61} = 1.73$$

Since value $|z_{\alpha/2}| = 1.96$, is more than calculated value $z_{cal} = 1.73$, the null hypothesis is accepted.

Confidence limits $\bar{x} \pm 1.96\dfrac{\sigma}{\sqrt{n}} = 3.4 \pm 1.96\dfrac{2.61}{\sqrt{900}} = 3.4 \pm 0.1705 = 3.5705$ and 3.2295.

Example 8.2: The mean life time of a sample of 400 fluorescent light bulbs produced by a company is found to be 1600 hours with a standard deviation of 150 hours. Test the hypothesis that the mean life time of the bulbs produced in general is higher than the mean life of 1570 hours at $\alpha = 0.01$ level of significance.

Solution: Let us take the null hypothesis that mean life time of bulbs is not more than 1570 hours, that is

$$H_0 : \mu \le 1570 \quad \text{and} \quad H_1 : \mu > 1570 \quad \text{(Right-tailed test)}$$

Given $n = 400$, $\bar{x} = 1600$ hours, $s = 150$ hrs and $\alpha = 0.01$. Thus using the z-test statistic.

$$z = \frac{\bar{x} - \mu}{\sigma_{\bar{x}}} = \frac{\bar{x} - \mu}{s/\sqrt{n}} = \frac{1600 - 1570}{150/\sqrt{400}} = \frac{30}{7.5} = 4$$

Since the calculated value $z_{cal} = 4$ is more than its critical value $z_\alpha = \pm 2.33$, the H_0 is rejected. Hence, we conclude that the mean lifetime of bulbs produced by the company may be higher than 1570 hours.

Example 8.3: A stenographer claims that she can take dictation at the rate of 120 words per minute. Can we reject her claim on the basis of 100 trials in which she demonstrates a mean of 116 words with a standard deviation of 15 words? Use 5% level of significance? *[Delhi Univ., BA Eco (Hons), 1990]*

Solution: Let us take the null hypothesis that the stenographer claim is true, that is

$$H_0 : \mu = 120 \quad \text{and} \quad H_1 : \mu \ne 120$$

Given $n = 100$, $\bar{x} = 116$, $\sigma = 15$ and $\alpha = 5$ per cent. Thus using the z-test statistic

$$z = \frac{\bar{x} - \mu}{\sigma/\sqrt{n}} = \frac{\bar{x} - \mu}{s/\sqrt{n}}, \text{ since } \sigma \text{ is not known}$$

$$= \frac{116 - 120}{15/\sqrt{100}} = -2.67$$

Since $|z_{cal}| = 2.67$ is more than its table value $|z_\alpha| = 1.96$ at 5 per cent level of significance, the null hypothesis H_0 is rejected, i.e. stenographer is claim is not true.

Example 8.4: A random sample of boots worn by 36 soldiers in a desert region showed an average life of 1.08 years with a standard deviation of 0.6 years. Under the standard conditions, the boots are known to have an average life of 1.28 years. Is there a reason to assert at 1% level of significance that use in desert causes the mean life of such boots to decrease? What will be your conclusion if the level of significance is 5%. Assume that life of boots is normally distributed.

[*Delhi Univ., BA Eco (Hons), 1997*]

Solution: Let us take the null hypothesis that the average life of boots is 1.28 years, i.e.

$$H_0 : \mu = 1.28 \quad \text{and} \quad H_1 < 1.28 \text{ (Left-tailed test)}$$

Given that $n = 36$, $\bar{x} = 1.08$, $s = 0.6$ and $\alpha = 5$ per cent. Thus applying z-test statistic as follows:

$$z = \frac{\bar{x} - \mu}{\sigma/\sqrt{n}} = \frac{\bar{x} - \mu}{s/\sqrt{n}} = \frac{1.08 - 1.28}{0.6/\sqrt{36}} = \frac{-0.20}{0.6/6} = -2.$$

(a) Since critical value of $|z_\alpha|$ at 1% level of significance for left tailed test is more than its calculated value $|z_{cal}| = 2$, therefore H_0 is accepted, i.e. use of boots in desert does not reduce the mean life of boots.

(b) Since critical value of $|z_\alpha| = 1.65$ at 5% level of significance for left tail test is less than its calculated value $|z_{cal}| = 2$, therefore H_0 is rejected, i.e. use of boots in the desert causes the mean life of the boots to decrease.

Example 8.5: An ambulance service claims that it takes, on the average 8.9 minutes to reach its destination in emergency calls. To check on this claim, the agency which licenses ambulance services has then timed on 50 emergency calls, getting a mean of 9.3 minutes with a standard deviation of 1.8 minutes. Does this constitute evidence that the figure claimed is too low at the 1 per cent significance level?

Solution: Let us consider the null hypothesis H_0 that 'the claim is same as observed' and alternative hypothesis is 'claim is different than observed'. These two hypotheses are written as:

$$H_0 : \mu = 8.9 \text{ and } H_1 : \mu \neq 8.9$$

Given $n = 50$, $\bar{x} = 9.3$, and $s = 1.8$. Using the z-test statistic, we get

$$z = \frac{\bar{x} - \mu}{s_{\bar{x}}} = \frac{\bar{x} - \mu}{s/\sqrt{n}} = \frac{9.3 - 8.9}{1.8/\sqrt{50}} = \frac{0.4}{0.254} = 1.574$$

Since $z_{cal} = 1.574$ in less than its critical value $z_{\alpha/2} = \pm 2.58$, at $\alpha = 0.01$, the null hypothesis is accepted. Thus, there is no difference between the average time observed and claimed.

Example 8.6: A radio shops sells, on an average, 200 radios per day, with a standard deviation of 50 radios. After an extensive advertising campaign, the management will compute the average sales for the next 25 days to see whether an improvement has occurred. Assume that the daily sales of radios is normally distributed.

(a) Write down null and alternative hypothesis.

(b) Test hypothesis at 5% level of significance if $\bar{x} = 126$.

(c) How large must $\bar{x}$ be in order that the null hypothesis is rejected at 5% level of significance.

[*Delhi Univ., BA Eco (Hons), 1998*]

Solution: Let us consider the null hypothesis that the average sales of radios is 200 per day. Then we may write as:

$$H_0 : \mu = 200 \quad \text{and} \quad H_1 : \mu > 200 \text{ (Right-tailed test)}$$

Given $n = 25$, $\bar{x} = 216$, $\sigma = 50$ and $\alpha = 0.05$. Applying z-test statistic as follows:

$$z = \frac{\bar{x} - \mu}{\sigma/\sqrt{n}} = \frac{216 - 200}{50/\sqrt{25}} = 1.6$$

Since calculated value of z is less than its critical value $z_{\alpha/2} = 1.645$ at $\alpha = 0.05$, therefore null hypothesis. H_0 is accepted. This implies that the average sales of radios is 200 per day and advertisement campaign does not improve the sales of radios.

Null hypothesis, H_0 will be rejected at $\alpha = 0.05$ level of significance provided calculated value of z is greater than its critical value $z = 1.645$, i.e.

$$z = \frac{\bar{x} - \mu}{\sigma/\sqrt{n}} > 1.645 \quad \text{or} \quad \frac{\bar{x} - 200}{50/\sqrt{25}} > 1.645$$

$$\frac{\bar{x} - 200}{10} > 1.645, \quad \text{i.e.} \quad \bar{x} > 216.45$$

Hence sample mean, $\bar{x}$ must be greater that 216.45 for H_0 to be rejected

8.6 HYPOTHESIS TESTING FOR DIFFERENCE BETWEEN TWO POPULATION MEANS

If we have two independent populations each having its mean and standard deviation as:

Population	*Mean*	*Standard Deviation*
1	μ_1	σ_1
2	μ_2	σ_2

then we can extend the hypothesis testing concepts developed in the previous section to test whether there is any significant difference between the means of these populations.

Let two independent random samples of large size n_1 and n_2 be drawn from the first and second population, respectively. Let the sample means so calculated be $\bar{x}_1$ and $\bar{x}_2$. The z-test statistic used to determine the difference between the population means $(\mu_1 - \mu_2)$ is based on the difference between the sample means $(\bar{x}_1 - \bar{x}_2)$ because sampling distribution of $\bar{x}_1 - \bar{x}_2$ has the property $E(\bar{x}_1 - \bar{x}_2) = (\mu_1 - \mu_2)$. This test statistic will follow the standard normal distribution for a large sample due to the central limit theorem. The z-test statistic is

$$\text{Test statistic: } z = \frac{(\bar{x}_1 - \bar{x}_2) - (\mu_1 - \mu_2)}{\sigma_{\bar{x}_1 - \bar{x}_2}} = \frac{(\bar{x}_1 - \bar{x}_2) - (\mu_1 - \mu_2)}{\sqrt{\dfrac{\sigma_1^2}{n_1} + \dfrac{\sigma_2^2}{n_2}}}$$

where $\sigma_{\bar{x}_1 - \bar{x}_2}$ = standard error of the statistic $(\bar{x}_1 - \bar{x}_2)$

$\bar{x}_1 - \bar{x}_2$ = difference between two sample means, that is, sample statistic

$\mu_1 - \mu_2$ = difference between population means, that is, hypothesized population parameter

If $\sigma_1^2 = \sigma_2^2$, the above formula algebrically reduces to:

$$z = \frac{(\bar{x}_1 - \bar{x}_2) - (\mu_1 - \mu_2)}{\sigma\sqrt{\dfrac{1}{n_1} + \dfrac{1}{n_2}}}$$

If the standard deviations σ_1 and σ_2 of each of the populations are *not known*, then we may estimate the standard error of sampling distribution of the sample statistic $\bar{x}_1 - \bar{x}_2$ by substituting the sample standard deviations s_1 and s_2 as estimates of the population standard deviations. Under this condition, the standard error of $\bar{x}_1 - \bar{x}_2$ is estimated as:

$$s_{\bar{x}_1 - \bar{x}_2} = \sqrt{\frac{s_1^2}{n_1} + \frac{s_2^2}{n_2}}$$

The standard error of the *difference between standard deviation of sampling distribution* is given by

$$\sigma_{\sigma_1 - \sigma_2} = \sqrt{\frac{\sigma_1^2}{2n_1} + \frac{\sigma_2^2}{2n_2}}$$

The null and alternative hypothesis are stated as:

Null hypothesis : $H_0 : \mu_1 - \mu_2 = d_0$
Alternative hypothesis :

One-tailed Test	*Two-tailed Test*
$H_1 : (\mu_1 - \mu_2) > d_0$	$H_1 : (\mu_1 - \mu_2) \neq d_0$
$H_1 : (\mu_1 - \mu_2) < d_0$	

where d_0 is some specified difference that is desired to be tested. If there is no difference between μ_1 and μ_2, i.e. $\mu_1 = \mu_2$, then $d_0 = 0$.

Decision rule: Reject H_0 at a specified level of significance α when

One-tailed test	*Two-tailed test*
• $z_{cal} > z_{\alpha}$ [or $z < -z_a$ when $H_1 : \mu_1 - \mu_2 < d_0$ • When p-value $< \alpha$	• $z_{cal} > z_{\alpha/2}$ or $z_{cal} < -z_{\alpha/2}$

Example 8.7: A firm believes that the tyres produced by process A on an average last longer than tyres produced by process B. To test this belief, random samples of tyres produced by the two processes were tested and the results are:

Process	*Sample Size*	*Average Lifetime (in km)*	*Standard Deviation (in km)*
A	50	22,400	1000
B	50	21,800	1000

Is there evidence at a 5 per cent level of significance that the firm is correct in its belief?

Solution: Let us take the null hypothesis that there is no significant difference in the average life of tyres produced by processes A and B, that is,

$$H_0 : \mu_1 = \mu_2 \text{ or } \mu_1 - \mu_2 = 0 \quad \text{and} \quad H_1 : \mu_1 \neq \mu_2$$

Given, $\bar{x}_1 = 22{,}400$ km, $\bar{x}_2 = 21{,}800$ km, $\sigma_1 = \sigma_2 = 1000$ km, and $n_1 = n_2 = 50$. Thus using the z-test statistic

$$z = \frac{(\bar{x}_1 - \bar{x}_2) - (\mu_1 - \mu_2)}{\sigma_{\bar{x}_1 - \bar{x}_2}} = \frac{\bar{x}_1 - \bar{x}_2}{\sigma_{\bar{x}_1 - \bar{x}_2}} = \frac{\bar{x}_1 - \bar{x}_2}{\sqrt{\frac{\sigma_1^2}{n_1} + \frac{\sigma_2^2}{n_2}}}$$

$$= \frac{22,400 - 21,800}{\sqrt{\frac{(1000)^2}{50} + \frac{(1000)^2}{50}}} = \frac{600}{\sqrt{20,000 + 20,000}} = \frac{600}{200} = 3$$

Since the calculated value $z_{cal} = 3$ is more than its critical value $z_{\alpha/2} = \pm 1.645$ at $\alpha = 0.05$ level of significance, therefore H_0 is rejected. Hence we can conclude that the tyres produced by process A last longer than those produced by process B.

Example 8.8: The mean weight of 50 male students who showed above average participation in school athletics was 68.2 kgs with a standard deviation of 2.5 kg. While 50 male students who showed no interest in such participation had a mean weight of 67.5 kgs with a standard deviation of 2.8 kgs. Test the hypothesis that male students who participate in school athletics are healthier than other male students.

Solution: Let us take the null hypothesis that there is no difference between the mean weight of male students who participate and do not participate in athletics. That

$$H_0 : \mu_1 = \mu_2 \quad \text{and} \quad H_1 : \mu_1 > \mu_2 \text{ (Right-tailed test)}$$

Given $n_1 = 50$, $\bar{x}_1 = 68.2$, $s_1 = 2.5$, and $n_2 = 50$, $\bar{x}_2 = 67.5$, $s_2 = 2.8$

Applying z-test statistic as follows:

$$z = \frac{\bar{x}_1 - \bar{x}_2}{\sqrt{\frac{s_1^2}{n_1} + \frac{s_2^2}{n_2}}} = \frac{68.2 - 67.5}{\sqrt{\frac{(2.5)^2}{50} + \frac{(2.8)^2}{50}}} = \frac{0.7}{0.5308} = 1.3188$$

The critical value of $z = 1.645$ at 5% level of significance is more than its calculated value, $z = 1.3188$, null hypothesis, H_0 is accepted. Hence, average weight of the male students who participate in school athletics is same as the average weight of other male students in school.

Example 8.9: The Educational Testing Service conduced a study to investigate difference between the scores of female and male students on the Mathematics Aptitude Test. The study identified a random sample of 562 female and 852 male students who had achieved the same high score on the mathematics portion of the test. That is, the female and male students viewed as having similar high ability in mathematics. The verbal scores for the two samples are given below:

	Female	*Male*
Sample mean	547	525
Sample stundard deviation	83	78

Do the data support the conclusion that given populations of female and male students with similar high ability in mathematics, the female students will have a significantly high verbal ability? Test at $\alpha = 0.05$ significance level. What is your conclusion?

Solution: Let us take the null hypothesis that the female students have high level verbal ability, that is,

$$H_0 : (\mu_1 - \mu_2) \geq 0 \text{ and } H_1 : (\mu_1 - \mu_2) < 0$$

Given, for female students: $n_1 = 562$, $\bar{x}_1 = 547$, $s_1 = 83$, for male students: $n_2 = 852$, $\bar{x}_2 = 525$, $s_2 = 78$, and $\alpha = 0.05$.

Substituting these values into the z-test statistic, we get

$$z = \frac{(\bar{x}_1 - \bar{x}_2) - (\mu_1 - \mu_2)}{\sqrt{\frac{s_1^2}{n_1} + \frac{s_2^2}{n_2}}} = \frac{547 - 525}{\sqrt{\frac{(83)^2}{562} + \frac{(78)^2}{852}}}$$

$$= \frac{22}{\sqrt{12.258 + 7.140}} = \frac{22}{\sqrt{19.398}} = \frac{22}{4.404} = 4.995$$

Using a one-tailed test with $\alpha = 0.05$ significance level, the critical value of z-test statistic is $z_\alpha = \pm 1.645$. Since $z_{cal} = 4.995$ is more than the critical value $z_\alpha = 1.645$, null hypothesis, H_0 is rejected. Hence, we conclude that there is no sufficient evidence to declare that difference between verbal ability of female and male students is significant

Self-Practice Problems 8A

8.1 The mean breaking strength of the cables supplied by a manufacturer is 1800 with a standard deviation of 100. By a new technique in the manufacturing process it is claimed that the breaking strength of the cables has increased. In order to test this claim a sample of 50 cables is tested. It is found that the mean breaking strength is 1850. Can we support the claim at a 0.01 level of significance?

8.2 A sample of 100 households in a village was taken and the average income was found to be Rs. 628 per month with a standard deviation of Rs. 60 per month. Find the standard error of mean and determine 99 per cent confidence limits within which the income of all the people in this village are expected to lie. Also test the claim that the average income was Rs. 640 per month.

8.3 A random sample of boots worn by 40 combat soldiers in a desert region showed an average life of 1.08 years with a standard deviation of 0.05. Under the standard conditions, the boots are known to have an average life of 1.28 years. Is there reason to assert at a level of significance of 0.05 that use in the desert causes the mean life of such boots to decrease?

8.4 An ambulance service claims that it takes, on an average, 8.9 minutes to reach its destination in emergency calls. To check on this claim, the agency which licenses ambulance services had them timed on 50 emergency calls, getting a mean of 9.3 minutes with a standard deviation of 1.8 minutes. At the level of significance of 0.05, does this constitute evidence that the figure claimed is too low?

8.5 A sample of 100 tyres is taken from a lot. The mean life of the tyres is found to be 39,350 km with a standard deviation of 3260 km. Could the sample come from a population with mean life of 40,000 km? Establish 99 per cent confidence limits within which the mean life of the tyres is expected to lie.

8.6 A simple sample of the heights of 6400 Englishmen has a mean of 67.85 inches and a standard deviation of 2.56 inches, while a simple sample of heights of 1600 Austrians has a mean of 68.55 inches and a standard deviation of 2.52 inches. Do the data indicate that the Austrians are on the average taller than the Englishmen? Give reasons for your answer.

8.7 A man buys 50 electric bulbs of 'Philips' and 50 electric bulbs of 'HMT'. He finds that 'Philips' bulbs gave an average life of 1500 hours with a standard deviation of 60 hours and 'HMT' bulbs gave an average life of 1512 hours with a standard deviation of 80 hours. Is there a significant difference in the mean life of the two makes of bulbs?

8.8 Consider the following hypothesis:

$$H_0: \mu = 15 \text{ and } H_1: \mu \neq 15$$

A sample of 50 provided a sample mean of 14.2 and standard deviation of 5. Compute the

p-value, and conclude about H_0 at the level of significance 0.02.

8.9 A product is manufactured in two ways. A pilot test on 64 items from each method indicates that the products of method 1 have a sample mean tensile strength of 106 lbs and a standard deviation of 12 lbs, whereas in method 2 the corresponding values of mean and standard deviation are 100 lbs and 10 lbs, respectively. Greater tensile strength in the product is preferable. Use an appropriate large sample test of 5 per cent level of significance to test whether or not method 1 is better for processing the product. State clearly the null hypothesis.

8.10 Two types of new cars produced in India are tested for petrol mileage. One group consisting of 36 cars averaged 14 kms per litre. While the other group consisting of 72 cars averaged 12.5 kms per litre.

(a) What test-statistic is appropriate if $\sigma_1^2 = 1.5$ and $\sigma_2^2 = 2.0$?

(b) Test whether there exists a significant difference in the petrol consumption of these two types of cars. (use $\alpha = 0.01$)

Hints and Answers

8.1 Let $H_0 : \mu = 1800$ and $H_1 : \mu \neq 1800$ (Two-tailed test)

Given $\bar{x} = 1850, n = 50, \sigma = 100, z_\alpha = \pm 2.58$ at $\alpha = 0.01$ level of significance

$$z = \frac{\bar{x} - \mu}{\sigma/\sqrt{n}} = \frac{1850-1800}{100/\sqrt{50}} = 3.54$$

Since $z_{cal} (= 3.54) > z_\alpha (= 2.58)$, reject H_0. The breaking strength of the cables of 1800 does not support the claim.

8.2 Given $n = 100, \sigma = 50; \sigma_{\bar{x}} = \frac{\sigma}{\sqrt{n}} = \frac{50}{\sqrt{100}} = 5.$

Confidence interval at 99% is: $\bar{x} \pm z_\alpha \sigma_{\bar{x}} = 628 \pm 2.58\ (5) = 628 \pm 12.9; 615.1 \leq \mu \leq 640.9$

Since hypothesized population mean $\mu = 640$ lies in the this interval, H_0 is accepted.

8.3 Let $H_0 : \mu = 1.28$ and $H_1 : \mu < 1.28$ (One-tailed test)

Given $n = 40, \bar{x} = 1.08, s = 0.05, z_\alpha = \pm 1.645$ at $\alpha = 0.05$ level of significance

$$z = \frac{\bar{x} - \mu}{s\sqrt{n}} = \frac{1.08-1.28}{0.05/\sqrt{40}} = -28.57$$

Since $z_{cal} (= -28.57) < z_{\alpha/2} = -1.64$, H_0 is rejected. Mean life of the boots is less than 1.28 and affected by use in the desert.

8.4 Let $H_0 : \mu = 8.9$ and $H_1 : \mu \neq 8.9$ (Two-tail test)

Given $n = 50, \bar{x} = 9.3, s = 1.8, z_{\alpha/2} = \pm 1.96$ at

$\alpha = 0.05$ level of significance

$$z = \frac{\bar{x} - \mu}{s/\sqrt{n}} = \frac{9.3-8.9}{1.8/\sqrt{50}} = 1.574$$

Since $z_{cal} (= 1.574) < z_{\alpha/2} (= 1.96)$, H_0 is accepted, that is, claim is valid.

8.5 Let $H_0 : \mu = 40{,}000$ and $H_1 : \mu \neq 40{,}000$ (Two-tail test)

Given $n = 100, \bar{x} = 39{,}350, s = 3{,}260$, and $z_{\alpha/2} = \pm 2.58$ at $\alpha = 0.01$ level of significance

$$z = \frac{\bar{x} - \mu}{s/\sqrt{n}} = \frac{39{,}350 - 40{,}000}{3260/\sqrt{100}} = -1.994$$

Since $z_{cal} (= -1.994) > z_{\alpha/2} (= -2.58)$, H_0 is accepted. Thus the difference in the mean life of the tyres could be due to sampling error.

8.6 Let $H_0 : \mu_1 = \mu_2$ and $H_1 : \mu_1 > \mu_2$; μ_1 and μ_2 = mean height of Austrians and Englishmen, respectively.

Given, Austrian : $n_1 = 1600, \bar{x}_1 = 68.55, s_1 = 2.52$ and Englishmen; $n_2 = 6400, \bar{x}_2 = 67.85, s_2 = 2.56$

$$z = \frac{x_1 - x_2}{\sigma_{\bar{x}_1 - \bar{x}_2}} = \frac{x_1 - x_2}{\sqrt{\frac{s_1^2}{n_1} + \frac{s_2^2}{n_2}}}$$

$$= \frac{68.55 - 67.85}{\sqrt{\frac{(2.52)^2}{1600} + \frac{(2.56)^2}{6400}}} = 9.9$$

Since $z_{cal} = 9.9 > z_\alpha (= 2.58)$ for right tail test, H_0 is rejected. Austrian's are on the average taller than the Englishmen.

8.7 Let $H_0 : \mu_1 = \mu_2$ and $H_1 : \mu_1 \neq \mu_2$; μ_1 and μ_2 = mean life of Philips and HMT electric bulbs, respectively

Given, Philips : $n_1 = 50, \bar{x}_1 = 1500, s_1 = 60$ and HMT: $n_2 = 50, \bar{x}_2 = 1512, s_2 = 80$

$$z = \frac{x_1 - x_2}{\sqrt{\frac{s_1^2}{n_1} + \frac{s_2^2}{n_2}}} = \frac{1500 - 1512}{\sqrt{\frac{(60)^2}{50} + \frac{(80)^2}{50}}}$$

$$= -\frac{12}{14.14} = -0.848$$

Since z_{cal} $(= -0.848) > z_{\alpha/2}$ $(= -2.58)$ at $\alpha = 0.01$ level of significance, H_0 is accepted. Mean life of the two makes is almost the same, difference (if any) is due to sampling error.

8.8 Given $n = 50$, $\bar{x} = 14.2$, $s = 5$, and $\alpha = 0.02$

$$z = \frac{\bar{x} - \mu}{s/\sqrt{n}} = \frac{14.2 - 15}{5/\sqrt{50}} = -1.13$$

Table value of $z = 1.13$ is 0.3708. Thus p-value $= 2\,(0.5000 - 0.3708) = 0.2584$. Since p-value $> \alpha$, H_0 is accepted.

8.9 Let $H_0 : \mu_1 = \mu_2$ and $H_1 : \mu_1 > \mu_2$; μ_1 and μ_2 = mean life of items produced by Method 1 and 2, respectively.

Given, Method 1: $n_1 = 64$, $\bar{x}_1 = 106$, $s_1 = 12$; Method 2: $n_2 = 64$, $\bar{x}_2 = 100$, $s_2 = 10$

$$z = \frac{\bar{x}_1 - \bar{x}_2}{\sqrt{\frac{s_1^2}{n_1} + \frac{s_2^2}{n_2}}} = \frac{106 - 100}{\sqrt{\frac{(12)^2}{64} + \frac{(10)^2}{64}}} = 3.07$$

Since z_{cal} $(= 3.07) > z_\alpha$ $(= 1.645)$ for a right-tailed test, H_0 is rejected. Method 1 is better than Method 2.

8.10 Let $H_0 : \mu_1 = \mu_2$ and $H_1 : \mu_1 \neq \mu_2$; μ_1 and μ_2 = mean petrol mileage of two types of new cars, respectively.

Given $n_1 = 36$, $\bar{x}_1 = 14$, $\sigma_1^2 = 1.5$ and $n_2 = 72$, $\bar{x}_2 = 12.5$, $\sigma_2^2 = 2.0$

$$z = \frac{\bar{x}_1 - \bar{x}_2}{\sqrt{\frac{\sigma_1^2}{n_1} + \frac{\sigma_2^2}{n_2}}} = \frac{14 - 12.5}{\sqrt{\frac{1.5}{36} + \frac{2}{72}}}$$

$$= \frac{1.5}{0.2623} = 5.703$$

Since z_{cal} $(= 5.703) > z_{\alpha/2}$ $(= 2.58)$ at $\alpha = 0.01$ level of significance, H_0 is rejected. There is a significant difference in petrol consumption of the two types of new cars.

8.7 HYPOTHESIS TESTING FOR SINGLE POPULATION PROPORTION

Sometimes instead of testing a hypothesis pertaining to a population mean, a population proportion (a fraction, ratio or percentage) p of values that indicates the part of the population or sample having a particular attribute of interest is considered. For this, a random sample of size n is selected to compute the proportion of elements having a particular attribute of interest (also called success) in it as follows:

$$\bar{p} = \frac{\text{Number of successes in the sample}}{\text{Sample size}} = \frac{x}{n}$$

The value of this statistic is compared with a hypothesized population proportion p_0 so as to arrive at a conclusion about the hypothesis.

The three forms of null hypothesis and alternative hypothesis pertaining to the hypothesized population proportion p are as follows:

Null hypothesis	*Alternative hypothesis*
• $H_0 : p = p_0$	$H_1 : p \neq p_0$ (Two-tailed test)
• $H_0 : p \geq p_0$	$H_1 : p < p_0$ (Left-tailed test)
• $H_0 : p \leq p_0$	$H_1 : p > p_0$ (Right-tailed test)

To conduct a test of a hypothesis, it is assumed that the sampling distribution of a proportion follows a standardized normal distribution. Then, using the value of the sample proportion $\bar{p}$ and its standard deviation $\sigma_{\bar{p}}$, we compute a value for the z-test statistic as follows:

$$\text{Test statistic } z = \frac{\bar{p} - p_0}{\sigma_{\bar{p}}} = \frac{\bar{p} - p_0}{\sqrt{\dfrac{p_0\,(1 - p_0)}{n}}}$$

The comparison of the z-test statistic value to its critical (table) value at a given level of significance enables us to test the null hypothesis about a population proportion based on the difference between the sample proportion $\bar{p}$ and the hypothesized population proportion.

Decision rule: Reject H_0 when

One-tailed test	*Two-tailed test*
• $z_{cal} > z_\alpha$ or $z_{cal} < -z_\alpha$ when $H_1 : p < p_0$ • p-value $< \alpha$	• $z_{cal} > z_{\alpha/2}$ or $z_{cal} < -z_{\alpha/2}$

8.7.1 Hypothesis Testing for Difference Between Two Population Porportions

Let two independent populations each having proportion and standard deviation of an attribute be as follows:

Population	*Proportion*	*Standard Deviation*
1	p_1	σ_{p_1}
2	p_2	σ_{p_2}

The hypothesis testing concepts developed in the previous section can be extended to test whether there is any difference between the proportions of these populations. The null hypothesis that there is no difference between two population proportions is stated as:

$$H_0 : p_1 = p_2 \text{ or } p_1 - p_2 = 0 \quad \text{and} \quad H_1 : p_1 \neq p_2$$

The sampling distribution of difference in sample proportions $\bar{p} - \bar{p}_2$ is based on the assumption that the difference between two population proportions, $p_1 - p_2$ is normally distributed. The standard deviation (or error) of sampling distribution of $p_1 - p_2$ is given by

$$\sigma_{\bar{p}_1 - \bar{p}_2} = \sqrt{\frac{p_1\,(1 - p_1)}{n_1} + \frac{p_2\,(1 - p_2)}{n_2}}\,;\; q_1 = 1 - p_1 \text{ and } q_2 = 1 - p_2$$

where the difference $\bar{p}_1 - \bar{p}_2$ between sample proportions of two independent simple random samples is the point estimator of the difference between two population proportions. Obviously expected value, $E(\bar{p}_1 - \bar{p}_2) = p_1 - p_2$.

Thus the z-test statistic for the difference between two population proportions is stated as:

$$z = \frac{(\bar{p}_1 - \bar{p}_2) - (p_1 - p_2)}{\sigma_{\bar{p}_1 - \bar{p}_2}} = \frac{\bar{p}_1 - \bar{p}_2}{\sigma_{\bar{p}_1 - \bar{p}_2}}$$

Invariably, the standard error $\sigma_{\bar{p}_1 - \bar{p}_2}$ of difference between sample proportions is not known. Thus when a null hypothesis states that there is no difference between the population proportions, we combine two sample proportions $\bar{p}_1$ and $\bar{p}_2$ to get one unbiased estimate of population proportion as follows:

$$\text{Pooled estimate } \bar{p} = \frac{n_1\bar{p}_1 + n_2\bar{p}_2}{n_1 + n_2}$$

The z-test statistic is then restated as:

$$z = \frac{\bar{p}_1 - \bar{p}_2}{s_{\bar{p}_1 - \bar{p}_2}}; \quad s_{\bar{p}_1 - \bar{p}_2} = \sqrt{\bar{p}\,(1-\bar{p})\left(\frac{1}{n_1} + \frac{1}{n_2}\right)}$$

Example 8.10: An auditor claims that 10 per cent of customers' ledger accounts are carrying mistakes of posting and balancing. A random sample of 600 was taken to test the accuracy of posting and balancing and 45 mistakes were found. Are these sample results consistent with the claim of the auditor? Use 5 per cent level of significance.

Solution: Let us take the null hypothesis that the claim of the auditor is valid, that is,

$$H_0 : p = 0.10 \quad \text{and} \quad H_1 : p \neq 0.10 \quad \text{(Two-tailed test)}$$

Given $\bar{p}$ = 45/600 = 0.075, n = 600, and α = 5 per cent. Thus using the z-test statistic

$$z = \frac{\bar{p} - p_0}{\sigma_{\bar{p}}} = \frac{0.075 - 0.10}{\sqrt{\dfrac{0.10 \times 0.90}{600}}} = -\frac{0.025}{0.0122} = -2.049$$

Since z_{cal} (= – 2.049) is less than its critical (table) value z_{α} (= – 1.96) at α = 0.05 level of significance, null hypothesis, H_0 is rejected. Hence, we conclude that the claim of the auditor is not valid.

Example 8.11: A manufacturer claims that at least 95 per cent of the equipments which he supplied to a factory conformed to the specification. An examination of the sample of 200 pieces of equipment revealed that 18 were faulty. Test the claim of the manufacturer.

Solution: Let us take the null hypothesis that at least 95 per cent of the equipments supplied conformed to the specification, that is,

$$H_0 : p \geq 0.95 \quad \text{and} \quad H_1 : p < 0.95 \text{ (Left-tailed test)}$$

Given $\bar{p}$ = per cent of pieces conforming to the specification = 1 – (18/100) = 0.91 n = 200 and level of significance α = 05. Thus using the z-test statistic,

$$z = \frac{\bar{p} - p_0}{\sigma_{\bar{p}}} = \frac{0.91 - 0.95}{\sqrt{\dfrac{0.95 \times 0.05}{200}}} = -\frac{0.04}{0.015} = -2.67$$

Since z_{cal} (= – 2.67) is less than its critical value z_{α} (= – 1.645) at α = 0.05 level of significance, the null hypothesis, H_0 is rejected. Hence we conclude that the proportion of equipments conforming to specifications is not 95 per cent.

Example 8.12: In two large population, there are 30% and 25% respectively of blue eyed people. Is this difference likely to be hidden in the sample of 1200 and 900 respectively from the two population.

[*Delhi Univ., B.Sc (G), 1998, 2000*]

Solution: Given p_1 = 0.30, n_1 = 1200 and p_2 = 0.25, n_2 = 900. Using z-test statistic,

$$z = \frac{|p_1 - p_2|}{\sqrt{\dfrac{p_1q_1}{n_1} + \dfrac{p_2q_2}{n_2}}} = \frac{0.30 - 0.25}{\sqrt{\dfrac{0.30 \times 0.70}{1200} + \dfrac{0.25 \times 0.75}{900}}} = 2.56$$

Since $z_{cal} = 2.56$ is more than its critical value $z = 196$, H_0 is rejected at 5% level of significance. Hence sample will reveal the difference in the population properties proportions. It is not likely to be hidden in sampling.

Example 8.13: In a simple random sample of 600 men taken from a big city, 400 are found to be smokers. In another simple random sample of 900 men taken from another city 450 are smokers. Do the data indicate that there is a significant difference in the habit of smoking in the two cities?

Solution: Let us take the null hypothesis that there is no significant difference in the habit of smoking in the two cities, that is,

$$H_0 : p_1 = p_2 \quad \text{and} \quad H_1 : p_1 \neq p_2 \quad \text{(Two-tailed test)}$$

where p_1 and p_2 = proportion of men found to be smokers in the two cities.

Given, $n_1 = 600$, $\bar{p}_1 = 400/600 = 0.667$; $n_2 = 900$, $\bar{p}_2 = 450/900 = 0.50$ and level of significance $\alpha = 0.05$. Thus using the z-test statistic

$$z = \frac{(\bar{p}_1 - \bar{p}_2) - (p_1 - p_2)}{s_{\bar{p}_1 - \bar{p}_2}} = \frac{\bar{p}_1 - \bar{p}_2}{s_{\bar{p}_1 - \bar{p}_2}}; \quad p_1 = p_2$$

$$\text{where } s_{\bar{p}_1 - \bar{p}_2} = \sqrt{\bar{p}(1 - \bar{p})\left(\frac{1}{n_1} + \frac{1}{n_2}\right)}; \quad q = 1 - p$$

$$= \sqrt{0.567 \times 0.433\left(\frac{1}{600} + \frac{1}{900}\right)} = \sqrt{0.245\,(0.002)} = 0.026;$$

$$\bar{p} = \frac{n_1\bar{p}_1 + n_2\bar{p}_2}{n_1 + n_2} = \frac{600\,(400/600) + 900\,(450/900)}{600 + 900}$$

$$= \frac{400 + 450}{1500} = \frac{850}{1500} = 0.567$$

Substituting values in z-test statistic, we have

$$z = \frac{0.667 - 0.500}{0.026} = \frac{0.167}{0.026} = 6.423$$

Since $z_{cal} = 6.423$ is greater than its critical value $z_{\alpha/2} = 2.58$, at $\alpha/2 = 0.025$ level of significance, the null hypothesis, H_0 is rejected. Hence we conclude that there is a significant difference in the habit of smoking in two cities.

Example 8.14: A die is thrown 9000 times and a throw of 3 or 4 is observed 3240 times. Show that the die can not be regarded as an unbiased one and find the limits between which the probability of a throw of 3 or 4 lies. *[Delhi Univ., BA (P), 2001]*

Solution: Given, $x = 3240$ and $n = 9000$. Then

$$\bar{p} = \frac{x}{n} = \frac{3240}{9000} = 0.36; \quad \bar{q} = 1 - p = 1 - 0.36 = 0.64, \text{ and}$$

Probability of getting 3 or 4 is: $\frac{1}{6} + \frac{1}{6} = \frac{1}{3}$

Let us consider the null hypothesis that die is unbiased, that is

$$H_0 : p = \frac{1}{3} \quad \text{and} \quad H_1 : p \neq \frac{1}{3}$$

Applying the z-test statistic as follows:

$$z = \frac{\bar{p} - p}{\sqrt{\frac{\bar{p}\bar{q}}{n}}} = \frac{0.36 - 0.333}{\sqrt{\frac{0.36 \times 0.64}{9000}}} = \frac{0.36 - 0.3333}{0.0049598} = 5.38$$

Since calculated value, $z_{cal} = 5.38$ is more than its critical value $z_\alpha = 1.645$ at $\alpha = 0.05$ level of significance, the null hypothesis, H_0 is rejected, i.e. die is biased. Since die is biased, therefore $p \neq 13$.

Then the probable limits for p are: $p \pm 3\sqrt{\frac{pq}{n}} = 0.36 \pm 3\sqrt{\frac{0.36 \times 0.64}{9000}} = 0.36 \pm 0.015 = 0.375$ and 0.345

Hence, probability of getting 3 or 4 lies between 0.345 and 0.375.

Example 8.15: In two large population, there are 30 per cent and 25 per cent people of blue eyed respectively. Is this difference likely to be hidden in the sample of 1200 and 900 respectively from the two population. *[Delhi Univ., BSc(G), 1998, 2000]*

Solution: Let us take the null hypothesis that the difference between two population is likely to be hidden in the given proportion. That is

$$H_0 : p_1 = p_2 \text{ and } H_1 : p_1 \neq p_2$$

Given, $\bar{p}_1 = 0.30$, $n_1 = 1200$, $\bar{p}_2 = 0.25$, $n_2 = 900$ and $\alpha = 5\%$. Applying the z-test statistic as follows:

$$z = \frac{\bar{p}_1 - \bar{p}_2}{\sqrt{\frac{\bar{p}_1\bar{q}_1}{n_1} + \frac{\bar{p}_2\bar{q}_2}{n_2}}} = \frac{0.30 - 0.25}{\sqrt{\frac{0.30 \times 0.70}{1200} + \frac{0.25 \times 0.75}{900}}} = 2.56$$

Since calculated value of $z = 2.56$ is more than its critical value $z_\alpha = 1.645$ at $\alpha = 5$ per cent, null hypothesis is rejected and hence difference between population proportion is not likely to be hidden in the sample.

Example 8.16: In a year there are 956 births in a town A of which 52.5% were males, while in town A and B combined, this proportion in a total of 1406 births was 0.496. Is there any significant difference in the proportion of male births in the two towns? *[Delhi Univ., BA (P), 2001]*

Solution: Let us take the null hypothesis that there is no difference in the proportion of male births in two towns. That is

$$H_0 : p_1 = p_2 \text{ and } H_1 : p_1 \neq p_2$$

Given, $n_1 = 956$, $n_1 + n_2 = 1406$; $n_2 = 1406 - 956 = 450$; $\bar{p} = 0.496$, $\bar{q} = 1 - 0.496 = 0.504$ and $\bar{p}_1 = 0.525$

Let $\bar{p}_2$ be the proportion of male births in the sample of size n_2 (i.e. town B). Then, we have

$$\bar{p} = \frac{n_1\bar{p}_1 + n_2\bar{p}_2}{n_1 + n_2}$$

$$0.496 = \frac{956 \times 0.525 + 450\bar{p}_2}{1406} \quad \text{or} \quad \bar{p}_2 = 0.434$$

Using the z-test statistic as follows:

$$z = \frac{\bar{p}_1 - \bar{p}_2}{\sqrt{\bar{p}\bar{q}\left(\frac{1}{n_1} + \frac{1}{n_2}\right)}} = \frac{0.525 - 0.434}{\sqrt{0.496 \times 0.504\left(\frac{1}{956} + \frac{1}{450}\right)}} = \frac{0.091}{0.027} = 3.363$$

Since $z_{cal} > |3|$, H_0 is rejected, i.e. there is a difference between the proportion of male births in town A and B.

Self-Practice Problems 8B

8.11 A company manufacturing a certain type of breakfast cereal claims that 60 per cent of all housewives prefer that type to any other. A random sample of 300 housewives contains 165 who do prefer that type. At 5 per cent level of significance, test the claim of the company.

8.12 An auditor claims that 10 per cent of a company's invoices are incorrect. To test this claim a random sample of 200 invoices is checked and 24 are found to be incorrect. At 1 per cent significance level, test whether the auditor's claim is supported by the sample evidence.

8.13 A sales clerk in the department store claims that 60 per cent of the shoppers entering the store leave without making a purchase. A random sample of 50 shoppers showed that 35 of them left without buying anything. Are these sample results consistent with the claim of the sales clerk? Use a significance level of 0.05.

8.14 A dice is thrown 49,152 times and of these 25,145 yielded either 4, 5, or 6. Is this consistent with the hypothesis that the dice must be unbiased?

8.15 A coin is tossed 100 times under identical conditions independently yielding 30 heads and 70 tails. Test at 1 per cent level of significance whether or not the coin is unbiased. State clearly the null hypothesis and the alternative hypothesis.

8.16 Before an increase in excise duty on tea, 400 people out of a sample of 500 persons were found to be tea drinkers. After an increase in the duty, 400 persons were known to be tea drinkers in a sample of 600 people. Do you think that there has been a significant decrease in the consumption of tea after the increase in the excise duty?

8.17 In a random sample of 1000 persons from UP 510 were found to be consumers of cigarettes. In another sample of 800 persons from Rajasthan, 480 were found to be consumers of cigarettes. Do the data reveal a significant difference between UP and Rajasthan so far as the proportion of consumers of cigarettes in concerned?

8.18 In a random sample of 500 persons belonging to urban areas, 200 are found to be using public transport. In another sample of 400 persons belonging to rural area 200 area found to be using public transport. Do the data reveal a significant difference between urban and rural areas so far as the proportion of commuters of public transport is concerned (use 1 per cent level of significance).

8.19 A machine puts out 10 defective units in a sample of 200 units. After the machine is overhauled it puts out 4 defective units in a sample of 100 units. Has the machine been improved?

8.20 500 units from a factory are inspected and 12 are found to be defective, 800 units from another factory are inspected and 12 are found to be defective. Can it be concluded that at 5 per cent level of significance production at the second factory is better than in first factory?

Hints and Answers

8.11 Let $H_0 : p = 60$ per cent and $H_1 : p <$ 60 per cent (One tailed test)

Given, sample proportion,

$\bar{p} = 165/300 = 0.55$;

$n = 300$ and $z_\alpha = 1.645$ at $\alpha = 5$ per cent

$$z = \frac{\bar{p} - p_0}{\sqrt{\frac{pq}{n}}} = \frac{0.55 - 0.60}{\sqrt{\frac{0.60 \times 0.40}{300}}} = -1.77$$

Since z_{cal} ($= -1.77$) is less than its critical value $z_\alpha = -1.645$, the H_0 is rejected. Percentage preferring the breakfast cereal is lower than 60 per cent.

8.12 Let $H_0 : p = 10$ per cent and $H_1 : p \neq$ 10 per cent (Two-tailed test)

Given, sample proportion, $\bar{p} = 24/200 = 0.12$; $n = 200$ and $z_{\alpha/2} = 2.58$ at $\alpha =$ 1 per cent

$$z = \frac{\bar{p} - p_0}{\sqrt{\frac{pq}{n}}} = \frac{0.12 - 0.10}{\sqrt{\frac{0.10 \times 0.90}{200}}} = 0.943$$

Since z_{cal} (= 0.943) is less than its critical value $z_{\alpha/2}$ = 2.58, the H_0 is accepted. Thus the percentage of incorrect invoices is consistent with the auditor's claim of 10 per cent.

8.13 Let $H_0 : p = 60$ per cent and $H_1 : p \neq$ 60 per cent (Two-tailed test)

Given, sample proportion, $\bar{p}$ = 35/60 = 0.70; n = 50 and $z_{\alpha/2}$ = 1.96 at α = 5 per cent

$$z = \frac{\bar{p} - p_0}{\sqrt{\frac{pq}{n}}} = \frac{0.70 - 0.60}{\sqrt{\frac{0.60 \times 0.40}{50}}} = 1.44$$

Since z_{cal} (= 1.44) is less than its critical value $z_{\alpha/2}$ = 1.96, the H_0 is accepted. Claim of the sales clerk is valid.

8.14 Let $H_0 : p = 50$ per cent and $H_1 : p \neq$ 50 per cent (Two-tailed test)

Given, sample proportion of success p = 25,145/49,152 = 0.512; n = 49,152

$$z = \frac{\bar{p} - p_0}{\sqrt{\frac{pq}{n}}} = \frac{0.512 - 0.50}{\sqrt{\frac{0.50 \times 0.50}{49{,}152}}} = \frac{0.012}{0.002} = 6.0$$

Since z_{cal} (= 6.0) is more than its critical value $z_{\alpha/2}$ = 2.58 at a = 0.01, the H_0 is rejected, Dice is biased.

8.15 Let $H_0 : p$ = 50 per cent and $H_1 : p \neq 50$ per cent (Two-tailed test)

Given, n = 100, sample proportion of success $\bar{p}$ = 30/100 = 0.30 and $z_{\alpha/2}$ = 2.58 at α = 0.01

$$z = \frac{\bar{p} - p_0}{\sqrt{\frac{pq}{n}}} = \frac{0.30 - 0.50}{\sqrt{\frac{0.50 \times 0.50}{100}}} = -\frac{0.20}{0.05} = -4$$

Since z_{cal} (= – 4) is less than its critical value $z_{\alpha/2}$ = – 2.58, the H_0 is rejected.

8.16 Let $H_0 : p$ = 400/500 = 0.80 and $H_1 : p <$ 0.80 (One-tailed test)

Given n_1 = 500, n_2 = 600, $\bar{p}_1$ = 400/500 = 0.80, $\bar{p}_2$ = 400/600 = 0.667 and z_α = 2.33 at α = 0.01

$$\bar{p} = \frac{n_1\bar{p}_1 + n_2\bar{p}_2}{n_1 + n_2} = \frac{400 + 400}{500 + 600} = 0.727;$$

$$q = 1 - 0.727 = 0.273$$

$$s_{\bar{p}_1 - \bar{p}_2} = \sqrt{\bar{p}\,\bar{q}\left(\frac{1}{n_1} + \frac{1}{n_2}\right)}$$

$$= \sqrt{0.727 \times 0.273\left(\frac{1}{500} + \frac{1}{600}\right)} = 0.027$$

$$z = \frac{\bar{p}_1 - \bar{p}_2}{s_{\bar{p}_1 - \bar{p}_2}} = \frac{0.80 - 0.667}{0.027} = 4.93$$

Since z_{cal} (= 4.93) is more than its critical value z_α = 2.33, the H_0 is rejected. Decrease in the consumption of tea after the increase in the excise duty is significant.

8.17 Let $H_0 : p_1 = p_2$ and $H_1 : p_1 \neq p_2$ (Two-tailed test)

Given, UP: n_1 = 1000, $\bar{p}_1$ = 510/1000 = 0.51; Rajasthan: n_2 = 800, $\bar{p}_2$ = 480/800 = 0.60

$$\bar{p} = \frac{n_1\bar{p}_1 + n_2\bar{p}_2}{n_1 + n_2} = \frac{510 + 480}{1000 + 800} = 0.55;$$

$$q = 1 - 0.55 = 0.45$$

$$s_{\bar{p}_1 - \bar{p}_2} = \sqrt{\bar{p}\bar{q}\left(\frac{1}{n_1} + \frac{1}{n_2}\right)}$$

$$= \sqrt{0.55 \times 0.45\left(\frac{1}{1000} + \frac{1}{800}\right)} = 0.024.$$

$$z = \frac{\bar{p}_1 - \bar{p}_2}{s_{\bar{p}_1 - \bar{p}_2}} = \frac{0.51 - 0.60}{0.024} = -3.75$$

Since z_{cal} (= – 3.75) is less than its critical value $z_{\alpha/2}$ = – 2.58, the H_0 is rejected. The proportion of consumers of cigarettes in the two states is significant.

8.18 Let $H_0 : p_1 = p_2$ and $H_1 : p_1 \neq p_2$ (Two-tailed test)

Given, Urban area: n_1 = 500, $\bar{p}_1$ = 200/500 = 0.40; Rural area: n_2 = 200, $\bar{p}_2$ = 200/400 = 0.50

$$\bar{p} = \frac{n_1\bar{p}_1 + n_2\bar{p}_2}{n_1 + n_2} = \frac{200 + 200}{500 + 400} = 0.44;$$

$$q = 1 - p = 0.55$$

$$s_{\bar{p}_1-\bar{p}_2} = \sqrt{\bar{p}\,\bar{q}\left(\frac{1}{n_1}+\frac{1}{n_2}\right)}$$

$$= \sqrt{0.44\times 0.55\left(\frac{1}{500}+\frac{1}{400}\right)} = 0.033$$

$$z = \frac{\bar{p}_1-\bar{p}_2}{s_{\bar{p}_1-\bar{p}_2}} = \frac{0.40-0.50}{0.033} = -3.03$$

Since $z_{cal} = -3.03$ is less than its critical value $z_{\alpha/2} = -2.58$, the H_0 is rejected. Proportion of commuters of public transport in urban and rural areas is significant.

8.19 Let $H_0 : p_1 \le p_2$ and $H_1 : p_1 > p_2$ (One-tailed test)

Given, Before overhaul: $n_1 = 200$, $\bar{p}_1 = 10/200 = 0.05$; After overhaul: $n_2 = 100$, $\bar{p}_2 = 4/100 = 0.04$

$$\bar{p} = \frac{n_1\bar{p}_1 + n_2\bar{p}_2}{n_1+n_2} = \frac{10+4}{200+100} = 0.047;$$

$$q = 1 - p = 0.953$$

$$s_{\bar{p}_1-\bar{p}_2} = \sqrt{0.047\times 0.953\left(\frac{1}{200}+\frac{1}{100}\right)}$$

$$= 0.026;$$

$$z = \frac{\bar{p}_1-\bar{p}_2}{s_{\bar{p}_1-\bar{p}_2}} = \frac{0.05-0.04}{0.026} = 0.385$$

Since z_{cal} (= 0.385) is less than its critical value $z_\alpha = 1.645$ at $\alpha = 0.05$, the H_0 is accepted.

8.20 Let $H_0 : p_1 \le p_2$ and $H_1 : p_1 > p_2$ (One-tailed test)

Given $n_1 = 500$, $\bar{p}_1 = 12/500 = 0.024$, $n_2 = 800$, $\bar{p}_2 = 12/800 = 0.015$

$$\bar{p} = \frac{n_1\bar{p}_1 + n_2\bar{p}_2}{n_1+n_2} = \frac{12+12}{500+800} = 0.018;$$

$$q = 1 - p = 0.982$$

$$s_{\bar{p}_1-\bar{p}_2} = \sqrt{\bar{p}\,\bar{q}\left(\frac{1}{n_1}+\frac{1}{n_2}\right)}$$

$$= \sqrt{0.018\times 0.912\left(\frac{1}{500}+\frac{1}{800}\right)} = 0.0076$$

$$z = \frac{p_1-p_2}{s_{\bar{p}_1-\bar{p}_2}} = \frac{0.024-0.015}{0.0076} = 1.184$$

Since $z_{cal} = 1.184$ is less than its critical value $z_\alpha = 1.645$ at $\alpha = 0.05$, the H_0 is accepted. Production in second factory is better than in the first factory.

8.8 HYPOTHESIS TESTING FOR POPULATION MEAN WITH SMALL SAMPLES

When the sample size is small (i.e., less than 30), the central limit theorem does not assure us to assume that the sampling distribution of a statistic such as mean $\bar{x}$, proportion $\bar{p}$, is normal. Consequently when testing a hypothesis with small samples, we must assume that the samples come from a normally or approximately normally distributed population. Under these conditions, the sampling distribution of sample statistic such as $\bar{x}$ and $\bar{p}$ is normal but the critical values of $\bar{x}$ or $\bar{p}$ depend on whether or not the population standard deviation σ is known. When the value of the population standard deviation σ is not known, its value is estimated by computing the standard deviation of sample s and the standard error of the mean is calculated by using the formula, $\sigma_{\bar{x}} = s/\sqrt{n}$. When we do this, the resulting sampling distribution may not be normal even if sampling is done from a normally distributed population. In all such cases the sampling distribution turns out to be the *Student's t-distribution*.

8.8.1 Hypothesis Testing for Single Population Mean

The test statistic for determining the difference between the sample mean $\bar{x}$ and population mean μ is given by

$$t = \frac{\bar{x}-\mu}{s_{\bar{x}}} = \frac{\bar{x}-\mu}{s/\sqrt{n}}; \quad s = \sqrt{\frac{\Sigma(x-\bar{x})^2}{n-1}}$$

where s is an unbiased estimation of unknown population standard deviation σ. This test statistic has a t-distribution with $n - 1$ degrees of freedom.

Decision Rule: Rejected H_0 at the given degrees of freedom n–1 and level of significance when

One-tailed test	*Two-tailed test*
• $t_{cal} > t_\alpha$ or $t_{cal} < -t_\alpha$ for H_1: $\mu < \mu_0$	$t_{cal} > t_{\alpha/2}$ or $t_{cal} < -t_{\alpha/2}$

Example 8.17: A machine puts out 16 imperfect articles in a sample of 500. After machine is overhauled, it puts out 3 imperfect articles in a batch of 100. Has the machine been improved.

Solution: Let us take the null hypothesis, that the machine has not been improved. That is

$$H_0 : p_1 = p_2 \text{ and } H_1 : p_1 > p_2$$

Given $n_1 = 500$, $x_1 = 16$, $p_1 = x_1/n_1 = 16/500 = 0.032$ and $n_2 = 100$, $x_2 = 3$, $p_2 = x_2/n_2 = 3/100 = 0.03$.

$$\text{Also } p = \frac{p_1n_1 + p_2n_2}{n_1+n_2} = \frac{500(0.032)+100(0.03)}{500+100} = \frac{16+3}{600} = 0.032$$

Thus $q = 1 - p = 1 - 0.032 = 0.968$. Using z-test statistic

$$z = \frac{p_1 - p_2}{\sqrt{pq\left(\frac{1}{n_1}+\frac{1}{n_2}\right)}} = \frac{0.032-0.03}{\sqrt{0.032\times0.968\left(\frac{1}{500}+\frac{1}{100}\right)}} = \frac{0.002}{\sqrt{0.0003716}} = 0.103$$

Since $z_{cal} = 0.103$ is less than its critical value $z = 1.645$ at $\alpha = 0.05$ level of significance, null hypothesis, is accepted. Hence machine has not been improved after overhauling.

Example 8.18: The average breaking strength of steel rods is specified to be 18.5 thousand kg. For this a sample of 14 rods was tested. The mean and standard deviation obtained were 17.85 and 1.955, respectively. Test the significance of the deviation.

Solution: Let us take the null hypothesis that there is no significant deviation in the breaking strength of the rods, that is,

$$H_0 : \mu = 18.5 \text{ and } H_1 : \mu \neq 18.5 \text{ (Two-tailed test)}$$

Given, $n = 14$, $\bar{x} = 17.85$, $s = 1.955$, $df = n - 1 = 13$, and $\alpha = 0.05$ level of significance. The critical value of t at $df = 13$ and $\alpha/2 = 0.025$ is $t_{\alpha/2} = 2.16$.

Using the t-test statistic,

$$t = \frac{\bar{x}-\mu}{\frac{s}{\sqrt{n}}} = \frac{17.85-18.5}{\frac{1.955}{\sqrt{14}}} = -\frac{0.65}{0.522} = -1.24$$

Since t_{cal} (= – 1.24) value is more than its critical value $t_{\alpha/2} = -2.16$ at $\alpha/2 = 0.025$ and $df = 13$, the null hypothesis H_0 is accepted. Hence we conclude that there is no significant deviation of sample mean from the population mean.

Example 8.19: An automobile tyre manufacturer claims that the average life of a particular grade of tyre is more than 20,000 km when used under normal conditions. A random sample of 16 tyres was tested and a mean and standard deviation of 22,000 km and 5000 km, respectively were computed. Assuming the life of the tyres in km to be approximately normally distributed, decide whether the manufacturer's claim is valid.

Solution: Let us take the null hypothesis that the manufacturer's claim is valid, that is,

$$H_0 : \mu \geq 20{,}000 \quad \text{and} \quad H_1 : \mu < 20{,}000 \text{ (Left-tailed test)}$$

Given, $n = 16$, $\bar{x} = 22{,}000$, $s = 5000$, $df = 15$ and $\alpha = 0.05$ level of significance. The critical value of t at $df = 15$ and $\alpha = 0.05$ is $t_\alpha = 1.753$. Using the t-test statistic,

$$t = \frac{\bar{x} - \mu}{s/\sqrt{n}} = \frac{22{,}000 - 20{,}000}{5000/\sqrt{16}} = \frac{2000}{1250} = 1.60$$

Since t_{cal} (= 1.60) value is less than its critical value $t_\alpha = 1.753$, $\alpha = 0.05$ and $df = 15$ at the null hypothesis H_0 is accepted. Hence we conclude that the manufacturer's claim is valid.

Example 8.20: A random sample of size 16 has the sample mean 53. The sum of the squares of deviation taken from the mean value is 150. Can this sample be regarded as taken from the population having 56 as its mean? Obtain 95 per cent and 99 per cent confidence limits of the sample mean.

Solution: Let us take the null hypothesis that the population mean is 56, i.e.

$$H_0 : \mu = 56 \quad \text{and} \quad H_1 : \mu \neq 56 \text{ (Two-tailed test)}$$

Given, $n = 16$, $df = n - 1 = 15$, $\bar{x} = 53$; $s = \sqrt{\dfrac{\Sigma (x - \bar{x})^2}{(n-1)}} = \sqrt{\dfrac{150}{15}} = 3.162$

- 95 per cent confidence limit

$$\bar{x} \pm t_{0.05} \frac{s}{\sqrt{n}} = 53 \pm 2.13 \frac{3.162}{\sqrt{16}} = 53 \pm 2.13\,(0.790) = 53 \pm 1.683$$

- 99 per cent confidence limit

$$\bar{x} \pm t_{0.01} \frac{s}{\sqrt{n}} = 53 \pm 2.95 \frac{3.162}{\sqrt{16}} = 53 \pm 2.33$$

Example 8.21: A random sample of 16 values from a normal population showed a mean of 41.5 inches and sum of squares of deviations from this mean equal to 135 square inches. Show that the assumption of mean of 43.5 inches for the population is not reasonable. Obtain 95 per cent and 99 per cent confidence limits for the same. *[Delhi Univ., BA (P), 2002]*

Solution: Let us take the null hypothesis (H_0) that the population mean (μ) is equal to 43.5 inches. That is $H_0 : \mu = 3.5$ and $H_1 : \mu \neq 43.5$ (Two-tailed)

Given, $n = 16$, $\bar{x} = 41.5$; $\Sigma (x - \bar{x}) = 135$, $\mu = 43.5$, so that

$$\sigma^2 = \frac{\Sigma(x - \bar{x})^2}{n-1} = \frac{135}{16-1} = 9$$

Applying t-test statistic, $$t = \frac{\bar{x} - \mu}{\sigma/\sqrt{n}} = \frac{41.5 - 43.5}{3/\sqrt{16}} = \frac{-2}{0.75} = -2.66.$$

Since calculated t_{cal} = 2.66 than its critical value t_{α} = 2.31 at df = 15 and α = 0.05 level of significance, the null hypothesis is rejected at 5% level of significance and we conclude that population mean is not 43.5.

However, table value of t at 15 $d.f.$ at α = 0.01 significance level is 2.947. Since calculated $t_{cal} = |-2.66| < 2.947$, H_0 is accepted and we conclude that population mean, μ = 43.5.

95 per cent confidence limit for μ:

$$\bar{x} \pm t_{0.05}\left(\frac{s}{\sqrt{n}}\right) = 41.5 \pm 2.131 \times (3/4) = 41.5 \pm 1.598 = 39.902 \text{ and } 43.098.$$

99 per cent confidence limit for μ:

$$\bar{x} \pm t_{0.01}\left(\frac{s}{\sqrt{n}}\right) = 41.5 \pm 2.947 \times (3/4) = 43.71 \text{ and } 39.29$$

Example 8.22: A random sample of size 10 has been drawn from a normal population and the observations are found to be 60, 62, 63, 64, 65, 67, 68, 69, 70 and 72. Obtain an unbased estimate of σ^2 and a 95 per cent confidence interval for μ. Given that upper 2.5% point of t-distribution with 9 d.f is 2.26.

[ICWA (Intermediate), June 2001]

Solution: Since n = 10(<30), we use t-test. The sample mean and an unbiased estimate of σ^2 is calculated as follows:

x	$(x - \bar{x}) = (x - 66)$	$(x - \bar{x})^2$
60	−6	36
62	−4	16
63	−3	9
64	−2	4
65	−1	1
67	1	1
68	2	4
69	3	9
70	4	16
72	6	36
660		132

$$\bar{x} = \frac{\Sigma x}{n} = \frac{660}{10} = 66 \quad \text{and} \quad s^2 = \frac{\Sigma(x-\bar{x})^2}{n-1} = \frac{132}{9} = 14.67$$

95% Confidence limits for μ:

$$\bar{x} \pm t_9(0.025)\frac{s}{\sqrt{n}} = 66 \pm 2.26\frac{\sqrt{14.67}}{\sqrt{10}}$$

$$= 66 \pm 2.26\sqrt{1.467} = 66 \pm 2.26 \times 1.211$$

$$= 63.263 \text{ and } 68.737$$

Hence, $63.263 < \mu < 68.737$

Example 8.23: Nine observations of a sample had the following value : 45, 47, 50, 52, 48, 47, 49, 53, 51. Does the mean of nine items differ significantly from the assumed population mean of 47.5.

Solution: Since $n = 9(< 30)$, we use t-test for single mean. The sample mean and an unbiased estimate of σ^2 is calculated as follows:

x	$d = x - 49$	d^2
45	−4	16
47	−2	4
50	1	1
52	3	9
48	−1	1
47	−2	4
(49) ← A	0	0
53	4	16
51	2	4
490	1	55

$$\bar{x} = A + \frac{\Sigma d}{n} = 49 + \frac{1}{9} = 49.11 \text{, where } A = 49 \text{ is the assumed mean.}$$

$$s^2 = \frac{1}{n-1}\left[\Sigma d^2 - \frac{(\Sigma d)^2}{n}\right] = \frac{1}{8}\left[55 - \frac{1}{9}\right] = 6.86 \quad \text{or} \quad s = \sqrt{6.86} = 2.62$$

Let us take the null hypothesis, H_0, that there is no difference between sample mean and population mean. That is,

$$H_0 : \mu = 47.5 \text{ and } H_1 : \mu \neq 47.5$$

Using t-test statistic

$$t = \frac{\bar{x} - \mu}{s/\sqrt{n}} = \frac{49.11 - 47.5}{2.62/\sqrt{9}} = 1.84.$$

Since calculated value of $t = 1.84$ is less than its critical value, $t = 2.30$ at $df = n - 1 = 9 - 1 = 8$ and $\alpha = 0.05$ level of significance, null hypothesis is accepted. Hence the difference between sample mean and population mean is only due to fluctuations in sampling.

Self-Practice Problems 8C

8.21 Ten oil tins are taken at random from an automatic filling machine. The mean weight of the tins is 15.8 kg and the standard deviation is 0.50 kg. Does the sample mean differ significantly from the intended weight of 16 kg?

8.22 Nine items of a sample had the following values: 45, 47, 50, 52, 48 47, 49, 53, and 50. The mean is 49 and the sum of the square of the deviation from mean is 52. Can this sample be regarded as taken from the population having 47 as mean? Also obtain 95 per cent and 99 per cent confidence limits of the population mean.

8.23 The electric bulbs of 10 random samples from a large consignment gave the following data:

Item	*Life in '000 hours*
1	4.2
2	4.6
3	3.9
4	4.1
5	5.2
6	3.8
7	3.9
8	4.3
9	4.4
10	5.6

Can we accept the hypothesis that the average life time of the bulbs is 4000 hours.

8.24 A random sample of size 16 has 53 as mean. The sum of the squares of the deviations taken from mean is 135. Can this sample be regarded as taken from the population having 56 as mean? Obtain 95 per cent and 99 per cent confidence limits of the mean of the population.

8.25 A drug manufacturer has installed a machine which automatically fills 5 gm of drug in each phial. A random sample of fills was taken and it was found to contain 5.02 gm on an average in a phial. The standard deviation of the sample was 0.002 gms. Test at 5% level of significance if the adjustment in the machine is in order.

Hints and Answers

8.21 Let $H_0 : \mu = 16$ and $H_1 : \mu \neq 16$ (Two-tailed test)

Given $n = 10$, $\bar{x} = 15.8$, $s = 0.50$. Using *t*-test

$$t = \frac{\bar{x}-\mu}{s/\sqrt{n}} = \frac{15.8-16}{0.50/\sqrt{10}} = -1.25$$

Since $t_{cal} = -1.25 >$ critical value $t_{\alpha/2} = -2.262$, at $df = 9$ and $\alpha/2 = 0.025$, the null hypothesis is accepted.

8.22 Let $H_0 : \mu = 27$ and $H_1 : \mu \neq 47$ (Two-tailed test)

Given $\bar{x} = 49$, $\Sigma(x - \bar{x})^2 = 52$, $n = 9$, and

$$s = \sqrt{\frac{\Sigma(x-\bar{x})^2}{(n-1)}} = \sqrt{\frac{52}{8}} = 2.55.$$

$$t = \frac{\bar{x}-\mu}{s/\sqrt{n}} = \frac{49-47}{2.55/\sqrt{9}} = 2.35$$

Since $t_{cal} = 2.35 >$ critical value $t_{\alpha/2} = 2.31$ at $\alpha/2 = 0.025$, $df = 8$, the null hypothesis is rejected.

8.23 Let $H_0 : \mu = 4{,}000$ and $H_1 : \mu \neq 4000$ (Two-tailed test)

$$s = \sqrt{\frac{\Sigma(x-\bar{x})^2}{(n-1)}} = \sqrt{\frac{3.12}{9}} = 0.589 \text{ and}$$

$\bar{x} = \Sigma x/n = 44/10 = 4.4$ (in Rs. 000's).

$$t = \frac{\bar{x}-\mu}{s/\sqrt{n}} = \frac{4.4-4}{0.589/\sqrt{10}} = \frac{0.4}{0.186} = 2.150$$

Since $t_{cal} = 2.150 <$ critical value $t_{\alpha/2} = 2.62$ at $\alpha/2 = 0.025$ and $df = n-1 = 9$, the null hypothesis is accepted.

8.24 Let $H_0 : \mu = 56$ and $H_1 : \mu \neq 46$ (Two-tailed test)

Given: $n = 16$, $\bar{x} = 53$ and $\Sigma(x - \bar{x})^2 = 135$. Thus

$$s = \sqrt{\frac{\Sigma(x-\bar{x})^2}{(n-1)}} = \sqrt{\frac{135}{15}} = 3$$

Applying *t*-test, $t = \dfrac{\bar{x}-\mu}{s/\sqrt{n}} = \dfrac{53-56}{3/\sqrt{16}} = -4$

Since $t_{cal} = -4 <$ critical value $t_{\alpha/2} = -2.13$ at $\alpha/2 = 0.025$, $df = 15$, the null hypothesis is rejected.

8.25 Let $H_0 : \mu = 5$ and $H_1 : \mu \neq 5$ (Two-tailed test)

Given $n = 10$, $\bar{x} = 5.02$ and $s = 0.002$.

Applying *t*-test, $t = \dfrac{\bar{x}-\mu}{s/\sqrt{n}}$

$$= \frac{5.02-5}{0.002/\sqrt{10}} = 33.33$$

Since $t_{cal} = 33.33 >$ critical value $t_{\alpha/2} = 1.833$ at $\alpha/2 = 0.025$ and $df = 9$, the null hypothesis is rejected.

8.9 HYPOTHESIS TESTING BASED ON F-DISTRIBUTION

In several statistical applications we might require to compare population variances. For instance, (i) variances in product quality resulting from two different production processes; (ii) variances in temperatures for two heating devices; (iii) variances in assembly times for two assembly methods, (iv) variance in the rate of return on investment of two types of stocks and so on, are few areas where comparison of variances is needed.

When independent random samples of size n_1 and n_2 are drawn from two normal populations, the ratio

$$F = \frac{s_1^2/\sigma_1^2}{s_2^2/\sigma_2^2}$$

follow F-distribution with $df_1 = n_1 - 1$ and $df_2 = n_2 - 1$ degrees of freedom, where s_1^2 and s_2^2 are two sample variances and are given by

$$s_1^2 = \frac{\Sigma (x_1 - \bar{x}_1)^2}{n_1 - 1} \text{ and } s_2^2 = \frac{\Sigma (x_2 - \bar{x}_2)^2}{n_2 - 1}$$

If two normal populations have equal variances, i.e. $\sigma_1^2 = \sigma_2^2$, then the ratio

$$F = \frac{s_1^2}{s_2^2}\,;\ s_1 > s_2$$

has a probability distribution in repeated sampling that is known as F-distribution with $n_1 - 1$ degrees of freedom for numerator and $n_2 - 1$ degrees of freedom for denominator. For computational purposes, a larger sample variance is placed in the numerator so that ratio is always equal to or more than one.

Assumptions: Few assumptions for the ratio s_1^2/s_2^2 to have an F-distribution are as follows:

(i) Independent random samples are drawn from each of two normal populations

(ii) The variability of the measurements in the two populations is same and can be measured by a common variance σ^2, i.e. $\sigma_1^2 = \sigma_2^2 = \sigma^2$

The F-distribution, also called *variance ratio distribution*, is not symmetric and the F values can never be negative. The shape of any F-distribution depends on the degrees of freedom of the numerator and denominator. A typical graph of a F-distribution is shown in Fig. 8.5 for equal degrees of freedom for both numerator and denominator.

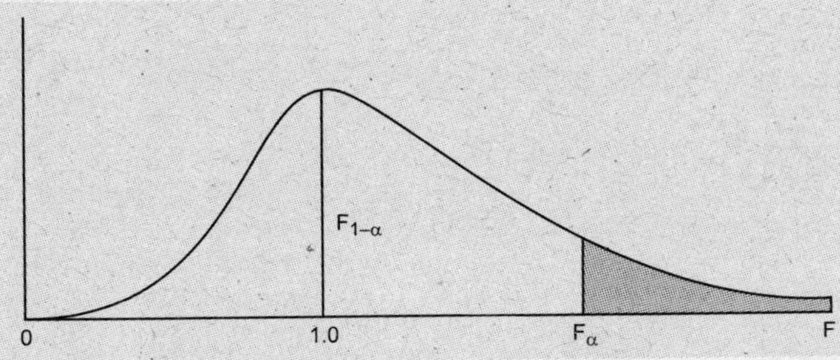

Figure 8.5 F-distribution for *n* Degrees of Freedom

8.9.1 Comparing Two Population Variances

How large or small must the ratio s_1^2/s_2^2 be for sufficient evidence to exist to the null hypothesis is stated below:

Null hypothesis	Alternative hypothesis	
$H_0 : \sigma_1^2 = \sigma_2^2$	$H_1 : \sigma_1^2 > \sigma_2^2$ or $\sigma_1^2 < \sigma_2^2$	(One-tailed Test)
$H_0 : \sigma_1^2 = \sigma_2^2$	$H_1 : \sigma_1^2 \neq \sigma_2^2$	(Two-tailed Test)

To conduct the test, random samples of size n_1 and n_2 are drawn from population 1 and 2 respectively. The statistical test of the null hypothesis H_0, uses the test statistic $F = s_1^2/s_2^2$, where s_1^2 and s_2^2 are the respective sample variances.

Decision rules: The criteria of acceptance or rejection of null hypothesis H_0 are as under:

1. Accept H_0 if the calculated value of F-test statistic is less than its critical value $F_{\alpha(v_1, v_2)}$, i.e. $F_{cal} < F_\alpha$ for one-tailed test.

   The critical value of F_α is based on degrees of freedom of numerator $df_1 = n_1 - 1$ and degrees of freedom of denominator $df_2 = n_2 - 1$. These values can be obtained from F-Tables (See appendix).

   As mentioned earlier, the population with larger variance is considered as population 1 to ensure that a rejection of H_0 can occur only in the right (upper) tail of the F-distribution curve. Even though half of the rejection region (the area $\alpha/2$ to its left) will be in the lower tail of the distribution. It is never used because using the population with larger sample variance as population 1 always places the ratio s_1^2/s_2^2 in the right-tail direction.

2. $H_0 : \sigma_1^2 = \sigma_2^2$ and $H_1 : \sigma_1^2 > \sigma_2^2$ (One-tailed test)

   The null hypothesis is setup so that the rejection region is always in the upper tail of the distribution. This helps us in considering the population with larger variance in the alternative hypothesis.

Example 8.24: A research was conducted to understand whether women have a greater variation in attitude on political issues than men. Two independent samples of 31 men and 41 women were used for the study. The sample variances so calculated were 120 for women and 80 for men. Test whether the difference in attitude toward political issues is significant at 5 per cent level of significance.

Solution: Let us take the hypothesis that the difference is not significant, that is,

$$H_0 : \sigma_w^2 = \sigma_m^2 \quad \text{and} \quad H_1 : \sigma_w^2 > \sigma_m \quad \text{(One-tailed test)}$$

The F-test statistic is given by $F = \dfrac{s_1^2}{s_2^2} = \dfrac{120}{80} = 1.50$

Since variance for women is in the numerator, the F-distribution with $df_1 = 41 - 1 = 40$ in the numerator and $df_2 = 31 - 1 = 30$ in the denominator will be used to conduct he one-tailed test.

The critical (table) value of $F_{\alpha = 0.05} = 1.79$ at $df_1 = 40$ and $df_2 = 30$. The calculated value of F = 1.50 is less than its critical value F = 1.79, the null hypothesis is accepted. Hence, the results of the research do not support the belief that women have a greater variation in attitude on political issues than men.

Example 8.25: The following figures relate to the number of units of an item produced per shift by two workers A and B for a number of days

A: 19 22 24 27 24 18 20 19 25

B: 26 37 40 35 30 30 40 26 30 35 45

Can it be inferred that worker A is more stable compared to worker B? Answer using the F-test at 5 per cent level of significance.

Solution: Let us take the hypothesis that the two workers are equally stable, that is,

$$H_0 : \sigma_A^2 = \sigma_B^2 \text{ and } H_1 : \sigma_A^2 \neq \sigma_B^2 \quad \text{(One-tailed test)}$$

The calculations for population variances σ_A^2 and σ_B^2 of the number of units produced by workers A and B, respectively are shown in Table 8.4.

Table 8.4 Calculation of σ_A^2 and σ_B^2

Worker A x_1	$x_1 - \bar{x}_1$ $= x_1 - 22$	$(x_1 - 22)^2$	*Worker B* x_2	$x_2 - \bar{x}_2$ $= x_2 - 34$	$(x_2 - \bar{x}_2)^2$
19	−3	9	26	−8	64
22	0	0	37	3	9
24	2	4	40	6	36
27	5	25	35	1	1
24	2	4	30	−4	16
18	−4	16	30	−4	16
20	−2	4	40	6	36
19	−3	9	26	−8	64
25	3	9	30	−4	16
			35	1	1
			45	11	121
198	0	80	374	0	380

$$\bar{x}_1 = \frac{\Sigma x_1}{n_1} = \frac{198}{9} = 22; \qquad \bar{x}_2 = \frac{\Sigma x_2}{n_2} = \frac{374}{11} = 34$$

$$s_A^2 = \frac{\Sigma (x_1 - \bar{x}_1)^2}{n_1 - 1} = \frac{80}{9-1} = 10; \qquad s_B^2 = \frac{\Sigma (x_2 - \bar{x}_2)^2}{n_2 - 1} = \frac{380}{11-1} = 38$$

Applying F-test statistic, we have

$$F = \frac{s_B^2}{s_A^2} = \frac{38}{10} = 3.8 \text{ (because } s_B^2 > s_A^2)$$

The critical value $F_{0.05(10,\,8)} = 3.35$ at $\alpha = 5$ per cent level of significance and degrees of freedom $df_A = 8$, $df_B = 10$. Since the calculated value of F is more than its critical value, the null hypothesis is rejected. Hence we conclude that worker A is more stable than worker B, because $s_A^2 < s_B^2$.

Example 8.26: It is known that the mean diameter of rivets produced by two firms A and B are practically the same, but the standard deviation may differ. For 22 rivets produced by firm A, the standard deviation is 2.9 mm, while for 16 rivets produced by firm B, the standard deviation is 3.8 mm. Test whether the rivets of firm A has the same variability as those of firm B.

Solution: Let us take the null hypothesis that the rivets of both the firms A and B have the same variability. That is,

$$H_0 : \sigma_1^2 = \sigma_2^2 \quad \text{and} \quad H_1 : \sigma_1^2 \neq \sigma_2^2$$

Given, $n_1 = 22, s_1 = 2.9$ and $n_2 = 16, s_2 = 3.8$. Thus

$$s_A^2 = \frac{n_1 s_1^2}{n_1 - 1} = \frac{22(2.9)^2}{22-1} = 8.805$$

$$s_B^2 = \frac{n_2 s_2^2}{n_2 - 1} = \frac{16(3.8)^2}{16-1} = 15.393$$

Since $s_B^2 > s_A^2$, applying F-test statistic

$$F = \frac{s_B^2}{s_A^2} = \frac{15.393}{8.805} = 1.74$$

Since calculated value of F = 1.74 is less than its critical value $F_{0.05} = 2.20$ at degree of freedom $df_A = 15$ and $df_B = 21$, the null hypothesis is accepted. Hence the rivets of both the firms A and B have the same variability.

Self-Practice Problems 8D

8.26 The mean diameter of a steel pipe produced by two processes, A and B, is practically the same but the standard deviations may differ. For a sample of 22 pipes produced by A, the standard deviation is 2.9 m, while for a sample of 16 pipes produced by B, the standard deviation is 3.8 m. Test whether the pipes produced by process A have the same variability as those of process B.

8.27 Tests for breaking strength were carried out on two lots of 5 and 9 steel wires respectively. The variance of one lot was 230 and that of the other was 492. Is there a significant difference in their variability?

8.28 Two random samples drawn from normal population are:

Sample 1	*Sample 2*
20	27
16	33
26	42
27	35
23	32
22	34
18	38
24	28
25	41
19	43
	30
	37

Obtain estimates of the variances of the population and test whether the two populations have the same variance.

8.29 In a sample of 8 observations, the sum of the squared deviations of items from the mean was 94.50. In another sample of 10 observations the value was found to be 101.70. Test whether the difference is significant at 5 per cent level of significance (at 5 per cent level level of significance critical value of F for $v_1 = 3$ and $v_2 = 9$ degrees of freedom is 3.29 and for $v_1 = 8$ and $v_2 = 10$ degrees of freedom, its value is 3.07).

8.30 Most individuals are aware of the fact that the average annual repair costs for an automobile depends on the age of the automobile. A researcher is interested in finding out whether the variance of the annual repair costs also increases with the age of the automobile. A sample of 25 automobiles that are 4 years old showed a sample variance for annual repair cost of Rs. 850 and a sample of 25 automobiles that are 2 years old showed a sample variance for annual repair costs of Rs. 300. Test the hypothesis that the variance in annual repair costs is more for the older automobiles, for a 0.01 level of significance.

8.31 The standard deviation in the 12-month earnings per share for 10 companies in the software industry was 4.27 and the standard deviation in the 12-month earning per share for 7 companies in the telecom industry was 2.27. Conduct a test for equal variance at $\alpha =$ 0.05. What is you conclusion about the variability in earning per share for two industries.

Hints and Answers

8.26 Let H_0 : There is no difference in the variability of diameters produced by process A and B, i.e.

$$H_0 : \sigma_A^2 = \sigma_B^2 \text{ and } H_1 : \sigma_A^2 \neq \sigma_B^2$$

Given $\sigma_A = 2.9, n_1 = 22, df_A = 21; \quad \sigma_B = 3.8, n_2 = 16, df_B = 21.$

$$s_A^2 = \frac{n_1}{n_1 - 1} \sigma_A^2 = \frac{22}{22-1} (2.9)^2$$

$$= \frac{22}{21} (8.41) = 8.81$$

$$s_2^2 = \frac{n_2}{n_2 - 1} \sigma_B^2 = \frac{16}{16-1} (3.8)^2$$

$$= \frac{16}{15} (14.44) = 15.40$$

$$F = \frac{s_2^2}{s_1^2} = \frac{15.40}{8.81} = 1.75$$

Since the calculated value $f = 1.75$ is less than its critical value $F_{0.05\,(15,\,21)} = 2.18$, the null hypothesis is accepted.

8.27 Let H_0 : No significant variability in the breaking strength of wires

Given $n_1 = 5, \sigma_1^2 = 230, df_1 = 4; n_2 = 9, \sigma_2^2 = 492, df_2 = 8$

$$F = \frac{\sigma_2^2}{\sigma_1^2} = \frac{492}{230} = 2.139$$

Since calculated value F = 2.139 is less its critical value $F_{0.05(8,\,4)} = 6.04$ the null hypothesis is accepted.

8.28 Let H_0 : Two populations have the same variance, i.e.

$$H_0 : \sigma_1^2 = \sigma_2^2 \text{ and } H_1 : \sigma_1^2 \neq \sigma_2^2.$$

Sample 1: $\bar{x}_1 = \dfrac{\Sigma x_1}{10} = 22;$

$$s_1^2 = \frac{\Sigma (x_1 - \bar{x}_1)^2}{n_1 - 1} = \frac{120}{9} = 13.33, df_1 = 9$$

Sample 2: $x_2 = \dfrac{\Sigma x_1}{12} = 35; \ df_2 = 11$

$$s_2^2 = \frac{\Sigma (x_2 - \bar{x}_2)^2}{n_2 - 1} = \frac{314}{11} = 28.54,$$

$$F = \frac{s_2^2}{s_1^2} = \frac{28.54}{13.33} = 2.14$$

Since calculated value F = 2.14 is less than its critical value $F_{0.05\,(11,\,9)} = 4.63$, the null hypothesis is accepted.

8.29 Let H_0 : The difference is not significant

Sample 1: $n_1 = 8, \Sigma(x_1 - \bar{x}_1)^2 = 94.50, v_1 = 7$

Sample 2: $n_1 = 10, \Sigma(x_2 - \bar{x}_2)^2 = 101.70, v_2 = 9$

$$\therefore \ s_1^2 = \frac{\Sigma (x_1 - \bar{x}_1)^2}{n_1 - 1} = \frac{94.50}{7} = 13.5;$$

$$s_2^2 = \frac{\Sigma (x_2 - \bar{x}_2)^2}{n_2 - 1} = \frac{101.70}{9} = 11.3$$

$$F = \frac{s_1^2}{s_2^2} = \frac{13.5}{11.3} = 1.195$$

Since the calculated value F = 1.195 is less than its critical value $F_{0.05\,(7,\,9)} = 3.29$, the null hypothesis is accepted.

8.30 Let H_0 : No significant difference in the variance of repair cost, $H_0 : \sigma_1^2 = \sigma_2^2$ and $H_1 : \sigma_1^2 > \sigma_2^2$

$s_1^2 =$ Rs. 850; $s_2^2 =$ Rs. 300

$n_1 = 25, df_1 = 24; n_2 = 25, df_2 = 24$

$$F = \frac{s_1^2}{s_2^2} = \frac{850}{300} = 2.833$$

Since the calculated value F = 2.833 is more than its critical value $F_{0.01(24,\,24)} = 2.66$, the null hypothesis is rejected.

8.31 Let H_0 :No significant difference of variability in earning per share for two industries, $H_0 : \sigma_1^2 = \sigma_2^2$ and $H_1 : \sigma_1^2 \neq \sigma_2^2$

Software industry : $s_1^2 = (4.27)^2 = 18.23,$ $n_1 = 10, df_1 = 9$

Telecom industry : $s_2^2 = (2.27)^2 = 5.15,$ $n_2 = 7, df_2 = 6$

$$\therefore \quad F = \frac{s_1^2}{s_2^2} = \frac{18.23}{5.15} = 3.54$$

Since the calculated value F = 3.54 is less than its critical value $F_{0.05\,(9,\,6)} = 4.099$, the null hypothesis is accepted.

Formulae Used

1. Hypothesis testing for population mean with large sample ($n > 30$)

   (a) Test statistic about a population mean μ

   - σ assumed known, $z = \dfrac{|\bar{x} - \mu|}{\sigma/\sqrt{n}}$
   - σ is estimated by s, $z = \dfrac{\bar{x} - \mu}{s/\sqrt{n}}$

   (b) Test statistic for the difference between means of two populations

   - Standard deviation of $\bar{x}_1 - \bar{x}_2$ when σ_1 and σ_2 are known

     $$\sigma_{\bar{x}_1 - \bar{x}_2} = \sqrt{\frac{\sigma_1^2}{n_1} + \frac{\sigma_2^2}{n_2}}$$

     Test statistic $z = \dfrac{(\bar{x}_1 - \bar{x}_2) - (\mu_1 - \mu_2)}{\sigma_{\bar{x}_1 - \bar{x}_2}}$

   - Standard deviation of $\bar{x}_1 - \bar{x}_2$ when $\sigma_1^2 = \sigma_2^2$

     $$\sigma_{\bar{x}_1 - \bar{x}_2} = \sigma\sqrt{\frac{1}{n_1} + \frac{1}{n_2}}$$

   - Point estimator of $\sigma_{\bar{x}_1 - \bar{x}_2}$

     $$s_{\bar{x}_1 - \bar{x}_2} = \sqrt{\frac{s_1^2}{n_1} + \frac{s_2^2}{n_2}}$$

   - Interval estimation for single population mean

     $\bar{x} \pm z_{\alpha/2}\, \sigma_{\bar{x}}$; σ is known

     $\bar{x} \pm z_{\alpha/2}\, s_{\bar{x}}$; σ is unknown

   - Interval estimation for the difference of means of two populations

     $(\bar{x}_1 - \bar{x}_2) \pm z_{\alpha/2}\sigma_{\bar{x}_1 - \bar{x}_2}$; σ_1 and σ_2 are known

     $(\bar{x}_1 - \bar{x}_2) \pm z_{\alpha/2} s_{\bar{x}_1 - \bar{x}_2}$; σ_1 and σ_2 are unknown

2. Hypothesis testing for population proportion for large sample ($n > 30$)

   (a) Test statistic for population proportion p

   $$z = \frac{\bar{p} - p}{\sigma_{\bar{p}}}; \quad \sigma_{\bar{p}} = \sqrt{\frac{p(1-p)}{n}}$$

   (b) Test statistic for the difference between the proportions of two populations

   - Standard deviation of $\bar{p}_1 - \bar{p}_2$

     $$\sigma_{\bar{p}_1 - \bar{p}_2} = \sqrt{\frac{p_1(1-p_1)}{n_1} + \frac{p_2(1-p_2)}{n_2}}$$

   - Point estimator of $\sigma_{\bar{p}_1 - \bar{p}_2}$

     $$s_{\bar{p}_1 - \bar{p}_2} = \sqrt{\frac{\bar{p}_1(1-\bar{p}_1)}{n_1} + \frac{\bar{p}_2(1-\bar{p}_2)}{n_2}}$$

   - Interval estimation of the difference between the proportions of two populations

     $$(\bar{p}_1 - \bar{p}_2) \pm z_{\alpha/2}\, s_{\bar{p}_1 - \bar{p}_2}$$

     where all n_1p_1, $n_1(1 - p_1)$, n_2p_2, and $n_2(1 - p_2)$ are more than or equal to 5.

   - Test statistic for hypothesis testing about the difference between proportions of two populations

     $$z = \frac{(\bar{p}_1 - \bar{p}_2) - (p_1 - p_2)}{\sigma_{\bar{p}_1 - \bar{p}_2}}$$

   - Pooled estimator of the population proportion

     $$\bar{p} = \frac{n_1\bar{p}_1 + n_2\bar{p}_2}{n_1 + n_2}$$

   - Point estimator of $\sigma_{\bar{p}_1 - \bar{p}_2}$

     $$s_{\bar{p}_1 - \bar{p}_2} = \sqrt{\bar{p}(1-\bar{p})\left(\frac{1}{n_1} + \frac{1}{n_2}\right)}$$

Chapter Concepts Quiz

True or False

1. A tentative assumption about a population parameter is called the null hypothesis.
2. As a general guideline, a research hypothesis should be stated as the alternative hypothesis.
3. The equality part of the expression (either $\geq$, $\leq$, or $=$) always appears in the null hypothesis.
4. Type I error is the probability of accepting null hypothesis when it is true.
5. Type II error is the probability of accepting null hypothesis when it is true.
6. The probability of making a Type I error is referred to as the level of significance.
7. The estimated standard deviation of sampling distribution of a statistic is called standard error.
8. Type I error is more harmful than Type II error.
9. For a given level of significance, we can reduce β by increasing the sample size.
10. If the cost of Type I error is large, a small level of significance should be specified.
11. For a given sample size n, an attempt to reduce the level of significance results in an increase in β. (T/F)
12. For a given level of significance, change in sample size changes the critical value.
13. The t-test statistic is used when $n \leq 30$ and the population standard deviation is known.
14. The value of the test statistic that defines the rejection region is called critical region for the test.

Concepts Quiz Answers

1. T	2. T	3. T	4. F	5. T	6. F	7. T	8. T	9. F
10. T	11. T	12. T	13. T	14. F				

Review Self-Practice Problems

8.32 A sample of size 25 yielded a mean equal to 33 and an estimated variance equal to 100. At the $\alpha = 0.01$ would we have reasons to doubt the claim that the population mean is not greater than 27?

8.33 An educator claims that the average IQ of American college students is at most 110, and that in a study made to test this claim 150 American college students selected at random had an average IQ of 111.2 with a standard deviation of 7.2. Use a level of significance of 0.01 to test the claim of the educator.
[*Delhi Univ., BA (H.Eco.), 1996*]

8.34 500 apples are taken at random from a large basket and 50 are found to be bad. Estimate the proportion of bad apples in the basket and assign limits within which the percentage most probably lies.

8.35 The election returns showed that a certain candidate received 46 per cent of the votes. Determine the probability that a poll of (a) 200 and (b) 1000 people selected at random from the voting population would have shown a majority of votes in favour of the candidate.

8.36 A simple random sample of size 100 has mean 15, the population variance being 25. Find an interval estimate of the population mean with a confidence level of (i) 99 per cent, and (ii) 95 per cent. If population variance is not given, what should be known to find out the required interval estimates?

8.37 A machine produced 20 defective articles in a batch of 400. After overhauling, it produced 10 defectives in a batch of 300. Has the machine improved? [*Madras Univ., MCom, 1996*]

8.38 Two samples of 100 electric bulbs each has a mean length of life 1500 and 1550 hours and standard deviation of 50 and 60 hours. Can it be concluded that two brands differ significantly at 1 per cent level of significance in equality?

8.39 A random sample of 100 mill workers in Kanpur showed their mean wage to be Rs. 3500 with a standard deviation of Rs. 280. Another random sample of 150 mill workers in Mumbai showed the mean wage to be Rs. 3900 with a standard deviation of Rs. 400. Do the mean wages of workers in Mumbai and Kanpur differ significantly ? Use $\alpha = 0.05$ level of significance.
[*Delhi Univ., MCom, 1999*]

8.40 As a controller of budget you are presented with the following data for budget variances (in Rs. 000's)

Department	*Budgeted sales*	*Actual sales*
A	1000	900
B	850	880
C	720	650
D	1060	860
E	750	820
F	900	1000
G	620	700
H	600	540
I	700	690
J	700	730
K	950	850
L	1100	1080

Is there any reason that achievements against budgets are slipping? Take $\alpha = 0.05$ level of significance.

8.41 A certain medicine given to each of 12 patients resulted in the following increase in blood pressure: 2, 5, 8, –1, 3, 0, –2, 1, 5, 0, 4, 6. Can it be concluded that the medicine will, in general, be accompanied by an increase in blood pressure?

8.42 The average monthly earnings for a women in managerial and professional positions is Rs. 16,700. Do men in the same positions have average monthly earnings that are higher than those for women? A random sample of $n=40$ men in managerial and professional positions showed $\bar{x}$ = Rs. 17,250 and s = Rs. 2346. Test the appropriate hypothesis using $\alpha = 0.01$.

8.43 The variability in the amount of impurities present in a batch of chemical used for a particular process depends on the length of time the process is in operation. A manufacturer using two production lines 1 and 2 has made a slight adjustment to line 2, hoping to reduce the variability as well as the average amount of impurities in the chemical. Samples of $n_1=25$ and $n_2=25$ measurements from two batches yield following means and variances: $\bar{x}_1 = 3.2$, $s_1^2 = 1.04$ and $\bar{x}_2 = 3.0$, $s_2^2 = 0.51$. Do the data present sufficient evidence to indicate that the process variability is less for line 2?

8.44 A media research group conducted a study of the radio listening habits of men and women. It was discovered that the mean listening time for men is 35 minutes per day with a standard deviation of 10 minutes in a sample of 10 men studied. The mean listening time for 12 women studied was also 35 minutes with a standard deviation of 12 minutes. Can it be concluded that there is a difference in the variation in the number of minutes men and women listen to the radio at $\alpha = 0.10$ significance level?

Hints and Answers

8.32 Let H_0 : No significant difference between the and hypothesized population means

Given, $\bar{x} = 33$, $s = \sqrt{100} = 10$,
$n = 25$, and $\mu = 27$.

$$t = \frac{\bar{x} - \mu}{s/\sqrt{n}} = \frac{33 - 27}{10/\sqrt{25}} = 3$$

Since $t_{cal} = 3$ is more than its critical value t = 2.064 at $\alpha/2 = 0.025$ and $df = 24$, the H_0 is rejected

8.33 Let H_0 : No significant difference between the claim of the educator and the sample results

Given $n = 150$, $\bar{x} = 111.2$,
$s = 7.2$ and $\mu = 110$

$$z = \frac{\bar{x}-\mu}{s/\sqrt{n}} = \frac{111.2-110}{7.2/\sqrt{150}} = 2.04$$

Since $z_{cal} = 2.04$ is less than its critical value $z_\alpha = 2.58$ at $\alpha = 0.01$, the H_0 is accepted.

8.34 Population of bad apples in the given sample, $p = 50/500 = 0.1; q = 0.9$

Standard error, $\sigma_p = \sqrt{\frac{pq}{n}}$

$$= \sqrt{\frac{0.1 \times 0.9}{500}} = 0.013$$

Confidence limits: $p \pm 3\,\sigma_p = 0.1 \pm 3(0.013)$;

or $0.081 \le p \le 0.139$

8.35 (a) Let $H_0 : p = 0.46$ and $H_1 : p \neq 0.46$
Given $p = 0.46, q = 0.54, n = 200$;

$$\sigma_p = \sqrt{\frac{pq}{n}} = \sqrt{\frac{0.46 \times 0.54}{200}} = 0.0352$$

Since 101 or more indicates a majority, as a continuous variable let us consider it as 100.5 and therefore the proportion is 100.5/200 = 0.5025

$$P(x \ge 101) = P\left[z \ge \frac{\bar{p}-p}{\sigma_p}\right]$$

$$= P\left[z \ge \frac{0.5025 - 0.46}{0.0352}\right]$$

$$= P[z \ge 1.21]$$

Required probability $= 0.5000 - 0.3869 = 0.1131$

(b) $$\sigma_p = \sqrt{\frac{0.46 \times 0.54}{1000}} = 0.0158$$

$$P(x \ge 1001) = P\left[z \ge \frac{\bar{p}-p}{\sigma_p}\right]$$

$$= P\left[z \ge \frac{0.5025 - 0.46}{0.0158}\right]$$

$$= P[z \ge 2.69]$$

Required probability $= 0.500 - 0.4964 = 0.0036$

8.36 Given $n = 100$, $\bar{x} = 15$, $\sigma_2 = 25$;
Standard error

$$\sigma_{\bar{x}} = \sigma/\sqrt{n} = 5/\sqrt{100} = 0.5$$

99 per cent confidence limits: $\bar{x} \pm 2.58\,\sigma_{\bar{x}}$

$15 \pm 2.58\ (0.5)$; 3.71 to 16.29

95 per cent Confidence limits: $\bar{x} \pm 1.96\,\sigma_{\bar{x}}$
$= 15 \pm 1.96(0.5)$; 14.02 to 15.98

8.37 Let H_0 : The machine has not improved after overhauling, $H_0 : p_1 = p_2$

Given, $p_1 = 20/400 = 0.050$,
$p_2 = 10/300 = 0.033$

$$\therefore \quad p = \frac{p_1 n_1 + p_2 n_2}{n_1 + n_2}$$

$$= \frac{20+10}{400+300} = 0.043;$$

$$q = 1 - p = 0.957$$

$$z = \frac{p_1 - p_2}{\sigma_{p_1 - p_2}} = \frac{p_1 - p_2}{\sqrt{pq\left(\frac{1}{n_1} + \frac{1}{n_2}\right)}}$$

$$= \frac{0.050 - 0.033}{\sqrt{0.043 \times 0.957\left(\frac{1}{400} + \frac{1}{300}\right)}}$$

$$= \frac{0.050 - 0.033}{0.0155} = 1.096$$

Since $z_{cal} = 1.096$ is less than its critical value $z_\alpha = 1.96$ at $\alpha = 5$ per cent, the H_0 is accepted.

8.38 Let H_0 : There is no significant difference in the mean life of the two makes of bulbs,

Given $n_1 = 100$, $\bar{x}_1 = 1500$, $\sigma_1 = 50$ and
$n_2 = 100$, $\bar{x}_2 = 1550$, $\sigma_2 = 60$

$$z = \frac{\bar{x}_1 - \bar{x}_2}{\sigma_{\bar{x}_1 - \bar{x}_2}} = \frac{\bar{x}_1 - \bar{x}_2}{\sqrt{\frac{\sigma_1^2}{n_1} + \frac{\sigma_2^2}{n_2}}}$$

$$= \frac{1500 - 1550}{\sqrt{\frac{(50)^2}{100} + \frac{(60)^2}{100}}}$$

$$= -\frac{50}{7.81} = -6.40$$

Since $z_{cal} = -6.40$ is less than its critical value $z_\alpha = -2.58$ at $\alpha = 1$ per cent, the H_0 is rejected.

8.39 Let H_0 : Overhauling has not improved the performance of the machine.

Given $p_1 = 10/200 = 0.05$; $p_2 = 4/100 = 0.04$;

$$\therefore \quad p = \frac{n_1 p_1 + n_2 p_2}{n_1 + n_2} = \frac{10+4}{200+100} = 0.047;$$

$$q = 1 - p = 0.953$$

$$\sigma_p = \sqrt{pq\left(\frac{1}{n_1} + \frac{1}{n_2}\right)} = \sqrt{0.047 \times 0.953\left(\frac{1}{200} + \frac{1}{100}\right)} = 0.027$$

$$z = \frac{p_1 - p_2}{\sigma_p} = \frac{0.05 - 0.04}{0.027} = 0.370$$

Since $z_{cal} = 0.370$ is less than its critical value $z = 1.96$ at $\alpha = 5$ per cent, the H_0 is accepted.

8.40 Let H_0 : Achievements in sales against budgets are slipping, i.e., $H_0 : \mu_1 = \mu_2$ and $H_1 : \mu_1 < \mu_2$

Department	*d*	d^2
A	–100	10,000
B	30	900
C	–70	4900
D	–200	40,000
E	70	4900
F	100	10,000
G	80	6400
H	–60	3600
I	–10	100
J	30	900
K	–100	10,000
L	–20	400
	–250	92,100

$$d = \frac{\Sigma d}{n} = \frac{250}{12} = 20.83;$$

$$s = \sqrt{\frac{\Sigma d^2}{n-1} - \frac{(\Sigma d)^2}{n\,(n-1)}} = \sqrt{\frac{92{,}100}{11} - \frac{(-250)^2}{12 \times 11}} = 88.87$$

$$\therefore \quad t = \frac{\bar{d}}{s/\sqrt{n}} = \frac{20.83}{88.87/\sqrt{12}} = 0.812$$

Since $t_{cal} = 0.812$ is less than its critical value $t = 1.79$ at $\alpha = 5$ per cent and $df = 11$, the H_0 is accepted.

8.41 Let H_0 : Medicine is not accompanied by an increase in blood pressure, i.e.

$H_0 : \mu_1 = \mu_2$ and $H_0 : \mu_1 < \mu_2$

d	d^2
2	4
5	25
8	64
–1	1
3	9
0	0
–2	4
1	1
5	25
0	0
4	16
6	36
31	185

$$\bar{d} = \frac{\Sigma d}{n} = \frac{31}{12} = 2.58;$$

$$s = \sqrt{\frac{\Sigma d^2}{n-1} - \frac{(\Sigma d)^2}{n\,(n-1)}} = \sqrt{\frac{185}{11} - \frac{(31)^2}{12 \times 11}} = 3.08$$

$$\therefore \quad t = \frac{\bar{d}}{s/\sqrt{n}} = \frac{2.58}{3.08/\sqrt{12}} = 2.89$$

Since $t_{cal} = 2.89$ is more than its critical value $t = 1.796$ at $\alpha = 5$ per cent and $df = 11$, the H_0 is rejected. Medicine increases blood pressure.

8.42 H_0: $\mu = 16{,}700$ and H_1: $\mu > 16{,}700$; μ = average monthly salary for men

Given $n = 400$, $\bar{x} = 17{,}250$ and $s = 2346$.

$$z = \frac{\bar{x} - \mu}{s/\sqrt{n}} = \frac{17{,}250 - 16{,}700}{2346/\sqrt{400}} = \frac{550}{117.3} = 4.68$$

Since z_{cal} (=4.68) > z_α = 2.58, H_0 is rejected and hence we conclude that the average monthly earnings for men are significantly higher than for women.

8.43 H_0: σ_1^2 and σ_2^2 and $H_1: \sigma_1^2 > \sigma_2^2$.

Given s_1^2 = 1.04, s_2^2 = 0.51, $n_1 = n_2$ = 25. Applying the test statistic

$$F = s_1^2 / s_2^2 = 1.04/0.51 = 2.04$$

Since f_{cal} (= 2.04) > f_α (= 1.70) at $df_1 = df_2$ = 24, reject H_0. Hence variability of line 2 is less than that of line 1.

8.44 H_0: $\sigma_L^2 = \sigma_L^2$ and H_0: $\sigma_L^2 \neq \sigma_L^2$

Given s_w^2 = 12, s_m^2 = 10, n_m = 10, n_w = 12. Applying the test statistic

$$F = s_1^2 / s_2^2 = (12)^2/(10)^2 = 1.44$$

Since F_{cal} (= 1.44) < f_α (= 3.10), accept H_0. Hence there is no difference in the variations of the two populations.

Glossary of Terms

Null hypothesis: The hypothesis which is initially assumed to be true, although it may in fact be either true or false based on the sample data.

Alternative hypothesis: The hypothesis concluded to be true if the null hypothesis is rejected.

Rejection region: The range of values that will lead to the rejection of a null hypothesis.

Critical value: A table value with which a test statistic is compared to determine whether a null hypothesis should be rejected or not.

One-tailed test: The test of a null hypothesis which can only be rejected when the sample test statistic value is in one extreme end of the sampling distribution.

Hypothesis testing: The process of testing a statement or belief about a population parameter by the use of information collected from a sample(s).

Type I error: The probability of rejecting a true null hypothesis.

Level of significance: The probability of rejecting a true null hypothesis due to sampling error.

Type II error: The probability of accepting a false null hypothesis.

Power of a test: The ability (probability) of a test to reject the null hypothesis when it is false.

Two-tailed test: The test of a null hypothesis which can be rejected when the sample statistic is in either extreme end of the sampling distribution.

***p*-value:** The probability of getting the sample statistic or a more extreme value, when null hypothesis is true.

***t*-test:** A hypothesis test for comparing two independent population means using the means of two small samples.

F-test: A hypothesis test for comparing the variance of two independent populations with the help of variances of two small samples.

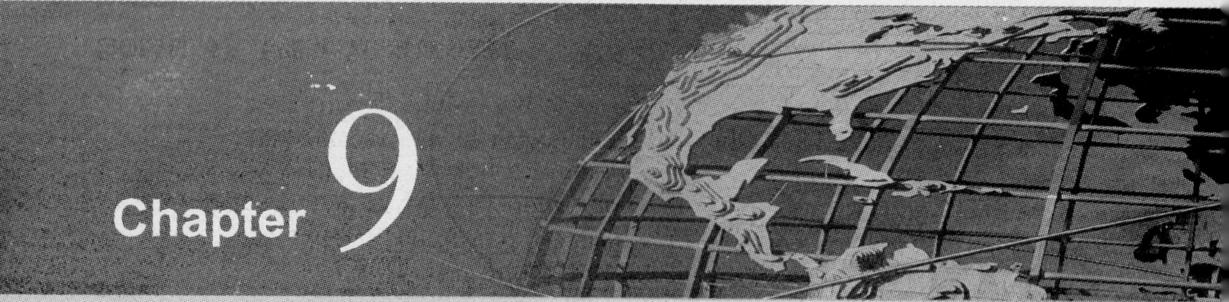

Correlation Analysis

LEARNING OBJECTIVES

After studying this chapter, you should be able to

- express quantitatively the degree and direction of the covariation or association between two variables.
- determine the validity and reliability of the covariation or association between two variables.
- provide a test of hypothesis to determine whether a linear relationship actually exists between the variables.

9.1 INTRODUCTION

The statistical methods, discussed so far, are used to analyse the data involving only one variable. Often an analysis of data concerning two or more quantitative variables is needed to look for any statistical relationship or association between them that can describe specific numerical features of the association. The knowledge of such a relationship is important to make inferences from the relationship between variables in a given situation. Few instances where the knowledge of an association or relationship between two variables would prove vital to make decision are:

- Family income and expenditure on luxury items.
- Yield of a crop and quantity of fertilizer used.
- Sales revenue and expenses incurred on advertising.
- Frequency of smoking and lung damage.
- Weight and height of *individuals*.
- Age and sign legibility distance.
- Age and hours of TV viewing per day.

A statistical technique that is used to analyse the strength and direction of the relationship between two quantitative variables, is called *correlation analysis*. A few definitions of correlation analysis are:

- An analysis of the relationship of two or more variables is usually called correlation.

— A. M. Tuttle

- When the relationship is of a quantitative nature, the appropriate statistical tool for discovering and measuring the relationship and expressing it in a brief formula is known as correlation.

— Croxton and Cowden

The **coefficient of correlation**, is a number that indicates the *strength (magnitude)* and *direction* of statistical relationship between two variables.

- The ***strength*** of the relationship is determined by the closeness of the points to a straight line when a pair of values of two variables are plotted on a graph. A straight line is used as the frame of reference for evaluating the relationship.
- The ***direction*** is determined by whether one variable generally increases or decreases when the other variable increases.

The importance of examining the statistical relationship between two or more variables can be divided into the following questions and accordingly requires the statistical methods to answer these questions:

(i) Is there an association between two or more variables? If yes, what is the form and degree of that relationship?

(ii) Is the relationship strong or significant enough to be useful to arrive at a desirable conclusion?

(iii) Can the relationship be used for predictive purposes, that is, to predict the most likely value of a dependent variable corresponding to the given value of independent variable or variables?

In this chapter the first two questions will be answered.

For correlation analysis, the data on values of two variables must come from sampling in pairs, one for each of the two variables. The pairing relationship should represent some time, place, or condition.

9.2 SIGNIFICANCE OF MEASURING CORRELATION

The objective of any scientific and clinical research is to establish relationships between two or more sets of observations or variables to arrive at some conclusion which is also near to reality. Finding such relationships is often an initial step for identifying causal relationships. Few advantages of measuring an association (or correlation) between two or more variables are as under:

1. Correlation analysis contributes to the understanding of economic behaviour, aids in locating the critically important variables on which others depend, may reveal to the economist the connections by which disturbances spread and suggest to him the paths through which stabilizing forces may become effective. —W. A. Neiswanger
2. The effect of correlation is to reduce the range of uncertainty of our prediction. The prediction based on correlation analysis will be more reliable and near to reality. — Tippett
3. In economic theory we come across several types of variables which show some kind of relationship. For example, there exists a relationship between price, supply, and quantity demanded; convenience, amenities, and service standards are related to customer retention; yield of a crop related to quantity of fertilizer applied, type of soil, quality of seeds, rainfall, and so on. Correlation analysis helps in quantifying precisely the degree of association and direction of such relationships.

4. Correlations are useful in the areas of healthcare such as determining the validity and reliability of clinical measures or in expressing how health problems are related to certain biological or environmental factors. For example, correlation coefficient can be used to determine the degree of inter-observer reliability for two doctors who are assessing a patient's disease.

9.3 CORRELATION AND CAUSATION

There are at least three criteria for establishing a causal relationship; correlation is one of them. While drawing inferences from the value of correlation coefficient, we overlook the fact that it measures only the strength of a linear relationship and it does not necessarily imply a causal relationship. That is, there are several other explanations for finding a correlation.

The following factors should be examined to interpret the nature and extent of relationship between two or more variables:

1. **Chance coincidence:** A correlation coefficient may not reach any statistical significance, that is, it may represent a nonsense (spurious) or chance association. For example, (i) a positive correlation between growth in population and wheat production in the country has no statistical significance. Because, each of the two events might have entirely different, unrelated causes. (ii) While estimating the correlation in sales revenue and expenditure on advertisements over a period of time, the investigator must be certain that the outcome is not due to biased sampling or sampling error. That is, he needs to show that a correlation coefficient is statistically significant and not just due to random sampling error.
2. **Influence of third variable:** If the correlation coefficient does not establish any relationship, it can be used as a source for testing null and allternative hypotheses about a population. For example, it has been proved that smoking causes lung damage. However, given that there is often multiple reasons of health problems, the reason of stress cannot be ruled out. Similarly, there is a positive correlation between the yield of rice and tea because the crops are influenced by the amount of rainfall. But the yield of any one is not influenced by other.
3. **Mutual influence:** There may be a high degree of relationship between two variables but it is difficult to say as to which variable is influencing the other. For example, variables like price, supply, and demand of a commodity are mutually correlated. According to the principle of economics, as the price of a commodity increases, its demand decreases, so price influences the demand level. But if demand of a commodity increases due to growth in population, then its price also increases. In this case increased demand make an effect on the price. However, the amount of export of a commodity is influenced by an increase or decrease in custom duties but the reverse is normally not true.

9.4 TYPES OF CORRELATIONS

There are three broad types of correlations:

1. Positive and negative,
2. Linear and non-linear,
3. Simple, partial, and multiple.

In this chapter we will discuss simple linear positive or negative correlation analysis.

9.4.1 Positive and Negative Correlation

A positive (or direct) correlation refers to the same direction of change in the values of variables. In other words, if values of variables are varying (i.e., increasing or decreasing) in the same direction, then such correlation is referred to as **positive correlation**.

A **negative (or inverse) correlation** refers to the change in the values of variables in opposite direction.

The following examples illustrate the concept of positive and negative correlation.

Positive Correlation

Increasing $\rightarrow x$	:	5	8	10	15	17
Increasing $\rightarrow y$	:	10	12	16	18	20
Decreasing $\rightarrow x$	:	17	15	10	8	5
Decreasing $\rightarrow y$	:	20	18	16	12	10

Negative Correlation

Increasing $\rightarrow x$	:	5	8	10	15	17
Decreasing $\rightarrow y$	:	20	18	16	12	10
Decreasing $\rightarrow x$	:	17	15	12	10	6
Increasing $\rightarrow y$	:	2	7	9	13	14

It may be noted here that the change (increasing or decreasing) in values of both the variables is not proportional or fixed.

9.4.2 Linear and Non-Linear Correlation

A linear correlation implies a constant change in one of the variable values with respect to a change in the corresponding values of another variable. In other words, a correlation is referred to as *linear correlation* when variations in the values of two variables have a constant ratio. The following example illustrates a linear correlation between two variables x and y.

x :	10	20	30	40	50
y :	40	60	80	100	120

When these pairs of values of x and y are plotted on a graph paper, the line joining these points would be a straight line.

A non-linear (or curvi-linear) correlation implies an absolute change in one of the variable values with respect to changes in values of another variable. In other words, a correlation is referred to as a *non-linear correlation* when the amount of change in the values of one variable does not bear a constant ratio to the amount of change in the corresponding values of another variable. The following example illustrates a non-linear correlation between two variables x and y.

x :	8	9	9	10	10	28	29	30
y :	80	130	170	150	230	560	460	600

When these pair of values of x and y are plotted on a graph paper, the line joining these points would not be a straight line, rather it would be curvi-linear.

9.4.3 Simple, Partial, and Multiple Correlation

The distinction between simple, partial, and multiple correlation is based upon the number of variables involved in the correlation analysis.

If only two variables are chosen to study correlation between them, then such a correlation is referred to as ***simple correlation***. A study on the yield of a crop with respect to only amount of fertilizer, or sales revenue with respect to amount of money spent on advertisement, are a few examples of simple correlation.

In ***partial correlation***, two variables are chosen to study the correlation between them, but the effect of other influencing variables is kept constant. For example (i) yield of a crop is influenced by the amount of fertilizer applied, rainfall, quality of seed, type of soil, and pesticides, (ii) sales revenue from a product is influenced by the level of advertising expenditure, quality of the product, price, competitors, distribution, and so on. In such cases an attempt to measure the correlation between yield and seed quality, assuming that the average values of other factors exist, becomes a problem of partial correlation.

In ***multiple correlation***, the relationship between more than three variables is considered simultaneously for study. For example, employer-employee relationship in any organization may be examined with reference to, training and development facilities; medical, housing, and education to children facilities; salary structure; grievances handling system; and so on.

9.5 METHODS OF CORRELATION ANALYSIS

The correlation between two ratio-scaled (numeric) variables is represented by the letter r which takes on values between -1 and $+1$ only. Sometimes this measure is called the '**Pearson product moment correction**' or the **correlation coefficient**. The correlation coefficient is scale free and therefore its interpretation is independent of the units of measurement of two varibles, say x and y.

In this chapter, the following methods of finding the correlation coefficient between two variables x and y are discussed:

1. Scatter Diagram method
2. Karl Pearson's Coefficient of Correlation method
3. Spearman's Rank Correlation method
4. Method of Least-squares

Figure 9.1 shows how the strength of the association between two variables is represented by the coefficient of correlation.

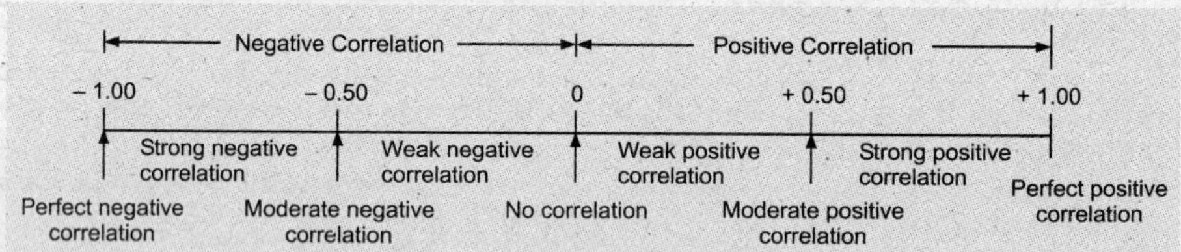

Figure 9.1 Interpretation of Correlation Coefficient

9.5.1 Scatter Diagram Method

The **scatter diagram** method is a quick at-a-glance method of determining of an apparent relationship between two variables, if any. A scatter diagram (or a graph) can be obtained on a graph paper by plotting observed (or known) pairs of values of variables x and y, taking the independent variable values on the x-axis and the dependent variable values on the y-axis.

It is common to try to draw a straight line through data points so that an equal number of points lie on either side of the line. The relationship between two variables x and y described by the data points is defined by this straight line.

In a scatter diagram the horizontal and vertical axes are scaled in units corresponding to the variables x and y, respectively. Figure 9.2 shows examples of different types of relationships based on pairs of values of x and y in a sample data. The pattern of data points in the diagram indicates that the variables are related. If the variables are related, then the dotted line appearing in each diagram describes relationship between the two variables.

The patterns depicted in Fig. 9.2(a) and (b) represent linear relationships since the patterns are described by straight lines. The pattern in Fig. 9.2(a) shows a *positive* relationship since the value of y tends to increase as the value of x increases, whereas pattern in Fig. 9.2(b) shows a *negative* relationship since the value of y tends to decrease as the value of x increases.

The pattern depicted in Fig. 9.2(c) illustrates very low or no relationship between the values of x and y, whereas Fig. 9.2(d) represents a curvilinear relationship since it is described by a curve rather than a straight line. Figure 9.2(e) illustrates a positive linear relationship with a widely scattered pattern of points. The wider scattering indicates that there is a lower degree of association between the two variables x and y than there is in Fig. 9.2(a).

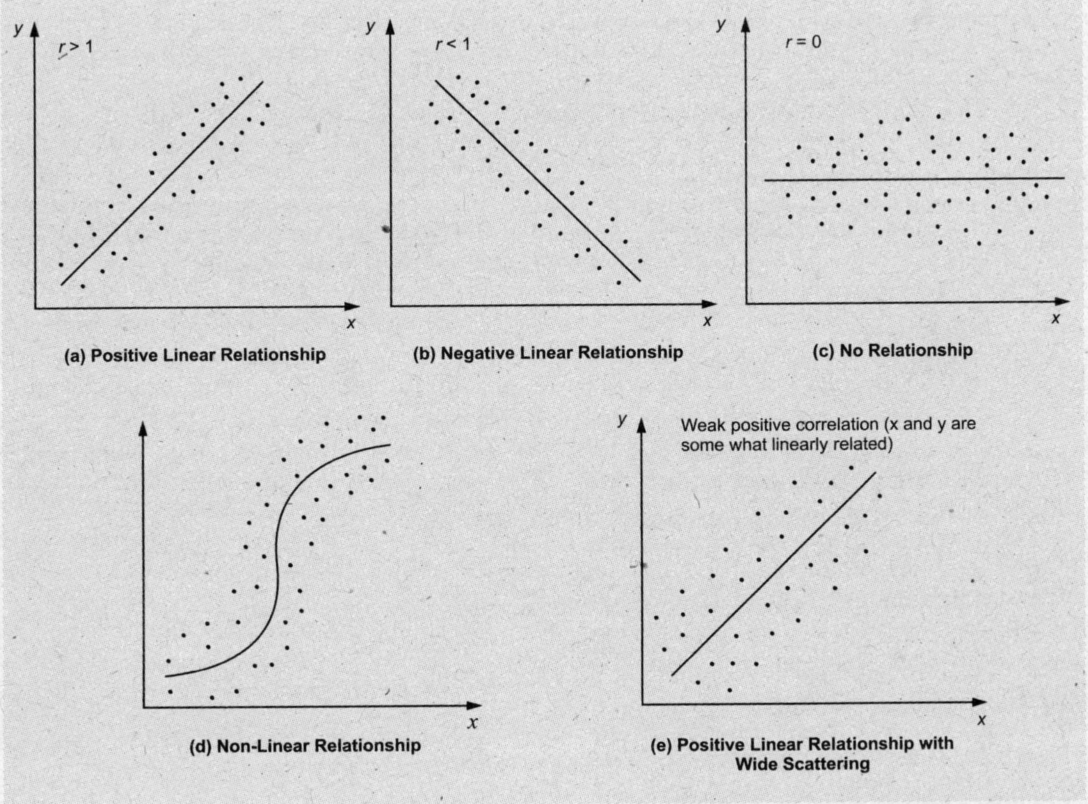

Figure 9.2 Typical Examples of Correlation Coefficient

Interpretation of Correlation Coefficients While interpretating correlation coefficient *r*, the following points should be taken into account:

(i) A low value of *r* does not indicate that the variables are unrelated but indicates that the relationship is poorly described by a straight line. A non-linear relatinship may also exist.
(ii) A correlation does not imply a *cause-and-effect* relationship, it is merely an observed association.

Specific Features of the Correlation Coefficient Regardless of the type of correlation coefficient we use, the following are the common among all of them.

(i) The value of *r* depends on the slope of the line passing through the data points and the scattering of the pair of values of variables *x* and *y* about this line (for detail see Chapter 10).
(ii) The sign of the correlation coefficient indicates the direction of the relationship. A positive correlation denoted by + (positive sign) indicates that the two variables tend to increase (or decrease) together (a positive association) and a negative correlation by – (minus sign) indicates that when one variable increases the other is likely to decrease (a negative association).
(iii) The values of the correlation coefficient range from + 1 to – 1 regardless of the units of measurements of *x* and *y*.
(iv) The value of $r = +1$ or -1 indicates that there is a perfect linear relationship between two variables, *x* and *y*. A perfect correlation implies that every observed pair of values of *x* and *y* falls on the straight line.
(v) The magnitude of the correlation indicates the strength of the relationship, which is the overall closeness of the points to a straight line. The sign of the correlation does indicates about the strength of the linear relationship.
(vi) Correlation coefficient is independent of the change of origin and scale of reference. In other words, its value remains unchanged when we subtract some constant from every given value of variables *x* and *y* (change of origin) and when we divide or multiply by some constant every given value of *x* and *y* (change of scale).
(vii) Correlation coefficient is a pure number independent of the unit of measurement.
(viii) The value of $r = 0$ indicates that the straight line through the data is exactly horizontal, so that the value of variable *x* does not change the predicated value of variable *y*.
(ix) The square of *r*, i.e., r^2 is referred to as *coefficient of determination*.

Further, from Fig. 9.2(a) to (e) we conclude that the closer the value of *r* is to either + 1 or – 1, the stronger is the association between *x* and *y*. Also, closer the value of *r* to 0, the weaker the association between *x* and *y* appears to be.

Example 9.1: Given the following data:

Student	:	1	2	3	4	5	6	7	8	9	10
Management aptitude score	:	400	675	475	350	425	600	550	325	675	450
Grade point average	:	1.8	3.8	2.8	1.7	2.8	3.1	2.6	1.9	3.2	2.3

(a) Draw this data on a graph paper.
(b) Is there any correlation between per capita national income and per capita consumer expenditure? If yes, what is your opinion.

Solution: By taking an appropriate scale on the *x* and *y* axes, the pair of observations are plotted on a graph paper as shown in Fig. 9.3. The scatter diagram in Fig. 9.3 with straight line represents the relationship between *x* and *y* 'fitted' through it.

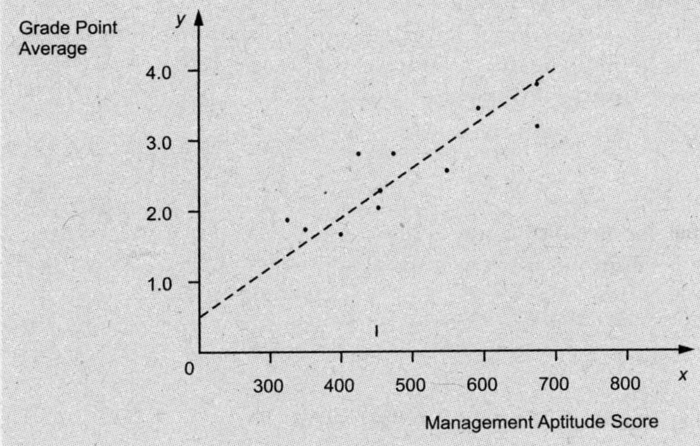

Figure 9.3 Scatter Diagram

Interpretation: From the scatter diagram shown in Fig. 9.3, it appears that there is a high degree of association between two variable values. It is because the data points are very close to a straight line passing through the points. This pattern of dotted points also indicates a high degree of linear positive correlation.

9.5.2 Karl Pearson's Correlation Coefficient

Karl Pearson's correlation coefficient measures quantitatively the extent to which two variables x and y are correlated. For a set of n pairs of values of x and y, Pearson's correlation coefficient r is given by

$$r = \frac{\text{Covariance}\,(x, y)}{\sqrt{\text{var}\,x}\,\sqrt{\text{var}\,y}} = \frac{\text{Cov}\,(x, y)}{\sigma_x\,\sigma_y}$$

where

$$\text{Cov}(x, y) = \frac{1}{n}\sum(x - \bar{x})\,(y - \bar{y})$$

$$\sigma_x = \sqrt{\frac{\sum(x - \bar{x})^2}{n}} \leftarrow \text{standard deviation of sample data on variable } x$$

$$\sigma_y = \sqrt{\frac{\sum(y - \bar{y})^2}{n}} \leftarrow \text{standard deviation of sample data on variable } y$$

Substituting mathematical formula for Cov (x, y) and σ_x and σ_y, we have

$$r = \frac{\frac{1}{n}\sum(x - \bar{x})\,(y - \bar{y})}{\sqrt{\frac{\sum(x - \bar{x})^2}{n}}\,\sqrt{\frac{\sum(y - \bar{y})^2}{n}}} = \frac{n\sum xy - (\sum x)\,(\sum y)}{\sqrt{n\sum x^2 - (\sum x)^2}\,\sqrt{n\sum y^2 - (\sum y)^2}} \qquad (9\text{-}1)$$

Step Deviation Method for Ungrouped Data When actual mean values $\bar{x}$ and $\bar{y}$ are in fraction, the calculation of Pearson's correlation coefficient can be simplified by taking deviations of x and y values from their assumed means A and B, respectively. That is, $d_x = x - A$ and $d_y = y - B$, where A and B are assumed means of x and y values. The formula (9-1) becomes

$$r = \frac{n\Sigma d_x d_y - (\Sigma d_x)(\Sigma d_y)}{\sqrt{n\Sigma d_x^2 - (\Sigma d_x)^2}\sqrt{n\Sigma d_y^2 - (\Sigma d_y)^2}} \qquad (9\text{-}2)$$

Step Deviation Method for Grouped Data When data on x and y values are classified or grouped into a frequency distribution, the formula (10-2) is modified as:

$$r = \frac{n\Sigma fd_x d_y - (\Sigma fd_x)(\Sigma fd_y)}{\sqrt{n\Sigma fd_x^2 - (\Sigma fd_x)^2}\sqrt{n\Sigma fd_y^2 - (\Sigma fd_y)^2}} \qquad (9\text{-}3)$$

Assumptions of Using Pearson's Correlation Coefficient

(i) Pearson's correlation coefficient is appropriate to calculate when both variables x and y are measured on an interval or a ratio scale.

(ii) Both variables x and y are normally distributed, and that there is a linear relationship between these variables.

(iii) The correlation coefficient is largely affected due to truncation of the range of values in one or both of the variables. This occurs when the distributions of both the variables greatly deviate from the normal shape.

(iv) There is a cause and effect relationship between two variables that influences the distributions of both the variables. Otherwise correlation coefficient might either be extremely low or even zero.

Advantage and Disadvantages of Pearson's Correlation Coefficient The correlation coefficient is a numerical number between – 1 and 1 that summarizes the magnitude as well as direction (positive or negative) of association between two variables. The chief limitations of Pearson's method are:

(i) The correlation coefficient always assumes a linear relationship between two variables, whether it is true or not.

(ii) Great care must be exercised in interpreting the value of this coefficient as very often its value is misinterpreted.

(iii) The value of the coefficient is unduly affected by the extreme values of two variable values.

(iv) As compared with other methods the computational time required to calculate the value of r using Pearson's method is lengthy.

9.5.3 Probable Error and Standard Error of Coefficient of Correlation

The probable error (PE) of coefficient of correlation indicates extent to which its value depends on the condition of random sampling. If r is the calculated value of correlation coefficient in a sample of n pairs of observations, then the standard error SE_r of the correlation coefficient r is given by

$$SE_r = \frac{1 - r^2}{\sqrt{n}}$$

The probable error of the coefficient of correlation is calculated by the expression:

$$PE_r = 0.6745\ SE_r = 0.6745\ \frac{1-r^2}{\sqrt{n}}$$

Thus with the help of PE_r we can determine the range within which population coefficient of correlation is expected to fall using following formula: $\rho = r \pm PE_r$ where ρ (rho) represents population coefficient of correlation.

Remarks

1. If $r < PE_r$ then the value of r is not significant, that is, there is no relationship between two variables of interest.
2. If $r > 6PE_r$ then value of r is significant, that is, there exists a relationship between two variables.

Illustration: If $r = 0.8$ and $n = 25$, then PE_r is

$$PE_r = 0.6745\ \frac{1-(0.8)^2}{\sqrt{25}} = 0.6745\ \frac{0.36}{5} = 0.048$$

Thus the limits within which population correlation coefficient (ρ_r) should fall are

$$r \pm PE_r = 0.8 \pm 0.048 \quad \text{or} \quad 0.752 \le \rho_r \le 0.848$$

Example 9.2: If covariance of 10 pairs of items is 7, variance of x is 36, $\Sigma(y-\bar{y})^2 = 90$. Find out co-relation coefficient, r. *[Delhi Univ., BCom (P), 2004]*

Solution: We know that $r = \dfrac{\text{Cov}(x, y)}{\sigma_x \sigma_y}$

Given, Cov $(x, y) = 7$, $n = 10$, $\sigma_x^2 = 36$, $\Sigma(y-\bar{y})^2 = 90$. Since Var$(x) = \sigma_x^2 = 36$, Std. dev $(\sigma_x) = 6$.

Also $$\sigma_y = \sqrt{\frac{\Sigma(y-\bar{y})^2}{n}} = \sqrt{\frac{90}{10}} = 3$$

Co-relation coefficient, $$r = \frac{\text{Cov}(x, y)}{\sigma_x\ \sigma_y} = \frac{7}{6 \times 3} = 0.39.$$

Example 9.3: Calculate Karl Pearson's coefficient of correlation from the following data. Interpret your result.

$$\sigma_x = 10,\ \sigma_y = 12,\ \bar{x} = 25 \text{ and } \bar{y} = 35$$

Summation of product of deviation from actual arithmetic means of two series is 24 and number of observations are 20. *[Delhi Univ., BCom (P), 2004]*

Solution: Given $\sigma_x = 10$, $\sigma_y = 12$, $\bar{x} = 25$, $\bar{y} = 35$, $\Sigma(x-\bar{x})(y-\bar{y}) = 24$ and $n = 20$. Then

$$\text{Cov}\ (x, y) = \frac{\Sigma(x-\bar{x})(y-\bar{y})}{n} = \frac{24}{20} = 1.2$$

We know that, $$r = \frac{\text{Cov}(x, y)}{\sigma_x \sigma_y} = \frac{1.2}{10 \times 12} = +0.01$$

Since magnitude of r is very small, correlation between x and y is negligible.

Example 9.4: If $r = 0.97$ and $n = 8$, find out the probable error of the coefficient of correlation and determine the limits for population correlation, r.

Solution: Given: $r = 0.97$, $n = 8$. Then

$$\text{P.E.}(r) = 0.6745\frac{1-r^2}{\sqrt{n}} = 0.6745\frac{(1-(0.97)^2)}{\sqrt{8}} = \frac{0.6745\times 0.0591}{2.828} = 0.014$$

Limits of population correlation $= r \pm \text{P.E.}(r) = 0.97 \pm 0.014 = 0.956$ to 0.984

Example 9.5: Test the significance of correlation for $r = +0.4$ on (a) $n = 10$ and (b) $n = 100$.

Solution: Given, $n = 10$, $r = 0.4$. Then,

$$\text{P.E.}(r) = 0.6745\frac{1-r^2}{\sqrt{n}} = 0.6745\frac{1-(0.4)^2}{\sqrt{10}} = 0.18$$

Also $$\frac{r}{\text{P.E.}(r)} = \frac{0.4}{0.18} = 2.22 < 6$$

Since the ratio is less than 6, r is not significant.

When $r = 0.4$ and $n = 100$. Then,

$$\text{P.E.}(r) = 0.6745\frac{1-r^2}{\sqrt{n}} = 0.6745\frac{1-(0.4)^2}{\sqrt{100}} = 0.06$$

Also $$\frac{r}{\text{P.E.}(r)} = \frac{0.4}{0.06} = 6.67 > 6.$$

Since the ratio is more than 6, r is highly significant.

Example 9.6: Given the following information: $r = 0.8$, $\Sigma xy = 60$, $\sigma_y = 2.5$, $\Sigma x^2 = 90$. Find the number of items.

Solution: We know that

$$\sigma_y = \sqrt{\frac{\Sigma(y-\bar{y})^2}{n}} = \sqrt{\frac{\Sigma y^2}{n}}$$

$$2.5 = \sqrt{\frac{\Sigma y^2}{n}} \text{ or } 6.25 = \frac{\Sigma y^2}{n}, \text{ i.e. } \Sigma y^2 = 6.25n$$

Given, $r = 0.8$, $\Sigma xy = 60$, $\Sigma y^2 = 6.25n$, $\Sigma x^2 = 90$. Apply the formula,

$$r = \frac{\Sigma xy}{\sqrt{\Sigma x^2 \times \Sigma y^2}}$$

$$0.8 = \frac{60}{\sqrt{90 \times 6.25n}}$$

$$\sqrt{90 \times 6.25n} = \frac{60}{0.8}$$

Squaring both sides, we get

$$90 \times 6.25n = \frac{3600}{0.64} \text{ or } n = \frac{3600}{0.64 \times 90 \times 6.25} = \frac{3600}{360}, \text{ i.e. } n = 10$$

Example 9.7: The coefficient of correlation between two variables x and y is 0.4 and their covariance is 10. If variance of x series is 9, find variance of y.

Solution: Given, $r = 0.4$, $\text{Cov}(x, y) = 10$, and $\sigma_x^2 = 90$. To find variance, σ_y^2 of y, apply the formula:

$$r = \frac{\text{Cov}(x, y)}{\sigma_x \sigma_y}$$

$$0.4 = \frac{10}{3\sigma_y} \quad \text{or} \quad \sigma_y = \frac{10}{3 \times 0.4}, \quad \text{i.e.} \quad \sigma_y = 8.33$$

or $$\sigma_y^2 = (8.33)^2 = 69.44$$

9.5.4 The Coefficient of Determination

The squared value of the correlation coefficient r is called **coefficient of determination**, denoted as r^2, It always has a value between 0 and 1. By squaring the correlation coefficient we retain information about the strength of the relationship but we lose information about the direction. *This measure represents the proportion (or percentage) of the total variability of the dependent variable, y that is accounted for or explained by the independent variable, x.* The proportion (or percentage) of variation in y that x can explain determines more precisely the extent or strength of association between two variables x and y.

- The coefficient of correlation r has been grossly overrated and is used entirely too much. Its square, coefficient of determination r^2, is a much more useful measure of the linear covariation of two variables. The reader should develop the habit of squaring every correlation coefficient he finds cited or stated before coming to any conclusion about the extent of the linear relationship between two correlated variables. —Tuttle

Interpretation of Coefficient of Determination: Coefficient of determination is preferred for interpreting the strength of association between two variables becuase it is easier to interpret a percentage. Illustrates the meaning of the coefficient of determination:

- If $r^2 = 0$, then *no variation* in y can be *explained* by the variable x. It is shown in Fig 9.2(c) where x is of no value in predicting the value of y. There is *no association* between x and y.
- If $r^2 = 1$, then values of y are *completely explained* by x. There is *perfect association* between x and y.
- If $0 \le r^2 \le 1$, the degree of explained variation in y as a result of *variation in values of* x depends on the value of r^2. Value of r^2 closer to 0 shows low proportion of variation in y explained by x. On the other hand value of r^2 closer to 1 show that variable x can predict the actual value of the variable y.

For example, let correlation between variable x (height) and variable y (weight) be $r = 0.70$. Now the coefficient of determination $r^2 = 0.49$ or 49 per cent, implies that only 49 per cent of the variation in variable y (weight) can be accounted for in terms of variable x (height). The remaining 51 per cent of the variability may be due to other factors, say for instance, tendency to eat fatty foods.

It may be noted that even a relatively high correlation coefficient $r = 0.70$ accounts for less than 50 per cent of the variability. In this context, it is important to know that 'variability' refers to how values of variable y are scattered around its own mean value. That is, as in the above example, some people will be heavy, some average, some light. So we can account for 49 per cent of the total variability of weight (y) in terms of height (x) if $r = 0.70$. The greater the correlation coefficient, the greater the coefficient of determination, and the variability in dependent variable can be accounted for in terms of independent variable.

Example 9.8: The following table gives indices of industrial production and number of registered unemployed people (in lakh). Calculate the value of the correlation coefficient.

Year :	1991	1992	1993	1994	1995	1996	1997	1998
Index of Production :	100	102	104	107	105	112	103	99
Number Unemployed :	15	12	13	11	12	12	19	26

Solution: Calculations of Karl Pearson's correlation coefficient are shown in the table below:

$$\bar{x} = \frac{\sum x}{n} = \frac{832}{8} = 104; \quad \bar{y} = \frac{\sum y}{n} = \frac{120}{8} = 15$$

Year	*Production* x	$dx = (x-\bar{x})$	d_x^2	*Unemployed* y	$d_y^2 = (y-\bar{y})$	d_y^2	$d_x d_y$
1991	100	− 4	16	15	0	0	0
1992	102	− 2	4	12	− 3	9	+ 6
1993	104	0	0	13	− 2	4	0
1994	107	+ 3	9	11	− 4	16	− 12
1995	105	+ 1	1	12	− 3	9	− 3
1996	112	+ 8	64	12	− 3	9	− 24
1997	103	− 1	1	19	+ 4	16	− 4
1998	99	− 5	25	26	+ 11	121	− 55
Total	832	0	120	120	0	184	− 92

Applying the formula, $r = \dfrac{n\Sigma d_x d_y - (\Sigma d_x)(\Sigma d_y)}{\sqrt{n\Sigma d_x^2 - (\Sigma d_x)^2}\sqrt{n\Sigma d_y^2 - (\Sigma d_y)^2}} = \dfrac{8\times -92}{\sqrt{8\times 120}\sqrt{8\times 184}}$

$$= \frac{-92}{10.954\times 13.564} = \frac{-92}{148.580} = -0.619$$

Interpretation: Since coefficient of correlation $r = -0.619$ is moderately negative, it indicates that there is a moderately large inverse correlation between the two variables. Hence we conclude that as the production index increases, the number of unemployed decreases and vice versa.

Example 9.9: Calculate coefficient of correlation between x and y

	X Series	Y Series
No. of items	15	15
Arithmetic Means	25	18
Sum of squares of deviations from arithmetic mean	136	138

Summation of product of deviations of x and y series from their respective means is: 122.

[*Delhi Univ., BCom(P) 1989, 2005, 2006*]

Solution: Given, $n = 15$, $\bar{x} = 25$; $\bar{y} = 18$, $\Sigma(x-\bar{x})^2 = 136$; $\Sigma(y-\bar{y})^2 = 138$; $\Sigma(x-\bar{x})(y-\bar{y}) = 122$,

Let, $x = x - \bar{x}$, $y = y - \bar{y}$.. Then $\Sigma x^2 = 136$, $\Sigma y^2 = 138$, $\Sigma xy = 122$. Then

$$\text{Co-relation coefficient, } r = \frac{\Sigma xy}{\sqrt{\Sigma x^2 \times \Sigma y^2}} = \frac{122}{\sqrt{136\times 138}} = 0.89$$

Example 9.10: The total of the multiplication of deviation of x and y is 3044. Number of pairs of observations are 10, Total of deviations of x are −170, total of deviations of y are −20. Total of squares of deviations of x = 8288. Total of squares of deviations of y = 2264. Find out coefficient of correlation when the arbitrary means of x and y are 82 and 68, respectively. [*Delhi Univ., BCom (P), 2001*]

Solution: Given $n = 10$, $A = 82$, $B = 68$, $\Sigma(x - A) = -170$, $\Sigma(y - B) = -20$, $\Sigma(x - A)^2 = 82$
$\Sigma(y - B)^2 = 2264$, and $\Sigma(x - A)(y - B) = 3044$,

Let $d_x = x - A$ and $d_y = y - B$. Then
$\Sigma d_x = -170$, $\Sigma d_y = -20$, $\Sigma d_x^2 = 8288$, $\Sigma d_x^2 = 2264$, $\Sigma d_x d_y = 3044$

Apply the formula, $r = \dfrac{n\Sigma d_x d_y - \Sigma d_x \Sigma d_y}{\sqrt{n\Sigma d_x^2 - (\Sigma d_x)^2}\ \sqrt{n\Sigma d_y^2 - (\Sigma d_y)^2}}$

$$= \frac{10(3044) - (-170)(-20)}{\sqrt{10(8288) - (-170)^2}\ \sqrt{10(2264) - (-20)^2}}$$

$$= \frac{30440 - 3400}{\sqrt{53980}\ \sqrt{22240}} = 0.78$$

Example 9.11: The following table gives the distribution of items of production and also the relatively defective items among them, according to size groups. Find the correlation coefficient between size and defect in quality.

Size-group	:	15–16	16–17	17–18	18–19	19–20	20–21
No. of items	:	200	270	340	360	400	300
No. of defective items	:	150	162	170	180	180	114

[*Delhi Univ., BCom, 1999*]

Solution: Let group size be denoted by variable x and number of defective items by variable y. Calculations for Karl Pearson's correlation coefficient are shown below:

Size–Group	*Mid-value* m	$d_x = m - 17.5$	d_x^2	*Percent of Defective Items*	$d_y = y - 50$	d_y^2	$d_x d_y$
15–16	15.5	−2	4	75	25	625	−50
16–17	16.5	−1	1	60	10	100	−10
17–18	17.5	0	0	50	0	0	0
18–19	18.5	1	1	50	0	0	0
19–20	19.5	2	4	45	−5	25	−10
20–21	20.5	3	9	38	−12	144	−36
		3	19		18	894	−106

Substituting values in the formula of Karl Pearson's correlation coefficient r, we have

$$r = \frac{n\Sigma d_x d_y - (\Sigma d_x)(\Sigma d_y)}{\sqrt{n\Sigma d_x^2 - (\Sigma d_x)^2}\ \sqrt{n\Sigma d_y^2 - (\Sigma d_y)^2}}$$

$$= \frac{6 \times -106 - 3 \times 18}{\sqrt{6 \times 19 - (3)^2}\ \sqrt{6 \times 894 - (18)^2}} = \frac{-636 - 54}{\sqrt{105}\ \sqrt{5040}}$$

$$= -\frac{690}{727.46} = -0.949$$

Interpretation: Since value of r is negative, and is moderately close to -1, statistical association between x (size group) and y (percent of defective items) is moderate and negative, we conclude that when size of group increases, the number of defective items decreases and vice versa.

Example 9.12: The following data relate to age of employees and the number of days they reported sick in a month.

Employees :	1	2	3	4	5	6	7	8	9	10
Age :	30	32	35	40	48	50	52	55	57	61
Sick days :	1	0	2	5	2	4	6	5	7	8

Calculate Karl Pearson's coefficient of correlation and interpret it. *[Kashmir Univ., BCom, 1997]*

Solution: Let age and sick days be represented by variables x and y, respectively. Calculations for value of correlation coefficient are shown below:

Age x	$dx = x - \bar{x}$	d_x^2	*Sick days* y	$d_y = y - \bar{y}$	d_y^2	$d_x d_y$
30	−16	256	1	−3	9	48
32	−14	196	0	−4	16	56
35	−11	121	2	−2	4	22
40	−6	36	5	1	1	−6
48	2	4	2	−2	4	−4
50	4	16	4	0	0	0
52	6	36	6	2	4	12
55	9	81	5	1	1	9
57	11	121	7	3	9	33
61	15	225	8	4	16	60
460	0	1092	40	0	64	230

$$\bar{x} = \frac{\Sigma x}{n} = \frac{460}{10} = 46 \text{ and } \bar{y} = \frac{\Sigma y}{n} = \frac{40}{10} = 4$$

Substituting values in the formula of Karl Pearson's correlation coefficient r, we have

$$r = \frac{n\Sigma d_x d_y - (\Sigma d_x)(\Sigma d_y)}{\sqrt{n\Sigma d_x^2 - (\Sigma d_x)^2}\sqrt{n\Sigma d_y^2 - (\Sigma d_y)^2}} = \frac{10 \times 230}{\sqrt{10 \times 1092}\sqrt{10 \times 64}}$$

$$= \frac{230}{264.363} = 0.870$$

Interpretation: Since value of r is positive, therefore age of employees and number of sick days are positively correlated to a high degree. Hence we conclude that as the age of an employee increases, he is likely to go on sick leave more often than others.

Example 9.13: Find the coefficient of correlation between price and sales from the following data.

Price (Rs.) :	103	98	85	92	90	84	88	90	94	95
Sales (units) :	500	610	700	630	670	800	800	570	700	680

[Delhi Univ., BCom, 2006]

Solution: Let price and sales be represented by variables *x* and *y*, respectively. Calculations for value of correlation coefficient are shown below:

Price (x)	$d_x = x - 90$	*Sales (y)*	$d_y = y - 700$	d_x^2	d_y^2	$d_x d_y$
103	13	500	– 200	169	40,000	– 2,600
98	8	610	– 90	64	8,100	– 720
85	– 5	(700) ← *B*	0	25	0	0
92	2	630	– 70	4	4,900	– 140
(90) ← *A*	0	670	– 30	0	900	0
84	– 6	800	100	36	10,000	– 600
88	– 2	800	100	4	10,000	– 200
90	0	570	– 130	0	16,900	0
94	4	700	0	16	0	0
95	5	680	– 20	25	400	– 100
	19		– 340	343	91,200	– 4360

Applying the formula of Karl Pearson's correlation coefficient, *r*, we have

$$r = \frac{n\Sigma d_x d_y - \Sigma d_x \Sigma d_y}{\sqrt{n\Sigma d_x^2 - (\Sigma d_x)^2}\ \sqrt{n\Sigma d_y^2 - (\Sigma d_y)^2}}$$

$$= \frac{10(-4360) - 19\,(-340)}{\sqrt{10(343) - (19)^2}\ \sqrt{10(91200) - (-340)^2}}$$

$$= \frac{-43{,}600 + 6{,}460}{\sqrt{3430 - 361}\ \sqrt{9{,}12{,}000 - 1{,}15{,}600}} = \frac{-37{,}140}{49{,}430} = -\,0.751$$

Example 9.14: The following table gives the frequency, according to the marks, obtained by 67 students in an intelligence test. Measure the degree of relationship between age and marks:

	Age in years				*Total*
Test Marks	*18*	*19*	*20*	*21*	
200–250	4	4	2	1	11
250–300	3	5	4	2	14
300–350	2	6	8	5	21
350–400	1	4	6	10	21
Total	10	19	20	18	67

[*Allahabad Univ., BCom, 1999*]

Solution: Let age of students and marks obtained by them be represented by variables x and y, respectively. Calculations for correlation coefficient for this bivariate data is shown below:

y \ x	d_y \ d_x	Age in years *18* *−1*	 *19* *0*	 *20* *1*	 *21* *2*	*Total, f*	fd_y	fd_y^2	fd_xd_y
200–250	−1	(4) 4	(0) 4	(−2) 2	(−2) 1	11	−11	11	0
250–300	0	(0) 3	(0) 5	(0) 4	(0) 2	14	0	0	0
300–350	1	(−2) 2	(0) 6	(8) 8	(10) 5	21	21	21	16
350–400	2	(−2) 1	(0) 4	(12) 6	(40) 10	21	42	84	50
Total, f		10	19	20	18	$n = 67$	$\Sigma fd_y = 52$	$\Sigma fd_y^2 = 116$	$\Sigma fd_xd_y = 66$
fd_x		−10	0	20	36	$\Sigma fd_x = 46$			
fd_x^2		10	0	20	72	$\Sigma fd_x^2 = 102$			
fd_xd_y		0	0	18	48	$\Sigma fd_xd_y = 66$			

where $d_x = x - 19$, $d_y = (m - 275)/50$

Substituting values in the formula of Karl Pearson's correlation coefficient, we have

$$r = \frac{n\Sigma fd_xd_y - (\Sigma fd_x)(\Sigma fd_y)}{\sqrt{n\Sigma fd_x^2 - (\Sigma fd_x)^2}\sqrt{n\Sigma fd_y^2 - (\Sigma fd_y)^2}}$$

$$= \frac{67 \times 66 - 46 \times 52}{\sqrt{67 \times 102 - (46)^2}\sqrt{67 \times 116 - (52)^2}}$$

$$= \frac{4422 - 2392}{\sqrt{6834 - 2116}\sqrt{7772 - 2704}}$$

$$= \frac{2030}{\sqrt{4718}\sqrt{5068}} = \frac{2030}{68.688 \times 71.19} = 0.415$$

Interpretation: Since the value of r is positive, therefore age of students and marks obtained in an intelligence test are positively correlated to the extent of 0.415. Hence, we conclude that as the age of students increases, score of marks in intelligence test also increases.

Example 9.15: Calculate the coefficient of correlation from the following bivariate frequency distribution:

Sales Revenue (Rs. in lakh)	*Advertising Expenditure (Rs. in '000)*				*Total*
	5–10	*10–15*	*15–20*	*20–25*	
75–125	4	1	—	—	5
125–175	7	6	2	1	16
175–225	1	3	4	2	10
225–275	1	1	3	4	9
Total	13	11	9	7	40

Solution: Let advertising expenditure and sales revenue be represented by variables x and y, respectively. The calculations for correlation coefficient are shown below:

Revenue y	*Mid-value* (m)	$x\rightarrow$ / *Mid-value* (m) / d_x / d_y	*Advertising Expenditure* *5–10*	*10–15*	*15–20*	*20–25*	*Total,* f	fd_y	fd_y^2	fd_xd_y
		Mid-value (m)	*7.5*	*12.5*	*17.5*	*22.5*				
		d_x	*−1*	*0*	*1*	*2*				
75–125	100	−2	(8) 4	(0) 1	(0) —	(0) —	5	−10	20	8
125–175	150	−1	(7) 7	(0) 6	(−2) 2	(−2) 1	16	−16	16	3
175–225	200	0	(0) 1	(0) 3	(0) 4	(0) 2	10	0	0	0
225–275	250	1	(−1) 1	(0) 1	(3) 3	(8) 4	9	9	9	10
		Total, f	13	11	9	7	$n = 40$	$\Sigma d_y = -17$	$\Sigma d_y^2 = 45$	$\Sigma fd_xd_y = 21$
		fd_x	−13	0	9	14	$\Sigma fd_x = 10$			
		fd_x^2	13	0	9	28	$\Sigma fd_x^2 = 50$			
		fd_xd_y	14	0	1	6	$\Sigma fd_xd_y = 21$			

where, $d_x = (m - 12.5)/5$ and $d_y = (m - 200)/50$

Substituting values in the formula of Karl Pearson's correlation coefficient, we have

$$r = \frac{n\Sigma fd_x d_y - (\Sigma fd_x)(\Sigma fd_y)}{\sqrt{n\Sigma fd_x^2 - (\Sigma fd_x)^2}\sqrt{n\Sigma fd_y^2 - (\Sigma fd_y)^2}} = \frac{40\times 21 - 10\times -17}{\sqrt{40\times 50 - (10)^2}\sqrt{40\times 45 - (-17)^2}}$$

$$= \frac{840+170}{\sqrt{1900}\sqrt{1511}} = \frac{1010}{1694.373} = 0.596$$

Interpretation: Since the value of r is positive, advertising expenditure and sales revenue are positively correlated to the extent of 0.596. Hence we conclude that as expenditure on advertising increases, the sales revenue also increases.

Example 9.16: A computer, while calculating the correlation coefficient between two variables x and y from 25 pairs of observations, obtained the following results:

$$n = 25,\ \Sigma x = 125,\ \Sigma x^2 = 650 \text{ and } \Sigma y = 100,\ \Sigma y^2 = 460,\ \Sigma xy = 508$$

It was, however, discovered at the time of checking that he had copied down two pairs of observations as:

x	y
6	14
8	6

instead of

x	y
8	12
6	8

Obtain the correct value of correlation coefficient between x and y.

[*MD Univ., MCom, 1998*]

Solution: The corrected values for termed needed in the formula of Pearson's correlation coefficient are determined as follows:

$$\text{Correct } \Sigma x = 125 - (6 + 8 - 8 - 6) = 125$$

$$\text{Correct } \Sigma y = 100 - (14 + 6 - 12 - 8) = 100$$

$$\text{Correct } \Sigma x^2 = 650 - \{(6)^2 + (8)^2 - (8)^2 - (6)^2\}$$

$$= 650 - \{36 + 64 - 64 - 36\} = 650$$

$$\text{Correct } \Sigma y^2 = 460 - \{(14)^2 + (6)^2 - (12)^2 - (8)^2\}$$

$$= 460 - \{196 + 36 - 144 - 64\} = 436$$

$$\text{Correct } \Sigma xy = 508 - \{(6\times 14) + (8\times 6) - (8\times 12) - (6 \times 8)\}$$

$$= 508 - \{84 - 48 - 96 - 48\} = 520$$

Applying the formula

$$r = \frac{n\Sigma xy - (\Sigma x)(\Sigma y)}{\sqrt{n\Sigma x^2 - (\Sigma x)^2}\sqrt{n\Sigma y^2 - (\Sigma y)^2}} = \frac{25\times 520 - 125\times 100}{\sqrt{25\times 650 - (125)^2}\sqrt{25\times 436 - (100)^2}}$$

$$= \frac{13{,}000 - 12{,}500}{\sqrt{625}\sqrt{900}} = \frac{500}{25\times 30} = 0.667$$

Thus, the correct value of correlation coefficient between x and y is 0.667.

Example 9.17: In order to find the correlation coefficient between two variables x and y from 12 pairs of observations, the following calculations were made:

$$\Sigma x = 30, \quad \Sigma x^2 = 670, \quad \Sigma y = 5, \quad \Sigma y^2 = 285, \quad \Sigma xy = 344$$

On subsequent verification, it was discovered that the pair (x = 11, y = 4) was copied wrongly, the correct values being x = 10, y = 14. After making necessary correction, find the correlation coefficient.

Solution: The corrected value for the pair (x, y) required in the formula of correlation coefficient is calculated as follows:

$$\text{Correct } \Sigma x = 30 - \text{wrong item} + \text{correct item} = 30 - 11 + 10 = 29$$

$$\text{Correct } \Sigma y = 5 - 4 + 14 = 15$$

$$\text{Correct } \Sigma x^2 = 670 - (11)^2 + (10)^2 = 670 - 121 + 100 = 649$$

$$\text{Correct } \Sigma y^2 = 285 - (4)^2 + (14)^2 = 285 - 16 + 196 = 465$$

$$\text{Correct } \Sigma xy = 344 - (11)(4) + (10)(14) = 344 - 44 + 140 = 440$$

Applying the formula,

$$r = \frac{n\Sigma xy - \Sigma x \Sigma y}{\sqrt{n\Sigma x^2 - (\Sigma x)^2}\sqrt{n\Sigma y^2 - (\Sigma y)^2}} = \frac{12(440) - (29)(15)}{\sqrt{12(649) - (29)^2}\sqrt{12(465) - (15)^2}}$$

$$= \frac{4845}{83.35 \times 73.18} = \frac{4845}{6099.5} = 0.794$$

Self-Practice Problems 9A

9.1 Making use of the data summarized below, calculate the coefficient of correlation.

Case	x_1	x_2	*Case*	x_1	x_2
A	10	9	E	12	11
B	6	4	F	13	13
C	9	6	G	11	8
D	10	9	H	9	4

9.2 Find the correlation coefficient by Karl Pearson's method between x and y and interpret its value.

x : 57 42 40 33 42 45 42 44 40 56 44 43
y : 10 60 30 41 29 27 27 19 18 19 31 29

9.3 Calculate the coefficient of correlation between x and y from the following data and calculate the probable errors. Assume 69 and 112 as the mean value for x and y respectively.

x :	78	89	99	60	50	79	68	61
y :	125	137	156	112	107	136	123	108

9.4 Calculate Karl Pearson's coefficient of correlation between age and playing habits from the data given below. Also calculate the probable error and comment on the value:

Age :	20	21	22	23	24	25
No. of students :	500	400	300	240	200	160
Regular players :	400	300	180	96	60	24

9.5 Find the coefficient of correlation between age and the sum assured (in '000 Rs.) from the following table:

Age Group (years)	*Sum Assured (in Rs.)*				
	10	*20*	*30*	*40*	*50*
20–30	4	6	3	7	1
30–40	2	8	15	7	1
40–50	3	9	12	6	2
50–60	8	4	2	—	—

9.6 Family income and its percentage spent on food in the case of one hundred families gave the following bivariate frequency distribution. Calculate the coefficient of correlation and interpret its value.

Food Expenditure (in percent)	*Monthly Family Income (Rs.)*				
	2000–3000	*3000–4000*	*4000–5000*	*5000–6000*	*6000–7000*
10–15	—	—	—	3	7
15–20	—	4	9	4	3
20–25	7	6	12	5	—
25–30	3	10	19	8	—

9.7 With the following data in 6 cities, calculate Pearson's coefficient of correlation between the density of population and death rate:

City	*Area in Kilometres*	*Population (in '000)*	*No. of Deaths*
A	150	30	300
B	180	90	1440
C	100	40	560
D	60	42	840
E	120	72	1224
F	80	24	312

[*Sukhadia Univ., BCom, 1998*]

9.8 The coefficient of correlation between two variables x and y is 0.3. The covariance is 9. The variance of x is 16. Find the standard deviation of y series.

Hints and Answers

9.1 $\bar{x}_1 = 80/8 = 10,\ \bar{x}_2 = 64/8 = 8;$

$$r = \frac{43}{\sqrt{32}\,\sqrt{72}} = 0.896$$

9.2 $r = -0.554$ **9.3** $r = 0.997$

9.3 $r = 0.014$ **9.5** $r = 0.780$

9.4 $r = 0.005$ **9.5** $r = -0.256$

9.6 $r = -0.438$ **9.7** $r = 0.988$

9.8 Given $\sigma_x = \sqrt{16} = 4;\quad r = \dfrac{\text{Cov}(x, y)}{\sigma_x \sigma_y}$

or $0.3 = \dfrac{9}{4\sigma_y}$ or $\sigma_y = 7.5$.

9.5.5 Spearman's Rank Correlation Coefficient

This method of finding the correlation coefficient between two variables was developed by the British psychologist Charles Edward Spearman in 1904. This method is applied to measure the association between two variables when only *ordinal* (*or rank*) *data* are available. In other words, this method is applied in a situation in which quantitative measure of certain qualitative factors such as judgement, brands personalities, TV programmes, leadership, colour, taste, cannot be fixed, but individual observations can be arranged in a definite order (also called rank). The ranking is decided by using a set of ordinal rank numbers, with 1 for the individual observation ranked first either in terms of quantity or quality; and n for the individual observation ranked last in a group of n pairs of observations. Mathematically, Spearman's rank correlation coefficient is defined as:

$$R = 1 - \frac{6\Sigma d^2}{n(n^2-1)}$$

where R = rank correlation coefficient

R_1 = rank of observations with respect to first variable

R_2 = rank of observations with respect to second variable

$d = R_1 - R_2$, difference in a pair of ranks

n = number of paired observations or individuals being ranked

The number '6' is placed in the formula as a scaling device, it ensures that the possible range of R is from – 1 to 1. While using this method we may come across three types of cases.

Advantages and Disadvantages of Spearman's Correlation Coefficient Method

Advantages

(i) This method is easy to understand and its application is simpler than Pearson's method.

(ii) This method is useful for correlation analysis when variables are expressed in qualitative terms like beauty, intelligence, honesty, efficiency, and so on.

(iii) This method is appropriate to measure the association between two variables if the data type is at least ordinal scaled (ranked)

(iv) The sample data of values of two variables is converted into ranks either in ascending order or decending order for calculating degree of correlation between two variables.

Disadvantages

(i) Values of both variables are assumed to be normally distributed and describing a linear relationship rather than non-linear relationship.

(ii) A large computational time is required when number of pairs of values of two variables exceed 30.

(iii) This method cannot be applied to measure the association between two variable grouped data.

Case I: When Ranks are Given

When observations in a data set are already arranged in a particular order (rank), take the differences in pairs of observations to determine d. Square these differences and obtain the total Σd^2. Apply, formula (10-4) to calculate correlation coefficient.

Example 9.18: The coefficient of rank correlation between debenture prices and share prices is found to be 0.143. If the sum of the squares of the differences in ranks is given to be 48, find the values of n.

Solution: The formula for Spearman's correlation coefficient is as follows:

$$R = 1 - \frac{6\Sigma d^2}{n(n^2 - 1)}$$

Given, R = 0.143, Σd^2 = 48 and n=7. Substituting values in the formula, we get

$$0.143 = 1 - \frac{6 \times 48}{n(n^2 - 1)} = 1 - \frac{288}{n^3 - n}$$

$$0.143\ (n^3 - n) = (n^3 - n) - 288$$

$$n^3 - n - 336 = 0 \quad \text{or} \quad (n - 7)\ (n^2 + 7n + 48) = 0$$

This implies that either $n - 7 = 0$, that is, $n = 7$ or $n^2 + 7n + 48 = 0$. But $n^2 + 7n + 48 = 0$ on simplification gives undesirable value of n because its discriminant $b^2 - 4ac$ is negative. Hence $n = 7$.

Example 9.19: When is rank correlation coefficient preferred to Karl Pearson's method? In a bivariate sample, the sum of squares of differences between the ranks of observed values of two variables is 231 and the correlation coefficient between them is –0.4. Find the number of pairs.

[*Delhi Univ., BCom, 2006*]

Solution: The association between two attributes such as Intelligence and Beauty, can be arranged in a serial order but the quantitative measurement of their value is difficult and cannot be calculated by the Pearson's coefficient of correlation because definite values cannot be assigned to such attributes.

Given, $\Sigma D^2 = 231$, $r = -0.4$.

Rank co-relation coefficient, $R = 1 - \dfrac{6\Sigma D^2}{n^3 - n}$, i.e. $-0.4 = 1 - \dfrac{6 \times 231}{n^3 - n}$

or
$$1.4\,(n^3 - n) = 6$$
$$n^3 - n = \frac{6 \times 231}{1.4} = 990$$
$$n^3 - n - 990 = 0$$
$$n^3 - n - 1000 + 10 = 0$$
$$n^3 - 10^3 - (n - 10) = 0$$
$$(n - 10)\,(n^2 - 10n - 99) = 0$$

That is, either $n = 10$ or $n^2 - 10n - 99 = 0$ which gives imaginary value of n, so $n = 10$.

Example 9.20: In a bivariate distribution, spearman's coefficient of correlation is –0.25. If the sum of the squares of differences of various ranks is 150. Find out the number of pairs of items.

[*Delhi, Univ., BCom (Pass), 2004*]

Solution: Given, $R = -0.25$, $\Sigma D^2 = 150$. We know that

$$R = 1 - \frac{6\Sigma D^2}{n^3 - n}$$

$$-0.25 = 1 - \frac{6(150)}{n^3 - n}$$

$$n^3 - n = \frac{900}{1.25} = 720$$

$$n^3 - n - 720 = 0$$
$$n^3 - n - 729 + 9 = 0$$
$$(n - 9)\,n^2 + 9n\,(n - 9) + 80\,(n - 9) = 0$$

This implies that either $n - 9 = 0$ or $n^2 + 9n + 80 = 0$. If $n - 9 = 0$, $n = 0$

But $n^2 + 9n + 80 = 0$ gives imaginary values of n. Hence $n = 9$

Example 9.21: The coefficient of rank correlation of the marks obtained by 10 students in Statistics and Accountancy was found to be 0.2. It was later discovered that the difference in ranks in the two subjects obtained by one of the students was wrongly taken as 9 instead of 7. Find the correct value of coefficient of rank correlation.

Solution: Given the incorrect rank correlation coefficient, $R = 0.2$. Applying the formula:

$$R = 1 - \frac{6\Sigma d^2}{n(n^2 - 1)}$$

$$0.2 = 1 - \frac{6\Sigma d^2}{10(10^2 - 1)} = 1 - \frac{6\Sigma d^2}{10 \times 99}$$

or
$$0.2 - 1.0 = -\frac{6\Sigma d^2}{990}$$

or $$-0.8 = -\frac{6\Sigma d^2}{990} \quad \text{or} \quad \Sigma d^2 = \frac{0.8 \times 990}{6} = 132$$

Corrected $\Sigma d^2 = 132 - (9)^2 + (7)^2 = 132 - 81 + 49 = 100$. Thus, correct value of

$$R = 1 - \frac{6\,(\text{Correct } \Sigma d^2)}{10\,(10^2 - 1)} = 1 - \frac{6 \times 100}{10 \times 99} = 1 - \frac{20}{33} = \frac{13}{33} = 0.39$$

Example 9.22: The ranks of 15 students in two subjects A and B, are given below. The two numbers within brackets denote the ranks of a student in A and B subjects respectively.

(1, 10), (2, 7), (3, 2), (4, 6), (5, 4), (6, 8), (7, 3), (8, 1),
(9, 11), (10, 15), (11, 9), (12, 5), (13, 14), (14, 12), (15, 13)

Find Spearman's rank correlation coefficient.

Solution: Since ranks of students with respect to their performance in two subjects are given, calculations for rank correlation coefficient are shown below:

Rank in A R_1	*Rank in B* R_2	*Difference* $d = R_1 - R_2$	d^2
1	10	−9	81
2	7	−5	25
3	2	1	1
4	6	−2	4
5	4	1	1
6	8	−2	4
7	3	4	16
8	1	7	49
9	11	−2	4
10	15	−5	25
11	9	2	4
12	5	7	49
13	14	−1	1
14	12	2	4
15	13	2	4
			$\Sigma d^2 = 272$

Apply the formula, $$R = 1 - \frac{6\Sigma d^2}{n^3 - n} = 1 - \frac{6 \times 272}{15\{(15)^2 - 1\}}$$

$$= 1 - \frac{1632}{3360} = 1 - 0.4857 = 0.5143$$

The result shows a moderate degree positive correlation between performance of students in two subjects.

Example 9.23: An office has 12 clerks. The long-serving clerks feel that they should have a seniority increment based on length of service built into their salary structure. An assessment of their efficiency by their departmental manager and the personnel department produces a ranking of efficiency. This is shown below together with a ranking of their length of service.

Ranking according to length of service :	1	2	3	4	5	6	7	8	9	10	11	12
Ranking according to efficiency :	2	3	5	1	9	10	11	12	8	7	6	4

Do the data support the clerks' claim for seniority increment?

Solution: Since ranks are already given, calculations for rank correlation coefficient are shown below:

Rank According to Length of Service R_1	*Rank According to Efficiency* R_2	*Difference* $d = R_1 - R_2$	d^2
1	2	− 1	1
2	3	− 1	1
3	5	− 2	4
4	1	3	9
5	9	− 4	16
6	10	− 4	16
7	11	− 4	16
8	12	− 4	16
9	8	1	1
10	7	3	9
11	6	5	25
12	4	8	64
			$\Sigma d^2 = 178$

Applying the formula, $R = 1 - \dfrac{6\Sigma d^2}{n(n^2-1)}$

$$= 1 - \frac{6\times 178}{12(144-1)} = 1 - \frac{1068}{1716} = 0.378$$

The result shows a low degree positive correlation between length of service and efficiency, the claim of the clerks for a seniority increment based on length of service is not justified.

Example 9.24: Ten competitors in a beauty contest are ranked by three judges in the following order:

Judge 1:	1	6	5	10	3	2	4	9	7	8
Judge 2:	3	5	8	4	7	10	2	1	6	9
Judge 3:	6	4	9	8	1	2	3	10	5	7

Use the rank correlation coefficient to determine which pair of judges has the nearest approach to common tastes in beauty.

Solution: The pair of judges who have the nearest approach to common taste in beauty can be obtained in ${}^3C_2 = 3$ ways as follows:

(i) Judge 1 and judge 2
(ii) Judge 2 and judge 3
(iii) Judge 3 and judge 1

Calculations for comparing their ranking are shown below:

Judge 1 R_1	*Judge 2* R_2	*Judge 3* R_3	$d^2 = (R_1 - R_2)^2$	$d^2 = (R_2 - R_3)^2$	$d^2 = (R_3 - R_1)^2$
1	3	6	4	9	25
6	5	4	1	1	4
5	8	9	9	1	16
10	4	8	36	16	4
3	7	1	16	36	4
2	10	2	64	64	0
4	2	3	4	1	1
9	1	10	64	81	1
7	6	5	1	1	4
8	9	7	1	4	1
			$\Sigma d^2 = 200$	$\Sigma d^2 = 214$	$\Sigma d^2 = 60$

Applying the formula

$$R_{12} = 1 - \frac{6\Sigma d^2}{n(n^2-1)} = 1 - \frac{6 \times 200}{10(100-1)} = 1 - \frac{1200}{990} = -0.212$$

$$R_{23} = 1 - \frac{6\Sigma d^2}{n(n^2-1)} = 1 - \frac{6 \times 214}{10(100-1)} = 1 - \frac{1284}{990} = -0.297$$

$$R_{13} = 1 - \frac{6\Sigma d^2}{n(n^2-1)} = 1 - \frac{6 \times 60}{10(100-1)} = 1 - \frac{360}{990} = 0.636$$

Since the correlation coefficient $R_{13} = 0.636$ is largest, the judges 1 and 3 have nearest approach to common tastes in beauty.

Case 2: When Ranks are not Given

When pairs of observations in the data set are not ranked as in Case 1, the ranks are assigned by taking either the highest value or the lowest value as 1 for both the variable's values.

Example 9.25: Quotations of index numbers of security prices of a certain joint stock company are given below:

Year	*Debenture Price*	*Share Price*
1	97.8	73.2
2	99.2	85.8
3	98.8	78.9
4	98.3	75.8
5	98.4	77.2
6	96.7	87.2
7	97.1	83.8

Using the rank correlation method, determine the relationship between debenture prices and share prices. [*Calicut Univ., BCom, 1997*]

Solution: Let us start ranking from the lowest value for both the variables, as shown below:

Debenture Price (x)	*Rank*	*Share Price* (y)	*Rank*	*Difference* $d = R_1 - R_2$	$d^2 = (R_1 - R_2)^2$
97.8	3	73.2	1	2	4
99.2	7	85.8	6	1	1
98.8	6	78.9	4	2	4
98.3	4	75.8	2	2	4
98.4	5	77.2	3	2	4
96.7	1	87.2	7	– 6	36
97.1	2	83.8	5	– 3	9
					$\Sigma d^2 = 62$

Applying the formula $R = 1 - \dfrac{6\,\Sigma d^2}{n^3 - n} = 1 - \dfrac{6 \times 62}{(7)^3 - 7}$

$$= 1 - \frac{372}{336} = 1 - 0.107 = -0.107$$

The result shows a low degree of negative correlation between the debenture prices and share prices of a certain joint stock company.

Example 9.26 An economist wanted to find out if there was any relationship between the unemployment rate in a country and its inflation rate. Data gathered from 7 countries for the year 2004 are given below:

Country	*Unemployment Rate (Percent)*	*Inflation Rate (Per cent)*
A	4.0	3.2
B	8.5	8.2
C	5.5	9.4
D	0.8	5.1
E	7.3	10.1
F	5.8	7.8
G	2.1	4.7

Find the degree of linear association between a country's unemployment rate and its level of inflation.

Solution: Let us start ranking from the lowest value for both the variables as shown below:

Unemployment Rate (x)	*Rank* R_1	*Inflation Rate* (y)	*Rank* R_2	*Difference* $d = R_1 - R_2$	$d^2 = (R_1 - R_2)^2$
4.0	3	3.2	1	2	4
8.5	7	8.2	5	2	4
5.5	4	9.4	6	– 2	4
0.8	1	5.1	3	– 2	4
7.3	6	10.1	7	– 1	1
5.8	5	7.8	4	1	1
2.1	2	4.7	2	0	0
					$\Sigma d^2 = 18$

Applying the formula,

$$R = 1-\frac{6\Sigma d^2}{n^3-n} = 1-\frac{6\times 18}{(7)^3-(7)} = 1-\frac{108}{336} = 0.678$$

The result shows a moderately high degree of positive correlation between unemployment rate and inflation rate of seven countries.

Case 3: When Ranks are Equal

While ranking observations in the data set by taking either the highest value or lowest value as rank 1, we may come across a situation of more than one observations being of equal size. In such a case the rank to be assigned to individual observations is an average of the ranks which these individual observations would have got had they differed from each other. For example, if two observations are ranked equal at third place, then the average rank of (3 + 4)/2 = 3.5 is assigned to these two observations. Similarly, if three observations are ranked equal at third place, then the average rank of (3 + 4 + 5)/3 = 4 is assigned to these three observations.

While equal ranks are assigned to a few observations in the data set, an adjustment is made in the Spearman rank correlation coefficient formula as given below:

$$R = 1 - \frac{6\left\{\Sigma d^2 + \frac{1}{12}\left(m_1^3 - m_1\right) + \frac{1}{12}\left(m_2^3 - m_2\right) + \ldots\right\}}{n(n^2-1)}$$

where m_i $(i = 1, 2, 3, \ldots)$ stands for the number of times an observation is repeated in the data set for both variables.

Example 9.27: Find the rank correlation coefficient from the following marks awarded by the examiners in statistics:

Examiner	*Marks Awarded by Examiner A*	*Marks Awarded by Examiner B*	*Marks Awarded by Examiner C*
1	24	37	30
2	29	35	28
3	19	16	20
4	14	26	25
5	30	23	25
6	19	27	30
7	27	19	20
8	30	20	24
9	20	16	22
10	28	11	29
11	11	21	15

[*Delhi Univ., BCom, 2005*]

Solution: Since ranks are not given, calculations for rank correlations coefficient are shown below:

Examiner	*Marks Awarded by Examiner A*	*Rank*	*Marks Awarded by Examiner B*	*Rank*	*Marks Awarded by Examiner C*	*Rank*	d_{AB}	d_{AC}	d_{BC}	d^2_{AB}	d^2_{AC}	d^2_{BC}
1	24	6	37	1	30	1.5	5	4.5	− 0.5	25	20.25	0.25
2	29	3	35	2	28	4	1	−1	−2	1	1	4
3	19	8.5	16	9.5	20	9.5	−1	−1	0	1	1	0
4	14	10	26	4	25	5.5	6	4.5	−1.5	36	20.25	2.25
5	30	1.5	23	5	25	5.5	−3.5	− 4	−0.5	12.25	16	0.25
6	19	8.5	27	3	30	1.5	5.5	7	1.5	30.25	49	2.25
7	27	5	19	8	20	9.5	− 3	−4.5	−1.5	9	20.25	2.25
8	30	1.5	20	7	24	7	−5.5	−5.5	0	30.25	30.25	0
9	20	7	16	9.5	22	8	−2.5	−1	1.5	6.25	1	2.25
10	28	4	11	11	29	3	−7	1	8	49	1	64
11	11	11	21	6	15	11	5	0	−5	25	0	25
										225	160	102.5

Applying the formulae:

$$R_{AB} = 1 - \frac{6\left[\Sigma d^2_{AB} + \frac{1}{12}(m_1^3 - m_1) + \frac{1}{12}(m_2^3 - m_2)\right]}{n(n^2 - 1)}$$

$$= 1 - \frac{6\left[225 + \frac{1}{12}(2^3 - 2) + \frac{1}{12}(2^3 - 2)\right]}{11 \times 120} = 1 - \frac{6 \times 226}{11 \times 120} = \frac{1356}{1320} = -0.027$$

$$R_{AC} = 1 - \frac{6\left[160 + \frac{1}{12}(2^3 - 2) + \frac{1}{12}(2^3 - 2) + 3\left\{\frac{1}{12}(2^3 - 2)\right\}\right]}{11 \times 120}$$

$$= 1 - \frac{6(160 + 2.5)}{11 \times 120} = 1 - \frac{975}{1320} = 0.261$$

Example 9.28: A financial analyst wanted to find out whether inventory turnover influences any company's earnings per share (in per cent). A random sample of 7 companies listed in a stock exchange were selected and the following data was recorded for each:

Company	*Inventory Turnover (Number of Times)*	*Earnings per Share (Per cent)*
A	4	11
B	5	9
C	7	13
D	8	7
E	6	13
F	3	8
G	5	8

Find the strength of association between inventory turnover and earnings per share. Interpret this finding.

Solution: Let us start ranking from lowest value forboth the variables. Since there are tied ranks, the sum of the tied ranks is averaged and assigned to each of the tied observations as shown below.

Inventory Turnover (x)	*Rank* R_1	*Earnings Per Share (y)*	*Rank* R_2	*Difference* $d = R_1 - R_2$	$d^2 = (R_1 - R_2)^2$
4	2	11	5	– 3.0	9.00
5	3.5	9	4	– 0.5	0.25
7	6	13	6.5	0.5	0.25
8	7	7	1	6.0	36.00
6	5	13	6.5	– 1.5	2.25
3	1	8	2.5	– 1.5	2.25
5	3.5	8	2.5	1.0	1.00
					$\Sigma d^2 = 51$

If may be noted that a value 5 of variable x is repeated twice (m_1 = 2) and values 8 and 13 of variable y is also reperated twice, so m_2 = 2 and m_3 = 2. Applying the formula:

$$R = 1 - \frac{6\left\{\Sigma d^2 + \frac{1}{12}(m_1^3 - m_1) + \frac{1}{12}(m_2^3 - m_2) + \frac{1}{12}(m_3^3 - m_3)\right\}}{n(n^2 - 1)}$$

$$= 1 - \frac{6\left\{51 + \frac{1}{12}(2^3 - 2) + \frac{1}{12}(2^3 - 2) + \frac{1}{12}(2^3 - 2)\right\}}{7(49 - 1)}$$

$$= 1 - \frac{6\{51 + 0.5 + 0.5 + 0.5\}}{336} = 1 - 0.9375 = 0.0625$$

The result shows a very week positive association between inventory turnover and earnings per share.

Example 9.29: Obtain the rank correlation coefficient between the variables x and y from the following pairs of observed values:

x :	50	55	65	50	55	60	50	65	70	75
y :	110	110	115	125	140	115	130	120	115	160

[*Mangalore Univ., BCom, 1997*]

Solution: Let us start ranking from lowest value for both the variables. Moreover, certain observations in both sets of data are repeated, the ranking is done in accordance with suitable average value as shown below.

Variable x	*Rank* R_1	*Variable* y	*Rank* R_2	*Difference* $d = R_1 - R_2$	$d^2 = (R_1 - R_2)^2$
50	2	110	1.5	0.5	0.25
55	4.5	110	1.5	3.0	9.00
65	7.5	115	4	3.5	12.25
50	2	125	7	– 5.0	25.00
55	4.5	140	9	– 4.5	20.25
60	6	115	4	2.0	4.00
50	2	130	8	– 6.0	36.00
65	7.5	120	6	1.5	2.25
70	9	115	4	5.0	25.00
75	10	160	10	0.0	00.00
					$\Sigma d^2 = 134.00$

It may be noted that for variable x, 50 is repeated thrice ($m_1 = 3$), 55 is repeated twice ($m_2 = 2$), and 65 is repeated twice ($m_3 = 2$). Also for variable y, 110 is repeated twice ($m_4 = 2$) and 115 thrice ($m_5 = 3$). Applying the formula:

$$R = 1 - \frac{6\left\{\Sigma d^2 + \frac{1}{12}(m_1^3 - m_1) + \frac{1}{12}(m_2^3 - m_2) + \frac{1}{12}(m_3^3 - m_3) + \frac{1}{12}(m_4^3 - m_4) + \frac{1}{12}(m_5^3 - m_5)\right\}}{n(n^2 - 1)}$$

$$= 1 - \frac{6\left\{134 + \frac{1}{12}(3^3 - 3) + \frac{1}{12}(2^3 - 2) + \frac{1}{12}(2^3 - 2) + \frac{1}{12}(2^3 - 2) + \frac{1}{12}(3^3 - 3)\right\}}{10(100 - 1)}$$

$$= 1 - \frac{6\,[134 + 2 + 0.5 + 0.5 + 0.5 + 2]}{990} = 1 - \frac{6 \times 139.5}{990} = 1 - \frac{837}{990}$$

$$= 1 - 0.845 = 0.155$$

The result shows a weak positive association between variables x and y.

Self-Practice Problems 9B

9.9 The coefficient of rank correlation of the marks obtained by 10 students in statistics and accountancy was found to be 0.2. It was later discovered that the difference in ranks in two subjects obtained by one of the students was wrongly taken as 9 instead of 7. Find the correct coefficient of rank correlation.

[*Delhi Univ., BCom, 1996*]

9.10 The ranking of 10 students in accordance with their performance in two subjects A and B are as follows:

A:	6	5	3	10	2	4	9	7	8	1
B:	3	8	4	9	1	6	10	7	5	2

Calculate the rank correlation coefficient and comment on its value.

9.11 Calculate Spearman's coefficient of correlation between marks assigned to ten students by judges x and y in a certain competitive test as shown below:

Student	*Marks by Judge x*	*Marks by Judge y*
1	52	65
2	53	68
3	42	43
4	60	38
5	45	77
6	41	48
7	37	35
8	38	30
9	25	25
10	27	50

9.12 An examination of eight applicants for a clerical post was taken by a firm. From the marks obtained by the applicants in the accountancy and statistics papers, compute the rank correlation coefficient.

Applicant :	A	B	C	D	E	F	G	H
Marks in accountancy:	15	20	28	12	40	60	20	80
Marks in statistics :	40	30	50	30	20	10	30	60

9.13 Seven methods of imparting business education were ranked by the MBA students of two universities as follows:

Method of Teaching :	1	2	3	4	5	6	7
Rank by students of Univ. A :	2	1	5	3	4	7	6
Rank by students of Univ. B :	1	3	2	4	7	5	6

Calculate the rank correlation coefficient and comment on its value.

9.14 An investigator collected the following data with respect to the socio-economic status and severity of respiratory illness.

Patient	:	1	2	3	4	5	6	7	8
Socio-economic status (rank)	:	6	7	2	3	5	4	1	8
Severity of illness rank)	:	5	8	4	3	7	1	2	6

Calculate the rank correlation coefficient and comment on its value.

9.15 You are given the following data of marks obtained by 11 students in statistics in two tests, one before and other after special coaching:

First Test (Before coaching)	*Second Test (After coaching)*
23	24
20	19
19	22
21	18
18	20
20	22
18	20
20	22
18	20
17	20
23	23
16	20
19	17

Do the marks indicate that the special coaching has benefited the students?

[*Delhi Univ., MCom, 1989*]

9.16 Two departmental managers ranked a few trainees according to their perceived abilities. The ranking are given below:

Trainee	:	A	B	C	D	E	F	G	H	I	J
Manager A	:	1	9	6	2	5	8	7	3	10	4
Manager B	:	3	10	8	1	7	5	6	2	9	4

Calculate an appropriate correlation coefficient to measure the consistency in the ranking.

9.17 In an office some keyboard operators, who were already ranked on their speed, were also ranked on accuracy by their supervisor. The results were as follows:

Operator	:	A	B	C	D	E	F	G	H	I	J
Speed	:	1	2	3	4	5	6	7	8	9	10
Accuracy	:	7	9	3	4	1	6	8	2	10	5

Calculate the appropriate correlation coefficient between speed and accuracy.

9.18 The personnel department is interested in comparing the ratings of job applicants when measured by a variety of standard tests. The ratings of 9 applicants on interviews and standard psychological test are shown below:

Applicant	:	A	B	C	D	E	F	G	H	I
Interview	:	5	2	9	4	3	6	1	8	7
Standard test	:	8	1	7	5	3	4	2	9	6

Calculate Spearman's rank correlation coefficient and comment on its value.

Hints and Answers

9.9 Given $R = 0.2, n = 10; R = 1 - \frac{6\Sigma\, d^2}{n(n^2-1)}$ or

$$0.2 = 1 - \frac{6\Sigma\, d^2}{10(100-1)} \text{ or } \Sigma d^2 = 100$$

Correct value of $R = 1 - \frac{6 \times 100}{10 \times 99} = 0.394$

9.10 $R = 1 - \frac{6\Sigma d^2}{n(n^2-1)} = 1 - \frac{6 \times 36}{10(100-1)} = 0.782$

9.11 $R = 1 - \frac{6\Sigma d^2}{n(n^2-1)} = 1 - \frac{6 \times 76}{10(100-1)} = 0.539$

9.12

$$R = 1 - \frac{6\left\{\Sigma d^2 + \frac{1}{12}\left(m_1^3 - m_1\right) + \frac{1}{12}\left(m_2^3 - m_2\right)\right\}}{n(n^2-1)}$$

$$= 1 - \frac{6\left\{81.5 + \frac{1}{12}(2^3 - 2) + \frac{1}{12}(3^3 - 3)\right\}}{8(64-1)} = 0$$

9.13 R = 0.50 **9.14** R = 0.477

9.15 R = 0.71 **9.16** R = 0.842

9.17 R = 0.006 **9.18** R = 0.817

Conceptual Questions

1. What is the meaning of the coefficient of correlation?
2. Explain the meaning and significance of the term correlation.
3. What is meant by 'correlation'? Distinguish between positive, negative, and zero correlation.
4. What are the numerical limits of r^2 and r? What does it mean when r equals one? zero? minus one?
5. What is correlation? Clearly explain its role with suitable illustration from simple business problems.
6. What is the relationship between the coefficient of determination and the coefficient of correlation? How is the coefficient of determination interpreted?
7. What is coefficient of rank correlation? Bring out its usefulness. How does this coefficient differ from the coefficient of correlation?
8. What is Spearman's rank correlation coefficient? How does it differ from Karl Pearson's coefficient of correlation?
9. (a) What is a scatter diagram? How do you interpret a scatter diagram?
   (b) What is a scatter diagram? How does it help in studying the correlation between two variables, in respect of both its direction and degree?
10. Define correlation coefficient 'r' and give its limitations. What interpretation would you give if told that the correlation between the number of truck accidents per year and the age of the driver is (–) 0.60 if only drivers with at least one accident are considered?

Formulae Used

1. Karl Pearson's correlation coefficient

$$r = \frac{\text{Covariance between } x \text{ and } y}{\sigma_x \, \sigma_y}$$

- Deviation from actual mean

$$r = \frac{\Sigma(x-\bar{x})(y-\bar{y})}{\sqrt{\Sigma(x-\bar{x})^2}\,\sqrt{\Sigma(y-\bar{y})^2}}$$

- Deviation from assumed mean

$$r = \frac{n\Sigma d_x\, d_y - (\Sigma d_x)(\Sigma d_y)}{\sqrt{n\Sigma d_x^2 - (\Sigma d_x)^2}\,\sqrt{n\Sigma d_y^2 - (\Sigma d_y)^2}}$$

$d_x = x - A$, $d_y = y - B$

A, B = constants

- Bivariate frequency distribution

$$r = \frac{n\Sigma fd_x d_y - (\Sigma fd_x)(\Sigma fd_y)}{\sqrt{n\Sigma fd_x^2 - (\Sigma fd_x)^2}\,\sqrt{n\Sigma fd_y^2 - (\Sigma fd_y)^2}}$$

- Using actual values of x and y

$$r = \frac{n\Sigma xy - (\Sigma x)(\Sigma y)}{\sqrt{n\Sigma x^2 - (\Sigma x)^2}\,\sqrt{n\Sigma y^2 - (\Sigma y)^2}}$$

2. Standard error of correlation coefficient, r

$$SE_r = \frac{1-r^2}{\sqrt{n}}$$

- Probable error of correlation coefficient, r

$$PE_r = 0.6745\,\frac{1-r^2}{\sqrt{n}}$$

3. Coefficient of determination

$$r^2 = \frac{\text{Explained variance}}{\text{Total variance}} = 1 - \frac{\Sigma(y-\hat{y})^2}{\Sigma(y-\bar{y})^2}$$

4. Spearman's rank correlation coefficient
- Ranks are not equal

$$R = 1 - \frac{6\Sigma d^2}{n(n^2-1)}$$

- Ranks are equal

$$R = 1 - \frac{6\left[\Sigma d^2 + \frac{1}{12}(m_i^3 - m_i)\right]}{n(n^2-1)}$$

$t = 1, 2, \ldots$

Chapter Concepts Quiz

True or False

1. There are several types of correlation coefficients, the selection of which is determined by the level of scaling of the two variables.
2. When both variables use measured on an interval or ratio scale, Pearson's correlation coefficient is most appropriate.
3. To use Pearson's correlation coefficient, it is assumed that both variables are continuous and normally distributed.
4. When there is no linear association between two variables, the value of r will be close to zero.
5. A correlation coefficient $r = -1$ represents a very low linear correlation.
6. The coefficient of determination is the square of the correlation coefficient.
7. As the correlation coefficient approaches zero, the possible error in linear prediction increases.
8. The closer the correlation coefficient is to zero, the greater the predictive validity of a test.
9. If a correlation coefficient for reliability of a test is close to 1, then the test is unreliable.
10. Even a high correlation is not necessarily indicative of a casual relationship between two variables.
11. As the value of r increases, the proportion of variability of one variable y that can be accounted for another variable x decreases.
12. If the relationship between two variables is nonlinear, the value of the correlation coefficient must be negative.
13. Spearman's correlation coefficient is used where one or both variables are at least of interval scaling.
14. A scatter diagram is used to help to decide if the relationship between two variables is linear or curvilinear.
15. When calculating Spearman's correlation coefficient, Σd^2 is the sum of the square of the difference between the means.

Concepts Quiz Answers

1. T	2. T	3. T	4. T	5. F	6. T	7. T	8. F	9. F
10. T	11. F	12. F	13. F	14. T	15. F			

Review Self-Practice Problems

9.19 The following are the monthly figures of the advertising expenditure and sales of a firm. It is generally found that advertising expenditure has its impact on sales generally after 2 months. Allowing for this time lag, calculate the coefficient of correlation.

Months	*Advertising Expenditure*	*Sales*	*Months*	*Advertising Expenditure*	*Sales*
Jan.	50	1200	July	140	2400
Feb.	60	1500	Aug.	160	2600
March	70	1600	Sep.	170	2800
April	90	2000	Oct.	190	2900
May	120	2200	Nov.	200	3100
June	150	2500	Dec.	250	3900

9.20 The coefficient of correlation between two variables x and y is 0.64. Their covariance is 16. The variance of x is 19. Find the standard deviation of y series.

9.21 Given $r = 0.8$, $\Sigma xy = 60$, $\sigma_y = 2.5$ and $\Sigma x^2 = 90$, find the number of observations, items. x and y are deviations from arithmetic mean. [*Delhi Univ., BCom, 1998*]

9.22 Calculate the Karl Pearson's coefficient of correlation between age and playing habits from the data given below. Comment on the value.

Age :	20	21	22	23	24	25
No. of students :	500	400	300	240	200	160
Regular players :	400	300	180	96	60	24

9.23 A survey regarding income and savings provided the following data:

Income (Rs.)	*Saving (Rs.)*			
	500	*1000*	*1500*	*2000*
40,000	8	4	—	—
6000	—	12	24	6
8000	—	9	7	2
10,000	—	—	10	5
12,000	—	—	9	4

Compute Karl Pearson's coefficient of correlation and interpret its value.

9.24 A company gives on-the-job training to its salesmen, followed by a test. It is considering whether it should terminate the services of any salesman who does not do well in the test. Following data give the test scores and sales (in '000 Rs.) made by nine salesmen during the last one year

Test scores : 14 19 24 21 26 22 15 20 19

Sales : 31 36 48 37 50 45 33 41 39

Compute the coefficient of correlation between test scores and sales. Does it indicate that termination of the services of salesman with low test scores is justified?

9.25 Calculate the coefficient of correlation and its probable error from the following:

Subject	*Per cent Marks in Final Year Exams*	*Per cent Marks in Sessions*
Hindi	75	62
English	81	68
Physics	70	65
Chemistry	76	60
Maths	77	69
Statistics	81	72
Botany	84	76
Zoology	75	72

9.26 Following figures give the rainfall in inches for the year and the production (in '00 kg) for the Rabi crop and Kharif crops. Calculate Karl Pearson's coefficient of correlation, between rainfall and total production.

Rainfall	:	20	22	24	26	28	30	32
Rabi production	:	15	18	20	32	40	39	40
Kharif production	:	15	17	20	18	20	21	15

9.27 President of a consulting firm is interested in the relationship between environmental work factors and the employees' turnover rate. He defines environmental factors as those aspects of a job other than salary and benefits. He visited to similar plants and gave each plant a rating 1 to 25 on its environmental factors. He then obtained each plant's turnover rate (annual in percentage) examined the relationship.

Environmental rating : 11 19 7 12 13 10 16 22 14 12

Turnover rate : 6 4 8 3 7 8 3 2 5 6

Compute the correlation coefficient between turnover rate and environmental rating and test it.

9.28 Sixteen companies in a state have been ranked according to profit earned during a particular financial year, and the working capital for that year. Calculate the rank correlation coefficient.

Company	*Rank(Profit)*	*Rank(Working capital)*
A	1	13
B	2	16
C	3	14
D	4	15
E	5	10
F	6	12
G	7	4
H	8	11
I	9	5
J	10	9
K	11	8
L	12	3
M	13	1
N	14	6
O	15	7
P	16	2

9.29 Following are the percentage figures of expenditure incurred on clothing (in Rs. '00 rupees) and entertainment (in Rs. '00 rupees) by an average working class family in a period of 10 years.

Year	:	1989	90	91	92	93	94	95	96	97	98
Expenditure on clothing	:	24	27	31	32	20	25	33	30	28	22
Expenditure on entertainment	:	11	8	5	3	13	10	2	7	9	2

Compute Spearman's rank correlation coefficient and comment on the result.

Hints and Answers

9.19 $r = 0.918$

9.20 $r = \dfrac{\Sigma xy}{n\sigma_x\sigma_y}$; $\sigma_x = \sqrt{9} = 3$;

$$0.64 = 16\frac{1}{3\sigma_y} \quad \text{or} \quad \sigma_y = 8.33$$

9.21 $r = \dfrac{\Sigma xy}{n\sigma_x\sigma_y}$ or $r^2 = \dfrac{(\Sigma xy)^2}{n^2\sigma_x^2\sigma_y^2}$;

$$(0.8)^2 = \frac{(60)^2}{n^2(90/n)\times 6.25} = \frac{3600}{90n\times 6.25};$$

$n = 10$

9.22 $r = -0.991$

9.23 $r = 0.0522$

9.24 $r = 0.947$

9.25 $r = 0.623$, $PE_r = 0.146$

9.26 $r = 0.917$

9.27 $r = -0.801$

9.28 $R = -0.8176$

9.29 $R = -0.60$

Regression Analysis

LEARNING OBJECTIVES

After studying this chapter, you should be able to

- use simple linear regression for building models to business data
- understand how the method of least squares is used to predict values of a dependent (or response) variable based on the values of an independent (or explanatory) variable
- measure the variability (residual) of the dependent variable about a straight line (also called regression line) and examine whether regression model fits to the data.

10.1 INTRODUCTION

In Chapter 9 we introduced the concept of statistical relationship between two variables such as: level of sales and amount of advertising; yield of a crop and the amount of fertilizer used; price of a product and its supply, and so on. The relationship between such variables indicate the degree and direction of their association, but fail to answer following question:

- Is there any functional (or algebraic) relationship between two variables? If yes, can it be used to estimate the most likely value of one variable, given the value of other variable?

The statistical technique that expresses the relationship between two or more variables in the form of an equation to estimate the value of a variable, based on the given value of another variable, is called *regression analysis*. The variable whose value is estimated using the algebraic equation is called *dependent* (or *response*) *variable* and the variable whose value is used to estimate this value is called *independent* (*regressor* or *predictor*) *variable*. The linear algebraic equation used for expressing a dependent variable in terms of independent variable is called *linear regression equation*.

The basic differences between correlation and regression analysis are summarized as follows:

1. Developing an algebraic equation between two variables from sample data and predicting the value of one variable, given the value of the other variable is referred to as regression analysis, while measuring the strength (or degree) of the relationship between two variables is referred as

correlation analysis. The sign of correlation coefficient indicates the nature (direct or inverse) of relationship between two variables, while the absolute value of correlation coefficient indicates the extent of relationship.

2. Correlation analysis determines an association between two variables x and y but not that they have a cause-and-effect relationship. Regression analysis, in contrast to correlation, determines the cause-and-effect relationship between x and y, that is, a change in the value of independent variable x *causes* a corresponding change (*effect*) in the value of dependent variable y if all other factors that affect y remain unchanged.
3. In linear regression analysis one variable is considered as dependent variable and other as independent variable, while in correlation analysis both variables are considered to be independent.
4. *The coefficient of determination r^2 indicates the proportion of total variance in the dependent variable that is explained or accounted for by the variation in the independent variable.* Since value of r^2 is determined from a sample, its value is subject to sampling error. Even if the value of r^2 is high, the assumption of a linear regression may be incorrect because it may represent a portion of the relationship that actually is in the form of a curve.

10.2 ADVANTAGES OF REGRESSION ANALYSIS

The following are some important advantages of regression analysis:

1. Regression analysis helps in developing a regression equation by which the value of a dependent variable can be estimated given a value of an independent variable.
2. Regression analysis helps to determine standard error of estimate to measure the variability or spread of values of a dependent variable with respect to the regression line. Smaller the variance and error of estimate, the closer the pair of values (x, y) fall about the regression line and better the line fits the data, that is, a good estimate can be made of the value of variable y. When all the points fall on the line, the standard error of estimate equals zero.
3. When the sample size is large ($df \geq 29$), the interval estimation for predicting the value of a dependent variable based on standard error of estimate is considered to be acceptable by changing the values of either x or y. The magnitude of r^2 remains the same regardless of the values of the two variables.

Remarks

1. The relationship between the dependent variable y and independent variable x exists and is linear. The average relationship between x and y can be described by a simple linear regression equation $y = a + bx + e$, where e is the deviation of a particular value of y from its expected value for a given value of independent variable x.
2. For every value of the independent variable x, there is an expected (or mean) value of the dependent variable y and these values are normally distributed. The mean of these normally distributed values fall on the line of regression.
3. The dependent variable y is a continuous random variable, whereas values of the independent variable x are fixed values and are not random.
4. The sampling error associated with the expected value of the dependent variable y is assumed to be an independent random variable distributed normally with mean zero and constant standard deviation. The errors are not related with each other in successive observations.
5. The standard deviation and variance of expected values of the dependent variable y about the regression line are constant for all values of the independent variable x within the range of the sample data.

6. The value of the dependent variable cannot be estimated for a value of an independent variable lying outside the range of values in the sample data.

10.3 PARAMETERS OF SIMPLE LINEAR REGRESSION MODEL

The fundamental aim of regression analysis is to determine a regression equation (line) that makes sense and fits the representative data such that the error of variance is as small as possible. This implies that the regression equation should adequately be used for prediction. J. R. Stockton stated that

- *The device used for estimating the values of one variable from the value of the other consists of a line through the points, drawn in such a manner as to represent the average relationship between the two variables. Such a line is called line of regression.*

The two variables x and y which are correlated can be expressed in terms of each other in the form of straight line equations called *regression equations*. Such lines should be able to provide the best fit of sample data to the population data. The algebraic expression of regression lines is written as:

- The regression equation of y on x

$$y = a + bx$$

is used for estimating the value of y for given values of x.

- Regression equation of x on y

$$x = c + dy$$

is used for estimating the value of x for given values of y.

Remarks

1. When variables x and y are correlated perfectly (either positive or negative) these lines coincide, that is, we have only one line.
2. Higher the degree of correlation, nearer the two regression lines are to each other.
3. Lesser the degree of correlation, more the two regression lines are away from each other. That is, when $r = 0$, the two lines are at right angle to each other.
4. Two linear regression lines intersect each other at the point of the average value of variables x and y.

10.3.1 Regression Coefficients

To estimate values of population parameter β_0 and β_1, under certain assumptions, the fitted or estimated regression equation representing the straight line regression model is written as:

$$\hat{y} = a + bx$$

where $\hat{y}$ = estimated average (mean) value of dependent variable y for a given value of independent variable x.

a or b_0 = y-intercept that represents average value of $\hat{y}$

b = slope of regression line that represents the expected change in the value of y for unit change in the value of x

To determine the value of $\hat{y}$ for a given value of x, this equation requires the determination of two unknown constants a (intercept) and b (also called regression coefficient). Once these constants are calculated, the regression line can be used to compute an estimated value of the dependent variable y for a given value of independent variable x.

The particular values of a and b define a specific linear relationship between x and y based on sample data. The coefficient 'a' represents the *level of fitted line* (i.e., the distance of the line above or below the origin) when x equals zero, whereas coefficient 'b' represents the *slope of the line* (a measure of the change in the estimated value of y for a one-unit change in x).

The regression coefficient 'b' is also denoted as:

- b_{yx} (*regression coefficient of y on x*) in the regression line, $y = a + bx$
- b_{xy} (*regression coefficient of x on y*) in the regression line, $x = c + dy$

Properties of regression coefficients

1. The correlation coefficient is the geometric mean of two regression coefficients, that is, $r = \sqrt{b_{yx} \times b_{xy}}$.
2. If one regression coefficient is greater than one, then other regression coefficient must be less than one, because the value of correlation coefficient r cannot exceed one. However, both the regression coefficients may be less than one.
3. Both regression coefficients must have the same sign (either positive or negative). This property rules out the case of opposite sign of two regression coefficients.
4. The correlation coefficient will have the same sign (either positive or negative) as that of the two regression coefficients. For example, if $b_{yx} = -0.664$ and $b_{xy} = -0.234$, then $r = -\sqrt{0.664 \times 0.234} = -0.394$.
5. The arithmetic mean of regression coefficients b_{xy} and b_{yx} is more than or equal to the correlation coefficient r, that is, $(b_{yx} + b_{xy})/2 \geq r$. For example, if $b_{yx} = -0.664$ and $b_{xy} = -0.234$, then the arithmetic mean of these two values is $(-0.664 - 0.234)/2 = -0.449$, and this value is more than the value of $r = -0.394$.
6. Regression coefficients are independent of origin but not of scale.

10.4 METHODS TO DETERMINE REGRESSION COEFFICIENTS

Following are the methods to determine the parameters of a fitted regression equation:

10.4.1 Least Squares Normal Equations

Let $\hat{y} = a + bx$ be the least squares line of y on x, where $\hat{y}$ is the estimated average value of dependent variable y. The line that minimizes the sum of squares of the deviations of the observed values of y from those predicted is the best fitting line. Thus the sum of residuals for any least-square line is minimum, where

$$L = \Sigma (y - \hat{y})^2 = \Sigma \{y - (a + bx)\}^2; \quad a, b = \text{constants}$$

Differentiating L with respect to a and b and equating to zero, we have

$$\frac{\partial L}{\partial a} = -2\,\Sigma\{y - (a + bx)\} = 0$$

$$\frac{\partial S}{\partial b} = -2\,\Sigma\{y - (a + bx)\}x = 0$$

Solving these two equations, we get the same set of equations as equations (10.1)

$$\Sigma y = na + b\Sigma x \qquad (10.1)$$

$$\Sigma xy = a\Sigma x + b\Sigma x^2$$

where n is the total number of pairs of values of x and y in a sample data. The equations (10.1) are called *normal equations* with respect to the regression line of y on x. After solving these equations for a and b, the values of a and b are substituted in the regression equation, $y = a + bx$.

Similarly if we have a least squares line $\hat{x} = c + dy$ of x on y, where $\hat{x}$ is the estimated mean value of dependent variable x, then the normal equations will be

$$\Sigma x = nc + d\,\Sigma y$$

$$\Sigma xy = n\,\Sigma y + d\,\Sigma y^2$$

These equations are solved in the same manner as described above for constants c and d. The values of these constants are substituted to the regression equation $x = c + dy$.

Alternative method to calculate value of constants

Instead of using the algebraic method to calculate values of a and b, we may directly use the results of the solutions of these normal equation.

The gradient 'b' (regression coefficient of y on x) and 'd' (regression coefficient of x on y) are calculated as:

$$b = \frac{S_{xy}}{S_{xx}}, \quad \text{where} \quad S_{xy} = \sum_{i=1}^{n}(x_i - \bar{x})(y_i - \bar{y}) = \sum_{i=1}^{n} x_i y_i - \frac{1}{n}\sum_{i=1}^{n} x_i \sum_{i=1}^{n} y_i$$

$$S_{xx} = \sum_{i=1}^{n}(x_i - \bar{x})^2 = \sum_{i=1}^{n} x_i^2 - \frac{1}{n}\left(\sum_{i=1}^{n} x_i\right)^2$$

$$\text{and } d = \frac{S_{yx}}{S_{yy}}, \quad \text{where} \quad S_{yy} = \sum_{i=1}^{n}(y_i - \bar{y})^2 = \sum_{i=1}^{n} y_i^2 - \frac{1}{n}\left(\sum_{i=1}^{n} y\right)^2$$

Since the regression line passes through the point $(\bar{x}, \bar{y})$, the mean values of x and y and the regression equations can be used to find the value of constants a and c as follows:

$a = \bar{y} - b\bar{x}$ for regression equation of y on x

$c = \bar{x} - d\,\bar{y}$ for regression equation of x on y

The calculated values of a, b and c, d are substituted in the regression line $y = a + bx$ and $x = c + dy$ respectively to determine the exact relationship.

Example 10.1: Use least squares regression line to estimate the increase in sales revenue expected from an increase of 7.5 per cent in advertising expenditure.

Firm	*Annual Percentage Increase in Advertising Expenditure*	*Annual Percentage Increase in Sales Revenue*
A	1	1
B	3	2
C	4	2
D	6	4
E	8	6
F	9	8
G	11	8
H	14	9

Solution: Assume sales revenue (y) is dependent on advertising expenditure (x). Calculations for regression line using following normal equations are shown in Table 10.1

$$\Sigma y = na + b\Sigma x \quad \text{and} \quad \Sigma xy = a\,\Sigma x + b\Sigma x^2$$

Table 10.1 Calculation for Normal Equations

Sales Revenue y	*Advertising Expenditure*, x	x^2	xy
1	1	1	1
2	3	9	6
2	4	16	8
4	6	36	24
6	8	64	48
8	9	81	72
8	11	121	88
9	14	196	126
40	56	524	373

Approach 1 (*Normal Equations*):

$$\Sigma y = na + b\Sigma x \quad \text{or} \quad 40 = 8a + 56b$$

$$\Sigma xy = a\Sigma x + b\Sigma x^2 \text{or} \quad 373 = 56a + 524b$$

Solving these equations, we get $a = 0.072$ and $b = 0.704$. Substituting these values in the regression equation

$$y = a + bx = 0.072 + 0.704x$$

For $x = 7.5\%$ or 0.075 increase in advertising expenditure, the estimated increase in sales revenue will be $y = 0.072 + 0.704\ (0.075) = 0.1248$ or 12.48%

Approach 2 (*Short-cut method*):

$$b = \frac{S_{xy}}{S_{xx}} = \frac{93}{132} = 0.704,$$

where $S_{xy} = \Sigma xy - \dfrac{\Sigma x \Sigma y}{n} = 373 - \dfrac{40 \times 56}{8} = 93$

$$S_{xx} = \Sigma x^2 - \frac{(\Sigma x)^2}{n} = 524 - \frac{(56)^2}{8} = 132$$

The intercept 'a' on the y-axis is calculated as:

$$a = \bar{y} - b\bar{x} = \frac{40}{8} - 0.704 \times \frac{56}{8} = 5 - 0.704 \times 7 = 0.072$$

Substituting the values of $a = 0.072$ and $b = 0.704$ in the regression equation, we get

$$y = a + bx = 0.072 + 0.704\,x$$

For $x = 0.075$, we have $y = 0.072 + 0.704\ (0.075) = 0.1248$ or 12.48%.

Example 10.2: The owner of a small garment shop is hopeful that his sales are rising significantly week by week. Treating the sales for the previous six weeks as a typical example of this rising trend, he recorded them in Rs. 1000's and analysed the results.

Week :	1	2	3	4	5	6
Sales :	2.69	2.62	2.80	2.70	2.75	2.81

Fit a linear regression equation to suggest to him the weekly rate at which his sales are rising and use this equation to estimate expected sales for the 7th week.

Solution: Assume sales (y) is dependent on weeks (x). Then the normal equations for regression equation: $y = a + bx$ are written as:

$$\Sigma y = na + b\Sigma x \quad \text{and} \quad \Sigma xy = a\Sigma x + b\Sigma x^2$$

Calculations for sales during various weeks are shown in Table 10.2.

Table 10.2 Calculations of Normal Equations

Week (x)	*Sales (y)*	x^2	xy
1	2.69	1	2.69
2	2.62	4	5.24
3	2.80	9	8.40
4	2.70	16	10.80
5	2.75	25	13.75
6	2.81	36	16.86
21	16.37	91	57.74

The gradient 'b' is calculated as:

$$b = \frac{S_{xy}}{S_{xx}} = \frac{0.445}{17.5} = 0.025; \quad S_{xy} = \Sigma xy - \frac{\Sigma x \, \Sigma y}{n} = 57.74 - \frac{21 \times 16.37}{6} = 0.445$$

$$S_{xx} = \Sigma x^2 - \frac{(\Sigma x)^2}{n} = 91 - \frac{(21)^2}{6} = 17.5$$

The intercept 'a' on the y-axis is calculated as

$$a = \bar{y} - b\bar{x} = \frac{16.37}{6} - 0.025 \times \frac{21}{6}$$

$$= 2.728 - 0.025 \times 3.5 = 2.64$$

Substituting the values $a = 2.64$ and $b = 0.025$ in the regression equation, we have

$$y = a + bx = 2.64 + 0.025x$$

For $x = 7$, we have $\quad y = 2.64 + 0.025\,(7) = 2.815$

Hence the expected sales during the 7th week is likely to be Rs. 2.815 (in Rs. 1000's).

10.4.2 Deviations Method

Calculations to least squares normal equations become lengthy and tedious when values of x and y are large. Thus the following two methods may be used to reduce the computational time.

(a) **Deviations Taken from Actual Mean Values of *x* and *y*** If deviations of actual values of variables x and y are taken from their mean values $\bar{x}$ and $\bar{y}$, then the regression equations can be written as:

- Regression equation of y on x

$$y - \bar{y} = b_{yx}(x - \bar{x})$$

where b_{yx} = regression coefficient of y on x.

The value of b_{yx} can be calculated using the using the formula

$$b_{yx} = \frac{\Sigma(x-\bar{x})(y-\bar{y})}{\Sigma(x-\bar{x})^2}$$

- Regression equation of x on y

$$x - \bar{x} = b_{xy}(y - \bar{y})$$

where b_{xy} = regression coefficient of x on y.

The value of b_{xy} can be calculated formula

$$b_{xy} = \frac{\Sigma(x-\bar{x})(y-\bar{y})}{\Sigma(y-\bar{y})^2}$$

(b) **Deviations Taken from Assumed Mean Values for *x* and *y*** If mean value of either x or y or both are in fractions, then we must prefer to take deviations of actual values of variables x and y from their assumed means.

- Regression equation of y on x

$$y - \bar{y} = b_{yx}(x - \bar{x})$$

$$\text{where } b_{yx} = \frac{n\Sigma d_x d_y - (\Sigma d_x)(\Sigma d_y)}{n\Sigma d_x^2 - (\Sigma d_x)^2}$$

n = number of observations

$d_x = x - A$; A is assumed mean of x

$d_y = y - B$; B is assumed mean of y

- Regression equation of x on y

$$x - \bar{x} = b_{xy}(y - \bar{y})$$

$$\text{where } b_{xy} = \frac{n\Sigma d_x d_y - (\Sigma d_x)(\Sigma d_y)}{n\Sigma d_y^2 - (\Sigma d_y)^2}$$

n = number of observations

$d_x = x - A$; A is assumed mean of x

$d_y = y - B$; B is assumed mean of y

(c) **Regression Coefficients in Terms of Correlation Coefficient** If deviations are taken from actual mean values, then the values of regression coefficients can be alternatively calculated as follows:

$$b_{yx} = \frac{\Sigma(x-\bar{x})(y-\bar{y})}{\Sigma(x-\bar{x})^2} = \frac{\text{Covariance}(x, y)}{\sigma_x^2} = r \cdot \frac{\sigma_y}{\sigma_x}$$

$$b_{xy} = \frac{\Sigma(x-\bar{x})(y-\bar{y})}{\Sigma(y-\bar{y})^2} = \frac{\text{Covariance}(x, y)}{\sigma_y^2} = r \cdot \frac{\sigma_x}{\sigma_y}$$

Example 10.3: Compute the two regression coefficients using the value of actual mean value of X and Y from the data given below and then work out the value of r.

X :	7	4	8	6	5
Y :	6	5	9	8	2

[GJU (Hisar), BBA, 2004]

Solution: Calculations for two regression coefficients are given below:

X	Y	$x = X - \bar{X}$	$y = Y - \bar{Y}$	xy	x^2	y^2
7	6	+1	0	0	1	0
4	5	−2	−1	2	4	1
8	9	+2	+3	6	4	9
6	8	0	+2	0	0	4
5	2	−1	−4	4	1	16
30	30	$\Sigma x = 0$	$\Sigma y = 0$	$\Sigma xy = 12$	$\Sigma x^2 = 10$	$\Sigma y^2 = 30$

$$\bar{X} = \frac{\Sigma X}{n} = \frac{30}{5} = 6 \quad \text{and} \quad \bar{Y} = \frac{\Sigma Y}{n} = \frac{\Sigma Y}{5} = 6$$

Regression coefficient of X on Y is: $b_{xy} = \dfrac{\Sigma xy}{\Sigma y^2} = \dfrac{12}{30} = 0.4$

Regression coefficient of Y on X: $b_{yx} = \dfrac{\Sigma xy}{\Sigma x^2} = \dfrac{12}{10} = 1.2$

Co-relation coefficient, $r = \sqrt{b_{xy} \times b_{yx}} = \sqrt{1.2 \times 0.4} = \sqrt{0.48} = 0.69.$

Example 10.4: Use following data to find out the two lines of regression and compute the Karl Pearson's coefficient of correlation.

$$\Sigma x = 250, \quad \Sigma y = 300, \quad \Sigma xy = 7900, \quad \Sigma x^2 = 6500, \quad \Sigma y^2 = 10000, \quad n = 10$$

Solution: Calculate $\bar{x}, \bar{y}$, b_{xy} and b_{yx} with the help of given information as follows:

$$\bar{x} = \frac{\Sigma x}{n} = \frac{250}{10} = 25; \quad \bar{y} = \frac{\Sigma y}{n} = \frac{300}{10} = 30$$

$$b_{xy} = \frac{n\Sigma xy - \Sigma x \Sigma y}{n\Sigma y^2 - (\Sigma y)^2} = \frac{10(7900) - (250)(300)}{10(10000) - (300)^2} = 0.4$$

Let the regression line of x on y be:

$$x - \bar{x} = b_{xy}(y - \bar{y})$$

$$x - 25 = 0.4(y - 30)$$

$$x = 0.4y - 12 + 25 = 0.4y + 13$$

Also

$$b_{yx} = \frac{n\Sigma xy - \Sigma x \Sigma y}{n\Sigma x^2 - (\Sigma x)^2} = \frac{10(7900) - (250)(300)}{10(6500) - (250)^2} = 1.6$$

Let the regression line of y on x be

$$y - \bar{y} = b_{yx}(x - \bar{x})$$

$$y - 30 = 1.6(x - 25)$$

$$y = 1.6x - 40 + 30 = 1.6x - 10$$

Hence, the coefficient of correlation is: $r = \sqrt{b_{xy} \times b_{yx}} = \sqrt{0.4 \times 1.6} = 0.8.$

Example 10.5: A departmental store gives training to its salesman which is followed by a test. The store is considering whether it should terminate the service of any salesman who does not do well in the test. The following data gives the scores and sales made by nine salesmen during a certain period:

Test Scores :	14	19	24	21	26	22	15	20	19
Sales ('00 Rs.) :	31	36	48	37	50	45	33	41	39

Calculate the correlation coefficient between test scores and the sales. Does it indicate that the termination of services of low test scores is justified? If the firm wants a minimum sales volume of Rs. 3000, what is the minimum test score that will ensure continuation of service? Also estimate the most probable sales volume of a sales making a score of 28. [*Delhi Univ., B.Com(Hons), 1998, 2002*]

Solution: Let test scores be x and sales be y. Calculation required to determine co-relation coefficient are shown below:

X	$d_x = X - 20$	d_x^2	Y	$d_y = Y - 40$	d_y^2	$d_x d_y$
14	–6	36	31	–9	81	54
19	–1	1	36	–4	16	4
24	4	16	48	8	64	32
21	1	1	37	–3	9	–3
26	6	36	50	10	100	60
22	2	4	45	5	25	10
15	–5	25	33	–7	49	35
20	0	0	41	1	1	0
19	–1	1	39	–1	1	1
180		120	360		346	193

$$\bar{x} = \frac{\Sigma x}{n} = \frac{180}{9} = 20 \quad \text{and} \quad \bar{y} = \frac{\Sigma y}{n} = \frac{360}{9} = 40$$

$$r = \frac{\Sigma xy}{\sqrt{\Sigma x^2 \times \Sigma y^2}} = \frac{193}{\sqrt{120 \times 346}} = 0.9476$$

The value of r shown that there is a high degree of correlation between test scores (x) and sales (y). This implies that the persons having low test scores will not be able to make good sales hence termination is justified.

Regression equation of X on Y is:

$$X - \bar{X} = b_{xy}(Y - \bar{Y}); \quad \text{where} \quad b_{xy} = \frac{\Sigma d_x d_y - (\Sigma d_x)(\Sigma d_y)}{\Sigma d_y^2 - (\Sigma d_y)^2} = \frac{193}{346} = 0.557$$

$$x - 20 = 0.557\,(y - 40)$$
$$x = 0.557\,y - 22.28 + 20 = 0.557\,Y - 2.28$$

When sales is Rs. 3000, i.e. $y = 30$, then $x = 0.557\,(30) - 2.28 = 14.43$

Hence, test score = 14.43 when sales volume is Rs. 3000.

Regression equation of Y on X:

$$y - \bar{y} = b_{yx}\,(x - \bar{x}); \quad \text{where} \quad b_{yx} = \frac{\Sigma xy}{\Sigma x^2} = \frac{193}{120} = 1.6$$

$$\therefore \quad y - 40 = 1.6\,(x - 20)$$
$$y = 1.6x - 32 + 40 = 1.6x + 8$$

When test score is 28, i.e. $x = 28$, then $y = 1.6(28) + 8 = 52.8$

Thus sales volume = 52.8 × 100 = Rs. 5280.

Example 10.6: The following data relate to the scores obtained by 9 salesmen of a company in an intelligence test and their weekly sales (in Rs. 1000's)

Salesmen :	A	B	C	D	E	F	G	H	I
Test scores :	50	60	50	60	80	50	80	40	70
Weekly sales :	30	60	40	50	60	30	70	50	60

(a) Obtain the regression equation of sales on intelligence test scores of the salesmen.

(b) If the intelligence test score of a salesman is 65, what would be his expected weekly sales.

[*HP Univ., MCom, 1996*]

Solution: Assume weekly sales (y) as dependent variable and test scores (x) as independent variable. Calculations for the following regression equation are shown in Table 10.3.

$$y - \bar{y} = b_{yx}\,(x - \bar{x})$$

Table 10.3 Calculation for Regression Equation

Weekly Sales, x	$dx = x - 60$	d_x^2	*Test Score, y*	$dy = y - 50$	d_y^2	$d_x d_y$
50	– 10	100	30	– 20	400	200
60	0	0	60	10	100	0
50	– 10	100	40	– 10	100	100
60	0	0	50	0	0	0
80	20	400	60	10	100	200
50	– 10	100	30	– 20	400	200
80	20	400	70	20	400	400
40	– 20	400	50	0	0	0
70	10	100	60	10	100	100
540	0	1600	450	0	1600	1200

(a) $\overline{x} = \dfrac{\Sigma x}{n} = \dfrac{540}{9} = 60;\quad \overline{y} = \dfrac{\Sigma y}{n} = \dfrac{450}{9} = 50$

$$b_{yx} = \frac{\Sigma d_x d_y - (\Sigma d_x)(\Sigma d_y)}{\Sigma d_x^2 - (\Sigma d_x)^2} = \frac{1200}{1600} = 0.75$$

Substituting values in the regression equation, we have

$$y - 50 = 0.75\,(x - 60) \text{ or } y = 5 + 0.75x$$

For test score $x = 65$ of salesman, we have

$$y = 5 + 0.75\,(65) = 53.75$$

Hence we conclude that the weekly sales is expected to be Rs. 53.75 (in Rs. 1000's) for a test score of 65.

Example 10.7: A company is introducing a job evaluation scheme in which all jobs are graded by points for skill, responsibility, and so on. Monthly pay scales (Rs. in 1000's) are then drawn up according to the number of points allocated and other factors such as experience and local conditions. To date the company has applied this scheme to 9 jobs.

Job :	A	B	C	D	E	F	G	H	I
Points :	5	25	7	19	10	12	15	28	16
Pay (Rs.) :	3.0	5.0	3.25	6.5	5.5	5.6	6.0	7.2	6.1

(a) Find the least squares regression line for linking pay scales to points.

(b) Estimate the monthly pay for a job graded by 20 points.

Solution: Assume monthly pay (y) as the dependent variable and job grade points (x) as the independent variable. Calculations for the following regression equation are shown in Table 10.4.

$$y - \overline{y} = b_{yx}\,(x - \overline{x})$$

Table 10.4 Calculations for Regression Equation

Grade Points, x	$d_x = x - 15$	d_x^2	Pay Scale, y	$d_y = y - 5$	d_y^2	$d_x d_y$
5	– 10	100	3.0	– 2.0	4	20
25	10	100	(5.0) ← B	0	0	0
7	– 8	64	3.25	– 1.75	3.06	14
19	4	16	6.5	1.50	2.25	6
10	– 5	25	5.5	0.50	0.25	– 2.5
12	– 3	9	5.6	0.60	0.36	– 1.8
(15) ← A	0	0	6.0	1.00	1.00	0
28	13	169	7.2	2.2	4.84	28.6
16	1	1	6.1	1.1	1.21	1.1
137	2	484	48.15	3.15	16.97	65.40

(a) $\bar{x} = \dfrac{\Sigma x}{n} = \dfrac{137}{9} = 15.22; \quad \bar{y} = \dfrac{\Sigma y}{n} = \dfrac{48.15}{9} = 5.35$

Since mean values $\bar{x}$ and $\bar{y}$ are non-integer value, therefore deviations are taken from assumed mean as shown in Table 10.4.

$$b_{yx} = \frac{n\Sigma d_x d_y - (\Sigma d_x)(\Sigma d_y)}{n\Sigma d_x^2 - (\Sigma d_x)^2} = \frac{9 \times 65.40 - 2 \times 3.15}{9 \times 484 - (2)^2} = \frac{582.3}{4352} = 0.133$$

Substituting values in the regression equation, we have

$$y - \bar{y} = b_{yx}(x - \bar{x}) \quad \text{or} \quad y - 5.35 = 0.133\,(x - 15.22) = 3.326 + 0.133x$$

(b) For job grade point x=20, the estimated average pay scale is given by

$$y = 3.326 + 0.133x = 3.326 + 0.133\,(20) = 5.986$$

Hence, likely monthly pay for a job with grade points 20 is Rs. 5986.

Example 10.8: Find two regression equations from the data given below:

x :	57	58	59	59	60	61	62	64
y :	77	78	75	78	82	82	79	81

[*GJU (Hisar), BBA, 2005*]

Solution: Calculations of two regression equations as shown below:

x	y	$d_x = x - 59$	$d_y = y - 82$	$d_x d_y$	dx^2	dy^2
57	77	–2	–5	+10	4	25
58	78	–1	–4	+4	1	16
59	75	0	–7	0	0	49
59	78	0	–4	0	0	16
60	82	+1	0	0	1	0
61	82	+2	0	0	4	0
62	79	+3	–3	–9	9	9
64	81	+5	–1	–5	25	1
480	632	8	–24	0	44	116

$$\bar{x} = \frac{\Sigma x}{n} = \frac{480}{8} = 60 \quad \text{and} \quad \bar{y} = \frac{\Sigma y}{n} = \frac{632}{8} = 79$$

We know that
$$b_{xy} = \frac{n\Sigma d_x d_y - \Sigma d_x \Sigma d_y}{N\Sigma d_y^2 - (\Sigma d_y)^2} = \frac{8(0) - (8)(-24)}{8(116) - (-24)^2} = \frac{192}{352} = 0.55$$

$$b_{yx} = \frac{n\Sigma d_x d_y - \Sigma d_x \Sigma d_y}{N\Sigma_x^2 - (\Sigma d_x)^2} = \frac{8(0) - (8)(-24)}{8(44) - (8)^2} = \frac{192}{288} = 0.67$$

Regression equation of x on y: $x - \bar{x} = b_{xy}(y - \bar{y})$

$$x - 60 = 0.55(y - \bar{y})$$

$$x = 0.55y - 43.45 + 60 = 0.55y + 16.55$$

Regression equation of y on x: $y - \bar{y} = b_{yx}(x - \bar{x})$

$$y - 79 = 0.67(x - 60)$$

$$y = 0.67x - 40.2 + 79 = 0.67x + 38.8.$$

Example 10.9: The following data give the ages and blood pressure of 10 women:

Age	:	56	42	36	47	49	42	60	72	63	55
Blood pressure	:	147	125	118	128	145	140	155	160	149	150

(a) Find the correlation coefficient between age and blood pressure.
(b) Determine the least squares regression equation of blood pressure on age.
(c) Estimate the blood pressure of a woman whose age is 45 years.

Solution: Assume blood pressure (y) as the dependent variable and age (x) as the independent variable. Calculations for regression equation of blood pressure on age are shown in Table 10.5.

Table 10.5 Calculations for Regression Equation

Age, x	$d_x = x - 49$	d_x^2	*Blood, y*	$d_y = y - 145$	d_y^2	$d_x d_y$
56	7	49	147	2	4	14
42	−7	49	125	−20	400	140
36	−13	169	118	−27	729	351
47	−2	4	128	−17	289	34
(49) ← A	0	0	(145) ← B	0	0	0
42	−7	49	140	−5	25	35
60	11	121	155	10	100	110
72	23	529	160	15	225	345
63	14	196	149	4	16	56
55	6	36	150	5	25	30
522	32	1202	1417	−33	1813	1115

(a) Coefficient of correlation between age and blood pressure is given by

$$r = \frac{n\Sigma d_x d_y - \Sigma d_x \Sigma d_y}{\sqrt{n\Sigma d_x^2 - (\Sigma d_x)^2}\sqrt{n\Sigma d_y^2 - (\Sigma d_y)^2}}$$

$$= \frac{10(1115)-(32)(-33)}{\sqrt{10(1202)-(32)^2}\sqrt{10(1813)-(-33)^2}}$$

$$= \frac{11150+1056}{\sqrt{12020-1024}\sqrt{18130-1089}} = \frac{12206}{13689} = 0.892$$

We may conclude that there is a high degree of positive correlation between age and blood pressure.

(b) The regression equation of blood pressure on age is given by

$$y - \bar{y} = b_{yx}(x - \bar{x})$$

$$\bar{x} = \frac{\Sigma x}{n} = \frac{522}{10} = 52.2; \quad \bar{y} = \frac{\Sigma y}{n} = \frac{1417}{10} = 141.7$$

and $$b_{yx} = \frac{n\Sigma d_x d_y - \Sigma d_x \Sigma d_y}{n\Sigma d_x^2 - (\Sigma d_x)^2} = \frac{10(1115)-32(-33)}{10(1202)-(32)^2} = \frac{12206}{10996} = 1.11$$

Substituting these values in the above equation, we have

$$y - 141.7 = 1.11\,(x - 52.2) \text{ or } y = 83.758+1.11x$$

This is the required regression equation of y on x.

(*c*) For a women whose age is 45, the estimated average blood pressure will be

$$y = 83.758+1.11(45) = 83.758+49.95 = 133.708$$

Hence, the likely blood pressure of a woman of 45 years is 134.

Example 10.10: The General Sales Manager of Kiran Enterprises—an enterprise dealing in the sale of readymade men's wear—is toying with the idea of increasing his sales to Rs. 80,000. On checking the records of sales during the last 10 years, it was found that the annual sale proceeds and advertisement expenditure were highly correlated to the extent of 0.8. It was further noted that the annual average sale has been Rs. 45,000 and annual average advertisement expenditure Rs. 30,000, with a variance of Rs. 1600 and Rs. 625 in advertisement expenditure respectively.

In view of the above, how much expenditure on advertisement would you suggest the General Sales Manager of the enterprise to incur to meet his target of sales?

Solution: Assume advertisement expenditure (y) as the dependent variable and sales (x) as the independent variable. Then the regression equation advertisement expenditure on sales is given by

$$(y - \bar{y}) = r\frac{\sigma_y}{\sigma_x}(x - \bar{x})$$

Given $r = 0.8$, $\sigma_x = 40$, $\sigma_y = 25$, $\bar{x} = 45{,}000$, $\bar{y} = 30{,}000$. Substituting these value in the above equation, we have

$$(y - 30{,}000) = 0.8\,\frac{25}{40}\,(x - 45{,}000) = 0.5\,(x - 45{,}000)$$

$$y = 30{,}000 + 0.5x - 22{,}500 = 7500 + 0.5x$$

When a sales target is fixed at $x = 80{,}000$, the estimated amount likely to the spent on advertisement would be

$$y = 7500 + 0.5\times 80{,}000 = 7500 + 40{,}000 = \text{Rs. } 47{,}500$$

Example 10.11: You are given the following information about advertising expenditure and sales:

	Advertisement (x) *(Rs. in lakh)*	*Sales (y)* *(Rs. in lakh)*
Arithmetic mean, $\bar{x}$	10	90
Standard deviation, σ	3	12

Correlation coefficient = 0.8

(a) Obtain the two regression equations.

(b) Find the likely sales when advertisement budget is Rs. 15 lakh.

(c) What should be the advertisement budget if the company wants to attain sales target of Rs. 120 lakh?

Solution: (a) Regression equation of x on y is given by

$$x - \bar{x} = r\frac{\sigma_x}{\sigma_y}(y - \bar{y})$$

Given $\bar{x} = 10, r = 0.8, \sigma_x = 3, \sigma_y = 12, \bar{y} = 90$. Substituting these values in the above regression equation, we have

$$x - 10 = 0.8\,\frac{3}{12}\,(y - 90) \quad \text{or} \quad x = -8 + 0.2y$$

Regression equation of y on x is given by

$$(y - \bar{y}) = r\frac{\sigma_y}{\sigma_x}(x - \bar{x})$$

$$y - 90 = 0.8\,\frac{12}{3}(x - 10) \quad \text{or} \quad y = 58 + 3.2x$$

(b) Substituting $x = 15$ in regression equation of y on x. The likely average sales volume would be

$$y = 58 + 3.2\,(15) = 58 + 48 = 106$$

Thus the likely sales for advertisement budget of Rs. 15 lakh is Rs. 106 lakh.

(c) Substituting $y = 120$ in the regression equation of x on y. The likely advertisement budget to attain desired sales target of Rs. 120 lakh would be

$$x = -8 + 0.2\,y = -8 + 0.2\,(120) = 16$$

Hence, the likely advertisement budget of Rs. 16 lakh should be sufficient to attain the sales target of Rs. 120 lakh.

Example 10.12: For 100 students of a class, the regression equation of marks in statistics (x) on marks in economics (y) is: $3y - 5x + 180 = 0$. If marks in economics is 50 and variance of marks in statistics is (4/9) of variance of marks in economics, find mean marks in statistics and the coefficient of correlation between them. *[Delhi Univ., BCom (Hons), 2005]*

Solution: Regression equation of x on y: $3y - 5x + 180 = 0$

$$x = \frac{3y}{5} + \frac{180}{5}$$

Thus, regression coefficient of x on y, $b_{xy} = \dfrac{3}{5}$

Also it is given that $\bar{y} = 50$. To find $\bar{x}$, put $y = 50$ in the regression equation we get

$$3(50) - 5x + 180 = 0 \quad \text{or} \quad x = 66, \text{ i.e. } \bar{x} = 66$$

It is given that $\sigma_x^2 = \frac{4}{9}\sigma_y^2$ i.e. $\sigma_x^2 = \frac{2}{3}\sigma_y$ or $\frac{\sigma_x}{\sigma_y} = \frac{2}{3}$

Since, $b_{xy} = \frac{3}{5}$ or $r \cdot \frac{\sigma_x}{\sigma_y} = \frac{3}{5}$

$$r\left(\frac{2}{3}\right) = \frac{3}{5} \quad \text{or} \quad r = \frac{3}{5}\times\frac{3}{2} = \frac{9}{10} = 0.9$$

Example 10.13: Given that

Regression euqation of y on x is: $y = 20 + 0.4\,x$

Mean of $x = 30$

Correlation coefficient $= 0.8$

Find regression equation of x on y. [*Delhi Univ., BCom, 2005*]

Solution: Given, regression equation of y on $x : y = 20 + 0.4x$. This implies that $b_{yx} = 0.4$.

Also, $\bar{x} = 30$, put $x = 30$ in the regression equation of y on x, we get

$$y = 20 + 0.4\,(30) = 20 + 12 = 32$$

Thus $\bar{y} = 32$

We know that, $r^2 = b_{xy} \times b_{yx}$

$$(0.8)^2 = b_{xy} \times 0.4 \quad [\text{since } r = 0.8, \quad b_{yx} = 0.4]$$

$$b_{xy} = \frac{0.64}{0.4} = 1.6$$

Regression equation of x on y is:

$$x - \bar{x} = b_{xy}(y - \bar{y})$$

$$x - 30 = 1.6\,(y - 32) = 1.6y - 51.2 + 30 = 1.6y - 21.2.$$

Example 10.14: Given:

	X Series	*Y Series*
Mean	18	100
Standard deviation	14	20

Coefficient of correlation $= 0.8$

Find the most probable value of Y if $X = 70$ and most probable value of X if Y $= 90$.

[*Delhi Univ., BCom (Hons), 2005*]

Solution: Given: $\bar{X} = 18$, $\bar{Y} = 100$, $\sigma_X = 14$, $\sigma_Y = 20$, and $r = 0.8$

Regression equation of X on Y: $X - \bar{X} = \frac{r\sigma_X}{\sigma_Y}(Y - \bar{Y})$

$$X - 18 = \frac{(0.8)(14)}{20}(Y - 100) = 0.56\,(Y - 100)$$

$$X = 0.56Y - 56 + 18 = 0.56Y - 38$$

If $Y = 90$, then $X = 0.56\,(90) - 38 = 12.4$

Regression equation of Y on X : $Y - \bar{Y} = \dfrac{r\sigma_Y}{\sigma_X}(X - \bar{X})$

$$Y - 100 = \frac{(0.8)(20)}{14}(X - 18) = 1.14(X - 18)$$

$$Y = 1.14\,X - 20.52 + 100 = 1.14\,X + 79.48$$

If $X = 70$, then $Y = 1.14\,(70) + 79.48 = 159.28$.

Example 10.15: Given $x = 4y + 5$ and $y = kx + 4$ are the lines of regression of x on y and y on x respectively. If k is positive, prove that it cannot exceed 1/4. If $k = 1/16$, find the means of two variable and correlation coefficient between them. [*Delhi Univ., BCom, 2006*]

Solution: Regression equation of x on y : $x = 4y + 5$. This implies that $b_{xy} = 4$

Regression equation of y on x : $y = kx + 4$. This implies that $b_{yx} = k$

We know that, $r^2 = b_{yx} \times b_{xy} = k \times 4$. Now if $r < 1$, then $r^2 < 1$ and hence $4k < 1$ or $k < \dfrac{1}{4}$

If $k = 1/16$, then $y = (1/16)x + 4$. Thus the regression coefficient of y on x, becomes, $b_{yx} = 1/16$. Then the correlation coefficient is

$$r = \sqrt{b_{yx} \times b_{xy}} = \sqrt{(1/16) \times 4} = \sqrt{1/4} = \pm\,0.5.$$

Since both b_{xy} and b_{yx} are positive, $r = +0.5$.

Solve two repression equations for x and y to get $\bar{x} = 28$ and $\bar{y} = 5.76$.

Example 10.16: In a partially destroyed laboratory record of an analysis of regression data, the following results only are legible:

Variance of $x = 9$

Regression equations : $8x - 10y + 66 = 0$ and $40x - 18y = 214$

Find on the basis of the above information:

(a) The mean values of x and y,

(b) Coefficient of correlation between x and y, and

(c) Standard deviation of y.

Solution: (a) Since two regression lines always intersect at a point $(\bar{x}, \bar{y})$ representing mean values of the variables involved, solving given regression equations to get the mean values $\bar{x}$ and $\bar{y}$ as shown below:

$$8x - 10y = -66$$
$$40x - 18y = 214$$

Multiplying the first equation by 5 and subtracting from the second, we have

$$32y = 544 \quad \text{or} \quad y = 17, \text{ i.e. } \bar{y} = 17$$

Substituting the value of y in the first equation, we get

$$8x - 10(17) = -66 \quad \text{or} \quad x = 13, \text{ that is, } \bar{x} = 13$$

(b) To find correlation coefficient r between x and y, we need to determine the regression coefficients b_{xy} and b_{yx}.

Rewriting the given regression equations in such a way that the coefficient of dependent variable is less than one at least in one equation.

$$8x - 10y = -66 \text{ or } 10y = 66 + 8x \text{ or } y = \frac{66}{10} + \frac{8}{10}x$$

That is, $b_{yx} = 8/10 = 0.80$

$$40x - 18y = 214 \text{ or } 40x = 214 + 18y \text{ or } x = \frac{214}{40} + \frac{18}{40}y$$

That is, $b_{xy} = 18/40 = 0.45$

Hence coefficient of correlation r between x and y is given by

$$r = \sqrt{b_{xy} \times b_{yx}} = \sqrt{0.45 \times 0.80} = 0.60$$

(c) To determine the standard deviation of y, consider the formula:

$$b_{yx} = r\frac{\sigma_y}{\sigma_x} \quad \text{or} \quad \sigma_y = \frac{b_{yx}\,\sigma_x}{r} = \frac{0.80 \times 3}{0.6} = 4$$

Example 10.17: There are two series of index numbers, P for price index and S for stock of a commodity. The mean and standard deviation of P are 100 and 8 and of S are 103 and 4 respectively. The correlation coefficient between the two series is 0.4. With these data, work out a linear equation to read off values of P for various values of S. Can the same equation be used to read off values of S for various values of P?

Solution: The regression equation to read off values of P for various values S is given by

$$P = a + bS \quad \text{or} \quad (P - \bar{P}) = r\,\frac{\sigma_p}{\sigma_s}(S - \bar{S})$$

Given $\bar{P} = 100$, $\bar{S} = 103$, $\sigma_p = 8$, $\sigma_s = 4$, $r = 0.4$. Substituting these values in the above equation, we have

$$P - 100 = 0.4\frac{8}{4}(S - 103) \text{ or } P = 17.6 + 0.8\,S$$

This equation cannot be used to read off values of S for various values of P. Thus to read off values of S for various values of P we use another regression equation of the form:

$$S = c + dP \quad \text{or} \quad S - \bar{S} = \frac{\sigma_s}{\sigma_p}(P - \bar{P})$$

Substituting given values in this equation, we have

$$S - 103 = 0.4\,\frac{4}{8}\,(P - 100) \quad \text{or} \quad S = 83 + 0.2P$$

Example 10.18: A panel of Judges A and B graded seven debators and independently awarded the following marks:

Debator	:	1	2	3	4	5	6	7
Marks of A	:	40	34	28	30	44	38	31
Marks of B	:	32	39	26	30	38	34	28

An eighth debator was awarded 36 marks by Judge A while Judge B was not present. If Judge B was also present, how many marks would you expect him to award to eighth debator assuming same degree of relationship exists in judgement? *[Delhi Univ., BCom (Hons) 1993]*

Solution: Let marks of A be denoted by x and that of B by y. A = 30 and B = 30 be assumed as mean value of x-series and y-series, respectively. The calculation required for regression equations are shown below:

Marks of $A(x)$	$d_x = x - 30$	d_x^2	Marks of $B(y)$	$d_Y = y - 30$	dy^2	$d_x d_y$
40	10	100	32	2	4	20
34	4	16	39	9	81	36
28	–2	4	26	–4	16	8
(30) ← A	0	0	(30) ← B	0	0	0
44	14	196	38	8	64	112
38	8	64	34	4	16	32
31	1	1	28	–2	4	2
245	35	381	227	17	185	206

$$\bar{x} = \frac{\Sigma x}{n} = \frac{245}{7} = 35 \quad \text{and} \quad \bar{y} = \frac{\Sigma y}{n} = \frac{227}{7} = 32.43$$

Regression coefficient of y on x:

$$b_{yx} = \frac{n\Sigma d_x d_y - \Sigma d_x \Sigma d_y}{n\Sigma d_x^2 - (\Sigma d_x)^2} = \frac{7(206) - (35)(17)}{7(381) - (35)^2} = \frac{1442 - 595}{2667 - 1225} = \frac{847}{1442} = 0.587$$

Regression equation of y on x is:

$$y - \bar{y} = b_{yx}(x - \bar{x})$$

$$y - 32.43 = 0.587(x - 35)$$

$$y = 0.587x - 20.545 + 32.43 = 0.587x + 11.885$$

Marks awarded to eighth debator by Judge B when marks awarded by Judge A is $x = 36$ is:

$$y = 0.587(36) + 11.885 = 33 \text{ marks}$$

Example 10.19: The lines of regression of a bivariate distribution are as follows: $5x - 145 = -10y$ and $14y - 208 = -8x$, variance of $x = 4$. Find out mean values of x and y and standard deviation of y. Also find correlation coefficient between x and y. *[Delhi Univ., BCom (Hons), 2001]*

Solution: Let the regression equation of x on y be:

$$5x - 145 = -10y$$

$$x = \frac{-10y}{5} + \frac{145}{5} = -2y + 29$$

Hence, regression coefficient of x on y becomes: $b_{xy} = -2$

Let the regression equation of y on x be:

$$14y - 208 = -8x$$

$$y = \frac{208}{14} - \frac{8x}{14}$$

Hence regression coefficient of y on x becomes: $b_{yx} = \frac{-8}{14}$

Now the coefficient of correlation r between x and y is given by

$$r = \sqrt{b_{yx} \times b_{xy}} = \sqrt{\frac{-8}{14} \times (-2)} = 1.06$$

Since value of r cannot exceed one, consider another set of regression equations:

Regression equation of x on y is

$$14y - 208 = -8x \quad \text{or} \quad x = \frac{208}{8} - \frac{14}{8}$$

Thus $b_{xy} = \dfrac{-14}{8}$

Regression equation of y on x is:

$$5x - 145 = -10y \quad 10y = 145 - 5x \quad \text{or} \quad y = \frac{145}{10} - \frac{5}{10}x$$

Thus $b_{yx} = \dfrac{-5}{10} = -\dfrac{1}{2}$

$$\text{Now} \quad r = \sqrt{b_{yx} \times b_{xy}} = \sqrt{-\frac{1}{2} \times \left(\frac{-14}{8}\right)} = \sqrt{0.875} = \pm 0.93$$

Since b_{xy} and b_{yx} both are negative, r should also be negative. Hence $r = -0.93$.

We know that, $\quad b_{yx} = \dfrac{r\sigma_y}{\sigma_x} \quad$ or $\quad -\dfrac{1}{2} = \dfrac{-0.93\sigma_y}{2}$, where $\sigma_x = 2$

or $$\sigma_y = \frac{2}{0.93 \times 2} = 1.075$$

Solve the two regression equations simultaneously to get $\bar{x}$ and $\bar{y}$.

$$5x - 145 = -10y \quad \text{or} \quad 5x + 10y = 145 \qquad (i)$$

$$14y - 208 = -8x \quad \text{or} \quad 8x + 14y = 208 \qquad (ii)$$

Multiply (*i*) by 8 and (*ii*) by 5 and subtracting, we get $10y = 120$ or $y = 12$

Substitute $y = 12$ is (*i*), we get $5x + 10(2) = 145$ or $x = 5$ Hence $\bar{x} = 5$ and $\bar{y} = 12$.

Example 10.20: The two regression lines obtained in a correlation analysis of 60 observations are:

$$5x = 6x + 24 \quad \text{and} \quad 1000y = 768x - 3708$$

What is the correlation coefficient and what is its probable error? Show that the ratio of the coefficient of variability of x to that of y is 5/24. What is the ratio of variances of x and y?

Solution: Rewriting the regression equations

$$5x = 6y + 24 \quad \text{or} \quad x = \frac{6}{5}y + \frac{24}{5}$$

That is, $b_{xy} = 6/5$

$$1000y = 768x - 3708 \quad \text{or} \quad y = \frac{768}{1000}x - \frac{3708}{1000}$$

That is, $b_{yx} = 768/1000$

We know that $b_{xy} = r\dfrac{\sigma_x}{\sigma_y} = \dfrac{6}{5}$ and $b_{yx} = r\dfrac{\sigma_y}{\sigma_x} = \dfrac{768}{1000}$, therefore

$$b_{xy} b_{yx} = r^2 = \frac{6}{5} \times \frac{768}{1000} = 0.9216$$

Hence $r = \sqrt{0.9216} = 0.96$.

Since both b_{xy} and b_{yx} are positive, the correlation coefficient is positive and hence $r = 0.96$.

$$\text{Probable error of } r = 0.6745 \frac{1-r^2}{\sqrt{n}} = 0.6745 \frac{1-(0.96)^2}{\sqrt{60}}$$

$$= \frac{0.0528}{7.7459} = 0.0068$$

Solving the given regression equations for x and y, we get $\bar{x} = 6$ and $\bar{y} = 1$ because regression lines passed through the point $(\bar{x}, \bar{y})$.

$$\text{Since } r\frac{\sigma_x}{\sigma_y} = \frac{6}{5} \text{ or } 0.96\frac{\sigma_x}{\sigma_y} = \frac{6}{5} \text{ or } \frac{\sigma_x}{\sigma_y} = \frac{6}{5 \times 0.96} = \frac{5}{4}$$

$$\text{Also the ratio of the coefficient of variability} = \frac{\sigma_x/\bar{x}}{\sigma_y/\bar{y}} = \frac{\bar{y}}{\bar{x}} \cdot \frac{\sigma_x}{\sigma_y} = \frac{1}{6} \times \frac{5}{4} = \frac{5}{24}.$$

Self-Practice Problems 10A

10.1 The following calculations have been made for prices of twelve stocks (x) at the Calcutta Stock Exchange on a certain day along with the volume of sales in thousands of shares (y). From these calculations find the regression equation of price of stocks on the volume of sales of shares.

$\Sigma x = 580$, $\Sigma y = 370$, $\Sigma xy = 11494$,
$\Sigma x^2 = 41658$, $\Sigma y^2 = 17206$.

10.2 A survey was conducted to study the relationship between expenditure (in Rs.) on accommodation (x) and expenditure on food and entertainment (y) and the following results were obtained:

	Mean	*Standard Deviation*
• Expenditure on accommodation	173	63.15
• Expenditure on food and entertainment	47.8	22.98

Coefficient of correlation $r = 0.57$

Write down the regression equation and estimate the expenditure on food and entertainment if the expenditure on accommodation is Rs. 200.

10.3 The following data give the experience of machine operators and their performance ratings given by the number of good parts turned out per 100 pieces:

Operator	1	2	3	4	5	6	7	8
experience (x)	16	12	18	4	3	10	5	12
Performance ratings (y)	87	88	89	68	78	80	75	83

Calculate the regression lines of performance ratings on experience and estimate the probable performance if an operator has 7 years experience.

10.4 A study of prices of a certain commodity at Delhi and Mumbai yield the following data:

	Delhi	*Mumbai*
• Average price per kilo (Rs.)	2.463	2.797
• Standard deviation	0.326	0.207
• Correlation coefficient between prices at Delhi and Mumbai $r = 0.774$		

Estimate from the above data the most likely price (a) at Delhi corresponding to the price of Rs. 2.334 per kilo at Mumbai (b) at Mumbai corresponding to the price of 3.052 per kilo at Delhi

10.5 The following table gives the aptitude test scores and productivity indices of 10 workers selected at random:

Aptitude scores (x) : 60 62 65 70 72 48 53 73 65 82

Productivity index (y) : 68 60 62 80 85 40 52 62 60 81

Calculate the two regression equations and estimate (a) the productivity index of a worker whose test score is 92, (b) the test score of a worker whose productivity index is 75.

10.6 A company wants to assess the impact of R&D expenditure (Rs. in 1000s) on its annual profit (Rs. in 1000's). The following table presents the information for the last eight years:

Year	*R & D expenditure*	*Annual profit*
1991	9	45
1992	7	42
1993	5	41
1994	10	60
1995	4	30
1996	5	34
1997	3	25
1998	2	20

Estimate the regression equation and predict the annual profit for the year 2002 for an allocated sum of Rs. 1,00,000 as R&D expenditure.

10.7 Obtain the two regression equations from the following bivariate frequency distribution:

Sales Revenue	*Advertising Expenditure (Rs. in thousand)*			
(Rs. in lakh)	*5–15*	*15–25*	*25–35*	*35–45*
75–125	3	4	4	8
125–175	8	6	5	7
175–225	2	2	3	4
225–275	3	3	2	2

Estimate (a) the sales corresponding to advertising expenditure of Rs. 50,000, (b) the advertising expenditure for a sales revenue of Rs. 300 lakh, (c) the coefficient of correlation.

10.8 The personnel manager of an electronic manufacturing company devises a manual test for job applicants to predict their production rating in the assembly department. In order to do this he selects a random sample of 10 applicants. They are given the test and later assigned a production rating. The results are as follows:

Worker	:	A	B	C	D	E	F	G	H	I	J
Test score	:	53	36	88	84	86	64	45	48	39	69
Production rating	:	45	43	89	79	84	66	49	48	43	76

Fit a linear least squares regression equation of production rating on test score.

10.9 Find the regression equation showing the capacity utilization on production from the following data:

		Average	*Standard Deviation*
• Production (in lakh units)	:	35.6	10.5
• Capacity utilization (in percentage)	:	84.8	8.5
• Correlation coefficient $r = 0.62$			

Estimate the production when the capacity utilization is 70 per cent.

10.10 Suppose that you are interested in using past expenditure on R&D by a firm to predict current expenditures on R&D. You got the following data by taking a random sample of firms, where x is the amount spent on R&D (in lakh of rupees) 5 years ago and y is the amount spent on R&D (in lakh of rupees) in the current year:

x : 30 50 20 80 10 20 20 40

y : 50 80 30 110 20 20 40 50

(a) Find the regression equation of y on x.

(b) If a firm is chosen randomly and $x = 10$, can you use the regression to predict the value of y? Discuss.

10.11 The following data relates to the scores obtained by a salesmen of a company in an intelligence test and their weekly sales (in Rs. 1000's):

Salesman intelligence	:	A	B	C	D	E	F	G	H	I
Test score	:	50	60	50	60	80	50	80	40	70
Weekly sales	:	30	60	40	50	60	30	70	50	60

(a) Obtain the regression equation of sales on intelligence test scores of the salesmen.

(b) If the intelligence test score of a salesman is 65, what would be his expected weekly sales?

[*HP Univ., M.Com., 1996*]

10.12 Two random variables have the regression equations:

$$3x + 2y - 26 = 0 \quad \text{and} \quad 6x + y - 31 = 0$$

(a) Find the mean values of x and y and coefficient of correlation between x and y.

(b) If the varaince of x is 25, then find the standard deviation of y from the data.

10.13 For a given set of bivariate data, the following results were obtained

$$\bar{x} = 53.2, \; \bar{y} = 27.9,$$

Regression coefficient of y on x = – 1.5, and Regression coefficient of x and y = – 0.2.

Find the most probable value of y when x = 60.

10.14 In trying to evaluate the effectiveness in its advertising compaign, a firm compiled the following information:

Calculate the regression equation of sales on advertising expenditure. Estimate the probable sales when advertisement expenditure is Rs. 60 thousand.

Year	*Adv. expenditure (Rs. 1000's)*	*Sales (in lakhs Rs.)*
1996	12	5.0
1997	15	5.6
1998	17	5.8
1999	23	7.0
2000	24	7.2
2001	38	8.8
2002	42	9.2
2003	48	9.5

Hints and Answers

10.1 $\bar{x} = \Sigma x/n = 580/12 = 48.33;$

$\bar{y} = \Sigma y/n = 370/12 = 30.83$

$$b_{xy} = \frac{\Sigma xy - n\bar{x}\,\bar{y}}{\Sigma y^2 - n(\bar{y})^2}$$

$$= \frac{11494 - 12 \times 48.33 \times 30.83}{17206 - 12(30.83)^2} = -1.102$$

Regression equation of x on y:

$$x - \bar{x} = b_{xy}(y - \bar{y})$$

$$x - 48.33 = -1.102\,(y - 30.83)$$

or $x = 82.304 - 1.102y$

10.2 Given $\bar{x} = 172$, $\bar{y} = 47.8$, $\sigma_x = 63.15$, $\sigma_y = 22.98$, and $r = 0.57$

Regression equation of food and entertainment (y) on accomodation (x) is given by

$$y - \bar{y} = r\,\frac{\sigma_y}{\sigma_x}(x - \bar{x})$$

$$y - 47.8 = 0.57\,\frac{22.98}{63.15}(x - 173)$$

or $$y = 11.917 + 0.207x$$

For x = 200, we have $y = 11.917 + 0.207(200) = 53.317$

10.3 Let the experience and performance rating be represented by x and y respectively.

$\bar{x} = \Sigma x/n = 80/8 = 10;$

$\bar{y} = \Sigma y/n = 648/8 = 81$

$$b_{yx} = \frac{n\Sigma d_x d_y - \Sigma d_x \Sigma d_y}{n\Sigma d_x^2 - (\Sigma d_x)^2} = \frac{247}{218} = 1.133;$$

where $d_x = x - \bar{x}$, $d_y = y - \bar{y}$

Regression equation of y on x

$$y - \bar{y} = b_{yx}(x - \bar{x})$$

or $y - 81 = 1.133\,(x - 10)$

or $y = 69.67 + 1.133x$

When $x = 7$, $y = 69.67 + 1.133\,(7) = 77.60 \cong 78$

10.4 Let price at Mumbai and Delhi be represented by x and y, respectively

(a) Regression equation of y on x

$$y - \bar{y} = r\,\frac{\sigma_y}{\sigma_x}(x - \bar{x})$$

$$y - 2.463 = 0.774 \frac{0.326}{0.207} (x - 2.797)$$

For x = Rs. 2.334, the price at Delhi would be y = Rs. 1.899.

(b) Regression on equation of x on y

$$x - \bar{x} = r \frac{\sigma_x}{\sigma_y} (y - \bar{y})$$

$$\text{or} \quad x - 2.791 = 0.774 \frac{0.207}{0.326} (y - 2.463)$$

For y = Rs. 3.052, the price at Mumbai would be x = Rs. 3.086.

10.5 Let aptitude score and productivity index be represented by x and y respectively.

$$\bar{x} = \Sigma x/n = 650/10 = 65;$$

$$\bar{y} = \Sigma y/n = 650/10 = 65$$

$$b_{xy} = \frac{n \Sigma d_x\, d_y - (\Sigma d_x)(\Sigma d_y)}{n \Sigma d_y^2 - \Sigma (d_y)^2} = \frac{1044}{1752} = 0.596;$$

where $d_x = x - \bar{x}$; $dy = y - \bar{y}$

(a) Regression equation of x on y

$$x - \bar{x} = b_{xy} (y - \bar{y})$$

or $\quad x - 65 = 0.596 (y - 65)$

or $\quad x = 26.26 + 0.596y$

When $y = 75, x = 26.26 + 0.596 (75) = 70.96 \cong 71$

$$\text{(b) } b_{yx} = \frac{n \Sigma d_x d_y - (\Sigma d_x)(\Sigma d_y)}{n \Sigma d_x^2 - (\Sigma d_x)^2}$$

$$= \frac{1044}{894} = 1.168$$

$$y - \bar{y} = b_{yx} (x - \bar{x})$$

or $\quad y - 65 = 1.168 (x - 65)$

or $\quad y = -10.92 + 1.168x$

When $x = 92, y = -10.92 + 1.168 (92) = 96.536 \cong 97$

10.6 Let R&D expenditure and annual profit be denoted by x and y respectively

$\bar{x} = \Sigma x/n = 40/8 = 5.625$; $\bar{y} = \Sigma y/n = 297/8 = 37.125$

$$b_{yx} = \frac{n \Sigma d_x d_y - (\Sigma d_x)(\Sigma d_y)}{n \Sigma d_x^2 - (\Sigma d_x)^2}$$

$$= \frac{8 \times 238 - (-3)(1)}{8 \times 57 - (-3)^2} = 4.266;$$

where $d_x = x - 6$, $d_y = y - 37$

Regression equation of annual profit on R&D expenditure

$$y - \bar{y} = b_{yx} (x - \bar{x})$$

$$y - 37.125 = 4.26 (x - 5.625)$$

or $\quad y = 13.163 + 4.266x$

For x = Rs. 1,00,000 as R&D expenditure, we have from above equation y = Rs. 439.763 as annual profit.

10.7 Let sales revenue and advertising expenditure be denoted by x and y respectively

$$\bar{x} = A + \frac{\Sigma fd_x}{n} \times h = 150 + \frac{12}{66} \times 50 = 159.09$$

$$\bar{y} = B + \frac{\Sigma fd_y}{n} \times k = 30 - \frac{26}{66} \times 10 = 26.06$$

$$b_{xy} = \frac{n \Sigma fd_x d_y - (\Sigma fd_x)(\Sigma fd_y)}{n \Sigma fd_y^2 - (\Sigma fd_y)^2} \times \frac{h}{k}$$

$$= \frac{66(-14) - 12(-26)}{66(100) - (-26)^2} \times \frac{50}{10} = -0.516$$

(a) Regression equation of x on y

$$x - \bar{x} = b_{xy} (y - \bar{y})$$

$$x - 159.09 = -0.516 (y - 26.06)$$

or $\quad x = 172.536 - 0.516y$

For $y = 50, x = 147.036$

(b) Regression equation of y on x

$$b_{yx} = \frac{n \Sigma fd_x d_y - (\Sigma fd_x)(\Sigma fd_y)}{n \Sigma fd_x^2 - (\Sigma fd_x)^2} \times \frac{k}{h}$$

$$= \frac{66(-14) - 12(-26)}{66(70) - (12)^2} \times \frac{10}{50} = -0.027.$$

$$y - \bar{y} = b_{yx} (x - \bar{x})$$

$$y - 26.06 = -0.027 (x - 159.09)$$

$$y = 30.355 - 0.027x$$

For $x = 300, y = 22.255$

$$\text{(c) } r = \sqrt{b_{xy} \times b_{yx}} = -\sqrt{0.516 \times 0.027}$$

$$= -0.1180$$

10.8 Let test score and production rating be denoted by x and y respectively.

$\bar{x} = \Sigma x/n = 612/10 = 61.2;$

$\bar{y} = \Sigma y/n = 622/10 = 62.2$

$$b_{yx} = \frac{n\Sigma d_x d_y - (\Sigma d_x)(\Sigma d_y)}{n\Sigma d_x^2 - (\Sigma d_x)^2}$$

$$= \frac{10\times3213-2\times2}{10\times3554-(2)^2} = 0.904$$

Regression equation of production rating (y) on test score (x) is given by

$$y - \bar{y} = b_{yx}(x - \bar{x})$$

$$y - 62.2 = 0.904\,(x - 61.2)$$

$$y = 6.876 + 0.904x$$

10.9 Let production and capacity utilization be denoted by x and y, respectively.

(a) Regression equation of capacity utilization (y) on production (x)

$$y - \bar{y} = r\frac{\sigma_y}{\sigma_x}(x - \bar{x})$$

$$y - 84.8 = 0.62\,\frac{8.5}{10.5}\,(x - 35.6)$$

$$y = 66.9324 + 0.5019x$$

(b) Regression equation of production (x) on capacity utilization (y)

$$x - \bar{x} = r\frac{\sigma_x}{\sigma_y}(y - \bar{y})$$

$$x - 35.6 = 0.62\,\frac{10.5}{8.5}\,(y - 84.8)$$

$$x = -29.3483 + 0.7659y$$

When $y = 70$, $x = -29.3483 + 0.7659(70) = 24.2647$

Hence the estimated production is 2,42,647 units when the capacity utilization is 70 per cent.

10.10 $\bar{x} = \Sigma x/n = 270/8 = 33.75;$ $\bar{y} = \Sigma y/n = 400/8 = 50$

$$b_{yx} = \frac{n\Sigma d_x d_y - (\Sigma d_x)(\Sigma d_y)}{n\Sigma d_x^2 - (\Sigma d_x)^2}$$

$$= \frac{8\times4800 - 6\times0}{8\times3592 - (6)^2} = 1.338;$$

where $d_x = x - 33$ and $d_y = y - 50$

Regression equation of y on x

$$y - \bar{y} = b_{yx}(x - \bar{x})$$

$$y - 50 = 1.338\,(x - 33.75)$$

$$y = 4.84 + 1.338x$$

For $x = 10$, $y = 18.22$

10.11 Let intelligence test score be denoted by x and weekly sales by y

$\bar{x} = 540/9 = 60;$ $\bar{y} = 450/9 = 50,$

$$b_{yx} = \frac{n\Sigma dx\,dy - (\Sigma dx)(\Sigma dy)}{n\Sigma d_x^2 - (\Sigma d_x)^2}$$

$$= \frac{9\times1200}{9\times1600} = 0.75$$

Regression equation of y on x :

$$y - \bar{y} = b_{yx}(x - \bar{x})$$

$$y - 50 = 0.75\,(x - 60)$$

$$y = 5 + 0.75x$$

For $x = 65$, $y = 5 + 0.75\,(65) = 53.75$

10.12 (a) Solving two regression lines:

$3x + 2y = 6$ and $6x + y = 31$

we get mean values as $\bar{x} = 4$ and $\bar{y} = 7$

(b) Rewritting regression lines as follows:

$3x + 2y = 26$ or $y = 13 - (3/2)x,$

So $b_{yx} = -3/2$

$6x + y = 31$ or $x = 31/6 - (1/6)y,$

So $b_{xy} = -1/6$

Correlation coefficient,

$$r = \sqrt{b_{xy}\times b_{yx}} = -\sqrt{(3/2)(1/6)} = -0.5$$

Given, Var(x) = 25, so $\sigma_x = 5$. Calculate σ_y using the formula:

$$b_{yx} = r\frac{\sigma_y}{\sigma_y}$$

or $$-\frac{3}{2} = 0.5\frac{\sigma_y}{5} \quad \text{or} \quad \sigma_y = 15$$

10.13 The regression equation of y on x is stated as:

$$y - \bar{y} = b_{xy}(x - \bar{x}) = r\cdot\frac{\sigma_y}{\sigma_x}(x - \bar{x})$$

Given, $\bar{x} = 53.20;$ $\bar{y} = 27.90,$ $b_{yx} = -1.5;$

$b_{xy} = -0.2$

Thus $y - 27.90 = -1.5(x - 53.20)$

or $y = 107.70 - 1.5x$

For $x = 60$, we have y

$= 107.70 - 1.5(60) = 17.7$

Also $r = \sqrt{b_{yx} \times b_{xy}} = -\sqrt{1.5 \times 0.2} = -0.5477$

10.14 Let advertising expenditure and sales be denoted by x and y respectively.

$\bar{x} = \Sigma x/n = 217/8 = 27.125$; $\bar{y} = \Sigma y/n = 58.2/8 = 7.26$

$$b_{yx} = \frac{n\sum dx\,dy - (\sum dx)(\sum dy)}{n\sum d_x^2 - (\sum dx)^2}$$

$$= \frac{8(172.2) - (25)(2.1)}{8(1403) - (25)^2} = \frac{1325.1}{10599} = 0.125$$

Thus regression equation of y on x is:

$$y - \bar{y} = b_{yx}(x - \bar{x})$$

or $y - 7.26 = 0.125(x - 27.125)$

$$y = 3.86 + 0.125x$$

When $x = 60$, the estimated value of $y = 3.869 + 0.125(60) = 11.369$

Conceptual Questions

1. (a) Explain the concept of regression and point out its usefulness in dealing with business problems.
   (b) Distinguish between correlation and regression. Also point out the properties of regression coefficients.
2. Explain the concept of regression and point out its importance in business forecasting.
3. Under what conditions can there be one regression line? Explain.
4. Why should a residual analysis always be done as part of the development of a regression model?
5. What are the assumptions of simple linear regression analysis and how can they be evaluated?
6. What is the meaning of the standard error of estimate?
7. What is the interpretation of y-intercept and the slope in a regression model?
8. What are regression lines? With the help of an example illustrate how they help in business decision-making.
9. Point out the role of regression analysis in business decision-making. What are the important properties of regression coefficients?
10. (a) Distinguish between correlation and regression analysis.
    (b) The coefficient of correlation and coefficient of determination are available as measures of association in correlation analysis. Describe the different uses of these two measures of association.
11. What are regression coefficients? State some of the important properties of regression coefficients.
12. What is regression? How is this concept useful to business forecasting?
13. What is the difference between a prediction interval and a confidence interval in regression analysis?
14. Explain what is required to establish evidence of a cause-and-effect relationship between y and x with regression analysis.
15. What technique is used initially to identify the kind of regression model that may be appropriate.
16. (a) What are regression lines? Why is it necessary to consider two lines of regression?
    (b) In case the two regression lines are identical, prove that the correlation coefficient is either + 1 or – 1. If two variables are independent, show that the two regression lines cut at right angles.

Formulae Used

1. Simple linear regression model
   $$y = \beta_0 + \beta_1 x + e$$
2. Simple linear regression equation based on sample data $y = a + bx$
3. Regression coefficient in sample regression equation $b = \hat{y}$
   $$a = \bar{y} - b\bar{x}$$

Chapter Concepts Quiz

True or False

1. A statistical relationship between two variables does not indicate a perfect relationship.
2. A dependent variable in a regression equation is a continuous random variable.
3. The residual value is required to estimate the amount of variation in the dependent variable with respect to the fitted regression line.
4. Standard error of estimate is the conditional standard deviation of the dependent variable.
5. Standard error of estimate is a measure of scatter of the observations about the regression line.
6. If one of the regression coefficients is greater than one the other must also be greater than one.
7. The signs of the regression coefficients are always same.
8. Correlation coefficient is the geometric mean of regression coefficients.
9. If the sign of two regression coefficients is negative, then sign of the correlation coefficient is positive.
10. Correlation coefficient and regression coefficient are independent.
11. The point of intersection of two regression lines represents average value of two variables.
12. The two regression lines are at right angle when the correlation coefficient is zero.
13. When value of correlation coefficient is one, the two regression lines coincide.
14. The product of regression coefficients is always more than one.
15. The regression coefficients are independent of the change of origin but not of scale.

Concepts Quiz Answers

1. T	2. T	3. T	4. T	5. T	6. F	7. T	8. T	9. F
10. F	11. T	12. T	13. T	14. F	15. T			

Review Self-Practice Problems

10.15 Given the following bivariate data:

x:	−1	5	3	2	1	1	7	3
y:	−6	1	0	0	1	2	1	5

(a) Fit a regression line of y on x and predict y if $x = 10$.

(b) Fit a regression line of x on y and predict x if $y = 2.5$.

10.16 Find the most likely production corresponding to a rainfall of 40 inches from the following data:

	Rainfall (in inches)	*Production (in quintals)*
Average	30	50
Standard deviation	5	10

Coefficient of correlation $r = 0.8$.

10.17 The coefficient of correlation between the ages of husbands and wives in a community was found to be + 0.8, the average of husbands age was 25 years and that of wives age 22 years. Their standard deviations were 4 and 5 years respectively. Find with the help of regression equations:

(a) the expected age of husband when wife's age is 16 years, and

(b) the expected age of wife when husband's age is 33 years.

10.18 You are given below the following information about advertisement expenditure and sales:

	Adv. Exp. (x) *(Rs. in crore)*	*Sales* (y) *(Rs. in crore)*
Mean	20	120
Standard deviation	5	25

Correlation coefficient 0.8

(a) Calculate the two regression equations.

(b) Find the likely sales when advertisement expenditure is Rs. 25 crore.

(c) What should be the advertisement budget if the company wants to attain sales target of Rs. 150 crore?

10.19 For 50 students of a class the regression equation of marks in Statistics (x) on the marks in Accountancy (y) is $3y - 5x + 180 = 0$. The mean marks in Accountancy is 44 and the variance of marks in Statistics is 9/16th of the variance of marks in Accountancy. Find the mean marks in Statistics and the coefficient of correlation between marks in the two subjects.

10.20 The HRD manager of a company wants to find a measure which he can use to fix the monthly income of persons applying for a job in the production department. As an experimental project, he collected data on 7 persons from that department referring to years of service and their monthly income.

Years of service :	11	7	9	5	8	6	10
Income (Rs. in 1000's):	10	8	6	5	9	7	11

(a) Find the regression equation of income on years of service.

(b) What initial start would you recommend for a person applying for the job after having served in a similar capacity in another company for 13 years?

(c) Do you think other factors are to be considered (in addition to the years of service) in fixing the income with reference to the above problems? Explain.

10.21 The following table gives the age of cars of a certain make and their annual maintenance costs. Obtain the regression equation for costs related to age.

Age of cars (in years)	:	2	4	6	8
Maintenance costs (Rs. in 100's)	:	10	20	25	30

10.22 An analyst in a certain company was studying the relationship between travel expenses in rupees (y) for 102 sales trips and the duration in days (x) of these trips. He has found that the relationship between y and x is linear. A summary of the data is given below:

$\Sigma x = 510$; $\Sigma y = 7140$; $\Sigma x^2 = 4150$; $\Sigma xy = 54{,}900$, and $\Sigma y^2 = 7{,}40{,}200$

(a) Estimate the two regression equations from the above data.

(b) A given trip takes seven days. How much money should a salesman be allowed so that he will not run short of money?

10.23 The quantity of a raw material purchased by ABC Ltd. at specified prices during the post 12 months is given below:

Month	*Price per kg (in Rs.)*	*Quantity (in kg)*	*Month*	*Price per kg (in Rs.)*	*Quantity (in kg)*
Jan	96	250	July	112	220
Feb	110	200	Aug	112	220
March	100	250	Sept	108	200
April	90	280	Oct	116	210
May	86	300	Nov	86	300
June	92	300	Dec	92	250

(a) Find the regression equations based on the above data.

(b) Can you estimate the approximate quantity likely to be purchased if the price shoots up to Rs. 124 per kg?

(c) Hence or otherwise obtain the coefficient of correlation between the price prevailing and the quantity demanded.

Hints and Answers

10.15 $\bar{x} = \Sigma x = 21/8 = 2.625$;

$\bar{y} = \Sigma y/n = 4/8 = 0.50$

$$b_{yx} = \frac{n\Sigma d_x d_y - (\Sigma d_x)(\Sigma d_y)}{n\Sigma d_x^2 - (\Sigma d_x)^2}$$

$$= \frac{8\times 30 - (-3)(-12)}{8\times 45 - (-1)^2} = 0.568;$$

$d_x = x - 3$; $d_y = y - 3$.

Regression equation:

$$y - \bar{y} = b_{yx}(x - \bar{x})$$

or $y - 0.5 = 0.568 (x - 2.625)$

$$y = -0.991 + 0.568x$$

(b) $$b_{xy} = \frac{n\Sigma d_x d_y - (\Sigma d_x)(\Sigma d_y)}{n\Sigma d_y^2 - (\Sigma d_y)^2}$$

$$= \frac{8\times 30 - (-3)(-12)}{8\times 84 - (-12)^2} = 0.386$$

Regression equation:

$$x - \bar{x} = b_{xy}(y - \bar{y})$$

or $x - 2.625 = 0.386 (y - 5)$

$$x = 0.695 + 0.386y$$

10.16 Let x = rainfall y = production by y. The expected yield corresponding to a rainfall of 40 inches is given by regression equation of y on x.

Given $\bar{y} = 50, \sigma_y = 10, \bar{x} = 30, \sigma_x = 5, r = 0.8$

$$y - \bar{y} = r\frac{\sigma_y}{\sigma_x}(x - \bar{x});$$

$$y - 50 = 0.8\ \frac{10}{5}\ (x - 30)$$

$$y = 2 + 1.6x$$

For $x = 40, y = 2 + 1.6\,(40) = 66$ quintals.

10.17 Let x = age of wife y = age of husband.

Given $\bar{x} = 25,\ \bar{y} = 22, \sigma_x = 4, \sigma_y = 5, r = 0.8$

(a) Regression equation of x on y

$$x - \bar{x} = r\frac{\sigma_x}{\sigma_y}(y - \bar{y})$$

$$x - 25 = 0.8\ \frac{4}{5}\ (y - 22)$$

$$x = 10.92 + 0.64y$$

When age of wife is $y = 16$; $x = 10.92 + 0.64\,(16) = 22$ approx.(husband's age)

(b) Left as an exercise

10.18 (a) Regression equation of x on y

$$x - \bar{x} = b_{xy}(y - \bar{y}) = r\frac{\sigma_x}{\sigma_y}(y - \bar{y})$$

$$x - 20 = 0.8\ \frac{5}{25}\ (y - 120)$$

$$x = 0.8 + 0.16y$$

Regression equation of y on x

$$y - \bar{y} = r\frac{\sigma_y}{\sigma_x}(x - \bar{x})$$

$$y - 120 = 0.8\frac{25}{5}\ (x - 20)$$

$$y = 40 + 4x$$

(b) When advertisement expenditure is of Rs. 25 crore, likely sales is

$$y = 40 + 4x = 40 + 4\,(25) = 140 \text{ crore.}$$

(c) For $y = 150$, $x = 0.8 + 0.16y$

$$= 0.8 + 0.16(150)$$

$$= 24.8$$

10.19 Let x = marks in Statistics and y = marks in Accountancy,

Given: $3y - 5x + 180 = 0$

or $x = (3/5)\,y + (180/5)$

For $y = 44$, $x = (3/5)\times 44 + (180/5) = 62.4$

Regression coefficient of x on y, $b_{xy} = 3/5$

Coefficient of regression

$$b_{xy} = r\frac{\sigma_x}{\sigma_y} = \frac{\sqrt{9}}{\sqrt{16}} \text{ (given)}$$

or $$\frac{3}{5} = r\frac{\sqrt{9}}{\sqrt{16}} \text{ or } \frac{3}{5} = \frac{3r}{4}$$

Hence $3r = 2.4$ or $r = 0.8$

10.20 Let x = years of service and y = income.

(a) Regression equation of y on x

$$b_{yx} = \frac{n\Sigma xy - (\Sigma x)(\Sigma y)}{n\Sigma x^2 - (\Sigma x)^2}$$

$$= \frac{7\times 469 - 56\times 56}{7\times 476 - (56)^2} = 0.75$$

$$y - \bar{y} = b_{yx}(x - \bar{x})$$

$$y - 8 = 0.75\,(x - 8)$$

$$y = 2 + 0.75x$$

(b) When x = 13 years, the average income would be

$$y = 2 + 0.75x = 2 + 0.75(13) = \text{Rs. } 11{,}750$$

10.21 Let x = age of cars and y = maintainance costs.

The regression equation of y on x

$\bar{x} = \Sigma x/n = 20/4 = 5;$

$\bar{y} = \Sigma y/n = 85/4 = 21.25$

and $$b_{yx} = \frac{n\Sigma xy - \Sigma x\,\Sigma y}{n\Sigma x^2 - (\Sigma x)^2} = \frac{7\times 490 - 20\times 85}{7\times 120 - (20)^2}$$

$= 3.25$

$$y - \bar{y} = b_{yx}(x - \bar{x})$$

$$y - 21.25 = 3.25\,(x - 5)$$

$$y = 5 + 3.25x$$

10.22 $\bar{x} = \Sigma x/n = 510/102 = 5;$

$\bar{y} = \Sigma y/n = 7140/102 = 70$

Regression coefficients:

$$b_{xy} = \frac{n(\Sigma xy) - (\Sigma x)(\Sigma y)}{n\Sigma y^2 - (\Sigma y)^2}$$

$$= \frac{102 \times 54900 - 510 \times 7140}{102 \times 740200 - (7140)^2} = 0.08$$

$$b_{yx} = \frac{n(\Sigma xy) - (\Sigma x)(\Sigma y)}{n\Sigma x^2 - (\Sigma x)^2}$$

$$= \frac{102 \times 54900 - 510 \times 7140}{102 \times 4150 - (510)^2} = 12$$

Regression lines:

$$x - \overline{x} = b_{xy}(y - \overline{y})$$

$$x - 5 = 0.08(y - 70) \text{ or } x = 0.08y - 0.6$$

and $y - \overline{y} = b_{yx}(x - \overline{x})$

$$y - 70 = 12(x - 5) \quad \text{or} \quad y = 12x + 10$$

When $x = 7, \quad \overline{y} = 12 \times 7 + 10 = 94$

10.23 Let price be denoted by x and quantity by y

$$\overline{x} = \Sigma x/n = 1200/12 = 100;$$

$$\overline{y} = \Sigma y/n = 2980/12 = 248.33$$

(a) Regression coefficients:

$$b_{xy} = \frac{n\Sigma d_x d_y - (\Sigma dx)(\Sigma dy)}{n\Sigma d_y^2 - (\Sigma d_y)^2} = -0.26$$

$$b_{xy} = \frac{n\Sigma d_x d_y - (\Sigma d_x)(\Sigma d_y)}{n\Sigma d_x^2 - (\Sigma d_x)^2} = -3.244$$

Regression lines:

$$x - \overline{x} = b_{xy}(y - \overline{y})$$

$$x - 100 = -0.26(y - 248.33)$$

or $x = -0.26y + 164.56$

and $y - \overline{y} = b_{yx}(x - \overline{x})$

$$y - 248.33 = -3.244(x - 100)$$

$$y = -3.244x + 572.73$$

(b) For $x = 124,$

$$y = -3.244 \times 124 + 572.73$$

$$= 170.474$$